D1395397

THE PRACTICE OF SOCIALIST
INTERNATIONALISM

The Practice of Socialist Internationalism

European Socialists and International Politics, 1914–1960

TALBOT C. IMLAY

OXFORD
UNIVERSITY PRESS

OXFORD
UNIVERSITY PRESS

Great Clarendon Street, Oxford, OX2 6DP,
United Kingdom

Oxford University Press is a department of the University of Oxford.
It furthers the University's objective of excellence in research, scholarship,
and education by publishing worldwide. Oxford is a registered trade mark of
Oxford University Press in the UK and in certain other countries

Published in the United States of America by Oxford University Press
198 Madison Avenue, New York, NY 10016, United States of America

British Library Cataloguing in Publication Data
Data available

Library of Congress Control Number: 2017944563

ISBN 978–0–19–964104–8

Printed and bound by
CPI Group (UK) Ltd, Croydon, CR0 4YY

Acknowledgements

My debts for this book run deep. The Social Sciences and Humanities Research Council of Canada and the Alexander von Humboldt Foundation both provided the financial support that made possible much of the research. I would like to thank Professor Clemens Wurm who acted as a gracious and discreet host during my Humboldt fellowship in Berlin. I am also grateful to the staff of the various archives and libraries in which I worked, all of whom were unfailingly helpful. The Université Laval's interlibrary loan office processed my requests with its usual efficiency; without its help I could not have written the same book.

At the Université Laval, I am extremely fortunate to be surrounded by a wonderful group of friends and colleagues: Aline Charles, Christel Freu, Didier Méhu, Arthur Ripoll, and Pierre-Yves Saunier. Donald Fyson deserves a special mention: his friendship, scholarly rigour, and sheer general competence are models for me. Beyond the Université Laval, I am thankful for the friendship of Andrew Barros, who works down the way in Montreal, as well as of Martin Thomas and Simon Kitson, both of whom are overseas, though Simon somewhat more so than Martin. As always, Peter Jackson has been a source of inspiration and (at times much-needed) encouragement; his belief that what we do is important is contagious. I am also grateful to Paul Miller, my graduate school friend, whose continued enthusiasm for historical research never seems to flag. Others have helped me in numerous ways over the years: Stefan Berger, Peter Carroll, Stephen Graham, Martin Horn, Nicolas Lépine, Tom Maulucci, Jenni Siegel, Glenda Sluga, and Till van Rahden. I would also like to thank the people at Oxford University Press and especially Cathryn Steele for her patience and gentle prodding.

My deepest debts are to my family. My parents, Robert and Camille Imlay, continue to provide all types of support, as do my two brothers, Pierre and Patrick, and their families. I am extremely grateful to them. My two children, Alicia Kate and Julian, have lived with this book all their lives, and I am thankful for everything they have brought to my own life. The extent of my debt to Alexandra is humbling. Throughout, she has encouraged me in the belief that I could indeed finish this book; and she has assumed far more than her share of family responsibilities, allowing me to do just that. Herta Müller's Lola might be right that goals are easier than wishes, but for me the two have fused together in my life with Alexandra and our children. This book is dedicated to them.

Talbot C. Imlay

Québec, Canada

Contents

List of Abbreviations

AABS	Arbetarrörelsens Arkiv och Bibliotek, Stockholm
AAOB	Arbeiderbevegelsens Arkiv og Bibliotek, Oslo
ABLP	Archives of the British Labour Party, Harvester microfilms
ACB	Anti-Colonial Bureau
ACImQ	Advisory Committee on Imperial Questions
ACIQ	Advisory Committee on International Questions
AdsD	Archiv der sozialen Demokratie
AFL	American Federation of Labor
AGM	Archives Guy Mollet
AILP	Archives of the Independent Labour Party
AMSAB	Institut voor Sociale Geschiedenis, Antwerp
AN	Archives nationales, Paris
APAC	All People's African Conference
APP	Archives de la Préfecture de Police, Paris
APS	Archives du Parti Socialiste
ASC	Asian Socialist Conference
BAK	Bundesarchiv Koblenz
BAL	Bundesarchiv Lichterfelde
BA-SAPMO	Stiftung Archiv der Parteien und Massenorganisationen der DDR im Bundesarchiv, Berlin
BASF	British-Asian Socialist Fellowship
BL	Bodleian Library
BLCAS	Bodleian Library of Commonwealth and African Studies, Oxford University
BLPES	British Library of Political and Economic Science, London
BSI	Bureau Socialiste International
CAP	Commission administrative permanente
CAS	Comité d'action socialiste
CCA	Churchill College Archives
CCF-NPD	Co-operative Commonwealth Federation/New Democratic Party of Canada
CGT	Confédération générale du travail
CHS	Centre d'histoire sociale du XXè siècle, Paris
COMISCO	Committee of the International Socialist Conference
CSP	Congress Socialist Party
DAPC	Direction des affaires politiques et commerciales (MAE)
DTMA	Draft Treaty of Mutual Assistance
EC	European Community
ECSC	European Coal and Steel Community
EDC	European Defence Community
EEC	European Economic Community
EFTA	European Free Trade Association
FCB	Fabian Colonial Bureau
FES	Friedrich Ebert Stiftung, Bonn

FLN	Front de libération nationale
FNSP	Fondation nationale des sciences politiques, Paris
FO	Foreign Office
GED	Groupe d'études doctrinales
GPS	Groupe parlementaire socialiste
GSPE	Groupe socialiste au parlement européen
GstA	Geheime Staatsarchiv Preuβischer Kulturbesitz, Berlin
HAEU	Historical Archives of the European Union, European University Institute, Florence
HIL	Hoover Institute Library, Stanford
IAR	International Authority for the Ruhr
IEV	Institute Emile Vandervelde, Brussels
IFTU	International Federation of Trade Unions
IISH	International Institute of Social History, Amsterdam
ILO	International Labour Office
ILP	Independent Labour Party
ISB	International Socialist Bureau
ISP	Indian Socialist Party
JO	Journal officiel de la République française. Débats parlementaires
JYUL	John Rylands University Library, Manchester
LAC	Library and Archives Canada, Ottawa
LAI	League Against Imperialism
LHASC	Labour History Archives and Study Centre (now the National Museum of Labour History), Manchester
LON	League of Nations Archives, Geneva
LPA	Labour Party Archive
LSI	Labour and Socialist International
MAE	Ministère des affaires étrangères
ME	Mouvement européen
MSEUE	Mouvement socialiste pour les états-unis d'Europe
MSPD	Mehrheitssozialdemokratische Partei Deutschlands
MUL	McGill University Libraries, Montreal
NAC	National Administrative Council
NAP	Norske Arbeiderparti
NEC	National Executive Committee
NL	Nachlass
OURS	Office universitaire de recherche socialiste, Paris
PAAP	Auswärtiges Amt—Politisches Archiv, Berlin
PCF	Parti communiste français
PLP	Parliamentary Labour Party
POB	Parti ouvrier belge
PRO	Public Records Office
PSA	Parti socialiste autonome
PSU	Parti socialiste unifié
RIIA	Royal Institute of International Affairs
SAI	Sozialistische Arbeiterinternationale
SFIO	Section française de l'Internationale ouvrière
SI	Socialist International
SII	Socialist International Information

SILO	Socialist Information and Liaison Office
SPD	Sozialdemokratische Partei Deutschlands
SPÖ	Sozialdemokratische Partei Österreichs
SPS	Sozialdemokratische Partei der Schweiz
Ssa	Sveriges socialdemokratiska arbetareparti
SSAZ	Schweizerisches Sozialarchiv, Zürich
TNA	The National Archives, Kew Gardens
TUC	Trades Union Congress
UCL	University College London
UEM	United Europe Movement
UGSOGB	Union of German Socialist Organisations in Great Britain
US	University of Sussex
USPD	Unabhängige Sozialdemokratische Partei Deutschlands
VDR	Verhandlungen des Deutschen Reichstags
VGA	Verein für die Geschichte der Arbeiterbewegung, Vienna

Wishes are difficult, writes Lola, goals are easier

Herta Müller, *The Land of Green Plums*,
trans. Michael Hofmann (1998).

Introduction
The Practice of Socialist Internationalism

In the summer of 1951 the Socialist International, grouping together socialist parties from over thirty countries and four continents, held its founding congress in Frankfurt am Main in Germany.* While the dominant tone was celebratory, the delegates found time to reflect on the meaning of internationalism for socialists. Some conceived of it in the traditional language of class. Internationalism, intoned Kurt Schumacher, the fiery leader of the German Social Democratic Party (SPD), aims at the 'equality of rights and status' for all peoples against the 'egotism of the wealthy classes, parading as internationalism'. Others, like the French socialist Salomon Grumbach, pointed to a number of guiding principles, among them the promotion of democracy, prosperity, and peace. Almost all delegates integrated the Cold War into their understanding of internationalism. Victor Larock, a Belgian socialist, thus spoke of 'the internationalism of the working masses who... fight for their liberation and their rights against Stalinist totalitarianism and capitalist exploitation.' But it was Morgan Phillips, the somewhat staid secretary of Britain's Labour Party, who offered the most revealing comments:

> Many of you, like myself, have attended every international Socialist gathering over the last six years and I think you will agree with me that we understand one another infinitely better now than we did at the end of the war. We have been through great international conflicts. There have been times when we have felt so irritated with the obstinacy of others that the whole framework of our movement seemed in danger. Yet our mutual faith as Socialists has pulled us through, and I believe that we have now more effective consultation one with another on the important issues which arise than was ever known in previous Socialist Internationals...[1]

For Phillips, internationalism signified a practice of regular consultation between socialist parties on international issues. The practice, he admitted, could be difficult: disagreements were common and consensus elusive. But rather than a liability,

---

* This introduction draws from two earlier publications: Talbot C. Imlay, 'The Practice of Socialist Internationalism during the Twentieth Century', *Moving the Social—Journal of Social History and of Social Movements* 55 (2016), 17–38; and 'Socialist Internationalism after 1914' in Glenda Sluga, Patricia Clavin, and Sunil Amrith, eds., *Internationalisms: A Twentieth-Century History* (Cambridge, 2017), 213–41.

[1] IISH, *Socialist International Information*, vol. 1, 1951, no. 27–8, 7 July 1951, 'First Congress of the Socialist International. Frankfurt am Main, 30 June–3 July 1951', Phillips, 19; vol. 1, no. 29–30, 21 July 1951, 'First Congress of the Socialist International', Schumacher, 4; Larock, 9; Grumbach, 14–17.

Phillips presented these difficulties as an asset that strengthened the bonds between parties. Indeed, conflict appears as part and parcel of a process by which socialists reaffirmed and renewed their commitment to the practice of internationalism—or to what Phillips called their 'mutual faith'. Socialist internationalism was thus both social and pragmatic: social in that it was a collective activity by socialists and pragmatic in that it centred on concrete issues of international politics.

Following Phillips, this book explores the practice of socialist internationalism. Based on archival research in twelve countries, it examines how European socialists collectively grappled with some of the most consequential issues of international politics from the First World War to circa 1960. Although a handful of studies have treated aspects of the subject, my book is the first to consider multiple international issues over a period lasting almost a half-century—a period that witnessed massive upheavals in Europe and beyond.[2] My aim is to contribute to the historical scholarship in three areas: socialism, internationalism, and international politics. But before discussing each of these areas, I should say something about several of the choices made in defining my subject. One choice concerns the emphasis on practical cooperation. Although socialist internationalism can be approached in several ways (as a doctrine, a political project, or a group identity, for example), I focus on practical cooperation between socialist parties because it was, as Phillips' comments suggest, a principal purpose of socialist internationalism. The delegates gathered in Frankfurt am Main believed that all socialists, whatever their party or national affiliations, were engaged in a joint endeavour to forge a better world—an endeavour whose ultimate success would be a collective one. 'Socialism', as a leading Belgian socialist wrote in 1944, 'cannot establish itself solidly and durably in only one country.'[3] For socialists it was accordingly imperative to work out common 'socialist' positions on issues of shared concern.

A second reason to emphasize practice is that it could have a galvanizing effect on socialists. In addition to the institutional structure provided by the Internationals (the Socialist International and its interwar predecessor, the Labour and Socialist International or LSI), socialists were bound together by a web of more informal elements—personal friendships, common understandings, mutual expectations, and responsibilities as well as shared experiences. In a speech to an international conference of socialist youth in 1926, Erich Ollenhauer, a future SPD leader, referred to the 'thousands of invisible links' uniting socialists.[4] Together, these formal and informal links constituted what can be called an international socialist community. Yet just as importantly, these links alone were insufficient

---

[2] For more focused studies, see Leonardo Rapone, *La socialdemocrazia europea tra le due guerre: Dall'organizzazione della pace alla resistenza al fascismo (1923–1936)* (Rome, 1999); Gerd-Rainer Horn, *European Socialists Respond to Fascism: Ideology, Activism and Contingency in the 1930s* (New York, 1996); and J.F. Wrynn, *The Socialist International and the Politics of European Reconstruction* (Uithoorn, 1976).

[3] Louis de Brouckère, 'Le caractère international du socialisme', reproduced in José Gotovitch, ed., *Camille Huysmans Geschriften en Documenten VIII. De Belgische Socialisten in London* (Antwerpen, 1981), 194.

[4] Christine Bouneau, 'La jeunesse socialiste et l'action internationale durant l'entre-deux-guerres', *Mouvement social* 223 (2008), 46.

to breathe life into this community. Something else was needed: the sustained practical cooperation between parties on international issues. Without this practice, the international socialist community risked becoming an empty shell, drained of much of its pertinence for the parties and individuals involved.

And this points to a final reason for emphasizing practice: doing so helps to illuminate the changing nature of twentieth-century socialist internationalism. The shared commitment of the parties to cooperate on international issues fluctuated over time, waxing in the wake of each of the two world wars and waning afterwards. Today, it has all but disappeared; for socialist parties the Socialist International is of marginal significance at most. This is not to say that socialists are no longer interested in international affairs. Rather, it appears that towards the end of the 1920s and again towards the end of the 1950s socialist internationalism underwent a process of nationalization as each party began to define its position on international issues increasingly on its own, independently of other parties. As the practice of internationalism became less of a collective enterprise between socialist parties, the international socialist community withered, its pertinence no longer apparent. One goal of this book is to understand how the practice of socialist internationalism became nationalized—or how, in Phillips' words, socialists lost their 'mutual faith'.

Another choice concerns the emphasis on international politics. Much of the scholarship on European socialism examines domestic political issues and especially the social and economic measures loosely grouped under the rubric of the welfare state.[5] But international politics also impinged on socialists, and no more so than in the period from 1914 to 1960—a period marked by the rippling effects of two world wars. These global conflicts profoundly shook the international political and economic order, infusing a sense of urgent pertinence into such issues as international security, European integration, and the future of empire. While these issues certainly had important domestic political implications, European socialists were convinced that they could not be adequately addressed in a national framework alone. And this conviction provided a powerful impetus to the practice of socialist internationalism.

A third choice was to confine the study to socialist (or social-democratic) parties.[6] There are two aspects to this choice. One is the focus on political parties. To be sure, the latter were never the sole arena of socialist political engagement, and many socialists were active outside of political parties. Nevertheless, political parties constituted a (if not *the*) principal site of socialist activity because they remained a vital organizational vehicle for contesting and gaining political power at the local and national levels.[7] A second aspect is the focus on socialist political parties. This

---

[5] Good examples are Sheri Berman, *The Primacy of Politics: Social Democracy and the Making of Europe's Twentieth Century* (Cambridge, 2006); and Gerassimos Moschonas, *In the Name of Social Democracy: The Great Transformation: 1945 to the Present* (London, 2002).

[6] Not all parties or individuals accepted the term socialist, preferring social democratic or labour, but for convenience's sake I use the term socialist throughout the book.

[7] This was true not only of socialists, a point that helps to explain the revival of interest among historians in political parties. See François Audigier, 'Le renouvellement de l'histoire des partis politiques', *Vingtième siècle* 96 (2007), 123–36.

choice is worth underscoring because socialist internationalism has been used to refer to the relations between communist parties and communist states.[8] International communism, however, was markedly different from international socialism. Created in the aftermath of the First World War, the Komintern evolved into a highly centralized, hierarchical, and authoritarian organization.[9] International socialism, by contrast, remained a much more loosely organized movement. Rather than a general staff, the Socialist Internationals operated as sites of interaction between parties that occurred on a voluntary basis. Internationalism was not something dictated to socialist parties; it was instead a self-imposed principle and practice. Just as pertinently, if international socialism was less centralized than communist internationalism, it was more structured than its Christian democratic rival. Wolfram Kaiser has examined the transnational network of leading Christian democratic politicians after 1945, which, he contends, decisively shaped the course of European integration. Yet the network he describes was remarkably nebulous, with little of the developed formal and even informal architecture of international socialism.[10] What distinguished the international socialist movement from its communist and Christian democratic counterparts was its combination of voluntarism and structure. And it is this combination that helped to make practical cooperation between socialist parties on international issues such a critical element of socialist internationalism.

In focusing on socialist parties, I have largely excluded trade unions from my definition of socialist internationalism. This decision is certainly questionable. In several countries close links existed between socialists and trade unionists: the Labour Party, for example, owed its creation to the desire of the British trade union movement to have its own political representation in Parliament. As scholars have shown, moreover, considerable practical cooperation took place between trade unionists from different countries and continents, particularly during the two post-war periods.[11] As we shall see in chapter 4 on interwar disarmament, the socialist and trade union Internationals sometimes worked together in the pursuit of common goals. Nevertheless, for several reasons, different dynamics operated within trade union internationalism: its greater emphasis on working conditions,

---

[8] For example, see John Dunn, 'Unimagined Community: The Deceptions of Socialist Internationalism' in *Rethinking Modern Political Theory* (Cambridge, 1986), 103–18. Also see the multi-university research project, 'Socialism Goes Global' at: http://socialismgoesglobal.exeter.ac.uk/

[9] There is some disagreement among scholars on the pace of the Komintern's subordination to Moscow but less so on its eventual extent. Compare Alexander Vatlin, *Die Komintern. Gründung, Programmatik, Akteure* (Berlin, 2009); and Tim Rees and Andre Thorpe, eds., *International Communism and the Communist International, 1919–1943* (Manchester, 1998).

[10] Wolfram Kaiser, *Christian Democracy and the Origins of European Union* (Cambridge, 2007); also see Paolo Acanfora, 'Christian Democratic Internationalism: The *Nouvelles Equipes Internationales* and the Geneva Circles between European Unification and Religious Identity, 1947–1954', *Contemporary European History* 24 (2015), 375–91.

[11] Geert Van Goethem, *The Amsterdam International: The World of the International Federation of Trade Unions (IFTU), 1913–1945* (Aldershot, 2006); Victor Silverman, *Imagining Internationalism in American and British Labor, 1939–49* (Urbana, IL, 2000); Denis Macshane, *International Labour and the Origins of the Cold War* (Oxford, 1992); and Wayne Thorpe, *The Workers Themselves: Revolutionary Syndicalism and International Labour, 1913–1923* (Dordrecht, 1989).

the prominent role of American trade unionists (American socialists, by contrast, were marginal to socialist internationalism), and the tense relations between socialist parties and trade unionists in some countries. In the end, socialist and trade union internationalism travelled along separate if at times parallel tracks. This separation, in turn, influenced relations with the International Labour Organization (ILO), created in 1919 to promote social and labour reform in Europe and beyond. While welcoming the ILO, socialist parties viewed its activities principally as the concern of organized labour, which had been instrumental in its emergence.[12]

Socialists, of course, did not operate in isolation. On several occasions, they cooperated with non-socialists in various organizations, for example, during the interwar years in the Union of Democratic Control and in the League of Nations Union in Britain and in the *Association française pour la Société des Nations* in France.[13] But much of this cooperation was ad hoc and temporary. Generally speaking, socialists kept their distance from non-socialist organizations, and nowhere was this truer than in the international realm. Indeed, socialists defined their internationalism in part in opposition to that of other political groups, most obviously the communists but also the Christian democrats after 1945. The practice of socialist internationalism, accordingly, remained very much a socialist affair. Interestingly, the exclusive nature of socialist internationalism contrasted with a growing tendency on the part of socialist parties to enter into electoral alliances and even coalition governments with non-socialist parties at home. The result, often enough, was considerable frustration among socialists with the compromises that invariably accompanied such alliances and coalitions. And this frustration arguably helps to explain the determination of socialist parties to exclude non-socialists from the practice of socialist internationalism. As the plausibility of a distinct socialist project faded at the national level, the practice of socialist internationalism became a means for socialists to reaffirm both their separate identities and the enduring pertinence of socialism.

Yet another choice is to concentrate on European as opposed to non-European socialists. If the resulting perspective is admittedly Eurocentric, it is also true that socialism was first and foremost a European phenomenon, even if its influence extended well beyond Europe. Writing in the 1970s, Asoka Mehta, a prominent Indian socialist, retrospectively described socialism as one of 'the two most powerful intellectual and social forces that have dominated recent centuries and shaped our lives [the other being nationalism]'; both, he added, 'arose in Europe, their ideas, inflexions and idioms have come from Europe; in considering them we cannot ignore that parentage.'[14] International socialism largely reflected its European origins. Thus, of the almost 600 delegates who attended the LSI's

---

[12] For a good introduction to recent scholarship on the ILO, see J. Van Daele et al., eds., *ILO Histories: Essays on the International Labour Organization and Its Impact on the World during the Twentieth Century* (Bern, 2010).

[13] See Helen McCarthy, *The British People and the League of Nations: Democracy, Citizenship and Internationalism, c. 1918–45* (Manchester, 2011); and Jean-Michel Guieu, *Le rameau et le glaive: Les militants français pour la Société des Nations* (Paris, 2008).

[14] Asoka Mehta, *Reflections on Socialist Era* (New Delhi, 1977), 17.

founding congress in 1923, all but eight were from European countries. Afterwards the proportions remained lopsided, even if less so: at the International's 1951 congress, only 18 of 102 delegates came from outside Europe. But while centred on Europe, the book does not ignore non-European socialists and socialist parties. Chapter 9 on decolonization devotes considerable attention to Asian socialists who, in 1951, formed the Asian Socialist Conference, an Asian counterpart to the Socialist International. Nevertheless, the role of Asian and other non-European socialists is largely refracted through a European lens. My primary interest is in the influence they exerted on European socialists.

Within the world of European socialism, I pay particular attention to British, French, and German socialists. This choice is explained by the combined weight of the parties involved: together the British, French, and German parties formed the core of international socialism during the twentieth century due to their size and to the political importance of their countries. As a Swiss socialist remarked, they constituted the 'big three'.[15] For much of the century the fortunes of international socialism would depend on the ability of British, French, and German socialists to work together. To be sure, other parties could sometimes exert influence, especially as intermediaries facilitating cooperation between the bigger parties. Following the First World War, Austrian and Swiss socialists contributed greatly to the reconstruction of the International, as did Belgian and Dutch socialists following the Second World War. At various points in the book, therefore, the smaller parties make an appearance. But they do so principally in terms of their impact on the interactions between the British, French, and German parties.

Methodological considerations also figured into my decision to privilege the 'big three'. International history arguably involves trade-offs between breadth and depth. There is an impetus to include ever more countries (and archives) in the analysis in order to highlight the complex multilateral dynamics at work in international politics;[16] at the same time, there is the need to examine closely the policymaking process within one country.[17] In choosing to emphasize the socialist parties of three countries, I hope to strike a reasonable balance between breadth and depth. I am interested in the many ways in which British, French, and German socialists influenced one another's policies on international issues. But I am also interested in the interplay between the international and domestic realms—between the practical cooperation among socialist parties and the political developments within each party. In a pioneering article, Robert Putnam modelled the relationship between domestic and international politics as a two-level game in which negotiators must take into account not only their international partners

---

[15] SSAZ, SPS, Ar 1. 111.12, 'Sitzung der Geschäftsleitung der SPS, 19 April 1952...', Hans Oprecht, 3.

[16] Examples include Lorenz Luthi, *The Sino-Soviet Split: Cold War in the Communist World* (Princeton, NJ, 2008); Patrick O. Cohrs, *The Unfinished Peace after World War I: America, Britain and the Stabilisation of Europe, 1919–1932* (Cambridge, 2006); and Jeremi Suri, *Power and Protest: Global Revolution and the Rise of Détente* (Cambridge, MA, 2003).

[17] For a valuable recent example of this approach, see Peter Jackson, *Beyond the Balance of Power: France and the Politics of National Security in the Era of the First World War* (Cambridge, 2013).

but also national actors.[18] Putnam's model works well for socialist internationalism, as the socialists involved had to consider the impact of their positions on other parties as well as on their own party. This interplay is perhaps most evident in the attempts to instrumentalize the practice of socialist internationalism—attempts that underscore the importance of internationalism to socialists. As we shall see, practical cooperation between parties on concrete issues offered opportunities to party leaders to strengthen their authority by invoking the approval of international socialism for their policies, a tactic they also used to undermine their internal critics; these critics, meanwhile, responded by claiming that their positions on international issues embodied the true spirit of socialist internationalism—a claim they often buttressed by citing the support of socialists abroad. The greater the number of socialist parties added to the mix, however, the harder it becomes to give the interplay between inter-party and intra-party politics its due.

If the book privileges the 'big three', it also highlights a fairly exclusive group within each party: the small number of leaders, prominent members, and officials at the forefront of inter-party relations and party policy on international issues. This 'high politics' approach admittedly neglects activity at a subnational level—activity that scholars have begun to investigate. Patrizia Dogliani, for example, has explored the international socialist municipal movement during the first half of the twentieth century in which networks of European socialists worked together to reform and modernize local government. In another example, Christine Collette has investigated grass-root forms of international socialist engagement in interwar Britain, including participation in sporting, tourist, and musical events. Seen from this vantage point, she insists, socialist internationalism was not simply 'the common philosophy of a handful of left European politicians' but also part of the lived experience of countless socialists.[19]

What might be called socialist internationalism from below certainly deserves more research, but for the moment its influence on the practice of socialist internationalism remains unclear. In 1945 the secretary of a local branch of the British Labour Party wrote to the Swedish Socialist Party asking to establish ties with a 'similar local party in your country'. 'I do sincerely believe', he noted, 'that the time has come when we should form a definite link between, not only the top dogs, but between the ordinary working class of the country.'[20] Such documents, however, are extremely rare in the archival records; revealingly, it does not appear that the Swedish party replied to the request. More generally, there are few signs that grass-roots activity trickled up to the 'top dogs', most likely because a small circle of men

---

[18] Robert Putnam, 'Diplomacy and Domestic Politics: The Logic of Two-Level Games', *International Organization* 42 (1988), 427–60.

[19] Patrizia Dogliani, 'European Municipalism in the First Half of the Twentieth Century: The Socialist Network', *Contemporary European History* 11 (2002), 573–96; Christine Collette, *The International Faith: Labour's Attitudes to European Socialism, 1918–39* (Aldershot, 1998), 99; and Christine Collette, '"Friendly Spirit, Comradeship, and Good-Natured Fun": Adventures in Socialist Internationalism', *International Review of Social History* 48 (2003), 225–44.

[20] AABS, Ssa, E 2B/01, letter from the Pelsall Labour Party, 7 September 1945.

(and they were almost exclusively male) dominated international policy.[21] Leading socialists, it is true, regularly referred to party sentiment, most often to claim that their position enjoyed popular support; but by this they frequently meant the opinion of the parliamentary group. And this is why several of the chapters pay particular attention to the factional politics within the socialist parliamentary groups in Britain, France, and Germany. If it is true that the practice of socialist internationalism involved a restrained cast of characters, it is an open question whether this constituted a weakness. On the one hand, the lack of a more solid anchoring within the parties probably factored into the eventual decline of the collective practice; on the other hand, the relative insulation of the 'top dogs' arguably facilitated the knitting of cross-party bonds between the members of this select group.

A final choice concerns periodization. As already mentioned, the book begins with the First World War and ends in 1960 or so. The starting point is explained by the fact that scholars have concentrated almost exclusively on the pre-1914 period, the golden age of socialist internationalism that supposedly came to a screeching halt with the outbreak of war. As we shall see, the practice of socialist internationalism survived and even flourished after August 1914. The end date is perhaps more questionable. It has been argued that socialist internationalism underwent a revival in the mid-1970s. If this revival is best embodied by Willy Brandt, the former chancellor of West Germany, who in 1976 became the Socialist International's president, it manifested itself most concretely within the European Community, which became a prominent site of inter-party cooperation.[22] As the conclusion will briefly discuss, however, this revival was limited not only in time but also in scope. From today's vantage point, it seems clear that the practice of socialist internationalism reached its twentieth-century high points in the years after the First and Second World Wars.

While covering the period from 1914 to 1960 or so, I am especially interested in the two post-war periods: 1918 to the early 1930s and 1945 to the late 1950s. Whereas scholars once described the aftermath of the two world wars in terms of reconstruction, the emphasis is now on upheaval and violence, loss and mourning.[23] Yet if the post-war years undoubtedly contained elements of tragedy, they can also be viewed as unique moments of heightened possibility. Geoff Eley has suggested

---

[21] In what amounted to an appendage to the International, female socialists from several countries met separately from their male counterparts, most often to discuss what were viewed as appropriately 'female' issues such as housing, education, health, and child care. See AAOB, NAP, D Db 1951, 'Bericht über die Internationale sozialistische Frauenkonferenz in Frankfurt/M. am 27./28 June 1951'; and Anette Eklund Hansen, 'Die internationale Konferenz socialistischer Frauen 1910 in Kopenhagen: Netzwerke, Walhrecht und Wohlfahrt', *Jahrbuch für Forschungen zur Geschichte der Arbeiterbewegung* 3 (2011), 5–33.

[22] Bernd Rother and Wolfgand Schmidt, eds., *Willy Brandt. Über Europa hinaus. Dritte Welt und Sozialistische Internationale* (Bonn, 2007); and Christian Salm, *Transnational Socialist Networks in the 1970s: European Community Development Aid and Southern Enlargement* (Houndmills, 2016).

[23] For example, see William I. Hitchcock, *The Bitter Road to Freedom: The Human Cost of Allied Victory in World War II Europe* (New York, 2008); István Deák, Jan T. Gross, and Tony Judt, eds., *The Politics of Retribution in Europe: World War II and its Aftermath* (Princeton, NJ, 2000); and Jay Winter, *Sites of Memory, Sites of Mourning: The Great War in European Cultural History* (Cambridge, 1995).

that the multiple and massive disruptions attendant on large-scale war fostered 'enabling indeterminacies'—situations in which people are able to conceive of change in ways they could not before.[24] Eley applies this perspective to change within countries, but it is also pertinent to international politics. Major war, as political scientists have argued, shakes the international system to its very roots, creating unparalleled opportunities for revising the status quo.[25] In 1918 and again in 1945 European socialists eagerly sought to contribute to the task of recasting international relations in a new mould in the aim of preventing a renewed cycle of interstate competition, tensions, and war.

THE HISTORY OF SOCIALISM

In exploring the practice of socialist internationalism, I hope to contribute to the history of twentieth-century socialism. Generally speaking, scholars have approached European socialism as a subject of national or subnational (regional and municipal) history. Prominent historical syntheses reflect and reinforce this neglect of socialism's international face insofar as they survey and compare developments in several national movements and parties.[26] Few studies consider the foreign policies of more than one party, and those that do most often adopt a comparative approach.[27] Rare are studies of the relations between two or more socialist parties;[28] and rarer still are those that broach the subject of socialist internationalism. To the extent that scholars consider the international dimensions of socialism, they investigate the foreign policies of particular parties, the international ideas of individual socialists, or the institutional workings of the different Internationals.[29]

[24] Eley, 'Europe After 1945', *History Workshop Journal* 65 (2008), 207–8.

[25] G. John Ikenberry, *After Victory: Institutions, Strategic Restraint, and the Rebuilding of Order after Major Wars* (Princeton, NJ, 2001); and Robert Gilpin, *War and Change in World Politics* (Cambridge, 1981).

[26] Berman, *The Primacy of Politics*; Geoff Eley, *Forging Democracy: The History of the Left in Europe, 1850–2000* (New York, 2002); Stefano Bartolini, *The Political Mobilization of the European Left, 1860–1980: The Class Cleavage* (Cambridge, 2000); Donald Sassoon, *One Hundred Years of Socialism: The West European Left in the Twentieth Century* (New York, 1996); and Marc Lazar, *La Gauche en Europe depuis 1945: invariants et mutations du socialisme européen* (Paris, 1996).

[27] See Dietrich Orlow, *Common Destiny: A Comparative History of the Dutch, French, and German Social Democratic Parties, 1945–1969* (New York, 2000); Detlef Rogosch, *Vorstellungen von Europa: Europabilder in der SPD und bei den belgischen Sozialisten 1945–1957* (Hamburg, 1996); Pascal Delwit, *Les partis socialistes et l'intégration européenne: France, Grande-Bretagne, Belgique* (Brussels, 1995); Stefan Berger, *The British Labour Party and the German Social Democrats, 1900–1931* (Oxford, 1994), 207–47; Kevin Featherstone, *Socialist Parties and European Integration: A Comparative History* (Manchester, 1988); and Michael Newman, *Socialism and European Unity: The Dilemma of the Left in Britain and France* (London, 1983).

[28] For studies of bilateral party relations, see Brian Shaev, 'Estrangement and Reconciliation: French Socialists, German Social Democrats and the Origins of European Integration, 1948–1957', PhD, University of Pittsburgh, 2014; Marc Drögemöller, *Zwei Schwestern in Europa. Deutsche und niederländische Sozialdemokratie 1945–1990* (Berlin, 2008); Nicolas Dohrmann, 'Les relations entre la SFIO et le SPD dans l'immédiat après-guerre (1945–1953)', thèse, École des Chartes, 2006; and Klaus Misgeld, *Sozialdemokratie und Außenpolitik in Schweden: Sozialistische Internationale, Europapolitik und die Deutschlandfrage 1945–1955* (Frankfurt, 1984).

[29] For examples of works on foreign policies, see R.M. Douglas, *The Labour Party, Nationalism and Internationalism, 1939–1951* (London, 2004); Stefan Feucht, *Die Haltung der Sozialdemokratischen*

The rare few who accord any attention to socialist internationalism tend to be dismissive. Thus for Wilfred Loth, socialist internationalism existed only 'on paper', while Rolf Steininger contends that socialist parties merely paid it 'lip service'.[30] For Donald Sassoon, the author of a panoramic history of twentieth-century European socialism, socialist internationalism amounted to empty rhetoric. 'Internationalism', he writes, 'was just a word... It was a feature of the verbal radicalism which was one of the characteristic traits of the [socialist] movement.'[31]

These dismissals of socialist internationalism reflect an influential reading of August 1914 as a revelation—as the moment when the major socialist parties, rallying to their country's war effort, confirmed their overriding attachment to the nation over class. The events of 1914, James Joll remarked long ago, revealed the 'unity of Socialists' to be a 'sham'.[32] Although this reading of 1914 is arguably misguided, in that the vast majority of European socialists had never rejected the duty of national defence,[33] it does explain the disinterest in socialist internationalism: why study something that did not exist? Tellingly, there is now a sizeable scholarly literature on the pre-1914 period, the supposed heyday of socialist internationalism, which emphasizes just how rooted socialist parties were in their respective nations. Socialist nationalism rather than internationalism seems to be the pertinent subject.[34] Equally telling, there is no similar body of scholarship for the period after 1914, as it is simply assumed that nationalism defined twentieth-century European socialism. Typical is the statement by the editors of a recent assessment of social democracy's past achievements and future potential. The principal lesson of 1914, they write, 'was that from then on lefts would be national'.[35]

Yet if the national loyalties of socialist parties were important, so too at times was their internationalism. To view twentieth-century European socialism simply as a

Partei Deutschlands zur Außenpolitik während der Weimarer Republik (1918–1933) (Frankfurt am Main, 1998); and Wilfried Loth, *Sozialismus und Internationalismus: Die französischen Sozialisten und die Nackkriegsordnung Europas 1940–1950* (Stuttgart, 1977). For individual socialists, see Marie-Dominique Cavaillé, *Rudolf Breitscheid et la France 1919–1933* (Frankfurt am Main, 1995); and Gilles Candar, *Jean Longuet, 1876–1938. Un internationaliste à l'épreuve de l'histoire* (Rennes, 2007). For the Internationals, see Guillaume Devin, *L'Internationale Socialiste: Histoire et sociologie du socialisme international (1945–1990)* (Paris, 1993); Werner Kowalski, ed., *Geschichte der Sozialistischen Arbeiter-Internationale (1923–1940)* (Berlin, 1985); and Julius Braunthal, *History of the International*, 3 volumes (London, 1967–1980).

[30] Loth, *Sozialismus und Internationalismus*, 269; and Rolf Steininger, *Deutschland und die Sozialistische Internationale nach dem Zweiten Weltkrieg* (Bonn, 1979), 98.

[31] Sassoon, *One Hundred Years of Socialism*, 29.

[32] James Joll, *The Second International, 1889–1914* (London, 1968), 1.

[33] For a recent reminder of this point, see Marc Mulholland, '"Marxists of Strict Observance": The Second International, National Defence, and the Question of War', *Historical Journal* 58 (2015), 615–40.

[34] See Kevin Callahan, '"Performing Inter-Nationalism" in Stuttgart in 1907: French and German Socialist Nationalism and the Political Culture of an International Socialist Culture', *International Review of Social History* 45 (2000), 51–87; Patrick Pasture and Johan Verberckmoes, eds., *Working-Class Internationalism and the Appeal of National Identity: Historical Debates and Current Perspectives* (Oxford, 1998); and Marcel van der Linden, 'The National Integration of European Working Classes (1871–1914): Exploring the Causal Configuration', *International Review of Social History* 33 (1983), 285–311.

[35] James Cronin, George Ross, and James Shoch, 'Introduction: The New World of the Center-Left' in *What's Left of the Left: Democrats and Social Democrats in Challenging Times* (Durham, NC, 2011), 2.

collection of 'national parties', as Sassoon proposes, cannot explain why socialists devoted so much time and energy to rebuilding the International after 1918 and again after 1945. It cannot explain why socialists felt it necessary to cooperate with one another for extended periods on international issues, nor how this cooperation affected politics within (as well as between) the parties. At weighty moments during the twentieth century, socialist parties operated simultaneously in distinct national contexts and in a larger collective socialist internationalist context extending beyond party and national borders. In recent years, transnational history has become increasingly popular among scholars, prompting talk of a transnational 'turn'. As with any field, the definition of transnational history is contested, but most scholars would likely agree that it challenges 'methodological nationalism'—the idea that national history can be studied in isolation.[36] In this sense, my book is inspired by transnational history in that its starting point is that socialist parties are best thought of not as separate containers but as a Venn diagram whose overlapping circles varied in size and significance over time. More concretely, it means that the policymaking of socialist parties sometimes possessed a prominent international socialist dimension. This latter dimension was never the only one, nor even the most influential. In some periods, especially when a socialist party participated in government, the international socialist dimension receded. Nevertheless, during the two extended post-war periods, the practice of socialist internationalism did encourage European socialists to consider one another's viewpoints, which in turn prodded socialist parties to look beyond their own parochial (national) perspectives.

THE HISTORY OF INTERNATIONALISM

If exploring the practice of socialist internationalism casts light on a significant yet neglected aspect of European socialism, it can also tell us something about twentieth-century internationalism more generally. Internationalism has received little scholarly attention, especially when compared to nationalism with which it is frequently paired. Most often, it is used to designate any activity that is not confined within the borders of a single country. To the extent that scholars attempt a more systematic treatment, they approach internationalism in one of three overlapping ways: as a complex and uneven process in which different regions and peoples of the world grow increasingly interconnected and different societies increasingly similar;[37] as a political project promoted by leading countries, groups, and prominent thinkers, comprising a set of principles and institutions aimed most often at encouraging

---

[36] For helpful discussions of transnational history, see Pierre-Yves Saunier, *Transnational History: Theory and History* (Houndmills, 2013); Margrit Pernau, *Transnationale Geschichte* (Göttingen, 2011); and Akira Irye, 'The Transnational Turn', *Diplomatic History* 31 (2007), 373–6.

[37] Jürgen Osterhammel, *Die Verwandlung der Welt: Eine Geschichte des 19. Jahrhunderts* (Munich, 2009); Karin Fischer and Susan Zimmermann, eds., *Internationalismen: Transformation weltweiter Ungleichheit im 19. und 20. Jahrhundert* (Wien, 2008); and C.A. Bayly, *The Birth of the Modern World, 1780–1914* (Malden, MA, 2004).

international cooperation and peace;[38] and as an individual or group identity that transcends national or subnational loyalties.[39] Though useful as starting points for discussion, none of these three approaches is entirely suitable for grasping the nature and significance of socialist internationalism.

As a process, internationalism is often depicted as progressing inexorably, especially when it is conflated with globalization; the latter, despite suffering temporary reverses, supposedly advanced with increasing speed and strength across the twentieth century, sweeping away all obstacles in its path.[40] But international cooperation between socialists resembled a fever more than a forward march, waxing in intensity in response to specific events (major war) before waning and almost disappearing altogether. This suggests that internationalism is best viewed not as an inexorable force but as clusters of activity, some interconnected and some not, occurring in multiple spaces, at various speeds and intensities, and with different durations. Far from being faceless, these clusters are directed by identifiable historical actors/agents (governments, corporations, NGOs, etc.), many of whom, moreover, are rooted in a particular state.[41] Equally important, the nature and extent of this rootedness vary not only with each particular case, but also in relation to changing patterns of internationalism during the twentieth century. From this perspective, socialist internationalism belonged to a distinct and seemingly transient category of international activity, one in which nationally rooted political parties assumed the leading role.

As a political project, internationalism frequently denotes a set of principles, the best-known example being liberal internationalism. One result is a tendency to judge an internationalist project in terms of the perceived fidelity of its promoters to its principles. The problem is that the principles involved are often open-ended and changing, leading to multiple and sometimes competing definitions. In the case of liberal internationalism, while Glenda Sluga emphasizes the 'realism' of a project that accepted a world based on nation states, Daniel Gorman identifies an array of Anglo-American internationalists imbued with an 'extremism of idealism' and who collectively constituted an 'international society' during the 1920s.[42] Given the

---

[38] Glenda Sluga, *Internationalism in the Age of Nationalism* (Philadelphia, PA, 2013); Akira Iriye, *Global Community: The Role of International Organizations in the Making of the Contemporary World* (Berkeley, CA, 2002); and John Boli and George M. Thomas, *Constructing World Culture: International Nongovernmental Organizations since 1875* (Stanford, CA, 1999).

[39] Whitney Walton, *Internationalism, National Identities, and Study Abroad: France and the United States, 1890–1970* (Stanford, CA, 2010); and Lisa Moses Leff, *Sacred Bonds of Solidarity: The Rise of Jewish Internationalism in Nineteenth-Century France* (Stanford, CA, 2006).

[40] This is evident in the dominant political-economic narrative of globalization, in which the growth of global exchanges and ties takes off at the end of the nineteenth century, suffers major setbacks with the First World War and the Depression, but regains momentum after 1945, before switching into overdrive, beginning in the 1970s. See Jeffrey Frieden, *Global Capitalism: Its Fall and Rise in the Twentieth Century* (New York, 2006).

[41] For internationalism as a cluster of activities, see Frederick Cooper's critique of the globalization paradigm in 'What is the Concept of Globalization Good For? An African Historian's Perspective', *African Affairs* 100 (2001), 189–213. For the national rootedness of one well-known international actor, see Alison Frank, 'The Petroleum War of 1910: Standard Oil, Austria, and the Limits of the Multinational Corporation', *American Historical Review* 114 (2009), 16–41.

[42] Sluga, *Internationalism in the Age of Nationalism*; and Daniel Gorman, *The Emergence of International Society in the 1920s* (Cambridge, 2012), 31.

project's malleable nature, it is perhaps not surprising that some scholars have sought to enfold socialist internationalism into liberal internationalism. In a recent article, Daniel Laqua presents interwar socialist internationalism as a variant of liberal internationalism because both championed democracy and peace.[43] That both did so is undoubtedly true; but much the same can be said for a large number of groups on the left and centre (and even some on the right) of European politics. Defining liberal (or socialist) internationalism as a project centred on such broad-based principles as peace and democracy makes almost everyone a liberal internationalist.

This being so, it is more useful to treat internationalism not as a fixed entity, goal, or destination but as a practice. For European socialists, this means focusing on their prolonged efforts to cooperate with one another on international issues. Although inspired by a handful of broad principles, the practice was not necessarily determined by them. Equally to the point, socialist internationalism as a project cannot be abstracted from its practice since the latter helped to define—and continuously redefine—the project's content and meaning for socialists. Whether socialist internationalism required one to support unilateral disarmament or multilateral arms limitations; free trade among European countries or the construction of a common market; or the national rights of colonial peoples versus the rights of minorities within colonies, were not questions that could be answered by reference to general principles. Instead, they were complex issues over which socialists debated, manoeuvred, and (sometimes) disagreed. For the study of liberal internationalism, which continues to dominate scholarship, an emphasis on practice directs attention towards the efforts of distinct groups of actors to translate open-ended principles into policy positions on issues.[44]

As an identity, internationalism is almost always associated with nationalism with which it is said to enjoy an intimate and even codependent relationship.[45] Much of the historical scholarship focuses on the construction of a cross-national sense of belonging and purpose, most often among politically engaged groups such as feminists, pacifists, and human rights advocates.[46] Interestingly, much of the theoretical work on identity supports the view that international and national identities are complementary. Indeed, in affirming that people possess multiple identities and that individual and group identities are constructed through social interaction, this work points to the promising possibility of transcending the

---

[43] Daniel Laqua, 'Democratic Politics and the League of Nations: The Labour and Socialist International as Protagonist of Interwar Internationalism', *Contemporary European History* 24 (2015), 175–92.

[44] A focus on practice need not be limited to liberal or socialist internationalism. For examples of other internationalisms, see Frank Wolff, *Neue Welten in der Neuen Welt: Die transnationale Geschichte des Allgemeinen Jüdischen Arbeiterbundes 1897–1947* (Köln, 2014); and Joachim Schröder, *Internationalismus nach dem Krieg: Die Beziehungen zwischen deutschen und französischen Kommunisten 1918–1923* (Essen, 2006).

[45] Perry Anderson, 'Internationalism: A Breviary', *New Left Review* 14 (2002), 5–25.

[46] See Leila J. Rupp, *Worlds of Women: The Making of an International Women's Movement* (Princeton, NJ, 1997); Sandi Cooper, *Patriotic Pacifism: Waging War on Europe, 1815–1914* (Oxford, 1991); and Margaret E. Keck and Kathryn Sikkink, *Activists beyond Borders: Advocacy Networks in International Politics* (Ithaca, NY, 1998).

exclusive national identities of individuals and groups from different countries.[47] Referring to research in social psychology, Jeffrey Checkel, examining the construction of a collective identity within European institutions, contends that 'discussion and persuasion within small groups consistently promote feelings of group identity'.[48]

Curiously, however, little attention has been paid to what happens after this shared cross-national group identity is said to exist. Thomas Risse, a prominent international relations scholar, assumes that social interaction reinforces collective identity: 'communicative action and its daily practices', he affirms, 'reproduce the common lifeworld [of groups].'[49] Yet the history of socialist internationalism indicates that such reproduction does not always occur. At the beginning of each of the two post-war periods, European socialists possessed a strong group identity that manifested itself in the commitment to practical cooperation between socialist parties. Over time, however, this shared commitment faded. Although socialists liked to claim there was no contradiction between their nationalism and internationalism, in reality they had difficulty reconciling the two over the long term. The problem was not simply that socialist parties sometimes disagreed with one another on international issues; it was also that the practice of socialist internationalism had the unintended effect of encouraging each party to define its position on its own, independently of the other parties. Rather than reproducing an 'international "we"', to borrow Leila Rupp's term, extended social interaction had a fissiparous effect, rooting the deliberations of each party more firmly in national and intra-party politics.[50] European socialists continued to identify themselves as internationalists and to interest themselves in international politics, but increasingly they did so alone. Put simply, the history of twentieth-century socialist internationalism suggests that if identities are socially constructed, they can also be socially deconstructed.

INTERNATIONAL HISTORY

Although international history is a vast and diverse field, it is possible, broadly speaking, to identify two distinct approaches. One approach is to focus on interstate relations in which state actors of various kinds—heads of government, ministerial departments, military services, etc.—assume the leading roles. Although sometimes denigrated as old-fashioned, this approach continues to produce new and innovative studies that are inspired by the obvious importance of states to international politics both today and in the past.[51] The other approach concentrates

---

[47] Manuel Castells, *The Information Age: Economy, Society, and Culture vol. II, The Power of Identity* (Malden, MA, 2004 edn.); Jeffrey T. Checkel, 'Why Comply? Social Learning and European Identity Change', *International Organization* 55 (2001), 553–8; and Thomas Risse, '"Let's Argue!": Communicative Action in World Politics', *International Organization* 54 (2000), 1–39.

[48] Checkel, 'Why Comply?', 563.   [49] Risse, '"Let's Argue!"', 11.

[50] Rupp, *Worlds of Women*, 129.

[51] Examples include Jackson, *Beyond the Balance of Power*; Cohrs, *The Unfinished Peace*; and Marc Trachtenberg, *A Constructed Peace: The Making of the European Settlement, 1945–1963* (Princeton, NJ, 1999).

on non-state actors and their transnational and transregional ties. A far from exhaustive list would include non-governmental organizations as well as anti-colonial, pacifist, anti-nuclear, environmental, and human rights movements.[52] Admittedly, the dividing lines between the two approaches can be porous: some non-governmental organizations were (and are) intimately tied to particular states, while within interstate organizations such as the League of Nations, officials could develop distinct corporate identities that coexisted uneasily with their purported loyalties to specific states.[53] That said, the two approaches are distinguishable if only because state and non-state actors differ in many ways (aims, functioning, resources); and if so, European socialist parties can be viewed as hybrid entities, incorporating aspects of both state and non-state actors. Well anchored in national political systems, the major socialist parties were attached to the state and its interests, however conceived. The depiction of socialists by their opponents as 'unpatriotic fellows' [*vaterlandslose Gesellen*] belonged far more to the realm of propaganda than to reality.[54] Yet at the same time and in a fashion similar to many non-state actors, socialist parties often adopted a critical stance towards their governments—and towards the understanding of state interests prevalent among their domestic political rivals. And nowhere perhaps was this stance more evident than in international politics. During the period covered by this book, European socialists aspired to remodel international relations between states so as to reduce the sources of recurrent tensions and conflict.

In some ways, the practice of socialist internationalism amounted to a concerted attempt to delineate the contours and contents of this remodelled international relations. Admittedly, success often proved elusive, if only because European socialists frequently disagreed among themselves on what the proper international socialist response should be to specific issues. Nevertheless, the extended efforts of socialists to forge collective positions on pressing international issues offer a different perspective on international history from the more state-centred and non-state-centred ones—a perspective, moreover, that throws into relief otherwise obscure aspects. The approach here is to offer not a general thesis but more precise arguments tied to the issues discussed in specific chapters. Thus in chapter 4 on interwar disarmament, the inability of socialists to agree to a workable programme underscores the intractability of the issue, as even some of disarmament's most fervent proponents could not reach a consensus. This lack of consensus, in turn, prompted the International to organize a petition campaign centred on a generic endorsement of disarmament, a step that can be viewed as an attempt to disguise failure. When it came to disarmament, popular mobilization did not necessarily represent

---

[52] For two examples, see Michael Goebel, *Anti-Imperial Metropolis: Interwar Paris and the Seeds of Third World Nationalism* (Cambridge, 2015); and Holger Nehring, *Politics of Security: British and West German Protest Movements and the Early Cold War, 1945–1970* (Oxford, 2013).

[53] For a useful overview, see Madeleine Herren, *Internationale Organizationen seit 1945: Eine Globalgeschichte der internationalen Ordnung* (Darmstadt, 2009). For a recent case study, see Patricia Clavin, *Securing the World Economy: The Reinvention of the League of Nations, 1920–1946* (Oxford, 2013).

[54] Dieter Groh and Peter Brandt, *'Vaterlandslose Gesellen': Sozialdemokratie und Nation, 1860–1990* (Munich, 1992).

an innovative broadening of politics. In the case of decolonization, chapter 9 examines the debates between European and Asian socialists during the 1950s on whether to assign priority to national, minority, or individual rights in newly independent postcolonial states. If these debates constituted a struggle to define socialist internationalism, they also lay bare some of the stakes involved in decolonization for international as well as national politics. In these and other chapters, the book provides a 'socialist' lens on the international history of the period, one that undoubtedly has its limits (as do all lenses) but one that has the advantage of being relatively unfamiliar.

STRUCTURE OF THE BOOK

The book is divided into two parts. Following the introduction and a first chapter on the First World War, which demonstrates that socialist internationalism did not die in 1914, Part I consists of four chapters on the first post-war period. Chapter 2 traces the developments that culminated in the founding of the Labour and Socialist International (LSI) in May 1923. Chapters 3 through 5 explore the practice of socialist internationalism, discussing in succession the issues of international security, disarmament, and colonialism. Following a short entr'acte on the nadir of socialist internationalism during the 1930s, Part II contains four chapters on the second post-war period. Chapter 6 tells the story of the International's resurrection during the wartime and post-war years, ending with the Socialist International's creation in 1951, while chapters 7 through 9 examine the practice of socialist internationalism through the issues of European unity, international security, and decolonization. A concluding chapter discusses the fate of socialist internationalism after 1960 and offers some brief remarks on a distinct category of internationalism—one centred on nationally based political parties. There is admittedly something artificial to the organization of Parts I and II in that, in each of the two post-war periods, European socialists grappled with the issues involved simultaneously. Considering them separately, however, allows me to distinguish the various ways in which the practice of socialist internationalism shaped and was shaped by the interactions of European socialists.

1

International Socialism at War, 1914–1918

In the autumn of 1912 the Balkans became engulfed in war as Bulgaria, Greece, Montenegro, and Serbia combined to attack the Ottoman Empire. In a Europe in which the great powers were heavily armed and grouped into rival alliance blocs, the danger of a regional war expanding into a general conflict was apparent to contemporary observers. It is in this context that over 550 European socialists gathered in November 1912 in the Swiss town of Basle to discuss the international socialist movement's response to the threat of war. After numerous speeches and some discussion, the delegates unanimously agreed on a resolution that was admittedly vague on specifics: socialists promised to do everything they could to prevent a European war but, should one nevertheless occur, they would strive to bring the conflict to 'a speedy end' and to 'hasten the downbreak [*sic*] of the predominance of the capitalist class'. The primary purpose of the conference, however, was not to draw up detailed plans for action but to impress upon socialists and non-socialists alike the strength and unity of the movement as well as its commitment to preserving peace. As the conference's president announced in his opening address:

> [Our gathering] indicates that the sentiments, convictions and determination that will be expressed during the debates are those not merely of a few hundred men and women...but the sentiments, convictions and determination of the masses. There is no doubt: behind the thousands of people demonstrating today in Basle against war and for peace are hundreds of thousands and millions of people who...think and feel as you do and are with us in their thoughts.[1]

Among those present at the Basle congress no one was more awed by this show of force than Jean Longuet, the French socialist and grandson of Karl Marx. In a hefty volume published in 1913, Longuet surveyed the international socialist movement, downplaying the tactical and theoretical differences between and within socialist parties and emphasizing its shared purpose. The reader of his survey, he projected, 'cannot but be profoundly struck by the profound unity, which is the essence of universal socialism'.[2]

Yet only one year later the international socialist movement was in disarray. The assassination in June 1914 of Francis Ferdinand, the heir to the Austro-Hungarian throne, triggered an international crisis that resulted in a general

---

[1] *Congrès international extraordinaire. Bâle 24–25 Novembre 1912* (Geneva, 1980 reprint), 31, 43, 53–63.

[2] Jean Longuet, *Le mouvement socialiste international* (Genève, 1976, reprint), 6. Also see Gilles Candar, *Jean Longuet (1876–1938): Un internationaliste à l'épreuve de l'histoire* (Rennes, 2007), 107–9.

conflict in early August. Rather than doing all in their power to end the conflict, as they had agreed to do at the Basle congress, the major socialist parties lined up to support their nation's war effort: the British, French, and German parties all voted to grant their government war credits. As indicated in the introduction, scholars generally view August 1914 as a damning indictment of the Second International and of socialist internationalism. At the moment of truth, the much-touted solidarity of socialists across national borders had shown itself to be an illusion—or even a 'sham'. The internationalist pretensions of socialists had been cruelly exposed, dealing a fatal blow to the international socialist community. In 1914, writes James Joll, '[t]he life had gone out of the Second International; and it was never to return.'[3]

This chapter challenges the view that socialist internationalism suffered a deadly blow in August 1914 by examining the efforts of European socialists to revive and recast the International during the war. The existing scholarship on the wartime history of international socialism focuses largely on the radical left, viewing the war years in terms of the origins of international communism and of the Third International.[4] Yet for much of the war the Bolsheviks and their allies remained a minority and even a marginal strain within the international socialist movement; the latter's history, in short, cannot be reduced to a prehistory of the Komintern. If the onset of war initially paralysed the Second International, it did not put an end to the practice of socialist internationalism. From early on, socialists from different parties met to discuss various aspects of the war. To be sure, these meetings were largely limited to socialists from the same alliance bloc; yet over time the pressure mounted within each of the major parties to organize an international socialist conference that would bridge the belligerent split. During the war, the French, German, and (to a lesser extent) British parties grew increasingly divided over the question of whether to favour a negotiated or victorious end to the war. As divisions deepened, socialists closely followed developments in other parties, with factions in one party drawing inspiration from those in others in what amounted to a struggle to define the meaning of socialist internationalism.

AUGUST 1914

As already mentioned, the received wisdom is that August 1914 sounded the death knell of international socialism. In voting to grant their governments war credits, the major European socialist parties presumably chose nation over class, decisively demonstrating the hollowness of their internationalist claims. That by 1914 European socialists were deeply attached to their nations is beyond doubt. Yet such an attachment was not incompatible with the sense of belonging to a larger

---

[3] Joll, *The Second International*, 183.
[4] Romain Ducoulombier, *Camarades! La naissance du parti communiste en France* (Paris, 2010); R. Craig Nation, *War on War: Lenin, the Zimmerwald Left, and the Origins of International Communism* (Durham, NC, 1989); David Kirby, *War, Peace and Revolution: International Socialism at the Crossroads 1914–1918* (New York, 1986); Annie Kriegel, *Aux origines du communisme français 1914–1920*, I (Paris, 1964); and Merle Fainsod, *International Socialism and the World War* (Cambridge, MA, 1935).

international community. To argue that a commitment to socialist internationalism demanded that socialists oppose their country's war efforts is to set the bar impossibly high—higher, indeed, than practically all socialists set it at the time. Well before the July crisis it was clear that there were no easy answers to the question of how to respond to an imminent threat of war or to war itself. If the resolution accepted at the Basle conference in 1912 remained vague on specifics it was because socialists disagreed on what should and could be done. Some socialists maintained that it was naïve to believe that socialist parties, which almost everywhere were excluded from political power, possessed the means to prevent a war. Others argued that the uneven development of working-class political and trade union organization across Europe blunted the potential effects of a general strike—the ultimate socialist weapon in any attempt to prevent or stop war. To be effective, the general strike had to be applied universally, for otherwise it would disadvantage those countries possessing the strongest labour movements. Not surprisingly, this argument was invoked by the Germans, whose labour movement was the envy of others.[5]

In addition to these disagreements regarding the capabilities of socialists, there is also the simple truth that the major European parties all recognized the principle of national defence in the event of foreign invasion. In this context, what is striking about the conflict that broke out in August 1914 is that almost all the belligerents could claim to be acting defensively. This was most obviously the case with France, whose north-eastern departments would soon be under German occupation. 'In the presence of aggression', intoned Édouard Vaillant, a prominent French socialist, 'Socialists will fulfill their duty to their country, to the [French] Republic and to the International.'[6] But the same also applied to Germany, whose eastern borders would be the site of major battles. 'We are threatened by the horrors of enemy invasion', the SPD declared in justifying its vote for war credits. 'Today we have decided neither for nor against war but rather the question of the necessary means for national defense.' Significantly, the declaration added that German socialists 'thus feel in conformity with the International, which has recognized the right of all peoples to national independence and self-defense'.[7] European socialists, in other words, did not understand their decisions in 1914 in terms of a stark choice between nationalism and internationalism. National defence was as much an international as it was a national right and duty.

This last point is important because it draws attention to the fact that European socialists did not completely abandon their commitment to the practice of socialist internationalism either during the July crisis or afterwards. Following Austria-Hungary's ultimatum to Serbia on 23 July, the Second International's Bureau (ISB) held emergency meetings in Brussels on 29 and 30 July. The participants agreed not only to call on all socialist parties to pursue and to intensify 'their [ongoing] organized activities against war', but also to move forward the International's

---

[5] See the comments of the Austrian socialist, Karl Renner, in his *Marximus, Krieg und Internationale* (Stuttgart, 1918), 354–7.
[6] 'Les socialistes français et la guerre', *L'Humanité*, 3 August 1914, 1–2.
[7] Cited in Suzanne Miller, *Burgfrieden und Klassenkampf: Die Deutsche Sozialdemokratie im Ersten Weltkrieg* (Düsseldorf, 1974), 62–3.

scheduled congress from late to early August. The first question on the agenda would be the 'war and the proletariat'.[8] To be sure, there is no reason to believe that the congress, had it met, would have been able to prevent a European war. But even if European socialists could not stop the rush to war in 1914, it is worth emphasizing that their reaction to the July crisis was to gather together in an effort to coordinate their responses. By 1914 practical cooperation had become something of a conditioned reflex for socialist parties. Having cooperated with one another for well over two decades under the aegis of the Second International, socialist parties could not imagine taking major decisions concerning international politics on their own, without consulting with their counterparts abroad. This explains why on 31 July the SPD dispatched Hermann Müller to Paris to discuss with French socialists the question of socialist approval of war credits. Together with Camille Huysmans, the Belgian socialist and secretary of the ISB, Müller met with members of the SFIO's parliamentary group, informing them of the divisions within the SPD's own group (*Fraktion*) on the question.[9] The SFIO's leaders, meanwhile, were no less eager to work with other parties. As Longuet explained at a rally on 2 August in Paris, while French socialists would do their duty to defend France, they also 'will do everything they can to maintain or to re-establish peace'. And they would do so together with German socialists whose willingness to cooperate provided 'an immense hope of reconciliation'.[10]

Müller's trip to Paris draws attention to another important point: if European socialists rallied behind their nation at war in August 1914, they did so reluctantly and sometimes only after agonizing debate. In the case of the SPD, the question of war credits triggered heated discussions within the *Fraktion*, with Haase, its co-chairman, and Georg Ledebour, a member of the party's executive committee, leading the charge in favour of a no vote. Until the last moment it appeared possible that the group would abstain. In the end, the *Fraktion*'s members voted 78 to 14 in favour of war credits; the principle of party discipline convinced the minority to support the majority within Parliament, with the result that in public the SPD offered its unanimous approval of the government's request.[11] Similar debates did not occur within the SFIO's parliamentary group, no doubt because the imminent threat of German invasion rendered the defensive nature of the war self-evident. But the SFIO was exceptional in this regard. In Britain the Labour Party appeared divided, with the chairman of its parliamentary party, Ramsay MacDonald, arguing in favour of British neutrality—a position stemming partly from a deep-seated suspicion of power politics that reflected his close ties to the pre-war international socialist community. The party's national executive endorsed MacDonald's position, condemning the government's support for France and Russia and demanding that everything be done 'to secure peace at the earliest

---

[8] The minutes and decisions of the meetings are reproduced in Georges Haupt, ed., *Le congrès manqué. L'Internationale à la veille de la Première Guerre mondiale* (Paris, 1965), 249–67.

[9] Joll, *The Second International*, 166–81.

[10] Longuet is cited in 'Les socialistes français et la guerre', *L'Humanité*, 3 August 1914, 2.

[11] Good accounts are in Dieter Groh, *Negative Integration und revolutionärer Attentismus: die deutsche Sozialdemokratie am Vorabend des Ersten Weltkrieges* (Frankfurt am Main, 1974), 653–60, 675–705; and Miller, *Burgfrieden und Klassenkampf*, 37–61.

possible moment'. The majority of Labour's parliamentary group, however, voted to support Britain's war effort, prompting MacDonald to resign.[12]

Significantly, MacDonald belonged to the Independent Labour Party (ILP), a political organization affiliated to the Labour Party. Although small in numbers with a declining local presence across Britain, the ILP exerted considerable influence on Labour. The ILP's self-assigned task was to prod Labour in a more socialist direction. In the domestic realm this meant campaigning for more ambitious measures of social reform than the more reformist-oriented Labour leadership proposed. But the ILP's mission also had an important international dimension. From its founding in the 1890s, the party took a particular interest in foreign policy, an interest that manifested itself in its active membership in the Second International. If ILP leaders hoped that Labour could be convinced to follow their example in working closely with Continental socialists, the need for practical cooperation between socialist parties informed the party's approach to the war. 'Across the roar of the guns, we send sympathy and greetings to the German Socialists...', an ILP manifesto announced in August 1914. 'They are no enemies of ours, but faithful friends.'[13] More concretely, during the war the ILP would lobby Labour to cooperate with European socialists. 'So far as Socialists are concerned', MacDonald wrote in November 1914, 'they must continue their efforts to keep the foundations of the International intact so that at the earliest possible moment they may begin to rebuild upon these foundations what the war has destroyed.'[14]

The decision of European socialists to support their governments in 1914 was thus neither straightforward nor uncontested. From the outset there could be found within each socialist party individuals and fledgling groupings deeply uncomfortable with the close association of socialism with the nation at war. If this was clearly the case with the SPD and Labour, it was also true of the SFIO, as Annie Kriegel made clear in her classic study of French socialism during the war.[15] To be sure, few socialists opposed the war outright. The need to defend the *patrie* and the *Vaterland* against the invader was widely accepted; in the British case, defending Belgium against German militarism and imperialism was enough. Initially, the unease of socialists expressed itself in criticism of the government's conduct of the war rather than the war itself. But as the conflict dragged on without any foreseeable end, some European socialists began to search for a path to peace via negotiation rather than military victory. Over time they grew in numbers, becoming in some cases the majority within their parties. Just as pertinently, many of these critics conceived of themselves as internationalists, a self-conception partly forged through confrontation with socialists committed to military victory. From early on, moreover, their internationalism manifested itself in calls for the renewal of international cooperation between socialists—including socialists from enemy countries.

---

[12] David Marquand, *Ramsay MacDonald* (London, 1977), 164–85.
[13] ILP, *Report of the Annual Conference...April 1915*, 115–16. Also see Robert E. Dowse, *Left in the Centre: The Independent Labour Party, 1893–1940* (Evanston, IL, 1966), 20.
[14] Cited in Marquand, *Ramsay MacDonld*, 182–3.
[15] Kriegel, *Aux origines du communisme français*, I.

WARTIME SOCIALIST INTERNATIONALISM: 1914–1917

After the war many European socialists castigated the pre-war Second International not because it did not prevent a conflict in 1914 but because it failed to organize a collective effort to end the conflict. Rather than work for a negotiated peace, European socialists, in the scathing words of the Swiss socialist Robert Grimm, had surrendered to 'dull resignation', 'chauvinism', and 'social patriotism'. In Grimm's account the true spirit of socialist internationalism had been kept alive during the war by a small and eclectic group of socialists who represented the revolutionary will of the international proletariat. Bucking party discipline, its members gathered together in Zimmerwald in September 1915 and again in Kienthal in April 1916, founding the Zimmerwald movement. The most prominent strand of this movement, dominated by the Bolsheviks, would pave the way for the creation of the Communist International after the war.[16] Grimm's version of events, however, downplayed the evolution of thinking about the war within the major socialist parties—an evolution that had important implications for the practice of socialist internationalism. If in 1914 few socialists were prepared to meet with their counterparts from enemy countries, this was no longer the case by 1917. By then the British, French, and German parties had all committed themselves to working together.

The outbreak of war divided the international socialist community, throwing up numerous obstacles to practical cooperation between the parties. In response to a British suggestion for a meeting of the Second International's Bureau, Camille Huysmans, the Belgian socialist and ISB secretary, wrote in December 1914 that 'it is quite impossible, useless, and even dangerous, to summon a meeting of the Bureau now. Impossible for most of our leading members are unable to come; useless, for we have no real power to do something; dangerous, because the conference would become a violent exchange of reproaches.'[17] The final concern was especially pertinent. Military developments in the opening phase of the war, most notably Germany's violation of Belgian neutrality and its invasion of France, created a gulf between French and German socialists. When, in October 1914, Scandinavian socialists had called a meeting of parties from the belligerent and neutral countries, the SFIO refused to attend. For Longuet, a meeting was simply impossible until the Allies had achieved a 'decisive [military] result' against 'Prussian militarism'.[18] The SFIO's intransigence, in turn, provided an excuse for the British and Germans to stay away. When the conference convened in Copenhagen in January 1915, the Scandinavian socialists found themselves alone.[19]

[16] SSAZ, SPS, Ar 1.260.3, Robert Grimm, *Der Wiener Konferenez der Internationalen Arbeitsgeimeinschaft sozialistischer Parteien* (Berne, 1921), 2. Also see Nation, *War on War*; Kirby, *War, Peace and Revolution*; and the documents collected in Horst Lademacher, ed., *Die Zimmerwalder Bewegung: Protokolle und Korrespondenz*, 2 volumes (The Hague, 1967).

[17] TNA Ramsay MacDonald Papers, PRO 30/69/1232, International Socialist Bureau, British Section, circular, Henderson, 28 December 1914, containing the text of Huysmans' reply. Also see AAOB, DNA, Forkrigsarkiv (1887–1940), Huysmans, ISB circular, December 1914.

[18] Jean Longuet, 'Initiative prématurée', *L'Humanité*, 19 October 1914, 1.

[19] Agnes Blänsdorf, *Die Zweite Internationale und der Krieg: Die Diskussion über die internationale Zusammenarbeit der sozialistischen Parteien 1914–1917* (Stuttgart, 1979), 109–33.

'Prudence', Huysmans had advised the British in December 1914, 'commands us to wait.' But soon many European socialists were becoming impatient for some form of international socialist cooperation. In response to the initiative of the Scandinavian parties, Belgian and French socialists lobbied for a meeting of socialists from the Allied nations, primarily in order to encourage the Labour Party to endorse the goal of an outright military victory. The resulting conference in London in February 1915 gathered together socialists from Belgium, Britain, France, and Russia. After considerable discussion the delegates agreed to a resolution in which they declared their shared determination to 'fight until victory' in order to defeat 'German imperialism'. Yet at the same time the delegates pledged their continued allegiance to the 'principles of the International' and expressed 'the hope that...the workers of all countries will find themselves reunited against militarism and capitalist imperialism'. Going further, a second resolution foresaw the reconstitution of the International after the war 'to impose on all nations the obligation to maintain peace'.[20] Two months later, German socialists organized their own conference in Vienna of socialist parties from the Central Powers. During the discussions several speakers criticized a single-minded policy of 'holding-out' [*Durchhalten*] until victory, suggesting instead the need for a peace policy behind which all socialists and socialist parties could rally. Reflecting these sentiments, the manifesto issued at the end of the conference, having declared the right of all peoples 'to defend their autonomy and independence', went on to assert that this right 'should not constitute an obstacle to maintaining international contact among all the socialist parties, as well as to continuing the activity of their international institutions'.[21]

The two conferences indicate that some life remained in the international socialist community. The war had not completely snuffed out the flame of solidarity between parties. Nevertheless, the fact that the two groups met separately in London and Vienna is noteworthy. Despite some signs of a willingness to cooperate together as well as several informal meetings in Switzerland between French and German socialists, over the next two years it proved impossible to organize a conference of parties from the two belligerent camps. In the spring–summer of 1915, the Swedish socialist Hjalmar Branting strove to arrange such a conference, shuttling between the different European capitals. Fairly quickly, however, he was forced to admit that the time was not yet ripe. The Labour Party refused to meet with socialists from enemy countries, citing the opposition of French socialists, while the SFIO insisted on preconditions that the SPD rejected—preconditions that amounted to an open break with the government and the nation at war. As for the SPD, if in principle the party expressed its willingness to cooperate with British and French socialists in the search for a negotiated end to the war, in practice a

[20] 'La conférence des socialistes des pays alliés. Les resolutions votées', *L'Humanité*, 16 February 1915, 1; and Blänsdorf, *Die Zweite Internationale und der Krieg*, 150–68.
[21] The manifesto is reproduced in Olga Hess Gankin and H.H. Fisher, *The Bolsheviks and the World War: The Origin of the Third International* (Stanford, CA, 1940), 284–5. Also see Blänsdorf, *Die Zweite Internationale und der Krieg*, 169–74.

majority of German socialists continued to support the government and thus a policy of peace through military victory.[22]

If the differences between the principal socialist parties proved insurmountable during 1915 and 1916, by early 1917 political developments within each party had combined with international events to place the question of practical cooperation on the agenda. The SFIO initially opposed any interaction with socialists from enemy countries: in December 1915 the party's congress voted against a proposal for an international socialist conference by 2,759 to 72.[23] At the same time, the SFIO was deeply committed to socialist internationalism—a commitment reflected not simply in its name (*Section française de l'Internationale ouvrière*) but also in the cult of Jean Jaurès, the party's leader who had been assassinated on the eve of war and whose prominence within the pre-war International had helped to transform socialist internationalism into a familiar practice for French socialists.[24] This ongoing commitment manifested itself during the war in growing calls for the renewal of cooperation with foreign socialists—from both allied and enemy countries. As early as May 1915, the SFIO's Haute-Vienne Federation openly criticized the party's intransigence on this score.[25] The following year, at the SFIO's national council in August, a resolution in favour of renewing relations with enemy socialists received over a third of the votes (1,075 of 2,899). By then an organized minority had formed within the party, whose members, despite their divisions over tactics and ultimate goals, were united in their opposition to the majority's support for the government and its pursuit of peace through military victory. In a lengthy circular in November 1916, the minority argued that in refusing to meet with enemy socialists the majority betrayed not only the International but also the hopes for peace. Interestingly, the circular pointed to developments within the SPD, arguing that a similar minority among German socialists needed to be encouraged: 'What real solidarity have we shown to those who, at the price of sacrifices that we ignore, struggle in Germany against the state of siege, of absolutism, of pangermanism? *Our silence and our distance deliver them to their enemies—who are our enemies.*'[26] That the minority's arguments were gaining ground became evident at the SFIO's annual congress in December 1916. This time a resolution calling for an immediate meeting of the International's bureau received almost half the votes: 1,407 for and 1,437 against.[27] In defending the resolution, Longuet underscored the SPD's willingness for a meeting, claiming

---

[22] See Labour Party, *Report of the Annual Conference of the Labour Party...January 26th, 1916, and two following days* (London, 1926), 31; and Ebert's comments in 'Protokoll der Sitzung des Parteiausschusses vom 7., 8. und 9 Januar 1916', reproduced in Dieter Dowe, ed., *Protokolle der Sitzungen des Parteiausschusses der SPD 1912 bis 1921*, Band I (Berlin/Bonn, 1980), 232–4.

[23] Kriegel, *Aux origines du communisme français*, I, 122–3.

[24] For Jaurès, see Gilles Candar and Vincent Duclert, *Jean Jaurès* (Paris, 2014), 414–30, 451–71; and Harvey Goldberg, *The Life of Jean Jaurès* (Madison, WI, 1962), 417–57.

[25] SFIO, Fédération de la Haute-Vienne, 'Rapport', 15 May 1915, reproduced in *Le mouvement ouvrier français contre la guerre, 1914–1918* vol. VI, *La minorité du Parti socialiste* (Paris, 1985).

[26] 'Circulaire de la Minorité du Parti socialiste Section française de l'Internationale aux Fédérations', November 1916, reproduced in ibid. Emphasis in original.

[27] Kriegel, *Aux origines du communisme français*, I, 113–42; and Fainsod, *International Socialism and the World War*, 110–11.

that 'German socialists…have made satisfactory declarations concerning the points that interest us the most.' The SFIO, he deplored, had become the sole obstacle to a revival of international socialist relations; it 'must end this attitude'.[28]

By the end of 1916 the resistance of the SFIO majority to a renewal of international socialist cooperation was frittering. Ironically, the majority found itself a prisoner of its earlier position. From the beginning, the majority had acknowledged the emergence of a minority within the SPD, admitting that its elements constituted potential interlocutors. As the majority's resolution at the SFIO's 1915 congress noted:

> The [French] Socialist party views as a reason for hope in the resumption of international socialist relations the growing distinction [within the SPD] between imperialist socialists and a minority.

> It is the growth of this minority which can save the honour of international socialism and which perhaps lays the groundwork, if this minority is energetic and far-seeing, for the renewal and salvation of the German people.[29]

To be sure, the majority sought to safeguard itself by attaching impossible conditions to any meeting with the German socialists: the latter must denounce Germany's sole responsibility for the origins and continuation of the war. As Pierre Renaudel, an SFIO majority leader, explained at Labour's annual conference in January 1916, '[u]ntil the best elements of [sic] the German Social Democracy take effective action…the position of the French Socialists cannot change, and the continuance of the war is inevitable.'[30]

The problem for Renaudel and his allies was that intransigence was losing its appeal within the SFIO. At the SFIO's congress in December 1916, a resolution, approved by 1,537 to 1,407 votes, softened the preconditions for a possible encounter with German socialists: rather than an open break with the German government, it simply asked the SPD to clarify its war aims.[31] Soon afterwards, at Labour's annual conference in January 1917, the weakness of the SFIO majority was apparent. Representing the latter, Renaudel sought to up the ante on discussions with enemy socialists, making them conditional on regime change in Germany—on the advent of what he called a 'real and powerful German democracy'. Renaudel, however, was challenged by Longuet, the minority's representative, who reminded the Labour conference that his faction 'had been growing and growing' and would likely soon become the majority. When it did so, moreover, the new majority would insist on an international socialist conference attended by all socialist parties. European socialism, Longuet explained, had 'been a little bit taken by the war' and 'had perhaps forgotten a little bit their constant pre-occupation of the past which had been to emphasize the link between the proletariat of all countries'.

---

[28] 'Au Congrès Socialiste. Le débat sur la politique générale', 29 December 1916, 1–2; and 'Au Congrès Socialiste. Les résolutions', 30 December 1916, 1, both in *L'Humanité*.

[29] See 'Manifeste du Congrès national', 29 December 1915, reproduced in SFIO, *Le Parti socialiste, la guerre et la paix* (Paris, 1918), 133.

[30] Labour Party, *Report of the Annual Conference of the Labour Party…January 26th, 1916*, Renaudel, 115.

[31] 'Au Congrès Socialiste. Le débat sur la politique générale', *L'Humanité*, 29 December 1916, 1–2.

The message was clear: socialists must unite across the belligerent divide to put an end to the war.[32]

As French and British socialists were well aware, dramatic developments were underway within the SPD. Within the SPD's parliamentary *Fraktion*, a growing minority criticized the government's purpose and conduct. In public expression of this disquiet, in June 1915 Karl Kautsky, Eduard Bernstein, and Hugo Haase issued a manifesto that questioned whether the war was in the best interests of German workers, given the signs of the government's expansionist war aims. If their manifesto fell short of calling for peace negotiations, across Germany a vocal minority demanded that socialists work actively for a clear break with the government. Indeed, at the local level a growing opposition movement to the SPD's support for the war effort could be detected. Although few socialists questioned the legitimacy of national defence, a growing minority protested what they perceived as the SPD's identification with a government and regime unwilling to consider any alternative to peace through military victory. By 1916 this minority had become the majority in Berlin. Meanwhile, in March 1916 the SPD's *Fraktion* expelled twenty dissidents for voting against war credits in the *Reichstag*, who promptly created their own parliamentary group. By now SPD divisions ran too deep to be patched over, and in early 1917 a split occurred with the creation of the Independent German Social Democratic Party (USPD).[33]

Although divided on doctrinal and tactical issues, the USPD's members were united by an ardent desire to work actively with foreign socialists for a negotiated peace. Speaking at the USPD's founding congress in April 1917, Hugo Haase, the party's chairman, accused the SPD of being insincere in its claims to favour peace through international socialist cooperation:

> Has the party leadership done anything for peace? Yes with declarations! But declarations are [useful] when one wants to talk about peace but does nothing to bring together the international representatives of the working class. [Or] when one wants to talk about peace and receive credit [for doing so] in order to make possible a war without end (enthusiastic applause) such talk of peace cannot have any effect.

The SPD, Haase continued, had sacrificed the 'confidence' of foreign socialists in German socialism. Kurt Eisner, a socialist leader from Munich, echoed Haase on this point, adding that the USPD's urgent task was to win back the International's trust. Approved by all but one delegate, the manifesto issued at the end of the congress confidently proclaimed that 'no insurmountable difficulty' stood in

---

[32] Labour Party, *Report of the Annual Conference of the Labour Party…January 23rd, 1917, and three following days* (London, 1917), 130–2.

[33] Robert E. Wheeler, *USPD und Internationale: Sozialistischer Internationalismus in der Zeit der Revolution* (Frankfurt am Main, 1975), 16–28; and Miller, *Burgfrieden und Klassenkampf*, 133–77. For Berlin, see Ottokar Luban, 'Der Kampf der Berliner SPD-Basis im ersten Kriegsjahr gegen die Kriegskreditbewilligung', *Jahrbuch für Forschungen zur Geschichte der Arbeiterbewegung* 2 (2014), 53–65. Also see David McKibben, 'Who Were the German Independent Socialists?: The Leipzig City Council Election of 6 December 1917', *Central European History* 25 (1992), 425–42.

the way of 'the renewed revival of the International and the activation of workers in its realm'.[34]

The emergence of a strong minority and then a breakaway party increased the pressure on the SPD to renew contacts with the Entente socialist parties. Faced with the deepening divisions among German socialists over the question of peace, SPD leaders organized a national conference in September 1916 to consider party policy. At the conference, leading dissidents and future USPD leaders such as Haase castigated the party for its support of the government's imperialist 'war of conquest'. The SPD, they argued, had a responsibility before the International not only to denounce Germany's expansionist war aims, but also to work with Entente socialists for a negotiated end to the war. Admittedly, the majority succeeded in forcing through a resolution declaring the SPD's determination to defend Germany against the 'destructive and conquering aims' of its enemies. But the resolution also proclaimed the SPD's readiness to cooperate with foreign socialists in the search for a negotiated peace, even if it blamed British and French socialists for the absence of such cooperation. In their speeches, Friedrich Ebert and Philipp Scheidemann, two of the majority's principal spokesmen, both emphasized the SPD's interest in reactivating the International. As Ebert intoned, 'all [socialist] forces must [unite] on one point: to concentrate on peace.'[35]

Although the USPD's creation removed the staunchest proponents of internationalism from their ranks, the majority socialists (MSPD) would continue to call for the renewal of international socialist cooperation. One reason they did so was to deny the USPD sole rights to the mantle of socialist internationalism. But the MSPD's interest in socialist internationalism was not simply instrumentalist. Before the war the Germans had been at the centre of the Second International: possessing the largest and best organized labour movement in Europe, the SPD was widely recognized as the pre-eminent party. To be sure, in assuming a leadership role, German socialists sought to shape the International's policy positions to their own advantage, provoking the ire of other parties, the SFIO among them. But the SPD's extensive pre-war engagement with international socialism also meant that the latter became an integral element of the party's understanding of socialism. Evidence for this comes from the wartime writings of Eduard Bernstein. Although best known as a father of Marxist reformism, Bernstein was also a fervent internationalist who during 1915–1916 sought to overcome the growing split within the SPD by appealing to the party's traditional commitment to socialist internationalism. The 'principal value' [*Hauptwert*] of the International, he explained, lay in its 'considerable moral effect'. The 'sense of belonging to an international movement' not only encouraged German socialists to look beyond their own narrow 'situation regarding state and society'; it also imbued them with an 'expansive

---

[34] *Protokoll über die Verhandlungen des Gründungs-Parteitages der U.S.P.D. von 6. bis 8. April 1917 in Gotha* (Berlin, 1921), reproduced in *Protokolle der Parteitage der Unabhängigen Sozialdemokratischen Partei Deutschlands. Band 1, 1917–1919* (Glashütten im Taunus, 1975), 13–14, 73, 79–82.

[35] SPD, *Protokoll der Reichskonferenz der Sozialdemokratie Deutschlands vom. 21., 22. und 23. September 1916* (1916), 18–22, 39–41, 73–5, 91–2. Also see Miller, *Burgfrieden und Klassenkampf*, 133–43.

idea or ideology' of solidarity that was vital to socialism's success as a mass political movement. Bernstein—like most German socialists—could not conceive of socialism in exclusively national terms, cut off from the larger international socialist community.[36] If the passions unleashed by the war certainly challenged this sense of community, they did not destroy it.

THE STILLBORN STOCKHOLM CONFERENCE (1917)

At the beginning of 1917 no end appeared to be in sight to a war that had already produced millions of casualties and was placing mounting strains on belligerent nations and societies. In Berlin food shortages provoked protests beginning in 1915, and in 1916 anti-war demonstrations occurred. Between 1916 and 1917 the number of French strikes more than doubled and the number of strikers increased sevenfold, jumping from 41,000 to 294,000. Britain also experienced rising strike activity.[37] Armies, meanwhile, were being pushed to breaking point and even beyond: in the fall of 1917 numerous French army units would refuse orders to occupy front-line positions. In this context, it is hardly surprising that the idea of a negotiated peace attracted growing support within the belligerent countries. Important here was Woodrow Wilson's 'peace without victory' speech in January 1917 in which the American president sought to prod the belligerent powers into negotiations by asking them to state their peace terms. In doing so, Wilson placed the issue squarely on the public agenda. But for European socialists at least, it would take the Russian Revolution in February 1917 to transform the mounting interest in a negotiated peace into a flurry of activity. A month after the revolution the Petrograd Soviet issued an appeal to the 'peoples of the entire world' to work together for peace, which by May became a call for 'an international conference of all Socialist parties and fractions of all countries'. Unwilling to leave matters to the Russians, Dutch and Scandinavian socialists jointly appealed for a meeting in Stockholm of all socialist parties and trade unions.[38]

The initial reaction to the Dutch-Scandinavian initiative was less than positive. Predictably, the SFIO's minority reacted favourably to what it perceived as an opportunity to end the war through negotiation.[39] Yet all its efforts could not prevent the SFIO's executive from rejecting the Dutch-Scandinavian invitation,

---

[36] Eduard Bernstein, 'Der Wert der Internationale der Arbeiter' in *Sozialdemokratische Völkerpolitik. Die Sozialdemokratie und die Frage Europa* (Leipzig, 1917), 73–82. For Bernstein's pre-war Marxist reformism, Manfred B. Steger, *The Quest for Evolutionary Socialism: Eduard Bernstein and Social Democracy* (Cambridge, 1997).

[37] Eley, *Forging Democracy*, 131–8. For comparative figures, see Leopold H. Haimson and Charles Tilly, eds., *Strikes, Wars, and Revolutions in an International Perspective: Strike Waves in the Late Nineteenth and Early Twentieth Centuries* (Cambridge, 1989).

[38] David Kirby, 'International Socialism and the Question of Peace: The Stockholm Conference of 1917', *Historical Journal* 25 (1982), 709–10; and Fainsod, *International Socialism and the World War*, 130–6.

[39] See '2e Circulaire de la Minorité du Parti Socialiste (Section française de l'Internationale) aux Fédérations', 6 May 1917, reproduced in *Le mouvement ouvrier français contre la guerre, 1914–1918* vol. VI.

principally because the majority of socialists suspected the neutral socialists of being instruments of the SPD's majority. Shortly afterwards, Labour's executive committee followed suit, voting nine to four with two abstentions against sending representatives to the proposed conference, prompting Ramsay MacDonald to rail privately against the 'stupidity of some of its [NEC's] members'.[40] Unlike the SFIO and Labour, the MSPD evinced considerable interest in a conference. Admittedly, many majority socialists remained committed to a military victory. Writing to Hjalmar Branting in March 1917, Albert Südekum, an SPD leader with close ties to the government, contended that the Entente powers (and their socialist allies) sought to 'knock Germany to the ground and to expel it from the ranks of the great powers'; for German socialists the choice was either 'to win [the war] or to perish'. But even Südekum expressed the hope for a post-war revival of the International, adding that this would require a strong SPD since German socialists had served as the pre-war International's 'backbone'.[41] Four months after Südekum's letter, the MSPD allied with several political parties in the *Reichstag* to issue a 'peace resolution' calling for a negotiated end to the war based on no annexations or indemnities.[42] Significantly, the previous month a high-level MSPD delegation had travelled to Stockholm to discuss the subject with Dutch and Scandinavian socialists, who, exploiting the Soviet proposal, had sent a questionnaire to all socialist parties with the intention of organizing a conference, most likely in Stockholm. In the preliminary talks in Stockholm, Ebert promised that the MSPD would be flexible.[43]

In reply to the questionnaire, the MSPD published a memorandum essentially proposing a peace based on the pre-war status quo—hence its rejection of all annexations and indemnities. Hence also, its ambivalence towards the principle of national self-determination. While accepting the principle, the MSPD did not necessarily equate it with national independence. Rather than the latter, the memorandum spoke of greater political autonomy for distinct groups within existing political structures. If the MSPD chiefly had in mind its own contested regions (Schleswig, Posen, Alsace-Lorraine), the Austrian socialists strongly endorsed this suggestion, no doubt with the multi-ethnic Austro-Hungarian Empire in mind. After outlining several principles for a post-war international order, including compulsory arbitration, disarmament, and freedom of communication, the MSPD's memorandum reiterated the party's readiness to attend an international

[40] For the French and British votes, see Rudolf Klepsch, 'Die britische Sozialdemokratie und das Projekt einer internationalen sozialistischen Friedenskonfernez im Frühjahr/Sommer 1917', *Archiv für Sozialgeschichte* 26 (1986), 240; and Marquand, *Ramsay MacDonald*, 212.

[41] AABS, Hjalmar Branting, 91/3/1/15, Südekum to Branting (Social-Demokraten), 24 March 1917, with attached: 'Deutschland und die Krieg. Ein Wort an die schwedischen Sozialdemokraten'.

[42] On this subject, see Wilhelm Rinhegge, *Frieden für Europa. Die Politik der deutschen Reichstagsmehrheit 1917/18* (Essen, 1988), 177–85. But also see Friedhelm Boll, *Frieden ohne Revolution? Friedenstrategien der deutschen Sozialdemokratie von Erfurter Programm 1891 bis zur Revolution 1918* (Bonn, 1980), 214–35.

[43] 'Sitzung der MSPD-Delegation in Stockholm, 4. Juni 1917', consulted online at: http://www.socialhistoryportal.org/stockholm1917/documents/111576.

socialist conference 'because we believe it to be the self-evident duty of every socialist who works for peace'.[44]

In its memorandum the MSPD urged other socialist parties to produce a similar document. The newly founded USPD proved eager to do so, submitting its own memorandum to the Dutch and Scandinavian socialists. Although the USPD's memorandum differed from the MSPD's in several respects, for example, in its call to determine Alsace-Lorraine's future by plebiscite, it too sought to focus attention on achieving peace. Indeed, for the USPD no principle or right justified prolonging the war. The USPD's memorandum thus called on socialist parties in all the belligerent countries to work together to forge a common 'peace programme' and to impose this programme on their respective governments, if necessary by refusing to vote war credits.[45] Any party that refused to do so, a parallel USPD document declared, 'betrays the international proletariat, international socialism [and] forfeits the right to cooperate with the proletarian International'.[46]

Although the SFIO's executive committee had rejected the initial Dutch-Scandinavian proposal for an international socialist conference, the invitation from the Petrograd Soviet was another matter. French socialists feared that the Russian revolution might lead to a separate Russo-German peace, and for this reason alone the SFIO could not simply spurn the Petrograd Soviet. Consequently, the party sent two majority socialists, Marius Moutet and Marcel Sembat, to Russia to strengthen the resolve of Russian socialists (the dominant element in the provisional Russian government) to remain in the war against the Central Powers. Significantly, on their return to Paris in May 1917 Moutet and Sembat both urged the SFIO to respond favourably to the idea of an international socialist conference in Stockholm. Although Albert Thomas, the minister of armaments and a leading *majoritaire*, warned that a conference would be a 'trap [*guet-apens*] for a peace on German terms', such warnings proved unavailing.[47] Following a lengthy debate at the SFIO's national council in May 1917, the minority triumphed, pushing through a resolution in which French socialists publicly joined their 'Russian comrades' in 'calling for a meeting of the International'. The SFIO's minority—the eclectic grouping in favour of a renewal of international socialist relations in order to bring about a negotiated peace—was on the verge of becoming the majority.[48]

---

[44] 'Die deutsche Sozialdemokratie und der Frieden. Erklärung der Delegation der deutschen Sozialdemokratie auf der internationalen sozialistischen Friedenskonferenz in Stockholm', 12 June 1917, reproduced in SPD, *Protokoll über die Verhandlungen des Parteitages der Sozialdemokratischen Partei Deutschlands. Abgehalten in Würzburg vom 14. bis 20. Oktober 1917* (Berlin, 1973 reprint), 39–44.

[45] 'Memorandum du Parti Socialdémocrate Indépendant', undated but June 1917, reproduced in *Conférence internationale socialiste de Stockholm 1917* (Geneva, 1980, reprint), 411–13.

[46] USPD, 'Erklärung der Delegation der USPD vor dem Holländisch-skandinavischen Komitee, o.D. [June 1917]', consulted online at: http://www.socialhistoryportal.org/stockholm1917/documents/111612.

[47] 'Lundi 18 Juin 1917—2e Journée de Stockholm' in 'Journal de Russie d'Albert Thomas', *Cahiers du monde russe et soviétique* 14 (1973), 189.

[48] 'Le Conseil National du Parti Socialiste. Cachin et Moutet retour de Russie rendent compte de ce qu'ils ont vu et entendu', 28 May 1917, 1–2; and 'Le Conseil National accepte d'enthousiasme la conférence internationale demandée par les socialistes russes', 29 May 1917, 1–2, both in *L'Humanité*. Also see Ducoulombier, *Camarades*, 31–121.

The majority's leaders were not prepared to accept defeat so easily. Writing to Branting in September 1917, Renaudel insisted that he and his 'French friends' fully supported the holding of an international conference, so long as one of its goals was to 'establish and to <u>punish</u> from an internationalist point of view' the responsibility of the Central Powers and their socialist parties for the war.[49] More concretely, the *majoritaires* worked hard to influence the commission established to draft the SFIO's response to the Dutch-Scandinavian questionnaire.[50] Predictably perhaps, the resulting document was somewhat confusing. Reflecting Wilson's influence, it sketched out a future international order in which arbitration, disarmament, freedom of commerce, and an international organization (*Société des nations*) would prominently figure. Much like the MSPD's memorandum, the SFIO's endorsed the principle of national self-determination in general, including Alsace-Lorraine. In proposing a plebiscite for the latter, however, French socialists sought to distinguish themselves from the MSPD, which was prepared at most to accept greater autonomy for the region within Germany. On the question of war responsibility, the SFIO offered a compromise: while identifying capitalism and imperialism as the principal long-term causes of conflict, the memorandum blamed the Central Powers for the immediate origins of the war and singled out Germany for its violations of international law, especially its invasion of neutral Belgium. For international socialism to have any moral authority, the SFIO insisted, all socialist parties must acknowledge these crimes. Going further, the memorandum suggested that a conference depended on regime change—on German socialists acting to create 'democratic institutions'. It then stepped back from this demand, claiming instead that the SFIO's participation in any conference required all socialists to recognize the right to national self-defence 'in the case of belligerent aggression'.[51]

The SFIO's ambivalence towards an international socialist conference made Labour's position on the subject all the more important. Indeed, both French and German socialists attached considerable importance to the British. That they did so is in some ways surprising. Before 1914 the Labour Party was a relatively minor actor within the international socialist community, viewed by many Continental socialists as parochial; some even believed that Labour was too pragmatic and reformist to be socialist. Admittedly, several scholars have questioned this portrait of Labour's isolation, arguing that before 1914 it was more closely involved with Continental socialist parties than is often thought.[52] Yet Labour's pre-war internationalism can be exaggerated. Much of Labour's international activity was

---

[49] AABS, Hjalmar Branting, 91/3/1/15, Renaudel to Branting, 10 September 1917. Also see AN, Papiers Albert Thomas, 94/AP/356, 'Le parti socialiste et la politique nationale', Thomas speech, 12 August 1917.

[50] See 'Parti socialiste. Commission du questionnaire', *L'Humanité*, 7 June 1917, 1.

[51] 'Réponse au questionnaire en vue de la conférence de Stockholm', reproduced in SFIO, *Le Parti socialiste, la guerre et la paix*, 7–65.

[52] Edward McNeilly, 'Labour and the Politics of Internationalism, 1906–1914', *Twentieth Century British History* 20 (2009), 431–53; Paul Bridgen, *The Labour Party and the Politics of War and Peace, 1900–1924* (Woodbridge, 2009); Berger, *The British Labour Party and the German Social Democrats*, 207–37; and Douglas J. Newton, *British Labour, European Socialism and the Struggle for Peace, 1889–1914* (Oxford, 1985).

undertaken by ILP members, who constructed their internationalist identity in opposition to what they understood as Labour's insularity. As Paul Ward has shown, moreover, patriotism ran deep in the pre-war British left. British socialists revelled in their uniqueness, using their sense of 'Englishness' as a means to denigrate foreign socialism.[53]

Labour's relative insularity before 1914 is worth underscoring because it throws into relief the sea change that occurred during the war. The party went from being a secondary player within the International into a major and even leading one, replacing the SPD as the dominant party. Although Labour's emergence was an evolutionary process, 1917 proved to be a decisive year. And here the question of a conference in Stockholm served as a springboard, helping to launch Labour to the fore of international socialist politics. Although Labour's executive had rejected the initial Dutch-Scandinavian proposal for a conference, party leaders readily endorsed the initiative of the Petrograd Soviet. Significantly, the key impetus came not from Ramsay MacDonald or the ILP but from Arthur Henderson, Labour's chairman and minister without portfolio in the British war cabinet. As late as early 1917, Henderson had been an outspoken proponent of peace through victory, declaring that this position had been agreed to among Allied socialists in February 1915. 'If that policy was right then', he contended in January 1917, 'it was right to-day.'[54]

Soon afterwards, however, Henderson's position changed. In May 1917 the British government sent Henderson to Russia to try to persuade Russian socialists to keep their country in the war on the Allies' side. Although Henderson had earlier been opposed to a renewal of relations with socialists from the Central Powers, on his return to London in July he quickly set out to overcome opposition to Labour participation in the proposed Stockholm conference. At a special Labour congress in August 1917, Henderson urged the party to accept the Petrograd Soviet's invitation to an international socialist congress, so long as the deliberations were merely consultative and not binding on the individual parties. After much debate the resolution encapsulating Henderson's position passed by 1,846,000 votes to 555,000.[55]

Why did Henderson push so hard for a conference? Jay Winter argued that during his mission to Russia the Labour leader concluded that the Stockholm conference was necessary to strengthen Russian socialists in order to keep the Bolsheviks at bay and Russia in the war on the Allies' side. Rudolf Klepsch, by contrast, places more emphasis on domestic political considerations. By the summer of 1917 Henderson had become uncomfortable with his party's support of the government, whose manpower policies were encountering growing opposition among rank-and-file trade unionists. Participation in the Stockholm conference, which

---

[53] Paul Ward, *Red Flag and Union Jack: Englishness, Patriotism and the British Left, 1881–1924* (Woodbridge, 1998). For the ILP, see McNeilly, 'Labour and the Politics of Internationalism'.

[54] Labour Party, *Report of the Annual Conference of the Labour Party...January 23rd, 1917*, Henderson, 87–8.

[55] Klepsch, 'Die britische Sozialdemokratie und das Projekt einer internationalen sozialistischen Friedenskonfernez im Frühjahr/Sommer 1917', 256–7, 267–70; and 'British Labour Conference', *London Times*, 11 August 1917.

the government opposed, would allow Labour to break with the coalition government as one part of a larger effort to refashion the party as an independent and avowedly socialist political organization.[56] If Winter and Klepsch's arguments have their merits, both downplay Henderson's interest in the Stockholm conference as a means of achieving a negotiated peace. By 1917 the war had entered its third year with no end in sight. Just as importantly, the Petrograd Soviet's call for a peace without annexations or indemnities—and the evasive responses of the British and French governments—raised suspicions about the nature of Allied war aims. For Henderson it was clear that the outcome of the war could not be left to armies alone; nor could the subsequent peace be left to governments. If the 'great British Labour and Socialist movement' chose 'not to use the political weapon to supplement our military activities', he declared in August 1917, 'I will venture to predict that you as a movement will regret it hereafter.'[57] What Henderson had in mind was for British—and Continental—socialists to launch a political process aimed at breaking the ongoing deadlock between the belligerent governments on the issue of peace negotiations.

Henderson was not proposing peace at any price. He believed in Germany's special responsibility for the war. That 'German tyranny and her [*sic*] scheme for world domination' had to be defeated was an article of faith.[58] Yet at the time, Henderson opposed those British and European socialists who sought the same peace through military victory. An international socialist conference would help to reconcile these two positions. A principal purpose of a conference would be to prod the SPD to move in the direction of the USPD, a party he admired. At the conference the delegates would draw up a peace programme that contained an implicit (and, more likely, explicit) condemnation of the German government's responsibility for the outbreak of war as well as of its war aims. This programme, Henderson believed, would help to convince the 'German people that it was the crime of their rulers that caused the war, and it is the crime of their rulers that now prevents its just settlement'.[59] More concretely, a conference would strengthen not only the USPD, but also those German socialists within the MSPD critical of their party's wartime policy. The result would be increased political and public pressure within Germany for substantial democratic reform, which Henderson viewed as a requirement for peace negotiations. Thus, while Henderson and the SFIO's *majoritaires* both sought to attach conditions to a conference, most notably that the question of responsibility for the war be included on the agenda, they did so for opposite reasons. Whereas the latter hoped that conditions would effectively sabotage any

---

[56] J.M. Winter, 'Arthur Henderson, the Russian Revolution and the Reconstruction of the Labour Party', *Historical Journal* 15 (1972), 753–73; Klepsch, 'Die britische Sozialdemokratie und das Projekt einer internationalen sozialistischen Friedenskonferenz im Frühjahr/Sommer 1917', 245–54; and Klepsch, *British Labour im Ersten Weltkrieg. Die Ausnahmesituation des Krieges 1914–1918 als Problem und Chance der britischen Arbeiterbewegung* (Göttingen, 1983), 69–202.

[57] 'British Labour Conference', *London Times*, 11 August 1917.

[58] MUL, Noel Edward Buxton Papers, carton 2, Henderson to Buxton, 2 January 1917; and Henderson, *The Aims of Labour* (New York, 1917), 49.

[59] 'British Labour Conference', *The London Times*, 11 August 1917, 4.

conference, Henderson envisaged them as a means to exert maximum pressure on German socialists.[60]

Henderson's initial hopes were stymied by the French and British governments, which refused to provide passports to socialists to travel to Stockholm. One sign of Henderson's displeasure and disappointment was his decision to resign from Lloyd George's government. Scholars contend that, even if it had occurred, the Stockholm conference would have failed because of the divisions within and between socialist parties. The conference, writes David Kirby, 'was doomed from the start by the inability of the socialist parties of the belligerent countries to return to the principles of internationalism enunciated by the Second International before 1914'.[61] There is something to be said for this. Sharp clashes would certainly have occurred on Alsace-Lorraine and, more generally, on the fraught question of how to apply the principle of national self-determination to the ethnically and linguistically mixed regions of Central and Eastern Europe.[62] That said, to view the Stockholm conference as a failure of socialist internationalism is questionable, if only because an emphasis on conflict obscures what is truly significant about the developments in 1917. Socialist parties from the two belligerent camps had begun talking to each other in a sustained fashion, even if through intermediaries (Scandinavian and Dutch socialists). However reluctantly and whatever their reservations, European socialists had rekindled the practice of socialist internationalism.

RENEWED EFFORTS FOR AN INTERNATIONAL SOCIALIST CONFERENCE: 1917–1918

The refusal of the Allied governments to grant passports for Stockholm did not mark the end of efforts to organize an international socialist conference. Henderson in particular remained determined to transform the international socialist community into an instrument for a negotiated peace. Now, however, he sought to proceed in two steps: the first would be for the Allied socialist parties to work out common peace terms; and the second to use the latter as the basis for forging a common peace programme with the socialist parties from the Central Powers, which each party would then pressure its government to adopt. Henderson accordingly took the initiative in organizing an inter-allied socialist meeting in London at the end of August 1917. At the meeting, three-quarters of the delegates approved a Labour resolution accepting an invitation to the Stockholm conference so long as it remained 'consultative and not mandatory'; as the conference was stillborn, the resolution had no immediate consequences even if it did testify to the mounting

---

[60] For the SFIO's *majoritaires*, see 'Lundi 18 Juin 1917—2e Journée de Stockholm' in 'Journal de Russie d'Albert Thomas', 187–91.

[61] Kirby, 'International Socialism and the Question of Peace', 713. Also see Klepsch, 'Die britische Sozialdemokratie und das Projekt einer internationalen sozialistischen Friedenskonferenz im Frühjahr/ Sommer 1917', 239.

[62] Jürgen Stillig, 'Das problem Elsaß-Lothringen und die Sozialistische Internationale im Jahr 1917', *Vierteljahrshefte für Zeitgeschichte* 23 (1975), 62–76.

support among Allied socialists for discussions with their counterparts from the Central Powers.[63]

More pertinent than the resolution was the memorandum presented by Labour on the subject of war aims. After an almost ritual denunciation of the 'ruthless imperialism of the autocratic governments', the memorandum asked 'whether it is not possible for the united action of the working classes to bring this monstrous conflict to a summary conclusion conformably to the principles of the International'. Continuing, it outlined several principles for peace, including the right to national self-determination for peoples in Europe (but not in the colonies), the creation of a League of Nations, the restoration of devastated areas, freedom of economic exchanges, and international arrangements for the protection of workers. The memorandum ended by declaring that these principles would be 'made more secure if the Socialist International is reconstituted'. Eager to proceed with an international socialist conference, the ILP accepted Labour's memorandum as a 'suitable basis for discussion', even if it added that there 'should be some grading and shading' on specific points.[64]

At the inter-allied socialist conference in London, MacDonald presented a report on the question of an international socialist conference. A peace based on 'justice and liberty', it maintained, could not be achieved by 'simple military victory' or by the 'secret diplomacy' of governments. Accordingly, socialists must organize an international conference to discuss 'the peace conditions that will bring a final end to militarism'—a conference in which minority as well as the majority groups in all parties would participate 'in order to assess the problem [of peace] from all points of view'. In his opening address, Henderson had emphasized the value of consensus, but agreement proved elusive. Not only did the Belgian party emphatically reject the idea of meeting with German socialists, but French socialists appeared divided on the subject. While Longuet backed MacDonald's report, Albert Thomas thought to preclude any gathering. Indeed, the SFIO's instructions to its delegates—instructions inspired if not written by Albert Thomas—insisted that the question of Germany's unique responsibility for the war must top the agenda of any international socialist conference.[65] Yet despite the support of Belgian socialists, Thomas and his fellow *majoritaire* delegates could not prevent the creation of an inter-party commission charged with preparing 'a new inter-allied conference in the aim of [organizing] an international [socialist] conference'.[66]

The lack of consensus among Allied socialists frustrated Henderson, who commented to MacDonald soon afterwards that 'we cannot risk a second failure'.[67]

---

[63] ILP, *Report of the Annual Conference...April 1918* (London, 1918), 10–11.

[64] For Labour's memorandum, see 'British Labour Conference', *London Times*, 11 August 1917, 4; for the ILP memorandum, see 'Rival Socialist War Aims', *London Times*, 29 August 1917, 8.

[65] AN, Fonds Albert Thomas, 94/AP/357, 'Directives pour la Conférence des socialistes', undated but in file of London inter-allied socialist conference, 28–29 August 1917.

[66] 'La Conférence socialiste interalliée de Londres', *L'Humanité*, 4 September 1917, 1–2.

[67] TNA, Ramsay MacDonald Papers, PRO/30/69/1161, Henderson to MacDonald, 18 September 1917.

But the Labour leader remained determined to advance with the aid of the Trades Union Congress (TUC), Britain's umbrella trade union organization. Taking Labour's original document as its starting point, a joint TUC-Labour committee soon produced a draft 'Memorandum on War Aims'. Although the memorandum did not explicitly mention an international socialist conference, this omission was unimportant to Henderson, who viewed the memorandum as a stepping stone towards just such a conference. In a letter to the SFIO's secretary in September 1917, he expressed the hope that the memorandum could provide a 'common working base' for their two parties. Together, he explained, Labour and the SFIO could advance:

> towards a common policy on war aims, rendering the principal question to consider that of the desire for the working class to exercise influence over a peoples' peace. It should thus be possible for the French and English soon to exchange memoranda and to continue our efforts to [discuss] the approach to other countries until we agree on the necessary shape of an agreement that will justify another attempt to organize an international [socialist] conference.[68]

Two noteworthy factors, meanwhile, reinforced Henderson's determination to organize an international socialist conference. The first concerned Russia. Following the Bolshevik revolution in November 1917, Lenin's call for an immediate end to the war rendered the question of a negotiated peace more pertinent than ever. Soon afterwards, Lloyd George and Wilson both issued famous statements on peace terms.[69] For Henderson, the possibility of peace negotiations in the near future made an international socialist conference all the more necessary. Such a conference, he told Branting in February 1918, constituted an 'important step to a people's peace'.[70] Meanwhile, the publication by the Bolsheviks of the secret peace treaties between the Allies stoked suspicions regarding the expansionist war aims of all the belligerents and not just the Central Powers. Writing to Lloyd George in January 1918, MacDonald pressed his case for allowing British socialists to meet with their German and Austrian counterparts. 'I fear this will shock old fashioned diplomats, but this is not an old-fashioned war & its settlement I hope will not be an old fashioned settlement.' Although Henderson was more prudent than MacDonald, he too questioned the aims of the Allied governments. Referring to Henderson, the *London Times* accurately reported in December 1917 that 'Labour is inclined to hold the British and other Allied Governments...under suspicion of designs which are variously called militarist, imperialistic, or annexationist.'[71]

---

[68] AN, Fonds Albert Thomas, 94/AP/406, Henderson (Labour) to Louis Delbreuilh, 29 September 1917. For the memorandum see LHASC, LPA, LSI 1/2–8, Labour and TUC, 'Memorandum on War Aims', 28 December 1917.

[69] For a classic and still valuable study, see Arno J. Mayer, *Political Origins of the New Diplomacy, 1917–1918* (New Haven, CT, 1959).

[70] AABS, Hjalmar Branting, 91/3/1/16, Henderson telegram, 19 February 1918; also see 'Les Délégués alliés reçus au groupe socialiste', *L'Humanité*, 16 February 1918, 1.

[71] TNA, Ramsay MacDonald Papers, PRO/30/69/1162, MacDonald (draft letter) to Lloyd George, 1 January 1918; and 'Labour and War Aims', *London Times*, 29 December 1917, 7.

The second and related factor concerned the SFIO and especially the growing strength of the minority. At the party's annual congress in October 1917, the *majoritaires* succeeded in defeating a minority resolution calling for an international socialist conference without any 'preliminary conditions'. But their victory was razor thin.[72] Time, moreover, clearly favoured the *minoritaires*. At the SFIO's National council in mid-February 1918, the two sides renewed the debate. While Renaudel's resolution in favour of approving war credits narrowly passed (1,548 votes to 1,415 with 19 abstentions), the vote approving Labour's 'Memorandum on War Aims' was strikingly one-sided (2,018 to 218, with 108 abstentions). No less significantly, the commission created to draft the corresponding resolution accepted the need for an international socialist conference without preconditions. Recognizing that opposition was futile, Thomas bowed to prevailing winds. 'In light of the present international situation in which popular movements are demonstrating in all countries', he told the congress, 'wisdom dictates to attend first an inter-allied conference and then an international [socialist] conference.'[73]

Together, the Russian Revolution and the growing strength of the SFIO's *minoritaires* set the stage for the inter-allied socialist conference in Paris in February 1918. Unlike the earlier conference in October, this one ended in consensus. The delegates approved a document based on the 'Memorandum on War Aims' submitted by Labour and the TUC. In addition to outlining positions on a variety of issues (the fate of the Austro-Hungarian and Turkish Empires, the future of the colonial world, and the principles for post-war political and economic relations), the new memorandum declared that an international socialist conference 'would at this stage render useful service to world democracy by assisting to remove misunderstandings as well as the obstacles which stand in the way of world peace'. It also laid out a procedure to follow. All socialist 'organisations' would be asked to make a 'public declaration' that their peace aims conformed to the principles of '[n]o annexations or punitive indemnities, and the right of all peoples to self-determination'. Though admitting that 'vital differences' persisted between the socialists from the two belligerent camps, the memorandum ended on an optimistic note, describing an international socialist conference as an 'opportunity for the delegates from the respective countries now in a state of war to make a full and frank statement of their present position and future intentions, and to endeavour by mutual agreement to arrange a programme of action for a speedy and democratic peace'.[74]

During the conference, Labour delegates sought to impart a sense of urgency. In his opening address, Henderson explained that the war would end in one of three ways: 'militarism', 'exhaustion', or 'conciliation'. While insisting that Labour was

---

[72] SFIO, *Congrès national de Bordeaux 6,7,8 et 9 Octobre 1917, Le Programme d'action du Parti Socialiste* (Paris, 1917); and 'Au Congrès de Bordeaux. Le texte de la motion Pressemane', *L'Humanité*, 11 October 1917, 2.

[73] 'Au Conseil National. Le vote sur le Memorandum britannique', *L'Humanité*, 19 February 1918, 1–2.

[74] LHASC, LPA, LSI 1/27, Inter-Allied Labour and Socialist Conference, 'Memorandum on War Aims agreed upon at the Central Hall, Westminister, London, S.W., on February 20th to 24th, 1918'.

not proposing peace at any price and certainly not a 'German militarist peace', he contended that 'sooner or later the last of these methods must be resorted to'. For conciliation to succeed, however, matters could not be left to 'the old methods of diplomacy'. Instead, socialists must act collectively: 'We must use…[an] inter-national [socialist] conference as an opportunity for removing every obstacle that stands in the way of an honourable[,] just, world settlement.' Going further, MacDonald underscored the importance of working closely with German socialists in the search for a negotiated peace. Though pointing to several individuals as '[o]ur German friends', including Haase, Kautsky, and Bernstein, MacDonald made it clear that Allied socialists must cooperate with all German socialists:

> Some say the German Social Democrats have fallen from grace. I tell you the only way to bring them back from [sic] grace is by facing them with the truth of democracy. Keep them away from us, keep them at arm's length, keep them under the influence of their own Imperialist Governments, keep them under the influence of the imperialism that is preached by certain sections of the Allies, and they will never find grace again; they will never come back to the road they left in 1914. Bring them face to face with ourselves, speak to them once again in the old international language of democratic liberty and democratic idealism, and I do not care how far they have fallen from grace: they will come back.[75]

Henderson was extremely pleased with the results. The conference, he cabled Branting, was a 'great success' and 'unanimity on british [sic] war aims practically secured on all points'. He now looked forward to an 'official agreement' among European socialists on an 'international conference as an important step to a peoples peace'. MacDonald, however, was less optimistic. 'Unanimity has been reached, but upon a very imperfect basis…' he noted in his diary. 'The danger is that it might be regarded as a defeatist document for Germany, & that instead of putting their case in reply the Germans may simply reject it & pull it to pieces as indeed they will find it far too easy to do.'[76]

MacDonald's pessimism soon proved to be well founded. In Paris, the Allied socialist delegates had decided to create a small committee tasked with organizing an international socialist conference. Along with Henderson, its members were Albert Thomas and Emile Vandervelde, both of whom were at best lukewarm towards an encounter with German socialists. As a first step, the committee arranged for copies of the new 'Memorandum on War Aims' to be sent to the social-ist parties of the Central Powers via the International's Bureau. The accompanying letter explained that it was essential to 'ascertain whether or not there exists between the labouring classes of the two groups of belligerent nations common opinions sufficient to make possible a common action against imperialism, and in favour of a democratic peace'. The recipient parties were invited to subject the memoran-dum to 'a conscientious and thorough examination' and to 'make a similar public

---

75 'Labour War Aims', *London Times*, 25 February 1918, 3–4. Also see 'À la Conférence socialiste de Londres', *L'Humanité*, 27 February 1918, 1–2.

76 AABS, Hjalmar Branting Papers, 91/3/1/16, Henderson telegrams, 19 and 26 February 1918; MacDonald is cited in Marquand, *Ramsay MacDonald*, 224.

declaration, either alone or jointly with all the Labour and Socialist organisations of Central Europe'.[77]

For the Allied socialists, it was the MSPD's response that would be decisive. Due to government censorship, the majority of German socialists did not receive an official copy of the letter until early June 1918, though party leaders were aware of the memorandum's content from other sources.[78] In any event, later that month Philip Scheidemann informed Pietre Troelstra, a Dutch socialist, that the MSPD remained committed to participating in an international socialist conference aimed at achieving a 'democratic peace of understanding'. At the same time, Scheidemann did not endorse the Allied socialist memorandum but instead reiterated the MSPD's approval of the peace terms outlined by the Dutch-Scandinavian socialists at Stockholm—terms that resembled closely the MSPD's own memorandum drawn up for the aborted Stockholm conference. To dispel any impression of intransigence, Scheidemann conceded that German socialists would be willing to discuss the issue of war guilt so long as they were given a fair hearing.[79] The following month the SPD replied officially to the Allied socialist memorandum. In a letter published in *Vorwärts*, the MSPD's newspaper, Hermann Müller reaffirmed the MSPD's readiness to participate in a conference. Regarding a 'public declaration', Müller stated that his party 'has always assented to a peace by agreement, which should be concluded without annexations and without contributions, upon the basis of the right of self-determination of the peoples'. For a more detailed exposition, he referred British and French socialists to the MSPD's Stockholm memorandum approved at the party's annual congress in August 1917.[80]

In the end, the Austrian (German), Hungarian, and Bulgarian socialist parties all indicated their general agreement with the Allied socialists' war aims memorandum. The MSPD alone did not offer explicit approval. In an article in *Le Populaire de Paris*, the newspaper of the SFIO's *minoritaires*, Huysmans claimed that the vital point was that the MSPD had accepted the proposals of the Dutch-Scandinavian socialists, something that 'constitutes a step forward and, I dare say, a big step'. In addition to remarking that Allied socialists had never demanded the unconditional acceptance of their memorandum, he pointed to practical political realities: it was too much to ask of the MSPD to endorse publicly a document drawn up by Allied socialists alone, just as the latter could not be expected to approve a German document. Basing his comments on conversations with German socialists, Huysmans insisted that the MSPD was prepared to make concessions on contentious issues, including the fate of Alsace-Lorraine. His conclusion was simple: the moment had

---

[77] LHASC, LPA, LSI 3/6, Letter dated March 1918 and signed by Huysmans and Vandervelde.

[78] See Ebert's comments in 'Kurzbericht über die Sitzung des Parteiausschusses vom 31. Mai 1918', reproduced in Dowe, ed., *Protokolle der Sitzungen des Parteiausschusses der SPD 1912 bis 1921*, II, 561.

[79] IISH, Pietre Jelles Troelstra, 443/1, 'Bericht über die Besprechungen Scheidemanns Troelstra's am 17 Juni [1918]', ms notes; also see LHASC, LPA, LSI 1/10, Huysmans' statement on Troelstra-Scheidemann conversation, undated.

[80] Müller to Huysmans, reproduced in *Vorwärts*, 16 July 1918. Also see Fainsod, *International Socialism and the World War*, 188–91.

come to hold an international socialist conference.[81] Not surprisingly, the SFIO's *minoritaires* agreed. While admitting that the MSPD could have been more forthcoming, Longuet pleaded that its response should not become an 'excuse...for perpetuating the paralysis and death of the International. This game has gone on for too long and the immense majority of the socialist proletariat are fed up with it.'[82]

FINAL EFFORTS FOR AN INTERNATIONAL SOCIALIST CONFERENCE: 1918

Notwithstanding Huysmans and Longuet's pleas, Henderson concluded that the MSPD's response was unsatisfactory. Interestingly, this was not his first reaction. In late July 1918 he wrote that the responses of the socialist parties of the Central Powers were 'most encouraging', adding in particular that 'the German socialists have adopted a new position in their relations with the Allied socialists'.[83] Similarly, in early August Labour's executive judged that the responses merited 'every effort' to organize an international socialist conference. Yet soon afterwards Henderson reversed his position. In a memorandum to Labour's executive, he pointed to inconsistencies concerning which set of peace terms German socialists endorsed, before concluding that the MSPD had adopted a 'definitely hostile attitude...towards the London [Allied socialist] Memorandum'. This being so, the question was whether to go ahead with an international conference without the MSPD but with the other socialist parties from the Central Powers. While admitting that there was 'much to be said' for this option, Henderson ultimately recommended the indefinite postponement of an international conference. One reason was his fear that a conference would 'provoke divisions' among Allied socialists and especially French socialists.[84] But another—and probably more important—reason was Henderson's belief that the MSPD had acted in bad faith. Writing to Branting in September 1918, Labour's chairman complained that German socialists had initially endorsed the Allied socialist memorandum as a starting point for negotiations, only to recant:

> it appeared to me that when one party had invited another to take part in conversations on the basis of socialist principles and the other party replied that they were willing to accept a certain document as the basis of discussion I was obliged to interpret the offer on the assumption that it had been made with a due sense of responsibility. It did not occur to me that the German Majority Socialists expected the Allied Socialists to pass through the furnace of political crises in their respective countries

[81] Huysmans, 'Les socialistes allemands et l'Internationale. Tout justifie l'espoir et l'optimisme', *Le Populaire de Paris*, 29 July 1918, 1.

[82] Longuet, 'Pour l'Internationale. Volonté ouvrière et opposition personnelles', *Le Populaire de Paris*, 24 August 1918, 1.

[83] Henderson, 'German Socialists and War Aims. Mr. Henderson's Reply', *London Times*, 27 July 1918, 8.

[84] Labour Party, NEC minutes, fiche 40, 'Inter-Allied Conference Decisions, February 20–24, 1918. Memorandum by Mr. Henderson', undated but autumn 1918. Also see Inter-Allied Socialist Conference, *The Replies of the Socialist Parties of the Central Powers to the 'Memorandum on War Aims'* (London, 1918).

in order to meet them and then find that they had decided in advance to close their minds to all arguments.[85]

For Henderson, it was not only German socialists but the German people who were not yet ready to 'join in an effort to conclude a peace by understanding'. In another memorandum to Labour's executive, he explained that:

> the process of disillusionment had not been carried far enough among the German people... Much additional work has yet to be done before the German people will be ready... to approach all the problems of peace in the interests of humanity and world democracy, and consistent with the principles of international socialism.[86]

Henderson was hardly alone in his attitude. During the spring–summer of 1918, distrust of the MSPD was widespread among Entente socialists. One reason was the peace of Best-Litovsk, signed between the German and Soviet governments in early March 1918, in which Germany exploited its military superiority and the principle of national self-determination to carve out a massive sphere of dominance in Eastern Europe. Whereas the USPD resolutely condemned the treaty, the MSPD's *Fraktion* agonized over what to do, with some members rejecting its expansionist thrust and others welcoming the prospect of an end to military hostilities on at least one front. But much of this debate was kept secret; what registered with foreign socialists was the final decision to abstain from the *Reichstag* vote—a decision seen as a repudiation of the principle of a peace without annexations and indemnities.[87] Adding fuel to the fire was the MSPD's decision to approve the Treaty of Bucharest between the Central Powers and Romania, which stripped the latter of territory; and perhaps even more influential were the German army's military offensives in the West (the *Kaiserschlacht*), which German and Entente socialists rightly viewed as an effort to impose a peace on German terms. Although the MSPD did not officially endorse the military offensive, its continuing support for war credits was damning. Not surprisingly, those Entente socialists who remained opposed to an international conference capitalized on these events to argue that the MSPD was once again complicit with German imperialism. Referring to the German military offensive in the West, a group of SFIO parliamentarians highlighted the MSPD's silence as proof that German socialists had 'abandoned socialism and international solidarity'—an abandonment already evident in the 'policy of August 4ᵗʰ [1918]'.[88]

As Henderson indicated to Branting, another reason for postponing an international socialist conference was the opposition of the American Federation of Labor (AFL). This factor is worth underscoring because 1917–1918 constituted one of the rare moments when the American labour movement (and American socialists) exerted palpable influence on European socialists. Led by Samuel Gompers, the

[85] AABS, Hjalmar Branting, 91/3/1/16, Henderson to Branting, 12 September 1918.

[86] IISH, BSI, 79, 'Inter-Allied Conference Decisions, February 20–24, 1918'.

[87] Miller, *Burgfrieden und Klassenkampf*, 358–70. Also see the debates in '18.3.1918: Fraktionssitzung' and '22.3.1918: Fraktionssitzung', both reproduced in Erich Matthias and Eberhard Pikart, eds., *Die Reichstagsfraktion der deutschen Sozialdemokratie 1914 bis 1918* (Düsseldorf, 1966), 386–92.

[88] AABS, Hjalmar Branting, 91/3/1/15, Groupe socialiste parlementaire to Branting, 20 April 1918.

AFL, which had initially endorsed American neutrality, reversed its position once the United States entered the war in April 1917, becoming a fervent advocate of peace through military victory. Gompers was thus firmly opposed to any talk of an international conference attended by German socialists, whom he denounced as instruments of the German government. 'Let the German Socialists...cease their false pretenses and underground plotting to bring about an abortive peace in the interest of Kaiserism and the ruling class', he fumed in May 1917. 'Let them cease calling pretended "international" conferences at the instigation or connivance of the Kaiser.'[89] Although the AFL generally sought to keep its distance from 'politics' and from political parties, the growing support among Entente socialists for an international socialist conference—calls echoed not only by the TUC but also by the French trade union organization (the *Confédération Générale du Travail* or CGT) at its July 1918 congress—persuaded Gompers to make an exception. Accordingly, in the autumn of 1918 he undertook a mission to Europe aimed at '[s]trengthening the hands of the pro-war socialists and labor men...'[90]

Having crossed the Atlantic, Gompers took the initiative in convoking an Inter-Allied Labour Conference in London in September 1918. While willing to discuss the terms of a possible peace programme based on Wilson's Fourteen Points, Gompers insisted an outright Allied military victory must be the starting point. As an AFL document circulated before the conference announced:

> We declare it to be our unqualified determination to do all that lies within our power to assist our allied countries in the marshalling of all of their resources to the end that the armed forces of the Central Powers may be driven from the soil of the nations which they have invaded and now occupy; and, furthermore, that these armed forces shall be opposed so long as they carry out the orders or respond to the control of the militaristic autocratic governments of the Central Powers which now threaten the existence of all self-governing people.[91]

Given the growing weight of the United States in international politics, it was all but impossible to ignore Gompers' wishes for an inter-allied conference. And Henderson, like most European socialists, was eager to integrate the American labour movement more fully into the larger international socialist movement. At the same time, he had no intention of allowing the AFL to set the agenda. 'I cannot say how much I regret the failure of the Majority Socialists to respond when the prospects [for an international socialist conference] were so good,' Henderson confided on the eve of Gompers' conference. 'The attitude of the German Majority

---

[89] Gompers to Executive Committee of the Council of Workmen's and Soldiers' Deputies, 6 May 1917, reproduced in Peter J. Albert and Grace Palladino, eds., *The Samuel Gompers Papers*, vol. 10 (Urbana, IL, 1986), 88–9.

[90] See the report on Gompers' mission in William Buckler to Irwin Laughlin, 29 October 1918, reproduced in Albert and Palladino, eds., *The Samuel Gompers Papers*, vol. 10, 549–54. Also see Martin Fine, 'Syndicalisme et réformisme. Samuel Gompers et le mouvement ouvrier français (1918–1919)', *Mouvement social* 68 (1969), 3–13; and Bernard Mandel, *Samuel Gompers: A Biography* (Yellow Springs, OH, 1963), 398–417.

[91] LHASC, LPA, LSI 2/12/12, 'Proposals of the American Federation of Labor Delegates to the Inter-Allied Labor Conference, London, September 17, 18, 19, 1918', undated.

makes it difficult for us to move the Americans in the right direction and I am afraid we shall find... Gompers rigid in his determination not to attend an International during the war.' Henderson, in fact, remained committed to an international socialist conference attended by German socialists, which he viewed as a necessary step towards a negotiated peace. 'We must... continue our efforts... for there is just a danger of feeling in Allied countries hardening in the direction of a fight to the finish which may mean years of war.'[92] From this perspective, a primary purpose of the inter-allied conference was not to close the door to an international conference but to place additional pressure on the MSPD to adopt what Henderson considered to be a more flexible attitude.

The competing conceptions of its purpose quickly manifested themselves during the inter-allied socialist conference itself. On the issue of an international conference with enemy socialists, a committee drafted a resolution based on a Labour party working paper. Having expressed its 'profound regret' at the MSPD's refusal to endorse the Allied socialist war aims memorandum, a position identified as an 'obstacle' to a conference, the resolution went on to recommend that exchanges on the subject continue with the socialist parties from the Central Powers who were more cooperative. The clear aim was to pressure the MSPD—an aim evident in the explicit appeal to the Bulgarian, Hungarian, and Austrian German parties 'to use their influence to modify the attitude of the [majority] Germans'. In the ensuing debate on the resolution, Albert Bourderon, a French *minoritaire*, proposed that the word 'obstacle' be replaced by the more conciliatory 'difficulty'; Longuet vigorously backed the amendment, asserting that he wanted the 'International to use its influence to end the war as soon as possible'. Longuet's speech provoked a reply from Henderson, who insisted that the amendment amounted to the approval of an international socialist conference without any conditions regarding participation. Not only did such a position supposedly contradict what had been agreed upon at the inter-allied socialist conference in February 1918; but it also carried the danger of 'a compromised peace'. With the Labour delegation voting en bloc, Bourderon's amendment was defeated even though 17 of 20 French socialists voted in favour—a vote that indicates the overwhelming support for an international socialist conference within the SFIO.[93]

But if Henderson opposed Bourderon's amendment, he refused to endorse Gompers' position. At the conference the AFL leader portrayed the war not as a struggle for socialism but as a crusade for democracy and freedom against autocracy and militarism. In practice, this meant unconditional support for the Allied governments in their pursuit of military victory. The American people, he intoned, 'wanted to stand unitedly behind the Allies, and were going to fight with them until the end, until democracy and opportunity for emancipation were assured'. In the aim of excluding any possibility of a meeting with German socialists, Gompers

[92] MUL, Noel Edward Buxton Papers, carton 2, Henderson to Buxton, 12 September 1918.
[93] AABS, Hjalmar Branting, 91/4/1/13, 'Inter-Allied Labour and Socialist Conference', undated draft report with minutes. Also see 'Les résolutions de la Conférence ouvrière et socialiste interalliée', *L'Humanité*, 21 September 1918, 1.

proposed that the following sentence be added to the resolution: 'That we will meet in Conference with those only of the Central Powers who are in open revolt against their autocratic governments.' Although Henderson did not comment directly on Gompers' proposal, the British delegation voted unanimously against the amendment, as did the French delegation. In the end, Gompers' proposed resolution won the backing of only the American and Canadian delegations (as well as three Italian socialists).[94]

Two points are worth emphasizing regarding the results of the inter-allied socialist conference. The first concerns the role of Gompers and the AFL. Gompers' experience in London reinforced his dislike of European socialists, whom he found too radical and doctrinaire for his liking. Afterwards, he would increasingly limit his cooperation with Europeans to trade unionists. The dislike, moreover, was mutual. For the French *minoritaires*, American trade unionists were non-socialist and even anti-socialist; they did not belong in an international gathering of socialists.[95] Even Henderson found it frustrating to work with Gompers. This divide between the Europeans and the Americans, evident at the London conference, together with the continued weakness of American socialists, helped to ensure that international socialism after 1918 would remain a predominately European affair.

In the meantime, and this is the second point, Henderson achieved his principal aim: keeping open the possibility of an international socialist conference that would include the German majority socialists. Almost immediately afterwards, moreover, Henderson was galvanized into action by the rapidly evolving course of the war. Beginning in the late summer of 1918, the tide of military and political developments shifted decisively in the Allies' favour. Following the failure of the German spring offensives, the Western allies began their own military offensives against which the German army, profoundly worn down, proved increasingly vulnerable. With its Austro-Hungarian ally on the brink of collapse, the German government at the beginning of October 1918 asked the United States for a ceasefire based on Wilson's Fourteen Points. Sensing the approaching end of the conflict, Henderson believed it imperative that international socialism be in a position to influence intergovernmental peace negotiations. The holding of an international socialist conference thus became more urgent than ever. With this goal in mind, Henderson worked to breathe life into the international executive committee created in London the previous month. Writing to the SFIO with a request for the names of possible members, he explained that 'I trust that I am not mistaken in my belief that we are hastening towards the end of the war, and that any Inter-Allied or International action associated with the present events must be taken without delay.'[96]

[94] AABS, Hjalmar Branting, 91/4/1/13, 'Inter-Allied Labour and Socialist Conference'; and 'War Aims of Allied Labour', *London Times*, 21 September 1918, 3.

[95] See the comments in Bricoux, 'La conférence de Londres', *Le Populaire de Paris*, 23 September 1918, 1.

[96] LHASC, LPA, LSI 3/101, Henderson to Frossard (SFIO), 17 October 1918. Also see ibid., ACIQ, memoranda: 1918–1920, Labour, 'Notes on Representation at the Peace Conference', Leonard Woolf, October 1918.

Henderson's renewed efforts for an international socialist conference received important backing from the SFIO. The SFIO's annual congress in mid-October 1918 marked the moment when the *minoritaires* officially became the *majoritaires* and thus in a position to determine party policy. In the final vote on general policy, the *minoritaire* resolution received 1,528 votes, outdistancing the *majoritaire* resolution by 316 votes. Although at stake in the vote was the SFIO's wartime policy in general—the support for war credits, ministerial participation—the issue of an international socialist conference figured prominently in the deliberations. In an editorial published during the congress, Paul Mistral, a prominent *minoritaire*, emphasized that the latter wanted an immediate conference and would not accept that it 'be indefinitely delayed due to a majority that contents itself with creating difficulties'. At the congress itself, Longuet accused the *majoritaires* 'of having paralyzed this powerful force for international action [i.e. international socialism]'.[97] The contending resolutions highlighted the differences between the two camps on this issue. Whereas the *majoritaire* resolution denounced the 'policies of the imperialist socialists', effectively making an international conference conditional on the MSPD openly revolting against the German government, that of the *minoritaires* called for an international socialist conference as 'rapidly as possible' without preconditions.[98] Immediately after the congress, Longuet announced triumphantly that the outcome represented 'first and foremost the definitive victory of International Socialism'. Two weeks later, L.O. Frossard, a prominent *minoritaire* and the SFIO's new secretary, informed Henderson of his complete support for Labour's efforts to breathe life into the inter-allied committee as a first step towards organizing an international socialist conference.[99]

If during the autumn of 1918 the British and French parties appeared eager to renew international socialist cooperation across the belligerent divide, German socialists were initially more restrained. While the independent socialists continued to agitate in this sense, their majority counterparts were more cautious. In August 1918 Ebert suggested to Victor Adler, the Austrian socialist leader, that he issue a renewed appeal for international socialist cooperation, pointing in particular to favourable developments within the SFIO.[100] Early the following month Ebert published a reply to Henderson's criticisms of the MSPD. Rejecting the Labour leader's accusation of insincerity, Ebert claimed that his party's Stockholm memorandum represented a good-faith effort to reply to the Allied socialist war aims memorandum. The fact that disagreement existed on several concrete issues

---

[97] Mistral, 'Les résolutions de Londres' and 'Au Congrès socialiste. La politique générale du parti', both in *L'Humanité*, 9 October 1918, 1–2.

[98] Interestingly, a third 'centrist' resolution sponsored by Léon Blum among others made no mention of an international socialist conference. For the three resolutions, see SFIO, 'Les motions proposées au vote des Fédérations en vue du prochain Congrès national', *L'Humanité*, 15 September 1918, 3; also see Albert Thomas, 'Les deux conceptions de la conférence internationale', *L'Humanité*, 9 September 1918, 1.

[99] Longuet, 'Ère nouvelle', *Le Populaire de Paris*, 12 October 1918; and LHASC, LPA, LSI 3/92, Frossard (SFIO) to Henderson (Labour), 31 October 1918.

[100] Ebert to Victor Adel, 7 August 1918, reproduced in Parteivorstand der Sozialistichen Partei Österreichs, ed., *Victor Adler. Briefewechsel mit August Bebel und Karl Kautsky* (Vienna, 1954), 662–3.

(the fate of Alsace-Lorraine, for example) should not be used as an excuse to rule out a conference—an argument, it is worth noting, that echoed that of the French *minoritaires*. Similarly, Ebert maintained that it was unfair for one side to attempt to dictate the bases of discussion.[101] Privately, however, party leaders judged the prospects of an international socialist conference to be practically nil. At a meeting of party officials and *Fraktion* members in September 1918, Scheidemann commented bitterly that proposals for international cooperation had met with 'scorn and derision' from Labour and the SFIO. Referring to French and British socialists, he added that: 'We do not want to judge prematurely... but all in all considering what we have experienced from them our hopes are very modest.' The bitter reality, he concluded, was that German socialists were on their own and should expect no help from socialists abroad.[102]

Events, though, quickly put an end to the MSPD's embittered isolation from the international socialist community. As it became clear not only that Germany would have to sue for peace but also that the political consequences of defeat would be far-reaching, German socialists desperately looked abroad for support. At the end of October 1918, the MSPD thus informed Dutch socialists that it accepted Wilson's Fourteen Points as a 'basis for a democratic peace'. 'The task of the International', it continued, 'is therefore to conquer the opposition to these negotiations on this basis wherever it appears... There is therefore an urgent need for an International Socialist Congress.'[103] Soon afterwards, Scheidemann published a lengthy article in *Vorwärts* explaining more fully the MSPD's position. While generally defending the party's wartime policy, he now admitted that German socialists (as with other European socialists) had been swept up in the 'chauvinist tide' unleashed in 1914. More pertinently perhaps, Scheidemann insisted that no convincing reasons now existed to postpone an international socialist conference. Pointing to the recent domestic political changes in Germany, chiefly, the advent of a parliamentary regime, he contended that Germany was no longer a military autocracy but had become a 'bourgeois democracy' with 'a strong socialist current'—similar to France and Britain. European socialists could once again stand united against the common enemy, which was imperialism. As he asked rhetorically: 'So what separates us now if the bourgeois press can no longer draw up a chauvinist caricature of our tactics, or now that imperialism rightly senses the reconstitution of the Red [Socialist] International as a danger for its limitless plans?' The 'entire fate of the world', Scheidemann concluded on a dramatic note, depended on the success of an international socialist conference.[104]

[101] Ebert, 'Zu Frage der Internationalen Konferenz', *Vorwärts*, 6 September 1918, 1.

[102] 'Protokoll der gemeinsamen Sitzung des Parteiausschusses und der Reichstagsfraktion. Montag, den 23 September 1918...', reproduced in Dowe, ed., *Protokolle der Sitzungen des Parteiausschusses der SPD 1912 bis 1921* tome II, 573–4. Also see the comments in BAL 901/55748, 'Die Rede Scheidemanns', *Hamburger Echo*, 24 September 1918.

[103] LHASC, LPA, LSI 3/87, Troelstra et al. to Henderson, 28 October 1918.

[104] Scheidemann, 'Der Frieden und die Internationale', *Vorwärts*, 2 November 1918, 1.

CONCLUSION

The outbreak of war in August 1914 undoubtedly dealt a serious blow to socialist internationalism. With each of the major parties lining up to support their country's war effort, the practice of international socialist cooperation necessarily suffered. The immediate priority became national defence in what British, French, and German socialists all viewed as a defensive war. As the conflict extended beyond the opening phase of military operations and as casualty tolls mounted, mutual bitterness and recriminations further widened the gulf between the socialist parties from the two warring camps. During the first two years of the war, a dominant majority of socialists in Britain, France, and Germany firmly supported their governments in the pursuit of peace through military victory.

Yet though serious, the blow to socialist internationalism was not fatal. From the beginning, dissident socialists in each country lamented the breakdown of international socialist relations. They argued not so much that transnational class solidarities should trump national loyalties but that the two were not mutually exclusive. As the dissidents grew in strength and influence over time, they also became more and more interested in a negotiated end to the war. The result was the creation of minority movements within the SPD and SFIO that challenged the majority's support of the government's war effort. The minority's critique contained several elements, prominent among them the charge that the majority had abandoned the practice of socialist internationalism. The path to a negotiated peace, French and German *minoritaires* maintained, lay through a revival of the international socialist community and, more concretely, an international conference attended by socialists from both the Entente and Central Powers. By early 1917 the widening split within the SPD resulted in the founding of a breakaway party, the USPD, which was self-avowedly socialist and internationalist. Meanwhile, if the SFIO did not split into two during the war, by October 1918 the *minoritaires* were numerous enough to become the new majority and to take over control of the party.

In both the French and German cases, the emergence of a strong minority movement prodded the majority socialists to reconsider not only their support for the government's war effort, but also their hesitations regarding an international socialist conference. Here, moreover, 1917 proved to be a critical year. The Russian and then Bolshevik revolutions placed the issue of a negotiated peace squarely on the agenda of international politics. With Russian (as well as Dutch and Scandinavian) socialists calling for an international socialist conference in Stockholm, the MSPD and the French *majoritaires* both endorsed the proposal. Indeed, French and German socialists found themselves engaged in indirect discussions regarding what, if any, preconditions to attach to a conference. Just as importantly, the issue of the Stockholm conference provided an opportunity for the British Labour Party, under Arthur Henderson's determined guidance, to assume a leadership role in international socialist relations. One of the striking developments in 1917, in fact, is the emergence of Labour as a major actor. Henderson's support for an international socialist conference, moreover, cannot be separated from his growing belief that a negotiated peace was urgently necessary. During 1917 and 1918 Henderson remained convinced that socialist parties from the two warring camps must come together to forge a common peace programme that each party would then press upon its government. And this meant working with enemy socialists—and German socialists above all.

In the end, the Stockholm conference was stillborn. In addition to the obstacles thrown up by the various governments, important differences existed between socialist parties on concrete issues. Chapter 3, which covers the efforts by European socialists to work out a peaceful post-war international order, will discuss these differences in greater detail. But for now the important point is that the flame of socialist internationalism continued to burn. Despite the failure of Stockholm, the British, French, and German parties remained interested in organizing an international socialist conference. Indeed, their interest in such a conference increased during the summer and autumn of 1918 as military and political developments accelerated, opening up the possibility of a rapid end to the war. It is impossible to say whether an international socialist conference would have occurred if the war had dragged on into 1919. But what can be said is that on the eve of the armistice in November 1918, a powerful and widespread desire existed within the major socialist parties for a revival of the practice of socialist internationalism. Once the guns fell silent on the Western Front this desire would manifest itself in efforts to reconstitute the International.

PART I

THE INTERWAR YEARS

2

Reconstituting the International, 1918–1923

As chapter 1 showed, in the autumn of 1918 British, French, and German socialists all called for an international socialist conference. Underpinning this clamour was a renewed commitment to the practice of socialist internationalism that had developed during the war. If anything, the armistice in November 1918 reinforced the collective determination of European socialists to renew their practical cooperation and, more ambitiously, to reconstitute the International. Rather than a negotiated end to the war, the urgent goal now became to influence the upcoming peace negotiations. Only if socialists spoke with one voice, it was assumed, could they help to shape the post-war international order. Initial efforts to cooperate culminated in an international socialist conference in Berne in February 1919 at which socialists from the two wartime camps met for the first time. In the end, however, it would take four years to reconstitute the International with the creation of the Labour and Socialist International (LSI) in 1923. That it took so long to do so is a testimony to the impact of the Great War and the Bolshevik revolution. Together, these two seismic events compelled socialists to reconsider the meaning and purpose of socialism. The search for answers sparked prolonged debates between and within the major parties, profoundly reconfiguring the pre-war world of European socialism. One prominent stake in this lengthy process, moreover, was the nature of socialist internationalism—both its content and its functioning.

This chapter examines this process, covering the period from the armistice in November 1918 to the LSI's founding congress in May 1923. Several points are worth underscoring. First, almost all European socialists during this period believed it to be urgently necessary to reconstitute an effective International. They disagreed, however, on what this entailed, with the result that for a brief moment three Internationals vied with each other for precedence. While multiple Internationals can be taken as a sign of division and weakness, they were evidence of the commitment of socialists to internationalism. Second, it is impossible to understand the period by looking at one party alone. Throughout, debates and developments in one party were influenced by, as well as influenced those in, other parties. If this interactive element was important during the war, it was even more so afterwards when the barriers to inter-party relations were fewer. Third, the Socialist International that emerged in 1923 was not a hollow shell. Although, unlike before 1914, international socialism was now divided into communist and socialist camps, the difficult process of renewal helped to forge close bonds between the member parties of the LSI. In a final and related point, the contents of socialist internationalism would be determined in great part by its practice—by the subsequent efforts of socialist parties to cooperate together on international issues.

TO BERNE: NOVEMBER 1918 TO FEBRUARY 1919

The armistice in November 1918 motivated European socialists to intensify their efforts to organize an international socialist conference. This was certainly true of Labour. Henderson was determined that his party—and the international socialist movement in general—should play a leading role in the making of the post-war international order. In pursuit of this goal, he pursued a two-track policy. One track was to try to get one or more Labour representatives appointed to the British delegation to the upcoming peace conference.[1] It was never likely, however, that Lloyd George would agree to separate representation for Labour at the peace conference. As a result, Henderson quickly focused on the second track—to organize an international socialist conference that would run alongside the intergovernmental peace conference and whose purpose would be to forge a programme of peace that the individual socialist parties would then pressure their governments to adopt. On the very day of the armistice, Labour and the TUC submitted a memorandum to the British government outlining plans for 'a World Labour and Socialist Conference to be held at the same time and in the same place as the Official Peace Conference'. In addition to pointing out that such a conference enjoyed the support of all socialist parties, the memorandum underscored international socialism's desire 'to bear its part in securing a lasting peace'. But while conciliatory in tone, the memorandum also indicated Labour's determination to proceed with or without official approval. 'We presume that the right of British Labour to attend a Conference at any time or place after the hostilities have ceased will not be challenged, but we regard it as important to lay the matter before you.'[2]

Having announced its intentions, Labour moved quickly to organize an international socialist conference. During November 1918 Henderson pressed Belgian, French, and Scandinavian socialists for their cooperation, emphasizing his impatience with delays. Efforts initially centred on Paris, which had been designated as the site for the official peace conference. But the Allied governments soon indicated that they would not allow an international socialist conference to take place in the French capital, principally because German socialists would presumably be present. With the SPD and the USPD both members of the governing coalition in Berlin, any German delegates to an international socialist conference could claim to represent the German government—a government that had not

---

[1] LHASC, LPA, ACIQ, Memorandums 1918–1920, Labour, ACIQ, 'Notes on Representation at the Peace Conference', Leonard Woolf, undated but 1918.

[2] LHASC, LPA, LSI 2/10/12, 'Memorandum on the World Labour and Socialist Conference to be held during Peace Negotiations', 11 November 1918.

been invited to the peace conference.[3] Bowing to reality, Henderson agreed to hold a conference in a neutral country, most likely Switzerland.

Interestingly, political developments within Britain reinforced Henderson's determination to organize an international socialist conference. At the end of November 1918 the government announced that Parliament would be dissolved and an election held in mid-December. For the first time, Labour campaigned as a truly independent party; no less importantly, socialist internationalism figured prominently in its campaign strategy. Labour, its election manifesto read, 'stands for the immediate restoration of the Workers' International', which was presented as an essential element in a 'Peace of International Cooperation'.[4] Early on, moreover, Henderson telegrammed socialist leaders abroad to issue statements 'conveying best wishes to British labour in its fight for ideals of labour international during present eventful general election', and asking them in particular to 'please emphasise importance for lasting puce [*sic*] of political victory for labour on the eve of the peace conference'. Clearly, Henderson sought to promote the association of Labour, socialist internationalism, and peace in the minds of voters.[5] Equally telling, during the election campaign Labour repeatedly committed itself to seeking international socialist approval for any peace treaty negotiated by governments. Given this pledge, Henderson wrote soon afterwards, 'We should be guilty of a betrayal if we did not take all possible measures to have the [international socialist] Conference called together without delay.'[6]

The election itself marked something of a defeat for Labour as the Conservative–Liberal coalition led by Lloyd George won a crushing majority of seats. Henderson even lost his seat, although another one was soon found for him. Labour's electoral defeat, however, did nothing to dampen Henderson's enthusiasm for an international socialist conference. Indeed, the opposite was truer: with Labour all but shut out of any direct influence on the government, more than ever it needed to mobilize international socialism if it were to have any influence on peacemaking. For Henderson, this logic was apparent even before the election results were announced at the end of December 1918. Writing to Émile Vandervelde, the Second International's president, he insisted on the urgency of an international socialist conference. 'The British working class movement is earnestly waiting the meeting of the Conference. The question is being asked on all sides, "Why has it not been called?"' As Henderson was well aware, prominent Belgian socialists, Vandervelde among them, resisted the prospect of a face-to-face meeting with German socialists. The cooperation of Belgian socialists was important, because they dominated the ISB which, in November 1918, had initially been assigned the

---

[3] MAE, Série Y Internationale 1918–1940, 395, Pichon (MAE) to Washington embassy, no. 4346, 22 December 1918; and LHASC, LPA, LSI 15/1/9, Geoff Barnes (FO) to Henderson, 4 December 1918.

[4] 'Labour's Call to the People', reproduced in 'Labour Manifesto', *London Times*, 28 November 1918, 8.

[5] AABS, Hjalmar Branting, 91/3/1/16, Henderson telegram to Branting, undated but November–December 1918.

[6] LHASC, LPA, LSI 3/152, Henderson to Vandervelde, 19 December 1918.

task of organizing a conference.[7] Increasingly impatient and with the opening of the Paris peace conference looming, Henderson in late December indicated that he was prepared to bypass the ISB if necessary. Thanks largely to Henderson's determination, Vandervelde found himself compelled to issue invitations for an international socialist conference. Originally scheduled for January in Lausanne, it would finally take place early the following month in Berne.[8]

One reason Henderson succeeded in imposing his will is that he received strong backing from French socialists. Although the wartime *minoritaires* became the majority in October 1918, the SFIO remained deeply divided. During the autumn of 1918 debate raged within the party over the goals of socialism and especially over its immediate revolutionary potential. Buoyed by their newly found dominance, the ex-*minoritaires* sought to use the issue of an international conference not only to confirm their victory over the ex-*majoritaires*, but also to place their stamp on French and European socialism. Thus the day after the armistice came into effect the SFIO's executive committee voted by thirteen to eleven to demand that the ISB organize a conference of all socialist parties, including those of the Central Powers.[9] Commenting on the decisions, Paul Faure, a prominent ex-*minoritaire*, announced that the time had come for all European socialists committed to revolutionary change to cooperate in a common enterprise. As Faure wrote:

> Today, it appears that nothing in the world can prevent socialist organizations from renewing contacts. Let us hurry up and wave aside any ploys. It is not with Belgian, English or other 'Allied' socialists with which we want to concert but with the proletariat of the entire world. It is possible that we will be more in agreement with German comrades than with socialists who are or have been ministers in bourgeois governments.[10]

For Faure and his ex-*minoritaire* comrades, working with German socialists meant, above all, working with the USPD, which during the war had repeatedly displayed its international socialist colours. The German independent socialists, Longuet proclaimed in November 1918, 'have never stopped opposing the barbaric acts of Prussian militarism'. But it was not only the USPD's wartime oppositional stance that recommended it to Longuet and Faure. Much like the ex-*minoritaires* and unlike the German majority socialists, the USPD was self-consciously internationalist and revolutionary. In the USPD, the French ex-*minoritaires* saw a reflection both of themselves and of the future of European socialism.[11]

---

[7] Ibid. For the POB, see the minutes of its Conseil général, 'Au Conseil général du Parti ouvrier', 19 December 1918, available at: http://www.amsab.be/bwpob/info_fr.htm.

[8] AABS, Hjalmar Branting, 91/3/1/16, Henderson to Branting, 19 December 1918. Also see Gerhard A. Ritter, ed., *Die II. Internationale 1918/1919. Protokolle, Memoranden, Berichte und Korrespondenzen* tome 1 (Berlin, 1980), 38–68.

[9] 'Comission administrative permanente. Séance du 12 novembre', *Le Populaire de Paris*, 14 November 1918, 2.

[10] Pax (Paul Faure), 'Et l'Internationale?', 15 November 1918, 1; and Paul Faure, 'En route pour l'Internationale', 14 January 1919, 1, both in *Le Populaire de Paris*.

[11] Longuet, 'La campagne des haines et l'Internationale', *Le Populaire de Paris*, 24 November 1918, 1. Longuet quickly established personal contacts with USPD leaders. See the military intelligence report in MAE, Série Y Internationale 1918–1940, 395, untitled report no. 3562/2, 8 March 1919.

Not surprisingly, the SFIO's ex-*majoritaires* were far from enthusiastic about the idea of an international socialist conference. Writing to Henderson in December 1918, Thomas remarked that he remained 'completely skeptical' about meeting German socialists.[12] For Thomas, a conference attended by German socialists amounted to a repudiation of the SFIO's wartime policy of support for the government—a policy with which he was closely identified. But more was at stake. For ex-*majoritaires*, the project of integrating the SFIO into a larger European internationalist and revolutionary movement had to be resisted since revolution meant bolshevism, whose aims and methods they rejected. The choice for the SFIO (and for France), Thomas insisted in November 1918, was between Bolshevik revolution and national reconstruction.[13] If the latter entailed 'profound reforms' at home, it excluded revolutionary upheaval. To be sure, some ex-*majoritaires*, like Paul Renaudel, spoke more easily of revolution, as did Léon Blum, who in 1918–1919 emerged as a leader of a centrist group that sought to chart a middle way between the warring factions. But they too preferred a reformist and parliamentary path for French socialism. For the ex-*majoritaires* in particular, their opposition to revolutionary bolshevism prompted them to privilege cooperation with socialist parties committed to reformism, chief among them Labour. The desire to stay close to Labour, in turn, left the ex-*majoritaires* with little choice but to agree to an international socialist conference—as Thomas admitted in his letter to Henderson.

From the start, German socialists supported Henderson's efforts to organize an international conference. For them, the autumn of 1918 was a period of breathtaking change: Germany sued for peace, its political regime was transformed, revolutionary strikes broke out in the major cities, and the MSPD and USPD both entered a coalition government. Although engrossed by developments at home, German socialists needed the international socialist community more than ever in order to safeguard the German people against draconian treatment by the Allies. Thus, on the day the armistice came into effect the MSPD and the USPD jointly appealed to Entente socialists to use their influence to put an end to the Allied blockade and to ensure that the German authorities could feed the population.[14] In the coming months, the focus for the MSPD shifted from the armistice to the upcoming peace terms. Writing in early 1919, Victor Schiff, who soon became *Vorwärts*' foreign policy editor, explained that if a 'just and democratic peace' (which he equated with Wilson's Fourteen Points) were to be achieved, international socialism would have to make its influence felt. During the war, Schiff noted, socialists had failed to organize an international conference; but the situation had changed. 'Now...the war is over and the peace conference looms before us, [and]...the International must collectively be victorious.'[15]

---

[12] LHASC, LPA, LSI 3/102, Thomas to Henderson, 25 December 1918.
[13] Thomas, 'Oui, il faut s'entendre', *L'Humanité*, 16 November 1918, 1.
[14] AABS, Hjalmar Branting, 91/3/1/16, telegram to Branting, 11 November 1918. Also see 'An die Völker der Entente. Ein Aufruf der Arbeiter und Soldaten', *Vorwärts*, 15 November 1918, 1.
[15] Schiff, 'Die Frage der Kriegsschuld in Bern', *Die Glöcke*, no. 43, 25 January 1919, 1342–7.

To be sure, German majority socialists were not naïve. A January 1919 editorial in *Vorwärts*, for example, cautioned against expecting too much from an international socialist conference. Even with the best of intentions, Labour and the SFIO simply lacked the 'effective means' [*Machtmittel*] to impose their will on their governments. Equally important, German majority socialists rejected any notion that the SPD's wartime conduct was uniquely blameworthy. Not only had the party consistently opposed imperialist war aims, but it had also transformed Germany into a parliamentary democracy along the lines of Britain and France. The MSPD, in other words, would not be lectured to by the Entente socialists.[16] The problem for the majority socialists, however, was that they lacked alternative allies abroad. As Karl Kautsky, a leading party theoretician, counselled, the SPD must place its trust in foreign socialists. 'In this trust [in socialists abroad] as well as in our own force must we base the strength of our foreign policy', Kautsky declared in a draft of the SPD's 'action program'. 'Happily [and] shoulder to shoulder with our foreign brothers will we embark on the democratization and socialization of the entire world.'[17] Concretely speaking, this dependence translated into an endorsement of Henderson's call for an international socialist conference, which the MSPD understood as part of the larger project to recreate an international socialist community in which German socialists would once again assume a prominent role.

If the MSPD endorsed the call for an international socialist conference with some reservations, the USPD did so with undisguised enthusiasm. At a meeting of parliamentary delegates in November 1918, the USPD members emphasized the importance of renewing links with socialists abroad. Meanwhile, prominent USPD figures, among them Hugo Haase and Rudolf Breitscheid, sought to enter into contact with French socialists through intermediaries in Switzerland. During 1918–1919, the independent German socialists were especially interested in cooperating with the SFIO now that the ex-*minoritaires* (who shared the USPD's self-conscious internationalism) had become dominant.[18] More generally, the USPD insisted that it was a more effective interlocutor with French and British socialists than the MSPD. Because of the latter's wartime betrayal of international socialism, the USPD's Kurt Eisner explained, the majority of socialists were widely distrusted by foreign socialists. For Eisner, only the USPD possessed the moral authority to speak for German socialism at the upcoming international socialist conference.[19]

---

[16] 'Bern', *Vorwärts*, 26 January 1919, 1–2; and 'Ja, wir haben die Kredite bewilligt!', *Vorwärts*, 3 December 1918, 1–2.

[17] BA-SAPMO, NL Karl Kautsky, NL 4055/2, 'Richtlinie für ein sozialistisches Aktions-Programm', Kautsky, 12 January 1919.

[18] See 'Montag, 15.11.1918: Reichskonferenz', reproduced in Erich Matthias and Susanne Miller, eds., *Die Regierung der Volksbeauftragten 1918/19*, I (Düsseldorf, 1969), 152–91; for contacts, see Harry Kessler, *Tagebücher, 1918–1937* (Frankfurt am Main, 1961), 13 November and 28 December 1918, 29, 85; and for the SFIO, see 'Französische Sozialisten gegen den Chauvinismus', *Die Freiheit*, 4 December 1918, 1.

[19] 'Rede in der 2. Sitzung des Provorischen Nationalrats am 13.12.1918', reproduced in Freya Eisner, ed., *Kurt Eisner. Sozialismus als Aktion: Ausgewählte Aufsätze und Reden* (Frankfurt, 1975), 93–5.

THE BERNE CONFERENCE, FEBRUARY 1919

In early February 1919, eighty delegates from twenty-one parties gathered in Berne. To be sure, there were notable absentees. In addition to the Belgian party, whose leaders refused to meet face-to-face with German socialists, Lenin and his fellow Bolsheviks stayed away, denouncing the proceedings in violent terms. Nevertheless, Berne was noteworthy: for the first time since before the war socialists from the Entente and Central Power countries met together as official delegates of their parties. Just as importantly, the agreements and disagreements between the delegates cut across both parties and belligerent camps.

In the opening address to the delegates, Henderson expressed his satisfaction that a conference was finally taking place as well as his hope that practical results would be achieved.[20] During the week-long conference, the delegates discussed numerous subjects, some of which will be discussed in subsequent chapters; but the focus of this chapter is on the reconstitution of an international socialist community. And here two issues dominated the exchanges between socialists. The first issue concerned the wartime conduct of socialist parties and particularly of the MSPD. Taking the lead, the French ex-*majoritaires* submitted a memorandum demanding an explicit condemnation of the German majority socialists:

> …it is not possible to reconstitute the International if, at the outset, the wartime conduct of socialist parties is not subject to judgement; if it is not made clear that these socialist parties, in the necessary conciliation between national defence and international [socialist] action, cannot…become the accomplices of governments that engaged in deliberate aggression.[21]

Elaborating on the memorandum, Albert Thomas explained that, unlike the USPD, the MSPD had betrayed the cause of international socialism during the war by becoming the 'accomplice' of German imperialism; the latter must accordingly admit 'the crimes' it had committed against 'socialism'. Similarly, Paul Renaudel argued that the question of the MSPD's wartime conduct was a 'moral problem' that international socialism must resolve before moving forward. In accusing the MSPD, Thomas and Renaudel likely had three aims in mind. One was to exclude the party from the international socialist community, at least temporarily; after all, both knew that the MSPD was unlikely to provide an unequivocal repudiation of its wartime policies. A second aim was to strengthen their own position within the SFIO vis-à-vis the ex-*minoritaires*. Any condemnation of the MSPD implied that the ex-*majoritaires* had been justified in supporting the French government's war effort. A third and related aim was to ensure that national loyalties remained a dominant aspect of socialist internationalism. It would be extremely dangerous, Thomas contended, to allow the 'class struggle' to take precedence over 'the national effort, the effort for the life and defense of the nation'. 'For us', he

---

[20] Ritter, ed., *Die II. Internationale 1918/1919*, I, Henderson, 192.
[21] IISH, Pietre Troelstra Papers, 450, 'La reconstitution de l'Internationale', signed Thomas, Renaude, E. Poisson, and Louis Dubreuilh, undated.

added, 'it is impossible to under-estimate the national factor at the present time.' That the German majority socialists said much the same thing was an irony that the French ex-*majoritaires* refused to recognize.[22]

Thomas and Renaudel's speeches provoked a chorus of responses. Speaking for the French ex-*minoritaires*, Paul Mistral noted that the question of responsibility for wartime policies should be extended to the International as a whole. Echoing Mistler, Longuet argued that all parties 'had been tempted more or less by chauvinism', even if the MSPD perhaps more so than others. But Longuet directed his chief criticism at Thomas and the ex-*majoritaires*, whom he accused of having consistently opposed the Stockholm conference and a negotiated peace during 1917–1918. The true representatives of international socialism, he continued, were neither the MSPD nor the SFIO's ex-*majoritaires* but rather the independent German socialists and the ex-*minoritaires*, who together would 'return socialism to the right path from which it had strayed'.[23]

Predictably, the MSPD delegates vigorously defended their party against Thomas' indictment. In supporting the government in 1914, Hermann Müller, who had been sent to Paris during the July crisis to consult with French socialists, argued the SPD had done the same as French and British socialists.[24] As with Müller, Otto Wels, who would soon be named the MSPD's co-chairman (along with Müller), maintained that German socialists—like all socialists—had simply sought to protect their nation and its people at a time of danger. But Wels' chief argument was that European socialists must look forward:

> The reconstitution of the International must be undertaken in cooperation with German social democracy. We must not ignore that in Paris imperialist forces are at work to endanger…a peace of justice and the League of Nations. It is thus our urgent duty…to turn our gaze towards the future…and not backwards where differences [between us] lie and that cause us to butt heads with one another…

If socialists were to exert any influence on the emerging post-war international order then they must be united, which meant setting aside their wartime conflicts. This argument was certainly self-serving: an extended debate on the SPD's wartime conduct would likely benefit the USPD, burnishing its reputation as the guardian of the internationalist flame. But Wels' plea to concentrate on the here and now also reflected a vision of socialist internationalism centred on practical cooperation; working together, socialists from different parties would forge socialist answers to the pressing questions of international politics.[25]

The MSPD's arguments received a frosty reception from the USPD. Kurt Eisner, minister-president of the Bavarian republic from November 1918 to January 1919, dismissed Wels' speech in particular as imbued with the 'completely old spirit' of

---

[22] Ritter, ed., *Die II. Internationale 1918/1919*, I, Thomas, 201–8; Renaudel, 220–9. Also see Pierre Renaudel, *L'Internationale à Berne. Faits et Documents* (Paris, 1919), 60.
[23] Ritter, ed., *Die II. Internationale 1918/1919*, I, Mistral, 208–9; Longuet, 271–4.
[24] Ibid., 243–4.   [25] Ritter, ed., *Die II. Internationale 1918/1919*, I, 210–20.

socialism; the new spirit was one in which nationalism and patriotism were absent and in which socialists were collectively committed to revolutionary change. Eisner thus lambasted the MSPD for having failed to fulfil its socialist duty during the war, which was 'to overthrow the German government, to conquer political power and to make peace'. Significantly, however, Eisner also criticized British and French socialists for failing to grasp the extent of the German revolution. Germany had not merely become a democracy; it was 'today the most radical state in the world' and 'on the verge of [becoming] a socialist state'. With Germany at the vanguard of socialism, the priority for all socialists (German and non-German) was to support the new German republic and the USPD. Indeed, the two were one and the same for Eisner. If this required a reconstituted International, it was one that must be oriented more towards 'immediate action' than towards 'a program for a distant future'.[26]

With French and German socialists divided both between and among themselves, it was left to the British to act as mediators. In a short speech, George Stuart-Bunning, a trade union leader, reminded the delegates that the purpose of the gathering was to influence the peace conference. 'Our object is that all eyes, all hearts, all souls and all forces should be turned to Paris, to Paris every day, to Paris every hour, to Paris every minute of this week.' The longer 'we may talk about responsibilities', he remarked, 'we shall not be influencing the conference in Paris in the direction of the democracy and peace of the world.' More concretely, he asked both the French ex-*majoritaires* and the German majority socialists to compromise on their positions, which, after much heated debate, they agreed to do. The resulting resolution shunted the question of responsibility to a future conference, though it also hinted that the question itself was no longer relevant as the 'old system responsible for the war' had been replaced by a 'new Germany' imbued with a 'revolutionary spirit'.[27] In the end, it is striking how quickly the issue of responsibility was neutralized—an issue that had stirred such bitterness within and between socialist parties since 1914. That the Berne conference succeeded in doing so highlights not only the widespread desire to overcome wartime divisions, but also a tacit consensus that all the major socialist parties had gone too far in supporting their nation's national war effort. One prominent sign of this consensus was the retreat from national politics of several socialists most closely identified with the pursuit of military victory, for example, the SFIO's Albert Thomas, who soon left to become director of the International Labour Office.

The second issue that dominated the proceedings at Berne was Bolshevism. The 1917 Bolshevik revolution had aroused considerable sympathy among European socialists, partly because of the hope that it might open a path towards a negotiated peace. The transformation of revolution into civil war, however, complicated matters. In addition to reports of mass violence and atrocities committed by all sides, socialists had to contend with the threat and then reality of foreign intervention in

---

[26] Ibid., Eisner, 230–43.
[27] Ritter, ed., *Die II. Internationale 1918/1919*, I, Stuart-Bunning, 264–5; and 'Resolution über die Schuldfrage', 316.

Russia's civil war. Exacerbating the confusion was the seeming paucity of reliable information. At the same time, European socialists had difficulty suspending judgement on the civil war. For the Bolshevik project—in terms both of its principles and of its concrete practice—raised questions about the nature of socialism and of socialist internationalism.

The question of attitudes towards Bolshevism initially cropped up during the debates on responsibility. But it was during the last day of the conference that the delegates tackled the issue head-on. And here Ramsay MacDonald took the lead in presenting a resolution on 'democracy and dictatorship'. Having welcomed the revolutions that overthrew 'imperialist and militarist governments' in Russia, Germany, and Austria-Hungary and having denounced all foreign military intervention, the resolution went on to appeal to workers in these countries to construct 'a democracy inspired by the political and economic principles of socialism and liberty'. In his introductory comments, MacDonald recognized that '[w]e are living in absolutely abnormal times' that demanded some flexibility on the part of socialists regarding their 'conception of democratic liberty'. That said, he made clear his belief that socialists could not accept the Bolshevik embrace of violence and dictatorship as legitimate political tools:

> We welcome all the revolutions that have been achieved in Europe, but these revolutions must not create conditions which might be accurately described as a transition from one form of tyranny to another. Liberty, democracy, freedom must be their steady and unchangeable goal. A revolution that does not establish liberty is not a revolution towards Socialism, and is not a revolution for which socialists ought to make themselves responsible or allow the outside bourgeois reaction to impose responsibility for it upon them.

Unlike socialism, MacDonald viewed Bolshevism as a desperate and destructive response to despair and chaos. 'The characteristic of Socialism', he intoned, 'is its constructive side, not its destructive side... Socialism is a construction of society, and the International must always place this before it as the special characteristic of the working class movement which it voices and solidifies.'[28] For MacDonald, moreover, Bolshevism underscored the need for an International capable of addressing concrete problems of post-war Europe. Indeed, responsibility for Bolshevism lay chiefly with the governments that had unleashed a world war and were incapable of dealing with the disastrous consequences.

MacDonald's criticism of Bolshevism was echoed by the French ex-*majoritaires* and German majority socialists, both of whom rejected Bolshevik aims and methods as un- and even anti-socialist. This position helped to counteract the divisive effects of the debate over responsibility, but also drew Labour closer to French and German socialists. Drawing on his experience in Russia in 1917, Henderson likened Bolshevism to anarchy, which was simply incompatible with socialist internationalism. The Bolshevists were absent from Berne, the Labour leader

---

[28] Ibid., untitled resolution, 503–4; and MacDonald, 508–10. Not long afterwards, MacDonald published an extended version of his views on Bolshevism in *Parliament and Revolution* (New York, 1920); also see Marquand, *Ramsay MacDonald*, 257–9.

explained, because 'they refused to come before the International to defend their methods, knowing that these methods are opposed to all the principles of the International.' Other delegates, however, proved less willing to condemn the Bolshevists. Eisner accused bourgeois governments of brandishing Bolshevism as a 'nightmare... in order to influence and decide the peace negotiations in a reaction-ary-imperialist sense', while Faure warned that fears of Bolshevism should not be exploited to sap socialism of its revolutionary potential.[29] But it was Faure's fellow ex-*minoritaire* (and future communist) Daniel Renoult who underscored the stakes involved in the debate on Bolshevism for those socialists who conceived of themselves as revolutionaries. Writing in *Le Populaire de Paris*, Renoult opined:

> The [ex-] *majoritaires* of France and the 'social-chauvinists' of all countries are trying, under the pretext of condemning Bolshevism, to replace the traditional International based on class struggle and the organization of the proletariat for the revolutionary conquest of power, with a new, reformist, ministerial, anti-revolutionary International that will be lifeless...[30]

Faced with these stark differences of opinion, Friedrich Adler, the Austrian social-ist whose opposition to war led him in 1916 to assassinate the Austrian prime minister, groped for a compromise. It was premature to proscribe Bolshevism, Adler argued, because socialists lacked reliable information about developments in Russia and because the nature of the present political situation remained unclear. If the recent world war had created the conditions for a revolutionary overturn of capitalism, then Bolshevik methods were justified and perhaps even necessary; if not, Bolshevik methods were wrong-headed. Until the situation became clearer, all socialists should strive to strengthen their 'international soli-darity' and work to create an International that gathered 'all the class conscious revolutionary socialist parties'—a category that included the Bolsheviks.[31] Unable to forge a consensus on Bolshevism, the delegates sought to buy time by sending an 'information commission' to Russia to prepare a detailed report to be submit-ted to a future international socialist congress.[32]

Overall, the Berne conference produced mixed assessments. An editorial in Labour's newspaper, *The Daily Herald*, praised Berne as 'one of the most important events in the world's history'.[33] The British Foreign Office was less positive, pre-dicting that Berne would be the 'swan song of the old International' as together wartime enmities and post-war challenges 'have finally destroyed the original ideal' of socialist internationalism.[34] Berne, however, was neither a stunning success nor a complete failure. Rather, it was, as Paul Faure cautiously commented, 'a first step' towards the reconstitution of the International. On all the important questions, he

---

[29] Ritter, ed., *Die II. Internationale 1918/1919*, I, Henderson, 548–50; Faure, 544; and Eisner, 505.
[30] Renoult, 'La Conférence internationale de Berne', *Le Populaire de Paris*, 4 February 1919, 1.
[31] Ritter, ed., *Die II. Internationale 1918/1919*, I, Adler, 527–33.
[32] 'La dernière séance de la Conférence de Berne. Décisions de la Commission permanente', *L'Humanité*, 12 February 1919, 1.
[33] 'Berne', *Daily Herald*, 15 February 1919, 7.
[34] TNA, FO 608/237, 'A Note on the Berne Conference', 28 February 1919.

added, 'the discussions will be continued with the seriousness they merit.' To facilitate ongoing discussions, the delegates had agreed to create a small executive commission charged with organizing a follow-up conference and with taking 'all...the necessary steps to achieve a reconstituted International as rapidly as possible'.[35]

THE KOMINTERN AND THE CHALLENGE OF COMMUNIST INTERNATIONALISM

If the majority of European socialists appeared content to postpone a judgement on Bolshevism, the Bolsheviks themselves soon pressed the issue with the creation of the Communist International (Komintern) in March 1919. The result was to complicate the debates among socialists regarding the purpose and nature of the International—and of socialist internationalism.

From the beginning of the war, Lenin denounced the 'opportunism and chauvinism' of the principal European socialist parties. In 'The Tasks of Revolutionary Social-Democracy in the European War', written in the autumn of 1914, the Bolshevik leader had declared that the 'betrayal of socialism by most political leaders of the Second International...signifies the ideological and political bankruptcy of the International'. Initially, Lenin's aim was to transform international socialism from within, purging the International of its corrupt leadership and replacing it with a new one that better reflected the 'revolutionary consciousness of the masses'.[36] Over the course of the war, however, the goal became to create a rival International. Following the creation of the Zimmerwald movement in September 1915, Lenin and his collaborators sought to steer it in this direction; at the Kienthal conference in April 1916 the Bolshevik delegates thus insisted that the Second International could not be saved and suggested it be replaced by a new (Third) International.[37] A year later Lenin was still more forthright. 'We must take the initiative', he declared in his April 1917 theses, 'in creating a revolutionary International, an International against the social-chauvinists and against the "Centre"', by which he meant socialists who sought a negotiated end to the war but who refused to endorse the Bolshevik formula of revolutionary defeatism.[38]

By 1917, then, Lenin believed that a new International was necessary. But what prompted him to act on this belief in March 1919 was the international socialist conference in Berne the previous month, which Lenin perceived as a threat.[39] In January 1919 the Bolsheviks thus issued an invitation to several parties and groups

[35] Faure, 'Après Berne', *Le Populaire de Paris*, 15 February 1919, 1; and Ritter, ed., *Die II. Internationale 1918/1919*, I, 'Resolution über die Forsetzung der Konferenzarbeit', 464.

[36] Reproduced in Lenin, *Collected Works* (Moscow, 1974), vol. 21, 15–19.

[37] For the Zimmerwald movement, see Craig Nation, *War on War*. For the Kienthal conference, see Lademacher, *Die Zimmerwalder Bewegung*, I.

[38] 'The Task of the Proletariat in the Present Revolution', reproduced in Lenin, *Collected Works*, vol. 24, 19–26.

[39] For helpful accounts of the Komintern's founding, see Vatlin, *Die Komintern*; Robert Service, *Comrades: A History of World Communism* (Cambridge, MA, 2007), 85–118; and Pierre Broué, *Histoire de l'Internationale communiste, 1939–1943* (Paris, 1997), 17–96.

to come to Moscow 'to convene the first congress of a new revolutionary international'. That this new International was meant to pre-empt the reconstitution of the pre-war socialist International was evident from the resolution announcing the Komintern's creation:

> The foundation of the Communist International is the more imperative since now at Berne, and possibly later elsewhere also, an attempt is being made to restore the old opportunist International and to rally to it all the confused and undecided elements of the proletariat. It is therefore essential to make a sharp break between the revolutionary proletariat and the social-traitor elements.[40]

In pursuit of this 'sharp break', the Komintern's platform included a number of principles designed not simply to underscore Bolshevism's revolutionary character but also to distinguish communist from socialist internationalism: an uncompromising commitment to revolution, to the dictatorship of the proletariat, and to the use of violence to gain political power.[41] At the Komintern's second congress in July 1920 Lenin presented the formal terms for adherence. Eventually known as the 'Twenty-One Conditions', they envisaged the creation of communist parties on the Bolshevik model grouped together in a highly disciplined, hierarchical, and centralized organization directed by Moscow and committed to the revolutionary conquest and exercise of power. Significantly, the Bolsheviks expressed their 'readiness to conduct negotiations with any party which leaves the Second International and wishes to approach the Communist International', though they added that these parties would first have 'to be cleansed of all elements which continue to act in the spirit of the Second International'.[42]

Even before the announcement of Lenin's terms it was apparent that the Komintern represented a fundamental challenge to socialist internationalism. Alexander Vatlin, a leading historian of the Komintern, argues that communist internationalism constituted a 'decisive break' with socialist traditions. If Lenin certainly framed the issue in these terms, many European socialists were less certain.[43] An initial opportunity for them to discuss this question came at the end of April 1919 when the permanent committee, established at the Berne conference, met in Amsterdam. Although there was almost no direct mention of Bolshevism, the newly formed Komintern influenced the discussions concerning the International. While Henderson proposed draft statutes that emphasized continuity with the pre-war Second International, others advocated a more thoroughgoing revision. MacDonald thus argued for 'a radical change in the form of the old organization', expressing in private his admiration for Lenin's administrative skills and political determination compared to the moderation of socialists. 'Fault of International',

---

[40] 'Invitation to the First Congress of the Communist International', 24 January 1919, reproduced in Jane Degras, ed., *The Communist International 1919–1943*, vol. I (London, 1971), 1–5.
[41] 'Platform of the Communist International, adopted by the first congress', 4 March 1919, reproduced in ibid., 17–24.
[42] 'Theses on the basic tasks of the Communist International adopted by the Second Comintern Congress', 19 July 1920, reproduced in ibid., 113–27.
[43] Vatlin, *Die Komintern*, 38–9.

he penned on his return from Amsterdam, 'is that it had become too parliamentary & has no vision.'[44] In Amsterdam, meanwhile, Haase, speaking for the USPD, maintained that a reconstituted International 'will only win back its [lost] influence when it assumes a revolutionary character'. Faced with these conflicting viewpoints, the permanent committee postponed discussion of the proposed statutes until a subsequent meeting scheduled for August 1919 in Lucerne.[45]

The newly created Komintern dominated the discussions in Lucerne. In his opening address as chairman, Henderson argued that 'the time has come when we must seriously overhaul our international organisation' but what he offered was something very similar to the pre-1914 International.[46] Earlier, in May 1919, a small 'action committee' made up of British and French socialists and chaired by Huysmans, had drawn up a revised draft of statutes for a reconstituted International, a copy of which was then circulated to the various parties. Much like its pre-war predecessor, the proposed International would be a 'federation of national sections' in which each party enjoyed considerable 'autonomy or independence'.[47] In response to Henderson, MacDonald insisted that much more was needed:

> The International should be 'energetic', should be 'on the spot', should be 'active'. I agree: but how? That is the whole question. It is not enough to create an organ of the International for these purposes. You must have a policy. The International must know with a great deal more accuracy than it now does exactly where it stands. What are to be our political declarations? Our economic declarations? ... In fact what we have to settle at Lucerne is whether the Second International is to live or to be buried.

For MacDonald, international politics were dominated by a struggle between revolution and reform, which he equated with reaction. Although sympathetic to Bolshevism's revolutionary aspirations, he rejected its version of revolution, chiefly because socialist internationalism should not renounce democracy. More generally, MacDonald continued to view Bolshevism as a baneful force. The Komintern, he argued, represented 'nothing but the vague upstirrings of revolution that always come after war, not constructive but destructive, not progressive but reactionary, for such a revolution can often be slavery on the one side; ruin on the other'. For MacDonald, the urgent task was to define a socialist internationalism that rejected violent evolution and reactionary reformism.[48]

At Lucerne, however, it quickly became clear that a third way between revolution and reform would be elusive. The bitter divisions between German socialists provided

---

[44] TNA, Ramsay MacDonald Papers, PRO 30/69/1753/1, diary entries, 2 and 22 May 1919.

[45] 'Bericht über die Konferenz in Amsterdam, 26. bis 29. April 1919', reproduced in Ritter, ed., *Die II. Internationale 1918/1919*, I, 585–8.

[46] 'Konferenz der Internationalen Permanenten Kommission in Luzern, 2. bis 9. August 1919', reproduced in ibid., I, Henderson, 613.

[47] For the 'action committee' meeting, see the file in IISH, BSI, 103. For the draft statutes, see AABS, Ssa, Socialistiska Internationalen, vol. 9, file 1919, 'Projet de Statuts de l'Internationale proposé par le Comité d'action', undated.

[48] 'Konferenz der Internationalen Permanenten Kommission in Luzern, 2. bis 9. August 1919', reproduced in Ritter, ed., *Die II. Internationale 1918/1919*, I, MacDonald, 614–17.

one source of difficulty. Speaking for the USPD, Arthur Crispien criticized the proposed statutes for their lack of 'revolutionary spirit'. Convinced that the present period would witness the decisive revolutionary struggle of international socialism against global capitalism, Crispien insisted that the International constituted the 'decisive question' for all socialist parties. He accordingly demanded an international organization capable of imposing a 'determined common front' of all socialist parties and dedicated to 'overturning the capitalist state and conquering political power'.[49] Equally critical of the proposed statutes, the USPD's Rudolf Hilferding called for an International assembling 'all proletarian and revolutionary forces in one unit for action'. Such an International would have to exclude the majority German socialists, whom Hilferding accused of 'crimes against the revolutionary proletariat' both before and after November 1918.[50] Although neither Crispien nor Hilferding proposed that socialists join the Komintern, their advocacy of an International actively committed to revolution paralleled the latter's programme. Not surprisingly, the MSPD highlighted this parallel. In his response to the USPD, Eduard Bernstein insisted that democracy must remain the 'foundation of the life of nations' and thus of socialist internationalism. Likening Bolshevism to anarchism, he described the Komintern as 'nothing but an International of Neo-Bakunism [anarchism] bent on violent upheaval'.[51]

With the USPD and the MSPD at loggerheads, it was left to Friedrich Adler to craft a consensus on the question of the Komintern, contending once again that a decision for or against was premature. That said, Adler did not disguise his hope of recreating socialist internationalism's pre-1914 unity by merging the Second and Third Internationals. Between the two Internationals, Adler proclaimed, 'a synthesis must be crafted that will lead to a single and united International.' Significantly, the idea of a 'synthesis' received a warm welcome from both the German independent socialists and the French ex-*minoritaires*. Speaking for the latter, Longuet expressed the hope that Lenin would listen to Adler 'and that the Bolsheviks would realise from the debates at that [*sic*] Conference that there existed no unbridgeable gulf between the two Internationals... and that there should be a single International even as there was a single proletariat throughout the world'.[52]

In his closing speech at Lucerne, Henderson lauded the 'magnificent spirit' of unity that had reigned throughout. But it was the differences that impressed most observers—differences that cut across national groupings. The inability of the participants to agree on a response to the Komintern resulted in two contending

---

[49] See ibid., Crispien, 622–3. For Crispien, see FES, AdsD, NL Arthur Crispien, 1/ACAA000001, 'Ein Proletarierleben für das Proletariat', 8. Also see Crispien, *Die Internationale. Vom Bund der Kommunisten bis zur Internationale der Weltrevolution* (Berlin, 1919).

[50] 'Konferenz der Internationalen Permanenten Kommission in Luzern, 2. bis 9. August 1919', reproduced in Ritter, ed., *Die II. Internationale 1918/1919*, I, Hilferding, 636–8.

[51] Ibid., Bernstein, 639–40.

[52] 'Konferenz der Internationalen Permanenten Kommission in Luzern, 2. bis 9. August 1919', reproduced in Ritter, ed., *Die II. Internationale 1918/1919*, I, Adler, 647–8; and Longuet, 648–9. USPD sympathy for Adler is evident from their pressure on him to attend the Lucerne meeting. See IISH, Fritz Adler Papers, 4, telegram from Haase and Hilferding, 22 July 1919.

resolutions on general policy, neither of which took a clear-cut position.[53] Instead, the issue of the International was deferred once again to a future international socialist conference. Yet the differences notwithstanding, it was clear that numerous European socialists, harbouring considerable misgivings towards both the pre-war Second International and the Third International, favoured some fusion of the two. At Lucerne, Adler emerged as the leading advocate of this idea.[54] But such a fusion proved impossible, partly because of Bolshevik intransigence but also because of developments within the British, French, and German parties.

DEVELOPMENTS IN BRITAIN, GERMANY, AND FRANCE

In early 1919 the German foreign ministry reported that the 'English Labour Party is the most important element in the international labour movement'.[55] Labour leaders, moreover, were determined to use this pre-eminence to oppose any adherence to (or fusion with) the Komintern. As Henderson explained to Huysmans in March 1920, within Labour:

> there is no belief in the dictatorship of a principle of action, nor have we any desire to incorporate it in our vocabulary as a synonym for democracy. Taking this view, we do not desire to compromise with the advocates of this doctrine by using their language about Soviets, Revolution or Dictatorship...[56]

Labour, in fact, proved allergic to Bolshevism, a condition rooted in a combination of factors: the prominent role of trade unions, the general appeal of reformism, and the party's commitment to parliamentary democracy. For international socialism, this allergy meant that Labour became the driving force behind a reconstituted Second International that was defined in good part in opposition to the Komintern.

Labour's firm stance on the issue of Bolshevism was not shared by the ILP. At the ILP's annual conference in April 1919, the delegates discussed the nature of a future International, eventually defeating a resolution that advocated an organization based on the principles of democracy and liberty. The primary reason for the defeat, it seems, was the fear that the resolution implied a condemnation of the Soviets.[57] Over the next year or so, a movement developed within the ILP in favour of affiliation with the Komintern, leading to a clash at the party's conference in April 1920. Following a speech by the party's chairman, Philip Snowden, in which international socialism and international democracy were presented as one and the same, the delegates debated the ILP's attitude towards the International. While the first speaker urged affiliation with the Komintern, warning that otherwise

---

[53] PAAP, Berne, 832, 'Internationale Sozialistenkonferenz Luzern 2. bis 9. August 1919 (Zusammenfassende Bericht)', 13 August 1919.
[54] Adler, 'Einheit oder Dreiteilung der Internationale', *Die Freiheit*, 24 September 1919, 1–2.
[55] PAAP, Bern 827, 'Die Internationale Arbeiterbewegung as weltpolitischer Faktor', undated but early 1919.
[56] BLPSE, ILP, 6/12/2, Henderson to Huysmans, 17 March 1920.
[57] ILP, *Report of the Annual Conference held at Huddersfield April, 1919* (London, 1919), 67–70.

the ILP 'would be brought to a state of absolute isolation from European Socialism', the next speaker, Ramsay MacDonald, recommended working with other parties to transform the International from within, thereby laying the basis for a 'real all-inclusive International'. While accepting the value of talking to the Komintern, MacDonald considered Bolshevism to be incompatible with the ILP's brand of socialism. But it was Fenner Brockway, an anti-conscription militant during the war, who best reflected prevailing opinion. Insisting that the International was 'near its deathbed, because it failed entirely to express the new spirit of the Socialist movement', Brockway urged the ILP to withdraw from the organization. Together with the German independent socialists and the French ex-*minoritaires*, he continued, the ILP should organize a 'Left Wing Conference, including Moscow' as a first step towards a new International based on 'true International principles'. In the final tally, almost 80 per cent of the delegates voted to leave the Second International while 70 per cent voted against affiliation with the Komintern.[58]

That a large majority of ILP delegates rejected affiliation with the Komintern is not surprising. The ILP's *raison d'être*, as Snowden reminded the conference, was to 'mould the opinion of the Labour Party on Socialist lines'; and as the *Daily Herald* made clear, a choice for Moscow would mean a definitive rupture with Labour.[59] But while rejecting any affiliation with the Komintern, Labour leaders recognized the need for flexibility on the issue of the International in order not to alienate the ILP—and its allies among Continental socialists. Hence the decision in November 1919 to appoint MacDonald to head the British section of the Second International with the task of reconstructing the latter. That someone as politically ambitious as MacDonald accepted the position points to the importance of socialist internationalism to Labour during the immediate post-war years. MacDonald, in any event, would infuse the efforts to reconstitute the International with renewed vigour and determination. No less pertinently, he served as a useful bridge between Labour and the ILP. MacDonald's continued influence within the ILP (he remained a member) would help to moderate the latter's position, distancing it from the Komintern. At the same time, MacDonald (and Labour) could exploit the ILP's close ties with the USPD and the French ex-*minoritaires* among other left-leaning socialists to steer them away from the dangers of communist internationalism.

German socialists were even more divided than British socialists on the issue of the International—and the nature of socialist internationalism. At the MSPD's annual congress in June 1919, Otto Wels, the party chairman, expressed considerable frustration with the criticisms of the USPD and of foreign socialists. But Wels' principal point was that German socialists must give their internationalism a more national (German) inflection—much as British and French socialists had supposedly done. It was imperative that:

> We remain attached to our people and our country to the end, we want to serve our country within the International, and we know that we can represent our national peculiarities and interests within the International...

---

[58] ILP, *Report of the Annual Conference held at Glasgow, April 1920* (London, 1920), 66–86.
[59] Ibid., 51; and 'The International', *Daily Herald*, 7 April 1920, 4.

that August 1914 had witnessed the 'spiritual collapse of international socialism'. The pressing task, consequently, was to forge a 'proletarian International' capable of advancing the 'revolutionary process' and the 'struggle against world capitalism'. For Stoecker and his supporters this could only mean the Komintern. In joining forces with the latter, he added, German socialists would not be separating themselves from Western European socialists because the decision to do so would help to persuade the 'real socialists' in France and Britain to follow the USPD's lead.[67]

Although nothing was decided at the September gathering, pressure mounted for a clear-cut choice. The International thus figured prominently on the agenda of the party's congress in Leipzig in early December 1919. Once again, both camps expounded their positions. Criticizing the Bolsheviks as nationalists, loyal only to the interests of Soviet Russia, Hilferding insisted that socialists must adopt a 'truly international standpoint' that required 'considering the situation of other socialist parties'. Hilferding in particular feared that a decision to join the Komintern would sharpen divisions within the SFIO, thereby weakening French (and international) socialism. Rather than the Komintern, socialists required an International that would allow each party to pursue its own revolutionary path. Here, moreover, Hilferding drew inspiration from the Labour Party, which had assumed the 'spiritual leadership' of the international socialist movement and which was supposedly close to gaining political power through parliamentary elections. In response, Stoecker sought to assuage fears that the USPD would be isolated from the West, suggesting that the majority of the SFIO would follow the USPD into the Komintern; with less justification, he even claimed that British workers were moving in this direction. As for the Komintern, he maintained that it would be a tool not of the Soviet government but of world revolution and that it would be sensitive to the particular needs of its member parties. In the end, the delegates opted to compromise, voting 227 to 54 to leave the Second International but not to affiliate with the Komintern—at least not for now.[68] As Crispien informed European socialist parties soon afterwards, the congress charged USPD leaders to take the initiative in organizing discussions with the Komintern and with all the social revolutionary parties in order to create an 'International capable of action'.[69]

Meeting with French socialists in Switzerland in January 1920, Crispien explained that a majority of the USPD favoured affiliation with the Komintern on certain conditions—conditions that would allow the party considerable autonomy in its internal affairs. Much, accordingly, would depend on Moscow's flexibility.[70]

---

[67] *Bericht über die Reichskonferenz der Unabhängigen Sozialdemokratischen Partei Deutschlands am 9. und 10. September 1919 im Abgeordnetenhaus zu Berlin*, reproduced in *Protokolle der Parteitage der Unabhängigen Sozialdemokratischen Partei Deutschlands*, Hilferding, 18–20; and Stoecker, 23–53.

[68] USPD, *Protokoll über die Verhandlungen des ausserordentlichen Parteitages in Leipzig vom 30. November bis 6. Dezember 1919*, reproduced in *Protokolle der Parteitage der Unabhängigen Sozialdemokratischen Partei Deutschlands*, Hilferding, 309–26; Stoecker, 326–42.

[69] BLPES, ILP Papers, 1919/97, USPD (Crispien) to ILP, 15 December 1919.

[70] SSAZ, SPS, Ar.1.111.1, 'Résumé über die Behandlungen zwischen der Geschäftsleitung der sozialdemokratischen Partei der Schweiz, den Genossen Frossard (Paris) und Crispien (Berlin) über

In an effort to gauge the latter, the USPD sent a delegation to Soviet Russia in the summer of 1920 to consult with the Bolsheviks. This comprised four members, two of whom favoured affiliation (Stoecker and Ernst Däumig) and two of whom harboured serious reservations (Crispien and Wilhelm Dittmann). The detailed story of their mission has been told elsewhere, but for our purposes the most important point is that the four returned in August 1920 profoundly divided on the question of affiliation.[71] All attempts to find a compromise failed. Not surprisingly, the sharpest point of contention concerned the nature of communist internationalism and the implications of affiliation with the Komintern—a contention fuelled by differing interpretations of Moscow's Twenty-One Conditions. But the two sides also clashed on the question of the potential impact of affiliation on other socialist parties, most notably the SFIO. While Crispien and Dittmann claimed that the majority of French socialists would reject the Komintern, leaving the USPD isolated, Däumig pointed out correctly (as we shall see) that the two delegates sent by the SFIO to Moscow had returned in favour of joining the Third International.[72]

With compromise impossible, USPD delegates gathered in Halle in October 1920 to take a decision. The lengthy and heated exchanges contained little that was new. Crispien and Hilferding, joined by Rudolf Breitscheid, an expert in foreign affairs and a fervent advocate of Franco-German rapprochement, insisted on the importance of remaining attached to British and French socialism, underscoring what they perceived to be a profound East–West divide. At the gathering, they received the support of Jean Longuet, who attended the conference as a fraternal delegate and who pleaded for British, French, and German socialists to cooperate in the construction of an 'international International' as opposed to a 'Russian International'. In the end, however, a considerable majority of the delegates rejected this plea, voting 236 to 156 to join the International (and the German Communist Party), leaving a much-reduced USPD.[73] The vote, as Robert Wheeler has shown, was largely the result of the influx of new members during 1919–1920, who constituted a powerful grass-roots movement championing a more radical and revolutionary course for socialism.[74] Relatively young, these militants had little roots in the pre-war world of international socialism. As a result, the members of the rump now found themselves in limbo, having rejected membership in both the Second and Third Internationals.

---

die Beurteilung der internationalen Verhältnisse und Vorbereitungen zur Wiederaufnahme der internationalen Beziehungen den sozialistischen Parteien…', 22 January 1920.

[71] See Arthur S. Lindemann, *The 'Red Years': European Socialism versus Bolshevism, 1919–1921* (Berkeley, CA, 1974), 148–216; and Bruno Naarden, *Socialist Europe and Revolutionary Russia: Perception and Prejudice, 1848–1923* (Cambridge, 1992), 386–97.

[72] USPD, *Protkoll der Reichskonferenz vom 1. bis 3. September 1920 zu Berlin*, reproduced in *Protokolle der Parteitage der Unabhängigen Sozialdemokratischen Partei Deutschlands*, Crispien, 6–7; Dittmann, 61; and Däumig, 44.

[73] USPD, *Protokoll über die Verhandlungen des ausserordentlichen Parteitages in Halle vom 12. bis 17. Oktober 1920*, reproduced in ibid.

[74] Wheeler, *USPD und Internationale*; and his '"Die 21 Bedingungen" und die Spaltung der USPD im Herbst 1920: Zur Meinungsbildung der Basis', *Vierteljahrshefte für Zeitgeschichte* 23 (1975), 117–54.

As USPD observers were well aware, the SFIO was deeply divided over the question of the International. That the creation of the Komintern helped to crystallize differences between French socialists was apparent at the party's annual congress in April 1919. In a fraternal address, Henderson praised the recently held Berne conference and declared that it was time for 'all democracies' to unite in an International. Taking his cue from Henderson, Paul Mistral, speaking for the ex-*majoritaires*, pointed to the Berne conference as proof that the pre-war International was alive and well. To join the Komintern, he added, would not only isolate the SFIO but also risked fracturing international socialism.[75] The majority of the delegates, however, adopted a more ambivalent attitude towards the Second International, which they associated with a reformist and anti-revolutionary stance. A resolution presented by Paul Faure on behalf of the ex-*minoritaires* thus denounced the 'policy of uncertainty and compromise' pursued by the ex-*majoritaires* during the war and expressed sympathy for 'all the revolutions that the great upheaval of war had provoked throughout the world'. The true International, the resolution concluded, was neither the League of Nations proposed by the victorious powers in Paris nor the one conceived of by the ex-*majoritaires* and their allies in Berne, but the International 'created by the workers of the world finally freed from capitalist oppression'.[76]

For all its revolutionary rhetoric, Faure's resolution did not directly address the issue of the Komintern. Instead, the delegates had to wait until the last night of the congress. In what turned out to be a raucous session, three different resolutions were debated: that the SFIO join the Komintern; that it remain in the Second International; or that it adopt a compromise position. Advocating the last resolution, Longuet proposed that the SFIO insist that all socialist 'sections' and not simply those present at Berne be invited to an upcoming international conference—an invitation that presumably included the Bolsheviks. No less importantly, the resolution called for the 'necessary purges' of socialists in each national section; the strict application of the principle of class struggle as well as 'uncompromising opposition to bourgeois political parties and governments'; and the 'clear and immediate orientation of the International towards social revolution'. On these conditions, the SFIO would remain for the time being in the pre-war International while retaining the right to enter into 'fraternal relations' with the Komintern. In the end, Longuet's proposal gained a plurality but not a majority of the votes (894 of 1,921).[77]

Longuet's resolution clearly represented a compromise position that avoided choosing either of the Second or Third Internationals. Sensitive to the dangers of division, many French socialists preferred to postpone a clear-cut decision.[78] But Longuet's compromise proved fragile. If an important minority of French socialists

---

[75] 'Au congrès socialiste. Séance de l'après-midi', *L'Humanité*, 21 April 1919, 2.
[76] 'Les derniers séances du Congrès national', *L'Humanité*, 23 April 1919, 2.
[77] 'Le dernier jour de Congrès. La discipline socialiste sera respectée', *Le Populaire de Paris*, 24 April 1919, 1–2.
[78] IISH, BSI, 103, SFIO to Huysmans, 30 June 1919; also see Longuet, 'Pour l'Internationale. L'action d'abord, le congrès après', *Le Populaire de Paris*, 20 June 1919, 1.

hoped to remain in a reconstituted International, a majority only agreed to do so under conditions that implied a transformation of the International—and of international socialism. Chief among the conditions would be a concerted effort to fuse socialist and communist internationalism, creating an International that resembled the Komintern far more than the pre-war Second International. As the French socialist Raoul Verfeuil explained in June 1919, 'our position at the...congress was very clear. We are heart and soul with the Third International.'[79] At the SFIO's special congress in September 1919, held to debate the party's platform for the upcoming national elections, L.O. Frossard, the party secretary, maintained that unity was only possible with those who 'are loyal to socialism and to class struggle and revolution'. Reflecting Frossard's anti-reformist rhetoric, the congress voted a resolution, modelled on the USPD's position, which refused to support bourgeois governments and rejected all electoral alliances with other political parties. The resolution contributed to the SFIO's poor showing in the November 1919 elections: although gaining 300,000 more votes than in 1914, the party's tally of parliamentary deputies dropped from 101 to 68.[80]

The election results, however, did nothing to heal the mounting divisions within the SFIO over the International. December 1919 saw the creation of a reconstruction committee within the SFIO, whose members included several proponents of affiliation with the Komintern. Indeed, at its opening meeting the committee favourably discussed a 'fusion' between the Komintern and the revolutionary elements of the Second International.[81] The USPD's decision earlier in the month to leave the latter and to negotiate with the Komintern served as a model for the committee. Arguing that the USPD had dealt the Second International a 'fatal blow', Daniel Renout, a prominent committee member, urged French socialists to ally with the independent German socialists in talks with the Communist International. As Longuet intimated to MacDonald in January 1920, the USPD's decision to leave the Second International made it impossible for the SFIO not to follow suit.[82]

The accuracy of Longuet's analysis became clear the following month at the SFIO congress in Strasbourg. Not only did the question of the International dominate the agenda, but the USPD's position clearly influenced the proceedings. Invoking the USPD's recent decision, Frossard and Longuet, two leading ex-*minoritaires*, both insisted that the SFIO must leave the Second International, though they differed in their assessments of the future. While Frossard, citing recent talks with Crispien, claimed that the independent German socialists would soon join the Komintern, Longuet suggested that they would remain outside, resulting in a small makeshift structure rather than a 'grand international socialist dwelling'.

[79] Verfeuil, 'Pour un congrès international', *Le Populaire de Paris*, 19 June 1919, 1.

[80] See 'Au Congrès—Le discours de Frossard', *Le Populaire de Paris*, 13 September 1919, 1; and 'La deuxième journée du Congrès national', *L'Humanité*, 13 September 1919.

[81] 'Comité pour la Reconstruction de l'Internationale', *Le Populaire de Paris*, 30 December 1919, 1; and Lindemann, *The 'Red Years'*, 93.

[82] Renoult, 'La Reconstruction de l'Internationale', *Le Populaire de Paris*, 17 December 1919, 1; and TNA, Ramsay MacDonald Papers, PRO 30/69/1164, Longuet to MacDonald, 8 January 1920.

Searching for a compromise, Faure insisted that a 'complete break' with the Second International was necessary, while adding that it was hard to conceive of an International without the British. This last remark is noteworthy in light of the speech of the ILP representative, who made it clear that his party would remain attached to Labour and that Labour would never join the Komintern. Continuing, Faure proposed that the SFIO cooperate with the USPD in negotiating acceptable conditions for affiliation with the Komintern. After prolonged debate, the delegates voted overwhelmingly to leave the Second International and to empower the party's executive committee to 'engage in negotiations without delay' with Moscow to organize an international socialist conference in the aim of uniting 'all parties committed to basing their action on the traditional principles of socialism'.[83]

Following the Strasbourg conference, the SFIO sought to cooperate with those socialist parties unhappy with both the Second and Third Internationals. It accordingly sent representatives to Britain and Italy to consult with the ILP and with the Italian Socialist Party. Meanwhile, in June 1920 Faure travelled to Switzerland to discuss the SFIO's position with a USPD representative. Although Faure pushed for an inclusive conference of parties, the USPD hesitated, fearing that such a step might be viewed by the Komintern as anti-Bolshevik. After some debate, it was agreed to give priority to negotiations with Moscow in the hope, as Frossard informed the ILP, that 'direct contact with our Bolshevik comrades will remove... all difficulties.'[84] Accordingly, in May 1920 Frossard and Marcel Cachin left for Moscow as the SFIO's delegates. Afterwards, both claimed that they took their decision 'in full accord with the independents [socialists] in Germany, present like us in Moscow'—a questionable claim in light of the division within the USPD's four-member commission.[85] But however arrived at, the essential point is that Frossard and Cachin recommended affiliation with the Komintern on their return in August 1920. This recommendation was all the more significant in that it came as a surprise—as a 'sensational reversal' in Léon Blum's words.[86] Before the voyage Frossard had expressed considerable ambivalence towards the Komintern; as for Cachin, he had been a strong supporter of the government's war effort during 1914–1918. For Annie Kriegel, the unexpected results of the mission underscored the accidental nature of the SFIO's schism, the product of short-term developments during 1919–1920. Yet as Romain Ducoulombier has argued more recently, the schism was also the culmination of efforts begun in August 1914 to regenerate socialism and socialist internationalism.[87]

[83] SFIO, *17e Congrès national tenu à Strasbourg les 25, 26, 27, 28 et 29 Février 1920. Compte rendu sténographique* (Paris, 1920), Frossard, 282–94; Longuet, 365–74; Faure, 452–70; and for the final resolution, 564–7.

[84] BLPES, ILP Papers, 1920/35, Frossard to Wallhead (ILP), 11 May 1920. For the meeting in Switzerland, see SSAZ, SPS, Ar.1.111.1, 'Sitzung der Geschäftsleitung Dienstag, den 8. Juni 1920', undated; and Faure, 'Le problème de l'Internationale', *L'Humanité*, 23 June 1920, 1.

[85] Frossard and Cachin, 'Retour de voyage', *L'Humanité*, 12 August 1920, 1. Also see Lindemann, *The 'Red Years'*, 109–15, 149–54, 174–80, 221–5.

[86] AN, Papiers Marcel Sembat, 637/AP/155, Blum to Sembat, undated but 1920.

[87] Kriegel, *Aux origines du communisme français*; and Romain Ducoulombier, 'Les socialistes devant la guerre et le scission (1914–1920)', *Cahiers Jaurès* 189 (2008), 33–55; also see the latter's *Camarades!*

By the end of 1920, in any case, a schism appeared inevitable. If any doubts existed among French socialists, the USPD's decision in October removed them. Our opponents within the SFIO, Renoult openly crowed, 'had counted greatly on the German Independents' but a 'considerable' majority had opted to join the Komintern; the SFIO, he promised, would do likewise at its next congress.[88] In many ways, the SFIO's congress at Tours in December 1920 merely confirmed the obvious. That said, the proceedings are interesting for what they reveal about the different understandings of socialist internationalism. Although there appeared to be some confusion about the precise meaning of the Komintern's Twenty-One Conditions, most speakers barely mentioned them, emphasizing instead the need to break with a recent past supposedly characterized by hesitancy, compromise, and hypocrisy—traits bundled together in the despised term 'reformism'. 'We are for the Third International', a delegate from the Vaucluse announced, 'because we condemn reformism.'[89] Those opposed to joining the Komintern likewise spoke in terms of a break, countering that communist internationalism was something not only new but also incompatible with traditional socialist internationalism. When Blum famously pleaded to preserve the 'veille maison', he had in mind the pre-war International that balanced international and national duties rather than insisted on subordinating one to the other.[90] Unmoved by Blum's nostalgia-tinged vision of socialist internationalism, a large majority of delegates voted to affiliate with the Komintern, leaving the SFIO to found the French Communist Party. Like the USPD, a greatly weakened French Socialist Party thus found itself in limbo.

MULTIPLE INTERNATIONALS

While French, German, and (to a lesser extent) British socialists argued passionately whether to join the Komintern, the proponents of the Second International strove to reinvigorate the latter. In a report presented at Labour's annual conference in June 1920, Huysmans, the International's secretary, complained that USPD and SFIO hostility hampered ongoing efforts to reconstruct the International. Dismissing proposals to create a new International, which would be a 'rival rump body' without any influence on international politics, the report pleaded with European socialists to work within rather than outside the Second International. If socialists were dissatisfied with the current International, they should cooperate to reconstitute it on new—and less reformist—bases. The Second International, the report concluded,

> has not excluded and it does not propose to exclude any section that accepts the essential principles of Socialism, and those who think that … it is not revolutionary as they

---

[88] Renoult, 'Les leçons du Congrès de Halle', *L'Humanité*, 23 October 1920, 1.
[89] The delegate was Denantes. See Jean Charles et al., eds., *Le Congrès de Tours (18e Congrès du Parti socialiste)* (Paris, 1980), 314.
[90] Ibid., Blum, 410–35.

The Geneva conference marked the official relaunch of the Second International. In a pamphlet published shortly afterwards, Adolf Braun, an MSPD delegate, enthused that the conference demonstrated that socialist unity was possible. 'The unity [manifest] at Geneva', he wrote, 'fills us with the hope that what binds us [socialists] is stronger than what divides us. The model of unity strikes us as urgent at home as within the International.'[98] Braun's enthusiasm notwithstanding, it was clear that the Second International was a shrunken version of its pre-war self, with the French and German parties notably absent. For MacDonald, in any case, the Geneva conference was one step in a much longer process. 'The International', he had remarked in June, 'was not to be constructed at one Conference by one resolution or one decision.'[99] But as MacDonald no doubt realized, little could be achieved in the immediate wake of the Geneva conference. Instead, the Second International would have to wait upon the outcome of the deepening divisions within the German and French parties.

By the end of 1920, with both the USPD and the SFIO having taken their decisions regarding the Komintern, MacDonald was ready to act. In particular, he feared that further delay might encourage other parties to leave the Second International. 'It will be a calamity', he explained to the Dutch socialist, Pietre Troelstra, in December, 'if any of the sections now affiliated to the 2nd International take independent action and leave the others in the lurch.' It was imperative, he added, that '[w]e should try and all act together'.[100] The following day the Labour party sent a lengthy circular to all the 'Socialist & Communist Parties of the World' that identified disunity as the greatest danger to socialism:

> The militant [socialist] forces have been divided and more attention is being paid to attacking each other upon tactics than to assaulting the common enemy. Every day that passes finds the old order re-establishing itself...The lack of a united International is allowing all our great opportunities to slip past, and the Socialist movement that ought to have been gathered together for a peace offensive will be dissipated in the futility of internal feuds.

But if Labour—and MacDonald in particular—sought unity, they did so on the Second International's terms, which included full autonomy for member parties and unequivocal support for the 'democratic method' in pursuing and exercising political power. Thus while calling upon all socialists to combat their governments' 'anti-Russian policy', the circular insisted that the Bolshevik brand of internationalism could only produce division and disaster. '[E]very Socialist who has any international instinct at all', it declared, 'will see that an International based upon Moscow principles can never represent more than the smallest and least influential fraction of the Socialist movement in the various countries. The Second International has therefore rejected Bolshevism as the basis of its existence.'[101]

---

[98] Adolf Braun, *Der Internationale Kongress zu Genf* (Berlin, 1920), 6.
[99] Labour, *Report of the Twentieth Annual Conference*, MacDonald, 173.
[100] IISH, Pietre Jelles Troelstra papers, 552, MacDonald to Troelstra, 29 December 1920.
[101] LHASC, LSI, 10/3/3, Labour party circular, 30 December 1920.

MacDonald hoped to convince the rump French and German parties (the SFIO and the USPD) as well as the ILP to join the Second International. But by then it was too late as the USPD and the SFIO were well on the way to creating their own international organization—the 'International Working Union of Socialist Parties' (or Vienna Union).[102] The latter's origins can be traced back to early 1920 when the ILP, prodded by the USPD, sought to organize a meeting of socialist parties that had left the Second International but had not joined the Komintern. Writing to the secretary of the Swiss party in February 1920, Frances Johnson, the ILP's chairman, urged him to take the initiative in this regard. The ILP, Johnson explained, 'does not feel that the best interests of Socialism can be served by the establishment of two, three or perhaps four international organisations', adding that it preferred 'one all-inclusive International, allowing the fullest autonomy and freedom of action and liberty of tactics to each Party connected with it'.[103] Initially, delays came from the USPD and the SFIO, both of whom were engaged in direct negotiations with Moscow. The ILP's persistence, however, paid off: in October 1920 the Swiss party issued an invitation for a meeting in Berne for early December. If the USPD readily agreed to go, the SFIO's decision to attend followed a razor-close vote in the party's executive committee, with those opposed arguing that the purpose of the proposed gathering was to forestall a decision in favour of the Komintern. Such suspicions were justified in the case of the ILP, which desperately sought to identify a third way between the Second and Third Internationals—a third way that would help it avoid a break with Labour.[104]

The continued hesitation of some socialists as well as difficulties obtaining permission from the Swiss authorities limited the size of the gathering in Berne in early December 1920. Nevertheless, representatives from the principal parties were present, including the SFIO, USPD, ILP, SPÖ (Austrian), and the SPS (Swiss). The immediate result was a declaration to the 'socialist parties of all countries'. Having failed to fulfil its 'historical duty' during the war, the Second International had become nothing more than a grouping of the 'purely reformist and nationalist current' of international socialism. The Declaration was also critical of the Komintern, accusing Bolsheviks of seeking to impose a single revolutionary model at the price of tearing apart socialist parties. What was needed, the declaration concluded, was an alternative path between the extremes of stultifying reformism and revolutionary violence. More concretely, the participants agreed to call an international socialist conference in Vienna in February 1921 to discuss the best means of pursuing the class struggle in the national and international realms.[105] The ultimate goal, declared an ILP memorandum that served as the basis for discussion, was a single

[102] For a general history, see André Donneur, *Histoire de l'Union des partis socialistes pour l'action internationale (1920–1923)* (Sudbury, ON, 1967).

[103] AILP, series III, Frances Johnson correspondence, reel 17, 1920/3, Johnson (ILP) to Swiss Socialist Party, 12 February 1920. Johnson returned to the charge in August. See SSAZ, SPS, Ar.1.260.4, Johnson (ILP) to Swiss Socialist Party, 26 August 1920.

[104] BLPES, ILP Papers, 1920/811, SPS to ILP, 29 October 1920; and 1920/106, Frossard (SFIO) to ILP, 16 November 1920.

[105] 'An die sozialistischen Parteien aller Länder', 7 December 1920, reproduced in *Die Freiheit*, 10 December 1920, 1. Invitations were sent out in January 1921. See the copy in SSAZ, SPS, Ar.1.260.3.

INITIAL ATTEMPTS AT UNITY

With the founding of the Vienna Union three international organizations now vied for pre-eminence among socialists. Although Adler preached patience, he quickly came under pressure from member parties of both the Vienna Union and the Second International. As mentioned, at the Vienna conference in February 1921 the SFIO had proposed that European socialists cooperate on the issue of reparations. During the opening months of 1921, the issue moved to the fore of international politics. In imposing the principle of reparations on Germany, the peace treaty had left the total amount uncertain until January 1921, when the Allies announced a figure of 226 billion gold marks, eventually reduced to 132 billion by the London agreements in May 1921. The intergovernmental negoti- ations bred considerable bitterness, with the Germans and the Allies (especially the French and British) clashing over Germany's capacity to pay as well as the methods of payment.[114] It is in this tense general climate that the SFIO invited the ILP and the USPD to a meeting in Amsterdam at the beginning of April 1921 to discuss 'practical solutions to the problems of reparations'.[115] Interestingly, the Second International got wind of the meeting and decided to organize its own gathering in Amsterdam on the subject. Although the leaders of the Second International sought to arrange joint discussions with the ILP, SFIO, and USPD delegates as well as with representatives of the trade union international (IFTU), their efforts only partially succeeded. While the IFTU agreed to a meeting, the Vienna Union refused on the grounds that any cooperation with the Second International was 'pointless' as any common position arrived at on reparations would be 'humbug' (*Spiegelfechterei*).[116]

Ironically, though they never met, the delegates of the Second International and the Vienna Union drew up reparations plans that resembled each other in notable respects. Both agreed that Germany had a duty to pay reparations, but both also made reparations tributary to the larger project of the economic reconstruction of regions devastated during the war—a project encompassing victors and van- quished. Looking further, both framed reparations as an opportunity to tighten the bonds of economic and financial interdependence not only between European countries but also with the United States. More concretely, both plans called for an international loan, guaranteed by the international community (i.e. the United States and/or the League of Nations), that would kick-start and lubricate the virtuous

---

[114] For an excellent account of the intergovernmental negotiations, see Zara Steiner, *The Lights that Failed: European International History 1919–1933* (Oxford, 2005), 193–206.

[115] For background, see 'Sozialistiche Wiedergutmachung', reproduced in *Nachrichten der Internationalen Arbeitsgemeinschaft Sozialistischer Parteien: Organ der II ½ Internationale Wien April 1921–Juni 1923* (Glashütten im Taunus, 1973), April 1921, 1–5; and Georg Ledebour, 'Die interna- tionale sozialistische Konferenz in Amsterdam', *Die Freiheit*, 8 April 1921, 1–2.

[116] BA-SAPMO, SPD, RY 20 II/145/16, SPD, *Bericht des Parteivorstandes über das Geschäftsjahr 1920/1921* (Berlin, 1921), 45–6; and 'Die sozialistische Wiedergutmachungspolitik', reproduced in *Nachrichten der Internationalen Arbeitsgemeinschaft Sozialistischer Parteien*, April 1921, 6–8. For the meeting with the IFTU, see IISH, SAI 2/51, 'Sitzung des Executivkomités der 2. Internationale mit dem Bureau des Internationalen Gewerkschaftsbundes am 1.IV 21...', undated.

cycle of payments and growing general prosperity. No less importantly, both plans sought to depoliticize reparations by handing contentious issues—Germany's capacity to pay, the distribution of funds, oversight of the international loan—to non-governmental bodies comprising financial and economic experts, though the Vienna Union alone demanded that workers be represented.[117] Afterwards, both the Second International and the Vienna Union advertised their respective plans as proof of socialist internationalism's continued pertinence. Thus, while the SFIO's Longuet applauded the 'fruitful character of the achievements' of socialists at Amsterdam, which he contrasted with 'lamentable shortcomings of governments', the SPD's newspaper trumpeted the results as proof that the 'dangerous division of the [international] workers' movement did not preclude 'positive work in the international realm'.[118]

In the wake of the Amsterdam meetings, MacDonald appeared more determined than ever to bring about international socialist unity, which he viewed as a precondition for the International's political effectiveness. 'Every good socialist', he confided in July 1921, 'must be convinced that something must be done without delay to bring divided forces together, so that Socialism may exercise some influence upon European affairs.'[119] From the beginning, MacDonald focused his efforts on the Vienna Union, efforts that benefited from two important advantages. One was his membership in the ILP, which provided MacDonald with direct ties to the organization; the second was his wartime record, which made it difficult to denounce him as a social patriot. Moving quickly, in June 1921 MacDonald shepherded a resolution through Labour's annual conference that called for the Second International to be strengthened in 'its democratic foundations as opposed to dictatorship'. This would be best achieved by working to overcome 'further division' with the Vienna Union and by inviting all 'Labour and Socialist bodies' to a conference 'from which a comprehensive International may arise'.[120] At a meeting later the same month, the Second International's executive committee approved a Labour proposal to take the initiative in organizing an international conference of socialist parties. MacDonald, accordingly, dispatched invitations to both the Vienna Union and its member parties for a conference to be held in London in October.[121]

MacDonald's invitation placed Adler in a difficult position. As the Vienna Union's chairman, Adler found himself buffeted by contending winds in the summer of 1921. On one side came pressure to negotiate with the Komintern. Writing

---

[117] For the Vienna Union's plan, see BLPSE, ILP Papers, 2/4, 'Joint Manifesto on Reparations', undated but April 1921; for the Second International's plan, see the documents attached to IISH, SAI 2/51, 'Sitzung des Executivkomités der 2. Internationale mit dem Bureau des Internationalen Gewerkschaftsbundes am 1.IV 21 . . .'

[118] Longuet, 'Au lendemain d'Amsterdam', *Le Populaire de Paris*, 8 June 1921, 1; and 'Die Internationale als Wegweiser', Vorwärts, no. 156, 4 April 1921, 1–2.

[119] IISH, Pietre Troelstra Papers, 552, MacDonald to Troelstra, 13 July 1921.

[120] Labour Party, *Report of the Twenty-First Annual Conference held in the Dome, Brighton, on June 21st, 22nd, 23rd and 24th 1921* (London, 1921), annex, 4.

[121] BA-SAPMO, SPD, RY 20 II/145/16, SPD, *Bericht des Parteivorstandes über das Geschäftsjahr 1920/1921*, 47; and LHASC, LPA, LSI 10/14/1, Labour (MacDonald) circular, 28 June 1921.

to Adler in June, the Swiss Socialist Party regretted that no effort had been made since the Vienna conference to cooperate with the Communist International and demanded 'a more determined and aggressive' policy in this sense. Although far from hostile to the Swiss party's demands, Adler replied that for the moment the Komintern evinced no signs of a willingness to cooperate. More generally, he once again counselled patience. The Vienna Union must avoid the type of 'insincere activity' [*Scheinaktion*]' that had reduced the Second International to an 'International of resolutions'. Its task was not to coordinate the activities of its members, let alone dictate a common position, but simply to encourage 'spontaneous action in certain countries'; for now, the Vienna Union should adopt a position of 'reserve'.[122] But if the Swiss party pressed for an opening towards the Komintern, the ILP insisted on the opposite—that the Vienna Union remain in contact with Labour and, by extension, with the Second International. Labour leaders barely tolerated the ILP's membership in the Vienna Union and they made it clear that the ILP's future in the Labour Party depended on its ability to act as a bridge with the Second International. The ILP, accordingly, underscored to Adler the 'importance of consultation with the Labour Party'.[123]

With the member parties of the Vienna Union tilting in separate directions, Adler was necessarily cautious in his response to MacDonald's invitation, even if his hostility towards the Second International was palpable. He began by chiding MacDonald for having communicated directly with the individual socialist parties, citing the resolution from the Vienna conference that prohibited member parties from negotiating separately with 'other international organisations'. Moving beyond reproaches, Adler emphasized the fundamental disagreement between the Second International and the Vienna Union—a disagreement he 'summarised as the opposition between the reformist and revolutionary conceptions of Socialism'. The Second International would have to undergo a conversion to revolutionary socialism for any merger to be possible:

> So long as this opposition [between reformist and revolutionary socialism] continues to exist, and so long as the parties affiliated to the 2nd International do not attain to greater insight into the conditions and possibilities of proletarian revolution, a basis of international proletarian unity is lacking, for fusion without fundamental ideas in common would be only formal unity, bereft of inner determination, without strength and capacity for action.

At the same time, Adler did not completely shut the door. Though rejecting an international conference, he welcomed 'consultations for informative [*sic*] purposes, which are not of a binding character', noting in particular the Vienna Union's readiness to meet with Labour's national executive.[124]

The upshot was a two-day meeting in mid-October 1921 in London between representatives of the Vienna Union and Labour. The latter lobbied for an international socialist conference, stressing the 'extremely painful' situation of

---

[122] SSAZ, SPS, Ar.1.260.3, SPS to Adler, 13 June 1921; and Adler to SPS, 18 June 1921. Emphasis in original.

[123] BLPSE, ILP Papers, 2/4, NAC minutes, 22–23 September 1921.

[124] Ibid., ILP Papers, 2/4, translated copy of Adler's reply, undated but July 1921.

international socialism, characterized, as Tom Shaw described, by 'warring sections, no unity of effort, division of energy, sections working against each other instead of helping each other'. Without a 'unified International on the political side' international socialism would be powerless. More concretely, Shaw proposed that the Second International and the Vienna Union begin by working together to overcome their differences. If this proposal did not rule out future negotiations with the Komintern, it was clear that Labour opposed unity with the communists. In response, Adler questioned the Second International's claim to speak for international socialism, labelling it a 'sectional movement'. The Second International 'represented a portion of the proletariat of the world with a special programme of its own', he explained. 'It was marked by a special sort of conduct during the war and it stood in a special position to other groups of socialist parties.' Echoing Adler, Georg Ledebour, a USPD leader, criticized Labour's wish to exclude the communists. The latter, he argued, 'were a proletarian organisation with a right to express their own conclusions and having a very definite historical development'. For both Adler and Ledebour, excluding the communists risked not only reinforcing the International's reformist tendencies; it would also entrench existing divisions among the workers in France, Germany, and other Continental countries, furthering weakening socialism at the national and international levels.[125]

The Labour delegates did not hide their disappointment. Henderson protested that 'further discussion seemed hopeless', prompting Emmanuel Shinwell, an ILP member, to claim that the Vienna Union's position contained some flexibility. But it was MacDonald, attending as a Labour delegate, who played the mediator. Insisting that the two organizations were not that far apart, he suggested that they work to 'lay down principles of common thought and common action'—principles that all parties would then be asked to accept. If the communists accepted them, so much the better; if not, they should be 'allowed to go on in their own way, but the other parties should not allow their own case to be weakened because the Communists were not prepared to come in now'. Since Adler rejected direct talks between the two organizations, MacDonald suggested that for now Labour and the Vienna Union together explore the possibility of 'common action' on concrete issues of international politics.[126] Adler promised a speedy reply.

When it arrived, Adler's reply indicated that MacDonald's hopes for a workable compromise were premature. In addition to ruling out a conference, Adler insisted that the Vienna Union was a more appropriate vehicle than the Second International (or Labour) for creating an 'all-inclusive International'. Labour's response, signed by Henderson, described the Vienna Union's position as 'indefensible'. In preventing 'any substantial progress' until the 'Communists have so modified their position as to make their cooperation with all other Socialist parties in the world possible', the Vienna Union effectively accepted the

---

[125] IISH, Pietre Troelstra Papers, 485, Labour Party, 'The Reconstruction of the International. Conference at the Clayton Hall, London, October 19th and 20th, 1921 between the Bureau of the International Working Union of Socialist Parties (Vienna Union) and the Executive Committee of the British Labour Party', undated.

[126] Ibid.

'indefinite postponement' of 'International Unity'.[127] MacDonald, meanwhile, was close to despair, admitting to Branting that:

> I am driven more and more to the conclusion that the international Socialist movement is so divided in policy and that some of the national sections are so anxious to use their International as a weapon with which to beat rival national sections that little can be done to unite us.

All that could be done, he lamented, was to 'hold the field and wait for a change'.[128]

THE SFIO SEIZES THE INITIATIVE

MacDonald proved to be overly pessimistic. Spurred by the activities of the SFIO, the Vienna Union soon proved to be more flexible. The French party emerged from the schism of the Tours congress in December 1920 in a pitiful state. Membership, which stood at 180,000 on the eve of the congress, fell to 50,000 at most. In voting to leave, the majority took with them most of the party funds and records as well as the flagship newspaper (*L'Humanité*). Although Blum typically remained optimistic, in many French departments the local organization either disappeared completely or led a shadow existence.[129] As Faure, the rump party's new secretary general, admitted in November 1921, 'everything has to be redone'. To be sure, the SFIO retained some advantages. Of its sixty-eight parliamentary deputies, fifty-five remained with the party. Arguably more importantly, in the larger towns and cities across France militants tended to remain loyal, providing the SFIO with the local tools to rebuild.[130] But in 1921–1922 the SFIO's potential for rebuilding lay in the future. What struck observers at the time—including foreign socialists— was the weakness of French socialism. One prominent sign of this weakness was the SFIO's repeated pleas to foreign socialist parties, including those belonging to the Second International, for help in financing *Le Populaire de Paris*, the party's principal newspaper.[131]

Significantly, the SFIO's weakness fuelled a keen interest in international socialist unity. Following Tours, the party shifted to the left, as many socialists who remained did so on the condition that the SFIO distance itself from its wartime 'reformist' course. At a meeting immediately following the vote at Tours, Blum reassured the ex-*minoritaires* such as Faure and Longuet, who had voted against affiliation with the Komintern, that he 'disagreed with any turn to the right'. It followed that the SFIO would join the Vienna Union, whose declared purpose was

[127] The two texts are reproduced in Robert Sigel, *Die Geschichte der Zweiten Internationale 1918–1923* (Frankfurt, 1986), 165–8.

[128] AABS, Hjalmar Branting, 91/3/1/22, MacDonald to Branting, 26 October 1921.

[129] AN, Papiers Marcel Sembat, 637/AP/155, Blum to Sembat, undated but early 1921.

[130] For the post-Tours party, see Tony Judt, *Marxism and the Left in France: Studies on Labour and Politics in France 1830–1981* (Oxford, 1989 edn.), 124–6. Faure is cited in SFIO, *XIXe Congrès national 29, 30, 31 Octobre–1er Novembre 1921. Rapports…*(Paris, 1921), Rapport moral, 4.

[131] OURS, Jean Longuet, 61 APO 7, Sidney Webb to Longuet, 27 December 1921; and AMSAB, POB, 'Séance du Bureau du Conseil général du 30-1-1922'.

to forge a united international socialist movement on a revolutionary basis.[132] That said, the SFIO remained divided on the question of an International: while a minority led by Renaudel sought to join the Second International, the majority led by Faure and Longuet were opposed. In this situation, the existence of several international social organizations fostered continuous tensions within the party— tensions that risked producing a renewed schism. Put simply, the unity of the post-Tours SFIO depended on creating a single International. Complicating matters were the divisions among French socialists on the question of whether cooperation with the communists was a practical possibility. If the partisans of the Second International predictably ruled out cooperation, others such as Longuet refused to reject the possibility outright, even if the 1920 schism had left deep scars.[133] Finally, with the SFIO too weak to exercise much influence on domestic politics, French socialists looked to the international realm and to the world of international socialism. Practical cooperation with foreign socialists on concrete issues offered a means not only to demonstrate the continued political relevance of French social-ism, but also to soothe ongoing tensions within the SFIO by building bridges with socialist parties across organizational divides.

The SFIO's interest in the practice of socialist internationalism was evident at its first post-schism congress in the autumn of 1921. Testifying to internal party divi-sions, the SFIO had invited fraternal delegates from member parties of both the Vienna International and the Second International. Speaking for Labour, Tom Shaw issued a fervent appeal for unity between the two socialist organizations—an appeal that received vigorous backing from Renaudel, who had been openly work-ing for a 'rapprochement' between the Second International and the Vienna Union.[134] Explicitly rejecting Shaw's appeal because it excluded the Komintern, the USPD's Ledebour proposed instead that the Vienna Union take the initiative in seeking practical cooperation with both the Second and Third Internationals. Ledebour's proposal for tripartite cooperation, however, met with a lukewarm response from Léon Blum, the SFIO's parliamentary leader, who questioned the Komintern's good faith. The 'great majority' of French socialists, he noted, were not prepared to wait until 'Moscow adopted a different attitude'. Reflecting Blum's growing influence within the SFIO, the final resolution favoured a joint initiative with the Second International: the Vienna Union was thus invited to work with Labour in forming an 'international action committee' comprising delegates from the three international organizations and charged with preparing a 'common pro-letarian front'.[135] In a published editorial the following day, Blum made it clear that the Vienna Union would be pressured to act in this sense.[136]

---

[132] 'Le congrès de la minorité', reproduced in Jean Charles et al., eds., *Le Congrès de Tours*, Blum, 678.

[133] For the deep scars, see the comments of the ex-*minoritaire* Paul Faure in his *La scission socialiste en France et dans l'Internationale* (Paris, 1921), 7.

[134] AABS, Hjalmar Branting, 91/3/1/22, Renaudel to Branting, 29 January 1921; and Renaudel, 'À Vienne', *Vie socialiste*, no. 32, 5 February 1921.

[135] 'Vive Internationale', 31 October 1921, 1–2; 'Troisième journée du Congrès National', 1 November 1921, 1; and 'Les résolutions du Congrès', 2 November 1921, 1, all in *Le Populaire de Paris*.

[136] Blum, 'Le Bilan du Congrès', *Le Populaire de Paris*, 3 November 1921, 1.

Adler was understandably unhappy with the results of the SFIO congress. Preferring to wait, he now faced a French party determined to galvanize developments. Writing to Ledebour soon afterwards, Adler emphasized the danger that 'we will soon be dragged against our will into a conference limited to the [Vienna Union] and the Second International.' To preclude such an event, he sought to pre-empt cooperation with Labour by informally contacting both the Second and Third Internationals; only if the two responded positively would work begin on organizing an international conference.[137] But SFIO leaders rejected this démarche. Seizing the initiative, in early December 1921 the SFIO proposed to organize a meeting of socialist parties from Western Europe to discuss 'questions of burning [international] relevance', identifying disarmament and the famine in Russia as well as reparations. Describing the overall international situation in bleak terms, Faure told Adler that European socialists could not wait but must forge a common response. Although Faure proposed to invite communist parties as well, the SFIO's move was rightly understood as an attempt to strengthen ties between Vienna and London. As the Swiss socialist Robert Grimm informed his party, the French sought first and foremost the 'resumption of relations' with the 'followers of the Second International'.[138]

Angry with the SFIO's initiative, Adler published a series of articles reiterating the mantra that a genuine International must be a synthesis of reform and revolution and that such a synthesis would take time to construct.[139] That the articles appeared in *Die Freiheit*, the USPD's newspaper, was no coincidence as Adler could count on the party's support in his efforts to counter the SFIO. At the USPD congress in January 1922, Salomon Grumbach, a German-speaking French socialist, read a letter from Faure in which the SFIO's general secretary asked the independent Germans to endorse his conference proposal. In response, Arthur Crispien, the USPD's chairman, rejected any idea of allying with a 'nationalist oriented' organization such as the Second International.[140] At the same time, however, Adler could not ignore the SFIO as it was a pillar of the Vienna Union. Reinforcing this factor was the ILP's influence. During late 1921 and early 1922, MacDonald increased his pressure on the ILP, demanding that it push Adler to cooperate with Labour. As a result, the ILP informed Adler that it backed the SFIO's proposal and expected the Vienna Union to do likewise.[141] At a meeting of the Vienna Union's executive bureau in mid-December 1921, Richard Wallhead, the ILP delegate, insisted that

---

[137] SSAZ, SPS, MFC 3, Adler to Ledebour, 9 November 1921; and Vienna Union circular to member parties, 9 November 1921, signed Adler.
[138] BLPSE, ILP Papers, 1921/3/8, Faure (SFIO) to Adler (Vienna Union), 1 December 1921; and SSAZ, SPS, AR.1.110.1, 'Sitzung des Geschäftsleitung. Dienstag des 6. Dezember 1921...', Grimm, 349.
[139] Adler, 'Die internationale Organisation der Arbeiterklasse', *Die Freiheit*, nos. 574 and 575, 9 December 1921, 1–2.
[140] USPD, *Protokoll über die Verhandlungen des Parteitages in Leipzig vom 8. bis 12. Januar 1922...*, reproduced in *Protokolle der Parteitage der Unabhängigen Sozialdemokratischen Partei Deutschlands Band 4, 1922–1923* (Glashütten im Taunas, 1976), Grumbach, 98–100; and Crispien, 121–8.
[141] AILP, series III, Frances Johnson correspondence, reel 18, 1920/279, MacDonald to Johnson, 25 October 1921; and BLPSE, ILP Papers, 4/1921/323, Johnson (ILP) to Faure (SFIO), 10 December 1921.

discussions take place not only with Labour but also with the Belgian and Dutch parties, both members of the Second International. Faced with a common SFIO-ILP front, Adler found himself compelled to give way, with the result that the Vienna Union's executive passed a resolution calling on the ILP and the SFIO 'to enter into relations with the English Labour Party' in order to organize a conference of parties from countries directly affected by the peace treaties.[142]

MacDonald replied to Faure that Labour would happily attend a conference of socialist parties to discuss concrete issues of international politics. He did, however, inform the SFIO through the ILP that Labour would insist on the exclusion of British communists, prompting Faure to reply that the SFIO wanted a conference with communist participation if possible but without it if necessary. For Faure, the essential point was that 'Labour be there. Without them it [the conference] is a failure.'[143] Attempts to exclude the communists provoked a heated debate at a meeting of the Vienna Union's executive bureau in mid-January 1922. Despite some grumbling, the bureau reiterated its approval of the SFIO's proposal on condition that parallel efforts be undertaken to organize an eventual conference with the executives of the Second and the Third Internationals. Accordingly, the SFIO in late January 1922 issued invitations to the 'proletarian parties' of Belgium, Britain, France, Germany, and Italy to a conference in early February to consider the subject of reparations—the subject, it is worth adding, that the member parties from the Vienna Union and the Second International had (separately) considered in Amsterdam in February 1921.[144]

The ensuing conference was a restrained affair. Aside from communists, the German socialists (the USPD and SPD) were absent due to railway strikes in Germany.[145] Consequently, it was decided to convoke another conference, this time in Frankfurt, for the end of the month. At the Frankfurt conference the delegates discussed reparations as well as disarmament, with the latter subject sparking some disagreement over the question of military alliances. Agreement on reparations, by comparison, proved to be relatively easy, no doubt because the subject had already been discussed at length. Indeed, the resolution on reparations, which was based on an SFIO draft, closely resembled the plans worked out the year before in Amsterdam: the close linkage between reparations and the reconstruction of devastated regions; international loans to kick-start the payment process; and the creation of an international organization to oversee the whole affair.[146]

---

[142] 'The Frankfurt Meeting of the Bureau of the Vienna Union', 17–18 December 1921, reproduced in *Nachrichten der Internationalen Arbeitsgemeinschaft Sozialistischer Parteien*, vol. 2, no. 1, January 1922; and BLPSE, ILP Papers, 4/1921/330, Wallhead (ILP) to Henderson (Labour), 21 December 1921.

[143] IISH, LSI (London Secretariat), 87, MacDonald to Faure, 29 December 1921; and Faure to MacDonald, 22 December 1921; and AILP, series III, Frances Johnson correspondence, reel 18, 1921/326, MacDonald to Johnson, 13 December 1921.

[144] For the executive bureau meeting, see the account in SSAZ, SPS, AR.1.110.11, 'Sitzung des Geschäftsleitung. Dienstag des 24. Januar 1922...', Grimm; and for the invitation, see BLPSE, ILP Papers, 2/4, Faure (SFIO) to Johnson (ILP), 25 January 1922.

[145] 'La Conférence internationale socialiste a suspendu hier ses travaux', *Le Populaire de Paris*, 7 February 1922, 1.

[146] LHASC, LPA, LSI, 11/4/13, 'The Five Party International Conference...Frankfurt, 25th, 26th and 27th February, 1922. Report', undated. A French police report, however, did indicate that a 'violent

Speaking for the SFIO, Longuet greeted the resolution as evidence that European socialists, working together, could find 'vigorous and subtle formulas' to concrete problems—a success he once again contrasted with governments which remained 'irremediably [and] stupidly divided'. Perhaps more importantly, some USPD members also welcomed the practical cooperation between parties regardless of institutional divides. Richard Breitscheid, a leading USPD voice on foreign policy, thus extolled the ability of socialists, despite 'differences of principle', to 'debate practical policy not only with calm and expertise, but also to arrive at unanimous results'. The 'ice has been broken', he continued, and if it was possible for socialists to reach an understanding on reparations then it was possible for them to forge common socialist positions on other policies.[147]

But perhaps the most important result of the SFIO's initiative was that it prodded Adler into one last attempt at uniting the three international socialist organizations. Earlier, in January 1922, the Vienna Union's secretary had formally invited the Second and Third Internationals to form a liaison committee with the Vienna Union to examine the possibility of an international conference. Taking advantage of the Frankfurt conference the following month, Adler arranged for parallel talks to take place between the executive committees of the Second International and the Vienna Union. The upshot was a decision to hold 'preliminary talks' between the executives of the three international organizations—talks that Adler promised to organize as quickly as possible.[148]

THE FAILURE OF TRIPARTITE NEGOTIATIONS

With the Second International's approval, Adler set about organizing tripartite talks. By mid-March 1922 he could announce that the executive committees of both the Second and Third Internationals had agreed to a joint meeting with the Vienna Union's bureau, which he hoped would occur at the end of the month in Berlin.[149] Although Adler feigned enthusiasm, he was privately pessimistic about the prospects. In meetings in Paris in early February 1922, Adler doubted that tripartite talks would lead to 'a reconstruction of the International of any kind', if only because the communists were participating for 'purely tactical reasons'. Yet, at the same time, he warned against creating an anti-communist International that would 'be used as an instrument to combat Bolshevism'. In part, Adler was motivated by the strength of communism at the national level, particularly in Central Europe. But probably a more important factor was his continuing antipathy for an International dominated by right-wing socialists—those whom he continued to

exchange' occurred between French and Belgian socialists over reparations. See AN F7/13425, 'Renseignements', no. 9855, 15 March 1922.

[147] Longuet, 'L'Internationale pour la paix du monde', *Le Populaire de Paris*, 2 March 1922, 1; and Breitscheid, 'Ein erster Schritt', *Der Sozialist*, no. 10, 11 March 1922, 153–4.
[148] 'La conférence socialiste', *Le Midi socialiste*, 28 February 1922, 2; and 'La réunion des deux bureaux exécutifs. La question de la Conférence générale', *Le Populaire de Paris*, 27 February 1922, 1.
[149] BLPSE, ILP Papers, 1922/44, Vienna Union circular, 10 March 1922, Adler.

label 'opportunists'. Unable to prevent the growing rapprochement between the Second International and the Vienna Union, Adler hoped to exploit tripartite talks to prevent a break with the Komintern—a break that would almost certainly lead to a fusion of the first two organizations. The Vienna Union's chief accordingly insisted that no conditions be attached to the Komintern's participation and that all 'questions of principle' be avoided. Instead, the talks should be 'limited to certain practical questions upon which action could be taken'.[150]

As Adler knew all too well, the Second International's executive committee did not share his views. Indeed, the Second International's willingness to participate in tripartite talks was circumscribed. First and foremost, none of its members believed it either desirable or possible to cooperate with the communists. The SPD was among the most outspoken in this regard: at the meetings in Frankfurt in late February 1922, Wels had opposed outright any talks with the Komintern.[151] But other parties, Labour among them, argued for a more subtle strategy of attaching political conditions to talks with the ostensible aim of testing communist goodwill but with the real goal of shifting responsibility for a break to the Komintern. And here the proposed conditions are revealing. While agreeing with Adler to avoid questions of principle, the Second International insisted that the Komintern provide satisfactory answers to questions concerning the independence of Georgia (menaced by the Red Army); the right of countries adjoining the Soviet Union to national self-determination; and the fate of political prisoners. Together, these questions raised issues that went to the heart of Bolshevik political doctrine and practice. Because it was all but impossible for the Bolsheviks to provide satisfactory answers without renouncing who they were, the questions were designed to underscore the fundamental incompatibility between socialist and communist internationalism. From the Second International's perspective, burdening the Komintern with the responsibility for a break would make it possible to win over much of the Vienna Union. As Renaudel had intimated to MacDonald in December 1921, if the 'refusal' to cooperate 'came from them [the communists] nothing could prevent a rapprochement between your organization and ours'.[152]

Some uncertainty surrounds why the Komintern agreed to Adler's proposal for tripartite talks. During most of 1921 the Komintern had steadily denounced the Vienna Union and the Second International, accusing both of 'helping the capitalist class in every country by encouraging a spirit of irresolution among the working class'.[153] Towards the end of the year, however, the Komintern shifted from an emphasis on civil war to a 'united front' policy that envisaged cooperation between

[150] AABS, Hjalmar Branting, 91/3/1/13, 'An International Socialist Conference Paris, 4th, 5th and 6th, February 1922', undated; and 'Auf dem Wege zu internationaler Kampffähigkeit', reproduced in *Nachrichten der Internationalen Arbeitsgemeinschaft Sozialistischer Parteien*, vol. 2, no. 3, March 1922.

[151] LHASC, LPA, LSI 11/4/11, 'International Unity. Proposed General Conference. A Report of the Discussions at Frankfurt', undated.

[152] For the insistence on conditions, see AMSAB, POB, 'Séance du Bureau du Conseil Général du 29-3-22'; and IISH, LSI (London Secretariat), 87, Renaudel to MacDonald, 24 December 1921.

[153] 'Extracts from the Theses on Tactics Adopted by the Third Comintern Congress', 12 July 1921, reproduced in Degras, ed., *The Communist International 1919–1943*, I, 256.

communists and socialists at the national level. As a result, the Komintern began to tone down its rhetoric, and in March 1922 its executive committee voted to participate in tripartite talks.[154] Two points are worth making regarding this decision. First, if the united front policy called for the unity of all workers, the call did not necessarily extend to the international organizations claiming to represent workers. The Bolsheviks, in other words, appealed to workers over the heads of their political and trade union leaders. Second, there is no reason to think that the Bolsheviks believed that a union with the Second International was feasible: too much—both in the past and in the present—divided them. If so, the Komintern likely had two related goals. One was to prevent a fusion of the Vienna Union and the Second International, the product of which would be anti-communist by definition, by keeping alive the possibility of communist cooperation. But if such a fusion proved unavoidable, the second goal would be to attract as much of the Vienna Union as possible to the Komintern. And for this reason, as Trotsky informed the Komintern's executive in February 1922, it was important that blame for a failure fall on European socialist leaders.[155]

With everyone in seeming accord, preliminary meetings between the executives of the three organizations took place in Berlin at the beginning of April 1922. Detailed accounts of the meetings already exist, but what is important for our purposes is that there was little chance of a consensus emerging on the International.[156] There was the clash of political cultures. The socialists, noted one outside observer, were shocked by the 'deliberately unkempt attitude' of the Komintern delegates who included 'young girls with short hair [and] men with long hair'.[157] More substantively, from the outset the Komintern and Second International delegates manoeuvred for advantage, each group accusing the other of intransigence. Meeting in private, the Second International's executive committee questioned whether it was even worth continuing the discussion, with Labour and SPD members expressing strong doubts on this score. After some debate, the committee members opted to submit a letter to the Komintern delegation reiterating their questions concerning communist policies and demanding that the Bolsheviks manifest 'the minimum of good faith and reciprocal sincerity'. Desperate to head off a failure, Adler proposed that the proceedings be adjourned and that a committee of nine be established with three representatives from each of the international organizations. Apparently unwilling to force a rupture, the three executive committees agreed to Adler's proposal, though the Second International continued to insist that at the next meeting the communists provide a 'definite written answer' to its questions.[158]

[154] Broué, *Histoire de l'Internationale communiste*, 252–5.

[155] '9. Sitzung (26. Februar. Abends)', reproduced in *Die Taktik der Kommunitischen Internationale gegen die Offensive des Kapitals. Bericht über die Konferenz der erweiterten Exekutive der Kommunistischen Internationale, Moskau, vom 24. Februar bis 4. März 1922* (Hamburg, 1922), Trotsky, 82–3.

[156] For accounts, see Donneur, *Histoire de l'Union des partis socialistes*, 225–78; and Sigel, *Die Geschichte der Zweiten Internationale*, 50–70.

[157] MAE, Série Y Internationale 1918–1940, 381, 'La Conférence des trois Internationales à Berlin 2–6 avril 1922', 11 April 1922.

[158] Notes on the various meetings can be found in LHASC, LPA, LSI Minutes, 1921–1937. Also see ibid., LSI 11/5/3, circular, 8 April 1922, MacDonald.

The first committee of nine meeting was scheduled for late May 1922 in Berlin. Two days before, the Second International's executive committee met to discuss tactics. Having once again overruled the SPD's proposal for an immediate break, the committee voted to submit a memorandum to the Komintern's delegates. In addition to reiterating its question regarding events in Georgia and the treatment of political prisoners, the memorandum underscored the profound differences between socialists and communists on the 'fundamental conception of Socialist liberty and methods'. The Second International, it declared, 'will be no party to deceiving the proletariat by appearing to take part in a unity which is a fraud, and is nothing more than an underhand tactic to allow noyautage and disruption to be pursued with greater effectiveness'. MacDonald read the memorandum at the committee of nine meeting, after which Karl Radek, the prominent Komintern leader, replied by accusing the Second International (and the SPD in particular) of seeking to sabotage efforts to organize an international socialist conference—an accusation that contained an implicit appeal to the member parties of the Vienna Union to enter into a 'united front' with the Komintern. To the undoubted surprise of all participants, however, Adler opined that both a prolongation of the meeting and a general conference appeared pointless. Clearly angry, Radek announced the Komintern's withdrawal from the committee of nine, blaming the failure of the tripartite talks on the Vienna Union.[159]

Despite his intervention at the meeting, Adler was not yet prepared to abandon hopes for a tripartite conference. In a public appeal to all workers one day after the committee of nine meeting, the Vienna Union blamed both the Second and Third Internationals for the failure to come to an agreement and reiterated its determination to create a united International.[160] Meeting in June 1922, the Vienna Union's executive bureau decided to call an international socialist conference for September 1922 in Karlsbad, Czechoslovakia. Meanwhile, in July 1922, Adler managed to arrange a meeting in Amsterdam of the Vienna Union, the Second International, and the IFTU to discuss the general situation. But though claiming international socialist unity to be a priority, Adler could not refrain from criticizing the Second International for refusing to cooperate with the Komintern.[161] By then, however, Adler's hopes for continued tripartite talks had become irrelevant. Following the collapse of the committee of nine meeting, an impatient MacDonald directed his anger at the Vienna Union, complaining in June 1922 (in an obvious reference to Adler) that 'international [socialist] co-operation' was being hindered 'by a few pontiffs who act as dancing masters'. The time had come, he concluded,

[159] Ibid., 'Report of Meeting of the Committee of Nine held in the Reichstag, Berlin, on Tuesday the 23rd of May 1922', undated. Emphasis in original. For Radek's response, see 'Erklärung der Delegation der Exekutive der Kommunistischen Internationale', reproduced in *Nachrichten der Internationalen Arbeitsgemeinschaft Sozialistischer Parteien*, vol. 2, no. 5, June 1922.

[160] 'An die Arbeiter aller Länder!', reproduced in ibid., vol. 2, no. 5, June 1922; and 'Bürositzung der I.A.S.P. in Frankfurt a.M. am 15 Juni 1922', reproduced in ibid., vol. 2, no. 6, July 1922.

[161] AABS, Hjalmar Branting, 91/4/1/3, 'Joint Meeting of the Executive Committees of the International Federation of Trade Unions (Amsterdam), the Second International (London) and the International Union of Socialist Parties (Vienna) held in Amsterdam on the 19th and 20th of July 1920'.

for European socialists to 'take matters into their own hands'.[162] The same month the Second International's executive committee decided to send an ultimatum to the Vienna Union: either it cooperate in organizing a 'general conference' or the Second International would go ahead on its own. In a circular letter a few days later, MacDonald insisted that the Second International would no longer wait for the Vienna Union:

> It is so determined however that international action shall not be crippled, and that the state of the world is so bad as to put to shame every influence that makes for Labour disunity, that it has decided to proceed itself with the Congress [general conference] if the Vienna Union refuses to co-operate.[163]

If MacDonald was determined to press forward with or without Adler's support, cautionary counsels now came from French socialists. During the summer of 1922 Faure sought to restrain the Labour leader. 'It is simply not possible for us to precipitate the fusion of our two organizations,' he wrote to MacDonald in June. 'Several steps are no doubt still necessary to bring together the international [socialist] forces.' The following month Faure asked him to 'make the effort to understand our difficulties and, in turn, the slowness of our action', while emphasizing his belief that 'international <u>socialist</u> unity is advancing well [*est en bon chemin*]'.[164] Faure's concern that hasty action could stoke tensions within the SFIO, possibly resulting even in a new schism, had some basis in reality. After all, wariness towards the 'reformist' Second International remained strong among French socialists. That said, the balance within the SFIO was tipping in favour of the Second International. In a series of articles in the early autumn of 1922, Longuet, hitherto a staunch backer of the Vienna Union, no longer ruled out a merger with the Second International but instead sought to attach conditions. For Longuet, the chief danger lay in a reconstituted International dominated by reformists who pursued a policy 'of compromise, of abdication, of abandonment of the class struggle'. Such an International would not only definitively alienate the left, including militants who might consider leaving the communists to rejoin the socialists; but it also risked strengthening the forces of 'socialist patriotism' within the SFIO. For these reasons, the Vienna Union must insist on a 'minimum of theoretical and practical guarantees' that a new International would be different from its predecessor. 'WE WILL NOT RETURN TO THE [pre-war] SECOND INTERNATIONAL,' Longuet emphatically proclaimed.[165]

---

[162] 'The Berlin Conference', *The Forward*, 3 June 1922, reproduced in MacDonald, *Wanderings and Excursions* (Indianapolis, 1925), 248–9.

[163] LHASC, LPA, LSI 14/4/1, Labour, 'International Labour & Socialist Conference held at...London on June 18th & 19th, 1922'; and BA-SAPMO, II. Internationale, RY 14 I 6/2/4, LSI, circular, MacDonald, 23 June 1922.

[164] IISH, LSI (London Secretariat), 88, Faure to MacDonald, 9 June 1922; and 102, Faure to MacDonald, 10 July 1922. Emphasis in original.

[165] Longuet, 'Le problème de l'unité internationale. Précisions et garanties nécessaires'; and 'Trois problèmes de l'unité internationale. Dictature, "social-patriotisme" et participation ministérielle', *Le Populaire de Paris*, 3 and 12 September 1922, 1. Emphasis in original.

While the SFIO havered, decisive events occurred in Germany. In the spring of 1922 the SPD and the USPD appeared to be as far apart as ever, with Crispien accusing the former of sabotaging efforts at international socialist unity.[166] Two months later, however, the assassination of Walter Rathenau, the German foreign minister, by nationalist extremists acted as a bridge between the two parties. In underscoring the existential threat to the Weimar Republic from within, Rathenau's murder prodded German socialists to cooperate in defence of the Republic and of democracy. At the international socialist meeting in Amsterdam in July 1922 Wels remarked that the 'situation in Germany was going from bad to worse', while Crispien reported that the 'two Socialist organizations [SPD and USPD] had come together in defence of the Republic, and were co-operating completely and loyally'.[167] Before long, USPD and SPD delegates were negotiating a merger between the two parties—negotiations that soon produced an agreement. At the USPD's congress in September, Ledebour passionately spoke against a merger with the SPD, objecting in particular to membership in the Second International. But Ledebour's objections were no match against the argument that the political effectiveness of German socialism was undermined by its continued divisions. On this point, even Adler agreed, remarking that the political situation in Germany no longer permitted 'a distinction between workers based on [political] parties'.[168]

The SPD and the USPD consummated their merger at a congress in Nuremburg in late September 1922. In welcoming the newly reunited SPD, Hermann Müller, the party's chairman, insisted that the immediate task of German socialism was to defend the Weimar Republic.[169] As the stronger party, with 1,175,000 members (compared to 300,000 for the USPD), the SPD could expect to be the dominant partner in the relationship. As one of its members triumphantly noted, the merger of the two parties demonstrated that it was impossible to pursue a socialist policy outside of the SPD.[170] Nevertheless, the integration of the USPD into the SPD would inject a powerful strain of internationalism into the latter's lifeblood. As Crispien explained at the Nuremburg congress, former USPD members like himself expected the SPD to cooperate closely with foreign parties to promote socialism in Germany and Europe.[171] No less importantly, some of the USPD's most

---

[166] Crispien, 'Einig – im revolutionären Sozialismus!', *Die Freiheit*, no. 179, 16 April 1922, 1–2.

[167] AABS, Hjalmar Branting, 91/4/1/3, 'Joint Meeting of the Executive Committees of the International Federation of Trade Unions (Amsterdam), the Second International (London) and the International Union of Socialist Parties (Vienna) held in Amsterdam on the 19th and 20th of July 1920'.

[168] *Protokoll über die Verhandlungen des Parteitages der Sozialdemokratischen Partei Deutschlands abgehalten in Gera vom 20. bis 23. September 1922*, reproduced in *Protokolle der Parteitage der Unabhängigen Sozialdemokratischen Partei Deutshlands* 4, Ledebour, 145–56, 166–70; Crispien, 131–45; Adler, 126. For USPD–SPD negotiations more generally, see Winkler, *Von der Revolution zur Stabilisierung*, 487–501.

[169] *Protokoll über die Verhandlungen des Einigungsparteitages abgehalten in Nürnberg am 24. September 1922*, reproduced in *Protokolle der Parteitage der Unabhängigen Sozialdemokratischen Partei Deutschlands* 4, Müller, 184.

[170] Bernd Braun and Joachim Eichler, eds., *Arbeiterführer Parlamentarier Parteiveteran. Die Tagebücher des Sozialdemokraten Hermann Molkenbuhr 1905 bis 1927* (Munich, 2000), 29 October 1922, 364.

[171] *Protokoll über die Verhandlungen des Einigungsparteitages abgehalten in Nürnberg am 24. September 1922*, Crispien, 187–8.

committed internationalists, among them Hilferding and Breitscheid, quickly assumed prominent roles in the SPD, placing them in a strong position to influence the party's future course.

The SPD–USPD merger also had immediate implications for the ongoing efforts to reconstitute a socialist International. For European socialists, the merger was widely interpreted as a precedent for the merger of the Vienna Union and the Second International. Indeed, a resolution at the Nuremburg congress presented socialism's newly found 'unity in Germany as a pledge and a certain promise for us of unity in the reconstituted International'.[172] But it was not only German socialists who perceived the international stakes involved in this sense. Writing to Kautsky in October 1922, Renaudel reported that his friends within the SFIO were 'all extremely happy to see the [SPD–USPD merger] realized' and that even Longuet accepted the 'fait accompli' and no longer opposed 'international [socialist] unity'. Consequently, Renaudel crowed, the fusion of the Vienna Union and the Second International could be achieved 'in the very near future'.[173] Similarly, the SPD–USPD merger ended any lingering doubts with the ILP regarding a merger between the Second International and Vienna Union. The 'two great wings of German socialism [had]…come together for the protection of the German Republic', the ILP's chairman explained, and that 'experience convinced him, even against his will, that further co-operation with the Third [International] had become impossible'.[174]

THE RECONSTITUTION OF THE INTERNATIONAL

Significantly, the merger of the SPD and USPD fortified MacDonald's belief that the Second International should forge ahead with or without Adler's support. 'Vienna is gasping,' he wrote in October 1922. 'We should continue to address all Socialist Parties on whatever is doing as though we alone were acting.'[175] By then, interestingly, MacDonald was no longer the head of the Second International's British section. Although claiming a desire to return to literary pursuits, MacDonald in fact wished to focus his political activities at home; he would soon become Labour's chairman. But if his choice to opt for national politics is noteworthy, so too is the fact that MacDonald remade his position within Labour, following his wartime political exile, through international socialist politics. In any case, MacDonald's replacement as the Second International's secretary, the trade unionist Tom Shaw, proved equally bent on moving forward with the reconstitution of the International. Writing to Renaudel in November 1922, Shaw complained of the Vienna Union's stalling tactics. 'Do you think we can dance attendance for ever on Vienna?' he remarked in frustration. The Second International, he insisted, would have 'to go

---

[172] FES, AdsD, NL Wilhelm Dittmann, 32, 'Arbeitendes Volk! Männer und Frauen!', 24 September 1922.

[173] Longuet to Kautsky, 11 October 1922, cited in Candar, *Jean Longuet (1876–1938)*, 268, fn. 11.

[174] ILP, *Report of the Annual Conference held at London, April 1923* (London, 1923), 84–5.

[175] IISH, LSI (London Secretariat), 89, MacDonald to Shaw, undated but October 1922. Emphasis in original.

on with its own work and to call it's [*sic*] Congress', bypassing Adler and appealing directly to the member parties of the Vienna Union.[176]

Faced with the Second International's determination to reconstitute the International, Adler conceded defeat. Although in October 1922 the Vienna Union's executive had announced its intent to continue working for an International that 'excluded no current of the world proletariat', its resolve soon crumbled. In early December the executive bureau voted six to three to ask the Second International to cooperate in organizing an international socialist conference. The Second International immediately accepted the offer, with the result that two days later delegates from the two organizations met in The Hague and agreed to create an 'action committee' whose 'principal task' was to prepare a conference. At the committee's opening meeting, held the same month, consensus was quickly reached for an international socialist conference to be held in May 1923 in Hamburg.[177] Although the various declarations made no mention of merging the two Internationals, the participants understood that this would be its principal purpose. Recognizing this reality, Adler could only bemoan that the International he had striven to create since 1918 would not emerge from the Hamburg conference. 'One cannot sweep aside the fact', he wrote in January 1923, 'that the International is destroyed and in no way can be reconstructed in a pinch.'[178]

Unable to stem the tide of developments sweeping towards a merger of the Vienna Union and the Second International, Adler and his supporters (such as Longuet) hoped to shape the nature of a reconstituted International. Aside from assurances that the latter would remain committed to the 'class struggle', they maintained that its decisions should be binding on all member parties. Only thereby could an effective International be created. During a two-day meeting in Cologne in early January 1923, the Vienna Union delegates managed to convince their Second International counterparts to endorse the principle that the International constituted the 'highest authority' between socialist parties and that membership signified a 'self-conscious reduction of the autonomy of parties'. Significantly, however, the final draft of the invitation to the Hamburg congress, sent out by both organizations, argued that consensus could not be expected to reign among the various parties from the outset but must be built through patient cooperation. As it read:

> The international organization of the working class…cannot, at the moment of its emergence, be the result of the principal agreement of all parties represented in it, but [such an organization] is one of the most important preconditions for achieving such a consensus. The proletarian parties, by sharing their experiences and by striving to apply in practice through energetic and collective efforts their agreements on the aims and methods of the international labour movement, will in ever greater measure construct the necessary basis for the common action of the world proletariat.[179]

---

[176] Ibid., Shaw to Renaudel, 27 November 1922.

[177] See the reports in *Nachrichten der Internationalen Arbeitsgemeinschaft Sozialistischer Parteien*, vol. 2, no. 9, December 1922.

[178] VGA, SPÖ, 118/713, Adler to Karl Cermak, 18 January 1923.

[179] 'Die Vorarbeiten für den Internationalen Sozialistenkongreß', reproduced in *Nachrichten der Internationalen Arbeitsgemeinschaft Sozialistischer Parteien*, vol. 3, no. 1, January 1923.

The invitation's contents reflected the opposition of the former MSPD and Labour to an International capable of dictating policy to its member parties. For both parties the principle of autonomy was sacrosanct. The task of the International, asserted Friedrich Stampfer, the *Vorwärts* editor, was not 'to direct and still less to command [but] to balance and to arbitrate. Only through joint persuasion and free will can collective action assume true force.'[180]

Adler fought hard against this conception of the International, lobbying the Vienna Union's member parties to insist on a more centralized organization. The Vienna Union, he explained to Swiss socialists in January 1923, must defend its 'agreed-upon principles' in negotiations with the Second International. But few if any parties were prepared to insist on the point. After considerable debate, Swiss socialists, for example, decided in March 1923 to attach no conditions to their membership in the new International.[181] The SFIO went even further. At the debate on the International at the party's national council in May 1923, Joseph Paul-Boncour, a leading advocate of national defence, expressed the fear that the International might try to dictate the SFIO's position in the event of war. In reply, Longuet insisted on the need for an 'International d'action' that would enable socialist internationalism to avoid the 'shortcomings' evident during 1914–1918. Blum, characteristically, tried to wish away the issue, asserting that 'there is no contradiction between national and international interests.' But if Longuet and Blum were arguably vague, Faure was unequivocal. 'In the International', he reassured Paul Boncour, 'there will be decisions taken on important issues by majority vote. In these cases, decisions that are not unanimous will have no force.'[182]

A week after the SFIO's national council, the international socialist conference opened in Hamburg. Over 600 delegates from 30 countries gathered to found a new International—the Labour and Socialist International (LSI). The gathering occurred against the backdrop of rising international tensions, marked most obviously by the occupation four months earlier of the Ruhr by French and Belgian troops. Yet international tensions only confirmed the need for international socialist unity. As Adler himself explained at the Vienna Union's final congress, 'the urgency of the moment compels us to combine all our forces.'[183] The threatening international situation also allowed the delegates gathered in Hamburg to skate over difficult issues. The emphasis instead was on unity. 'From this congress one concrete fact can be recognized', Wels enthused in his opening address, 'the reappearance of international [socialist] unity...It means the overcoming of divisions, the end of conflict between brothers.' To be sure, Adler insisted that the International's resolutions would be binding on member parties, arguing that international socialism

---

[180] Stampfer, 'Zum Weltkongreß der Sozialistichen Arbeiter Internationale', no. 233, 20 May 1923, 1.
[181] SSAZ, SPS, AR.1.110.12, 'Sitzung der Geschäftsleitung. Dienstag den 9. Januar 1923...', 2; and 'Sitzung des Parteivorstandes 24./25 März 1923...'
[182] 'Le Conseil National du Parti socialiste unanime pour la reconstruction de l'Internationale', *Le Populaire de Paris*, 14 May 1923, 1, 3.
[183] 'Schlußkonferenz der I.A.S.P. im Hamburg am 20. Mai 1923', reproduced in *Nachrichten der Internationalen Arbeitsgemeinschaft Sozialistischer Parteien*, vol. 3, no. 3, June 1923.

must not allow itself to be paralysed by divisions as it had during 1914–1918.[184] None of the other speakers, however, saw the need to contradict Adler, for it was evident that the LSI would be, as a French socialist remarked elsewhere, 'a federation' of parties 'free and equal between themselves'.[185]

The LSI's federalist structure is worth underscoring for several reasons. First and most obviously, it amounted to a defeat for Adler and his supporters within the Vienna Union, who wanted a more centralized organization capable of imposing a common line on its member parties.[186] Another and more important reason is that the federalist structure would profoundly shape the LSI's functioning and thus the nature of socialist internationalism. From its beginning, the majority of European socialists conceived of the LSI as an instrument for cooperation between socialist parties. Such cooperation would centre on concrete international issues, partly because of the scope and urgency of such issues during the post-war period, but also because theoretical or doctrinal questions were deemed to be too divisive. For socialists, in other words, internationalism was above all a practice, and the LSI would be judged on these terms. Now that international socialist unity had been achieved, the SPD's *Vorwärts* announced, socialists must turn to the task of 'solving today's practical [international] problems'. If the International was to succeed, it could not satisfy itself with 'forceful but also easy critiques' but must 'identify paths [to follow] and propose solutions' to concrete problems.[187]

[184] *Protokoll des ersten Internationalen Sozialistischen Arbeiterkongresses. Hamburg, 21. bis 25. Mai 1923* (Glashütten im Taunus, 1974), Wels, 13; Adler, 49.

[185] CHS, Fonds Jean Zyromski, 1 AS/67, 'Après le Conseil National', undated ms notes.

[186] For this reason, it is difficult to agree with André Donneur's conclusion that the Vienna Union profoundly influenced the nature of the LSI. See Donneur, *Histoire de l'Union des partis socialistes pour l'action internationale*, 371.

[187] 'Hamburg', *Vorwärts*, no. 243, 27 May 1923, 1.

3

European Socialists and the International Order, 1918–1925

Chapters 1 and 2 discussed the efforts of European socialists to reconstruct an international community following the outbreak of war in August 1914. Their efforts, which began during the war itself, culminated in May 1923 with the reconstitution of the International as the Labour and Socialist International (LSI). Socialists viewed the new International not as an end in itself but as an instrument to facilitate the practice of socialist internationalism. As they repeatedly intoned, the LSI must be an 'International of action' and not merely of words. The emphasis on practice, however, did not begin in 1923. From the moment of the armistice in November 1918, British, French, and German socialists struggled to cooperate with one another in placing a socialist stamp on the emerging post-war political order both within and between countries. The present chapter traces this struggle from the end of the war to the mid-1920s, a moment that several recent scholars have identified as marking the end of the post-war period and the 'making [of] real peace'.[1] It does so by examining socialist positions on a series of interlocking issues underpinning international politics from 1918: the peace treaties; the principle of national self-determination; reparations and economic reconstruction; and the League of Nations and security arrangements.

Given the prominence of these issues at the time, they have understandably attracted considerable scholarly attention. Until recently, the dominant approach has been to concentrate on decision-making by governments. Scholars have closely examined the perceptions, calculations, and choices of national leaders and their advisors as well as how the decision-making process in one country interacted with those in other countries.[2] While this approach remains alive and well, in recent years scholars have begun to pay attention to non-governmental actors and their projects to reform if not transform international politics. A sizeable body of scholarship now exists that highlights the activities of organized groups (partisans of disarmament, the League of Nations, anti-colonialism, European unity), many of which sought to mobilize popular support behind their cause and some of which

---

[1] The citation is from William Mulligan, *The Great War for Peace* (New Haven, CT, 2014), 339–69. For a similar argument, see Cohrs, *The Unfinished Peace after World War I*; and Adam Tooze, *The Deluge: The Great War and the Remaking of Global Order* (New York, 2014).

[2] For recent studies, see Robert Boyce, *The Great Interwar Crisis and the Collapse of Globalization* (London, 2009); and Steiner, *The Lights that Failed*.

operated across national borders.[3] Only rarely, however, is any attempt made to integrate the two approaches.[4] This being so, socialists are intriguing actors because they straddled the government/non-government divide. The principal socialist parties were not governmental actors for the most part, even if Labour's brief minority government in 1924 was an important exception. Yet at the same time, socialist parties were often close to power. Deeply engaged in national politics, British, French, and German socialists generally adopted a stance of responsible opposition with an onus on constructive criticism. Their goal was to influence the contours of government policy. It is the insider–outsider status of socialist parties that makes the practice of socialist internationalism a useful lens through which to consider the possibilities for—but also the limits of—alternative approaches to international politics during the early post-war period.

As an international actor, European socialists are almost entirely absent from the scholarship both on government decision-making and on non-governmental organizations. This absence reflects the perception of European socialism as a domestic political phenomenon. To the extent that scholars examine the international aspects of post-war European socialism, they focus on the foreign policies of individual parties and of the Labour Party above all.[5] Little effort is made to place the policies of one party in a larger, international socialist context. As for the International, the dominant impression is one of failure. Writing during the 1970s from a Cold War perspective, Julius Braunthal, the International's semi-official historian, portrayed an international labour movement paralysed by the split between communists and socialists; from the communist side, Werner Kowalski also denounced this split but placed the blame entirely on the socialists.[6] Less influenced by the Cold War, J.F. Wrynn, in a study of the LSI and European reconstruction, bemoaned the inability of the individual socialist parties to rise above their parochial interests and to adopt a truly internationalist viewpoint. 'Though one cannot deny their good will and the

---

[3] Good examples include Sluga, *Internationalism in the Age of Nationalism*, 45–78; Daniel Laqua, ed., *Internationalism Reconfigured: Transnational Ideas and Movements between the World Wars* (London, 2011); Helen McCarthy, *The British People and the League of Nations: Democracy, Citizenship and Internationalism, 1918–1945* (Manchester, 2011); Verena Schöberl, *'Es gibt ein grosses und herrliches Land, das sich selbst nicht kennt..Es heisst Europa': Die Diskussion um die Paneuropaidee in Deutschland, Frankreich und Grossbritannien, 1922–1933* (Berlin, 2008); Jean-Michel Guieu, *Le Rameau et le glaive: les militants français pour la Société des Nations* (Paris, 2008); and Thomas Richard Davies, *The Possibilities of Transnational Activism: The Campaign for Disarmament between the Two World Wars* (Leiden, 2007).

[4] One notable exception is Jackson, *Beyond the Balance of Power*, which argues for the growing influence of internationalist groups on the evolution of French security policy.

[5] For examples, see Thierry Hohl, *À Gauche! La Gauche socialiste, 1921–1947* (Dijon, 2004); and Stefan Feucht, *Die Haltung der Sozialdemokratischen Partei Deutschlands zur Außenpolitik während der Weimarer Republik (1918–1933)* (Frankfurt am Main, 1998). For Labour, see Paul Bridgen, *The Labour Party and the Politics of War and Peace, 1900–1924* (Woodbridge, 2009); Lucien M. Ashworth, *International Relations and the Labour Party: Intellectuals and Policy Making from 1918–1945* (London, 2007); Henry R. Winkler, *Paths Not Taken: British Labour and International Policy in the 1920s* (Chapel Hill, NC, 1994); and Wolfgang Krieger, *Labour Party und Weimarer Republik. Ein Beitrag zur Außenpolitik der britischen Arbeiterbewegung zwischen Programmatik und Parteitaktik (1918–1924)* (Bonn, 1978).

[6] Braunthal, *History of the International* II; and Kowalski, *Geschichte der Sozialistischen Arbeiter-Internationale*, 9.

persistence of their efforts in the cause of European reconciliation and reconstruction,' he explained, '... their work, so piecemeal and so weighted with compromise, often exhibited the same want of a basic international vision which was the great weakness of the pre-war Second International.'[7]

In judging the International a failure, the focus all too often is on what socialist internationalism should have been rather than on what it was. Instead of positing an abstract standard of internationalism against which reality can be compared, this chapter examines how European socialists collectively constructed their internationalism through cooperation on international issues. In so doing, it demonstrates that the policymaking of socialist parties possessed an important international socialist dimension; the debate on international issues occurred between as well as within socialist parties, with the one influencing the other. Consequently, the content and significance of socialist internationalism was a subject of ongoing negotiation between parties. In practising their internationalism, European socialists sought to shape the post-war order by forging solutions to the pressing international issues that they would then lobby their national governments to adopt. In this they arguably enjoyed some success. On the issues of reparations and Western European security, European socialists claimed with justice to have pointed the way forward to intergovernmental arrangements, most notably with the Dawes Plan and the Locarno accords, respectively. But if socialists could rightly boast of their role as trailblazers, their deliberations during the early post-war years also exposed the conditional and therefore fragile nature of the much-vaunted 'real peace' achieved by mid-decade.

BEFORE THE VERSAILLES PEACE TREATY

At the moment of the armistice in November 1918, European socialists were ill-prepared to provide a practical outline of the post-war international order. To be sure, during the last two years of the war the issue of peace terms became a preoccupying subject within and between socialist parties. Nevertheless, the priority on organizing an international socialist conference encouraged socialists to limit themselves to broad principles for fear that detailed definitions would exacerbate existing divisions. The majority of German socialists thus declared their support for a Wilsonian peace because it supposedly promised 'non-partisan justice', preferring not to dwell on the potential tensions between their views of justice and those of Wilson. Similarly, the Entente socialists embraced Wilson's proposed League of Nations since it would make 'the world safe for democracy' while also ensuring that 'there should be henceforth on earth no more War.' Left undiscussed was how exactly the League would do so.[8]

---

[7] Wrynn, *The Socialist International and the Politics of European Reconstruction*, 10.

[8] For the SPD, see '17.10.1918: Fraktionssiztung', reproduced in Matthias and Pikart, eds., *Die Reichstagsfraktion der deutschen Sozialdemokratie 1914 bis 1918*, 482; and for the Entente socialists, see LHASC, LPA, LSI 1/27, Inter-Allied Labour and Socialist Conference, 'Memorandum on War Aims agreed upon at the Central Hall, Westminister, London, S.W., on February 20th to 24th, 1918'.

With the armistice, European socialists were forced to consider more closely possible peace terms if they hoped to exert any influence on the peace conference that would eventually open in Paris in January 1919. The first opportunity for them to do so came at the international socialist conference in Berne in February 1919. For Arthur Henderson, Labour's chairman, the purpose of the Berne conference was to make international socialism's voice heard in favour of a Wilsonian peace. 'We desire to sustain the demand for a Wilsonian Peace,' he wrote to the Belgian socialist Emile Vandervelde in December 1918.[9] Just what a Wilsonian peace would look like remained unclear, though Henderson predictably emphasized a League of Nations, describing it to a German diplomat as the 'principal point' [*Hauptsache*] of any international order.[10] Within the SFIO, the ex-*minoritaires*, who hoped to focus the Berne conference on the question of how to reinforce the revolutionary wave they saw cresting across Europe, conceived of a Wilsonian peace in vague terms of a rapprochement with Germany now that it had undergone a political revolution. Underpinning this rapprochement would be the sustained cooperation of all socialists committed to social revolution, a group that included the USPD and the ILP but likely not the SFIO's ex-*majoritaires*.[11] The latter, by contrast, interpreted a Wilsonian peace in terms that reflected the fact of Allied victory and their belief in Germany's responsibility for the war. Punishment (and guarantees against future German aggression) and not rapprochement were the dominant themes.[12]

German socialists, meanwhile, welcomed the Berne conference as a promising sign of international socialist solidarity. In November 1918 the majority of independent German socialists had jointly appealed to the 'proletariat of all countries' to cooperate with them in the 'work for peace'.[13] The joint appeal stemmed from the calculation that the support of Entente socialists was indispensable to avoid a draconian peace for Germany. Yet just as importantly, they disagreed on how best to ensure this support. For the MSPD, the new democratic Germany that had emerged from the wreckage of war represented a decisive break with the past. Representing this new Germany, German socialists would attend the Berne conference as equals, working with their European comrades to identify a Wilsonian peace favourable to their country.[14] More concretely, the MSPD demanded that the right of national self-determination be applied to Germans, which would limit potential territorial losses in the east while allowing a union (*Anschluß*) with Austria; that Germany be admitted as a full member of any League of Nations; and that it not be forced to pay indemnities. The duty of socialist internationalism was to back these demands.[15]

[9] AMSAB, Camille Huysmans Archive, I 650, Henderson to Vandervelde, 6 December 1918.
[10] PAAP, Berne 828, unsigned report, 27 January 1919.
[11] L.O. Frossard, 'À Lausanne pour quoi faire?', *Le Populaire de Paris*, 9 January 1919, 2.
[12] LHASC, LSI 3/102, Thomas to Henderson, 25 December 1918.
[13] AABS, Hjalmar Branting, 91/3/1/16, German socialists to Branting, 11 November 1918. Austrian socialists also appealed to the Entente socialists for help. See VGA, SPÖ, Sitzungsprotokolle des Parteivorstandes, 12 December 1918.
[14] 'Internationale Sozialistenkonferenz am 6. Januar in Lausanne', *Vorwärts*, 22 December 1918, 1.
[15] See Phlipp Scheidemann, 'Friedenswahlen', *Vorwärts*, 19 January 1919, 1; also see 'Entwurf für einer Aktionsprogramm' attached to '6.2.1919: Fraktionssitzung', reproduced in Potthoff et al., eds., *Die SPD Fraktion in der Nationalsammlung 1919–1920*, 11–14.

The USPD, by comparison, believed that Germany must do more to demonstrate its bona fides abroad if it were to avoid a draconian peace. And this entailed
a more decisive break with the past. If we want to appeal to the 'pacifist and socialist
elements' abroad, Heinrich Ströbel, a leading USPD member, explained, Germany
must exclude all the political forces tarnished by the sins of the old regime, the
MSPD among them.[16] Indeed, the USPD repeatedly claimed that independent
German socialists alone possessed the moral authority to ask for a peace of rapprochement because they alone had worked for such a peace during the war. At the
same time, the independent socialists were less confident concerning the nature
of a Wilsonian peace, partly because they viewed the American president as the
leader of the most developed capitalist country in the world; and for independent
socialists, capitalism and a peace of rapprochement were incompatible.[17] But their
doubts regarding Wilson also stemmed from the USPD's greater willingness to
consider Germany's (partial) responsibility for the war, a viewpoint that facilitated
a more realistic assessment of the peace terms that the victorious powers were
likely to impose.

It was with these diverse perspectives on peace that European socialists gathered
together in Berne in February 1919. More than anything, the proceedings highlighted the continued reluctance of European socialists to address concrete issues.
This reluctance was evident in the discussions on the League of Nations. British
socialists insisted that a League must assume absolute priority: it was imperative, a
Labour delegate asserted, 'not only to make the League of Nations a part of the
peace settlement, but to make it the foundation upon which the peace settlement
itself is built; and unless that is done, there is no hope for the future'.[18] In response,
French socialists sought to steer debate towards the question of how such a league
would function in practice and, more to the point, how it would enforce decisions
on recalcitrant countries. Labour participants, however, dismissed these concerns
as secondary. Rather than details, Ramsay MacDonald spoke vaguely of a new
international politics. 'The League must not be a mere footnote to the last four
years of European history,' he exclaimed. 'It must be an entirely new volume. The
old series must be finished, bound up, and placed away upon the shelves. We must
start a new volume with a totally new spirit, with a new set of writers drawn from
the democracies of the free nations of the world.'[19] The league's success, in short,
would depend on a transformation of international politics. But the problem, as
several delegates remarked, was that this transformation had yet to occur.

A recourse to imprecision was also evident in the discussions of territorial issues.
All the delegates at Berne agreed on the right to national self-determination as a

---

[16] See the discussion in 'Montag, 15.11.1918: Reichskonferenz', reproduced in Matthias and
Miller, eds., *Die Regierung der Volksbeauftragten 1918/19*, tome I (Düsseldorf, 1969), 164–83.

[17] 'Wilson', *Die Freiheit*, no. 71, 23 December 1918, 1.

[18] 'Arbeiter- und Sozialistenkonferenz in Bern, 3. bis 10. Februar 1919', reproduced in Ritter, ed.,
Die II. Internationale 1918/1919, I, James H. Thomas, 288. Also see Ulrich Hochschild, *Sozialdemokratie und Völkerbund. Die Haltung der SPD und S.F.I.O. zum Völkerbund von dessen Grundung
bis zum deutschen Beitritt (1919–1926)* (Karlsruhe, 1982), 27–30.

[19] Ibid., MacDonald, 309–12.

guiding principle for the post-war political order. But as the SFIO's Pierre Renaudel remarked, consensus quickly vanished 'as soon as we touch upon concrete cases and we leave aside general propositions'.[20] This was especially true for Alsace-Lorraine: the question of whether and how to consult the will of the people provoked lengthy and contentious exchanges, principally but not solely between French and German socialists. Only slightly less tense were the discussions regarding the fate of the ex-Austrian-Hungarian empire. While Austrian socialists demanded support for a plebiscite in Austria, which would almost certainly result in a vote in favour of *Anschluß*, Czech socialists contended that plebiscites were unnecessary either in the Slovakian part of the new Czechoslovak state or in the German-speaking areas of the Czech part (later known as the Sudetenland).[21] Behind the opposing positions lurked disagreements about the precise weight to assign to linguistic, historical, geo-strategic, and economic factors in drawing national boundaries. After much debate within the territorial commission, it was decided to 'exclude the discussion of concrete cases and to stick to [general] principles'.[22]

INITIAL REACTIONS TO THE PEACE TREATY

Following the Berne conference, European socialists did not have to wait long for news from the peacemakers in Paris. A draft of the League of Nations covenant was published in February 1919, followed in April by the initial version of what would become the Versailles Treaty. The first opportunity for an exchange of views came at the end of April when the permanent commission, created by the Berne conference, met in Amsterdam to discuss a response. Much of the discussion centred on the League of Nations, with the British delegates in particular denouncing the proposed version as an 'alliance of governments'. Explaining Labour's position, Henderson insisted that the League contradicted the conditions established at the Berne conference, which included membership for all states (and thus for Germany and Russia) and democratic representation that would make it an organization of peoples and not governments. Others, including Renaudel, presented the League as a promising beginning whatever its weaknesses. Predictably perhaps, the final resolution represented a compromise. While admitting that the League 'contains the first germ' of an organization to achieve a 'permanent peace', it also highlighted the absence of authority to arbitrate disputes between states, to impose disarmament on all its members, to encourage international commerce, and to ensure the

---

[20] Ibid., Renaudel, 398.

[21] In the run-up to Berne, Austrian socialists had been lobbying European socialists on these issues. See OURS, Fonds Jean Longuet, 61 APO 4, Otto Bauer to Longuet, 9 January 1919; and AABS, Hjalmar Branting 91/4/1/3, untitled note from the SPÖ, 1 February 1919. For the positions of Central and Eastern European socialists more generally, Lee Blackwood, 'Socialism, Nationalism and the "German Question" from World War I to Locarno and Beyond', unpublished PhD, Yale University, 1995, 88–131.

[22] 'Arbeiter- und Sozialistenkonferenz in Bern, 3. bis 10. Februar 1919', reproduced in Ritter, ed., *Die II. Internationale 1918/1919*, I, Mistral, 472–5; and 'Allgemeine Resolution die territorialen Fragen betreffend', 343–4.

application of the peace treaties.[23] When the commission met again in Paris in mid-May 1919 it was more critical but still circumspect. Though commenting that 'this peace is not our peace', the commission preferred to defer an overall assessment to a future international socialist conference.[24]

The individual parties, however, were not prepared to wait. In Germany, both the SPD and the USPD not only fiercely denounced the treaty as a 'peace of violence of the worst kind', they also pleaded with the Entente socialists to pressure their governments for better terms.[25] But for German socialists the more immediate question was whether or not to sign the treaty. The majority of the USPD answered with a reluctant yes. Although viewing the treaty as a repudiation of Wilson's Fourteen Points, the independent socialists concluded that the German government (a coalition including the MSPD) must sign it, chiefly because the alternative would be far worse for the German people: the renewal of war and even the occupation of the country. For the USPD, however, signing the treaty was simply a first step in a longer strategy of treaty revision—a strategy that it conceived of as an international socialist project. 'Only international socialism can speak the words of living peace', the USPD's leadership announced in May 1919, adding that it had confidence in the 'victorious forward march' of the 'progressive proletarian revolution' that would 'destroy' the Versailles treaty, just as the wartime treaties of Best-Litovsk and Bucharest had been destroyed.[26] But while waiting for revolution, the USPD looked to European socialists for help. Speaking in June, Hugo Haase proclaimed that the independent socialists 'have full confidence...that the peace treaty will be eventually be revised through the solidarity of the international proletariat'.[27] For Haase and his allies, the collective project of treaty revision presupposed a good-faith attempt on Germany's part to fulfil the terms of the peace treaty—to pursue a policy of fulfilment (*Erfüllungspolitik*). In cooperation with their comrades abroad, German socialists would demonstrate Germany's commitment to peace as well as the treaty's fundamental unworkability.[28] Once the need of treaty revision had become apparent, the task of European socialism would be to point the way forward by offering 'socialist' solutions to the pressing problems of international politics.

The debate within the MSPD over the treaty was considerably more contentious. Far less convinced of Germany's particular responsibility for the war than the USPD, the majority of socialists found the peace treaty all the more iniquitous. In his diary, Hermann Molkenbuhr, a co-chairman of the SPD's *Fraktion*, condemned

---

[23] 'Bericht über die Konferenz in Amsterdam, 26. bis 29. April 1919', reproduced in Ritter, ed., *Die II. Internationale 1918/1919*, I, 575–80; and 'Resolution über die Gesellschaft der Nationen', 604–5.

[24] 'Siztung des Aktions-Komités', 10–12 May 1919, reproduced in Ritter, ed., *Die II. Internationale 1918/1919*, II, 859–60; and 'Déclarations de l'Internationale. Un exposé de la Commission d'action', *L'Humanité*, 13 May 1919, 1.

[25] 'Die U.S.P.D. und der Friede', *Die Freiheit*, no. 225, 12 May 1919, 1; and 'An die Sozialisten aller Länder', *Vorwärts*, 10 May 1919, 1.

[26] 'Friedensultimatum und U.S.P.', *Die Freiheit*, no. 282, 18 June 1919, 1.

[27] Vehandlungen des Deutschen Reichstags, 40. Sitzung, 22 June 1919, Haase, 1129. Also see Haase to Else, 8 July 1919, reproduced in Haase, ed., *Hugo Haase*, 183–4.

[28] 'Friede', *Die Freiheit*, no. 19, 11 January 1920, 1.

the 'shamelessness' of Entente imperialists, claiming that even a militaristic Germany would not have imposed such 'perfidy' on its defeated foes.[29] Meanwhile, within the *Fraktion*, Scheidemann passionately argued against signing, threatening to resign from the government if it did so. 'Which hand would not wither', he later declared, 'which placed this chain upon itself and upon us.'[30] Heinrich Cunow, editor of *Die Neue Zeit*, the SPD's theoretical journal, offered another argument: the SPD's approval would undercut socialist (and other) voices in neutral and enemy countries that opposed the peace terms.[31] After agonized debate, the *Fraktion* voted by a slim majority to accept the treaty, clearing the way for the government's signature, even if Scheidemann did resign. The reasons for accepting the treaty resembled those of the USPD: the alternative would be worse. To reject the treaty, explained Carl Severing, would produce chaos of the kind as to make the upheaval of November 1918 appear as 'pure child's play'.[32]

Like the USPD, the MSPD openly announced its intention to pursue a policy of treaty revision. Unlike the independent socialists, however, the majority of socialists were initially uncertain whether or not to cooperate with international socialism. Initially, many German socialists reacted angrily to what they viewed as the lukewarm response of the Entente socialists. In the pages of *Vorwärts*, Victor Schiff claimed that the majority of French socialists had greeted the publication of the peace terms in a way that poured 'scorn' on 'the spirit of socialism and internationalism'. 'Think of Jaurès', he scolded them.[33] In the end, however, the MSPD had little choice but to adopt a policy closely resembling that of the USPD. Along with voting for the peace treaty, the party endorsed an '*Erfüllungspolitik*', with Müller claiming that German majority socialists would fulfil its terms 'to the limit of their abilities' while also working 'loyally' for its revision.[34] Efforts to implement the treaty would demonstrate the impossibility of doing so. Like the USPD, moreover, the SPD looked to international socialism as an ally in this enterprise. If German majority socialists arguably did so with less enthusiasm than their independent counterparts, they too understood that treaty revision required a renewed commitment to the practice of socialist internationalism. As Wels told an international socialist gathering in August 1919, 'We know that the revision of the peace treaty can only come from the strength of the well organised masses of workers' at home and abroad.[35]

[29] Braun and Eichler, eds., *Arbeiterführer Parlamentarier Parteiveteran*, 14 May 1919, 338–9.

[30] '19.6.1919, vorm.: Fraktionssitzung', reproduced in Potthoff et al., eds., *Die SPD Fraktion in der Nationalsammlung 1919–1920*, Scheidemann, 91–2; and Breitman, *German Socialism and Weimar Democracy*, 49.

[31] Cunow, 'Die Versailler Friedensbedingungen', *Die Neue Zeit*, vol. 2, no. 8, 23 May 1919, 173.

[32] '23.6.1919, vorm.: Fraktionssitzung', reproduced in Potthoff et al., eds., *Die SPD Fraktion in der Nationalsammlung 1919–1920*, Severing, 112. Also see Miller, *Die Bürde der Macht*, 274–87.

[33] Schiff, 'Artikel 231. Ein zweiter Brief an die französischen Sozialisten', *Vorwärts*, no. 265, 25 May 1919, 1–2.

[34] Vehandlungen des Deutschen Reichstags, 64. Sitzung, 23 July 1919, Müller, 1853.

[35] 'Konferenzen der Internationalen Permanenten Kommission in Luzern, 2. bis 9. August 1919', reproduced in Ritter, ed., *Die II. Internationale 1918/1919*, I, Wels, 617.

As with the two German socialist parties, Labour voted reluctantly in Parliament for the peace treaty with Germany. Unlike their German counterparts, however, Labour leaders did so chiefly for domestic political reasons: they feared the political backlash at home of voting against a treaty that was popular among the public.[36] Nevertheless, British socialists did not disguise their dislike. In April 1919 Labour's advisory committee on international questions (ACIQ) claimed in a draft memorandum that the treaty contradicted Wilson's Fourteen Points as well as the positions expressed by international socialism at the Berne conference. The treaty was 'defective' not simply in its details:

> but fundamentally, in that it accepts, and indeed is based on the very political principles or premises which were the ultimate cause of this war, and which must, if adhered to, produce not only other wars, but a perpetuation in peace time of those economic and social conditions which it is the objects of workers to abolish.

The ACIQ's draft provided the basis for a joint statement the following month by Labour's parliamentary party and national executive.[37]

Having denounced the treaty as 'defective' while endorsing it in Parliament, the question for Labour became what position to adopt for the immediate future. The ILP's answer was to work for treaty revision with other socialist parties. In June 1919 an editorial in the ILP's principal publication thus described the 'so-called Peace Treaties' as a 'challenge to Labour and to International Socialism'. British and international socialism, it continued, must 'make it unmistakably clear and definite that it opposes these terms root and branch; that it accepts no responsibility for them; and that it will work might and main to secure the complete revision of them'.[38] Although sometimes frustrated with the ILP's brand of socialist militancy, on this subject at least Labour officials and leaders agreed. The ACIQ, for example, advised Labour's executive that treaty revision was essential for the future of international socialism:

> If the pledges [of treaty revision] are not fulfilled the International will certainly lose its influence with those peoples who suffer from the defects of the Treaty, and who will consequently lose faith in this form of political action and be driven to support either nationalist and militarist effort within their own states or some internationalist effort other than the present Socialist International.[39]

Henderson needed little convincing. Emphasizing the need for treaty revision, in June 1919 he announced Labour's 'determination to inaugurate at once a great national and international campaign in favour of a speedy and drastic revision'. At Labour's annual conference the same month MacDonald sponsored a resolution calling 'upon the Labour Movement in conjunction with the International to

---

[36] Krieger, *Labour Party und Weimarer Republik*, 128–43.

[37] LHASC, LPA, ACIQ, Memorandums 1918–1920, untitled memorandum, May 1919, Norman Angell; and Labour Party, Executive Committee of the Parliamentary Party, minutes, fiche 156, 5 June 1919, 'Labour and the Peace'.

[38] 'The Challenge to International Socialism', *Labour Leader*, 5 June 1919, 6.

[39] LHASC, LPA, ACIQ, Memorandums 1918–1920, 'The International and the Treaties', undated but 1919.

undertake a vigorous campaign for the winning of popular support for this policy'—a resolution 'carried with enthusiasm'.[40]

Unlike the British and German parties, the SFIO decisively rejected the peace treaty in Parliament. That it would do was not self-evident: the deepening divisions within the party between ex-*majoritaires* and ex-*minoritaires* rendered a shared position on any issue extremely difficult. A lengthy debate on the peace treaty occurred at the SFIO's national council in mid-July 1919. At the gathering, a group led by Albert Thomas, a prominent ex-*majoritaire*, argued for ratification and presented the stakes in terms of revolution versus reformism: the treaty, like the bourgeois state, should be modified not rejected.[41] Thomas's pleas, however, met with little sympathy. The debate at the council centred not on rejection or acceptance but on rejection or abstention. Several ex-*majoritaires*, Renaudel among them, pleaded for socialist deputies to abstain during the parliamentary vote, no doubt because they realized that no majority could be won for acceptance. But the vast majority of delegates clearly favoured a more uncompromising stand. It was an illusion, Paul Faure proclaimed, 'to believe that a peace drawn up by bourgeois [statesmen] could embody the end of militarism, justice and international peace'; Longuet more succinctly denounced the peace treaty as the 'consecration of the logic of imperialist war'. The final vote reflected Faure and Longuet's sentiments: over 70 per cent of the delegates refused ratification.[42] Victor Schiff, *Vorwärts'* foreign affairs editor who had earlier denounced the SFIO's lukewarm response to the peace terms, praised the vote as a sign of international socialism's support for the MSPD's position.[43]

Schiff's optimism was partly misplaced. The debate among French socialists on the peace treaty became entangled in the growing split within the SFIO on the nature and goals of socialism. Many of those opposed to the treaty were far more interested in revolution than treaty revision. 'Real [treaty] revision', declared Fernand Loriot, a future communist, 'can only be achieved by revolution.'[44] When deepening divisions finally produced a schism, with the majority of socialists leaving to join the Communist Party, the SFIO found itself not only much reduced in strength but also separated from its most radical elements. To be sure, the SFIO continued to reject reformism, claiming to be a revolutionary socialist (non-communist) party. Nevertheless, when it came to international policy in particular the SFIO pursued a reformist as opposed to revolutionary orientation, influenced in part by its ongoing interactions with other European socialists, including Labour. The result was that French socialists quietly replaced their rejectionist stance towards the peace treaties with a revisionist one, thereby bringing

[40] Henderson, 'The Peace Treaty', *Daily Herald*, 30 June 1919, 4; and Labour Party, *Report of the Nineteenth Annual Congress… on June 25th, 26th and 27th, 1919*, 'The Peace Treaty and the League of Nations', 139–42.

[41] For Thomas, see TNA PRO FO 608/125, Grahame (Paris) to Curzon (FO), no. 697, 15 July 1919; and 'Le Parti Socialiste et la Paix', *L'Humanité*, 15 July 1919, 2.

[42] For the debates, see ibid. as well as 'Le Conseil National du Parti Socialiste examines les clauses du Traité de paix', *L'Humanité*, 14 July 1919, 1–2.

[43] Schiff, 'Die französischen Strömungen', *Vorwärts*, 23 July 1919, 1.

[44] 'Le Parti Socialiste et la Paix', *L'Humanité*, 15 July 1919, 2.

them closer to British and German socialists. No less importantly, the SFIO viewed treaty revision as a collective socialist endeavour. It was the duty of all European socialists, explained an SFIO memorandum circulated to the other parties, to work together to revise the peace treaty (and the League of Nations first and foremost) in order to construct a more peaceful post-war order.[45]

THE COMPLEXITIES OF NATIONAL
SELF-DETERMINATION: THE CASE OF UPPER SILESIA

Although the international socialist movement emerged from the war deeply divided, by early 1920 the British, French, and German parties had endorsed a policy of treaty revision. Just as importantly, they all agreed that this policy required a concerted effort on the part of socialist parties to work together. Over the course of the following year, however, the collective commitment to international socialist cooperation was threatened by the issue of Upper Silesia. Part of the pre-war German Empire, this heterogeneous region was claimed in 1918–1919 by both Germany and the newly reconstituted Poland. Torn between German and Polish claims, the peacemakers in Paris decided that Upper Silesia would be administered by an inter-allied commission pending a plebiscite to determine its fate on the understanding that the entire region would be attached either to Poland or to Germany. Held in March 1921, the results of the plebiscite were a victory for Germany, though not an overwhelming one: 706,820 people voted for Germany and 479,418 for Poland. Following the plebiscite, the issue was thrown into the lap of the League of Nations' Council which in October 1921 decided, under heavy French lobbying, to partition the region. Although two-thirds of the territory and 55 per cent of its population went to Germany, Poland received 90 per cent of Upper Silesia's known coal reserves as well as 75 per cent of its industry.[46] Not surprisingly, the Council's decision provoked a storm of criticism within Germany.

Well before the Council's decision in October 1921 the future of Upper Silesia had become a subject of debate and disagreement among European socialists. On the German side, the SPD and USPD both insisted that the region should go to Germany. Consistent with their self-image, German independent socialists strove to adopt an 'internationalist' perspective. Writing in *Der Sozialist*, the USPD's weekly, Eugen Prager called for popular consultation through a free and unbiased plebiscite. Local socialists, Prager continued, should vote as neither Poles nor Germans but as international socialists; at the same time, Prager inadvertently revealed just how elusive such an internationalist perspective could be in arguing that a vote for Germany would provide a powerful fillip to the 'freedom struggle of the German working class' whereas a vote for Poland would strengthen the Polish

---

[45] IISH, Second International, 360, SFIO, 'Bericht ueber den Frieden und den Voelkerbund', undated but 1920.
[46] Guido Hitze, 'Die oberschlesische Frage im Jahre 1921', *Die Politische Meinung*, no. 397, December 2002, 6–67; and Steiner, *The Lights that Failed*, 356–7.

bourgeoisie.[47] The SPD, meanwhile, underscored both the principle of national self-determination and the economic costs to Germany and Europe of detaching Upper Silesia. An article in *Vorwärts* in July 1921 thus insisted that Upper Silesia had nothing to do with France's strategic position or with the health of Poland's economy; instead, it was simply a question of 'the will of its inhabitants'.[48] At the SPD's annual congress several months later Müller described Upper Silesia as a 'vital [economic] area' for Germany. The SPD, he continued, had undertaken a campaign to convince '[foreign] party comrades and friends of peace' of the 'immense importance' of the problem for the German and European economies.[49]

In arguing for awarding Upper Silesia to Germany, the SPD could count on Labour's support. An ACIQ memorandum, for example, warned its transfer to Poland would result in both a 'strengthening of French capitalist and militarist influence in Poland' and a 'further weakening and impoverishment of Germany'. The economic and political consequences would be far-reaching, weakening Germany economically and thus its ability to pay reparations. Germany's default on reparations, in turn:

> will reopen the whole question of the occupation of the Ruhr, or the alternative pro-posal which has been made in Paris of French control of German industry. In either event the great dislocation of industry, social unrest, the rapid fall of the Mark...the depression of the standard of life and the extension of French militarist domination will be inevitable.

With the stakes so high, the memorandum concluded that Labour should mobilize the international socialist community by launching 'a campaign of meetings on a comprehensive and constructive programme, making its aim the restoration of European security, credit and trade'.[50]

The historian Lee Blackwood has accused Western European socialists of parrot-ing the views of German socialists in their wilful ignorance of Central and Eastern Europe's ethno-national complexities.[51] But if this criticism might apply to Labour, it does not to the SFIO. French socialists were sensitive to the inherent difficulties involved in categorizing a mixed region in national terms. Upper Silesia, one wrote in this respect, 'is not a [simple] math problem solvable by the rules of math'.[52] This sensitivity manifested itself in calls for negotiations between Poles and Germans (and between Polish and German socialists) to work out a solution acceptable to both—for what Salomon Grumbach, an SFIO expert on Germany, termed a

---

[47] Prager, 'Der Kampf um Oberschlesien', *Der Sozialist*, vol. 7, 19 March 1921, 241–4. Also see Prager, 'Oberschliesen', *Die Freiheit*, no. 131, 19 March 1921, 1–2.

[48] Adolf Köster, ' "Self-Determination" ', *Vorwärts*, no. 333, 17 July 1921, 1–2.

[49] SPD, *Protokoll über die Verhandlungen des Parteitages der Sozialdemokratischen Partei Deutschlands abgehalten in Görlitz vom 18. bis 24. September 1921*, Müller, 274, 295.

[50] LHASC, LPA, ACIQ, Memorandums 1922–1924, 'Proposed Memorandum on the Economic Situation', D.F. Buxton, 12 October 1921.

[51] Blackwood, 'Socialism, Nationalism and the "German Question" from World War I to Locarno and Beyond', 130–1.

[52] F. Caussy, 'La question silésienne. Solution allemande ou solution polonaise', *Le Populaire de Paris*, 20 July 1921, 1.

'transactional solution'. In pursuit of the latter, French socialists took advantage of their contacts with USPD leaders to urge them to negotiate, while the SFIO's executive committee exploited its close ties with Polish socialists to counsel flexibility.[53] More generally, leading French socialists questioned the wisdom of national self-determination as an organizing principle for the post-war European order. In the midst of debates over Upper Silesia's fate, a frustrated Longuet remarked that the principle has 'everywhere created new injustices as serious if not worse than those existing before'.[54]

Complexity, however, was not a feature of international politics that interested MacDonald, who directed Labour's efforts to reconstitute a socialist International. Once the League decision to partition Upper Silesia became known, MacDonald took the lead in proposing a collective protest on the part of European socialist parties. If he hoped that such a protest might build bridges between the Second International and the Vienna Union, MacDonald also sought to focus socialist attention on what he deemed to be a clear-cut issue—the non-respect of national determination. Regarding Upper Silesia, he lectured socialists that international socialism must publicly proclaim that 'a majority having voted for a union with Germany that decision should have been accepted'.[55] But if the SPD was predictably enthusiastic, MacDonald's own party proved less so. Tom Shaw, who would soon replace MacDonald as the International's chairman, warned that it was 'impossible to deal in such a cursory way with a question of such great importance'. Undaunted, MacDonald drafted a resolution for the Second International that strongly denounced the League's decision as 'unfortunate and ill-advised'. The draft prompted Shaw to rebuke MacDonald for attempting to speak on behalf of the International's executive on 'a delicate question like that of Upper Silesia'. No doubt to MacDonald's frustration, the Second International refrained from condemning the League's decision on Upper Silesia—as did the Vienna Union to which the SFIO belonged.[56]

All told, the fate of Upper Silesia helped to convince British and French socialists of the complexity of the situation. Part of this complexity stemmed from the awkward fact that the socialist parties most directly involved—the German and Polish parties—sharply disagreed. But the complexity was also rooted in the inherent difficulties of applying the principle of national self-determination to ethnically mixed regions. For European socialists, who were seeking to renew international socialism in order to shape the post-war order, a preoccupation with national self-determination promised to stir rancour and division. Writing in the

[53] Grumbach, 'On reprendra aujourd'hui la discussion du problème de la Haute-Silésie', *Le Populaire de Paris*, 11 August 1921, 1; and Renaudel, 'Die internationale Aktion', *Der Sozialist*, no. 21, 28 May 1921, 489–91.

[54] Longuet, 'Le droit des peuples et ses applications', *Le Populaire de Paris*, 26 May 1919, 1.

[55] IISH, Pietre Troelstra Papers, 552, MacDonald to Troelstra, 14 October 1921; also see AABS, Hjalmar Branting, 91/3/1/22, MacDonald to Branting, 14 October 1921.

[56] The letters as well as MacDonald's draft resolution are in IISH, LSI (London Secretariat), 85. For the Vienna Union, see 'Sitzung des Exekutivkomitees in London no, 17. bis 21. Oktober 1921', reproduced in *Nachrichten der Internationalen Arbeitsgemeinschaft Sozialistischer Parteien*, no. 6, November 1921, 1.

immediate aftermath of the League's decision, Léon Blum, who was emerging as the leading French socialist, suggested that any solution to the Upper Silesian question—and, by extension, to ethnic-territorial questions in general—was bound to be unsatisfactory. Blum accordingly urged European socialists to direct their attention to other issues presumably more amenable to agreement.[57] Chief among these would be reparations.

THE BREWING INTERNATIONAL CRISIS: REPARATIONS

Chapter 2 discussed reparations in the context of efforts to create a single International. Particular attention was paid to the role of the SFIO: the existence of two rival international organizations (the Second International and the Vienna Union) threatened the party's fragile unity in the wake of the December 1920 schism. In this context, French socialists seized on reparations as a unifying issue, one that could foster cooperation between socialist parties across organizational divides. But as important as the SFIO's calculations were, the interest of European socialists in reparations also needs to be understood in terms of their recent experience with the plebiscite in Upper Silesia and its effects on their thinking about treaty revision. In 1919 European socialists were committed to working collectively to revise the peace treaties. But several aspects of treaty revision were fraught with difficulties and dangers, not least the conjoined questions of territorial borders and the principle of national self-determination. Focusing on reparations, by comparison, possessed several potential advantages for socialists. First and foremost, the issue possessed immense relevance for international politics. Following the London schedule in May 1921, which nominally fixed Germany's total reparations obligations at 132 billion gold marks, the question of whether the Germans could or would pay the amounts due at regular intervals quickly came to dominate European politics.[58] If socialist internationalism was to be relevant, it had to address this issue. But another advantage of reparations is that it offered ample scope for cooperation between socialists. The British, French, and German parties all agreed that Germany should contribute to the reconstruction of the devastated regions in Belgium and France, which meant that discussion could centre on how and how much to pay as well as on the larger political framework for payment. These questions, moreover, could be presented as technical issues in a way that territory and peoples, tied closely as they were to national identity, could not. Reparations, in short, appeared to be a promising test case for the practice of socialist internationalism.

When it came to international socialist cooperation on reparations, the SPD initially took the lead. From early on, the German majority socialists strove to convince

---

[57] Blum, 'En Haute-Silésie', *Le Populaire de Paris*, 14 October 1921, 1.

[58] The scholarship on reparations is vast but good starting points are Steiner, *The Lights that Failed*, 182–250; Bruce Kent, *The Spoils of War: The Politics, Economics and Diplomacy of Reparations 1918–1932* (Oxford, 1989); and Marc Trachtenberg, *Reparations in World Politics: France and European Economic Diplomacy, 1916–1923* (New York, 1980).

socialist parties abroad of the need for clear limits on Germany's reparations obligations—an effort that met with some success at the international socialist conference in Lucerne in August 1919. On his return home, Otto Wels explained that, in response to SPD arguments, the delegates had agreed that reparations should not be so high as to reduce the living standards of German workers.[59] Afterwards, reparations became the chief element of the SPD's fulfilment strategy in regards to the peace treaty: Germany must try to pay as much as it could in order to demonstrate that it could not and that treaty revision was therefore urgent. While urging a genuine effort at repayment, the MSPD also sought to frame reparations in the wider context of post-war economic reconstruction. In addition to recognizing Germany's responsibility to help rebuild the devastated regions in France and Belgium, German socialists floated proposals that envisaged financial as well as non-financial contributions; if they were hardly alone in doing so, German socialists distinguished themselves in the role they accorded to concrete cooperation between German and French construction workers.[60] More generally, the MSPD viewed reparations and reconstruction as offering a promising path to Franco-German and European rapprochement precisely because economic issues were presumed to be especially conducive to cooperation. The task of international socialism was to take the lead in working for a rapprochement in this sense. Because reparations risked ending in a 'European catastrophe', the MSPD's parliamentary group declared in February 1921, European socialists must propose a 'salutary solution' to the issue.[61] Despite the bitter feelings between German majority and independent socialists, moreover, the MSPD could count on the USPD's support. Revision of the reparations terms, an editorial in *Die Freiheit* announced, can only come through the combined efforts of the 'international proletariat'. Our 'chief task', the editorial dilated, 'is to strengthen the international ties between the proletariat of all countries and to do our best to demonstrate to our foreign comrades just how unreasonable, unachievable and inhumane the so-called peace terms really are.'[62]

In casting their eyes abroad, German socialists looked especially to British socialists as possible allies in the quest for treaty revision. In the immediate wake of the war, some Labourites welcomed the idea of reparations. Speaking at the party's 1919 conference, J.R. Clynes defended reparations, remarking that if Labour 'said Germany was to pay nothing they would hear something from the Socialists of France and Belgium'.[63] Majority sentiment within Labour, however, quickly shifted due principally to two factors. The first one was evidence that post-war Germany was crippled by hardship—evidence provided by prominent Labour and

---

[59] 'Sitzung des Parteiausschusses am 28. und 29. August 1919 in Berlin...', reproduced in Dowe, ed., *Protokolle der Sitzungen des Parteiausschusses der SPD 1912 bis 1921*, II, Wels, 688. For the Lucerne conference's resolution, see 'Konferenzen der Internationalen Permanenten Kommission in Luzern, 2. bis 9. August 1919', reproduced in Ritter, ed., *Die II. Internationale 1918/1919*, I, 'Wirtschaftliche Fragen', 663–4.

[60] For example, see A. Ellinger, 'Deutschland und der Wiederaufbau Nordfrankreichs', *Die Neue Zeit*, 17 October 1919, 49–57.

[61] 'Erklärung der Sozialdemokraten', *Vorwärts*, 2 February 1921, 1.

[62] 'Spa', *Die Freiheit*, no. 262, 6 July 1920, 1–2.

[63] Clynes is cited in Bridgen, *The Labour Party and the Politics of War and Peace*, 125.

trade union travellers. Passing through Berlin in August 1919, MacDonald remarked in his diary on '[t]he terrible impression of suffering—too great even for punishment.'[64] The second factor was the growing conviction that German economic weakness—a weakness blamed largely on reparations—constituted a general calamity. Here, moreover, the ACIQ played a major role in disseminating this view. A memorandum in 1921 directly linked the impoverishment of Europe to the impoverishment of Germany. 'That the biggest productive machine in Europe should be lamed in a time of world shortage is a general disaster,' it insisted. Still more to the point, the memorandum identified the principal culprit as the 'reparations problem', which not only hampered Europe's recovery but also Britain's economic health as Germany had to reduce its purchases of British goods to pay for its indemnity. The result was a growing hostility towards reparations in principle. In 1921 an official Labour statement demanded a 'drastic revision of the economic clauses of the Treaty' and especially of its reparations clauses.[65] The flipside to this hostility was a growing suspicion of France, which appeared to be the staunchest supporter of reparations among the great powers. The 'impossible Reparation claims', noted Charles Rhoden Buxton, an ACIQ member, 'are made to be used as a pretext for further measures and are calculated to place Germany under the heel of France.'[66]

French socialists were well aware of Labour's growing suspicion of France—suspicion that strained Labour–SFIO relations. In June 1921, Longuet had attended a meeting of Labour's ACIQ during which he 'dwelt on the need of understanding French views in the Reparation and other questions'; French socialists, he added, 'thought that some of the British criticisms of French policy were made from a narrowly British point of view'. At the meeting, Longuet pressed Labour to support a renunciation of Britain's claim to reparations—a claim based on German responsibility for pensions and allowances rather than for material damage. The ACIQ agreed to recommend such a renunciation to the national executive, and at the end of the year Labour publicly announced its intention to waive almost all British claims.[67] Afterwards, as international tensions sharpened as the British, French, and German governments disagreed on reparations, the SFIO redoubled its efforts to mobilize European socialists behind a comprehensive reparations plan involving loans to Germany, credits for industrial reconstruction, fiscal controls, and schemes for the distribution of raw materials and safeguards for working conditions. The urgent task for European socialists, explained an SFIO memorandum circulated in early 1922, was to unite behind such a plan:

> In order that this... [plan] may be effectively carried out, there must be complete agreement between the Socialist Parties interested. This agreement is indispensable, in

[64] TNA, James Ramsay MacDonald Papers, PRO/30/69/1753/1, diary, 7 August 1919.

[65] LHASC, LPA, ACIQ, Memorandums 1918–1920, 'Draft Memorandum on Labour's Foreign Policy', no. 226, November 1921. Emphasis in original; and Labour Party, *Report of the Twenty-First Annual Conference*, 233.

[66] BLCAS, Charles Roden Buxton, MSS Brit.Emp. s 405, 2/4, 'Causes of the Present Situation', undated but 1922.

[67] US, Leonard Woolf Papers, 1D1c, ACIQ minutes, 22 June 1921; and see Bridgen, *The Labour Party and the Politics of War and Peace*, 153–4.

order that the efforts made by each individual party...should agree and converge with the efforts of its sister parties, so that the strength of each may increase and arm itself with the united strength of the others. It is indispensable in order that the Socialist ideal may exercise its full powers of persuasion or of pressure on the whole of the opinion of the world.[68]

The immediate result of the SFIO's efforts was a conference of British, French, and Belgian socialists in Brussels in May 1922. The differences between the French and British participants were palpable. Led by MacDonald and Henderson, Labour not only insisted on the economic damage caused by reparations but also portrayed French policy as unrestrained militarism: '[T]o English eyes France was seen as the obstacle to the general reconstruction of Europe, which was a matter of life and death to the British people, and was pursuing a militarist policy for the sake of reparations and security, which was leading to new combinations and future wars.' Led by Blum, the SFIO delegates offered a partial defence of French policy, reiterating France's need for financial help in reconstructing its devastated regions while also pointing to Germany's rapid post-war economic recovery, which induced fears of German revenge. At the same time, they agreed to a resolution that not only urged a negotiated solution to the looming reparations crisis, but also firmly rejected France's right to occupy the Ruhr in response to German non-payment— an occupation that the French government was threatening to undertake.[69]

At the conference, all three parties pledged to 'begin immediately a campaign in their respective countries' along the lines of their joint resolution. Back in Paris, an enthusiastic Blum cited the conference as evidence of 'international proletarian solidarity [and] of the mutual good will and knowledge that preceded common action'.[70] European socialists, however, appeared helpless to hinder the brewing international crisis over reparations. Writing to Eduard Bernstein in December 1922, Renaudel could only express the hope that the French and German governments would do nothing to aggravate the situation.[71] But such hopes were soon shattered: at the beginning of January 1923 the long-anticipated crisis crystallized as French and Belgian troops occupied the Ruhr.

INTERNATIONAL SOCIALISM AND THE OCCUPATION OF THE RUHR

European socialists wasted little time in reacting to the occupation. At the end of January 1923, delegates from the Second International, the Vienna Union, and the

---

[68] IISH, LSI (London Secretariat), 23/7, 'Memorandum by the French Socialist Party (S.F.I.O.): The Economic Situation and Reparations', undated but February 1922.
[69] LHASC, LPA, LSI 14/1/1/2, 'Franco-British-Belgian Relations', undated but May 1922. Belgian socialists also agreed that as a 'creditor' France did not have 'the right to reduce [Germany] to slavery or to cut it up into pieces'. See AMSAB, POB, 'Séance du Conseil général du 17-5-1922'.
[70] Blum, 'La Conférence de Bruxelles a affirmé la fraternité du prolétariat mondial', *Le Populaire de Paris*, 24 May 1922, 1.
[71] FES, AdsD, NL Eduard Bernstein, D.582, Renaudel to Bernstein, 29 December 1922.

IFTU met in Amsterdam to discuss possible joint action. Opening the meeting, Edo Fimmen, speaking for the IFTU, threw cold water on the idea of a coordinated general strike in several countries, arguing that 'the possibility of the masses responding to an appeal for any form of direct action was not very great'; for similar reasons, he ruled out an international boycott campaign of French and Belgian goods. Léon Jouhaux, the French trade union leader, confirmed Fimmen's assessment, adding that the majority of public and parliamentary opinion in France believed the occupation to be necessary to force Germany to pay reparations. Jouhaux's comments provoked a passionate response from Wels. Along with denouncing French policy, which supposedly exploited the issue of reparations to detach the Rhineland, the SPD leader insisted on the need for a 'complete revision of the [Versailles] Treaty'. That said, Wels admitted that German socialists could not oppose attempts to dismember Germany alone. As he remarked, 'it was the support of other comrades that they [German socialists] needed.'[72]

In view of Wels' plea for support, what could socialists (and trade unionists) do? In his opening remarks, Fimmen had proposed a collective appeal to the governments concerned for a 'settlement by arbitration'. Clearly dissatisfied, J.R. Thomas, a Labour delegate, asked whether British troops could be withdrawn from the Rhineland and, more immediately, whether 'international [socialist] demonstrations' within Germany would be helpful. Wels replied that the SPD favoured a continued British troop presence as a guarantee against French efforts to annex both the Rhineland and the Ruhr. As for international demonstrations, Wels hesitated, pointing to the dangers of provoking a nationalist reaction; but he soon relented, claiming that 'the holding of big demonstrations with speakers from other countries would have a good moral effect in Germany'. Fimmen then proposed that speaking events should be held not only in Germany but also in Britain, France, and Belgium. While the delegates all agreed that this was a good idea, one SFIO delegate warned that 'French and Belgian speakers would have a rough time in Germany'. In the end, the delegates promised to 'carry on a vigorous campaign...in all countries by means of the Press, meetings and demonstrations' against 'methods of force and violence'.[73]

Having rejected a collective strike or boycott action, it remained for European socialists to work out the nature of their 'vigorous campaign'. An initial attempt came in early February 1923 in Lille during the SFIO's congress. At a parallel meeting of European socialists, Blum sketched an optimistic portrait of the short-term prospects: with the SFIO and French workers both united in opposition to the Ruhr occupation, the French government would confront mounting 'protests' to its policy inside and outside of Parliament. The SPD's Rudolf Hilferding drew a darker picture: the French government, he insisted, aimed at a lengthy occupation in order to separate the Rhineland from Germany, and the longer the occupation lasted the weaker would become German socialists. For this reason, 'intervention'

---

[72] For the conference, see LHASC, LPA, LSI 14/8/1/1, 'The Situation in the Ruhr. International Conference', undated. Emphasis in original. For the IFTU, also see Van Goethem, *The Amsterdam International*, 35–6.

[73] LHASC, LPA, LSI 14/8/1/1, 'The Situation in the Ruhr. International Conference'.

was necessary to bring about negotiations between the French and German governments. Vincent Auriol, the principal author of the SFIO's reparations policy, fully agreed with Hilferding. Socialist parties, he argued, must pressure national governments to negotiate a solution to the reparations crisis based on the socialist plan worked out in 1921–1922 and discussed in chapter 2. The delegates, accordingly, drew up a manifesto that highlighted the socialist reparations plan as a guide for international negotiations.[74] In his speech to the larger SFIO congress, Hilferding praised the manifesto and declared that international socialism 'alone can make heard the grand words of reason and fraternity'.[75]

The following month Belgian, British, French, and Italian socialists met in Paris to discuss how to overcome what MacDonald described as the 'danger of present drift'. Denied visas to travel, German socialists were absent. Accordingly, the participants agreed to send a delegation to Germany to discuss with the SPD how to adapt the socialist reparations plan 'to present needs' as well as the 'conditions under which national security can be attained'.[76] The following week they met again to discuss an SPD memorandum on reparations. The Germans accepted Germany's obligation to pay reparations for reconstruction, but proposed to reduce the total to 30 billion gold marks, which would be paid either all at once or in a short series of transfers. This would be achieved through 'loans directly guaranteed and rapidly issued, the annual payments and liquidation of which would be paid by Germany'. In return for an international credit operation of this kind, Germany would offer several security guarantees, including a 'solemn pledge' not to declare war for several decades, participation in an international security pact, and entry into the League of Nations. At the second meeting at the end of the month, the participants accepted the SPD's memorandum 'on its general lines . . . as affording a basis for negotiations to end the present situation' and agreed that each of the parties, including the SPD, would bring the document 'to the attention of their governments by all possible means'.[77]

The seeming consensus on reparations, however, soon appeared to be fragile. At the first Bureau meeting of the recently founded International in July 1923, the Ruhr occupation dominated the agenda. Untypically pessimistic, Blum remarked that the situation 'had gone from bad to worse', citing French opinion that viewed evacuation from the Ruhr as 'an intolerable national humiliation'. On the question of reparations, the SFIO leader now insisted that Germany's obligations could not be determined independently of the needs of reconstruction, the final amount of

---

[74] Labour Party, NEC minutes, fiche 76, TUC and Labour Party, Joint International Department, 'The Ruhr and Reparations. International Meeting held during the French Socialist Congress, Lille, February, 1923', undated.

[75] 'La deuxième journée du Congrès national a été une éclatante manifestation de solidarité internationale', *Le Populaire de Paris*, 5 February 1923, 2.

[76] IISH, LSI (London Secretariat), 60, TUC and Labour Party, Joint International Department, 'The Situation in the Ruhr. Inter-Parliamentary Conference in the Chamber of Deputies, Paris, 20th March 1923', undated. Also see MacDonald's extensive notes of the meeting in TNA, Ramsay MacDonald Papers, PRO 30/69/1753/4.

[77] IISH, LSI (London Secretariat), 60, 'The Situation in the Ruhr. Inter-Parliamentary Conference at Paris'.

which was necessarily unknown.[78] Unable to agree, European socialists met again in London at the end of the month, this time with the SPD present. Opening the meeting, the SPD's Adolf Braun, emphasizing the 'highly fevered condition' at home, maintained that international socialism must work for the 'moral strengthening of Germany and her working classes', which could best be achieved by formulating 'practical proposals'. Braun then suggested a trade-off: German agreement to promise to pay reparations out of future revenue as well as to end passive resistance (strike action) in return for French agreement to reduce its occupation to the barest minimum possible. Blum, however, held out little hope for an agreement on these terms. The French government would not abandon the occupation without 'at least a semblance of success'—i.e. a guarantee of 'real payments' of reparations. With no consensus in sight, Vandervelde revived an earlier proposal by Henderson to send an international socialist commission to the Ruhr. After some debate it was decided that Tom Shaw, the LSI's secretary, would visit the Ruhr to investigate what the International could do 'on behalf of the working classes of the Ruhr district'.[79]

Ready in August 1923, Shaw's report highlighted the difficult material conditions of Ruhr workers—conditions that all socialists agreed the LSI should strive to alleviate.[80] But its more important effect was to refocus attention on the imperative need for a negotiated solution to the Ruhr crisis if an 'explosion' were to be avoided. It was therefore of 'decisive importance' that European socialists do everything possible to bring about intergovernmental negotiations on the basis of the socialist reparations plan.[81] Although French and German socialists questioned the usefulness of renewed socialist pressure on Paris and Berlin, events soon intervened to change the situation, particularly the appointment of Gustav Stresemann as German Chancellor in August and his decision in September to end passive resistance in the Ruhr.[82]

It is at this moment that it becomes possible to detect international socialism's influence on international politics. The most obvious case is that of the SPD, a central element in Stresemann's new coalition government. From the beginning of the Ruhr occupation, the SPD pressed the German government to offer concrete proposals for a settlement, and claimed some credit when the government did so in June 1923.[83] But as a member of Stresemann's government the SPD found itself in a far stronger position to shape policy: the decision to end passive resistance was not simply a response to the catastrophic economic situation in the Ruhr (and Germany more generally); it was also a sign of SPD influence. With the German government on board, attention now turned to the French. 'It is absolutely

---

[78] IISH, SAI, 599, TUC and Labour, Joint International Department, 'The Ruhr Question', undated minutes of meeting, 11 July 1923.

[79] IISH, SAI, 854, LSI, 'International Party Conference on the Ruhr Question held at Easton Lodge (London) July 22nd 1923', undated. Emphasis in original.

[80] In November 1923 the LSI created a monetary fund to aid German workers. See LHASC, LPA, LSI minutes 1921–1937, LSI circular to parties, November 1923, Adler and Shaw.

[81] VGA, SPÖ, 191/1364, LSI circular, 20 August 1923, which includes 'Bericht ueber die Lage im Ruhrgebiet', Shaw.

[82] For French and German doubts, see IISH, SAI, 1662, Adler to Henderson, 15 September 1923.

[83] See LHASC, LPA, LSI minutes 1921–1937, Wels, Müller, Crispien (SPD) to Labour, 8 June 1923.

essential', Shaw wrote Henderson, 'that pressure should be brought to bear...on [French Premier] Poincaré at once.'[84] Neither Henderson nor Shaw had to wait long, as the SFIO mounted a concerted effort to persuade the French government— and Poincaré in particular—to agree to negotiations. Meeting with Poincaré in September 1923, Blum and Bracke urged him to make concrete proposals, under-scoring the worsening political-economic crisis in Germany that strengthened the communists and the nationalists while weakening the democratic forces. Beyond the corridors of power, the SFIO launched a parliamentary and public campaign emphasizing the imminent danger of a German political and economic collapse in the absence of a negotiated settlement of the Ruhr crisis.[85]

Poincaré, admittedly, proved less susceptible to socialist solicitation than Stresemann. But political developments favoured the socialists. In the British gen-eral elections in December 1923 Labour gained sufficient seats to form a minority government with MacDonald as prime minister. Unhappy with what he regarded as the International's passivity in the Ruhr crisis, MacDonald was determined to push British policy in a more activist direction, which essentially meant applying greater pressure on Paris to make concessions.[86] In spring 1924, moreover, French elections also beckoned. As European socialists realized, the most promising way to alter French policy was through a change of government. In preparation for the elections, the SFIO appealed to the international socialist community for financial help, particularly for its newspaper, *Le Populaire de Paris*. For the International, Faure explained, the '"fighting front" is now in France, so far as present politics are concerned' and socialist parties must 'help at once financially' so that French socialists 'may not only keep their paper but also fight the elections next year'. Adler and Shaw duly issued an appeal for funds that met with a favourable response from several parties, including the Belgian and the Austrian.[87] To be sure, such aid did not determine the outcome of the elections, which saw Poincaré defeated and his government replaced by a centre-left coalition (*Cartel des gauches*) that the SFIO supported within Parliament. Nevertheless, it did provide a much-needed material and especially moral fillip to French socialists, reinforcing their sense of belonging to a larger international community that was united around the goal of resolving the Ruhr crisis through intergovernmental negotiations.

DEVELOPMENTS WITHIN THE BRITISH, GERMAN, AND FRENCH PARTIES

The occupation of the Ruhr provoked perturbations within the principal European socialist parties. Although these perturbations threatened the willingness of British,

---

[84] IISH, SAI, 1662, Shaw to Henderson, 20 August 1923.
[85] A copy of the report of the meeting is in LHASC, LPA, LSI 4/4/19. Also see IISH, SAI, 1589, Bracke to Shaw, 14 September 1923.
[86] IISH, SAI, 1804, MacDonald to Shaw, 31 August 1923.
[87] IISH, SAI, 1566, Shaw circular, 20 October 1923. For the Belgians, see AMSAB, POB, 'Séance du Bureau du Conseil Général du 22 Mai 1924'; and for the Austrians, see VGA, SPÖ Alteparteiarchiv, Sitzungsprotokolle des Parteivorstandes, 14 November 1923.

French, and German socialists to cooperate with each other, in the end the Ruhr crisis produced a renewed collective commitment to the practice of socialist internationalism.

From the beginning, Labour strongly denounced the occupation of the Ruhr. A draft statement submitted to the International in January 1923 thus described the occupation as an 'act of war'. In a letter the same month, MacDonald lamented that the crisis 'is not only destroying what little beginnings had been made towards a settlement and reconstruction in Central Europe, but is intensifying the dislocation of the world's trade and must result in serious damage and a deepened industrial distress to ourselves'.[88] There was much sympathy within Labour for Germany's plight and especially the deleterious effects of the occupation on German workers. This sympathy reinforced suspicions of the French. 'The more France fails in securing Reparations payment', an ACIQ memorandum predicted, 'the more ruthless must we expect to be the pursuit of her political aims: the detachment of the Rhineland, the disruption of Germany.' Another memorandum described the French as the 'most convinced believers' in the creed of force. 'A large circle of the most influential politicians of France believe in force with the zeal and ardour of religious fanatics.'[89] Everything possible must be done, the ACIQ accordingly insisted, to pressure the French government, going so far as to warn Labour's executive in July 1923 against creating 'a false impression that the Party supports the French Ruhr policy'.[90] The ACIQ's dislike of French policy spilled over into criticism of the SFIO, which stood accused of opposing its government with insufficient vigour. Reflecting this thinking, a joint Labour–TUC statement in August 1923 declared that the SFIO must be compelled to place more pressure on 'the French Government and the French people' to adopt 'a more conciliatory attitude'.[91]

Surprisingly perhaps, MacDonald strove to dampen anti-French sentiment. Rather than denunciations of the French, he told Labour's annual conference in June 1923, the party should offer 'proposals and propositions that had a precise bearing upon the problem [Ruhr occupation] as it was at the moment, and that, if carried out, would help to solve the problem'. No less importantly, MacDonald pointed out that this was precisely what European socialists sought to do when they met together in 'Conference after Conference'.[92] To be sure, MacDonald had little sympathy for French policy: in an article reproduced in *Vorwärts* the following month he asserted that Labour should not shrink from a 'confrontation' with France.[93] That said, a hard-headed calculation tempered MacDonald's own anti-French inclinations. He recognized that the Ruhr crisis could only be resolved

[88] IISH, LSI (London Secretariat), 107, 'Draft Manifesto', January 1923; and TNA, James Ramsay MacDonald Papers, PRO/30/69/1167, MacDonald to Bonar Law, 29 January 1923.

[89] LHASC, LPA, ACIQ, Memoranda 1922–1924, 'Memorandum on Ruhr Situation', January 1923; and BLCAS, Charles Roden Buxton, MSS Brit.Emp. S 405, 2/4, 'Causes of the Present Situation', undated but 1923.

[90] BLEPS, Charles Roden Buxton Papers, 7/3, ACIQ, untitled memorandum, no. 229, July 1923.

[91] Labour Party, NEC minutes, fiche 80, untitled resolution, 23 August 1923.

[92] Labour Party, *Report of the 23rd Annual Conference held in…London, on June 26th, 27th, 28th, and 29th, 1923* (London, 1923), MacDonald, 221–2.

[93] MacDonald, 'Englands Arbeiter und Frankreich', *Vorwärts*, no. 339, 22 July 1923, 1.

through negotiations, and for these to occur French participation was necessary. Even the ACIQ admitted as much. Any Labour proposals for a settlement, the committee members agreed in August, must 'bear the stamp of generosity towards them [the French]' because it 'is the power of the French people which alone can induce the French Government to relax its hold on the Ruhr and the Rhineland'.[94] For both Labour leaders and the ACIQ, moreover, French socialists served as an indispensable intermediary between the French people and the French government— and hence the need to work with the SFIO. Indeed, throughout the crisis Labour remained in touch with the SFIO via the International, via personal relations (Longuet, for instance, corresponded regularly with several Labourites), and via inter-party exchanges. Regarding the latter, Labour's parliamentary group organized a meeting with French and Belgian socialists in March 1923 to discuss the Ruhr crisis. As MacDonald's personal diary indicates, the meeting helped to sensitize him to the SFIO's good-faith efforts to work out proposals politically acceptable to all concerned.[95] This greater sensitivity, in turn, had a moderating effect on Labour leaders, helping to counter the temptation to provoke a rupture with France and with the SFIO.

More generally and notwithstanding some frustration with French socialists, Labour never seriously entertained the idea of withdrawing from the practice of socialist internationalism. True, in public, Labour leaders sometimes sought to distance themselves from the International, worried that their domestic political opponents would succeed in tarring the party as the instrument of a foreign organization.[96] But for party leaders and officials, the relevant question was always how best to mobilize international socialism behind the party's policy goals—in this case a negotiated settlement. If anything, the Ruhr crisis reinforced the relevance of this general question.

The Ruhr occupation potentially endangered the SFIO's commitment to the practice of socialist internationalism. Put simply, a strong temptation existed to support the government's policy. French socialists had never questioned the legitimacy of reparations for reconstruction, and many believed that Germany was deliberately evading its responsibility in this regard. As Blum had made clear to foreign socialists in July 1923, moreover, the SFIO faced the political reality that the government's hard-line policy enjoyed considerable public support. For a party under constant attack from the right and left (communists) and facing general elections in 1924, the prospect of escaping from its isolation by embracing the government's Ruhr policy was no doubt appealing. Reinforcing the appeal was the assumption that France's goals remained limited. Although the historical debate on Poincaré's ultimate intentions continues, French socialists generally disagreed with their British and German counterparts that the government's ambitions extended

---

[94] LHASC, LPA, ACIQ, minutes, 23 August 1923.
[95] See the diary notes in TNA, Ramsay MacDonald Papers, PRO/30/69/1753/4. Also see Labour Party, Executive Committee of the Parliamentary Party, minutes, fiche 166, 21 March 1923.
[96] LHASC, LPA, LSI, 12/10/3, 'Notes to be adapted for Mr. Henderson', undated but 1923. On Conservative propaganda efforts to highlight Labour's dependence on the International, see Laura Beers, *Your Britain: Media and the Making of the Labour Party* (Cambridge, MA, 2010), 56, 76.

beyond reparations to include the annexation of German territory. As Vincent Auriol informed European socialists in February 1923, Poincaré 'only wants guarantees' for the payment of reparations—a claim Blum reiterated in July.[97]

Yet notwithstanding the temptation to support the government, the SFIO adopted an oppositional stance from the outset. Several days after the start of the occupation, Blum announced in Parliament his party's 'categorical' opposition. 'We repeat our refusal to endorse for one moment this nefarious policy before national and international opinion.'[98] French socialists went beyond mere statements. In January 1923 the SFIO's executive instructed the regional federations to begin a public campaign against the 'foreign policy insanities of the French government'. Over the coming months the SFIO vigorously pursued this campaign, working with German socialists, for example, to organize a 'propaganda week' in the autumn of 1923.[99] For Blum, a central theme of the SFIO's campaign was the occupation's 'bilan' (assessment of results). In numerous articles he sought to highlight the occupation's counterproductive nature, not least because Germany's economic ruin would preclude any reparations. One purpose of the campaign was to prod Poincaré's government to the negotiating table. To do so, the SFIO outlined its own bases for a possible agreement that resembled closely the reparations plan worked out by European socialists during 1921–1922 in its call for international oversight but that also innovated in according a vital role to the League of Nations and to the United States.[100] But another and related purpose was to demonstrate to European socialists the SFIO's continued commitment to working together to bring about a negotiated solution. The SFIO's ability to present its reparations proposals as part of an international socialist plan lent more heft to the former: French socialists could credibly argue that their proposals were not the product of a small and isolated political party inside France but instead a serious project that enjoyed considerable support abroad, especially in Britain and Germany, whose socialist parties were comparatively stronger. Only by cooperating with other socialist parties could the SFIO—and international socialism—influence international politics.

In the case of the SPD, the historian Stefan Feucht has argued that the Ruhr crisis endangered its political independence as the party found itself pulled towards a 'united front' with either the communists or the nationalists.[101] But the crisis also threatened the SPD's commitment to international socialism. At an international

[97] LHASC, LPA, LSI 14/8/1/1, 'The Situation in the Ruhr. International Conference'; and IISH, SAI, 599, TUC and Labour, Joint International Department, 'The Ruhr Question', undated minutes of meeting, 11 July 1923. For recent studies that argue that Poincaré's aims expanded as the occupation lengthened, see Jackson, *Beyond the Balance of Power*, 391–426; and Stanislas Jeannesson, *Poincaré, la France et la Ruhr (1922–1924). Histoire d'une occupation* (Strasbourg, 1998).

[98] 'L'abomindable séance de la Chambre: frénésie, injures, violence, esprit de guerre', *Le Populaire de Paris*, 12 January 1923, 1–2.

[99] 'La paix en danger', *Le Populaire de Paris*, 18 January 1923, 1; and FES, AdsD, Nachlass Wilhelm Dittmann, Moskaufilm, Fonds 215, 34, SFIO (secrétaire adjoint) to Dittmann, 28 July 1923.

[100] Paul Renaudel, 'Vers l'abime' and 'En réponse au "Vorwaerts". Pour des solutions positives', *Le Populaire de Paris*, 15 and 22 February 1923.

[101] Feucht, *Die Haltung der Sozialdemokratischen Partei Deutschlands zur Außenpolitik während der Weimarer Republik*, 241–6.

socialist gathering in late 1922 Otto Wels announced that if the Ruhr were occupied it would become 'impossible' for German socialists to continue to support an *Erfüllungspolitik*.[102] As this policy constituted a fundamental element of consensus among the principal European socialist parties, it is hard to see how the practice of socialist internationalism could survive its abandonment. With the occupation, moreover, divisions sharpened within the SPD, a process that risked turning Wels' warning into reality. On the left the group around Paul Levi, a former communist, viewed the occupation as an opportunity for European workers to unite in a common struggle against their class enemies.[103] For Levi this common struggle had to be waged not only against all bourgeois political parties and governments, which were militarist and chauvinist by definition, but also against the leaders of European socialist parties who, as a group, were supposedly too compromised by national political calculations to be genuine internationalists.[104]

If Levi's group criticized the SPD and, indeed, all socialist leaders for being insufficiently internationalist, others insisted that German socialism was excessively internationalist. Early on, Friedrich Adler, who was close to German socialists, voiced the fear that the Ruhr occupation would propel the SPD into a version of the wartime *Burgfrieden* in which internationalism had been sacrificed on the nationalist altar.[105] For evidence, Adler could have pointed to Wilhelm Sollmann, an SPD deputy who would serve briefly as Interior Minister in Stresemann's government from August to November 1923. Writing in February, Sollmann called for German socialists to lead a national uprising in response to the Ruhr occupation; the SPD, he contended, should not be swayed by those who denounced such a call as 'nationalism' because the right of national resistance belonged to all workers. Several months later his comments were even more pointed. The International, he explained, was built on the principle that socialism was internationalist because the struggle against capitalism could not be confined to the national realm. Yet, in reality, the International was too weak to help German socialists, and 'foreign comrades' could offer nothing but 'expressions of sympathy'. Given this reality and in what amounted to a rejection of socialist internationalism, Sollmann urged German socialists to embrace a positive nationalism—what he called a 'socialist love of the fatherland'.[106]

That the Ruhr crisis involved the occupation of German territory by foreign troops no doubt heightened the temptation to follow Sollmann's course. Nevertheless, from the outset the SPD adopted a balanced position, seeking to

---

[102] Wels cited in SPD Parteivorstand, *Sozialdemokratische Parteikorrespondenz für die Jahre 1923 bis 1928 (Ergänzungsband)* (Berlin, 1930), 5–6.

[103] Robert Dißmann, 'Ruhrkampf und Internationale', *Sozialistische Politik und Wirtschaft*, no. 3, 22 February 1923, 2–3.

[104] For Levi's group, see Hans-Ulrich Ludewig, 'Die "Sozialistische Politik und Wirtschaft". Ein Beitrag zur Linksopposition in der SPD 1923 bis 1928', *Internationale Wissenschaftliche Korrespondenz zur Geschichte der Deutschen Arbeiterbewegung* 17 (1981), 14–41. For Levi more generally, see Frédéric Cyr, *Paul Levi: Rebelle devant les extrêmes* (Québec, 2013).

[105] Adler, *Die Besetzung des Ruhrgebietes und die Internationale* (Vienna, 1923), 14–15.

[106] Sollmann, 'Kampf und Ziel', 19 February 1923, 1189–92 and 'Zu neuen Aufstieg', 3 December 1923, 883–93, both in *Die Glocke*.

reconcile a national perspective, which demanded outright opposition to the occupation, with its obligations as a member of the international socialist community.[107] In the first instance, this meant support for the government's policy of passive resistance, which the SPD's executive described in February 1923 as the duty of German workers. Interestingly, SPD leaders insisted that such resistance enjoyed international socialism's full backing; one German socialist even designated Ruhr workers as the 'prizefighters of the International'.[108] At the same time, the SPD, consistent with its statements at international socialist gatherings, openly opposed all forms of active resistance, whether it be sabotage of material or attacks on French (and Belgian) personnel, and demanded that the German government repudiate such activities. Equally pertinent, with explicit reference to international socialist agreements, the party launched a campaign in favour of international negotiations, repeatedly pressing the German government to make concrete and reasonable proposals to France and other interested countries. The straightest path to negotiations, declaimed Hermann Müller in the Reichstag in April 1923, was via a 'direct offer' to the Allied governments on the basis of the reparations plan worked out by European socialists.[109]

There can be little doubt that the SPD sincerely believed a negotiated settlement to be the wisest option. As German socialists told their British and French counterparts during a meeting in April 1923, prolonged resistance amounted to '*Katastrophepolitik*' for German workers.[110] But international socialism also figured as a factor in the SPD's thinking. Well before the Ruhr crisis, the party had committed itself to working with other socialist parties—a commitment it reaffirmed at the outset of the occupation.[111] Domestic political considerations, moreover, reinforced this commitment. As scholars have shown, German socialists feared that the mounting economic and financial distress in the Ruhr and in Germany would provide a boost to the political extremes and might even destroy Weimar democracy. Party leaders, accordingly, were interested in a political coalition that could shore up the Republic and (more immediately) form a government capable of finding a way out of the crisis.[112] Existing studies, however, overlook the fact that the SPD needed the cooperation of the international socialist community to demonstrate to its potential coalition partners that a negotiated end to the occupation was feasible, both because a roadmap existed (the socialist reparations plan) and because it enjoyed the support of political forces abroad. If the prospects for

[107] Feucht terms this a 'moderate national position'. See Feucht, *Die Haltung der Sozialdemokratischen Partei Deutschlands zur Außenpolitik während der Weimarer*, 245.

[108] 'Sozialdemokratie und Ruhrkampf. Einstimmige Entschließung des Parteiausschusses', *Vorwärts*, no. 65, 7 February 1923, 1; and FES, Nachlass Carl Severing, 96, 'Haltet aus! Kämpft für das internationale und deutsche Recht!', *Freie Presse*, 12 March 1923.

[109] VDR, Reichstagsprotokolle, 16 April 1923, Müller, 10550; for SPD pressure on the government, also see Conan Fischer, *The Ruhr Crisis, 1923–1924* (Oxford, 2003), 182–3.

[110] See the secret report on the meeting in BAL R 43/I/2661, Auswärtiges Amt to Reichskanzlei, 13 April 1923, with attachment 'Agent F meldet am 9.4.23'.

[111] Crispien, 'Internationale Pflichten', *Vorwärts*, no. 74, 14 February 1923, 1. Also see Dieter Groh and Peter Brandt, '*Vaterlandslose Gesellen*', 180–5.

[112] Winkler, *Von der Revolution zur Stabilisierung*, 553–669; and Breitman, *German Socialism and Weimar Democracy*, 93–113.

such a coalition initially appeared bleak, by the end of the summer the SPD had concluded that one was possible. In August 1923, the SPD thus withdrew its support from Wilhelm Cunow's government and agreed to enter a new government led by Stresemann. And as already noted, SPD ministers wasted little time in pressing the Chancellor to end passive resistance and to enter into negotiations with the French government.[113]

To be sure, the SPD's relationship with the international socialist community during the crisis was sometimes tense. German socialists found especially frustrating the SFIO's seeming inability to influence Poincaré's policy; at times, this frustration boiled over into suspicions of the SFIO's commitment to socialist internationalism. One German socialist thus complained to Adler of the 'very calm but very weak and mendacious promises' of French socialists.[114] But rather than abandon socialist internationalism, this frustration prompted the SPD to move closer to Labour. As Breitscheid commented in March 1923, Labour held the key to resolving the Ruhr crisis. Labour leaders, moreover, encouraged these expectations: along with providing financial help to the SPD, they kept German socialists informed of their efforts to pressure the British government to intervene to compel Paris and Berlin to negotiate. Citing the 'thousands of demonstrations' organized in Britain for this purpose, Tom Shaw even suggested that Labour was doing more than most socialist parties to fulfil its international socialist obligations.[115] Whatever the merits of Shaw's suggestion, German socialists viewed Labour as an invaluable ally. It is therefore hardly surprising that the SPD greeted the creation of Labour's minority government in early 1924 with immense enthusiasm. While the new government might not be able to pursue a 'purely socialist policy', a *Vorwärts* editorial predicted, it would undoubtedly be inspired by a 'socialist spirit', thereby ensuring that 'international problems…will be approached from another perspective'.[116]

EUROPEAN SOCIALISTS AND THE DAWES PLAN

The SPD's enthusiastic welcome of Labour's electoral success points to the interaction of developments at the national and international levels, which combined to resolve the Ruhr crisis. Under strong SPD pressure, Stresemann's government decided to call for an end to passive resistance, well aware that the Ruhr and Germany as a whole were on the brink of chaos. Although it would soon quit the government, the SPD continued to press Stresemann to pursue a negotiated

---

[113] 'Besprechung mit den Parteienführen vom 25. September 1923', reproduced in Karl Dietrich Erdmann and Martin Vogt, eds., *Akten der Reichskanzlei Weimarer Republik. Die Kabinette Stresemann I u II. 13 August bis 6. Oktober 1923* (Boppard am Rhein, 1978), 356–61.

[114] IISH, Fritz Adler Papers, 9, Otto Braun to Adler, 6 September 1923.

[115] For money, see Labour Party, NEC minutes, fiche 87, Joint International Committee, 21 May 1924; for Shaw, see 'Was soll England tun!', *Vorwärts*, no. 421, 9 September 1923, 1.

[116] 'Nach Baldwins Sturz', *Vorwärts*, no. 36, 22 January 1924, 1.

end to the Ruhr crisis.[117] The change of governments in Britain and Germany, together with the deteriorating situation in Germany marked by collapse of the currency, provided the background at the end of 1923 for the creation of two international experts' committees, the most important of which was the one chaired by Charles Dawes, an American banker, which began work in January 1924. Although given a limited mandate to investigate Germany's capacity to pay reparations, the Dawes Committee set its sights on what Stephen Schuker termed a 'comprehensive plan for the readjustment of the entire reparations burden'.[118] The Committee would issue its report in April 1924, but before then it was clear that its proposals would include guaranteed but reduced reparations payments in return for a French withdrawal from the Ruhr.

The international history of what would become the Dawes Plan has been told before.[119] While less known, the international socialist aspects of the story merit attention because European socialists would help to determine their country's response to the Dawes Plan. Interestingly, European socialists initially reacted with hesitation to the news of the Dawes Committee's creation. At a meeting of the LSI's executive in mid-February 1924, the Austrian socialist Otto Bauer warned that the committee 'concealed great dangers to the international workers' and especially to German workers. Admitting that what he called the 'Capitalist solution' to the crisis might be the only one possible for the time being, Bauer nevertheless added that the 'International must not identify itself with it in any way'. In response, the SPD's Otto Braun argued that German socialists 'could not take up a purely negative attitude towards the Capitalist attempts at a solution'. The resulting resolution was predictably ambiguous. While welcoming the apparent willingness of governments to seek a negotiated solution to the 'Reparations problem', it went on to admonish that such a solution must not become a 'serious menace to the international proletariat' in general and to German workers in particular.[120]

European socialists believed that much would depend on their British counterparts, whose electoral victory had reinforced Labour's prominence within international socialism. MacDonald dominated Labour policy: supremely confident in his ability to find a reasonable settlement to the Ruhr crisis, he became British foreign secretary as well as prime minister. From the outset, he presumed that French policy posed the primary obstacle to this goal, noting in early 1924 that the 'French are terrible, but I am sticking to them like a leech'.[121] At the same time, MacDonald recognized that France could not simply be bullied, which rendered necessary some consideration of French views. MacDonald, in effect,

---

[117] In addition to Winkler, *Von der Revolution zur Stabilisierung*, 625–32, see Günter Arns, 'Die Linke in der SPD-Reichstagsfraktion im Herbst 1923', *Vierteljahrshefte für Zeitgeschichte* 22 (1974), 191–203.

[118] Stephen A. Schuker, *The End of French Predominance in Europe: The Financial Crisis of 1924 and the Adoption of the Dawes Plan* (Chapel Hill, NC, 1976), 28.

[119] In addition to Schuker, *The End of French Predominance in Europe*, which remains indispensable, see Steiner, *The Lights that Failed*, 237–50; and Cohrs, *The Unfinished Peace after World War I*, 129–53.

[120] IISH, SAI, 198, Labour Party, Joint International Department, 'The Labour and Socialist International. Executive Committee, Luxemburg, 16 & 17 February 1924'.

[121] BLEPS, E.D. Morel Papers, F8/106, MacDonald to Morel, March–April 1924.

pursued a more balanced diplomacy than his anti-French bias might indicate. The need for balance, however, set him at odds with his party. 'Some of us', a Labourite wrote Longuet in April 1924, 'are not quite sure whether MacDonald in his efforts to gain French goodwill is not too much neglecting the German Socialists...' Reflecting these concerns, the ACIQ urged the Labour government to exert the utmost pressure on Paris even at the risk of provoking a rupture in Anglo-French relations.[122] The ACIQ received support from Labour's parliamentary party, which declared that a final settlement should remove any obligation on Germany's part to pay reparations—a condition unacceptable not only to the French government but also to the SFIO. MacDonald found himself forced to defend his policy, in part by arranging for more positive coverage of his efforts in Labour publications. While his success is difficult to measure, it is clear that Labour was divided on the nature of a reparations settlement.[123]

Mention has already been made of the French elections in May 1924 that produced the *Cartel des gauches* government. In the run-up to the elections, the SFIO made the end of Poincaré's coalition (*bloc national*) the priority; for the SFIO, moreover, a key (if not the key) element of its programme was a negotiated settlement of the Ruhr crisis. Having jettisoned any faith in Poincaré's moderate aims, French socialists castigated the government for its disastrous and dishonest reparations policy, which they warned aimed at Germany's disintegration.[124] During the opening months of 1924, as the crumbling franc exposed France's financial weakness, Blum repeatedly emphasized the negative 'bilan' of the Ruhr crisis, arguing that France would have to accept the Dawes Committee's proposals even if they came from capitalist bankers. For socialists at least, Blum sought to sugar the pill by associating the proposals with the socialist reparations plan outlined in 1921–1922. If only the government had followed socialist advice, he contended, France could have negotiated a reparations settlement without the humiliation of having one imposed on it by outside experts.[125]

Following the elections and after a lengthy and anguished debate in which the example of Labour's minority government figured prominently, the SFIO decided not to participate in the *Cartel des gauches* government but to offer parliamentary support. Over the coming months the SFIO's steady pressure helped to ensure that Premier Edouard Herriot would accept the Dawes Committee's report, even if France's desperate financial situation was undoubtedly the decisive factor. But the French elections had an impact on European socialists more generally. The SFIO presented the Bloc's defeat not just as a victory for French and for international socialism but also as a turning point in international politics in general and in

---

[122] OURS, Jean Longuet, 61 APO/4, James Hudson to Longuet, 9 April 1924; and LHASC, LPA, ACIQ, Memorandums 1922–1924, 'Memorandum on Policy re: Reparations, Ruhr and Inter-Allied Debts', January 1924.

[123] Labour Party, Executive Committee of the Parliamentary Party, minutes, fiche 14, minutes, 3 July 1924. For MacDonald's efforts to defend himself, see TNA, Ramsay MacDonald Papers, PRO/30/69/28, R. Rosenberg (MacDonald's secretary) to Stephenson, 18 April 1924.

[124] See 'Aux travailleurs, aux démocrates de la France', *Le Populaire de Paris*, 10 February 1924, 1.

[125] See the collection of Blum's editorials in *l'Oeuvre de Léon Blum*, III–1, *1914–1928* (Paris, 1972), 307–30 and especially those of 7 and 24 April 1924.

Franco-German relations in particular. The new French government, Paul Faure promised German socialists, would discuss issues with Germany 'in an entirely new language'.[126] That French socialists waxed enthusiastic is not surprising; but arguably more surprising is that German socialists did so as well. Soon after the election, Breitscheid, who only recently had been encouraging the SPD to concentrate on Labour, pointed to the Cartel's victory as proof that French and German socialists were united in their determination to remove the obstacles to a settlement of the Ruhr crisis.[127] Similarly, at the SPD's annual congress in June 1924, Crispien explained that the French elections revealed 'another France, that of the socialists and working masses with whom German workers could cooperate in the general reconstruction of the devastated areas... and in substituting [international] reconciliation for war'.[128]

The enthusiastic response of SPD leaders to the French elections, while no doubt sincere, also constituted a means to disarm internal criticism regarding the Dawes Committee's proposals. Despite or more likely because of the merger of the SPD with the rump USPD, the united SPD was prey to divisions during 1923–1924, especially on the issue of participation in coalition governments. A sizeable minority existed that opposed participation, for fear that German socialism would be corrupted by the exercise of power with bourgeois parties. In this situation, the party leadership in November 1923 deemed it best to leave the coalition government formed the previous August. Tensions nevertheless continued to exist, threatening the SPD's endorsement of the Dawes Plan. If some on the party's right were unhappy with what they viewed as Germany's continued servitude in the form of reparations, considerable grumbling also came from the left and especially from Levi's group. While welcoming the projected end of the Ruhr occupation, Levi criticized the proposed settlement for defending the interests of the bourgeoisie (German and international), pointing in particular to the relatively low tax burden imposed on German industry. Levi's thinking on the Dawes Committee's report reflected his oppositional stance on the issue of participation in government: in both cases, the task was to define distinct socialist positions in opposition to those of non-socialists. This being so, the efforts of party leaders to wrap the Dawes Plan in the mantle of Franco-German and European rapprochement—a rapprochement embodied in international socialist cooperation—provided a means to mollify those socialists who were wary of any association with the work of bourgeois capitalists.[129]

A similar logic, moreover, operated with Labour. During the summer of 1924, complaints about the Dawes Committee's report continued to be voiced. In July,

---

[126] Faure, 'Frankreich nach den Wahlen vom 11. Mai', *Die Glocke*, 19 June 1924, 383.

[127] 'Ce que notre camarade Breitscheid pense des élections françaises', *Le Populaire de Paris*, 15 May 1924, 1; and Breitscheid, 'Die Stunde der Demokratie', *Vorwärts*, no. 280, 17 June 1924, 1–2.

[128] SPD, *Sozialdemokratischer Parteitag 1924. Protokoll mit dem Bericht der Frauenkonferenz* (Berlin, 1924), Crispien, 46.

[129] Levi, *Sachverständigen-Gutachten und was dann?* (Berlin, 1924), 29–31. That Levi's group was impressed by the prospects of Franco-German rapprochement is clear from J. Vetrich, 'Deutschland und Frankreich', *Sozialistische Politik und Wirtschaft*, no. 33, 23 May 1924, 2–3.

MacDonald, who was preoccupied with the international negotiations surrounding the report, received a lengthy letter from the secretary of Labour's executive expressing 'certain doubts'. In addition to the request to be kept better informed about the ongoing negotiations, Labour's executive underscored its dislike of any settlement that included reparations, regardless of French (or SFIO) wishes. If reparations were imposed, the letter made clear, Britain should not be bound to act with France in the event of a default.[130] Faced with pressure from his own party, MacDonald imitated SPD leaders in emphasizing the larger prospects of European rapprochement. As he explained in Parliament in August in comments directed as much to Labour as to non-Labour MPs:

> The question which the Government had to consider when the Dawes Report was issued was a very simple one, namely, whether we could take the Report as a whole, with all its faults and with all its doubtful provisions, and use the opportunity which its issue gave us to try to begin a new chapter in the history of the relations, first of the Allies with each other, and, secondly, of the Allies with Germany.[131]

Although MacDonald did not mention international socialism in his speech, he underscored the point that France accepted the plan—an acceptance he, the NEC, and the ACIQ all realized was the result in part of SFIO pressure. In any event, as with the SPD, MacDonald's arguments helped to dampen dissent, and Labour as a whole eventually supported the report.

As a result, the LSI's approval of the Dawes Plan was all but certain. Indeed, as early as June 1924, LSI and IFTU leaders, meeting in Amsterdam to consider the committee's report, agreed that the latter corresponded to international socialism's own plan, especially in its provision for a reduction in Germany's obligations and for an international credit operation to jump-start payments. Accordingly and notwithstanding its 'defects and omissions' (notably the non-linkage of reparations and inter-allied war debts), the report was judged acceptable as the best available option given that its rejection 'would not be followed by something better in its place, but would on the contrary, merely serve to intensify the European crisis'.[132] But for European socialists at least, the Dawes report was more than a stopgap measure. The report held out the promise not only of ending the international crisis triggered by the Ruhr occupation; but also of opening a new era of European and international conciliation. And with Labour in government and with both the SFIO and the SPD in a position to pressure their governments, European socialists were more determined than ever to work together to place their stamp on international politics.

---

[130] TNA, Ramsay MacDonald Papers, PRO/30/69/128, H.S. Lindsay (Labour) to MacDonald, 4 July 1924.

[131] Hansard 1803–2005, House of Commons, 5 August 1924, MacDonald, 2823–4.

[132] LHASC, LPA, LSI minutes 1921–1937, Labour Party, 'The Labour and Socialist International. Reparations: The Dawes Report', undated. Also see the file in IISH, SAI, 602.

EUROPEAN SOCIALISTS AND EUROPEAN SECURITY: INITIAL DIFFICULTIES

In an assessment of the June 1924 LSI–IFTU meeting, Blum regretted that the issue of European security had not been discussed. During the Ruhr crisis, socialists had understandably focused on the financial and economic aspects of European politics. The issue of security, however, was difficult to avoid. Indeed, it was inextricably connected to the Ruhr occupation if only because the French government had never viewed reparations merely in terms of reconstruction. For Paris, reparations (and the application of the Versailles Treaty more generally) constituted a safeguard against a renewed German threat. As a result, the question of how to ensure France's security loomed over the Ruhr crisis—and sometimes surfaced in international socialist discussions. Yet as Blum recognized, the issue risked provoking a 'long and difficult debate' among European socialists.[133]

That European security would be a fraught issue for European socialists was apparent well before the Ruhr crisis. The Versailles Treaty had contained American and British guarantees of France's security. With the American Senate's refusal to endorse the treaty, the US guarantee became defunct, whereupon the British government chose to renounce its own guarantee. Given France's understandable dissatisfaction with this turn of events, the question inevitably arose: with what, if anything, to replace the stillborn guarantees? During 1921–1922, the British (both the government and the informed public) debated the possibility of a bilateral pact with France that would offer some security. Pertinent here is the growing body of scholarship on Labour's international policy after 1918. Despite some differences of nuance, the consensus is that the policy underwent a process of maturation in which Labour discarded its naïve assumptions about international politics and embraced a more reasonable and realistic approach. Supposedly propelling this evolution was a small group of intellectuals, many of whom sat on the ACIQ, as well as Henderson and MacDonald.[134] A notable facet of this scholarship is the treatment of Labour's international policy in isolation. When, however, Labour's policy during the first half of the 1920s is placed in an international socialist context, it appears far more dogmatic, contradictory, and even duplicitous.

From the beginning, Labour adamantly rejected any idea of a security guarantee to France. Asked in late 1919 whether Britain should maintain its guarantee in the absence of an American one, the ACIQ responded with an unequivocal no. One reason given was Labour's opposition to military alliances in principle, which the ACIQ equated with the 'old-world diplomacy' that had led to war in 1914. Not surprisingly, a deep-seated mistrust of France constituted another reason. The ACIQ

---

[133] Blum, 'La résolution d'Amsterdam et le Conférence de Londres', *Le Populaire de Paris*, 31 July 1924, 1.

[134] See Winkler, *Paths Not Taken*; Lucian Ashworth, *International Relations and the Labour Party: Intellectuals and Policy Making from 1918–1945* (London, 2007); Bridgen, *The Labour Party and the Politcs of War and Peace*; and Casper Sylvest, 'Interwar Internationalism, the British Labour Party, and the Historiography of International Relations', *International Studies Quarterly* 48 (2004), 409–32.

viewed the French government's professed security concerns as a veil to disguise its domineering aims: 'The plain fact is...that her [France's] ruling groups, probably the most reactionary and militarist party now in power in Europe, intends quite consciously to continue in a policy of violence and exploitation.' A final and related reason offered for rejecting a guarantee to France was that it would undermine the League of Nations' universalism by creating separate alliances. Speaking to an American journalist, Henderson claimed that the League's collective guarantee under article X provided 'ample security' to France. The danger of a 'special [Anglo-French] Treaty', he insisted, 'is that it seems to cast doubt on this general obligation.'[135]

The passage of time did nothing to attenuate Labour's opposition. At the beginning of 1922, in the context of renewed discussions of a possible British guarantee to France, Leonard Woolf, a prominent ACIQ member, prepared a draft resolution for Labour's national executive. Woolf began by distinguishing between two options: a general military alliance with France; and a more limited guarantee of military aid in the event of unprovoked German attack. The first option was dismissed on the grounds that a military alliance would render British policy dependent on Paris and that it was 'fundamentally inconsistent' with a League-centred policy. As for the second option, Woolf admitted that it might be useful as a means of influencing French policy. Nevertheless, with the pre-1914 precedent in mind, he rejected a limited guarantee, arguing that it would be impossible in practice to restrict Britain's obligations to France and to Europe. 'It would be disastrous', he concluded, 'for the people of this country again to allow themselves to be entangled in such vague obligations and military commitments on the Continent of Europe.' Instead of a guarantee, the 'only safe policy is that of a real League of Nations in which all countries would reciprocally guarantee one another against unprovoked aggression and invasion'.[136]

The problem, as Woolf himself admitted, was that this 'real' League did not yet exist. Several months later, in a report prepared for an upcoming meeting of European socialists, Woolf emphasized the League's inadequacies as a genuine security institution. '[N]either in its membership, nor its constitution, nor its procedure' was it 'the real League for which Labour stands'. Instead, the League had been 'perverted from the first into an instrument of the short-sighted, one-sided, and vindictive policy of the victors in a war'. Woolf listed a number of measures designed to reform the League: an expanded membership to include Germany and the Soviet Union; more power to the Assembly as opposed to the Council; and an end to the rule of unanimity. But Woolf's more basic point concerned the need for a fundamental transformation on the part of national governments. Labour, he asserted, 'holds that if the Governments which compose the League genuinely renounced imperialistic, capitalist, nationalist and belligerent policy, the existing

---

[135] LHASC, LPA, ACIQ memorandums 1918–1920, ACIQ, 'An Interview with Mr. Arthur Henderson—circulated for the information of members', December 1919.

[136] MUL, Noel-Buxton Papers, MS 951, 16, Labour, ACIQ, 'Draft Resolution for Submission to the Executive Committee', Woolf, 15 January 1922; and LHASC, LPA, ACIQ Minutes, Joint International Committee, 1 February 1922.

League provides a framework which...might become a powerful instrument of pacific internationalism'. One is tempted to reply that, if all governments did so, there would be little need for a League. For Woolf, the pressing question was what to do in an imperfect world. Given the League's inadequacies, it behoved the international socialist movement to 'look around for any other instrument which it may have ready to its hand' to prevent war. Yet, having firmly rejected military guarantees, Woolf (and Labour) had little to offer aside from a plea for the International to use 'the immense power of passive resistance to war which lies in the workers of the world'.[137]

As Woolf's memorandum suggests, Labour discussed the question of a military guarantee to France with other socialist parties, the SFIO among them. An initial exchange occurred at the international socialist conference in Frankfurt in February 1922. While reparations were the principal item on the agenda, the issue came up during the discussions on disarmament during which the Labour delegates proposed a resolution containing an 'explicit and outright condemnation of military alliances and conventions'. The Belgian delegates took the lead in objecting to a declaration along these lines, pointing to the POB's support for the recent Franco-Belgian military convention. Vandervelde promised to abide by the International's decisions, but warned that opposition to the convention would leave Belgian socialists vulnerable at home to attacks from 'Jingoes'. Faced with this opposition, the Labour delegates withdrew their proposal while reserving the right 'to oppose all these military alliances involving a return to the pre-war conditions of a balance of power'. With no consensus in sight, Léon Blum suggested a 'consultation' between British and French socialists on the matter. The British delegates agreed but insisted that the purpose of any such consultation was to consider 'how we [Labour] may best cooperate with them [the SFIO] in our respective countries and Parliaments in a condemnation of the proposed pact between Great Britain and France'.[138]

The immediate result was a meeting of British and French socialists in Paris in mid-March 1922. Unsurprisingly, the British delegates sought a joint denunciation of military alliances. In response, Blum strove to minimize the differences between the two parties, suggesting that it was a question not of principle but of 'expediency'—of determining a policy for what he identified as a transitional period between the pre-war balance of power politics and the post-war's new diplomacy. Speaking for Labour, Shaw proposed that French socialists draw up a memorandum that the delegates would discuss at a meeting in the near future. Longuet readily acquiesced on the SFIO's behalf, though he cautioned Labour against adopting an intransigent position.[139] Although some French participants were frustrated at what they saw as Labour's tendency to blame all of Europe's problems on French militarism, the British were comparatively optimistic.

[137] LHASC, LPA, ACIQ memorandums 1918–1920, ACIQ, 'Draft Report for the International Socialist Conference. The League of Nations and Disarmament', Woolf, 25 July 1922.

[138] LHASC, LPA, LSI, 11/4/13, 'The Five Party International Conference...Frankfurt, 25th, 26th and 27th February, 1922. Report', undated. Emphasis in original.

[139] IISH, LSI (London Secretariat), 146, 'Anglo-French Pact', 15 March 1922.

In a report on the meeting, Ben Tillet, the trade union leader, expressed confidence that continued cooperation could produce 'some practical results' despite the tensions between the two parties.[140] If Shaw was more circumspect, informing Labour MPs that 'complete agreement' might prove elusive, he did think it possible to achieve 'a perfect understanding' of the attitudes of various European socialist parties.[141]

Wasting no time, French socialists drafted a memorandum outlining their position. The SFIO, it began, shared Labour's dislike of military alliances, associating them with a balance of power policy that engendered rivalry, tensions, and war. Like Labour, the SFIO promised to direct 'all its energies towards an organisation of Europe which pending the peace desired by Socialism, will reduce the risk of war to a minimum'. Elaborating on Blum's previous remarks, the memorandum maintained that the differences between Labour and the SFIO were 'of a purely practical nature': it was a question of what 'attitude' to adopt during the present transitional period 'between the policy of the past, which cannot and must not be revived, and the organisation of the future which is not yet realised'. Given the intermediacy of the present, the SFIO proposed as an alternative to Labour's 'rigid and uniform' position a more flexible approach that would judge each case on its own merits in order to determine 'whether it is... in the nature of a step backward towards the past which we all agree to condemn, or of progress towards the future for which we're all preparing'. From this perspective, the memorandum maintained, European socialists should endorse a limited Anglo-French military guarantee as it would reduce the security fears of the French people, weaken 'militarist tendencies', and strengthen French socialists. The SFIO, it concluded, 'could not, therefore, take up an attitude of complete hostility against this Pact without injuring the interests, not only of the French working class, but of International Socialism'.[142]

In an assessment for Labour's parliamentary party, Woolf characterized the SFIO's memorandum as 'extraordinarily inconsistent and self-contradictory'. What French socialists failed to understand, he insisted, was that 'non-Labour Governments' in Britain and France simply could not be trusted 'to pursue a non-imperialist, non-militarist policy, a policy in harmony with the principles of international socialism'.[143] Although French socialists recognized that Labour was unlikely to budge, they agreed to meet with their British and Belgian counterparts in May 1922 to debate security issues. The result did little to bridge differences. The Labour delegates opened with a lengthy critique of France's militarist policy regarding both reparations and security and which, if continued, would 'inevitably

[140] Sembat, 'Visites', *Le Populaire de Paris*, 19 March 1922, 1; and IISH, LSI (London Secretariat), 146, 'Report of Delegation to French Socialist and Parliamentary Party', Tillet, undated.

[141] Labour Party, Executive Committee of the Parliamentary Party, minutes, fiche 164, 21 March 1922.

[142] IISH, LSI (London Secretariat), 146, 'Anglo-French Pact', SFIO, undated but March 1922.

[143] LHASC, LPA, ACIQ memorandums 1918–1920, 'Anglo-French Pact', Woolf, April 1922. Having heard Paul Faure's arguments in favour of a military guarantee, another ACIQ member wrote that on 'this question French logic appears singularly wanting'. See MUL, Noel-Buxton Papers, MS 951, 16, 'France, Reparations and the Pact', undated but spring 1922.

bring about a new war'; they also dismissed French security concerns with the argument that the 'British public did not believe that France was in any real danger'. While conceding that French fears of Germany amounted to a 'morbid condition of the nerves', the SFIO's representatives maintained that the French public was unwilling to entrust national security to an organization such as the League of Nations. This being so, both the French and Belgian delegates rehearsed the case for limited military agreements that would 'be truly pacific in their spirit'. When this argument predictably fell on deaf ears, French socialists could only plead for mutual understanding: they were not asking Labour to approve the SFIO's policy but merely to refrain from publicly condemning it.[144]

If French socialists harboured any lingering hopes regarding British flexibility, they were put to rest the following month at Labour's annual conference. Introducing the resolution on foreign policy, Shaw emphasized the efforts of the two parties to 'come to a common agreement...on questions like the very important question of the Anglo-French Pact'. But while implying that such efforts would continue, Shaw also made it clear that any agreement must reflect Labour's position. 'It was for the Labour Party', he insisted, 'to show them [French social-ists] the futility of the Pact.' The SFIO must be made to understand that the 'real remedy for international quarrels, disputes and dislocations was a purified and extended League of Nations, and there could be no real League of Nations so long as they had individual agreements'. MacDonald, who seconded the motion, indicated that Labour would continue to pressure French socialists to abandon their militarist ideas. Labour, he promised, will ask 'our French friends':

> Why do you go back to your military ideas of pacts and force and so on? Have they ever defended you? It is perfectly true that you are afraid trouble may come. It is per-fectly true that you see a cloud beyond the Rhine. It is perfectly true that you want security; but will you tell us when an Army ever made you secure?[145]

Initially, Labour could count on the SPD's tacit support in its rejection of all military alliances. Although the SPD acted largely as a bystander in the dispute over military guarantees, its overall position appeared closer to Labour than to the SFIO. Generally speaking, German socialists evinced little understanding of French security fears, perceiving France as a direct threat to Germany. 'France's current hegemony over the European heartland', a German socialist journal asserted in 1921, 'means the death by starvation of millions of Germans, the dis-memberment of Germany, and the persistent threat of war in Europe.'[146] Rather than military alliances, German socialists during 1921–1922 increasingly centred their international policy on the League. SPD spokesmen thus advocated not only Germany's membership on equal terms but also the mandatory arbitration of all disputes. Backed by clear-cut procedures for robust economic sanctions, the

---

[144] For the meeting, see LHASC, LPA, LSI 14/1/1/2, 'Franco-British-Belgian Relations', undated. For the POB, see AMSAB, POB, 'Séance du Conseil Général du 17–5–1922'.

[145] Labour Party, *Report of the Twenty-Second Annual Conference held...on June 27th, 28th, 29th and 30th 1922* (London, 1922), Shaw, 188–9; MacDonald, 189–90.

[146] M Beer, 'Die Frage der Internationale', *Die Glocke*, 25 September 1920, 703–6.

League would guarantee the security of all states.[147] Significantly, however, the SPD's position began to change during the Ruhr occupation as German socialists were compelled to confront the fact that France's security concerns could not simply be wished away. Groping for ways to reassure the French, in March 1923 the SPD proposed to European socialist parties a 'solemn undertaking' on Germany's part not to wage war for ninety-eight years; if that proved insufficient, the SPD promised to support 'a pact, signed by the United States and England, and guaranteeing the security of France and Belgium'.[148] An editorial the same month in *Vorwärts* went even further, announcing the SPD's willingness to work for an 'Anglo-French guarantee pact' even against the 'opposition of our English comrades'.[149] By early 1923, in other words, Labour found itself increasingly isolated within the world of international socialism.

EUROPEAN SOCIALISTS AND EUROPEAN SECURITY: ONGOING DIFFICULTIES

During 1924–1925, Labour's isolation became more marked. One sign was the growing support among European socialists to move the LSI's secretariat from London to the Continent. In May 1924, Adler, the LSI's secretary, wrote to Vandervelde in favour of such a move. Family reasons aside, Adler gave as his principal reason his frustration with Labour, which he faulted for its insufficient Marxism and internationalism: in this regard, he remarked, Labour appeared stuck in the 'childhood stage' in comparison to Continental parties.[150] Labour officials vigorously opposed the proposal, in part because they remained committed to the practice of socialist internationalism. As Labour's international secretary wrote to MacDonald in early 1924, the party's foreign policy programme 'is, in part, the result of consultation and agreements with the Labour Parties of other countries. To that extent it is more likely to contribute to the solution of international difficulties.'[151]

But if Labour succeeded in keeping the LSI's secretariat in London, it could not prevent the deepening rift over the issue of European security. Indeed, in early 1924 the issue reappeared with the Draft Treaty of Mutual Assistance (DTMA). Closely identified with Robert Cecil, Britain's chief representative at Geneva, the DTMA sought to fill so-called 'gaps' in the edifice of collective security by enhancing the authority of the League of Nations' Council and by permitting regional

---

[147] BA-SAPMO, NL Hermann Müller, N 2200/194, 'Völkerbeziehungen und Internationale' in SPD, *Programmentwurf der S.P.D. Ein Kommentar*, 79; and BAL, NL Paul Löbe, N 2178/108, 'Friedenswarte und Völkerbund', 21 December 1922.

[148] IISH, LSI (London Secretariat), 60, Labour and TUC, 'The Situation in the Ruhr. Inter-Parliamentary Conference in the Chamber of Deputies, Paris, 20th March, 1923'. Also see Hochschild, *Sozialdemokratie und Völkerbund*, 105, 117.

[149] 'Frankreichs beste Sicherheit', *Vorwärts*, np. 142, 25 March 1923, 1–2.

[150] IISH, SAI, 1293, Adler to Vandervelde, 18 May 1924.

[151] TNA, Ramsay MacDonald Papers, PRO/30/69/226, Gillies to Rosenbery (MacDonald's secretary), 8 February 1924, which includes 'The Labour and Socialist International', undated.

security agreements under League aegis. With a view to upcoming discussions within the League's assembly, Adler in March 1924 asked the LSI's member parties for their thoughts. Although few appear to have responded, the Dutch party submitted a lengthy article by Pietre Troelstra that Adler circulated to all the parties. Well aware of disagreements between socialist parties on the issue of security, Troelstra sought to focus attention on general disarmament, a goal all socialists could presumably support. From this perspective, the DTMA was dangerous not simply because it allowed military agreements, but also because such agreements implied an acceptance of some level of armaments. Disarmament being the priority, Troelstra insisted that the 'first duty' of socialist parties was to support MacDonald's government, which he claimed was pursuing a 'policy of peace' in Geneva.[152] At the LSI Executive meeting in early June 1924, however, the participants refused to endorse Troelstra's position, preferring to postpone a decision on military pacts in general and on the DTMA in particular.[153]

For European socialists, the decisive debate on the DTMA would occur within Labour. The ACIQ considered the treaty at a meeting in February 1924. Surprisingly, given its previous opposition to an Anglo-French military agreement, the committee was divided regarding its recommendation: some wanted outright rejection while others wanted the Labour government to propose alternatives. Eventually, the committee rejected by seven votes to six a resolution condemning any treaty that contained the 'principle of Mutual Military Guarantees'.[154] Reflecting this division, the ACIQ charged two members (Lowes Dickinson and E.D. Morel) with drafting possible alternative proposals. Unable to agree, Dickinson and Morel submitted two papers. The first one, while criticizing military alliances, argued that the Labour government should aim to improve the DTMA, contending that simple rejection would deprive the government of a 'valuable instrument' to push France 'to change its policy, and accept a reasonable settlement with Germany'. Among the proposed improvements were a stricter definition of aggression; a more robust system of obligatory arbitration of international disputes; and precise conditions concerning military guarantees. The second paper, by contrast, reiterated the ACIQ's doctrinaire hostility to military alliances, equating them with French policy. Rather than the DTMA, it advocated a security policy centred on an inclusive League of Nations (including Germany and the Soviet Union), all of whose members renounced war and accepted the obligation to disarm. The Labour government would lead by example, pledging Britain to submit all international disputes for binding arbitration. As the paper confidently asserted: 'We believe that it is in the power of British diplomacy directed by a British Labour Government to win over the opinion of the whole civilised world by willingness to give such striking proofs of honesty and determination.'[155]

[152] IISH, SAI, 1171, LSI circular, 27 March 1924, Adler; and Trolestra, 'Völkerbund und Garantieverträge'.

[153] IISH, SAI, 201, 'Siztung der Executive der S.A.I. am 5., 6. und 7. Juni 1924 in Wien'.

[154] US, Leonard Woolf Papers, 1D1c, ACIQ minutes, 6 and 18 February 1924.

[155] TNA, Ramsay MacDonald Papers, PRO/30/69/21, ACIQ, 'The Draft Treaty of Mutual Assistance', memoranda I and II, May 1924.

In April 1924 the ACIQ met to consider the two papers. After some debate, a 'small majority' voted in favour of accepting the DTMA, including the possibility of 'Complementary Agreements'.[156] Much now depended on MacDonald. The ACIQ did not have to wait long. Three days after receiving the papers, MacDonald's secretary informed the committee that the prime minister had 'thoroughly explored' the issue and 'has now made up his mind upon it. He is of the opinion that the true alternative is the general policy of His Majesty's Government.' MacDonald, in effect, had decided to kill the DTMA. With the cabinet's approval, MacDonald in July 1924 officially repudiated the treaty in an open letter to the League's Secretary-General. '[P]artial treaties...' such as the DTMA, it read, 'by one group of States is likely to bring about the formation of competing groups, and that the result will be a reappearance of the former system of alliances and counter-alliances, which in the past has proved such a serious menace of the peace of the world.'[157]

MacDonald's swift action put an end to the developing debate within Labour regarding possible security guarantees to France. No less pertinently, it pre-empted any further consideration of the DTMA by the International. The ACIQ had submitted copies of both papers to the International for discussion at its executive meeting in June 1924—an act, incidentally, that illustrates Labour's continued attachment to the practice of socialist internationalism. But in light of the Labour government's obvious hostility, which was well-known even before its announcement in July, the LSI's executive opted to defer discussion of security pacts to a subsequent meeting.[158]

The DTMA's demise, however, left unresolved the problem of France's security demands. Something else would be needed. Accordingly, towards the end of 1924 attention shifted to the Geneva Protocol (Protocol for the Settlement of International Disputes). A result of negotiations between the governmental delegates gathered in Geneva in September 1924 for the League's fifth assembly, the Protocol sought to combine security, arbitration, and disarmament. States refusing international arbitration would be designated as aggressors, a designation that entailed the automatic imposition of sanctions by other states, including military measures. The resulting general security would pave the way for disarmament: all states were to ratify the Protocol by 1 May 1925 and a general disarmament conference was to open on 15 June. Peter Jackson has shown that the Protocol reflected French thinking on security, which explains its popularity in Paris.[159] British motives in negotiating the Protocol are perhaps less clear. No doubt the belief within Whitehall that Paris must be offered something played a role. So too

---

[156] US, Leonard Woolf Papers, 1D1c, ACIQ minutes, 30 April 1924; and IISH, SAI 1170, Labour and TUC, ACIQ, 'The Draft Treaty of Mutual Assistance', no. 327, May 1924.

[157] TNA, Ramsay MacDonald Papers, PRO/30/69/21, MacDonald (secretary) to Gillies (Labour), 19 May 1924. For MacDonald's repudiation, see 'The Rejected Pact', *Manchester Guardian*, 22 July 1924, 14, copy in IISH, SAI, 1172.

[158] For the papers, see the file in IISH, SAI, 1170. Incomplete minutes of the executive meeting are in SAI, 201, 'Sitzung der Exekutive der S.A.I. am 5., 6. und 7. Juni 1924 in Wien'.

[159] Jackson, *Beyond the Balance of Power*, 457–68.

did the minority Labour government's desire to appease Liberals who, like Cecil, lobbied incessantly for a more active British policy at Geneva.[160] But the world of international socialism also figured into the equation. MacDonald's abrupt and unilateral dispatch of the DTMA had done nothing to reverse his party's growing isolation among European socialists. With French, German, and Belgian socialists lobbying for military guarantees, if not necessarily for the DTMA, Labour came under pressure from the international socialist community to offer something.

As is well-known, the Protocol quickly encountered opposition in Britain. The government's military advisors claimed that it would impose unbearable military burdens on the country and would transform its armed forces (and especially the navy) into the world's police force. Given this resistance, it is unlikely that a Labour minority government could have approved of the Protocol. In any event, no decision was necessary as the government's parliamentary defeat triggered general elections in October 1924 that resulted in a Conservative majority government, which quickly repudiated the Protocol. But Conservative opposition aside, it is noteworthy that from the outset Labour appeared less than enthusiastic about the Protocol. Having returned to London before the end of negotiations, MacDonald instructed the British delegation in Geneva not to sign. During the election campaign, moreover, Labour spokesmen offered a half-hearted and disingenuous defence of the Protocol against Conservative attacks. Henderson, for example, contended that the envisaged sanctions on aggressor states were a 'last resort' the need for which would likely never arise.[161] After the elections, Labour leaders offered little sign that they were prepared to support the Protocol.

In this situation of uncertainty, the issue of the Protocol was placed on the agenda of the LSI's executive meeting in Brussels in January 1925. To guide the discussion and in an effort to find a consensus, Adler asked Blum and H.N. Brailsford, an ILP member and prolific writer on international affairs, to prepare a joint report on the Protocol.[162] A single report proved impossible, and so Brailsford submitted one for Labour and the trade unionist Léon Jouhaux (presumably at Blum's request) one for the French. Jouhaux's report praised the DTMA as 'an important stage on the road towards European and world organisation' before going on to argue that the Protocol's defeat 'would mean a grave peril, and would be a terrible blow to the cause of peace'. It 'is the duty of the Labour Movement', it accordingly concluded, 'to give its support in every country to its acceptance, and to put pressure upon the governments to prevent the scheme from being defeated'. Brailsford's report, by contrast, was far more ambivalent. While 'in abstract [and] on paper worthy of support', the Protocol supposedly possessed numerous practical dangers stemming from Germany and the Soviet Union's non-membership in the League as well as from the continued existence of national armaments. Brailsford thus argued that the surest path to security lay not in the Protocol but in far-reaching

[160] See Yearwood, *Guarantee of Peace*, 289–97; and Steiner, *The Lights that Failed*, 380–3.

[161] 'New Peace Plan: Mr. Henderson on the Protocol', *Times Digital Archive*, 13 October 1924, 15. For MacDonald's instructions, see Bridgen, *The Labour Party and the Politics of War and Peace*, 184.

[162] IISH, SAI, 1715, LSI to Brailsford, 13 December 1924.

treaty revision. 'It is the duty of every Socialist Party', his paper proclaimed, 'to foster the development of a public opinion which will demand the revision of these Treaties, in the name not only of justice but of peace.'[163]

At the Brussels meeting, Labour delegates sought to distance themselves from the Protocol. Opening the discussion, Josiah Wedgwood, a former Labour cabinet minister, made it clear that his party viewed the Protocol unfavourably. In addition to imposing huge military burdens, the Protocol risked dragging Britain 'into another war unless the force of the League was so overwhelming that none would defy it'—a condition impossible to fulfil. Expressing 'astonishment' at Wedgwood's comments, Blum pointed out that the Protocol had been in good part the work of the Labour government. The SFIO, he continued, had been greatly disappointed with MacDonald's 'hostile decision' against the DTMA; presenting the Protocol as an improved version of the treaty, especially in terms of defining aggressors, Blum could not understand Labour's hostility to its own handiwork. While admitting that the Protocol was impractical for the time being, given the Conservative government's opposition, Blum insisted that this reality reinforced the need for 'special agreements'—for military guarantees. The SFIO leader thus renewed the plea for a purely defensive Anglo-French pact, adding that it would provide French socialists with 'an opportunity...to work in France in favour of a reduction of armaments'. Not only the Belgian but also the German delegates backed Blum. Speaking for the SPD, Wels thus echoed Blum's astonishment at Labour's efforts to disown the Protocol, insisting that MacDonald and Henderson had given 'pledges...to the whole of Social Democracy' on the subject. Like Blum, Wels assured Labour that his party preferred the Protocol to 'special agreements' between countries. But with the Protocol now moribund, he declared that the SPD would not regard an Anglo-French pact as a 'hostile act'.[164]

Clearly taken aback by the general frustration of their Continental comrades, the Labour delegates struggled to clear up the 'misunderstanding about the British attitude'. Labour, one of them explained, 'was wholeheartedly in favour of the general principles of the Protocol, but it was not committed in detail'. The Labour delegation then listed several conditions for accepting the Protocol, including Soviet membership in the League of Nations and provisions for general treaty revision. If the second condition subordinated support for the Protocol to the wholesale transformation of the post-war order, the first one, as the Belgian socialist Vandervelde irritatedly remarked, was no more feasible in the immediate term, as the Soviets refused to enter the League. After further debate, the majority of participants chose to override Labour objections and to vote a resolution describing the Protocol as 'a fundamental advance towards the goal of world peace'. The 'duty' of all socialist parties was 'to direct their efforts to ensure the [parliamentary]

---

[163] Ibid., 'The Geneva Protocol', Jouhaux, undated; and 'Draft of Memorandum on the Geneva Protocol', Brailsford, undated.

[164] LHASC, LPA, LSI minutes 1921–1937, Labour Party, Joint International Department, minutes of LSI Bureau and executive committee meeting, Brussels, January 1925.

ratification of the Geneva Peace Protocol and to ensure that the projected disarmament conference was organized as quickly as possible'.[165]

EUROPEAN SOCIALISTS AND EUROPEAN SECURITY: DIFFERENCES EXACERBATED

Blum sought to apply a favourable gloss to the Brussels meeting, writing soon afterwards that European socialists had reaffirmed the importance of cooperating together to 'ensure a concordance [and] convergence' of positions.[166] If Blum's roseate perspective said more about him than the meeting, it is nonetheless true that a general desire for conciliation existed among socialists. In Labour's case, soon after the Brussels meeting its leaders created a committee to consider the Protocol, with the bulk of the work falling to the ACIQ. After an exhaustive exchange in early February 1925, the committee members agreed to recommend that Labour endorse the Protocol 'on the ground that it furnished the only practical plan at present for obtaining disarmament and substituting arbitration for war as the method of settling disputes'. Labour, accordingly, 'should do everything in its power to obtain acceptance of these principles of the Protocol'. The ACIQ's conciliatory impulses, however, had clear boundaries. While accepting the Protocol, the recommendation remarked that 'certain modifications might be necessary' before reiterating Labour's opposition to 'any form of limited military alliances or guarantees'. The following week, both the Labour and the TUC executives approved the proposed resolution.[167]

Whether Labour's somewhat grudging endorsement of the Protocol would have been sufficient to forge a consensus among European socialists is impossible to say, for international developments soon intervened to alter the situation. In January–February 1925, the German government officially proposed a Rhineland security pact combining non-aggression, arbitration, and security agreements. The proposal eventually led to the famous Locarno Accords in October 1925. There are numerous international histories of the accords, with scholars disagreeing on the latter's significance: while some present Locarno as a new beginning and even as a second and more viable structure for peace than the peace treaties, others view it as a house of cards that fostered the dangerous illusion of peace.[168] From the perspective of European socialists, Locarno is important because the prospect of a Rhineland pact exacerbated tensions between Labour and the Continental parties.

---

[165] Ibid. For the resolution, see AABS, Hjalmar Branting, 91/4/1/4, SAI, Bulletin, vol. 2, no. 1, January 1925, 'Resolutionen beschlossen bei der internationalen Tagung in Brüssels vom 2. bis 6. Januar 1925'.

[166] Blum, 'À Bruxelles', *Le Combat Social*, 9 January 1925, 1.

[167] US, Leonard Woolf Papers, 1D1c, ACIQ minutes, 11 February 1925; and Labour Party, NEC minutes, fiche 96, Joint meeting of the executives of Labour and the TUC, 25 February 1925.

[168] For positive assessments, see Mulligan, *The Great War for Peace*, 339–69; Cohrs, *The Unfinished Peace after World War I*; and Peter Krüger, *Die Aussenpolitik der Republik von Weimar* (Darmstadt, 1985), 269–301. For negative assessments, see Boyce, *The Great Interwar Crisis*, *passim*; and Jon Jacobson, *Locarno Diplomacy: Germany and the West, 1925–1929* (Princeton, NJ, 1972).

Examining these tensions, moreover, casts an interesting light on the larger stakes involved in Locarno. The International would eventually endorse Locarno in what amounted to a tacit admission that consensus on an alternative was unreachable. But this endorsement was also rooted in the hope that Locarno would provide the basis for general disarmament. For socialists (and perhaps also for many non-socialists), Locarno was an expedient whose ultimate justification would depend on the fate of a far more ambitious project.

Almost from the beginning, Labour opposed the German government's pro-posal for a multinational Rhineland security pact. One reason involved domestic politics: with their party now in opposition and with the Conservative-led British government emerging as a major actor in the ensuing international negotiations, Labour leaders had an incentive to criticize the projected outcome. But another reason for Labour's opposition was its visceral dislike of anything resembling a military alliance. And here, not surprisingly, MacDonald took the lead. The pro-posed pact, he wrote in March 1925, 'is a mere salve...and not a cure. It is also being used to mislead people from a comprehensive agreement which really affects the root causes of war.' The pressing task for the champions of peace, MacDonald insisted several months later, was 'to try to eradicate the military idea of alliances as the basis of security and to put in its place a conception of trust based upon a real and passionate desire for peace'.[169] Ironically, the flipside of opposition to the security pact was a warm embrace of the Protocol, despite the recent attempts to disown it. Referring to the Protocol, MacDonald wrote to a Canadian correspond-ent in May 1925 that he was 'terribly disappointed' at the government's 'lack of vision'. 'I am perfectly certain', he asserted the following month, 'that all effective work to secure peace will have to begin with the Protocol.'[170]

Under MacDonald's leadership, Labour launched a propaganda campaign built around opposition to the security pacts and support for the Protocol. A pamphlet written by MacDonald categorically rejected the argument that the proposed Rhineland pact would contribute to security, equating all 'pacts' with the balance of power—with military alliances, arms races, and war. The only security that Pacts offered was that 'possessed by a suicidal mania'. The contrast with the Protocol was stark. MacDonald now presented the latter not simply as a reasonable structure for security but as the very embodiment of peace:

> Its [the Protocol] essential characteristic is that it, for the first time in international policy, embodies the idea of national security of a general kind by provisions which derogate from neither the honour nor the sovereignty of nations. The Protocol strikes at war as a method of settling grievances; it is not a temporary settlement of this or that difficulty but the sub-stitution of a peace system for a war system: it is the Peace Movement in an international compact.

---

[169] TNA, Ramsay MacDonald Papers, PRO/30/69/1170-2, MacDonald to Sir Daniel Stevenson, 25 March 1925; and MacDonald to Chairman of the International Peace Congress, 6 August 1925.

[170] Ibid., PRO/30/69/1170-1, MacDonald to Dandurand, 13 May 1925; and Bodleian, Gilbert Murray Papers, 153, MacDonald to Murray, 16 June 1925.

A similar pamphlet by Henderson, while admitting that the Protocol 'requires revision', insisted that it offered the surest path to security and peace. The Protocol, he wrote, provides:

> the nations with the very means which we hope all peace-loving nations would naturally use to the full in order to avoid war. It was not a theoretical admiration for the principle of arbitration which animated the framers of the Protocol, but the practical and urgent need of seeking to organise the world for peace.

Claiming that the Protocol was not dead, Henderson insisted that Labour was determined to work for its revival.[171]

Labour's campaign reached a crescendo at the party's annual conference in September 1925. In the debate on foreign policy, the national executive's resolution lauded the Protocol and declared that Labour 'will strongly oppose any Pacts of Guarantee of a limited character which are of the nature of Alliances of Groups of Nations and are not based on the principles of the Protocol'. Interestingly, Wedgwood, who had attended the LSI's executive meeting in January, objected that the resolution did not go far enough in denouncing pacts in general and the emerging Rhineland pact in particular:

> To his mind, any system of Pacts of Guarantee backed by military force must inevitably lead to a Europe divided into two parties. If the Pact went through they would see England, France and Germany welded together, and inevitably they would have in the East of Europe another set of Powers getting together, with dangerous results to the whole of Europe.

Though admitting that he had never approved of the Protocol, Wedgwood reluctantly accepted that it might be better than a pact; but his real purpose was to keep the focus on opposition to military guarantees. Accordingly, he demanded that Labour publicly pledge itself not to be bound by any pact signed by the Conservative government. Replying for the national executive, MacDonald reassured Wedgwood that Labour 'had made their position perfectly clear' regarding the proposed Rhineland pact. 'They had opposed it'—and would continue to do so.[172]

At the conference, MacDonald remarked that Labour's ultimate position on the Rhineland pact would have to await not only information on its final provisions but also consultations with socialist parties abroad. These remarks point to the international socialist dimension of Labour's propaganda campaign. From the beginning, Labour leaders sought to mobilize the International in support of the Protocol and against any security pact. In mid-March 1925, MacDonald's secretary wrote to Shaw, the LSI's secretary, to ask whether 'something more through the International [could be done] to maintain the Protocol'; the 'very greatest activity', he added, 'should be shown'. When Shaw replied that European socialists and trade unionists were frustrated with Labour's somersaults on the Protocol,

---

[171] MacDonald, *Protocol or Pact: The Alternative to War* (London, 1925), emphasis in original; and Henderson, *Labour and the Geneva Protocol* (London, 1925), copies of both in IISH, SAI, 1175.

[172] For the resolution and debate, see Labour Party, *Report of the 25th Annual Conference held . . . on September 29th and 30th, and October 1st and 2nd, 1925* (London, 1925), 252–60.

MacDonald pretended not to understand why anyone could be confused. MacDonald, in any case, insisted 'that the most active steps should be taken without delay to get the Protocol put in the forefront of the subjects that the political and industrial Internationalists should fight [for]'.[173] Clearly impatient, MacDonald had already sought to take matters into his own hands. With an eye on an upcoming parliamentary debate on foreign policy, MacDonald in July asked French and German socialist leaders to sign a joint declaration calling on governments to ratify the Protocol and warning that if the latter died, countries would be pushed to seek security in 'a system of opposed alliances that would heighten the risk of war'.[174]

If MacDonald hoped to score domestic points against the Conservatives by showing that the Protocol enjoyed considerable political support in Europe, his request was also an attempt to impose Labour's position on the International. Keen to soothe tensions with Labour, the SFIO responded favourably to MacDonald's request, though Faure did complain about the short notice period that precluded any discussion. In private, French socialists found it 'rather curious' that Labour— the only socialist party to reject the Protocol—'today requests with so much urgency the signature of a joint manifesto in favour of the Protocol'.[175] The SPD, however, proved less obliging. Along with refusing to be rushed into a decision, Wels contended that the declaration did not reflect the SPD's position as expressed at the January 1925 meeting in Brussels. In particular, German socialists could not accept the proposition that guarantee treaties necessarily increased the risks of war. Wels also referred to Germany's domestic political situation in which nationalists fiercely denounced the government's proposed Rhineland pact; from this perspective, Labour's proposed declaration would be used by the SPD's domestic opponents (the communists) as proof that it had allied with the 'German ultra-nationalists' against the government's security pact proposal. While the Protocol remained 'our goal', Wels told Labour, the SPD viewed the security pact as a 'positive step' towards its revival. Having received a copies of Wels' response, the SFIO's executive retracted its approval of the declaration, deferring a decision to the upcoming LSI executive meeting in May 1925.[176]

At the May meeting, Henderson sought to deflect attention from the German government's offer, contending instead that the International should do 'everything in its power to keep the principles of the Protocol alive'. Speaking for the SFIO, Blum countered that socialists must consider alternatives to the Protocol such as the Rhineland pact which, he remarked, resembled ideas that European socialists had been discussing among themselves since 1923. Wels seconded Blum while also reiterating that for domestic political reasons alone the SPD could not

---

[173] TNA, Ramsay MacDonald Papers, PRO/30/69/1170-2, MacDonald (secretary) to Shaw, 18 March 1925; Shaw to MacDonald, 24 March 1925; and MacDonald (secretary) to Shaw, 26 March 1925; and IISH, SAI, 1804, Shaw to MacDonald, 27 March 1925.

[174] IISH, SAI, 1175, Labour to SPD, 19 March 1925.

[175] 'Commission administrative permanente. Séance du mercredi 25 mars 1925', *Le Populaire de Paris*, 1 April 1925, 3.

[176] See the file in IISH, SAI, 1175.

reject guarantee pacts. After Henderson interjected that Labour could not vote for a resolution endorsing 'pacts of guarantee of a more limited character', the participants decided to charge Adler with organizing an 'emergency meeting' of socialist parties to attempt to forge a common position on the subject.[177] Henderson, however, made it clear that Labour would not budge. While happy to consult with European socialists, Labour, he told Shaw, 'entertain[ed] serious objections on political grounds to any action which may appear to substitute the Pact for the Protocol'.[178] Not surprisingly, the emergency meeting in London in early July 1925 produced little consensus—a reality reflected in the final resolution. While urging socialists to make the 'greatest efforts... to obtain the definitive ratification of the Geneva Protocol', it tacitly sanctioned 'partial pacts' as an intermediary measure.[179] Commenting on the meeting, a German socialist fretted that a permanent division appeared to be emerging within the International between British and Continental socialists.[180]

A final effort to forge a common socialist position took place at the LSI's congress in Marseille in August 1925. In preparation for the congress, Labour circulated a lengthy memorandum rehearsing its arguments against alliances—and thus against the proposed security pact. But Belgian, French, and German socialists were not prepared to bend: in late July representatives from the three parties had met in Brussels to coordinate their position on the subject of security pacts.[181] True to form, at the Marseille congress Henderson lauded the Protocol as the 'best plan' for security and peace and declared that it 'must remain the guiding principle of international [socialist] activity and of the individual [socialist] parties'. Addressing himself directly to Henderson, the SPD's Hilferding, while praising the Protocol, insisted that security pacts could also represent a 'step' towards peace. Interestingly, Hilferding pitched his argument in terms of socialist internationalism. In earlier years, he explained, German socialists had rallied to the reparations proposals of their French and British comrades, despite the domestic political costs involved in accepting the principle of Germany's obligation to pay something. Socialist internationalism now required Labour to support the Continental socialists on the issue of security pacts: '...I believe... that the international spirit will move Labour to join with us in the same front. For us continental socialists, it is vital that we take a step forward in order to overcome the poisonous hatred afflicting the foreign policies of Germany and France.' Blum, the next speaker, argued that security pacts should be viewed not as an 'obstacle' to the Protocol but as 'a step consistent

[177] LHASC, LPA, LSI 28, Labour Party, 'Labour and Socialist International', report on the meeting of the LSI executive in Paris, 9–10 May 1925. Also see the file in IISH, SAI, 221.

[178] IISH, SAI, 1664, Henderson to Shaw, 22 May 1925.

[179] BA-SAPMO, II. Internationale, RY 14 I6/2/25, 'Siztung des Bureau der S.A.I. in London, am 4. Juli 1925', in SAI Bulletin, vol. 2, no. 3, July 1925, 7–8; also see the file in IISH, SAI, 611.

[180] Felix Stössinger, 'Deutschland und Frankreich in Marseille', *Die Glocke*, 22 August 1925, 645–6.

[181] For Labour's memorandum, see LHASC, LPA, LSI 28, 'Security Pacts', LSI, Marseilles, 1925. For the Continental socialists, see 'Dans l'Internationale. Une conférence des socialistes d'Allemagne, de Belgique et de France sur le Pacte de sécurité', *Le Populaire de Paris*, 1 August 1925, 3; and IISH, SAI 1615, Renaudel to Adler, 5 July 1925.

with the logic of the Protocol'. Like Hilferding, moreover, the SFIO's leader appealed to Labour's socialist internationalism: when the International's history will be written, he declared, it will be a tale of how 'differences [between member parties] were always overcome'. The final resolution, which Labour only reluctantly approved, postponed a final decision until the Rhineland pact was concluded, at which time the International would undertake a 'detailed examination' of its terms.[182]

EUROPEAN SOCIALISTS AND LOCARNO

European socialists would not have to wait long for the terms of the Rhineland pact. In October 1925 the details of the Locarno accords were made public. The heart of the accords consisted of mutual pledges of non-aggression between Belgium, France, and Germany, with Britain and Italy acting as guarantors. As part of this structure of pledges and guarantees, Germany would become a full member of the League of Nations. Although Poland and Czechoslovakia would be associated through arbitration conventions, Locarno drew a clear distinction between Western Europe and Eastern Europe. With a Rhineland pact now a reality, Adler sought to convoke a meeting of European socialists as quickly as possible in order to pressure Labour to abandon its hostility to separate pacts.[183] The resulting two-day meeting in London in early November 1925 witnessed an 'exhaustive debate' at the end of which the delegates unanimously (with the sole exception of those from the ILP, who abstained) voted a resolution approving the Locarno accords 'as a first step towards the pacification of Europe'. 'Without being under any illusion as to the imperfect character of particular clauses of the Pact [Locarno]', it continued, the International nevertheless considers this step 'as a partial success in the great fight of the international working-class against the methods of violence in relations between states'. As for the Protocol, the resolution expressed regret that it 'has been for the time being wrecked by the attitude of the British Tory Government'.[184] As a French socialist reported, all socialist parties had agreed to support the Locarno accords within their national Parliaments, even if some did so more reluctantly than others.[185]

Of the principal socialist parties, the SFIO greeted Locarno with the most enthusiasm. Speaking to a parliamentary commission, Renaudel exulted that

---

[182] *Zweiter Kongreß der Sozialistischen Arbeiter-Internationale. Marseille, 22. bis 27. August 1925. Bericht des Sekretariats und Verhandlungsprotokoll* (Glashütten im Taunus, 1974), Henderson, 238–9, 319–20; Hilferding, 263–5; Blum, 270–1; and for the resolution, 'Internationale und Sonderverträge', 360–2.

[183] IISH, SAI, 1589, Adler to Bracke, 17 October 1925.

[184] CCA, Phillip Noel Baker Papers, NBKR 2X/2, NEC, 'Labour and Socialist International Executive Meeting, 4th and 5th November, 1925', undated; IISH, SAI, 244, contains an incomplete copy of the minutes. Also see LHASC, LPA, LSI Minutes 1921–1937, 'The International on Locarno', *International Information*, vol. 2, no. 43, 12 November 1925.

[185] 'Commission administrative permanente. Séance du mercredi 11 novembre 1925', *Le Populaire de Paris*, 27 November 1925, 3.

French socialists shared the government's 'joyful satisfaction' with the result.[186] That French socialists would vote for ratification was thus a foregone conclusion; indeed, Blum had said as much at the party's national congress in August 1925. A prominent reason for the SFIO's enthusiasm lay in the additional security that the accords provided for France. But, as so often, domestic political calculations also entered into the equation. During 1924–1925 a debate raged within the SFIO over the question of whether to participate in the government as a coalition partner. Eventually, a majority of French socialists followed Blum's recommendation to remain outside the government but to support it within Parliament. In this context, Locarno was critical because it helped to bind the SFIO with the government parties, especially the Radicals: while the two disagreed on social and economic issues (taxes most prominently), foreign policy offered promising terrain for consensus. Just as importantly, Locarno's binding function also applied to the SFIO. The debate over participation threatened a party whose unity remained fragile. Yet if there was one thing that all French socialists could agree on, it was Locarno. Jean Zyromski, a fierce opponent of participation, thus welcomed the accords as an 'instrument of international détente', while Joseph Paul-Boncour, an equally outspoken proponent of participation, greeted them as an 'idea...that can unite nations'.[187] Finally, Locarno also strengthened the ties binding French socialists to the International. In the parliamentary debate on ratification, the SFIO's Charles Spinasse claimed that Locarno was the work of international socialism: European socialists had pointed the way forward first on the issue of reparations and then on the issue of security. Referring to the practice of socialist internationalism, Spinasse explained that 'We find there all the ideas partially realized since 1922...as tomorrow we will find those ideas that must be realized if we want to return to a normal and healthy [international] life.'[188]

Domestic political considerations also factored into the SPD's response to the Locarno accords. The party's leadership was unambiguously in favour. At the beginning of 1925, prominent German socialists had urged Stresemann to offer a Rhineland pact; afterwards, the party praised what it considered to be its handiwork. An official party pamphlet thus welcomed Locarno as a sharp break with the past: rather than the 'spirit of national hatreds and war' that had infused the Versailles treaty, Locarno constituted 'a step forward in the direction of general peace and the expansion of democracy'.[189] That SPD leaders felt the need to campaign for Locarno reflected the fact that not all German socialists were convinced of its merits. On the party's left, Paul Levi rejected the argument that Locarno was an instrument of peace, describing it (ironically, in terms similar to Labour) as a military alliance whose purpose could only be war. Meanwhile on the party's right,

---

[186] AN C//14763 Commission des Affaires Étrangères, Renaudel, 19 December 1925.

[187] Zyromski, 'La vie internationale', *Le Combat Social*, 30 October 1925, 3; and AN C//14763 Commission des Affaires Étrangères, Paul-Boncour, 23 February 1926.

[188] 'Discours de Spinasse sur les accords de Locarno', *Le Populaire de Paris*, 5 March 1926, 1–2.

[189] SPD, *Völkerbund oder Bündnis mit Sowjetruβland. Der Kampf um den europäischen Frieden* (Berlin, 1925), 3. Also see Klaus E. Rieseberg, 'Die SPD in der "Locarnokrise" Oktober/November 1925', *Vierteljahrshefte für Zeitgeschichte* 30 (1982), 134.

critics complained either that it was too pro-British or that it would freeze the status quo in Europe, thereby removing any possibility of treaty revision.[190] For SPD leaders, Locarno offered an opportunity to draw critics from the left and right towards the centre—and hence the emphasis on German membership in the League of Nations. As a member, Germany would be better placed to promote peace, which all German socialists (including those on the left) sought, while also pursuing treaty revision, a goal especially cherished on the SPD's right.

For SPD leaders, in any event, the biggest domestic political problem was not so much internal party dissent as it was the reaction of German nationalists, particularly the German Nationalist People's Party (DNVP). In response to Locarno, the DNVP quit the government coalition, threatening the latter's existence. Unwilling to allow the DNVP to exploit the nationalist card to the SPD's detriment, the party's *Fraktion* was initially determined to force the nationalists to take responsibility for rejecting Locarno. The ensuing scenario would see German socialists voting against ratification, resulting in the government's defeat and new elections in which the SPD would campaign in favour of Locarno. On sober second thought, however, a majority of *Fraktion* members opted to vote for ratification for several reasons.[191] One reason was to avoid the scenario outlined above, which risked confusing voters. Another and related one was the risk that the nationalists might succeed in improving their tally in federal elections, which in turn might torpedo Locarno. And for SPD leaders, this prospect was unacceptable precisely because they identified so closely with Locarno, seeing it as the product of socialist foreign policy since 1919. 'Locarno', Breitscheid wrote in this sense, 'is the continuation of the *Erfüllungspolitik* that we have supported and that [the government] has pursued.' It was a policy, moreover, that German socialists had worked out in 'numerous congresses and conferences with foreign socialist parties'. For Breitscheid (and for the SPD leadership in general), socialist internationalism required that the party do all it could to uphold the Locarno accords—even if doing so left it vulnerable to attacks from German nationalists.[192]

Unsurprisingly, the International's endorsement of the Locarno accords sat uneasily with many Labourites. If MacDonald pretended in public that he had never opposed security pacts, he privately grumbled about the revival of 'the wily old diplomatist in Europe'.[193] The ACIQ also appeared unimpressed. One memorandum thus bemoaned the absence of criticism of Locarno, which it attributed to a naïve 'will to peace'; another complained that the accords amounted to a military alliance that not only imposed potentially unlimited burdens on Britain, but also

---

[190] For the left, see Levi, 'Locarno', *Sozialistische Politik und Wirtschaft*, no. 3, vol. 41, 15 October 1925, 1; for the right, see Ludwig Quessel, 'Genf, Heidelberg und Locarno', *Sozialistische Monatshefte*, 25 October 1925, 598–605; and Rieseberg, 'Die SPD in der "Locarnokrise"', 140.

[191] Rieseberg, 'Die SPD in der "Locarnokrise"', 139–49; and Heinrich August Winkler, *Der Schein der Normalität: Arbeiter und Arbeiterbewegung in der Weimarer Republik 1924 bis 1930* (Berlin, 1985), 250–9.

[192] Breitscheid, 'Locarno', *Die Gesellschaft* 2 (1925), 508–9; also see Breitscheid, 'Locarno et la politique allemande', *Nouvelle Revue Socialiste*, 5 December 1925, 17–22.

[193] Bodleian Library, Arthur Ponsonby Papers, MS. Eng.Hist. c 669, MacDonald to Ponsonby, 10 November 1925.

risked being exploited 'for purposes other than those specified in them'.[194] Reflecting this widespread disgruntlement, the parliamentary party debated the question of whether Labour should vote for ratification of the Locarno accords. At a meeting in mid-November 1925, Wedgwood introduced a resolution that amounted to a repudiation of the accords; with MacDonald presiding, the resolution was narrowly defeated by two votes. Afterwards, a majority voted for a resolution that called for ratification of the accords.[195] The following day, in the parliamentary debate on ratification, Shaw admitted that it was only after a 'great deal of heart-searching' that Labour decided to vote in favour, notwithstanding its principled opposition to 'any partial pacts or alliances'. In a last effort to register its unhappiness, Labour proposed an amendment to the government's resolution in favour of Locarno that warned of the possible dangers involved. When the amendment was defeated, Labour MPs reluctantly voted to ratify the accords.[196]

Why, in the end, did Labour accept the Locarno accords after having putting up such staunch opposition to security pacts? One reason, no doubt, is that Locarno was a fait accompli accepted by all the governments concerned: there was little to be gained at home or abroad by obstinate resistance. But another reason was rooted in its attachment to the practice of socialist internationalism. Despite its obvious differences with other socialist parties on the issue of security, Labour never turned its back on the International but instead sought to convince Continental socialists to revise their position. This effort proved largely unsuccessful, and Labour found itself increasingly isolated (and criticized) within the international socialist community. From this perspective, to continue its opposition, to refuse to endorse the Locarno accords, risked not only deepening its isolation but also creating a permanent fracture within the International. And that was something most Labourites were unwilling to do. As David Mitrany, an ACIQ member, had warned in the summer of 1925, Labour could not 'oppose an arrangement which French and German and Belgian Socialists are desperately anxious to put through'.[197] However begrudgingly, MacDonald ultimately agreed.

In the end, European socialists managed to forge a fragile consensus in favour of ratifying the Locarno accords. The SFIO accepted the result with enthusiasm, the SPD with resolve, and Labour with some ill will. Yet however fragile the consensus, European socialists had demonstrated a persistent commitment to working together on pressing international issues—to the practice of socialist internationalism. Indeed, this commitment marked the entire period from armistice in November 1918 to the Locarno accords in 1925. With Locarno

---

[194] TNA, Ramsay MacDonald Papers, PRO/30/69/1273, ACIQ, 'Memorandum on the Reactionary Attitude of the Government in International Affairs', no. 341, Angell, November 1925; and CCA, Phillip Noel Baker Papers, NBKR 2X/2, ACIQ, 'Memorandum on the Pact of Locarno', no. 340 A, November 1925.

[195] Labour Party, Executive Committee of the Parliamentary Party, minutes, fiche 18, 16 November 1925; and fiche 168, 17 November 1925.

[196] Hansard 1803–2005, House of Commons, 18 November 1925, Thomas, 507; and 540–1 for the vote.

[197] TNA, Ramsay MacDonald Papers, PRO/30/69/1170-2, Gillies to MacDonald, 23 June 1925, which includes Mitrany to Gillies, 23 June 1925.

ratified, attention would quickly shift to the issue of disarmament. For Labour, in fact, disarmament had long been a priority. The party's attachment to the Protocol stemmed partly from its provision for a general disarmament conference. Afterwards, Labour leaders all but made their grudging acceptance of Locarno conditional on a collective effort on the part of European socialists to promote disarmament. 'The Labour Party', insisted its memorandum on security pacts submitted to the LSI's Marseille congress, 'regard it as vital that there should be at an early date such a Disarmament Conference as the Geneva Protocol would have brought about this year.'[198] For their own reasons, French and German socialists proved eager to sign up to the cause of disarmament. As chapter 4 will show, however, disarmament posed a difficult, divisive, and ultimately unmasterable challenge to socialist internationalism.

[198] LHASC, LPA, LSI 28, 'Security Pacts', LSI, Marseilles, 1925.

4

The Quest for Disarmament, 1925–1933

In retrospect, few enterprises in international politics appear as futile as the quest for disarmament following the First World War. For well over a decade this quest occupied—and sometimes preoccupied—national governments and their officials, producing countless proposals and counterproposals that were exhaustively discussed in countless meetings. The overall results were meagre. If disarmament got off to a promising start with the naval arms limitation treaty signed in Washington in 1922, attempts to control the international armaments trade, the private production of armaments, and the use of chemical and biological weapons all stalled due to the resistance of leading states. Afterwards, success proved still more elusive. The effort to extend the limits on naval armaments in 1927 and 1928 led to bitter wrangling between the French, British, and Americans, and the agreement hammered out at the 1930 London Naval Conference did little to alleviate tensions. Meanwhile, during the second half of the 1920s attention increasingly focused on the League of Nations under whose aegis preparatory discussions began in 1926 for a world disarmament conference. After four years of work, a draft disarmament convention was finally ready in December 1930, allowing the conference to open in February 1932. But the conference failed miserably. Nazi Germany's decision to leave the conference (and the League of Nations) in October 1933 dealt a fatal blow, but well before then it had become evident that an agreement on general disarmament was unlikely.[1] Adding insult to injury, the 1930s would become the decade not of disarmament but of rearmament.[2]

The reasons for the failure of disarmament after 1919 are not hard to find. Disarmament itself was a vague concept. Should it be total or partial? Was it best approached in quantitative terms (number of soldiers or weapons) or in qualitative terms (types of weapons or types of armies)? Should it encompass what Joseph Paul-Boncour, a French socialist, termed a nation's 'war potential'—its demographic, industrial, and other resources? More fundamentally, as Andrew Webster has argued, failure stemmed from the 'inability to rise above the specific concerns

---

[1] For excellent accounts of interwar disarmament, see Andrew Webster, 'From Versailles to Geneva: The Many Forms of Interwar Disarmament', *Journal of Strategic Studies* 29 (2006), 225–46; Andrew Webster, 'Making Disarmament Work: The Implementation of International Disarmament Provisions in the League of Nations Covenant', *Diplomacy & Statecraft* 16 (2005), 551–69; and Steiner, *The Lights that Failed*, 565–97.

[2] Joseph Maiolo, *Cry Havoc: How the Arms Race Drove the World to War, 1931–1941* (New York, 2010).

of each nation-state'.[3] When it came to security, no government was willing to transfer authority to an international organization such as the League of Nations or to place confidence in international agreements whose provisions were difficult to verify and even harder to enforce. During the 1920s, various governments might consider some mutually agreed limits on armaments in order to reduce spending and to avoid unnecessary arms races, but they resisted anything more ambitious. In negotiations, each nation sought to convince others to make a greater effort to disarm while minimizing its own.

National case studies dominate the scholarship on interwar disarmament. Several excellent works trace the elaboration of American, British, French, and German policies, showing how these reflected various negotiating strategies as well as the perceived national interests of each country. This national-centred approach, in turn, provides the building blocks for international histories that highlight the fundamental differences in national approaches to—and under-standings of—disarmament.[4] More recently, scholars have begun to examine the activities of pacifist and other non-governmental groups that lobbied for disarmament—activities that Thomas Richard Davies has labelled a 'trans-national non-governmental campaign for general disarmament'. While Davies concluded that the campaign had little effect on national policies, Cecelia Lynch, in her study of interwar American and British peace movements, argued that they diffused and strengthened norms in favour of international cooperation and disarmament, even if the policy effects of such norms were not immediate.[5] But whatever the precise influence of pro-disarmament groups, their very exist-ence helps to explain why disarmament remained on the agenda of international politics for so long. Because of the widespread conviction that disarmament enjoyed considerable popular support, no government wished to be seen as being responsible for its failure.

Generally overlooked is that international socialism also grappled with the issue of disarmament after 1919. From the outset, European socialists supported the quest for disarmament, and during the second half of the 1920s they not only pressured governments to pursue international negotiations but also strove

---

[3] Webster, 'The Transnational Dream: Politicians, Diplomats and Soldiers in the League of Nations' Pursuit of International Disarmament, 1920–1938', *Contemporary European History* 14 (2005), 494.

[4] For national studies, see Carolyn J. Kitching, *Britain and the Geneva Disarmament Conference: A Study in International History* (Basingstoke, 2002); idem, *Britain and the Problem of International Disarmament* (London, 1999); Dick Richardson, *The Evolution of British Disarmament Policy in the 1920s* (London, 1989); Maurice Vaïsse, *Sécurité d'abord. La politique française en matière de désarmement 9 décembre 1930–17 avril 1934* (Paris, 1981); and Edward W. Bennett, *German Rearmament and the West, 1932–1933* (Princeton, NJ, 1979). For international histories, see Andrew Webster, 'Anglo-French Relations and the Problem of Disarmament and Security, 1929–1933', PhD, Cambridge University, 2001; Phillips P. O'Brien, *British and American Naval Power: Politics and Policy, 1900–1936* (London, 1998); Richard Fanning, *Peace and Disarmament: Naval Rivalry and Arms Control, 1922–1933* (Lexington, KY, 1995); and Christopher Hall, *Britain, America and Arms Control, 1921–1937* (Basingstoke, 1987).

[5] Davies, *The Possibilities of Transnational Activism: The Campaign for Disarmament between the Two World Wars* (Leiden, 2007), 14; and Cecelia Lynch, *Beyond Appeasement: Interpreting Interwar Peace Movements in World Politics* (Ithaca, NY, 1999). Also see Marta Petriciolo and Donatella Cherubini, eds., *Pour la paix en Europe. Institutions et société civile dans l'entre-deux-guerres* (Brussels, 2007).

to work out their own proposals. The effort to do so, however, proved to be a fraught one for European socialists. As one British socialist remembered:

> I have rarely spent hours more futile than these long discussions in the International [LSI] Executive, debating whether reductions in armaments should be applied to material or men or budgets and whether Socialists should be encouraged to go to the Disarmament Conference if they could get appointed to delegations from capitalist governments. I became so impatient that I found it difficult to stop myself from bursting into protests. Guns so many inches shorter, ships so many tons lighter, bombs so many pounds less—what was the practical value of all this in preventing war.[6]

Ultimately, the issue greatly contributed to undermining the collective commitment to the practice of socialist internationalism. Why it did so is interesting for several reasons. First and most obviously, the inability of socialists to work out a practical programme for disarmament underscores the near-impossibility of anyone doing so: European socialists all agreed to make disarmament a priority, and if they could not reach a consensus on a detailed programme then who could? But the experience of socialists also highlights the complex ways in which the national and international realms interacted. For European socialists, disarmament was maddeningly complex not only because it was inseparable from other issues, most notably security, but also because it raised unresolved questions regarding the meaning of international socialism. Prominent among these questions was that of how socialists should respond to the possibility of war and especially of the (non-socialist) nation at war. The more they wrestled with disarmament, the more difficult it became for European socialists to disentangle disarmament from the domestic political disputes over such questions—disputes both within individual socialist parties as well as between them and non-socialist parties at home. Overall, the practice of socialist internationalism had the paradoxical effect of rooting socialist parties more firmly in national politics.

INTERNATIONAL SOCIALISM AND DISARMAMENT: INITIAL VIEWS

The international socialist movement had long been a prominent proponent of disarmament. At the Second's International's 1907 Congress in Stuttgart, for example, the resolution on militarism declared that it was 'the duty' of all socialists to 'combat with all their force land and naval armaments'. If the resolution papered over important differences over the question of what action (if any) to attempt in the event of a war, all socialists agreed on the goal of transforming 'permanent armies' into militia forces. Echoing the arguments of the French socialist Jean Jaurès, the resolution claimed that militia forces would render 'aggressive wars impossible'

[6] Fenner Brockway, *Inside the Left: Thirty Years of Platform, Press, Prison and Parliament* (London, 1947), 170.

while also facilitating the 'disappearance of national antagonisms'.[7] During the war itself socialists from both belligerent camps envisaged a post-war world in which national armed forces would be significantly reduced. The SPD's memorandum prepared for the aborted Stockholm conference argued that a peace treaty must contain provisions for limiting naval and land armaments, whose aim would be to establish a 'peoples' army...for national defence against military aggression and [internal] repression by force'. Similarly, the Allied socialists memorandum on war aims drafted in early 1918 charged a future League of Nations with taking 'steps for the prohibition of fresh armaments on land and sea, and for the common limitation of the existing armaments by which all the peoples are already overburdened'. These measures would pave the way for the 'concerted abolition of compulsory military service', providing countries with a choice between 'a voluntarily recruited force or to organise the nation for defence without professional armies for long terms of military service'.[8]

Following the armistice in November 1918, European socialists continued to call for disarmament. Initially, however, they did not view it as a priority issue. For much of the first half of the 1920s, socialists directed their attention elsewhere—to reconstructing the International, to resolving the reparations puzzle, and to finding a viable formula for security. As a result, the discussions of disarmament both between and within the principal socialist parties were characterized by imprecision and emerging tensions. At the international socialist conference in Berne in February 1919, for example, participants disagreed on the value of professional versus militia (or peoples') armies.[9] Soon after the Berne conference, European socialists learned of the peace terms. Part V of the Versailles treaty imposed drastic limits on German military forces, including an army reduced to 100,000 men, a rump navy, and no air force; this enforced disarmament was presented as the precondition for 'a general limitation of armaments of all nations'. Meanwhile, article 8 of the League Covenant spoke of the 'reduction of national armaments to the lowest point consistent with national safety'.[10] Rather than work out their own proposals, European socialists, at a meeting in May 1919, accepted these provisions as a 'necessary condition for general rearmament', before going on to insist that one-sided disarmament would not by itself result in 'a weakening of general European militarism'. International socialism must thus pressure governments 'to abandon [their] militarist policies and to reduce their land and naval armaments without delay'.[11]

[7] 'La motion sur le militarisme', *L'Humanité*, 25 August 1907, 1. More generally, see Milorad M. Drachkovitch, *Les socialismes français et allemand et le problème de la guerre, 1870–1914* (Geneva, 1953), 323–43.

[8] 'Die deutsche Sozialdemokratie und der Frieden. Erklärung der Delegation der deutschen Sozialdemokratie auf der internationalen sozialistischen Friedenskonferenz in Stockholm', 12 June 1917; and LHASC, LPA, LSI 1/27, Inter-Allied Labour and Socialist Conference, 'Memorandum on War Aims', February 1918.

[9] 'Arbeiter- und Sozialistenkonferenz in Bern, 3. bis 10. Februar 1919', reproduced in Ritter, ed., *Die II. Internationale 1918/1919*, vol. I, 292–310.

[10] Webster, 'The Transnational Dream', 494–5.

[11] AABS, Socialistiska Internationalen 1918–1922, 9, 'Deklaration des Internationalen Aktions-Komités über die Pariser Friedensbedingungen' in *Bulletin der Zweiten Internationale*, May 1919, 6–7.

Afterwards, European socialists evinced little interest in disarmament during the first half of the 1920s. At the LSI's founding congress in 1923, disarmament remained an afterthought. The resolution on the 'imperialist peace and the tasks of the working class' added nothing new: after declaring that only disarmament could ensure a 'lasting peace', it called on socialist parties 'to exert steady pressure on governments to compel them...to propose general disarmament'.[12] At the International's second congress two years later, European socialists manifested more interest in disarmament but little more precision. While Labour's Arthur Henderson insisted that the priority must be on 'general disarmament', both the SPD's Rudolf Hilferding and the SFIO's Léon Blum spoke in terms of a triptych: security, arbitration, and disarmament. The resulting resolution predictably fudged the question of priorities: in addition to enjoining European socialists to strive through 'legal-parliamentary means' to bring about 'disarmament or armaments limitations', it declared that peace and security required a system of international arbitration as well as 'universal and total disarmament'.[13]

EUROPEAN SOCIALIST PARTIES AND DISARMAMENT

If the International's position on disarmament lacked precision, a chief reason was that the issue risked exacerbating tensions within the principal socialist parties. From early on, the SFIO presented itself as a staunch advocate of disarmament. In a lengthy memorandum circulated to socialist parties in early 1922, the SFIO identified Germany's disarmament as the necessary 'prelude' to general disarmament—a disarmament, it added, that had been accomplished thanks in large part to the persistent efforts of German socialists to ensure their country's compliance with the peace terms. The time had thus come to move forward with 'methodical disarmament', which the memorandum defined as a reduction by France (and other countries) of armaments and military budgets to the levels imposed on Germany. This process would include the creation of an international military force, most likely under the League of Nations' control, to apply international sanctions if and when necessary.[14] Although still vague, what the SFIO proposed as its 'positive action program' announced the following year, was a disarmament process that would be 'progressive, universal and simultaneous'. Or, as Blum had written in *Le Populaire de Paris*: 'Disarm Germany. Disarm ourselves. Disarm Europe.'[15]

---

[12] 'Der imperialistische Friede und die Aufgaben der Arbeiterklasse', reproduced in *Beschlüsse des Internationalen Sozialistischen Arbeiterkongresses in Hamburg*, 6–7.

[13] *Zweiter Kongreß der Sozialistischen Arbeiter-Internationale in Marseille*, Henderson, 238; Hilferding, 263; Blum, 277; and 'Die Internationale Sozialistische Friedenspolitik', 360.

[14] BLEPS, ILP, 6/12/3, 'International Socialist Conference of the Five Countries...Memorandum by the French Socialist Party. Disarmament', undated but February 1922.

[15] SFIO, *XXe Congrès National 3,4,5 et 6 Février 1923. Rapports...* (Paris, 1923), 19; and Blum, 'Désarmez. Désarmons', *Le Populaire de Paris*, 4 April 1922, 1.

The SFIO's support for disarmament, however, could not disguise emerging internal tensions on the issue. If disarmament constituted a future goal there remained the question of national defence in the immediate and short term—a question that had so divided French socialists during the recent war. The question was made all the more urgent by the government's project in the early post-war years of revamping the French military, most notably by fixing the length of military service at eighteen months. Suspicious of the government's intentions, the SFIO countered with its own proposed army project. Principally the work of Joseph Paul-Boncour, a deputy from Paris and party expert on military affairs, the SFIO's counter-project unequivocally recognized the need for national defence. While general disarmament might be the ideal, France must be defended in the meantime. As Paul-Boncour explained in Parliament in March 1922:

> I don't think that in order to avoid it [war] the socialist party should abandon its traditional support for national defence. I am profoundly convinced that it is not because of us [France] that in neighbouring and rival countries there are... antagonistic forces. Our socialist policy and our fundamental internationalism should serve... to encourage all peaceful forces but we must also be confident that if war forces gain pre-eminence that we have the means to defend ourselves.

Dismissing as a 'stupid doctrine' the claim that national defence and capitalism were incompatible, Paul-Boncour, referring explicitly to Jean Jaurès' pre-war study, *l'Armée nouvelle*, outlined a militia army organized around local and regional recruitment with a short-term military service. Unlike a professional army, this militia would be a defensive force, incapable of waging aggressive war.[16] No less conspicuous was Paul-Boncour's concept of the 'armed nation'. In a future war, he contended, all resources (manpower, economic, industrial) would have to be mobilized to defend France. If this concept had the benefit for socialists of undermining military claims for political independence, it also demanded considerable peacetime preparations for a possible war. The task of political authorities, Paul-Boncour intoned, was to forge in advance 'the instrument for the defense... [of what] is the armed nation'.[17]

Paul-Boncour rightly claimed that the SFIO's leadership had approved of his 'positive project of national defence'. This approval, however, stemmed more from his advocacy of a militia army than from support for significant peacetime preparations for war. Paul-Boncour's public pronouncements on the subject of national defence, in fact, soon stirred grumbling within the SFIO. In a pamphlet published in 1922, Anatole Sixte-Quenin, a former deputy, addressed the question of national defence. If one aim was to defend Paul-Boncour against communist charges that he was a social-patriot, Sixte-Quenin also sought to restrain the former's enthusiasm for national defence. There could be no socialism, he remarked in an obvious

---

[16] JO, Chambre des Députés, 28 March 1922, Paul-Boncour, 1185, 1189–90; and Paul-Boncour, 'La loi militaire à la Chambre', *Le Populaire de Paris*, 15 March 1922.

[17] JO, Chambre des Députés, 28 March 1922, Paul-Boncour, 1185, 1189–90. In the Chamber's army commission, Paul-Boncour lobbied steadily for a 'plan of industrial mobilization'. See AN, Commission de l'armée, C//14642, 16 November 1921.

warning to Paul-Boncour, if national defence became an 'absolute dogma'.[18] With less circumspection, Jean Longuet voiced concern regarding Paul-Boncour's 'viewpoint that appears narrowly national'. Numerous French socialists, Longuet added, *consider the international duty to the working class as superior to national duty*. Vigorously defending himself, Paul-Boncour countered that, while disarmament might be an inspiring ideal, the priority must be on national defence for the time being. French socialists, he concluded, must appear 'determined to assure the security of the country they seek to govern'.[19] With the SFIO's unity still fragile in the wake of the December 1920 schism, French socialists tacitly agreed for now not to press the matter. But tensions over disarmament were evident.

If Paul-Boncour's proposal revealed latent tensions among French socialists regarding disarmament, German socialists appeared to be more united on the issue. The one-sided disarmament of Germany certainly rankled many majority socialists: an editorial in *Vorwärts* in August 1919 thus accused the Allies of seeking to render Germany powerless so that they could dominate Central Europe. Well aware of this frustration, MSPD leaders sought to exploit Germany's unilateral disarmament as a moral club with which to pressure the Allies to fulfil their promise to disarm. Disarmament will be a 'blessing for the whole world', Hermann Müller, the SPD leader and German foreign minister, declared in August 1919, when it has been extended to all countries. Success in this endeavour, Müller added in a comment directed to both socialists and non-socialists, would be realized 'when all military reasoning had been completely abandoned'.[20] The independent socialists likewise reminded the Allies of their pledge to follow Germany in disarming, even if they too expressed doubts about the likelihood of capitalist countries ever disarming. But however they judged the prospects of disarmament, German socialists could all agree that European socialists had a duty to pursue this goal. Identifying Germany's unilateral disarmament as a 'danger to peace', Hilferding insisted at the SPD's 1924 congress that socialists must find 'a way' to bring about the 'general disarmament' promised by the peace treaty.[21]

Two issues, however, threatened to disturb the SPD's unity over disarmament. The first concerned a militia army. Immediately following the peace treaty, some German socialists expressed regret that the Allies had imposed on Germany a professional army rather than a militia-type army. Indeed, at the SPD's 1920 congress, the reporter for the parliamentary *Fraktion* defended a 'people's army' in much the same terms as Paul-Boncour would.[22] Nevertheless, the SPD quickly made a virtue of necessity: party leaders accepted that in principle a small professional army could

[18] Sixte-Quenin, *La Défense nationale et l'unité socialiste* (Paris, 1922), 4–5, 7. Also see Jean Zyromski, 'Défense nationale et Socialisme', *L'Avenir*, no. 70, April 1922, 180–90.

[19] Longuet, 'Dictature, "social-patriotisme" et participation ministérielle', 12 September 1922, 1; and Paul-Boncour, 'Parlons clair', 18 September 1922, 1, both in *Le Populaire de Paris*. Emphasis in original.

[20] Bernhard Rausch, 'Auf dem Wege zur Abrüstung?', *Vorwärts*, no. 414, 15 August 1919, 1–2; and Verhandlungen des Deutschen Reichstags, 23 July 1919, Müller, 1852.

[21] SPD, *Sozialdemokratischer Parteitag 1924. Protokoll mit dem Bericht der Frauenkonferenz* (Berlin, 1924), Hilferding, 173.

[22] SPD, *Protokoll über die Verhandlungen des Parteitages der Sozialdemokratischen Partei Deutschlands abgehalten im Kasse von 10. bis 16. Oktober 1920* (Berlin, 1920), Hildebrand, 92.

provide a better bulwark against a revival of German militarism than the universal military service associated with a militia army. If this raised the question of what type of safeguards were needed to prevent a professional army from becoming an instrument of reaction, it also set the SPD on a possible collision course with the SFIO, which was the most prominent champion of militia armies (and of short-term military service) within the LSI. That the potential for tensions existed on this score, moreover, was apparent from criticisms of Paul-Boncour's 'armed nation'. In a 1924 pamphlet, Paul Levi argued that Paul-Boncour's conception not only consti-tuted the culmination of militarism but would also effectively preclude any possibil-ity of disarmament.[23] Although Levi belonged to the SPD's far left, his argument that Paul-Boncour's 'armed nation' could not be reconciled with disarmament was one that many socialists would find persuasive—in both Germany and France.

Another potentially troubling issue concerned national defence. German socialists initially agreed to seek security through general disarmament. At an international socialist conference in 1922, they promised to monitor Germany's compliance with its disarmament obligations and to denounce any suspected breaches, in return for the pledge of French socialists in particular to press their government to move forward with disarmament.[24] Yet many German socialists also possessed a sense of Germany's vulnerability, surrounded as it was by neighbours that had not disarmed. At least two factors exacerbated this sense of vulnerability. One was the belief in France's determination to dominate Germany—a belief seemingly confirmed by its military occupation of the Ruhr in 1923. The other factor concerned domestic politics. SPD leaders feared the political costs at home of appearing to be unwilling to defend Germany. For now, the party sought to gloss over the issue of national defence by vague references to 'international disarmament'.[25] But the question of the SPD's attitude towards Germany's current military needs remained unresolved.

The approach of British socialists to disarmament was no clearer than that of their French and German counterparts. Initially, Labour appeared to favour far-reaching disarmament. In June 1919, for instance, a joint Labour–TUC conference regretted that the League covenant mentioned 'national armaments' as amounting to an implicit approval of national defence.[26] Predictably, the ILP sought to encourage Labour in this sense, insisting that Britain (and Labour) take 'the initia-tive in making a definite proposal...for immediate universal disarmament by general agreement'.[27] Behind the scenes, however, Labour thinking revealed considerable

[23] Levi, 'Über realistischen Pazifismus' (1924), reproduced in Charlotte Beradt, ed., *Paul Levi. Politische Texte: Zwischen Spartakus und Sozialdemokratie* (Frankfurt, 1969), 270–93.
[24] See the comments in Franz Künftler, 'Internationale Abrüstung', *Die Freiheit*, no. 104, 22 March 1922, 1–2.
[25] See the SPD's 1925 programme in Dowe and Klotzbach, eds., *Programmatische Dokumente der deutschen Sozialdemokratie*, 216–24.
[26] TNA PRO 608/24/18, Labour-TUC, 'Special National Conference to Consider the Allies' Proposals for the League of Nations...April 3rd, 1919', undated.
[27] Labour Party, *Report of the Twenty-Second Annual Conference held...on June 27th, 28th, 29th and 30th 1922* (London, 1922), 192–3. Also see BLEPS, ILP Papers, ILP/5/1920/6, Fenner Brockway, *Can Britain Disarm? A Reasoned Case in Fourteen Points* (London, undated).

uncertainty. During 1922–1923, Labour submitted two papers on disarmament to European socialist parties. The first one, written by Leonard Woolf, a prominent ACIQ member, rejected 'complete disarmament' as impractical for the time being, and instead urged socialists to treat the question in a 'severely practical manner'. States could negotiate reductions in armaments by 'fixing ratios of land and naval forces' and perhaps also by agreements to abolish certain types of weapons, most notably the blockade, the submarine, and aeroplanes. In his conclusion, however, Woolf cast doubt on the likelihood of such 'practical' measures, placing his confidence instead in the 'immense power of passive resistance to war which lies in the workers of the world'. He thus encouraged European socialist parties to 'agree to oppose any war entered into by any Government, whatever the ostensible object of the war'.[28] The second paper, written by Arthur Ponsonby, another ACIQ member, was far more pessimistic. Disarmament, it contended, was impossible in the absence of popular control of foreign policy in all countries and of a League of Nations acting as a 'supreme international body' capable of dealing with the 'inevitable disputes which may arise between nations'. Until these two conditions were met, Labour should not 'make itself responsible for any detailed scheme of proposals for the regulation and reduction of armaments as a preliminary to disarmament'.[29]

Clearly aware of the reigning uncertainty over disarmament, Labour and the TUC's joint research and information department sought to impose some clarity. In a 1923 memorandum the department warned that a future Labour government would likely have to deal with the issue. The absence of clear principles was dangerous, as Labour 'risks being led by humanitarian sentiment into supporting such schemes as are unsound in principle and to a large extent [are] camouflage for militarist programmes'. Just what principles Labour should base its policy on, however, remained unclear. Having claimed that disarmament could not be achieved through the League of Nations, which was 'merely a committee of victorious and highly armed powers', the memorandum nevertheless suggested that Labour, together with 'foreign Labour [parties]', should work to reconstruct the League in order to pursue several measures, including the '[r]eciprocal reduction of naval, air and military establishments' as well as the '[a]bolition of conscription or its conversion into annual militia training'. At the same time, the authors did not disguise their dislike of arms limitation (as opposed to general disarmament), whose effect was supposedly to 'stabilize armaments already excessive and to stultify pressure for their radical revision'. In the end, the memorandum offered bromides rather than clear principles: the 'road to disarmament will necessarily be a long one and need not be a single one'.[30]

While European socialists all proclaimed their support for disarmament, neither the SFIO, the SPD, nor Labour had worked out a clear-cut position by mid-decade.

---

[28] LHASC, LPA, ACIQ memoranda 1922–1924, 'Draft Report for the International Socialist Conference. The League of Nations and Disarmament', Woolf, 25 July 1922. A version was submitted to the LSI's 1923 Hamburg congress. See LPA, LSI 12/4/1, The League of Nations and Disarmament.

[29] IISH, LSI (London Secretariat), 158, ACIQ, 'Disarmament', Ponsonby, May 1923.

[30] LHASC, LPA, ACIQ memoranda 1922–1924, TUC–Labour, Joint Research and Information Department, 'Memorandum on Disarmament. Principles of a Disarmament Policy', undated but 1923.

However, with the opening of intergovernmental negotiations at Geneva in 1926, European socialists would be forced to confront hard questions.

DISARMAMENT MOVES TO THE FOREFRONT OF INTERNATIONAL POLITICS

With the Locarno accords in October 1925, the world's attention turned towards disarmament. The previous month, the League of Nations' sixth assembly had asked the League Council to begin preparations for a world disarmament conference. In December, the Council created a preparatory commission, which included delegates from three non-League members at the time (Germany, the Soviet Union, and the United States). Charged with drawing up a draft disarmament convention covering naval, air, and land armaments, the preparatory commission held its first meeting in May 1926. These developments encouraged hope among disarmament's proponents, prominent among them European socialists. In an interview in *Vorwärts* in October 1925, Ramsay MacDonald declared:

> The great task of socialist parties is to do everything to ensure that a well-prepared disarmament conference is convened as soon as possible by the League of Nations. The idea of the disarmament conference should be embraced by the Socialist International and the socialist parties of all countries must make their most important international goal the pursuit of disarmament.[31]

Although MacDonald could not speak for the International, in the wake of Locarno, European socialists generally agreed to make disarmament a priority for international socialism. And this meant that socialist parties would have to work out a common position.

But first European socialists would have to address the question of their position towards the League of Nations. As chapter 3 showed, European socialists had manifested considerable ambivalence towards the new organization: while some denounced the League as a tool of capitalist and imperialist powers, others maintained that it could become an instrument of lasting peace, but for it to do so socialists would have to inspire the organization with international socialist principles. Aware of the need to clarify the International's position, Friedrich Adler, its secretary, circulated a memorandum in August 1926 on the subject. The early scepticism of socialists, Adler recounted, had begun to change with MacDonald's minority government and the Protocol, which underlined the League's potential 'as an instrument of progress towards the pacification of the world'. Germany's projected membership, meanwhile, removed the League's 'worst congenital defect'—that it was a victor's club. If the absence of the Soviets and Americans limited the League's 'effective action...especially in the disarmament question', for Adler the more important point was the need to resist the return of the 'old

---

[31] 'Unterredung mit MacDonald. Locarno ein Schritt – Die Abrüstung das Ziel', *Vorwärts*, no. 508, 27 October 1925, 1.

diplomacy' characterized by armaments, rivalry, and war. To defeat the 'old diplomacy', European socialists required an 'international organization of the nations', and the League was the only available one at the moment. Working with the League, international socialism could advance its international agenda—an agenda in which disarmament featured conspicuously.[32]

Adler had drafted his memorandum in preparation for the LSI's executive meeting in August 1926. At the meeting, the discussion centred on the question of whether socialists should be allowed to serve as League delegates of non-socialist governments. As we shall see in the section on European socialists and the Paul-Boncour case, the activities of Paul-Boncour, who was intimately involved in disarmament negotiations at Geneva, provoked particular problems on this score. But the noteworthy point for now is that none of the participants proposed that the International shun the League.[33] As disarmament gained in importance, the League increasingly became the epicentre of international politics, and for this reason alone European socialists accepted the need to work with (and even through) it. Soon afterwards, the International created a special commission on disarmament chaired by Johann Willem Albarda, an energetic and determined Dutch socialist. The commission's stated mandate was somewhat vague: to consider the 'problems of disarmament in so far as they assume actuality through the official disarmament conference of the League of Nations'.[34] But, in reality, the commission had the more challenging task of working out a collective socialist position on disarmament. As Hilferding observed, the commission must move beyond generalities to elaborate a 'concrete political action program' that socialist parties could then pressure their governments to pursue in Geneva.[35]

The first meeting of the LSI's disarmament commission in August 1926 revealed just how challenging this task would be. While everyone agreed on the need to 'leave the theoretical side of disarmament' and to focus on practical proposals, agreement did not extend much further. Opening the proceedings, the Belgian socialist de Brouckère, a member of Belgium's delegation to the League's preparatory commission, explained that the negotiations at Geneva had highlighted the difficulty of defining 'what is meant by disarmament'. Speaking next, the SPD's Wels voiced pessimism that the League negotiations would achieve 'any practical results' before reiterating his party's opposition to militia-type armies—the type favoured by the SFIO. Clearly upset with the tone of the discussions, de Brouckère emphasized the need for European socialists to find some common ground, pointing to the 'danger of reaching the conclusion that the Labour Parties had as much difficulty in reaching agreement as the Governments'. Similarly, Albarda warned against scepticism and insisted that it was up to the International to give a

[32] IISH, SAI, 249, 'The League of the Nations and the Labour and Socialist International', LSI Secretary, undated but August 1927.

[33] CCA, Philip Noel-Baker Papers, 2X/2, 'Labour and Socialist International. Meetings, Zurich, August 26–29, 1926', undated.

[34] LHASC, LPA, LSI, 14/21/1/1, minutes of LSI Bureau meeting, 11–12 April 1926, Zurich; and IISH, SAI, 1665, LSI circular to parties, 22 April 1926.

[35] Hilferding, 'Krieg, Abrüstung und Milizsystem', *Die Gesellschaft*, no. 5, May 1926, 386.

lead to its member parties. More concretely, he supported de Brouckère's proposal that socialist parties undertake 'a close technical study' of disarmament that could be used as the basis for the LSI's programme. The meeting accordingly ended with the decision to send a questionnaire to each party with the aim of soliciting concrete proposals.[36]

The questionnaire was not a great success. By mid-January 1927 only the Austrian and Dutch parties had provided answers, prompting Albarda to postpone a planned meeting of the LSI's disarmament commission.[37] A reminder by Adler prodded Labour and the SPD to submit responses. Labour's response, drafted by Philip Noel-Baker, one of the party's leading disarmament advocates, adopted a practical tack. Having identified comprehensive disarmament as the ideal option, it accepted that a more limited effort in terms of types of armaments and regions covered might be necessary. More concretely, it proposed that the restrictions on land and air forces imposed on Germany be applied to all countries, and that the Washington naval accords be extended to encompass further reductions in the number and size of warships as well as the abolition of submarines.[38] Although the response made no mention of security or arbitration, the same month Arthur Henderson submitted a draft convention for the 'all-inclusive pacific settlement of international disputes' to Adler, urging the International to recommend its adoption by the League of Nations.[39] Conveyed by Otto Wels, the SPD's response, while announcing its support for all measures of international disarmament, abstained from offering any 'detailed proposals' on the grounds that Germany had already been significantly disarmed by the 'Diktat von Versailles'. That said, Wels requested an international socialist meeting as quickly as possible to discuss the question of military organization, adding that the International must choose between a Jaurès-type militia army and a small (professional) army. That the SPD favoured the latter and the SFIO the former helps to explain perhaps the absence of a response from French socialists.[40]

After much delay, the LSI's disarmament commission finally met again in late August 1927 to discuss a report by Albarda. The report began by emphasizing how difficult disarmament would be, if only because of the resistance of most governments and many vested interests. But Albarda was no pessimist. In addition to summarizing the various responses to the questionnaire, he identified several principles that the LSI might champion: that disarmament be linked to a system of

---

[36] CCA, Philip Noel-Baker Papers, 2X/2, 'Labour and Socialist International. Meetings, Zurich, August 26–29, 1926'.

[37] See the file in IISH, SAI, 760, and especially Albarda to Adler, 16 January 1927.

[38] For the draft, see CCA, Philip Noel-Baker Papers, 2X/2, 'Draft Reply Proposed by Professor Philip Noel Baker', undated; and US, Leonard Woolf Papers, 1D1c, ACIQ minutes, 7 December 1926. A copy of the final version is in IISH, SAI, 760.

[39] IISH, SAI, 1666, Henderson to Adler, 8 February 1927; and LHASC, LPA, LSI minutes 1921–1937, LSI circular, 21 February 1927, which contains Labour, 'Commentary on the Draft Convention of Pacific Settlement', undated.

[40] IISH, SAI, 760, Wels (SPD) to Adler, 17 February 1927. In July 1927 Renaudel, the SFIO's delegate on the LSI's disarmament commission, was still promising a response to the questionnaire. See ibid., 760, Renaudel to Adler, 26 July 1927.

international arbitration; that it not be 'one-sided' but involve equal obligations and guarantees for all countries; that national armed forces come under the democratic control of Parliaments; and that soldiers not be allowed to 'become estranged from the people'. This last principle is particularly noteworthy because it appeared to assume that militia-type armies were the preferred model. Appended to Albarda's report was a lengthy draft resolution for the LSI's executive. If the resolution reiterated Albarda's principles, it also reinforced the perceived bias for militia-type armies by emphasizing the need for all socialist parties to work to reduce the period of military service. Avoiding precise proposals, the memorandum maintained instead that the 'problem of disarmament must pass out of the realm of technical discussion into the realm of politics'. And for Albarda this meant a public campaign in favour of disarmament. Socialist parties were thus encouraged 'to rouse public opinion within their ranks by a propaganda at once methodical, intensive and systematic'.[41]

That Albarda's report and the commission's draft resolution would not create a consensus became evident at the LSI's executive meeting the following month at which SFIO and SPD participants clashed on the relative merits of professional armies versus militia-type armies. Although the SPD opposed Albarda's proposal for a public campaign, with Hermann Müller claiming that it would be inappropriate for a country such as Germany that had been 'forcefully disarmed', the meeting concluded with a resolution calling for limited 'propaganda activity' in favour of disarmament as well as for continued study of the issue by the LSI's disarmament commission.[42] The resulting propaganda effort proved to be a mitigated success at best: the keenest participants were Belgian socialists, who grafted a pro-disarmament strain onto their ongoing campaign to reduce military service to six months.[43] But this did not discourage Albarda from drafting an updated report on disarmament that the LSI commission discussed in February 1928. In addition to reiterating the principles outlined by its predecessor, the new report sought to avoid disputes by insisting the choice of 'military system must be left open to all nations'. Just as importantly, it dismissed disagreements between socialist parties as 'technical' issues that could be easily resolved through political activity in favour of disarmament:

> The technical difficulties presented by disarmament can only be surmounted by the strongest political pressure. It is the business of socialist parties to exert such pressure. Therefore the L.S.I. must not lose itself in discussions on matters of technical detail, but must rather by means of the utmost pressure on all governments prevent the technical difficulties from being used as a pretext to wreck all efforts at disarmament.[44]

[41] IISH, SAI, 760, LSI, 'Report of the Committee on Disarmament, to be submitted to the L.S.I. Executive, Brussels, 10. Sept. 1927', undated.

[42] For the minutes of the meeting, see IISH, SAI, 291, 'Protokoll', undated; for the final resolution, see AABS, Ssa, F 02 B:03, 'Tagungen der Sozialistische Arbeiter-Internationale', *Internationale Information*, no. 48, 13 September 1927, 387–8.

[43] See IISH, SAI, 763, Van Roosbroeck (POB) to Adler, 5 December 1927; and SAI, 296, 'Propaganda Action for Disarmament', undated but February 1928. Also see AMSAB, POB, 'Séance du Conseil Général du 28-11-27'.

[44] IISH, SAI, 765, 'Report of the Disarmament Commission of the L.S.I.', undated but February 1928. Also see Wrynn, *The Socialist International and the Politics of European Reconstruction*, 96–7.

Approving the report several days later, the LSI's executive decided that the issues of 'militarism and disarmament' would top the agenda of the LSI's congress scheduled for August 1928 in Brussels.[45]

After such a build-up, the discussion at the Brussels congress proved to be anti-climactic. The resolution presented by the LSI's executive was a reworked version of the disarmament committee's February 1928 report. In a gesture to socialist doctrine, it declared that total disarmament was impossible in a world dominated by capitalism: only socialism's victory could abolish war—and armaments. Until then, the LSI and its member parties would continue to exert the 'strongest possible pressure' on governments to agree to compulsory arbitration of international disputes as well as to an international disarmament conference that would arrive at agreed-upon reductions and restrictions on national armed forces and their armaments. Significantly, the choice of military system (militia versus professional army) was once again left to each country—and to each socialist party.[46] In a report on the congress, the German ambassador in Brussels noted that 'behind the scenes' it took 'serious and difficult work' to arrive at resolutions replete with 'contradictions'.[47] The ambassador was well informed: the unanimous approval of Albarda's resolution did little to hide persistent differences, not least on the question of military systems. In another assessment, the Austrian socialist Karl Renner regretted the decision to leave the choice of military system to each party, predicting that disunity would be the inevitable result as socialists lacked the shared theoretical foundation needed to forge a common position.[48] But the problem was not simply that each party was on its own; it was also that the practice of socialist internationalism possessed real limits. The issue of disarmament would challenge the determination of European socialists to balance their internationalist obligations with their rootedness in national politics.

EUROPEAN SOCIALISTS AND THE PAUL-BONCOUR CASE

The potential for disarmament to shift the balance between national and international perspectives was apparent early on in the case of French socialists. Mention has already been made of Paul-Boncour. In 1924 he became vice-president of the study commission of the *Conseil supérieur de le défense nationale* (CSDN), a political-military institution charged with preparing France for a future war.[49]

[45] SSAZ, SPS, Ar 1.260.5, 'Zur Abrüstungsfrage' in LSI, *Dokumente und Diskussionen*, vol. 5, no. 5, 28 February 1928.

[46] *Kongreß-Protokolle der Sozialistischen Arbeiter-Internationale*, vol. 3, no. 1, *Dritter Kongreß der Sozialistischen Arbeiter-Internationale. Brüssel, 5. bis 11. August 1928* (Glashütten im Taunus, 1974), 'Der Vorschlag der Exekutive der S.A.I. für den Brüssler Kongreß', I, 104–7.

[47] PAAP Pol 19 R 98559, Brussels to AA, no. A. 431, 15 August 1928.

[48] Renner, 'Auf dem Wege zur großen Erneuerung. Ein Nachwort zum Brüsseler Kongress', *Die Gesellschaft* 2 (1928), 296.

[49] For the CSDN's activities, see Talbot C. Imlay, 'Preparing for Total War: Industrial and Economic Preparations for War in France between the two World Wars', *War in History* 15 (2008), 43–71.

Around the same time, the *Cartel des gauches* government appointed him to the French delegation at the League of Nations, where he quickly distinguished himself by his activism on the preparatory commission for the world disarmament conference. Although approved by the SFIO, Paul-Boncour's appointment soon provoked problems due to his outspoken positions on disarmament. Along with his emphasis on the need to consider a country's 'war potential', Paul-Boncour subordinated disarmament to arbitration and above all to security. As he wrote in a May 1926 report for the preparatory commission, 'countries [like France] threatened by aggression cannot desist... from tying together the questions of security and armaments, not only by making disarmament conditional on security but also in disarming only *to the extent* that security guarantees are obtained.'[50] Paul-Boncour's views, moreover, were well known thanks to his numerous public statements. If such views mirrored French government policy, his insistence on additional security guarantees for France was bound to rankle with both French and non-French socialists.

Unhappiness with Paul-Boncour's activities at Geneva quickly manifested itself within the International. The LSI executive meeting in April 1926 had seen a brief discussion of the conduct of socialists serving on national delegations to the League of Nations. But at the Bureau meeting the following month, Otto Bauer, the Austrian socialist, trained his sights directly on Paul-Boncour. Pointing to recent speeches by the latter, Bauer complained that they caused 'extraordinary difficulties' for socialist parties in other countries, precisely because domestic political opponents claimed these speeches reflected the position of international socialism. Echoing Bauer, Adler commented on the confusion caused by socialists who represented bourgeois rather than socialist governments: Paul-Boncour's case, he added, 'easily gives rise to difficulties, because the public views these delegates in the League of Nations as also representatives of the L.S.I.'. With Paul-Boncour's activities in Geneva now on the table, the participants decided to inform the SFIO that the larger question of socialist membership on national delegations would be discussed more thoroughly at the next meeting of the International's executive.[51]

In the meantime, the issue of Paul-Boncour's League of Nations mandate was raised at the SFIO's annual congress at the end of May 1926. Following a report by Bracke on the LSI's activities, Jean Zyromski suggested that Paul-Boncour's presence at Geneva presented dangers for the SFIO. 'Our comrade [Paul-Boncour] risks finding himself caught between the decision of our party and the International and the instructions of a bourgeois government.'[52] Interestingly, Zyromski's opposition stemmed not from any intrinsic hostility to armaments or to national defence but from his unequivocal opposition to socialist participation in a non-socialist government. This opposition informed Zyromski's views on the League of Nations. While willing to admit that the League might serve as an instrument for peace, Zyromski rebelled against what he termed the 'mystique' of the organization

[50] LON R 265, Preparatory Commission, Memorandum de M. Paul-Boncour à l'appui de ses propositions (document C.P.D./C.R./7.), undated but May 1926. Emphasis in original.
[51] IISH, SAI, 249, Adler to SFIO, 15 May 1926. For the April 1926 executive meeting, see the incomplete minutes in IISH, SAI, 244.
[52] 'Le XXIIIe Congrès nationale socialiste', *Le Populaire de Paris*, 28 May 1926, Zyromski, 2.

among socialists. Fundamentally, the League was a club of great powers that reflected their nationalist and imperialist orientations. For this reason, nothing was to be expected from the League concerning disarmament: socialists should not become the 'dupes' of 'sterile discussions and disputes' between governments.[53] Rather than the League, Zyromski championed international socialism, calling for more coordination among socialist parties as well as a more centralized International. Zyromski, moreover, was not alone in his beliefs. In early May 1926 an impressive list of French socialists, including Bracke and Faure, the SFIO's secretary general, joined Zyromski in founding a socialist newspaper, *La Correspondance socialiste*, whose mission was to counter what they perceived as the national rootedness of socialist parties. The first issue thus opened with a call for a strong International that could prevent socialist parties from operating 'without cohesion in international politics and solely preoccupied with the particular political conditions of their [national] milieu'.[54]

At the SFIO's congress, Zyromski's criticism of Paul-Boncour's mandate provoked a response from leading proponents of the SFIO's participation in government. Salomon Grumbach, a party expert on Franco-German relations, maintained that Paul-Boncour's presence did not contradict 'the fundamental principles of socialism'. The International, he continued, should cooperate with the League, which, however bourgeois it might be, constituted 'at present the greatest factor for peace' in the world. Echoing Grumbach, Renaudel contended that the International's policy was to support the League and that, as a delegate at Geneva, Paul-Boncour was advancing the cause of socialism and peace.[55] Although the debate ended inconclusively, two weeks later Jean-Baptiste Sévérac, the SFIO's assistant secretary, informed Adler that the party's executive commission would address the issue of Paul-Boncour's mandate at a meeting in July 1926. In his letter, Sévérac included a lengthy defence by Paul-Boncour who expressed surprise at the LSI's reservations. Regarding his activities as a member of the League preparatory commission, Paul-Boncour argued that his position was inspired by the Geneva Protocol, which the LSI supposedly supported and which explicitly linked disarmament to security.[56] The SFIO's executive committee, however, was not completely convinced. After considerable debate, the committee in July 1926 voted twenty-one to eight (with four abstentions) to refer the question of socialist delegates to the League to the International. Although Zyromski's proposal to terminate Paul-Boncour's mandate was defeated, the majority agreed that the SFIO representative on the LSI's executive should vote in favour of forbidding socialist membership in national delegations to the League of countries with bourgeois

[53] Zyromski, 'La vie internationale', *Le Combat social*, 11 June 1926, 3.

[54] 'Déclaration', *La Correspondance socialiste*, 1 May 1926, 1. For Zyromski's views, see his series of articles in *Le Combat* and *La Correspondance socialiste* during the first half of 1926. More generally, see Hohl, *À Gauche!*, 43–58.

[55] 'Le XXIIIe Congrès nationale socialiste', 2.

[56] IISH, SAI, 249, Sévérac (SFIO) to Adler, 17 June 1928.

governments. The vote amounted to a tacit repudiation by the SFIO of Paul-Boncour's claim that disarmament must be subordinated to security.[57]

As a result of the SFIO's request, the Paul-Boncour case figured on the agenda of the LSI's executive meeting in August 1926. The resulting discussion was somewhat confusing—and inconclusive. While de Brouckère praised Paul-Boncour's work (as well as his own) at Geneva, Bauer emphasized the tensions between international and national perspectives, condemning Paul-Boncour's position as 'the point of view of Nationalism'. Bauer's charge, in turn, prompted Renaudel to insist that Paul-Boncour sincerely (and justifiably) believed that France's national interests could never 'conflict with the international interest of peace'. After Wels remarked in frustration that the International was grappling with the Paul-Boncour case only because French socialists could not settle their 'difficulties' themselves, the participants approved a resolution deferring to the upcoming LSI congress the task of establishing 'principles of action' for international socialism in its relations with the League. In the meantime, it would be up to individual parties to define the conditions of appointment for socialist delegates as well as to ensure that the activities of socialist delegates were 'reconcilable with the general interests of the labour movement and the decisions of the L.S.I.'.[58]

With the ball back in its court, the SFIO debated anew the Paul-Boncour case at its national council in the autumn of 1926. After a lengthy debate, Paul Faure, the party's administrative secretary, reluctantly concluded that the SFIO should endorse Paul-Boncour's presence in Geneva because of the urgency of the work being done there—work that centred on preparing for a world disarmament conference. His argument proved persuasive, and the majority of participants voted to extend Paul-Boncour's mandate for the time being on condition that he cooperate closely with the International and with the socialist members of other national delegations.[59] Soon afterwards, however, Paul-Boncour was once again in the spotlight due to the government's proposed law on the 'organization of the nation in wartime'. Not only was Paul-Boncour influential in drafting the law, but he also served as its parliamentary reporter—hence the moniker the 'Paul-Boncour law'. The decision of the SFIO's parliamentary group to support the bill provoked considerable criticism at the party's annual congress in April 1927. If the SFIO and the International endorsed national defence, Zyromski claimed, both also recognized the need for socialists to act 'independently and autonomously of bourgeois governments'; other delegates feared that the law would preclude international socialist cooperation in wartime. Zyromski and his allies succeeded in forcing the party

---

[57] 'Le Parti et la Société des Nations' in SFIO, *XXIVe Congrès National 17, 18, 19 et 20 Avril 1927. Rapports* (Paris, 1927), 16–17; and 'Commission administrative permanente plenière. Séance du 18 juillet 1926', *Le Populaire de Paris*, 22 July 1926, 6.

[58] CCA, Philip Noel-Baker Papers, 2X/2, 'Labour and Socialist International. Meetings, Zurich, August 26–29, 1926'. Emphasis in original.

[59] 'Conseil National du Parti Socialiste S.F.I.O. Séances des 31 Octobre et 1er Novembre 1926', *Le Populaire de Paris*, 18 November 1926, 4–5. Also see the summary in 'Le Conseil National', *Le Combat Social*, 5 November 1926.

to accept a national council to discuss the Paul-Boncour law.[60] Interestingly, at the council meeting at the end of June 1927 both Blum and Faure threw their support behind Paul-Boncour and his law. While Blum justified his decision on procedural grounds (that the parliamentary group possessed the authority to approve the law), Faure appealed to party unity, warning against a renewed schism, while also pointing to the upcoming national elections in 1928. The immediate result was a triumph for Paul-Boncour.[61]

The triumph would be short-lived. But this time the opposition came not only from within the SFIO but also from foreign socialists. Writing to Renaudel in October 1927, Adler insisted that it was contradictory for socialists to advocate both disarmament and war preparations.[62] But perhaps more damaging were attacks by German socialists. During 1927, Léon Blum had repeatedly called for a French evacuation of the Rhineland, arguing that the occupation 'perpetuates war measures [and] the spirit of war... it has no purpose.'[63] Reflecting this position, at the SFIO's extraordinary congress in December Longuet denounced the continued occupation as 'scandalous' and declared that the party was 'unanimous' in demanding an immediate French evacuation. Clearly angry, Paul-Boncour responded that Longuet's demand did not reflect the International's policy. Referring to the international socialist conference in Luxembourg the previous year, Paul-Boncour maintained that German socialists had agreed to subordinate a French withdrawal from the Rhineland to security conditions and, more precisely, to an international control of the region.[64] Paul-Boncour's claim, in turn, prompted an angry response from the SPD. In a lengthy article two days later in *Vorwärts*, the SPD's executive committee offered a different account of the Luxembourg conference to that of Paul-Boncour. Aware that a simple end to the occupation was politically realistic, French and German socialists had agreed for 'psychological' reasons that a French withdrawal would be accompanied by the establishment of a minimal system under the League's aegis to monitor the region's demilitarization. Just as importantly, this system would not be permanent but would last only as long as the projected occupation (fifteen years). Abandoning niceties, the SPD's executive openly accused Paul-Boncour of deforming the meaning of the agreement by transforming a 'practical [and] precise' goal (an end to the Rhineland occupation) into a permanent international control of the Rhineland.[65]

Soon afterwards, the SPD's Otto Wels wrote to the SFIO's executive commission to explain why German socialists were so upset with Paul-Boncour. However 'awkward' his letter might be, Wels began, the 'international [socialist] sentiment and international tradition' binding the two parties meant that the SPD had a duty

[60] SFIO, *XXIVe Congrès National tenu... les 17, 18, 19 et 20 Avril 1927. Comptre rendu sténographique* (Paris, 1927), Maurin, 138; Zyromski, 147–51; and final resolution, 450.
[61] 'Le Conseil National du Parti Socialiste', *Le Populaire de Paris*, 27 June 1927, 1–3.
[62] IISH, SAI, 1615, Adler to Renaudel, 22 October 1927.
[63] Blum, 'La contribution de la France à la paix', *Le Populaire de Paris*, 18 December 1927, 1. For an earlier call, see Blum, 'Pour la paix. La question rhénane', *Le Populaire de Paris*, 24 January 1927, 1.
[64] 'Le deuxième journée du Congrès National du Parti', *Le Populaire de Paris*, 28 December 1927, 2–3.
[65] 'Die Luxemburger Resolution. Räumungsfrage und Abrüstungsproblem', *Vorwärts*, no. 616, 30 December 1927, 1–2.

to inform the SFIO of the 'embarrassing impression' Paul-Boncour's statement had made. If at the Luxembourg conference German socialists had agreed to link the evacuation of the Rhineland with the issues of security and disarmament, it was 'completely and exclusively on the grounds of practical politics':

> In view of the fact that the bourgeois parties are governing at present, in view of the opposition and prejudice of the non-socialist masses of France against evacuation [of the Rhineland] without something in return [and] in view of the necessity for us *socialists*... to help the *bourgeois* governments to reach an agreement, we [socialists] had ourselves worked out suggestions for 'compensation' for an early evacuation.

The proposed concessions aimed to make a French withdrawal politically feasible rather than to provide additional security guarantees. International control, in short, was meant to be limited in time and scope. In publicly declaring that the Rhineland could not be evacuated without far-reaching and permanent international control, Wels charged, Paul-Boncour had betrayed not only the spirit of the Luxembourg conference, but also the principles of socialist internationalism that required socialist parties to consider the effects of their activities on the domestic political situation of other parties. Paul-Boncour's statement, Wels complained, had been exploited by nationalists and communists as proof that the SPD was indifferent to Germany's national interests. Worse still, all this occurred on the eve of German elections. The message was clear: the SFIO must rein in Paul-Boncour.[66]

Paul-Boncour was furious with the SPD's response, charging that German socialists had engaged in an 'unspeakable attack on me'. From now on, he would refuse to meet with German socialists.[67] Meanwhile, in a letter to the SFIO's executive, he once again insisted that the SPD had committed itself to an extensive system of international control as a counterpart to a French withdrawal from the Rhineland. If German socialists now sought to wriggle out of their commitments, it was because they had not properly prepared German 'public opinion in favour of international control as we have prepared our [French] opinion for an evacuation'. But Paul-Boncour did not simply contest the claims of German socialists. Well aware of the larger stakes involved, he used the letter to reiterate his position on the question of 'the positive organization of peace'. The SFIO, Paul-Boncour maintained, must remain attached to the Geneva Protocol whose 'centre-piece' consisted of 'international control and international sanctions'. Disarmament, in this approach, played little if any role.[68]

The SFIO's executive was not convinced by Paul-Boncour's arguments. At a meeting in early February 1928, the members decided to reassure the SPD that

---

[66] BA-SAPMO, NL Hermann Müller, N 2200/87, 'An die Mitglieder des Parteivorstandes der Sozialistischen Partei Frankreich!' Emphasis in original. This is a draft of the letter; the original has not been found. The letter is undated and the finding aid indicates 1926, but this is clearly wrong: it dates from early 1928.

[67] AN, Papiers Joseph Paul-Boncour, 424/AP/14, dr. 1, Paul-Boncour to Grumbach, 23 January 1928.

[68] Ibid., Paul-Boncour to Faure, 23 January 1928.

French socialists favoured an evacuation of the Rhineland 'without "preconditions"'.[69] More strikingly still, Blum publicly repudiated Paul-Boncour on the issue. In an editorial in *Le Populaire de Paris*, Blum maintained that an immediate French withdrawal had become a 'moral and political necessity'. The SFIO's parliamentary leader dismissed efforts to exploit the occupation for security purposes as misguided. As for a regime of international control, Blum, echoing the SPD, maintained that it must operate under the League of Nations' aegis and be limited in scope and time.[70] Blum's public repudiation of Paul-Boncour was uncharacteristic of someone dedicated to avoiding further splits within the SFIO. Why, then, did he do it? One explanation is that the SPD's position reflected his own inclinations. Blum was never comfortable with an emphasis on security: unlike Paul-Boncour, who remained suspicious of Germany's ultimate intentions, he appears to have sincerely believed that the continued occupation of the Rhineland endangered Franco-German rapprochement. But international socialist solidarity also factored into his thinking. German socialists, Blum argued, had loyally cooperated with the International after 1918, thereby creating bonds of mutual obligation that required French socialists to support the SPD's call for an end to the Rhineland occupation. As he wrote in July 1928:

> All Germany—socialist included—is imbued with the conviction that the military occupation is incompatible with the acceptance and application of the Dawes plan, with the Locarno accords and with Germany's entry into the League of Nations. This conviction is all the more natural and legitimate among German socialists as the acceptance of the Dawes plan and the signing of the Locarno accord are in fact their work—and, indeed, the work of the whole [socialist] International.

That the SPD at the time was the leading member of a coalition government in Germany constituted another—and related—factor. For Blum, the future of Franco-German relations and of European peace more generally hinged on the health of Weimar democracy, which in turn hinged on the strength of German socialism—the regime's principal backer. To keep the internal enemies of democracy at bay, the SPD required foreign policy successes and this, in turn, required a French withdrawal from the Rhineland.[71]

The implications of Blum's repudiation of Paul-Boncour also involved disarmament. During the autumn of 1927 Blum had written a revealing series of editorials on the subject. As so often, he avoided clear-cut positions, preferring to blur differences; nevertheless, it is possible to identify certain themes. One was his growing frustration with the lack of progress at Geneva on disarmament. The deliberations in Geneva, he opined in September, reflected a 'slow and careful formalism that eventually becomes unbearable'.[72] Similarly, Blum exhibited irritation with the

---

[69] 'Commission administrative permanente. Séance du 8 février 1928', *Le Populaire de Paris*, 9 February 1928, 3; also see 'Sozialsten für sofortige Räumung. Eine unzweideutige Erklärung des französischen Parteivorstandes', *Vorwärts*, no. 68, 9 February 1928, 1.

[70] Blum, 'L'évacuation de la Rhénanie. Que dira Briand?', *Le Populaire de Paris*, 2 February 1928, 1.

[71] Blum, 'Le rapprochement franco-allemand', *Le Populaire de Paris*, 5 July 1928, 1.

[72] Blum, 'Les dangers de la prudence' and 'Où en sommes-nous?', *Le Populaire de Paris*, 23 September and 8 October 1927, 1. Also see Gombin, *Les socialistes et la guerre*, 142–3.

French government, whose willingness to disarm he increasingly called into question. Another theme was that France owed it to Germany to disarm, not only because of the promises made in 1919 but also to strengthen German socialists in their struggle against reactionary forces. If disarmament continued to be delayed, he warned, 'we will have provided German reaction...with the most dangerous means of propaganda.'[73] Together, these themes prompted Blum to conclude that a bold proposal was needed to break the logjam at Geneva. It was wrong to believe that anything could be achieved 'by small steps [and] by slow, accumulative progress'. 'We will only reach our goal by big leaps and by forceful measures,' Blum announced. 'One must be imprudent.'[74]

Although Blum refrained from criticizing Paul-Boncour directly, the latter understood that the series of editorials represented a potential challenge. Accordingly, in an open letter to Blum in October 1927, Paul-Boncour insisted on the pre-eminence of security over disarmament: 'only *the adoption of a clear and honest international system of security can permit a real and general reduction of armaments.*'[75] That Paul-Boncour had reason to be concerned became evident at the SFIO's national council in July 1928. In the run-up to the gathering, the opponents of Paul-Boncour's League mandate sought to focus attention on disarmament policy. Writing in June, Zyromski, denouncing the 'circle of reciprocal impotence and hypocrisy' at Geneva, declared that the International must take the initiative in proposing 'general plan for disarmament'. Clearly targeting Paul-Boncour, he added that any plan must break with 'the false belief in *security as a precondition to disarmament*'.[76] At the national council, Zyromski, joined by others, reiterated their criticisms of Paul-Boncour's positions.[77] In a lengthy intervention, Paul-Boncour strove to reduce the differences with his critics, arguing that there existed a 'concomitance' and not an order of priority between security, arbitration, and disarmament: the three constituted an 'indissoluble trilogy'. In a tacit response to Blum, Paul-Boncour argued that disarmament could not be achieved by bold moves but only in stages, the first being the careful preparatory work at Geneva. While promising to work 'hard as steel' for disarmament, he also refused to accept any concrete constraints on his activities.[78] With Blum remaining silent in the debate, a reluctant Faure once again urged French socialists to endorse Paul-Boncour's continued presence in Geneva, pointing to the critical intergovernmental negotiations scheduled for September. With Faure's grudging blessing, just over 70 per cent of the delegates voted to renew Paul-Boncour's mandate.[79]

---

[73] Blum, 'Pourquoi il faut désarmer', *Le Populaire de Paris*, 6 October 1927, 1.

[74] Blum, 'Les dangers de la prudence', *Le Populaire de Paris*, 27 September 1927, 1.

[75] Paul-Boncour, 'Lettre à Léon Blum. Le "Protocole ouvert"', *Le Populaire de Paris*, 10 October 1927, 1. Emphasis in original.

[76] Zyromski, 'Le problème du désarmement', *Le Populaire de Paris*, 16 June 1928, 1–2. Emphasis in original. Also see his 'La participation directe des socialistes à la Société des Nations', *Nouvelle Revue Socialiste*, no. 24, 15 June–31 July 1928, 330–7.

[77] 'Le Conseil National Socialiste', *Le Populaire de Paris*, 15 July 1928, 2.

[78] See ibid. as well as the longer version of his speech in AN, Papiers Joseph Paul-Boncour, 424/AP/14, dr. 1, 'Discours Conseil Nal Juillet 1928', undated.

[79] 'Dernière séance du Conseil National', *Le Populaire de Paris*, 16 July 1928, 1–2.

Paul-Boncour's fate now rested on the course of disarmament negotiations in Geneva, with Faure remarking that socialists expected 'rapid and effective solutions'.[80] Events in the Swiss city soon forced a confrontation. In September, Paul-Boncour delivered a speech in which he openly contested Germany's right to demand general disarmament due to its disarmed state. According to the peace treaty and the League covenant, he claimed, the promise of 'arms reductions' depended on 'minimal guarantees of national security' for nations that felt threatened. As a result, the construction of a 'general structure of international security' constituted an indispensable precondition to disarmament. For Blum, this was too much, and he openly disavowed Paul-Boncour. The latter's arguments, Blum wrote in *Le Populaire de Paris*, implied that France lacked the security to disarm—an implication that supposedly contradicted the SFIO's position. 'We have always held', Blum stated, 'that the present state of security permitted France...a real [and] tangible reduction of our present armaments.'[81]

Blum's renewed disavowal rendered Paul-Boncour's position untenable. In a bitter letter to the SFIO's leadership, he decried the 'carefully concerted plot' against him. The French government, he insisted, sincerely sought disarmament and was being unfairly attacked by socialists at home and abroad. As for his activities in Geneva, Paul-Boncour claimed he was only doing what German socialists did—defending his country's interests. The mere fact that the SPD headed a coalition in Germany, he added tellingly, could not justify France's 'abdication' on disarmament. This time, however, SFIO leaders decided to provoke a break.[82] Seeking to involve the International in the campaign against Paul-Boncour, they urged Adler to organize a conference to discuss international issues, the most pressing of which they deemed to be disarmament.[83] Aware of prevailing winds, Paul-Boncour preempted matters by resigning from France's delegation to the League, informing Briand that to remain 'would cause inconvenience to my friends on the Left'.[84]

Paul-Boncour's resignation from the French delegation put an end for now to the controversy surrounding his activities in Geneva. Yet the controversy is important because it helped to define French socialist policy on disarmament. In response to Paul-Boncour's position in favour of careful steps centred on the principle of security first, the SFIO, led by Blum, moved towards an approach that favoured immediate and even bold steps—steps that envisaged some measure of unilateral disarmament on France's part. Another noteworthy difference between Blum and

[80] Faure, 'Les bienfaits du désarmement', *Le Populaire de Paris*, 18 July 1928, 1.

[81] For Paul-Boncour, see 'Un grand débat sur le désarmement à l'Assemblée de la S.D.N.', *Le Figaro*, 26 September 1928, 3; and for Blum, see his 'Le discours de Paul-Boncour', *Le Populaire de Paris*, 27 September 1928, 1.

[82] AN, Papiers Joseph Paul-Boncour, 424/AP/14, undated letter to 'Mon Cher Ami'; and 'Réunion commune de la C.A.P. plénière et du Groupe parlementaire', *Le Populaire de Paris*, 14 November 1928, 4.

[83] See the file in IISH, SAI, 909. The SPD understood the link between the SFIO's request and the Paul-Boncour case. See Wels (SPD) to Adler, 23 November 1928.

[84] SSAZ, SPS, Ar 1.260.6, 'La lettre de Paul-Boncour à M. Briand', SAI, *Dokumente und Diskussionen*, vol. 17, no. 3, 1928; and AN, Papiers Joseph Paul-Boncour, 424/AP/14, Paul Ramadier to Paul-Boncour, 28 October 1928.

Paul-Boncour concerned the role of international socialism. Unlike Paul-Boncour, who consistently championed a national perspective that called upon French socialists to focus on France's interests, Blum favoured a more internationalist perspective: not only was he more sensitive to the domestic political realities of other socialist parties (and the SPD in particular), but he also possessed more confidence in foreign socialists. Thus, whereas Paul-Boncour expected nothing from Labour, confiding to a friend that Labourites would always pursue Britain's narrow interests, Blum eagerly anticipated the prospect of a Labour government, confident that Labour was as committed as the SFIO to disarmament.[85]

THE *PANZERKREUZER* AFFAIR

After quitting the coalition in November 1925, the SPD remained in opposition for the next two and a half years. This opposition was not categorical: a majority of delegates at the party's annual congress in 1924 endorsed the principle of governmental participation if it was judged necessary in the interests of workers.[86] More concretely, in Parliament, the SPD tolerated the government due principally to its support for Stresemann's policy of European reconciliation. The SPD's ambivalence was evident in its position on the issue of socialist membership in national delegations to the League of Nations—the issue that so exercised the SFIO. Following a request from Stresemann, SPD leaders in the summer of 1927 decided to accept Rudolf Breitscheid's appointment to the German delegation. They did so with considerable reluctance, as doubts existed within the party about the wisdom of such an appointment. Nevertheless, the SPD was sensitive to Stresemann's concerns that a refusal on the SPD's part would be interpreted abroad as a rejection of the government's foreign policy. To Breitscheid, meanwhile, Müller confided that the SPD did not want to be blamed for the failure of disarmament negotiations at Geneva, even if Müller himself believed that such a failure was likely. The result was that Breitscheid went to Geneva with a circumscribed mandate from the SPD: the latter reserved the right to disavow his activities and positions.[87]

Interestingly, Breitscheid found his experience as a member of Germany's delegation to be a trying one. In a confidential report in the autumn of 1928, he complained that his role was 'completely unclear': did he represent the government or his party? More concretely, Breitscheid underscored the issue of the Rhineland. Whereas the German delegation (along with the SPD) demanded an immediate and unconditional French withdrawal, Breitscheid suspected that such a demand was not feasible in terms of French domestic politics. It would be wiser, he

---

[85] AN, Papiers Joseph Paul-Boncour, 424/AP/14, dr. 1, Paul-Boncour to Bertrand de Jouvenal, 17 October 1928; and Blum, 'Bonne année à l'Internationale', *Le Populaire de Paris*, 1 January 1928, 1.

[86] Winkler, 'Klassenkampf versus Koalition: Die französische Sozialisten und die Politik der deutschen Sozialdemokratie 1928–1933', *Geschichte und Gesellschaft* 17 (1991), 191–2.

[87] BA-SAPMO, NL Hermann Müller, N 2200/2, Stresemann to Müller, 30 July 1927; and Müller to Breitscheid, 3 and 10 August 1927.

remarked, to link an end to the occupation to other issues such as reparations.[88] Breitscheid's doubts on this score suggest that Paul-Boncour's version of SPD–SFIO negotiations on possible conditions for a French withdrawal was perhaps closer to the truth than the SPD publicly claimed. That said, the Rhineland issue appears to have been the exception and, generally speaking, Breitscheid supported the German delegation's positions. And on no subject was this more true than with disarmament. At Geneva, Breitscheid and his colleagues insisted that Germany had been disarmed by the victorious powers at Versailles and that the latter were obliged to disarm to its level.

The SPD and the government thus appeared to be of one mind on disarmament. It is ironic, therefore, that it was precisely on the subject of armaments that a political crisis erupted in 1928. In the opening months of the year the government decided to approve the construction of a pocket-battleship (*Panzerkreuzer*), whose displacement of 10,000 tons fell within the range permitted by the peace treaty. Consistent with its position of keeping Germany disarmed as a prelude to universal disarmament, SPD deputies voted against the navy budget in the *Reichstag* in March 1928, thereby helping to postpone a final decision on construction. During the election campaign soon afterwards, the SPD denounced the proposed construction as unnecessary, insisting that the money would be better spent on social programmes. 'First bread, then battleships,' the party's propaganda declared.[89] The SPD made important gains in the election, increasing its share of the popular vote by almost 4 per cent and its seat tally by twenty-two. As a clear winner and the single largest party in Parliament, the SPD formed a coalition government with Müller as Chancellor and Stresemann as Foreign Minister. Following a demand from the Defence Minister General Wilhelm Groener, the cabinet decided in August 1928 to go ahead with the construction of the pocket-battleship, chiefly because of Groener's threat to resign in the event of a refusal. The news of the cabinet's decision, however, unleashed a wave of opposition within the SPD. In addition to local protests across Germany, the party's parliamentary group and its executive committee expressed their regret that SPD cabinet ministers had approved construction. SPD leaders found themselves forced to backtrack, voting in November for a parliamentary motion against the pocket-battleship. As Wels informed the Reichstag, the SPD favoured general disarmament and thus judged new armaments spending to be 'mistaken'.[90]

The intra-party and inter-coalition aspects of the *Panzerkreuzer* crisis have been told before.[91] Less well known, however, is the international socialist dimension. The Müller government's decision came just days after the LSI congress in Brussels. Though not explicitly mentioning naval armaments, the congress

[88] AdsD, NL Carl Severing, 148, 'Vertraulicher Bericht von Rudolf Breitscheid', undated but September–October 1928.

[89] Breitman, *German Socialism and Weimar Democracy*, 148–9.

[90] Verhandlungen des Deutschen Reichstags, 15 November 1928, Wels, 328.

[91] See Breitman, *German Socialism and Weimar Democracy*, 148–51; Winkler, *Der Schein der Normalität*, 521–55; Donna Harsch, *German Social Democracy and the Rise of Nazism* (Chapel Hill, NC, 1993), 46–51; and Wolfgang Wacker, *Der Bau des Panzerschiffes 'A' und der Reichstag* (Tübingen, 1959).

had not only reaffirmed international socialism's support for universal disarmament, but also enjoined socialist parties to ensure that states 'eliminated or reduced' armaments.[92] In this context, it is not surprising that foreign socialists reacted strongly to the decision. In a letter to Müller, Albarda, the chairman of the LSI's disarmament commission, complained that the decision undermined the ongoing efforts of socialists in favour of disarmament.[93] But the most fervent protests came from French socialists. Writing in *Le Populaire de Paris*, Oreste Rosenfeld, a close observer of German politics, insisted that the issue did not concern German domestic politics alone. At a time when the prospects of international conciliation looked promising, the decision to build a pocket-battleship risked strengthening socialism's 'common enemies' who were all too ready to exploit the spectre of German nationalism to sabotage disarmament. Echoing Rosenfeld, Blum claimed that the SPD had an obligation to the International and to the SFIO to reject the pocket-battleship:

> [German] Social Democracy owes it to all the other parties of the International, and especially to the French party, to act when in government in favour of peace, in favour of general disarmament, in favour of a definitive rapprochement between France and Germany. It must abstain... from any measure that fosters doubts about its pacific intentions. It owes us never to provide to nationalist polemicists the argument that they use: 'You see German socialists are in power and nothing changes'... [94]

While the effects of the pressure from foreign socialists are uncertain, it is clear that socialist internationalist considerations figured prominently in the unfolding crisis within the SPD. Faced with a deeply divided party, the SPD's executive committee sought to sidestep the question of the battlecruiser by enfolding it into the larger question of the SPD's position towards national defence and armed forces—precisely the question that European socialists had recently discussed at the LSI's congress in Brussels. Accordingly, in September the executive committee appointed a commission to prepare a report for the upcoming annual congress in May 1929. The army commission, whose seventeen members represented a cross-section of political currents within the SPD, held its first meeting in early October 1928. As one member remarked, three possible attitudes towards Germany's armed forces emerged from the discussion: approval, rejection, or reluctant toleration. But another division is also apparent from the deliberations. On the one side stood those who emphasized the imperative need to cooperate with the International and to use the LSI Brussels disarmament resolution as the basis for the SPD's policy. 'Our task', so announced Heinrich Ströbel, 'is to embrace the International's disarmament program and to work for its practical application.' On the other side stood those who argued that the size and nature of the German military must be

---

[92] *Dritter Kongreß der Sozialistischen Arbeiter-Internationale. Brüssel*, 'Der Militarismus und die Abrüstung', IX, 11.

[93] AdsD, NL Hermann Müller-Franken, 1/HAMG000034, Albarda to Müller, 27 September 1928.

[94] Rosenfeld, 'Le croiseur allemand', *Le Populaire de Paris*, 18 August 1928, 1; and Blum, 'L'affaire du crosieur allemand. Fausse note', ibid., 19 August 1928, 1.

determined by Germany's situation, both internal and external. From this perspective, the LSI's disarmament resolution was either irrelevant or unhelpful—or both.[95]

So divided, the commission decided to ask four non-members (Otto Bauer, Eduard Bernstein, Julius Deutsch, and Karl Kautsky) to submit memoranda on the SPD's military policy. The four agreed on several points. One was the importance of the LSI Brussels resolution on 'militarism and disarmament': with the exception of Bernstein, they all cited the resolution as a key marker in guiding their thinking. The difficulty, of course, was that the LSI's resolution was deliberately imprecise, leaving it to the individual parties to determine what military policy to recommend. All expressed reservations about the traditional socialist support for militia-type armies and the universal military service they implied, though Bauer added that, so long as French and Belgian socialists endorsed such a system, the SPD should avoid any principled rejection.[96] More pertinently for this chapter, there was general agreement that the SPD must cooperate with the International in pursuit of general and universal disarmament. In this context, Bauer identified Germany as a 'pioneer' in disarmament, pointing the way forward for other countries. This pioneer status, in turn, helps to explain the general silence regarding the battlecruiser. None of the respondents declared in its favour, even if all four accepted the need for Germany to possess some armed forces for national defence. Kautsky alone mentioned the battlecruiser in recommending against its approval. Indeed, he argued that Germany could make a major contribution to peace by embracing its 'disarmed state' [*Waffenlosigkeit*] and voluntarily abstaining from arming to treaty limits. 'Germany's example', he asserted, 'provides the most powerful propaganda for general disarmament and world peace.'[97]

Furnished with copies of the four memoranda and the LSI's Brussels resolution, the commission members met over three days in early December 1928 to draft 'guidelines on military policy'. The resulting document explicitly referred to the LSI resolution in favour of compulsory arbitration of international disputes and of 'complete disarmament' through international agreement. Germany's 'historical mission', it affirmed, was to be the 'pioneer of international disarmament'—a mission that precluded both one-sided disarmament and efforts to surpass or to circumvent the armaments limits imposed by the peace treaty. If the guidelines recognized the principle of national defence and thus the need for armed forces, they refrained from pronouncing on the merits of professional versus militia armies—a subject that risked deepening differences with French socialists, among others. Instead, they emphasized another point common to the four memoranda: the importance of democratizing the armed forces to ensure that they became a reliable instrument

---

[95] IISH, Karl Kautsky Papers, H 38, 'Sitzung der Wehrkommission am 2. Oktober 1928', undated, Ströbel, 3–4; and Hünlich, 8. Also see Wilhelm Dittmann, *Erinnerungen*, ed. Jürgen Rojhan, vol. III (Frankfurt, 1995), 949–50.

[96] See AdsD, NL Paul Levi, 76/158, Bauer, 'Gutachten über ein Wehrprogramm der Deutschen Sozialdemokratie'; Bernstein, 'Die Sozialdemokratie und die Wehrfrage'; and Deutsch, 'Gutachten über ein Wehrprogramm der Deutschen Sozialdemokratie'. Also see Kautsky, *Wehrfrage und Sozialdemokratie* (Berlin, 1928).

[97] Kautsky, *Wehrfrage und Sozialdemokratie*, 62.

of the democratic Weimar Republic. If this point reflected the tradition of socialist suspicion towards the army and naval officer corps, it was also one that figured prominently in the LSI Brussels resolution.[98]

Rather than calming matters, the publication of the draft guidelines in December 1928 fuelled a further polarization of debate within the party. From the outset, the guidelines came under fierce attack from the left, particularly from those close to Paul Levi, whose anti-militarism translated into a rejection of the principle of national defence and armed forces of any kind. Levi and his supporters also opposed all class collaboration, whether this meant participation in coalition governments or cooperation with the League of Nations. In an article in August 1928, an ally of Levi argued that the Paul-Boncour case and the vote of SPD ministers for the battlecruiser were two examples of the same dangerous phenomenon: of socialists being co-opted by their class enemies.[99] Levi was situated on the SPD's left and even extreme left, but his arguments enjoyed a larger echo. One example is Toni Sender, a *Reichstag* deputy and member of the SPD's army commission, who publicly criticized the guidelines on military policy. For Sender, the opposition movement within the SPD to the battlecruiser amounted to a 'levée en masse' behind disarmament and peace. In addition to ignoring this movement, the SPD's guidelines contradicted the LSI's Brussels resolution. The latter not only identified 'complete disarmament' as the goal of international socialism; it also called upon socialist parties in each country to undertake 'permanent action' in favour of a 'reduction of armaments'. For the LSI's disarmament campaign to possess any meaning, Sender insisted, all socialists must work tirelessly 'to limit and finally eliminate armaments'. In practice, this precluded German socialists from supporting the battlecruiser, and still less additional spending on armaments even within treaty limits. Sender's interpretation of the LSI resolution was certainly questionable: after all, it had left the issue of military systems to each socialist party to determine— a decision that implied the existence of some military forces. But the more pertinent point concerns Sender's use of socialist internationalism to legitimate and justify an oppositional position in favour of disarmament and against military forces in general.[100]

Criticism of the SPD's guidelines provoked a strong reaction from other German socialists. Julius Deutsch, for example, castigated 'Levi-like contentions' as 'crazy phantasies' [*Spintisiererei*] whose sole result was to produce 'confusion' among the masses.[101] Significantly, the critics increasingly championed the principle of

---

[98] 'Richtlinien der Sozialdemokratie zur Wehrpolitik', *Vorwärts*, 27 December 1928. In private, SPD leaders remained opposed to a militia army, equating the reintroduction of universal (male) military service with rearmament. See BA-SAPMO, SPD, RY 20/II/145/14, Crispien to Eduard Zachert, 8 November 1928. For the tradition of socialist suspicion, see Wacker, *Der Bau des Panzerschiffes 'A'*, 12–24.

[99] Paul Levi, *Wehrhaftigkeit und Sozialdemokratie* (Berlin, 1928), especially 3–10; and Hans-Erich Kaminski, 'Diziplin', *Sozialistische Politik und Wirtschaft*, 17 August 1928, 3.

[100] Toni Sender, 'Kritik an den Richtlinnien zur Wehrpolitik', *Die Gesellschaft* 1 (1929), 113–24. For Sender more generally, see William Smaldone, *Confronting Hitler: German Social Democrats in Defense of the Weimar Republic* (Lanham, MD, 2009), 163–77.

[101] AdsD, NL Paul Levi, 76/158, Deutsch, 'Schlusswort zum Wehrprogramm', undated. Deutsch was, in fact, Austrian.

national defence as well as Germany's practical need for armed forces. Julius Leber, a *Reichstag* deputy and commission member, thus argued that it would be irresponsible for Germany not to possess the military strength allowed by the Versailles treaty. Otherwise, he warned, Germany risked becoming the 'powerless object' in the 'chess game' of European politics. Similarly, Carl Severing denounced the critics as pacifists and pacifism as unsocial: the SPD, he emphasized, had always recognized the duty of national defence. As for 'general disarmament', while it might be the ultimate goal of socialists, considerable time and potential dangers stood between the present and the 'achievement of this ideal'.[102] Writing on the eve of the SPD's annual congress in May 1929, Friedrich Stampfer, the editor of *Vorwärts* and yet another commission member, explained that the German people required an army if Germany was not to become a 'parade and recruiting ground' for 'warring states'.[103] What is striking in all these pronouncements, especially when compared to Sender's, was the scant attention accorded not only to disarmament but also to the International. The perspective adopted was very much a German one.

Vying perspectives were on display at the SPD's annual congress in May 1929. In defending the decision to approve the pocket-battleship, Müller underscored the danger of an end to the coalition government: 'The political was decisive', he declared in this regard. But also noteworthy was Müller's evident frustration with the complaints of foreign socialists. The peace treaty had forcefully disarmed Germany, and thus for them to speak of German imperialism was beyond the 'understanding of normal people'. German socialists, he added, had repeatedly told their '[foreign] party comrades' that if their countries did not disarm then 'nationalism among us will only grow stronger'. As for the criticism of the SPD's participation in government, Müller contended that war in 1914 might have been prevented if the Second International's resolutions had allowed Jaurès to join a French government. Müller's barely disguised attack on international socialism drew a sharp response from Kurt Rosenfeld, a former USPD member, who described the approval of the battlecruiser as a blow to the International and to the SPD's 'internationalist obligations'. Not only did Rosenfeld insist that the SPD had a duty to encourage 'international [socialist] convictions', he also contended that war could be prevented not by socialists participating in government but only 'through the proletariat organized by the socialist International'.[104]

With the SPD so divided, the last word belonged to Wilhelm Dittmann, the chairman of the SPD's army commission. Although identified with the party's left, having earlier belonged to the USPD, Dittmann lined up squarely behind Müller. He began by defending the SPD's participation in government as the best means to exert 'influence on the question of war and peace'. If this required approving the battlecruiser and accepting the reality of armed forces, then so be it. Interestingly,

---

[102] Leber, 'Zur Klärung des Wehrproblems', *Die Gesellschaft* 2 (1929), 125–30; and Severing, 'Randbemerkungen zu den Richtlinien', ibid., 3 (1929), 197–205.

[103] Stampfer, 'Der Weg ins Neuland', *Vorwärts*, no. 241, 26 May 1929, 1.

[104] SPD, *Protokoll Sozialdemokratischer Parteitag Magdeburg 1929 vom 26. bis 31 Mai in der Stadthalle* (Berlin, 1929), Müller, 8–85; and Rosenfeld, 88–90.

Dittmann said little about disarmament except to criticize Paul-Boncour's notion of 'war potential', which he dismissed as an attempt to 'sabotage' any disarmament; and to reiterate Müller's argument that the refusal of the victor powers to disarm undermined the SPD and strengthened nationalist forces in Germany. Ignoring Rosenfeld, Dittmann mentioned neither the International nor international socialism. To the extent that socialist internationalism figured in his presentation, it took the form of an implicit criticism of foreign socialists, who were not doing enough to pressure their governments to disarm. After considerable debate, the guidelines were accepted by just over 60 per cent of the delegates.[105] More importantly, the overall effect of the *Panzerkreuzer* affair was to strengthen the tendency within the SPD to consider disarmament from a national as opposed to socialist internationalist perspective.

HOPES SHATTERED: LABOUR'S MINORITY GOVERNMENT

By 1928, French and German socialists appeared to be drifting apart: while the SFIO favoured a more internationalist perspective in which immediate and even unilateral measures of disarmament occupied a central place, the SPD moved towards a more national perspective in which calls for disarmament served domestic political needs first and foremost. The activities of Labour's second minority government would only exacerbate the tensions between European socialists. In the general election in May 1929, Labour increased its seat total by 136: with its 287 seats it became the leading party in Parliament though still short of a majority. As a result, in June 1929 Labour formed its second minority government with MacDonald once again as prime minister and with Henderson as Foreign Secretary.

Ironically, in light of what would happen, European socialists greeted Labour's electoral victory with considerable enthusiasm. Writing to MacDonald in early June, Müller welcomed the prospect of close cooperation between the British and German governments on international issues. 'I know', he claimed, 'that we are in perfect harmony, that all must be done, to save the peace of Europe, which guarantees the welfare of nations.' Significantly, in an interview in *Vorwärts* a few days earlier, MacDonald had indicated that an international agreement on disarmament would be at the top of his government's priority list.[106] A similar excitement was evident among French socialists and especially Blum. The SFIO knows, the latter wrote in early June, that one priority will animate the Labour government's international policy: 'I make peace... I make peace... and again I make peace.'[107] And for Blum, the path to peace lay through disarmament.

---

[105] Ibid., Dittmann, 105–19; and 262 for the vote.

[106] TNA, James Ramsay MacDonald Papers, PRO/30/69/1174/1, Müller (SPD) to MacDonald, 8 June 1929; and 'Unterredung mit MacDonald', *Vorwärts*, no. 255, 4 June 1929, 1.

[107] Blum, 'Le Labour Party au pouvoir, servira la cause de la Paix', *Le Populaire de Paris*, 2 June 1929, 1.

The hopes of German and French socialists, however, rested on shaky foundations. The Labour government's positions on international politics and on disarmament in particular, were deliberately imprecise—and even deceitful. Beginning in 1927, Labour trumpeted the defunct Geneva Protocol as part of its preparations for possible elections. Ignoring his earlier scepticism regarding the document, MacDonald wrote to a confidant in September that 'the Protocol will sooner or later have to be the basis of further consideration' at the League of Nations, adding that it was a 'remarkable document as a first draft'. The Protocol, he continued, constituted the 'very definite centre for the embodiment of our ideas' and 'on every Labour platform during the coming autumn and winter campaign, it will be advocated.'[108] Determined to have Labour adopt the Protocol as part of its 'official policy', MacDonald scored a notable success at Labour's annual congress in October 1927: the conference resolution on foreign policy not only deplored the Protocol's abandonment but also championed it as the key to disarmament.[109] Beyond Labour, MacDonald sought to persuade potential sympathizers of the Protocol's importance. In letters to C.P. Scott, the *Manchester Guardian*'s editor, he declared that the Protocol 'is going to be thrust into the whirlpool of party politics, because we shall certainly have a great deal to say about it in the autumn and winter campaign'. Asking Scott to study the document closely, MacDonald stressed that disarmament was intricately bound up with the Protocol, pointing out that the latter's application was dependent on the success of an international disarmament conference.[110]

MacDonald's championing of the Protocol did not go uncontested within Labour. Indeed, in September 1927 the *Manchester Guardian* published a letter by Philip Snowden, a future Chancellor of the Exchequer, criticizing the Protocol for imposing onerous military burdens on Britain. If such burdens were unacceptable, so too was what Snowden perceived as the Protocol's emphasis on security at the expense of disarmament:

> Disarmament is the only way to get security, and the only way by which peaceful acceptance of arbitration can be ensured.
> It is on disarmament that I think all desirous of seeing war relegated to the limbo of ancient brutalities should concentrate. When there is no longer the means to do ill deeds ill deeds will not be done.[111]

In reply, MacDonald reaffirmed his belief that Labour was committed to the Protocol, even if the latter was only a 'first draft'. Refusing to back down, Snowden replied that the Protocol had never been 'seriously discussed' either by the Labour government or by the party. Denouncing the Protocol as a 'French inspiration, a

---

[108] Bodleian, Gilbert Murray Papers, 153, MacDonald to Murray, 12 September 1927; and TNA, James Ramsay MacDonald Papers, PRO/30/69/1172/1, MacDonald to Murray, 11 October 1927.

[109] Labour Party, *Report of the 27th Annual Conference held in...Blackpool October 3rd to 7th, 1927* (London, 1927), 237–8, 243–4.

[110] JYUL, C.P. Scott Correspondence, 336/203, MacDonald to Scott, 13 September 1927; and Guardian Archive, A/M7/11, MacDonald to Scott, 19 September 1927.

[111] 'The Principles of the Protocol. Letter by Mr. Philip Snowden', *Manchester Guardian*, 16 September 1927.

further attempt on their part to get us [Britain] to underwrite the [peace] Treaties', he insisted that Britain could not be expected to 'settle with our arms and cash every quarrel which arose'. The Protocol, in any case, was now a 'dead letter', freeing Labour to consider the 'problem of security afresh'. For Snowden, who rejected any possible military obligations on Britain's part, a new approach meant privileging disarmament over security. The latter 'is a mental condition and it can never be effective without disarmament'.[112]

In his efforts to contain Snowden's challenge, MacDonald could count on the support of Henderson, who agreed that the Protocol was central to Labour's policy.[113] But MacDonald faced a greater problem: the growing dissatisfaction within Labour with the vagueness of MacDonald's statements on the Protocol and disarmament. Towards the end of 1927, Arthur Ponsonby, who had served as parliamentary under-secretary of state for foreign affairs in Labour's first government, submitted a memorandum to MacDonald arguing that a peace policy centred on disarmament would enjoy considerable appeal to electors. The difficulty was the lack of clarity regarding Labour's position, not least in terms of the Protocol, which fostered competing interpretations. It was thus imperative that before the next elections Labour work out a 'constructive policy which can easily be understood, and will unite the party in a thoroughly advanced line'.[114] Not long afterwards, George Middleton, the chairman of Labour's organization of electoral candidates, recommended to MacDonald that:

> the policy of the Party towards the problem of international security and disarmament might with advantage be clearly stated—or, rather, re-stated—not only for the benefit of Labour candidates who are called upon to meet all kinds of misrepresentations about Labour's policy, but also that the electorate in general may know what the Labour Party's position is in regard to the settlement of international disputes.

What Middleton wanted was a clear and concise statement of Labour policy.[115]

MacDonald, however, wanted to avoid greater precision. It would be a 'mistake', he told Ponsonby, to 'formulate with any finality, so far as the next general election is concerned, any precise and exclusive formula regarding our Peace policy'. As he explained: 'We are in the fortunate position at present of enjoying so much confidence, both at home and abroad, that when we get into office we shall continue—in relation to whatever may be our circumstances—to pursue a policy of settlement and peace, and it would be most short-sighted of us to do anything to disturb that confidence.'[116] Middleton refused to be fobbed off, but if MacDonald found

---

[112] TNA, James Ramsay MacDonald Papers, PRO/30/69/1172/2, MacDonald to Snowden, 26 September 1927; and Snowden's response, 28 September 1927. Also see PRO/30/69/1743, diary, 16 September 1927.

[113] Labour Party, Executive Committee of the Parliamentary Party, minutes, fiche 24, 7 November 1927.

[114] TNA, James Ramsay MacDonald Papers, PRO/30/69/1172/2, Ponsonby to MacDonald, 17 November 1927.

[115] Ibid., PRO/30/69/1173/2, George Middleton to MacDonald, 20 February 1928.

[116] Bodleian, Arthur Ponsonby Papers, MS. Eng. Hist. c 670, MacDonald to Ponsonby, 18 November 1927.

himself compelled to be more expansive, he remained vague. Labour, he wrote, favoured the 'triple road' of security, arbitration, and disarmament. As to the question of what priority to assign to each one, MacDonald admitted that some security guarantees to France and other Continental countries were necessary to persuade them to disarm, only to insist that such a guarantee would not add to Britain's existing obligations. Any security guarantee, he contended, would remove 'of itself every reasonable risk that it will ever have to be made effective in the form of armed intervention. It is not a step into further obligations but towards arbitration and disarmament.' MacDonald, in effect, argued that security guarantees by Britain would be conditional on the countries concerned carrying out an international disarmament scheme. Left unclear was just how such a scheme would be achieved.[117]

MacDonald's studied vagueness was on full display at Labour's annual congress in October 1928. In introducing the resolution on world peace and disarmament, the Labour leader described it as a 'full-blooded, unqualified condemnation' of Britain's current disarmament policy. Unlike the government, which supposedly based its disarmament policy on a 'war assumption' (that wars were likely and armed forces therefore necessary), Labour began from a 'peace assumption'. A Labour government would 'go back to Geneva...to change not merely the proportions of the figures on the stage, but to change the whole stage itself and give a new outlook and a new point of view'. Rather than details, MacDonald invoked the Protocol. If 'Europe and the nations of Europe continued to believe in peace and continued to value peace', he intoned, 'they would have to go back to where they stood in 1924.' Recognizing that the 'total abolition of armaments' could not be imposed on others but only achieved through international negotiations, MacDonald pledged that a Labour government would provide a new impetus to such negotiations, though he carefully refrained from offering any details on Labour's position. Instead, he offered fiery rhetoric: a Labour government would send delegates to Geneva who would ensure that 'Labour's international ideas would thrash Capitalist international ideas and make them so much ashamed of themselves that they would not voice themselves in the League.'[118]

Why did MacDonald opt for vagueness? Domestic political factors certainly entered into his thinking. As his repeated references to upcoming elections indicate, MacDonald feared anything that might jeopardize Labour's prospects. Equally pertinent, a clear-cut position risked deepening the divisions within Labour between those who demanded what MacDonald termed an 'absolute disarmament policy' and those willing to settle for something less.[119] But there were also considerations more closely tied to the anticipated disarmament negotiations themselves. In the run-up to the 1929 elections, Labourites in general were convinced that a Labour government could have a decisive influence on international politics—a conviction

---

[117] TNA, James Ramsay MacDonald Papers, PRO/30/69/1173/2, MacDonald to Middleton, 27 February 1928.
[118] Labour Party, *Report of the 28th Annual Conference held in... Birmingham October 1st to 5th, 1928* (London, 1928), 183–94.
[119] See fn 116.

fuelled partly by a sense of Britain's great power status. Writing to MacDonald in November 1928, Philip Noel-Baker pleaded for a future Labour government to make 'serious and radical proposals' regarding disarmament, remarking that the 'peace forces of Europe' would rally behind 'British leadership'.[120] Similarly, in a book published the same year, Hugh Dalton, who would become under-secretary for foreign affairs in 1929, wrote that in 'international affairs there is still tremendous force behind a British example...Our country can, if she will, lead the world far, along new paths of constructive peace and international righteousness.' For Dalton, moreover, on no international issue was a British initiative more urgent than on disarmament: only a Labour government could break the impasse at Geneva.[121]

MacDonald possessed an enormous confidence in his own ability to persuade the leaders of other countries to negotiate a disarmament agreement. From this perspective, the process of negotiation itself was of decisive importance rather than any principles or fixed positions, as these risked exacerbating differences. For MacDonald, vagueness was an effective bargaining strategy. This does not mean that he lacked strong ideas. When it came to disarmament, MacDonald (like Snowden) had little patience for arguments concerning security, especially from the French—whether socialists or non-socialists. He was convinced that such arguments were at best misguided and at worst insincere. When praising the Protocol, MacDonald emphasized disarmament and arbitration and never sanctions. He was committed to disarmament by international agreement—hence his disinterest in Ponsonby's call for 'disarmament by example'.[122] And he believed that an international disarmament agreement would take time: at Labour's 1928 conference he let slip that a world disarmament conference would probably require two years of preparatory negotiations. But whatever his own views, MacDonald resolutely cultivated an ambiguity regarding disarmament. Labour stood by the Protocol but what this meant concretely remained unclear. The Protocol, as MacDonald liked to claim, should not be taken as 'a verbally inspired gospel' but rather as 'a basis of consideration'.[123]

Whatever its justification, MacDonald's vagueness regarding disarmament had the unfortunate effect of stifling reflection within Labour on the relationship between disarmament and sanctions—a reflection initiated within the ACIQ. In a memorandum to the committee in March 1927, Charles Rhoden Buxton asked whether the time had come for the party to reconsider its hostility to naval and military sanctions. Although Buxton found the prospect of military force appalling, he suggested that Labour's support for the Protocol and for disarmament entailed the possibility of sanctions. In a commentary on Buxton's memorandum,

---

[120] TNA, James Ramsay MacDonald Papers, PRO/30/69/1173/1, Noel-Baker to MacDonald, 1 November 1928.

[121] Dalton, *Towards the Peace of Nations: A Study of International Politics* (London, 1928), xi.

[122] Ponsonby, 'Disarmament by Example', *Journal of the Royal Institute of International Affairs* 7 (1928), 225–32. Also see Martin Ceadel, *Semi-Detached Idealists: The British Peace Movement and International Relations, 1854–1945* (Oxford, 2000), 268–70.

[123] Bodleian, Gilbert Murray Papers, 153, MacDonald to Murray, 12 September 1927.

Arnold Forster went further, arguing that to eliminate sanctions would deal a death blow to the League: a League incapable of sanctioning an aggressor was powerless.[124] In an ACIQ memorandum the following year, David Mitrany, a Rumanian-born expert on international politics, highlighted the link between security and disarmament. 'The countries who insist on strong sanctions are...those most fearful for their security and therefore most anxiously nursing their armed strength,' he reasoned. 'To refuse to provide sanctions would undoubtedly put an end to all hope of early disarmament.' This being so, the task for Labour was to make sanctions effective on those countries being punished as well as tolerable for those countries applying them.[125] All talk of sanctions, however, was anathema to MacDonald, which helped to ensure that the debate on them remained cloistered within the ACIQ.

In his memorandum, Mitrany remarked that Labour would never succeed in convincing the socialist International to endorse a repudiation of all sanctions. His reference to the International directs attention to two further points. One is the relative absence of international socialism in the thinking of MacDonald: there is no evidence that he felt in any way bound by the LSI's resolutions, regardless of how open-ended they were. The second point, which also constitutes another unfortunate effect of MacDonald's vagueness regarding disarmament, concerns the expectations of foreign socialists. Mention has already been made of the enthusiasm with which French and German socialists greeted Labour's electoral success in 1929. But the sentiment went much deeper. For the international socialist movement as a whole, the advent of a Labour government marked a decisive moment in international politics. In a report to the LSI's executive in July 1929, Adler argued that Labour's second minority government would produce a 'decisive change' in foreign policy. Referring to the 'disarmament question' in particular, he expected MacDonald to seize the 'initiative' to solve the 'difficult problem' of naval and land disarmament and make sure that the League preparatory commission 'finally engaged in fruitful work'.[126] Given such expectations, European socialists were bound to be disappointed. Yet it is also true that Labour, and MacDonald in particular, did much to stoke the expectations of European socialists.

THE TRAVAILS OF NAVAL DISARMAMENT

From the viewpoint of European socialists, Labour's government made a promising start. Unlike its Conservative predecessor, the new government signed the Optional Clause, thereby recognizing the jurisdiction of the Permanent Court of

---

[124] LHASC, LPA, ACIQ, memoranda: 1924–36, 'Sanctions in the Convenant and the Protocol', no. 358, Buxton, March 1927; and BLPES, David Mitrany Papers, 47, ACIQ, 'Sanctions', no. 365, Arnold Forster, May 1927.

[125] BLPES, David Mitrany Papers, 47, ACIQ, 'A Labour Policy on Sanctions', no. 366, Mitrany, May 1928. Mitrany had long been arguing the case for sanctions. See his *The Problem of International Sanctions* (London, 1925).

[126] IISH, SAI, 328, 'Bericht des Sekretariates der S.A.I.', July 1929.

International Justice, and it adhered to the general scheme for international arbitration of disputes. Equally important as a signal, it appointed Robert Cecil, a Liberal and long-time champion of disarmament, to head Britain's delegation to the League of Nations. Cecil was assisted by two Labourites: Noel-Baker, a fervent disarmament advocate, and Dalton, who wrote in 1928 that 'total disarmament... is the only sane objective'.[127] Tensions between European socialists, however, soon manifested themselves over the issue of naval disarmament. Although intergovernmental talks between the British and Americans on the subject in the summer of 1927 had ended in failure, two years later both sides were prepared to try again. On a visit to the United States in October 1929, MacDonald arrived at a preliminary agreement with the American President Herbert Hoover for parity between the two navies. With this agreement in hand, the Labour government organized the London naval conference that opened in January 1929 and brought together delegations from Britain, France, Italy, Japan, and the United States.[128] Labour leaders were understandably excited. At the party's annual conference in October 1929 Henderson contended that success in the naval realm would clear 'the way to the early summoning of a general Disarmament Conference on which the hopes of the world have so long been centred in vain. If that conference comes up to our hopes and expectations', he added, 'we shall have opened a new era, in which the vast sums previously spent on Armaments will be put to better purposes.'[129]

Continental socialists, however, appeared less enthused with the announcement of the naval conference. In a lengthy parliamentary speech at the end of December 1929, Paul-Boncour described the upcoming conference as unfortunate. Having done nothing to advance the cause of general disarmament at the League, he contended, the Labour government had opted to pursue disarmament through the narrow prism of British interests that focused exclusively on naval arms limitations and on an Anglo-American entente. The British initiative, Paul-Boncour continued, threatened the larger project of disarmament—a project, he claimed, that the work of the League's preparatory commission was carefully advancing. The Anglo-American agreement on parity, which would effectively authorize the Americans to build beyond present levels, promised not arms limitation but a return to the old diplomacy—'to alliances, to bilateral encounters [and] to limited [disarmament] accords'. Paul-Boncour's biggest fear was that the London conference would abandon the principle, which supposedly underpinned efforts at Geneva, that disarmament required a 'serious international organization for security'. Ironically, Paul-Boncour echoed MacDonald in calling for a return to the Protocol, thus highlighting the competing meanings assigned to the latter:

---

[127] Ceadel, *Semi-Detached Idealists*, 278; and Dalton, *Towards the Peace of Nations*, 146.

[128] See Steiner, *The Lights that Failed*, 568–70, 587–92; Fanning, *Peace and Disarmament*, 106–32; and David Carlton, *MacDonald versus Henderson: The Foreign Policy of the Second Labour Government* (London, 1970), 119–43.

[129] Labour Party, *Report of the Annual Conference held in... Brighton, September 30–October 4, 1929* (London, 1929), Henderson, 210.

I don't think it unfriendly to remind one's friends [the Labour government] of the work we did together...I don't think it unfriendly to remind them of concepts we elaborated together...because there are words that must be constantly repeated: 'Protocol! Protocol! Protocol'...as without the Protocol disarmament becomes a caricature.[130]

Equally concerned about the Labour government's priorities, the Dutch socialist Albarda lobbied for a meeting of the LSI disarmament commission to discuss the naval conference.[131] The resulting meeting in early January 1930 proved contentious, particularly between the French and British participants. Citing passages from Paul-Boncour's parliamentary speech, William Gillies, Labour's international secretary, demanded to know if it represented the SFIO's views. Defending the naval conference, Gillies explained that the Protocol 'could not be resurrected' and that 'it was bad policy for Socialists to avoid doing what was practicable because the irrealisable could not be attained.' In response, Renaudel claimed not only that the SFIO supported the Protocol but also that the International had always advocated general disarmament and not 'local treaties' such as the Anglo-American naval agreement. Continuing, he criticized the latter as a quasi-alliance that achieved no reduction in armaments because parity entailed a significant increase in American naval construction. But perhaps Renaudel's sharpest criticism was that the Labour government was selfishly pursuing British interests. Evidently angry, Gillies countered that France had security aplenty through Locarno and that it was Britain that justly felt threatened—not least by France's fleet. After considerable discussion, the participants agreed to a resolution that thanked the Labour government for calling a naval conference while also expressing hope that the conference would provide a spur to ongoing efforts to realize general disarmament through the League.[132]

To Labour's executive, Gillies reported that the meeting 'was successful in clearing up many misunderstandings' among 'continental comrades'. A joint meeting of the LSI and IFTU executives two months later, however, showed Gillies' optimism to be misplaced. The SFIO's delegates found themselves on the defensive due to the recent demand by the French government for increases in its own naval programme. Both Renaudel and Blum agreed that the French demand was unacceptable, with Blum adding that France possessed sufficient security to envisage a reduction of naval and land armaments. Moving on, Blum echoed Renaudel's critique of the Anglo-American naval agreement: that it sanctioned increases in armaments. But the SFIO leader's principal point concerned the Protocol. French socialists, he argued, were deeply disappointed to learn that MacDonald had seemingly abandoned the Protocol as it 'had a greater hold than any other idea' on the

---

[130] JO, Débats parlementaires, Chambre des députés, 19 December 1929, Paul-Boncour, 4492–6.

[131] IEV, Archives Emile Vandervelde, EV/III/75, Adler to Vandervelde, 4 January 1930; and IISH, SAI, 768, Albarda to Adler, 20 December 1929.

[132] LHASC, LPA, LSI minutes 1921–1937, Labour, 'Meeting of the Disarmament Commission of the Labour and Socialist Internationale', Gillies, undated; and AABS, Ssa, F 02 B: 07, 'Tagung der Abrüstungskommission der S.A.I.' in *Internationale Information*, vol. VII, no. 2, 7 January 1930, 15–16.

French public: 'A certain sentimentalism, mysticism, certain hopes and desires gathered round the Protocol in France,' Blum explained. 'If the Protocol is not taken up again, the British will put themselves in a bad position as regards disarmament.' As in January, Gillies insisted that there was no returning to the Protocol, and all but demanded that Blum repudiate Paul-Boncour's insistence on arbitration and security. More generally, he maintained that the SFIO had a duty to follow Labour's lead. French socialists, Gillies sermonized, 'must adapt themselves to the new situation with regard to the organisation of peace by international agreement and give the fullest support to the Geneva policy of the British Labour Government'.[133]

Once again, the published resolution welcomed the Labour's government initiative in organizing a naval disarmament conference and expressed the hope that it would lead to 'real and tangible' reductions in naval armaments. At the same time, it declared that the naval conference would be 'completely fruitless' unless it led to a 'general reduction of armaments in all categories'. Soon afterwards, Blum wrote that much depended on the naval disarmament conference: success would invigorate the negotiations in Geneva whereas failure would remove any remaining hope of progress towards general disarmament.[134] These conditional endorsements, however, barely veiled important differences among European socialists regarding the Protocol and its larger significance. In distancing itself from the Protocol and in focusing on a naval armaments limitation agreement, the Labour government effectively announced its disinterest in a more general disarmament agreement that encompassed the fraught issue of security. French socialists, by contrast, resurrected the Protocol in the hope that it would provide additional security to France, but also because they preferred a general disarmament agreement that would include land—and not just naval—armaments.

The Labour government also faced resistance from within its own party. Just days after the contentious meeting of the LSI's disarmament commission in January 1930, an editorial in the *Daily Herald*, Labour's unofficial newspaper, warned that the International was 'perfectly right in its assumption . . . that naval disarmament cannot stand by itself as a separate question'. Labour's government must consider 'the whole question of the limitation of armaments on land and sea and air'. In a cleverly framed article in the same newspaper the following week, Paul-Boncour denounced separate agreements (i.e. the Anglo-American naval accord) as a relapse into power politics—the 'old habits of playing at alliances and combinations'. The quest for disarmament, he insisted, must be recentred on the League.[135] Although the *Daily Herald* could bring little direct pressure to bear on Labour leaders, the same was less true of the party's parliamentary group, which in

---

[133] LHASC, LPA, LSI minutes 1921–1937, Labour, 'Joint Meeting of the Bureau of the Labour and Socialist International and the Executive of the International Federation of Trade Unions, Paris, March 7, 1930', undated.

[134] AABS, Ssa, F 02 B: 07, 'Manifest der gemeinsamen Sitzung des Bureau der S.A.I. und das I.G.B., Paris, 7 März 1930' in *Internationale Information*, vol. VII, no. 15, 10 March 1930, 140–1; and Blum, 'Étroite solidarité', *Le Populaire de Paris*, 9 March 1930, 1.

[135] 'A Lead for Peace', *Daily Herald*, 8 January 1930, 4; and 'Paul-Boncour discusses the Master Key to Disarmament', *Daily Herald*, 13 January 1930, 4.

January and again in March 1930 informed MacDonald of its unhappiness with the government's approach to naval disarmament. In February 1930, meanwhile, the ACIQ informed Labour's national executive that 'some anxiety' existed in the party regarding the naval disarmament conference 'and in some quarters [there is] a feeling that a bolder policy on the part of the Government might produce better results'. Although eschewing precise proposals, the committee recommended that the executive consider steps to mobilize public opinion and to cooperate more closely with French socialists.[136] The following month 100 MPs (97 from Labour) issued a declaration emphasizing the need for an 'energetic policy' by the Labour government to achieve 'a definite reduction' and 'limitation of naval armaments'.[137] Adler worked behind the scenes to encourage similar declarations from Continental socialists.[138]

Clearly irritated by this pressure, Gillies wrote a blistering letter to Adler that underscored the tensions between Labour and the SFIO on disarmament. Categorically rejecting Adler's suggestion for an informal approach to Blum or other French socialists to work out a common position, Gillies sneered that it would only be 'misunderstood'. He also questioned the SFIO's understanding of its 'international duty' before accusing French socialists of lacking 'moral courage'. While the Labour Party strove to influence the Labour government when it came to disarmament, the SFIO offered nothing but criticism even though it was in opposition and even though the French government proposed to expand naval construction. A French 'manifesto', in any case, would be worse than useless as the 'non-signatories would be more significant than the signatories'. The basic problem was that French socialists were not truly committed to disarmament, whether of naval or land armaments. Gillies accordingly rebuffed Adler's proposal to organize an international socialist conference on disarmament in the spring of 1930; for Labour's international secretary there was no point in discussing the subject with French—or other European—socialists.[139]

The relative failure of the London naval conference did not help matters. In April 1930, Britain, the United States, and Japan signed a treaty that foresaw limits to naval construction on a comparative rather than absolute scale (10: 10: 7); neither France nor Italy signed the treaty. '[W]hat a waste', a despondent Blum commented on the results, adding that it was difficult to see how the 'work of Geneva' could be effectively restarted.[140] At a meeting of the LSI's executive in May 1930, the general sentiment was equally downcast. A memorandum prepared for the meeting bemoaned the 'evident bad faith of the vast majority of governments' that

---

[136] Labour Party, Executive Committee of the Parliamentary Party, minutes, fiche 31, H.S.L. to Prime Minister, 28 January and 7 March 1930; and US, Leonard Woolf Papers, ID1c, ACIQ minutes, 19 February 1930.

[137] IEV, Archives Emile Vandervelde, EV/III/75, 'Déclaration sur la Conférence navale', undated but mid-March 1923.

[138] Ibid., Adler to Vandervelde, 20 March 1930.

[139] Ibid., Gillies to Adler, 4 April 1930; and ISH, SAI, 640, Adler circular to LSI Bureau, 9 April 1930.

[140] Blum, 'L'échec de la Conférence navale', *Le Populaire de Paris*, 12 April 1930, 1.

had worked to sabotage any real progress on disarmament over the last ten years. If the ensuing resolution once again thanked the Labour government for its initiative on behalf of naval disarmament, it also made clear that European socialists were at a loss regarding what to do. Instead of a socialist programme, the International's executive simply urged socialist parties to redouble their efforts in favour of international disarmament and against all 'peace-threatening rearmament' at home.[141]

THE LSI'S PETITION CAMPAIGN

Considerable pessimism reigned among European socialists in the summer of 1930 regarding the prospects for disarmament. The London naval conference proved to be a disappointment, while negotiations in Geneva appeared to be bogged down in discussions over technical issues. This pessimism provides the context for the LSI's initiative to mobilize public opinion behind disarmament, principally through a petition campaign. To be sure, the idea was not new. As part of the effort to increase the pressure on governments to negotiate in good faith, in February 1929, the LSI's executive had agreed to collect signatures for a petition urging the League's preparatory commission to fulfil its promise to work out an international agreement for the anticipated world disarmament conference.[142] In April 1929, an LSI delegation submitted the petition to the commission. Although the LSI's propaganda spoke of a 'storm of petitions', the lack of time and of proper preparation meant that the results were meagre: 11,000 or so signatures, the vast majority coming from Holland and Belgium. The response of the British, French, and German parties ranged from feeble to non-existent. In his speech to the League's disarmament commission, the Belgian socialist de Brouckère declared that the petition 'truly reflects [international] public opinion', but the commission's members had good reason to question this claim.[143]

In any event, Albarda, who remained the chairman of the LSI's disarmament commission, was disappointed by the response of socialist parties to the petition campaign. 'I have the impression', he wrote Adler in April 1929, 'that in most countries little was done.'[144] Albarda, however, refused to be deterred. In October 1929, he drafted a lengthy memorandum for the International. Pointing to the 'divergence of views' on disarmament among European socialists, it urged a concerted attempt to arrive at a common disarmament programme that would provide a 'line of conduct' for the International and its member parties. Although not criticizing the petition campaign directly, the memorandum contended that,

---

[141] Copies of both the memorandum and the resolution are in IISH, SAI, 347.

[142] IISH, SAI, 313, 'Programme of Action for Disarmament', undated but February 1929.

[143] AABS, Ssa, F 02 B: 06, 'Wir fordern die Abrüstung. Eine Deputation der S.A.I. in Genf', *Internationale Information*, vol. VI, no. 12, 13 April 1929, 143–5; 'De Kampf um die Abrüstung', *Internationale Information*, vol VI, no. 13, 16 April 1929, de Brouckère, 148; and SSAZ, SPS, AR 1.260.7, 'Die Petitionskampagne geht weiter', *Internationale Information*, vol. VI, no. 15, 6 May 1929, 174.

[144] IISH, SAI, 1178, Albarda to Adler, 2 April 1929.

if socialists continued to mask their differences behind 'vaguely worded proclamations', they would condemn themselves to 'participate as powerless and passive in the discussion of questions that are of the greatest interest to people'. It went on to discuss possible positions on issues of military organization: the nature and size of armed forces, militia-type versus professional armies, the length of military service. But for Albarda, the overriding point concerned the need for socialist parties to make 'positive concessions' to arrive at a 'common program'. Without a willingness to do so, he admonished, the International would fail in its duty to dissipate the 'confusion' surrounding disarmament at Geneva and to 'indicate a way out'.[145]

Albarda's plan was to have the LSI's disarmament commission discuss and endorse his memoranda, after which the difficult task of working out a 'common program' could begin. But organizing a commission meeting proved to be extremely difficult as several members maintained that their political activities at home made it difficult to get away, prompting an irritated Adler to remark that 'international meetings are only possible if, in favour of these latter, comrades suspend their obligations in their respective countries'.[146] Not helping matters was the fact that Albarda broke his leg in December 1929, making a further postponement all but inevitable. While it would be too much to argue that the difficulties in fixing a meeting reflected a lack of willingness among socialist parties to make the kind of concessions Albarda had in mind, it is true that the prospects of forging a common programme on disarmament appeared dim. As Albarda himself recognized in his memorandum, the differences between European socialists on the issue were considerable. In any case, Albarda's proposal was soon overtaken by events, most notably the London naval conference. When the LSI's disarmament commission finally met in early January 1930, the result was (as we saw) a contentious encounter between the French and British delegates. Albarda's ambitious proposal, in short, was dead on arrival.

Albarda once again refused to give up. But this time, the focus would be on mobilizing the International through a new petition campaign—the very type of activity he had scorned because it supposedly 'masked' differences between socialists. In preparation for the LSI executive meeting in August 1930, Albarda prepared two documents. The first, subtitled 'Next Steps in the Action of Disarmament', called upon socialists 'of all countries' to take 'energetic action in favour of peace and disarmament'. More concretely, it spoke of organizing international 'demonstrations' in leading countries with a view to influencing the deliberations of the League's preparatory commission scheduled for November. The second document proposed a massive petition campaign. Referring to the relative failure of the 1929 campaign in Britain, France, and Germany, Albarda suggested that the search for signatures be expanded beyond socialist parties to include trade union organizations

[145] IISH, Johan Willem Albarda Papers, 4, 'Rapport sur la question du désarmement', Albarda, 22 October 1929.
[146] IISH, SAI, 767, Albarda to Adler, 12 November 1929; and SAI, 768, Adler to Renaudel, 12 December 1929.

as well as women and youth groups.[147] At the executive meeting, the participants approved Albarda's first document, and a number of demonstrations occurred in several countries over the coming weeks. Overall, though, the response was again disappointing: while the SFIO promised a 'journée de masse' at the end of October 1930, the SPD reported that its 'hands were full' with domestic politics; as for Labour, it did not even bother to reply.[148]

'Energetic action' having failed, Albarda in the spring of 1931 renewed his argument for a petition campaign:

> The international petition campaign is not only a splendid method of securing that the will of the people shall be expressed in an imposing manner, it is also a first-rate method of arousing and increasing the interest of the workers in disarmament. It is, in addition, a wonderful means of educating the organised workers in the carrying out of international actions.

In a bid to improve on the 1929 results, Albarda repeated the suggestion that socialist parties cooperate with various socialist organizations (women, youth, musical groups, etc.) as well as trade unions.[149] Helpful, here, was the decision in February 1931 to create a joint disarmament commission with the IFTU to coordinate 'common action' between the socialist and trade union Internationals. At a meeting of the joint commission in June 1931, the members approved a 'program of action' drafted by Albarda that centred on a petition campaign. In addition to an 'energetic propaganda' in the socialist press, the plan envisaged a special 'Bureau' that would 'control the entire organisation down to the smallest detail, supervise the manner in which the campaign is carried out and be of assistance, so that not a single country is left behind'. As in 1929, the collected petitions would be presented at Geneva, this time to the president of the world disarmament conference due to begin in February 1932.[150] The joint commission approved a slightly revised version of the plan, which was then submitted to the LSI's congress in Vienna in the summer of 1931. Following a brief debate, the delegates overwhelmingly endorsed the plan.[151]

Given the disagreements among European socialists, there was little chance of a special bureau being created along the lines suggested by Albarda. This became clear in the autumn of 1929 when Albarda wrote to Adler to complain that the International's lack of authority made cooperation difficult with the IFTU. In his lengthy reply, a vexed Adler basically argued that the executive could not impose

---

[147] IISH, SAI, 365, 'Draft Resolution by Albarda on: Next Steps in the Action on Disarmament', undated but August 1930; and BA-SAPMO, II. Internationale, RY 14 I 6/2/37, 'Vorschläge des Genossen Albarda betreffend Abrüstungsaktion', undated but August 1930.

[148] IISH, SAI, 773, LSI (Adler) circular, 24 October 1930.

[149] IISH, SAI, 777, 'Proposal by J.W. Albarda for an international disarmament petition to the League of Nations', undated but June 1931.

[150] See AABS, Ssa, F 02 B: 08, 'Internationale Beratungen in Zürich', *Internationale Information*, vol VIII, no. 6, 28 February 1931, 89–90; and ibid., 'Zur Abrüstungsaktion der beiden Internationalen', *Internationale Information*, vol. VIII, no. 26, 27 June 1931, 348.

[151] *Kongreß-Protokolle der Sozialistischen Arbeiter-Internationale*, vol. 4, no. 2, *Vierter Kongreß der Sozialistischen Arbeiter-Internationale Wien, 25. Juli bis 1. August 1931. Berichte, Verhalndlungen und Beschlüsse* (Glashütten im Taunus, 1974), VI, 22–80, X, 4–7.

its will on the International's member parties, especially if the latter were not of one mind.[152] Nevertheless, the petition campaign enjoyed some success even in the absence of a bureau. The petition itself was short and simple: it called on governments to negotiate a 'Convention...which will ensure an immediate and substantial reduction of effectives and all forms of war material and expenditure, and lead to complete, universal and controlled disarmament at the earliest possible moment'. Together, the LSI and the IFTU collected considerably more signatures than in 1929: a report in early 1932 cited 630,604 from Germany, almost 900,000 from France, and close to 5 million from Britain. Bolstering (and, indeed, inflating) these numbers was the decision to solicit signatures not from individuals but from local party and trade union organizations en bloc.[153] In February 1932 a joint LSI–IFTU delegation submitted the petitions to a plenary session of the world disarmament conference with Vandervelde declaring that they expressed the 'collective will of the vast majority of the world proletariat'.[154]

Whether the delegates at the League's plenary commission were any more convinced by such declarations than they had been in 1929, is impossible to say. But what can be said is that the petition campaign amounted to an admission of defeat. European socialists (either alone or with others) had not been able to persuade governments to make meaningful progress towards disarmament; and few, if any, socialists, expected the petitions to have an effect. 'In no way are we illusionary enough to believe that our demands will be fully and speedily accepted in the present situation,' Vandervelde admitted in his speech to the conference. The petition campaign, in any case, could not disguise the absence of a collective socialist position on disarmament. After several years of concerted effort, European socialists could agree on little beyond the rather banal point that armaments reduction and general disarmament were desirable goals. To be sure, working out a shared programme for such a complex issue as disarmament was inherently difficult, perhaps too difficult. But the failure of European socialists to do so ensured that each party would be left to itself to determine its position in what everyone agreed was a time of mounting international tensions.

SEPARATE PATHS

That socialist parties would adopt separate paths on the issue of disarmament first became evident with the SFIO. During 1930–1931, Blum developed a position in favour of unilateral armaments reductions on France's part—or what was known as disarmament by example. Arguing that disarmament was an 'essential element' of security and that France already possessed considerable security, Blum argued in

---

[152] IEV, Archives Emile Vandervelde, EV/III/75/2, Albarda to Adler, 24 September 1929; and Adler to Albarda, 17 October 1929.
[153] AABS, Ssa, F 02 B: 09, 'Bericht über die Abrüstungspetition', *Für die Abrüstung*, 6 February 1932, 14–18; and Davies, *The Possibilities of Transnational Activism*, 97–8.
[154] AABS, Ssa, F 02 B: 09, 'Rede von Emile Vandervelde', *Für die Abrüstung*, 7 February 1932, 19–21.

May 1930 that additional discussions among 'diplomats and technicians' would produce no results. Instead, something more striking was needed:

> What we need are big initiatives, big examples that will induce others to do likewise. There is no doubt that this duty falls basically to the victorious powers of the last war, especially those most strongly armed. France should provide the example in disarmament and it should do so because it can do so. The task of French socialism is to steer its propaganda in this direction and to exert a growing influence on [public] opinion.[155]

Over the coming months Blum expounded on the argument that France must provide an example, eventually publishing a book in 1931 entitled *The Problems of Peace*. In the book, Blum described disarmament as 'the dominant problem that determined all others', explaining that an emphasis on security was self-defeating because it only produced more armaments, greater insecurity, and eventually war. While recognizing progressive and simultaneous disarmament of all nations to be the ultimate goal, Blum insisted that France must give a lead by embarking on immediate and significant armaments reductions. When it came to disarmament, audacity not prudence was imperative.[156]

Several factors influenced Blum to advocate disarmament by example. One obvious factor was the lack of tangible progress in intergovernmental discussions on disarmament—a lack highlighted by the failure of the London naval conference. Indeed, the timing of Blum's campaign suggests that the naval conference acted as a powerful spur. Heightening this effect was Blum's continued frustration with the French government, whose determination to expand France's naval construction programme had greatly complicated the negotiations in London. Another (and less obvious) factor concerned the SPD. Blum was extremely sensitive to the SPD's difficult domestic political position caused by the growing polarization of German politics and the rise of anti-republican forces, among them the Nazis. During 1930–1931, Blum defended the SPD's policy of tolerating conservative governments in Germany against those French socialists who sought to exploit the German case in their battle against the SFIO's own participation in government.[157] Underpinning Blum's defence was the belief that the SPD constituted the strongest pillar of the Weimar Republic, a regime on whose continued existence European peace depended. It was German socialists, Blum wrote in June 1931, who stood in the way of 'Hitler's national-fascism'. In this context, the duty of French (and international) socialism was to do everything possible to assist the SPD in its defence of the Weimar regime.[158] And one way of doing so was to signal the SFIO's (and France's) willingness to disarm, as this could aid the SPD in countering the accusation of their domestic political opponents that German socialists, in calling for disarmament, were collaborating in their country's ongoing mistreatment

---

[155] Blum, 'Le devoir d'exemplarité', *Le Populaire de Paris*, 15 May 1930, 1.
[156] Blum, *Les problèmes de la paix* (Paris, 1931), 70, 154.
[157] On this subject, see Winkler, 'Klassenkampf versus Koalition', 193–205.
[158] Blum, 'L'Allemagne actuelle et la Social-démocratie', *Le Populaire de Paris*, 4 June 1931, 1; and *Vierter Kongreß der Sozialistischen Arbeiter-Internationale Wien*, Blum, VI, 106–17.

by the victor powers. That German socialists understood Blum's move is suggested by their decision to issue his book in German translation, with an introduction by Hilferding stressing the SFIO's influence on French politics.[159]

By the early 1930s, Blum's interest in disarmament by example centred more on its indirect effects. There is little evidence that he believed the French government would take the initiative in disarmament. Yet in seeking to bolster the SPD indirectly, Blum unintentionally exacerbated tensions within his own party. This became clear over the fraught question of whether socialists should support national defence. Blum wanted to keep the issue of disarmament off the agenda of the SFIO's annual congress in June 1930 on the purported grounds that the party's position had been 'clearly fixed in principle and practice'. But this is unconvincing. As Blum knew, for many French socialists the issues of disarmament and national defence were inextricably tied together, making it impossible to consider one in isolation from the other. If Blum sought to avoid a debate on disarmament it is because he recognized the subject's divisive potential. The problem for Blum was that those socialists who sympathized with his advocacy of disarmament by example tended to hold two additional political positions: a marked pacifism and a prin-cipled rejection of participation in coalition governments. When combined, these two positions translated into a marked suspicion of the principle of national defence and its corollary that France's defences needed to be prepared for a possible war. By comparison, those socialists who opposed disarmament by example, which they understood as disarmament without additional security guarantees, sought to identify socialism with national defence. Neither group was willing to separate the issues of disarmament and national defence, and so Blum found himself forced to promise that the entire subject would top the programme at the SFIO's next congress.[160]

Unsurprisingly, deep divisions were on display at SFIO's congress in May 1931. In the run-up to the congress, Paul-Boncour, Renaudel, and several other socialists distributed a memorandum outlining their position. Invoking both Jaurès and the International for support, it argued that socialists could not separate the question of national defence from that of disarmament, which was itself inseparable from a larger 'organization of peace' that included security and arbitration. In an obvious reference to Blum, the memorandum warned that this whole should not be sacri-ficed to 'audacious acts'.[161] At the congress itself, Renaudel submitted a lengthy resolution that effectively argued against any initiative on France's part, chiefly by subordinating disarmament to the attainment of additional security guarantees. But it also did so by emphasizing national defence. In his comments on the reso-lution, Renaudel maintained that socialists could not be in favour of national defence while ignoring its implications—the need for armed forces to defend against attack. In an opposing resolution, Faure echoed Blum in insisting that it

[159] Blum, *Ohne Abrüstung keine Friede. Die französische Sozialdemokratie im Kampf um die Organisation des Friedens* (Berlin, 1931), Hilferding, 3–5.

[160] Blum, 'Désarmement et socialisme', *Le Populaire de Paris*, 12 May 1930, 1; and SFIO, *XXVIIe Congrès National tenu...les 8,9,10 et 11 juin 1930* (Paris, 1930), 382–3.

[161] AN, Papiers Joseph Paul-Boncour, 424/AP/14, 'Projet de memorandum', undated.

was up to France 'to seize the initiative in disarmament measures'. More striking, however, was its position on national defence. Having accepted national defence in principle, the resolution rejected it in practice: French socialists were called upon to refuse not only all 'collaboration or solidarity' with the policies of bourgeois governments, but also all military credits. 'Not one penny, not one man for the bourgeoisie's military machine.' The vote on the two resolutions clearly indicated the balance of opinion within the party: 2,486 for Faure and 824 for Renaudel.[162]

Renaudel and Faure both insisted that their resolutions corresponded to the positions of the International and of socialist internationalism. Striving, as usual, to blur differences between rival factions, Blum proposed that the SFIO work to strengthen the coordination between parties within the International regarding national defence and disarmament. Yet by 1931 it was highly unlikely that European socialists could forge a common programme on these issues. Instead, the coming months saw two related developments within French socialism. One was the growing suspicion of national defence in general. Tellingly, Paul-Boncour would quit the SFIO at the end of 1931, denouncing French socialism's alienation from 'national sentiment'; two years later, Renaudel would follow him.[163] The second development was an inward turn on the SFIO's part, as French socialists became increasingly preoccupied with the related issues of participation in government and national defence, especially in the event of war. The SFIO continued to advocate disarmament, but more in a symbolic and even utopian sense than as practical politics.

Labour also turned inwards at the beginning of the 1930s. The bitter end of Labour's government in August 1931 provided the impetus: the cabinet's inability to agree to cuts in social spending in response to the Depression led to the government's downfall and its replacement by a 'national government' with MacDonald as prime minister. Worse still, in the general elections in October 1931 Labour lost 231 seats, leaving it with a mere 46. Digesting MacDonald's 'betrayal' and the subsequent electoral disaster would preoccupy Labour for several years. Meanwhile, with Labour decimated, the trade unions were able to increase their influence within the labour movement, reinforcing the party's inward turn. Although the trade unions were by no means uninterested in foreign affairs, their primary focus was on domestic issues—a focus the Depression only sharpened.

To be sure, Labour did not completely ignore foreign affairs in general or disarmament in particular. The ACIQ, for example, continued to study the question of disarmament, and in a memorandum in December 1932 even argued that Labour 'cannot consistently object' to French demands for greater security.[164] By then the world disarmament conference had opened in Geneva, ensuring that the subject remained front-page news. Moreover, the fact that Arthur Henderson

---

[162] SFIO, *XXVIIIe Congrès National tenu…les 24, 25, 26 et 27 Mai 1931* (Paris, 1931), Renaudel, 433–2; Faure, 403–7; and 444 for the vote.

[163] AN, Papiers Joseph Paul-Boncour, 424/AP/14, Paul-Boncour to Séverac, undated but late 1931; also see ibid., 'Déclaration' signed by Paul-Boncour, Renaudel, and others, undated but issued following the May 1931 congress.

[164] LHASC, LPA, ACIQ memoranda, 1924–1936, 'Disarmament', no. 429 (a), December 1932.

presided over the conference provided Labour with an additional reason to follow the proceedings. Yet, as with the SFIO, disarmament for Labour soon
became more of an ideal than a practical proposition: support for disarmament
was ritualistically intoned but without much expectation that it could be realized
in any foreseeable future. Instead, as pacifism gained in strength within Labour,
attention shifted to the larger subject of war prevention. Speaking at Labour's
annual congress in October 1932, Ponsonby declared that 'I am afraid that I
have no hopes in disarmament coming under the capitalist system', adding that
'what you can do [though] is to prevent war' by a pacifist refusal to fight. Labour,
he explained, should announce that 'the workers of Great Britain refuse to take
up arms against their fellow workers...or any other country in the world.' If
pacifism remained a minority movement within Labour, the following year the
ACIQ warned of the rise of isolationism within the party evident in the widespread disenchantment with the League of Nations—a disenchantment the
ACIQ partly attributed to the 'long drawn-out failure...of the League's
Disarmament Conference'.[165] Henderson, meanwhile, cut a lonely figure—both
within Labour and at Geneva. All but abandoned by the British government and
even by his own party, he would, in a sad irony, seek solace in the petitions he
received (from socialists and non-socialists) as the disarmament conference's
president.[166]

As with the SFIO and Labour, the SPD also turned inwards during the 1930s,
even before the disaster of the Nazi seizure of power in early 1933. The polarized
political situation within Germany, which left the SPD increasingly isolated, prodded German socialists to amplify their calls for other countries to disarm to
Germany's level. Germany, Breitscheid announced in February 1932, had been
'unjustly treated, as we were forced to disarm while others were only beginning to
disarm'. To be sure, Breitscheid insisted that the SPD was not demanding (as
German nationalists were) the 'freedom to arm' [*Wehrfreiheit*], but he did insist
that Germany's unequal status was unacceptable. Several months later, Breitscheid
repeated the point at a joint LSI/IFTU conference:

> Overall the defeated countries face a wall of armaments.
>
> Germany demands equality of rights concerning armaments; but German workers
> want this equality to manifest itself not in Germany's rearmament but in the disarma-
> ment of victor states.[167]

By the autumn of 1932, however, the SPD's commitment to equality through disarmament was less clear. Following the German government's announcement of its
intention to seek equality by rearming, the LSI's bureau gathered in Zurich at the

---

[165] Labour, *Report of the 32nd Annual Conference...Leicester, October 3rd to 7th, 1932* (London,
1932), Ponsonby, 230–1; and LHASC, LPA, ACIQ memoranda, 1924–1936, 'The Labour Party's
Policy Regarding the League of Nations', no. 433A, April 1933.
[166] LON, R 475, Henderson to David Thurston Smith, 21 October 1933.
[167] 'Abrüstung, Reparationen, Friede. Eine Rede Dr. Rudolf Breitscheids' in *Sozialdemokratische
Parteikorrespondenz*, no. 2, February 1932, 75–87; and AABS, Ssa, F 02 B: 09, 'Die Beschlüsse der
Züricher Abrüstungskonferenz', *Für die Abrüstung*, vol. IX, no. 8, 28 May 1932, 43–4.

end of September to discuss the situation. Adler opened the meeting by voicing his concern with events in Germany and his 'unease' at the SPD's response to the nationalist/Nazi threat. Echoing Adler's implicit criticism of the SPD, Blum expressed astonishment at 'the facility and docility with which Germany had slid back into the old Imperialist system', pointing in particular to the recent removal of the SPD government in Prussia, Germany's largest state. Representing Labour, Gillies suggested that the rise of German nationalism was the predictable result of a misguided policy: Labour had always believed that 'the Germans were being pressed too hard, and that they would inevitably kick'. But no more than Blum or Adler was Gillies willing to concede Germany's right to rearm. Socialist policy, he dubiously contended, had never rested 'upon any principle of equality in arma-ments or on any Treaty promises'. Germany must remain disarmed, even if the victor countries refused to disarm to any significant extent:

> Any treaty of disarmament which provided for the controlled re-armament of Germany and a slight reduction in the armaments of other States would be a treaty to be opposed. Support for the re-arming of Germany now, whatever the conditions and circumstances, would carry with it responsibility for the fatal consequences which would ensue. The fight for disarmament would be lost.

Albarda and Renaudel, among others, pressed for a resolution denouncing any form of German rearmament. In response, Otto Wels contended that it would be wrong 'to pass a resolution and tie ourselves down to a definite form of words which might not be applicable in rapidly changing conditions'. The International, the SPD chief argued, could not ignore Germany's tense political situation in which an uncompromising resolution risked weakening the SPD's against its domestic opponents. Like Wels, Breitscheid also pleaded for understanding. 'It was always very difficult for them [German socialists] to hold the line that equal-ity lies through the disarmament of others' when the latter refused to disarm. The SPD, he added, was vulnerable to attacks not only from German nationalists but also from 'many of their own people'. In the end, no resolution emerged from the meeting.[168]

In the wake of the meeting, Blum sought to downplay the absence of a resolution, claiming that one was unnecessary because international socialism's disarmament policy had not changed.[169] But the claim was questionable. By 1932, the SPD faced considerable pressure to distinguish its position from that of the International. In a highly nationalized domestic political context, German socialists found the advocacy of equality through disarmament increasingly difficult, especially when the prospects of general disarmament were so dim. The result was growing tensions between the SPD on the one hand and the other socialist parties on the other. Reporting on the recent Zurich meeting, Gillies remarked that the 'Nationalist

---

[168] LHASC, LPA, LSI minutes 1921–1937, Labour Party, 'Labour and Socialist International. Meeting of the Enlarged Bureau. Zurich, September 27, 28, 1932', undated.
[169] IISH, SAI, 653b, Blum, 'La rencontre de Zurich'.

wave is washing the shores of the German Party'; the SPD, he intimated, could no longer be counted on to oppose Germany's rearmament.[170]

The tensions between the SPD and the other parties were again on display at the LSI bureau meeting in Berlin in mid-December 1932, the last international socialist gathering before Hitler's appointment as Chancellor. Revealingly, the SPD initially sought to remove disarmament from the agenda, well aware of its fraught nature both for German domestic politics and for its relations with other socialist parties. But the subject could not be avoided, principally because the French government had proposed a disarmament plan at Geneva (the *Plan constructif*), one of whose principal authors was Paul-Boncour.[171] If the plan predictably tied disarmament to additional security guarantees, it also promised equality of armaments for all participating countries, thereby implicitly accepting some German rearmament, as France would never disarm to Germany's level; finally, the plan appeared to favour militia armies. At the Berlin meeting the participants initially focused on this last aspect, reprising debates about the relative merits of militia versus professional-type armies. Faced with calls from some French socialists for an end to obligatory military service, SFIO delegates sought an endorsement of militia systems by the International as a means to silence such calls: in a militia army, all (male) citizens would presumably serve. While Wels refrained from pronouncing on the subject, Gillies made it clear that Labour would never approve of militia systems.[172]

But the more fundamental issue concerned German rearmament. Wels explained that a 'tremendous propaganda [was] going on' in Germany in favour of rearmament, which made it difficult for the SPD to take a clear stand on armaments and even military systems. As at the preceding meeting, Gillies sought to persuade the SPD to remain committed to German disarmament as the first step towards general disarmament. In addition to reiterating the dubious claim that the International had never promised 'full equality' to Germany, he appealed to the SPD delegates to have faith in the eventual victory of international socialism. It was imperative to 'remember...what it is that they, the German socialists, were guarding for their comrades in other lands. "If you hold fast, our victory outside will not be long delayed."' Besieged as they were at home, however, such appeals understandably rang hollow to German socialists. The SPD, Wels commented in this sense, 'had to keep contact with the [German] people, and act accordingly'. By the end of 1932, European socialists could no longer even agree on the principle of disarmament. To be sure, the SPD's Hilferding was more sensitive to the concerns of non-German socialists—as well as to the stakes involved in German rearmament. As with Gillies and Blum, Hilferding deplored the fact that equality of armaments effectively meant acquiescing in German rearmament, something, he insisted, the SPD and the International had always resisted in the name of general disarmament. The 'adoption

---

[170] LHASC, LPA, LP/ID/WG/NEC-PCE, box 5, Gillies to Philip Noel Baker, 17 October 1932.

[171] Vaïsse, *Sécurité d'abord*, 292–302.

[172] LHASC, LPA, LSI 4/15/10, Labour Party, 'Labour and Socialist International. Meeting of the Bureau, Berlin, December 11, 12, 1932', undated. For the SPD's reluctance to discuss disarmament, see IISH, SAI, 654, Adler circular to Bureau members, 10 November 1932.

of the point of view that national security requires a certain degree of defensive armaments', he lamented, rendered 'it utterly impossible to achieve the radical programme which they had advocated in the past'. But Hilferding was realistic enough to understand that nothing could be done. The 'international situation', he noted, 'would lead to its [German rearmament] adoption'.[173]

European socialists would remain publicly committed to the success of the world disarmament conference. The latter, a joint LSI and IFTU resolution declared in August 1933, 'can neither come to an end nor fail, so as to leave the road open to re-armament, to a new competition in armed peace and to a world catastrophe'.[174] But the resolution's beseeching tone betrayed despair not confidence. Hilferding had been right to predict German rearmament. In fact, the 1930s would witness a galloping international arms race rather than disarmament. Although French and British socialists would initially oppose this development, during the second half of the 1930s, both the SFIO and Labour would reluctantly endorse national rearmament in response to the looming menace posed by the aggressor states.[175]

This depressing dénouement stands in stark contrast to the hopes invested in disarmament during the previous decade. During the second half of the 1920s, the socialist International had identified disarmament as a priority and socialist parties had sought to pressure their national governments to take the necessary steps to ensure that the negotiations in Geneva ended in success. European socialists, however, found it far more difficult to forge a collective position on disarmament, let alone to devise a practical programme. Despite a prolonged and concerted effort, the differences between the major parties—differences rooted in particular national contexts—remained too great to overcome. In what amounted to a tacit admission of failure, European socialists turned to a petition campaign, seeking refuge in admonishment.

It is tempting to see the failure of European socialists to forge a workable disarmament programme as confirmation of what one scholar described as socialist internationalism's lack of 'a basic international vision'.[176] But there is more to the story. European socialists did possess an 'international vision', one, moreover, that manifested itself in the practice of internationalism—in the prolonged attempt to work out a common position on disarmament. The problem is that this practice proved self-defeating. When it came to disarmament, it did not simply expose pre-existing differences between socialist parties; it also fortified them, thereby helping to anchor each party more firmly in its national context. In exacerbating tensions over the issues of national defence and participation in non-socialist governments, Blum's appeal for disarmament by example, conceived

---

[173] LHASC, LPA, LSI 4/15/10, Labour Party, 'Labour and Socialist International. Meeting of the Bureau, Berlin, 11, 12 December 1932'.

[174] IISH, SAI, 778, 'Resolution', 24 August 1933.

[175] For the arms race, see Maiolo, *Cry Havoc*. For Labour and the SFIO, see Talbot C. Imlay, *Facing the Second World War: Strategy, Politics, and Economics in Britain and France, 1938–1940* (Oxford, 2003), 137–66, 188–216.

[176] Wrynn, *The Socialist International and the Politics of European Reconstruction*, 10.

partly to help the SPD, had the unintended effect of turning the SFIO inwards as it became increasingly preoccupied with its own problems. Similarly, the SPD's close association with international socialism left it vulnerable to accusations from German nationalists that it was betraying Germany's interests—accusations that German socialists could not easily ignore. Labour's attempt to instrumentalize the International for its own purposes, meanwhile, provoked a reaction from the Continental socialist parties, which in turn reinforced the tendency to consider disarmament through the prism of Labour's own immediate needs. As the British, French, and German parties all grew more self-absorbed, the practice of socialist internationalism necessarily suffered.

5

European Socialists and Empire
between the Wars

For a long time the international history of the interwar years neglected the colonial world, focusing instead on intra-European rivalries and on transatlantic relations.[1] More recently, however, scholars have turned their attention to empire, prompted in part by a growing sensitivity to the imperial aspects of World War I. Rather than merely a European affair, the war is now framed as an imperial conflict fought by and for empires.[2] The war's effects, moreover, reverberated well beyond Europe. The two major European victors, France and Britain, both emerged from the conflict with larger empires than in 1914; indeed, the French and British Empires reached their peak of expansion in 1919. Germany, by contrast, lost its overseas empire in Africa, Asia, and the Pacific. At the same time, the war generated the disintegration of three European empires: the Austrian-Hungarian, Ottoman, and Russian. No less importantly, the experience of war fuelled nationalist movements within the remaining empires. Erez Manela has argued that the immediate post-war period witnessed a 'Wilsonian moment' as Egyptians, Indians, Chinese, and Koreans all insisted that national self-determination, proclaimed as a basic right by the American president, applied not just to Europe but also to the non-European world. Although in the short term this clamour produced few concrete results, anti-colonial movements would continue to operate within and between empires, assuming different forms and embodying a range of goals stretching from assimilation with or integration into the metropole to outright national independence.[3] That the Bolsheviks under Lenin's leadership championed national self-determination for the colonial world helped to weave anti-colonialism further into the fabric of interwar international politics.

With the ebbing of the immediate post-war tide of anti-colonial activism, what might be called a new framework came to dominate European thinking about empire. This framework is encapsulated in the term 'trusteeship' and embodied in the League of Nations' mandate system. Conjured as a solution to the vexing problem

---

[1] Recent examples include Boyce, *The Great Interwar Crisis*; Cohrs, *The Unfinished Peace after World War I*; and René Girault and Robert Frank, *Turbulente Europe et nouveaux mondes 1914–1941* (Paris, 2004 edn.).

[2] For an overview, see Robert Gerwarth and Erez Manela, eds., *Empires at War: 1911–1923* (Oxford, 2014).

[3] Manela, *The Wilsonian Moment*. For a useful introduction, see Jane Burbank and Frederick Cooper, *Empires in World History: Power and the Politics of Difference* (Princeton, NJ, 2010), 369–404.

of what to do with the colonial possessions of the defeated belligerents (Germany and the Ottoman Empire), the mandates were conceived of as a trust: as article 22 of the League's covenant famously read, their 'well-being and development...form a sacred trust of civilisation'. The mandatory power was responsible for administering the territory in the best interests of the native inhabitants while preparing them for self-government in some unspecified future. Although applied only to ex-enemy colonies, the mandates were widely understood to be a model for all colonial powers. Underpinning the mandate system was the belief that all nations and colonies could be ranked in hierarchical terms ranging from advanced civilizations (European countries) to primitive ones, and that a territory's aptness for self-government depended on its ranking. If this assumption meant that self-government was deemed to be a distant prospect at best for many territories, the League's mandate system, as Susan Pedersen argues, contributed to the process of decolonization by opening colonialism to 'international scrutiny', which in turn fostered the dissemination of new international norms regarding the means and ends of colonial rule.[4] From this perspective, the interwar years appear as a transitional period between the imperial rivalries of the great powers before 1914 and the dissolution of empires into separate nation states after 1945.

Generally speaking, interwar European socialists adopted the trusteeship framework and its underlying assumptions. As Partha Sarathis Gupta and Manuel Semidei among others have shown, British and French socialists espoused a reformist approach that emphasized improvements in colonial practice while de-emphasizing self-government, let alone national independence.[5] Both Semidei and Gupta criticized this reformism, maintaining that it left socialists ill-equipped to understand developments after 1945. No less critical of European socialists was the East German historian, Werner Kowalski, who accused the International of 'justifying the colonial system' and of echoing 'imperialist ideologues'.[6] Other scholars have been more sympathetic to European socialists, pointing to the complexity of a colonial world that defied one-size-fits-all solutions; to the progressive aspects of socialist colonial policy, especially when compared to the pro-imperial currents on the right; and to the open-ended nature of reformism that left space for more determined anti-colonialist voices.[7] But whether critical or sympathetic, scholars

---

[4] Susan Pedersen, 'The Meaning of the Mandate System: An Argument', *Geschichte und Gesellschaft* 32 (2006), 560–82; and Pedersen, *The Guardians*. Also see Véronique Dimier, *Le Gouvernement des colonies, regards croisés franco-britanniques* (Brussels, 2004), 199–271; Nadine Méouchy and Peter Sluglett, eds., *The British and French Mandates in Comparative Perspective* (Leiden, 2004); and Michael D. Callahan, *Mandates and Empire: The League of Nations and Africa, 1914–1931* (Brighton, 1999). For civilizational ranking, see Mark Mazower, 'An International Civilization? Empire, Internationalism and the Crisis of the Mid-Twentieth Century', *International Affairs* 82 (2006), 553–66; and Gerrit W. Gong, *The Standard of 'Civilization' in International Society* (Oxford, 1984).

[5] Semidei, 'Les socialistes français et le problème colonial entre les deux guerres (1919–1939)', *Revue français de science politique* 18 (1968), 1115–54; and Gupta, *Imperialism and the British Labour Movement, 1914–1964* (London, 1975).

[6] Kowalski, *Geschichte der Sozialistischen Arbeiter-Internationale*, 118–20.

[7] Braunthal, *History of the International* II; Emmanuelle Sibeaud, 'La gauche et l'empire colonial avant 1945' in Jean-Jacques Becker and Gilles Candar, eds., *Histoires des gauches en France* II (Paris, 2004), 345–50; and Howe, *Anti-Colonialism in British Politics*.

generally agree that European socialists promoted a reformed colonialism aimed at improving rather than ending colonial rule.

This chapter does not deny the influence of the trusteeship framework on European socialists after 1919 but argues instead that support for reformist colonialism was more uncertain and contested than is often contended. Although the existing scholarship focuses on individual socialist parties, empire was a subject of debate between as well as within parties.[8] To be sure, the debate occurred essentially among Europeans. Scholars have recently highlighted the efflorescence of political and cultural activism among colonial subjects in the metropoles and especially in London and Paris.[9] But European socialists stood outside much of this activity: unlike after 1945 (as we shall see), during the interwar period they talked largely among themselves, lending their debates on empire an abstract if not detached quality. Yet however Eurocentric it was, the International provided a forum for the articulation of a socialist anti-colonialism. One prominent aspect of this anti-colonialism was calls for a policy of more active support for anti-colonial movements in the colonies. Socialist proponents of this policy, moreover, expressed considerable sympathy for the idea of national independence, a point worth emphasizing given recent studies that locate the immediate origins of decolonization in the post-1945 period.[10] While the transformation of empires into nation states was not pre-programmed, national independence did appear as a conceivable and even desirable prospect for some European socialists at least. Socialist anti-colonialism also harboured a more systemic opposition to the global political and economic order in which colonialism was embedded—an opposition rooted in pre-1914 debates. After 1919, however, this systemic opposition would be pushed towards the margins of European socialism, a process facilitated by the Komintern's outspoken anti-colonialism. At the International's 1928 congress this marginalization produced a vague reaffirmation of the trusteeship framework that papered over differences; the longer-term result was a narrowing of vision. After 1945 European socialists would become vocal advocates of colonial development, but absent from their advocacy was any overhaul of the international political-economic order. In the end, the trusteeship framework functioned not as a well-defined political programme nor even as an open-ended vista of possibilities, so much as a means to close off more far-reaching proposals.

---

[8] For single-party studies, see Billy Frank et al., eds., *The British Labour Movement and Imperialism* (Newcastle upon Tyne, UK, 2010); Owen, *The British Left and India*; Ahmed Koulakssis, *Le Parti socialiste et l'Afrique du Nord: de Jaurès à Blum* (Paris, 1991); Henri Bangou, *Le Parti socialiste français face à la décolonisation de Jules Guesde à François Mitterand. Le cas de Guadeloupe* (Paris, 1985); and Georges Oved, *La gauche française et le nationalisme marocain 1905–1922* vol. I (Paris, 1984).

[9] See Marc Matera, *Black London: The Imperial Metropolis and Decolonization in the Twentieth Century* (Berkeley, CA, 2015); Michael Goebel, *Anti-Imperial Metropolis: Interwar Paris and the Seeds of Third World Nationalism* (New York, 2015); Susan D. Pennybacker, *From Scottsboro to Munich: Race and Political Culture in 1930s Britain* (Princeton, NJ, 2009); and Jonathan Derrick, *Africa's 'Agitators': Militant Anti-Colonialism in Africa and the West, 1918–1939* (New York, 2008).

[10] See Frederick Cooper, *Citizenship between Empire and Nation: Remaking France and French Africa, 1945–1960* (Princeton, NJ, 2014); and Todd Shepard, 'A l'heure des "grands ensembles" et la guerre d'Algérie: l'État-nation en question', *Mondes(s): Histoires, Espaces, Relations* 1 (2012), 113–34.

A final reason to highlight the uncertain and contested nature of socialist support for the trusteeship framework concerns the fate of the more systemic critics of colonialism. Having been marginalized during the 1920s, several of them would reappear during the 1930s as colonial appeasers. As war clouds gathered, they contended that another European conflict could only be avoided by renegotiating the principles of the international economic order with Nazi Germany in particular—a renegotiation that involved a redistribution of colonies. The appeal of colonial appeasement extended well beyond socialists to include prominent government officials in London and Paris, and Pedersen argues that the episode served ultimately to discredit the internationalist approach to empire exemplified by the League mandates.[11] For European socialists, however, the debate on colonial appeasement inflicted a final blow not to the trusteeship framework but to systemic critiques of colonialism—and to more ambitious visions of a postcolonial international politics.

THE PRE-1918 LEGACY

European socialists inherited an ambivalent attitude towards colonialism from the pre-1914 years that would influence their approach to the issue after 1918. This ambivalence manifested itself at the Second International's Stuttgart congress in August 1907, the first one to consider the 'colonial question' at length. As part of the proceedings, the delegates nominated a commission to draft a policy statement on colonialism. The commission's deliberations, however, revealed deep divisions that precluded any consensus, resulting in majority and minority statements. The majority statement, presented to the congress by Henri Hubert van Kol, a Dutch socialist and commission chairman, denounced capitalist colonial policy for its violence and exploitation as well as for fuelling tensions between European countries. Socialists had a duty both to combat these practices in their national parliaments and to work for reforms aimed at bettering the conditions of native inhabitants. None of this would likely have surprised the delegates; after all, European socialists figured among the leading critics of colonial abuses.

More novel, however, was Kol's plea for European socialists to embrace a 'socialist colonial policy' that was realistic and responsible. The world was divided into empires, he maintained in his oral presentation, and colonies were a fact that could not be ignored. As with European countries the colonies must pass through a capitalist phase before reaching socialism. But if capitalism was necessary, so was reform. At home, Kol explained, socialists did not confine themselves to an unconditional opposition to capitalism but instead worked to improve the situation of workers; they must do the same for colonial peoples by offering a colonialism that would do away with the exploitative abuses of its current capitalist variant. During the plenary discussion, Kol received the backing of several delegates, most notable among them Eduard Bernstein, the pre-eminent proponent of German reformist

[11] Pedersen, *The Guardians*, 325–93. Also see Andrew J. Crozier, *Appeasement and Germany's Last Bid for Colonies* (London, 1988).

socialism. Making the case for a 'positive socialist colonial policy', Bernstein dismissed as 'utopian' the idea that the colonies could be abandoned, commenting that it amounted to returning the United States to 'the Indians'. A 'capitalist colonial policy must be replaced by a socialist one'.[12]

Within the colonial commission, the most determined opposition to Kol came from Georg Ledebour, the German socialist who would later become a founder of the Independent Social Democratic Party (USPD). The minority statement, inspired by Ledebour, insisted that capitalist colonial policy in its 'innermost nature' led to the 'servitude, forced labour or eradication' [*Ausröttung*] of native peoples; that it led not to the economic development of colonies but to their 'enslavement and pauperization'; and that the 'civilizing mission' was a 'cloak for the lust for conquest and exploitation'. In justifying the minority statement, Ledebour contended that so long as capitalist societies existed colonial policy would necessarily be brutally exploitative. In European countries workers could organize to place limits on capitalist exploitation, but in the colonies native peoples supposedly possessed little 'oppositional force'. This being so, all socialists must categorically oppose colonialism in all its forms.[13] Significantly, Ledebour received powerful backing from Karl Kautsky, the 'pope of socialism', who enjoyed immense influence on German and European socialists. Declaring a 'socialist colonial policy' to be a 'complete logical contradiction', Kautsky insisted that socialists could not endorse colonialism, which he equated with 'the conquest and forceful occupation of an overseas country'. With Kautsky's backing, Ledebour succeeded in winning a small majority in the plenary session for the minority statement.[14]

The historian Sebastian Schikl argues that the differences between European socialists on the issue of colonialism can be exaggerated: all were reformists insofar as they denounced colonial abuses; and all shared the Eurocentric assumption that colonial civilizations were backward, if not inferior.[15] That said, it is possible to identify two fairly distinct socialist approaches to colonialism in the immediate pre-war years—approaches that had notable implications for how socialists conceived of the future of empire. Ramsay MacDonald, the British socialist and Independent Labour Party (ILP) leader, sketched out one approach in a booklet published in 1907, *Labour and the Empire*. A delegate at the Stuttgart congress, MacDonald, in voting for Kol's majority statement, urged socialists to work out a 'determined program for colonial policy'. His booklet, which aimed to offer

---

[12] *Internationaler Sozialisten-Kongreß zu Stuttgart 18. bis 24. August 1907* (Glashütten im Taunus, 1976), 24 for the majority resolution; Kol, 25–8, 36–7; and Bernstein, 28–9. Also see F. Tichelman, 'Pays Bas: La social-démocratie hollandaise et l'Indonésie' in Georges Haupt and Madeleine Reberioux, eds., *La Deuxième Internationale et l'Orient* (Paris, 1967), 212–40.

[13] *Internationaler Sozialisten-Kongreß zu Stuttgart*, 24–5 for the minority resolution; and Ledebour, 29–30, 110–11.

[14] Ibid., Kautsky, 34–5; Kamar (India), 38.

[15] Sebastian D. Schikl, *Universalismus und Partikularismus: Erfahrungsraum, Erwartungshorizont und Territorialdebatten in der diskursiven Praxis der II. Internationale 1889–1917* (St. Ingbert, 2012), 112, 123; and Roger Fletcher, *Revisionism and Empire: Socialist Imperialism in Germany, 1897–1914* (Boston, MA, 1984). But also see Jen-Uwe Guettel, 'The Myth of the Pro-Colonialist SPD: German Social Democracy and Imperialism before World War I', *Central European History* 45 (2012), 452–84.

precisely such a programme, focused on trusteeship or what MacDonald termed the 'imperial standard'. Taking the British Empire as a case study, MacDonald emphasized its diversity, with some members closer to self-government than others. For those dependencies unable to govern themselves, the British had a dual duty to develop them economically while also safeguarding the interests and well-being of native populations. The 'more developed nations', he wrote in this regard, 'are brought into the position of something like guardian and teacher of the less well developed nations.' An underlying assumption was that empire would endure well into the future and that even the White Dominions would eschew outright political independence. MacDonald's scheme included the possibility of international agreements on colonial administration to provide an element of oversight. Interestingly, he suggested that the 'political organisations of Labour and Socialism all the world' could provide an added element of oversight to ensure that the colonial powers respected the principles of trusteeship.[16]

If MacDonald sketched out one approach, Kautsky outlined another in a booklet also published in 1907: *Sozialismus und Kolonialpolitik*. Unhappy with the course of the debate at the Stuttgart congress, Kautsky decided to develop his arguments for a wider public. As expected, he reiterated the argument that a 'positive' or 'socialist' colonial policy was oxymoronic: capitalism and colonialism were inseparable, rendering a benign version of the former illusory. While accepting the diversity of empire, Kautsky nevertheless insisted that the imperial expansion of the last few decades had been almost entirely exploitative, working to the detriment of native populations. The civilizing mission, he tellingly commented, belonged to capitalist and not to socialist ethics. But if all this was familiar from the Stuttgart congress, Kautsky went on to make two related points. The first point concerned socialist policy. *Pace* his critics, Kautsky did not contend that the colonies should be abandoned, something he assumed capitalist powers would never do. Instead, he insisted that socialists should not only oppose any further colonial acquisitions but should also 'energetically' support all colonial independence movements. 'Our goal must be: the emancipation of the colonies; the freeing of the nations living within them.'[17] Unlike MacDonald (and Kol), who deferred self-government to a distant future, Kautsky claimed that European socialists must strive to bring about a rapid end of colonialism by supporting what he termed elsewhere 'the resistance forces of native peoples'.[18]

Kautsky's second point stemmed from his commitment to Marxism. A leading biographer attributes Kautsky's anti-colonialism to 'humanistic values' that provoked him to rebel against the brutal exploitation of native peoples.[19] But Kautsky's Marxism led him to embed his rejection of colonialism in a global perspective that divided the world into developed and undeveloped (or underdeveloped) regions. Kautsky shared the widely held belief that development was necessary for the latter;

[16] MacDonald, *Labour and the Empire* (London, 1907), 46–7, 99.
[17] Kautsky, *Sozialismus und Kolonialpolitik* (Berlin, 1907), 39.
[18] Kautsky, 'Methoden der Kolonialverwaltung', *Die Neue Zeit* 26 (31 January 1908), 621.
[19] Gary P. Steenson, *Karl Kautsky, 1865–1938: Marxism in the Classical Years* (Pittsburgh, PA, 1991 edn.), 174–80.

but unlike many contemporary commentators he argued that the primary obs-tacles were not so much the supposed cultural or racial shortcomings of colonial peoples as they were the lack of access to resources and expertise of various kinds—an access that colonialism closed off rather than opened. Instead of colonialism, Kautsky envisioned development as a mutually beneficial process of voluntary and peaceful exchanges between the developed and independent non-developed nations. Here, in barest outline, was a vision of a postcolonial (and post-capitalist) international order in which economic development became a collective project linking the developed and underdeveloped regions and countries.[20]

If the outbreak of war in 1914 placed the issue of colonialism on the back-burner for European socialists, it would re-emerge in connection with the discus-sions on war aims during 1917–1918. Once again, it is possible to discern two approaches. One approach, that of trusteeship, proved popular among Allied socialists. Their February 1918 war aims statement thus declared that the peace treaty 'ought to secure to the natives in all colonies and dependencies effective pro-tection against the excesses of capitalist colonialism'. Singling out sub-Saharan Africa, it advocated a 'system of control, established by international agreement under the League of Nations and maintained by its guarantee' that would be 'con-cerned to safeguard the rights of natives under the best conditions for them'.[21] Among Allied socialists, the only dissenting note came from the ILP, which expressed doubts about the effectiveness of international supervision, warning that it should not become a cover for the perpetuation of colonial rule.[22]

The second approach, that of a more determined and systematic opposition to colonialism, resonated more with socialists from the Central Powers and espe-cially German socialists. During the war, the Allies had seized Germany's overseas colonies, and the SPD realized that, short of an overwhelming German victory, there was little likelihood of their return. This realization prodded the party towards a strong anti-colonialist position, if only as a means to score propaganda points against Allied socialists. In its 1917 war aims statement the SPD proclaimed the right to national self-determination of the Irish, Egyptians, Moroccans, Tripolitanians, Indians, and Koreans among others, all of whom conveniently belonged to the empires of Germany's enemies. German socialists, the statement continued, invited socialists from countries with colonies to raise their voices 'in favour of the freedom of all nations [suffering] under the weight of foreign domination'.[23] If the opportunism of the SPD's wartime anti-colonialism is difficult

---

[20] Kautsky, *Sozialismus und Kolonialpolitik*, *passim*. Also see Marc Michielson, 'The Missing Link: The Views of the Second International School of Thought on Development, Underdevelopment and Dependency', *Itineraio* 14 (1990), 61–6.

[21] Inter-Allied Labour and Socialist Conference, *Memorandum on War Aims* (London, 1918), 12–13.

[22] 'Note du Parti Ouvrier Indépendant (I.L.P.) au Memorandum sur les buts de guerre, publié par le Comité exécutif du Labour Party', reproduced in *Conférence internationale socialiste de Stockholm 1917* (Geneva, 1980 reprint), 392–5.

[23] 'Die deutsche Sozialdemokratie und der Frieden. Erklärung der Delegation der deutschen Sozialdemokratie auf der internationalen sozialistischen Friedenskonferenz in Stockholm', 12 June 1917, reproduced in SPD, *Protokoll über die Verhandlungen des Parteitages der Sozialdemokratischen Partei Deutschlands. Abgehalten in Würzburg vom 14. bis 20. Oktober 1917* (Berlin, 1973 reprint), 40.

to deny, the same cannot be said of the independent German socialists. Perceiving itself as the true representative of revolutionary socialism, the USPD from the beginning espoused a clear anti-colonial message. Denouncing all policy of 'colonial conquest and foreign domination', the party's 1917 war aims memorandum rejected any legal or economic arguments for colonialism and declared anything short of self-determination—what it called 'autonomous administration'—to be irreconcilable with socialist principles.[24]

When it came to the colonial world, socialists from the Allied countries leaned towards a trusteeship approach that presumed the continued existence of colonial rule well into the future. With some justice, an Indian observer accused socialists of betraying their principles. The preparations for the aborted 1917 Stockholm conference, he wrote, demonstrate 'that for West-European socialists, as well as for all Imperialists, the world of mankind means only Europe'.[25] But the accusation was also unjust, for German socialists were clearly tempted by another approach, one that envisaged independence in the near future for some colonies at least. Wartime politics prevented socialist parties from the two belligerent blocs from meeting and thus from confronting their two approaches to colonialism. As a result, the two approaches would continue to coexist into the post-war period.

1918–1919: THE RESPONSE TO THE PEACE TREATIES

As soon as its terms were known, the SPD denounced the peace treaty as evidence of the Allies' imperialist designs. The treaty, noted Hermann Molkenbuhr, a German socialist, revealed 'to the full light of day [*in voller Nacktheit*] the shamelessness of French, English and American imperialists'.[26] As chapter 2 showed, the SPD's criticism echoed among numerous Allied socialists who expressed disappointment with the peace terms. If much of this disappointment centred on the treaty's European dimension, socialists also questioned its clauses dealing with the colonial world. In particular, two related aspects provoked discussion: the fate of Germany's overseas colonies and the League of Nations' mandate system.

Not surprisingly, the SPD maintained that Germany's colonies seized by the Allies during the war should be returned. In February 1919, even before the publication of the peace terms, the SPD submitted a resolution to the international socialist conference in Berne: citing the fifth of Wilson's Fourteen Points calling for an 'absolutely impartial adjustment of all colonial claims', it insisted that this ruled out the 'principle of conquest'. German colonies, the resolution continued, constituted part of the 'national property of the [new] social-democratic German Republic', which could be trusted to administer the colonies in the interests of native peoples far more than could the 'imperial powers'—i.e. Britain and France.

---

[24] 'Memorandum du Parti Socialdémocrate Indépendant', reproduced in *Conférence internationale socialiste de Stockholm 1917*, 414–15.

[25] Cited in Schikl, *Universalismus und Partikularismus*, 403.

[26] Braun and Eichler, eds., *Arbeiterführer Parlamentarier Parteiveteran*, 14 May 1919, 338.

The resolution ended with a call for an international accord that would guarantee open and equal access to colonial economic resources for all countries.[27] The SPD's insistence on the return of German colonies drew a blistering response from the independent German socialists. An article in *Die Freiheit*, the USPD's newspaper, pointed to the demand as a sign of the majority socialists' 'capitulation' to 'bourgeois colonial policy'. Referring to the 1907 Stuttgart congress resolution, it maintained that socialists must oppose all colonialism and champion instead the rapid 'construction' of self-government in the colonies. Going further, the article suggested that an active socialist colonial policy centred on the 'international emancipation of the native peoples' could serve as a bridge uniting socialists across the wartime divide. Speaking in the German national assembly the following month, Alfred Henke, a USPD member, proclaimed that no capitalist country possessed a right to colonies. As with the USPD's newspaper, Henke pointed to the 1907 Stuttgart resolution to claim that this position reflected that of international socialism.[28]

Allied socialists, meanwhile, responded with ambivalence to the SPD's demand for the return of Germany's colonies, sensitive as they were to the charge that a double standard was at work. Interestingly, warnings of hypocrisy came from socialists who before 1914 had promoted a socialist colonial policy. Speaking at Labour's annual congress in June 1919, Paul Renaudel, a prominent figure on the SFIO's pre-war pro-colonial right, criticized 'the wrongs' done to Germany and mentioned in particular the 'clauses of the Treaty of Peace relating to colonial territory'. The 'matter had been settled in a way which enabled countries to take those territories solely for their own profit', Renaudel deplored, 'instead of allowing Germany colonial territory.' Similarly, the Belgian socialist Emile Vandervelde told the Labour audience that European socialists 'must undo what Versailles had done badly', adding: 'There was no peace when Great Britain had a right to Colonies and other countries had not.'[29] This embarrassment helps to explain the silence on the subject at the international socialist conference in Berne in 1919. Over SPD protests, the majority of the delegates agreed not to address the issue of Germany's colonies directly, preferring instead to defer discussion to a subsequent conference. The only mention of colonies was tucked away in a general resolution on territorial questions which, consistent with the principles of trusteeship, emphasized the responsibility of imperial states to protect native peoples and to guide them as quickly as possible towards 'national self-determination'.[30]

The SPD did not have to wait long for a more extended discussion of the return of Germany's colonies. At the Berne conference it was agreed to create a permanent commission that held its first meeting in Amsterdam in April 1919. Opening the

[27] 'Resolution, betreffend die Rückgabe der deutschen Kolonien', undated but February 1919, reproduced in Ritter, ed., *Die II. Internationale 1918/1919* II, 803.

[28] 'Kolonial-Fanfaren', *Die Freiheit*, 4 February 1919, 1–2; and Verhandlungen des Deutschen Reichstags, 1 March 1919, 414, Henke.

[29] Labour, *Report of the Nineteenth Annual Conference... June 25th, 26th and 27th, 1919*, Renaudel, 150; Vandervelde, 151. Also see GstA, 1 HA Rep. 90A/3786, German embassy, Holland, to AA, no. 20795, 23 July 1919.

[30] 'Arbeiter- und Sozialistkonferenz in Bern, 3. bis 10. Februar 1919', reproduced in Ritter, ed., *Die II. Internationale 1918/1919* I, 343–4 for the resolution.

discussion on the issue of Germany's colonies, Pieter Troelstra, a Dutch socialist on close terms with several German socialists, criticized the SPD's position as reflecting the 'interests of a particular country' rather than 'our international [socialist] principles'. At the same time, he insisted that socialists must oppose any 'open or hidden annexation' and must therefore support the return of Germany's colonies. Answering Troelstra, MacDonald rejected Troelstra's position as 'inadequate', proposing instead a resolution endorsing trusteeship—a resolution, he added, that was consistent with Allied socialist war aims and with a Wilsonian peace. Explaining what he meant by trusteeship, MacDonald outlined an approach that opposed all 'oppression and exploitation of colonial peoples' and any 'open or hidden imperialist policy', that guaranteed the commercial 'open door' in all colonies, and that 'educated native inhabitants for political independence'. To ensure the application of this approach, colonial administration should be subjected to international oversight through the League of Nations. The ex-German colonies would not be returned but Germany would possess a 'claim' to a colonial 'patronage mandate' once it became a member of the League.[31]

Troelstra, in turn, opposed MacDonald's text, insisting that the return of Germany's colonies involved a 'question of rights' and warning that League oversight could easily become the fig leaf behind which countries pursued their 'annexation policy'. Still stronger criticism came from the USPD's Hugo Haase, who maintained that the real question concerned not the fate of Germany's colonies but the position of European socialists towards colonialism in general. In effect, the USPD leader maintained that socialists must pursue an unrelenting opposition to colonialism in principle by exposing the 'real nature of all colonial policy and its exploitative character'. As the USPD had declared in the German national assembly the month before, a socialist colonial policy was impossible under capitalism. From this perspective, colonialism amounted to the international version of capitalist domination within the nation. Only by overthrowing capitalism could socialists end colonialism—and the exploitation of one part of the world by another. Even those socialists who did not share Haase's (and the USPD's) revolutionary politics disliked MacDonald's outline. Referring to the latter, Camille Huysmans, the International's wartime secretary, caustically remarked that in practice it amounted to an endorsement not only of Britain's Empire but also of the 'principle of capitalism'.[32]

The resulting resolution reflected the reigning ambivalence towards colonialism. In addition to denouncing any attempt to 'rob Germany of its colonies' as well as all 'imperialist annexationist policies', it condemned the 'oppression of all peoples' and the subordination of one people to another. But while proclaiming socialism's opposition to colonialism, the resolution also cautiously welcomed the international supervision of colonial administration as a means to protect 'the rights of [colonial] peoples' and to prepare them for the 'exercise of autonomy'. Aware that

[31] 'Bericht über die Konferenz in Amsterdam, 26. bis 29. April 1919', reproduced in Ritter, ed., *Die II. Internationale 1918/1919* I, 592–4.

[32] Ibid., 592–4. For the USPD also see *Verhandlungen des Deutschen Reichstags*, 1 March 1919, 414.

this did not amount to a well-defined position, the participants added the promise that the 'socialist conception of the colonial question' would be thoroughly discussed at a future congress of the International. A subsequent meeting of the permanent commission in August 1919 in Lucerne did little to clarify matters; instead its resolution declared that socialist colonial policy remained that fixed at the 1907 Stuttgart congress.[33]

The position of European socialists towards the fate of Germany's colonies remained in flux, and this flux influenced their response to the second and related aspect of colonial policy—the trusteeship approach embodied in the League of Nations' mandate system. Interestingly, some of the strongest opposition to the emerging system came from colonial voices seeking to influence the deliberations of European socialists. In early 1919, for example, a group of Syrian Arabs wrote to British and French socialist leaders complaining that Syria, Palestine, and Mesopotamia were to be placed under Anglo-French protectorate without consulting the local inhabitants. As the 'sincere champions of justice, equity and equality', the group intoned, European socialists must support national self-determination, thereby demonstrating that they 'do not belong to the number of those who simply make use of words "justice, civilisation and humanity" to prepare all the better the triumph of imperialism and who are advocates of the weak nations only to disguise their capitalist projects'.[34] Similarly, the Egyptian national party demanded that European socialists recognize Egypt's right to independence. Although Egypt was not designated as a mandate, the Egyptians implicitly criticized the principle of trusteeship, arguing that British rule, 'far from being a blessing', had been exploitative of the Egyptian people and economy. Indian nationalists, among others, also petitioned European socialists along these lines.[35] Several people from the colonial world were permitted to speak at the February 1919 Berne conference, but their influence appears to have been minimal. At the Lucerne meeting soon afterwards European socialists welcomed the League's mandate system on several conditions: that all colonies (and not just former enemy colonies) be included; that the responsibility for the mandates be transferred to the League and not to the individual mandatory powers; that Germany retain the possibility of becoming a mandatory power; and that the 'equality of economic opportunity' be guaranteed by the League for all mandates.[36]

But behind this welcome lurked considerable hesitations. Surprisingly perhaps, British socialists figured prominently among the doubters. The problem for many

---

[33] 'Resolution über die Deutschen Kolonien', reproduced in Ritter, ed., *Die II. Internationale 1918/1919* I, 602. For the resolution of the Lucerne meeting, see ibid., 664–5.

[34] IISH, Pieter Troelstra Papers, 448, undated letters to Arthur Henderson (Labour) and Jean Longuet (SFIO).

[35] AABS, Hjalmar Branting, 9/1/4/1/3, 'Memorandum zur aegyptischen Frage des Internationalen Sozialisten Kongress in Bern von dem Komites des Aegyptischen Nationalen Partei überreicht', undated; and Europäisches Zentralkomitee der Indischen Nationalisten to Secretary of Bern conference, 3 February 1919. Also see IISH, Pieter Troelstra Papers, 448, undated letter from same asking to be allowed to participate in the Berne conference.

[36] 'Kolonien', reproduced in Ritter, ed., *Die II. Internationale 1918/1919* I, 664–5. Also see IISH, BSI, 103, 'Report on the General Situation', undated but June 1919.

Labourites was not the principle of trusteeship but the perceived deficiencies in the emerging mandate system. An ACIQ memorandum in the spring of 1919, for example, regretted that the system did not provide concrete provisions for the protection of native populations.[37] Soon afterwards Leonard Woolf went further, publicly questioning the very basis of the mandate system. Arguing that under capitalism colonialism had resulted in '[p]olitical subjection, exploitation, and economic slavery' for native populations, Woolf dismissed the notion that the mandates represented a fundamental change. 'The League, as it exists to-day, and its Mandate system', he wrote, 'are both shams, and Article 22 is simply being used to obscure the fact that France and Britain are obtaining large accessions of territory for economic exploitation in Africa and Asia.' At the same time, Woolf refused to despair, holding out the hope that European socialists could help to transform the mandate system into a global development effort overseen by the League and involving the investment of considerable capital, technology, and political and economic expertise.[38] As with Kautsky, Woolf envisaged development as an expanding net of mutually beneficial exchanges between the developed world and the non-developed and underdeveloped world, with members of the latter moving quickly towards political independence.[39]

But if Woolf and other Labourites viewed the mandate system as a cynical cloak for continued colonial exploitation, the party as a whole remained wary of anti-colonialism, not least for electoral reasons. As the ACIQ candidly admitted in 1920, Labour 'could not choose a more effective method of political suicide' than by calling for an end to empire.[40] Partly in reaction to this ambivalence, the ILP, whose members viewed themselves as Labour's avant-garde, espoused a strongly anti-colonialist line. At the ILP's annual conference in 1920, Philip Snowden, the chairman, castigated the 'infamy of British Imperialism' in Egypt and India before going on to criticize the League as an instrument of power and imperial policies.[41] But it was Fenner Brockway, rapidly emerging as a tireless anti-colonial activist, who offered the clearest statement of the ILP's position in a pamphlet published the same year. For Brockway, imperialism amounted to the 'economic, political and social exploitation of the underdeveloped peoples of the earth'. Needed was not trusteeship and League mandates but another approach to the economic development of underdeveloped regions, one located in a postcolonial world and based on international cooperation and exchanges between independent countries. In both the developed and developing worlds, moreover, socialism (and trade unionism) would assume a vital role in building a global 'Socialist Community' by providing inspiration and leadership at the

[37] LHASC, LPA, ACIQ: memoranda 1918–1920, 'Memorandum on the Draft Treaty of Peace', May 1919.

[38] Woolf, *Economic Imperialism* (London, 1920), 100–11. Also see his pamphlet, *Mandates and Empire* (London, 1920), in which Woolf emphasizes the need for a massive investment in education.

[39] LHASC, LPA, ACIQ: memoranda 1918–1920, 'Draft Policy on International Economic Policy', Woolf, October 1919.

[40] LHASC, LPA, ACIQ, 'Memorandum on Draft Pamphlet on Empire Government', H. Duncan Hall, September 1920.

[41] ILP, *Report of the Annual Conference...April, 1920* (London, 1920), Snowden, 52–3.

national level. The urgent task for European socialists was thus to help socialists in the colonies to organize themselves. For Brockway, a rapid end to colonial rule constituted a precondition for this community.[42]

In its opposition to colonialism and thus to trusteeship, the ILP resembled the independent German socialists, who also found themselves on the left of mainstream European socialism. Thus, whereas the majority German socialists (MSPD) basically approved the League's mandate system, insisting only that it be extended to all colonies and that Germany become a mandatory power, the USPD roundly rejected it. The League, Arthur Crispien, the party's co-chairman, declared in late 1919, 'is nothing other than…the international instrument of domination of international capital for the repression of peoples of all countries'. As for the mandate system itself, Crispien dismissed it as an 'arrangement' by imperialist states to safeguard their 'imperialist gains'.[43] Elaborating on the USPD's position, Kautsky in March 1919 insisted that the priority be on preparations for the rapid attainment of self-determination for colonial peoples, even if some might not yet be 'ripe' for this fundamental right. Echoing his pre-war writings, Kautsky argued that the issue of colonial policy must be considered in the larger context of international economic relations. Colonialism must be replaced by an international development project tying together the developed and underdeveloped regions and countries. Afterwards, Kautsky strove to sensitize German (and other European) socialists to what he viewed as the awakening of colonial peoples, especially but not solely in Asia. The International, he intoned, cannot remain indifferent to the 'aspiring nations of the East' but must instead actively back their 'energetic struggle', even if the latter was more nationalist than socialist in nature.[44]

Like the USPD, the SFIO initially embraced an anti-colonialism incompatible with the League's mandate system and its underlying trusteeship principles. In April 1919 the SFIO's national council called on European socialist parties to 'combat' all imperialist ventures whether in 'colonial or metropolitan territories'.[45] The tone was even shaper at a subsequent meeting in July, with Longuet asserting that the 'imperialist peace' offered nothing to colonial peoples in Asia and Africa. The final resolution excoriated the League as a 'caricature' of wartime hopes. Not least among the League's faults was its supposed imperialist purpose, evident in the 'scandalous partition' of Germany's colonies as well as in its camouflage of Britain's continued 'domination' of Egypt.[46] Not surprisingly, French socialists had little

[42] BLEPS, LSI, 5/1920/7, Brockway, *How to End War: I.L.P View on Imperialism and Internationalism* (London, 1920); and Brockway, *Inside the Left* (London, 1947), 165–7.

[43] 'Protokoll über die Verhandlungen des ausserordentlichen Parteitages in Leipzig vom 30. November bis 6. Dezember 1919', reproduced in *Protokolle der Parteitage der Unabhängigen Sozialdemokratischen Partei Deutschlands* vol. II, Crispien, 171; and 'Amerika gegen den Völkerbund', *Die Freiheit*, no. 563, 20 November 1919, 1–2.

[44] 'Protokoll über die Verhandlungen des ausserordentlichen Parteitages vom 2. bis 6. März 1919 in Berlin', reproduced in *Protokolle der Parteitage der Unabhängigen Sozialdemokratischen Partei Deutschlands* vol. I, Kautsky, 118; and Kautsky, *Vergangenheit und Zukunft der Internationale* (Vienna, 1920), 62.

[45] Daniel Renoult, 'Contre l'impérialisme', *L'Humanité*, 8 February 1919, 1; and 'Contre la paix de violence. Pour la pais de droit', *L'Humanité*, 24 April 1919.

[46] 'Le Parti socialiste et la paix', *L'Humanité*, 15 July 1919, 1; and 'La motion Renoult adoptée par le Parti au Conseil National', *Le Populaire de Paris*, 17 July 1919, 2.

good to say about the mandates system. Speaking in February 1920, Marius Moutet, an SFIO colonial expert and future colonial minister in Léon Blum's Popular Front government, depicted them as a cover for direct occupation and rule by the imperial powers.[47]

THE COMMUNIST CHALLENGE

In the wake of the First World War, European socialists appeared uncertain about their position towards the colonial world. Whereas some endorsed a trusteeship approach with varying degrees of enthusiasm, others argued for a more oppositional stance, including active support for anti-colonial movements. There was nothing inherently unstable about this uncertainty; after all, a well-established tradition existed among socialists of toleration for multiple viewpoints. This uncertainty would nevertheless dissipate by the late 1920s, replaced by a more consensual (and vague) commitment to trusteeship. Significantly, events in the colonial world played almost no role in this development; instead, a dominant factor was the emergence of the Bolsheviks as champions of anti-colonialism.

From the beginning, the Bolsheviks framed their anti-colonialism in opposition to European socialists. At the Komintern's founding conference in Moscow in March 1919, Grigori Zinoviev, the chair of its executive committee, remarked contemptuously that European socialists 'did not dare to subject it [colonial policy] to a detailed examination'; on the subject of trusteeship he added sarcastically: 'One can imagine how the League of Nations might safeguard the colonies.' More generally, the Komintern's resolution on the February 1919 socialist international conference in Berne declared that the 'discussion on the colonial question' revealed that European socialists were 'treading the same path as the bourgeois-liberal colonial politicians, who believe the imperialist bourgeoisie's policy of colonial exploitation and subjugation is justified and wish only to dress it up with humanitarian and philanthropic phrases'. Soon afterwards, Nikolai Bukharin, another leading Bolshevik and member of the Komintern's executive committee, wrote that the proletariat welcomed 'the uprisings of the colonial people'. Bukharin contrasted the Komintern's stance with that of European socialists, grouped together in the 'Bern[e] Yellow "International"', who accepted the 'transfer of colonies to the thieves in the "League of Nations" so that the fate of hundreds of millions of people may be decided by the bankers of New York, London, and Paris'.[48]

Although the Komintern's second conference in the summer of 1920 is best known for its elaboration of conditions for membership, Bolshevik leaders also found time to reiterate their opposition to colonialism. In his lengthy comments

---

[47] AN, C//14632, Commission des affaires étrangères, Chambre des députés, 19 February 1920, Moutet.

[48] John Riddell, ed., *Founding the Communist International: Proceedings and Documents of the First Congress, March 1919* (New York, 1987), 193–4, 203, 307–8.

on the report on the national and colonial questions, Lenin insisted that the 'characteristic feature of imperialism consists in the whole world... being divided into a large number of oppressed nations and an insignificant number of oppressor nations, the latter possessing colossal wealth and powerful armed forces'. This being so, Lenin echoed Bukharin's earlier admonition to Bolsheviks to support 'bourgeois liberation movements' in the colonies, overriding the doubts of the Indian communist M.N. Roy regarding their revolutionary potential. In defining this position, Lenin juxtaposed it with that of the Second International that showed 'no sign of genuine revolutionary work or of assistance to the exploited and dependent nations in their revolts against the oppressor nations'. In his closing remarks to the conference, Zinoviev once again underscored the differences between communist and socialist internationalism. Pointing to the Second International's 1907 Stuttgart resolution, he claimed that European socialists had endorsed 'a so-called cultural colonial policy that is, in fact, the piratical policy of imperialism'. Unlike the socialist International, the Komintern 'had to say and it did say that it did not want to be an International only of the working people with white skin, but also an International of the working people with black and yellow skins, and International of the working people of the whole world'.[49]

Few if any non-Europeans attended the post-war international socialist gatherings as delegates. This was an aspect that the Bolsheviks strove not to emulate. Indeed, in June 1920, a month before its second conference, the Komintern's executive issued a call to the peoples of Asia to send representatives to a congress in Baku to discuss 'how to unite the efforts of the European proletariat with yours in order to struggle against the common enemy'. The congress, which met in October 1920, assembled almost three thousand delegates, the vast majority of them non-Europeans. Presenting the Komintern's report on national and colonial questions, Mikhail Pavlovich (Tomsky), a high-ranking Bolshevik, announced a commitment to 'fight for the liberation of the East', adding that this contradicted the 'current line of action of the Yellow traitor International headed by Kautsky, Vandervelde, and other agents of imperialism'. European socialists, Tomsky continued, were incapable of 'taking the initiative in bringing revolution to the black and yellow continents, or even simply in making propaganda for ideas of liberation among the suffering masses of Asia and Africa. The Second International did not and does not want to know the East from that angle.' Zinoviev, meanwhile, attacked the notion of trusteeship, supposedly encapsulated in the 1907 Stuttgart resolution, and the 'view that "civilized" Europe can and must act as a tutor to "barbarous" Asia'. Rather than tutorship, Zinoviev offered an alliance between anti-colonial nationalists and Bolsheviks in Asia and beyond in favour of national

---

[49] For Lenin, see John Riddell, ed., *Workers of the World and Oppressed Peoples, Unite! Proceedings and Documents of the Second Congress, 1920* vol. I (New York, 1991), 211, 216; for Zinoviev, see vol. II, 798–801. Also see Michael Weiner, 'Comintern in East Asia, 1919–39' in Kevin McDermott and Jeremy Agnew, eds., *The Comintern: A History of International Communism from Lenin to Stalin* (Houndmills, 1996), 158–63.

self-determination. 'There must be no colonies,' Tomsky insisted in this regard. 'All nations have equal rights.'[50]

Robert Young, a prominent scholar of postcolonialism, claims that the Komintern offered the 'first systematic programme for global decolonization'.[51] This is certainly an exaggeration: as much of the recent scholarship on the Komintern indicates, its interest in anti-colonialism was largely rhetorical; and during the early post-war years the Bolsheviks' attention remained riveted on Europe and especially on Germany—a Eurocentrism that persisted until the organization's abolition in 1943.[52] Closer to home, the Soviet authorities strove to establish a revamped version of the Tsarist Empire that had dissolved under the strains of war and revolution.[53] Nevertheless, the Bolsheviks' anti-colonial rhetoric cannot be dismissed merely as cynical posturing, if only because it reverberated within and beyond Europe. In the case of European socialists, the Komintern demanded a 'well-defined and clear-cut policy in respect of colonies and oppressed nations' as a condition for admittance.[54] In insisting on anti-colonialism, the Bolsheviks helped to ensure that the issue became embroiled in the larger and divisive debate among European socialists on whether to join the Komintern. In September 1920, Marcel Cachin, a French socialist and proponent of adhesion to the Komintern, celebrated the Baku congress as proof of the gulf that separated the Communist and Socialist Internationals. Whereas the latter limited itself to useless protests, the Komintern advocated 'action, direct and vigorous action'. Two months later, at the SFIO's Tours congress, which saw a majority of delegates vote to join the Komintern, Cachin proclaimed that imperialism was on the march in Asia and the Middle East, preparing new conquests and wars. Only by 'lining up immediately and enthusiastically behind the [sole] great power in the world that has declared war on imperialism', the Soviet Union, could European socialists defeat imperialism.[55]

The influence of the Bolsheviks' anti-colonial position would also be felt on the European socialists who refused to join the Komintern. To recall from chapter 2, the USPD, the SFIO, and the ILP all joined the Vienna Union, an association that sought to unite the communist and socialist Internationals under the banner of revolutionary socialism. This aim influenced its position on anti-colonialism. Not only did the Vienna Union insist that European socialists must support 'the

---

[50] John Riddell, ed., *To See the Dawn: Baku, 1920—First Congress of the Peoples of the East* (New York, 1993), Tomsky, 146–7, 154; and Zinoviev, 50, 66–7, 72–3.

[51] Robert J.C. Young, *Postcolonialism: An Historical Introduction* (Oxford, 2001), 10.

[52] The best history of communist internationalism is Silvio Pons (translated by Allan Cameron), *The Global Revolution: A History of International Communism, 1917–1991* (Oxford, 2014), 7–42. Also see Vatlin, *Die Komintern*, 158–200.

[53] Terry Martin, *The Affirmative Action Empire: Nations and Nationalism in the Soviet Union, 1923–1939* (Ithaca, NY, 2001); and Dominic Lieven, *Empire: The Russian Empire and its Rivals from the Sixteenth Century to the Present* (London, 2003), 288–329.

[54] Lenin, 'Terms of Admission into Communist International', available at: https://www.marxists.org/archive/lenin/works/1920/jul/x01.htm.

[55] Cachin, 'La Révolution russe et la libération des peuples', *L'Humanité*, 1 September 1920, 1; and Charles, ed., *Le Congrès de Tours*, Cachin, 380–3.

freedom of struggling nationalities and colonial peoples against the dominant system of capitalism', but its anti-colonialism resembled the Komintern's in its emphasis on imperialism as a global framework of relations between classes, countries, and regions.[56] As with the Komintern, moreover, the Vienna Union's member parties evinced hostility towards trusteeship and the League of Nations' mandate system in particular. At the Vienna Union's founding congress in February 1921, the ILP's R.C. Wallhead denounced the peace treaty's colonial provisions as a dangerous continuation of pre-war imperialism. All peoples had a right to national self-determination, Wallhead exclaimed, and urged European socialists to join with the oppressed masses of the world to overthrow capitalism and colonialism.[57] The Vienna Union's anti-colonialism is worth highlighting because it represented one possible path for interwar European socialism in terms of colonial policy. In the end, however, it was a path not taken because the Vienna Union (as chapter 2 showed) was eventually forced to merge with the Second International largely on the latter's terms. And these terms included the downplaying of anti-colonialism.

By the time of the Vienna Union's merger with the Second International, the latter, with Labour in the lead, had moved closer to an endorsement of trusteeship—a shift in which the Bolsheviks played a major part. The Komintern's drumbeat of criticism of the Second International's colonial policy helped to fuse Bolshevism and anti-colonialism in the eyes of many European socialists, resulting in efforts to distance international socialism from anti-colonialism. In Labour's case, the ACIQ turned its back on the party's (admittedly) lukewarm support for Indian self-government, concluding in 1922 that 'a rapid advance, on democratic lines, is impossible.' Instead of self-government, the British, together with cooperative Indians, should concentrate on the lengthy and 'constructive work' of creating 'a sound, well-balanced, and instructed electorate'. Behind this recommendation lurked the fear of what the ACIQ identified as 'chaos' and 'despotism'—terms connoting dangerous and uncontrollable development and often associated with Bolshevism. Two years later, Rudolf Hilferding, a former USPD stalwart and now SPD leader, referred to the Bolshevik danger in calling for a prudent colonial policy. Extremely wary of 'Russian [Soviet] imperialism', he explained that while socialists must welcome the 'awakening' of Asians and Africans, 'we believe it would be dangerous if this progress assumed forms incompatible with the security and culture of Western Europe...' For Hilferding, a radical anti-colonialism of the kind championed by the Bolsheviks—and earlier by the Vienna Union—had become anathema.[58]

The flipside to a rejection of a more radical-cum-Bolshevik anti-colonialism was a growing interest in the trusteeship framework among European socialists. A good

---

[56] 'Aufruf der Berner Konferenz. An die sozialistischen Parteien aller Länder!', reproduced in *Protokoll der Internationalen Sozialistischen Konferenz in Wien vom 22. bis 27. Februar 1921*, 5–8.

[57] *Protokoll der Internationalen Sozialistischen Konferenz in Wien vom 22. bis 27. Februar 1921*, Wallhead, 17–19, 104–5.

[58] LHASC, LPA, ACIQ memoranda: 1922–1924, 'Memorandum on India', no. 247, Col. B. Williams, June 1922; and SPD, *Sozialdemokratischer Parteitag 1924. Protokoll mit dem Bericht der Frauenkonferenz*, Hilferding, 196.

example is a 1923 pamphlet on foreign policy written by Arthur Henderson, who had shaped Labour's wartime policy and would become party leader in 1931. While admitting that the mandate system was flawed, Henderson refused to abandon it, arguing that '[i]n principle it is the right one' because it 'gives a legal basis for international criticism and control'. European socialists, he elaborated, should work to improve the system by placing mandates under a strengthened League of Nations administration and by extending them to all colonies 'which are, for the time being, incapable of standing alone and governing themselves'.[59] That Henderson expressed a widely shared position became evident at the LSI's founding congress in May of the same year. Having reiterated socialist opposition to colonial expansion and exploitation and having identified 'democratic self-administration' to be the desired goal for colonial peoples, the principal resolution on international policy indicated that these prescriptions did not apply to all colonies. For those lacking the necessary conditions, European socialists were exhorted to pressure governments to prepare for eventual self-government. The complete absence of any time frame suggested that this entailed a prolonged effort.[60]

EUROPEAN SOCIALISTS AND THE RIF WAR

Partly in reaction to Bolshevik anti-colonialism, European socialists during the early 1920s were moving towards an embrace of the trusteeship framework for the colonial world. But this embrace was never complete. During the mid-1920s a growing number of European socialists evinced dissatisfaction with trusteeship: while some maintained that it was too vague, others complained that it left unanswered the question of what, if any, support to offer anti-colonial movements in the colonies. The result was sometimes heated discussions both within and between socialist parties. The Rif War provided an important impetus for this burgeoning interest in colonial policy.

Although unrest had been evident for several years in the Spanish zone of Morocco, the Rif War began in 1921 when armed inhabitants from the mountainous Rif region under the leadership of Abd-el Krim destroyed a Spanish army numbering some 15,000. Following the creation of an independent Rif republic, a violent conflict ensued over the next several years between Abd-el Krim's supporters and Spanish military forces. At the end of 1924, the conflict spilled over into the French zone, leading to a Franco-Spanish military alliance to defeat Abd-el Krim. With over 100,000 French troops engaged in Morocco by mid-1925, the Rif War quickly became an international event.[61]

---

[59] Henderson, *Labour and Foreign Affairs* (London, 1923), 11.

[60] 'Der imperialistische Friede und die Aufgaben der Arbeiterklasse', reproduced in *Beschlüsse des Internationalen Sozialistischen Arbeiterkongresses in Hamburg 21. bis 25. Mai 1923*, 7.

[61] On the Rif War, see Vincent Courcelle-Labrousse and Nicolas Marmié, *La Guerre du Rif: Marco 1921–1926* (Paris, 2008); Dirk Sasse, *Franzosen, Briten und Deutsche in Rifkrieg 1921–1926: Spekulanten und Sympathisanten, Deserteure und Hasardeure im Dienste Abdelkrims* (Munich, 2006), 21–53; and Tayeb Boutbouqalt, *La Guerre du Rif et la réaction de l'opinion internationale 1921–1926* (Tangier, 1992).

The Bolsheviks contributed greatly to politicizing the Rif War. During 1924 and especially 1925 Komintern leaders seized upon the war as an opportunity to pursue an anti-colonial and anti-militarist agenda. Instructions accordingly went out to communists to support Abd-el Krim and his cause. The Komintern, moreover, focused much of its energy on France. From the outset, the PCF was divided between a militant core that championed anti-colonialism and a more reticent party leadership influenced by a combination of anti-Arab prejudices and fears of alienating the patriotic sentiments of French workers. But whatever its internal dissensions, the PCF took the lead in a public campaign against the Rif War centred on the call for an immediate peace, a French military evacuation, the independence of the Rif region and, perhaps most controversially, 'fraternization' between French military forces and Abd-el Krim's army. As part of the campaign, the PCF not only organized rallies and petition drives, published pamphlets and posters, and led a failed general strike in October 1925; it also lobbied for a united front (*front unique*) of political parties, movements, and trade unions on the left that would include French socialists.[62]

Communist attempts to ally with French socialists utterly failed, chiefly because of the SFIO's distrust of the PCF—a distrust exacerbated by calls for fraternization, which socialists (with some justice) interpreted as an incitement to desertion. But it is also worth noting that French communists continued to heap scorn on socialist leaders.[63] Indeed, the PCF's strategy was to appeal to socialist militants over the heads of their leaders, a strategy that predictably infuriated the latter. Whatever the precise reasons for the SFIO's hostility, its refusal to cooperate with communists does not mean that it endorsed the French government's pursuit of military operations against Abd-el Krim. As Charles Robert-Ageron showed, the SFIO's position during 1925–1926 evolved from hesitant support of the government's policy to opposition. Although the SFIO offered parliamentary backing to the centre-left *Cartel des gauches* government formed after the May 1924 general elections, by the spring–summer of 1925 a substantial minority of SFIO deputies refused to endorse its Moroccan policy by declining to vote war credits. In justifying his party's stance, Blum explained that 'by principle [and] tradition we are the adversaries of colonialism'. Over the next several months, the SFIO maintained its critical stance, pressuring the government to seek a negotiated settlement and to accept the principle of the Rif Republic's political independence and League of Nations membership. Abd-el Krim's capitulation in May 1926 did nothing to alter the party's opposition. In a gesture fraught with political symbolism at a time when the French army continued to bask in the glory of victory in 1918, the SFIO abstained from the parliamentary vote of gratitude to French troops that had fought in the Rif War.[64]

---

[62] For the PCF's campaign, see Oved, *La gauche française et le nationalisme marocain 1905–1922* vol. I, 227–317; David H. Slavin, 'The French Left and the Rif War, 1924–25: Racism and the Limits of Internationalism', *Journal of Contemporary History* 26 (1991), 5–32; and Nicole Le Guennec, 'Le Parti communiste et la guerre du Rif', *Movement social* 78 (1972), 39–64.

[63] Le Guennec, 'Le Parti communiste et la guerre du Rif', 50.

[64] Ageron, 'Les socialistes français et la guerre du Rif' in *Abd el-Krim et la République du Rif: actes du colloque international d'études historiques et sociologiques 18–20 janvier 1973* (Paris, 1976), 273–92.

Ageron focused on the exchanges between French socialists and French com-munists. But the Rif War also possessed an international socialist dimension. Under pressure not only from the PCF but also from socialist militants, Blum took advantage of a meeting of SFIO and Labour parliamentarians in January 1925 to raise the issue of colonial policy and especially that of the European administration of the 'coloured and conquered races'. Insisting on the need for Labour and the SFIO to work out 'some general lines' of policy, Blum proposed to centre efforts on the trusteeship framework: French and British socialists 'might make common propaganda to generalise the idea of mandates, widening the supervisory powers of the League, and making it a body through which disputes arising out of colonial possessions might be settled'. Speaking for Labour, Josiah Wedgwood accepted the principle of extending the mandate system but hesitated when it came to protect-orates, of which Morocco was one, suggesting that the French and British should 'go slowly in the direction of control through the League of Nations'. For Blum, who sought Labour's help in framing the Rif War and Morocco's future in trusteeship terms, Wedgwood's hesitant approval was more important than his reservations.[65] With Labour's backing, the SFIO the following month issued a statement attributing Abd-el Krim's armed opposition not to colonialism per se but to the wrong-headed nature of French (and Spanish) rule. French colonial policy, accordingly, needed to be infused with trusteeship principles. For socialists, the statement proclaimed, 'colonialism can be justified only if it brings the aid of a superior civilization to the native peoples and only if nations possessing colonies act as mandatories of civilization and humanity as a whole.'[66]

Having placed the Rif War on the agenda of international socialist politics, SFIO leaders found it difficult to control the ensuing discussions. At a meeting of the LSI's bureau in early July 1925, Pierre Renaudel came under pressure to clarify the SFIO's position. Otto Bauer, the Austrian socialist, warned that the issues involved in the conflict risked reproducing pre-1914 divisions within and between socialist parties. Although Bauer agreed to postpone a debate on the subject, citing 'our complete confidence' in French socialists, it was evident that the SFIO would need a clearer position on the Rif War—one that went beyond invocations of a civilizing mission.[67] At a meeting of Spanish, French, and British socialists in Paris later the same month, Spanish and Labour participants pressed French socialists to be more forthcoming, resulting in a common position that combined precise recommendations regarding the Rif War with far-reaching suggestions for the future of colonialism in Morocco and beyond. On the Rif War, the joint resolution called for an end to military hostilities and the opening of negotiations based on

---

The Blum citation is from p. 282. For the SFIO and the PCF, see Judt, *La reconstruction du Parti socialiste*, 149–64.

[65] LHASC, LPA, LSI Minutes, minutes of SFIO-Labour meeting, 1 January 1925. Also see US, Leonard Woolf Papers, 1D2c, Advisory Committee on Imperial Questions, minutes, 25 February 1925.

[66] JO, *Débats*, 5 February 1925, Henry Fontanier, 580–1.

[67] BA-SAPMO, II. Internationale, RY 14 I 6/2/25, 'Sitzung des Bureaus des S.A.I. in London am 4. Juli 1925' in *Bulletin der Sozialistischen Arbeiter-Internationale* 3 (July 1925), 7–8. Also see IISH, SAI, 1615, Renaudel to Friedrich Adler, 5 July 1925.

the principle of independence for the Rif Republic; on Morocco, the Spanish and French protectorates were to be transferred to the League which would apply 'a regime analogous to that of the mandates already instituted by it'. As for colonialism more generally, the resolution, reflecting Marxist belief in the economic underpinnings of imperialist rivalries, envisaged a 'collective economic system of the world' overseen by the League of Nations.[68]

Several weeks later, in August 1925, the LSI's second congress opened in Marseille. Following remarks from a Spanish socialist, the delegates unanimously approved a resolution underscoring the need for a negotiated settlement to the Rif War, and for an independent Rif Republic.[69] Yet, just as significantly, the consensus did not extend much further. As with previous international socialist gatherings, various colonial voices lobbied European socialists to adopt a more determined anti-colonial stance, including national independence for existing mandated territories.[70] While European socialists were unprepared to go this far, they appeared equally unwilling to endorse the trusteeship framework. Consequently, and in time-honoured fashion, they decided not to decide. Opening the debate on colonialism, Louis Piérard, a Belgian socialist, admitted that this 'big, important question' merited a thorough discussion because the position of European socialists remained unclear. The choice, Piérard added, was the same as that at the 1907 Stuttgart congress: either a socialist colonial policy, which he associated with a 'policy of colonial mandates', or opposition to colonialism, which implied working actively for its end. Rather than choose, however, Piérard proposed to defer the debate on colonial policy to the next LSI congress—a proposal the delegates unanimously accepted.[71] Writing soon after the congress, the SFIO's Paul Faure urged European socialists to define a colonial policy that avoided both the 'Muscovite theses' of abandonment and a naïve reliance on the League of Nations.[72] Faure did not, however, offer any indication of what this policy might look like.

QUESTIONING COLONIALISM

The Rif War produced ripples among European socialists, prompting them to consider anew the question of a socialist colonial policy. This process was clearly evident with the SPD. Although German socialists directed most of their attention to Europe, the colonial world also attracted their interest during the mid-1920s. This was especially true of left-leaning German socialists. The *Sozialistische Politik und Wirtschaft*, the newspaper of Paul Levi, a founder of the KPD who had migrated

---

[68] LHASC, LPA, LSI 4/10/1, 'Moroccan Situation', undated; and 'Pour la Paix au Maroc. Une Conférence socialiste internationale', *Le Populaire de Paris*, 1 August 1925, 1.

[69] *Zweiter Kongreß der Sozialistischen Arbeiter-Internationale. Marseille, 22. bis 27. August 1925*, 328–9; and IISH, SAI, 29, 'Resolution on Morocco'.

[70] IISH, SAI, 44, Edouard Khoury to the LSI congress, 24 August 1925. Also see the file in SAI 40.

[71] *Zweiter Kongreß der Sozialistischen Arbeiter-Internationale. Marseille, 22. bis 27. August 1925*, Piérard, 329–31; and IISH, SAI, 30, 'The Colonial Question'.

[72] Faure, untitled editorial, *Le Populaire de Paris*, 31 August 1925, 6.

back to the SPD, devoted considerable space to the Rif War, urging French and European socialists to view it as proof of the revolutionary potential of non-European peoples. More generally, Levi and his supporters urged the SPD to take the lead in the anti-colonial cause—to demonstrate that German and European socialists are 'the real friends and allies of the millions of colonial slaves' in Asia and Africa. 'There is no colonial rebellion', Levi's newspaper declared in this sense, 'that is unjustified'; the only way to douse the flames of revolt, it added, was for socialists to work actively for 'the freedom of [all] colonial peoples'.[73]

Admittedly, Levi was something of a gadfly and his influence on the SPD relatively minor. The same, however, could not be said of the former USPD leaders who had reintegrated the SPD in 1923. Reporting on the recent LSI congress in Marseille, Arthur Crispien told the SPD's annual congress in September 1925 that international socialism must make a collective effort to end the Rif War because French socialists and trade unionists alone lacked the 'strength and the means' to do so. Casting his gaze more widely, Crispien argued that the present period witnessed the 'awakening of the working masses in the Chinese, Indian and Muslim world'. While admitting that this awakening did not amount to the desired 'proletarian revolution', he nevertheless insisted that European socialists must support the national aspirations of the colonial world: 'We demand the right of national self-determination for peoples of Asia and Africa.' Anti-communism, moreover, figured in Crispien's thinking. If European socialists did not become the champions of the colonial peoples, the communists would exploit 'these national revolutionary upheavals' for their own destructive ends. Echoing Crispien in identifying what he termed the 'awakening of nations without history', Hilferding, another former USPD luminary, maintained that European socialists must embrace anti-colonialism in order 'to influence, to oversee and to direct [it] . . . so that the process does not culminate once again in a catastrophic, warlike fashion'. If Hilferding's primary fear concerned the danger of war more than Bolshevism, the former USPDers all agreed that the SPD must adopt a more active anti-colonial policy.[74]

To be sure, the SPD was not prepared to renounce the trusteeship framework. Its 1925 programme, approved at the party's congress, spoke not of an end to colonialism but of opposition to 'the exploitation of colonial people and to the violent destruction of their economic and cultural life'. A gloss on the programme repeated the earlier demand that the mandate system be extended to all colonies and that the League of Nations' authority over the mandatory powers be increased.[75] That said, even mainstream SPD leaders found a stronger anti-colonial stance attractive for political reasons. Writing to a confidant in early 1927, Hermann Müller, soon to become Chancellor, argued that for 'practical reasons' Germany should not pursue its political and moral right to colonies. Not only could the resources involved in maintaining colonies be better invested at home, but the dispossession of its

[73] BA-SAPMO, SPD, RY 20/II/144 1/7, B.M. Huber, 'Kolonialpolitik und Sozialismus', *Sozialistische Politik und Wirtschaft* 3 (7 August 1925).
[74] SPD, *Sozialdemokratischer Parteitag 1925 in Heidelberg*, Crispien, 238–41; and Hilferding, 282.
[75] SPD, *Das Heidelberger Programm. Grundsätze und Forderungen der Sozialdemokratie* (Berlin, 1925), 65–70.

colonies freed Germany from any association with colonial exploitation. Germany consequently enjoyed a 'great reputation' among colonial peoples, a reputation, Müller suggested, that it could exploit for commercial and political benefits. Accordingly, Müller recommended that Germany use its position on the League's mandates commission to strengthen ties to colonial peoples striving for independence. However instrumentalist Müller's view, it did point to the SPD's willingness to consider a more active anti-colonial policy.[76]

French socialists also questioned the trusteeship framework during the mid-1920s. As we saw, the SFIO's growing opposition to the French government's pursuit of the Rif War during 1925–1926 did not simply reflect domestic political dynamics but also a response to international socialist pressure. Yet this is not all. The Rif War, together with a major rebellion in Syria during the second half of the 1920s, triggered a debate among French socialists on the nature of colonialism—a debate that not only involved international socialism but also echoed pre-1914 disagreements within the Second International.[77]

With the flames of revolt blazing in Morocco and Syria, the delegates at the SFIO's congress in August 1925 agreed to create a 'commission d'études coloniale' to consider party policy.[78] A prominent member of the newly minted commission was Jean Zyromski, a founder of the *Bataille socialiste*, a leftist group within the SFIO, and an outspoken critic of colonialism. Impressed by events in Morocco, Syria, and beyond, Zyromski believed that the colonial world was crumbling under the combined weight of revolts against exploitation and servitude—a revolt that European socialists must support.[79] A committed internationalist, Zyromski sought to mobilize the International behind an anti-colonial campaign. Insisting that it would be a 'deplorable and disastrous error' to ignore the 'colonial problem', he lobbied for colonial policy to be placed on the LSI's agenda. The International, Zyromski asserted in May 1926, 'must pay greater attention to the oppressed nationalities', adding that socialists must not allow international communism to enjoy the monopoly on the issue. But for the LSI to play this role, he wrote the following month, European socialists must first forge a 'homogenous policy' towards the colonial world.[80] If Zyromski pushed French socialists to take the lead within the International, he also sought to use the latter to influence the SFIO's policy. At the SFIO's national council in November 1926, for example, he argued that France should give up its Syrian mandate, pointing to the LSI's 1925 resolution in

---

[76] BA-SAPMO, NL Hermann Müller, N 2202/2, Müller to Institut für Auswärtige Politik (Dr Köstler), 19 September 1927.

[77] For the Syrian revolt, see Daniel Neep, *Occupying Syria under the French Mandate: Insurgence, Space and State Formation* (Cambridge, 2012); Michael Provence, *The Great Syrian Revolt and the Rise of Arab Nationalism* (Austin, TX, 2005); and Lenka Bokova, *La confrontation franco-syrienne à l'époque du Mandat 1925–1927* (Paris, 1990).

[78] SFIO, CAP, 'Séance du 14 octobre 1925', *Le Populaire de Paris*, 21 October 1925, 3.

[79] Zyromski, 'La vie internationale', *Le Combat social*, 12 June 1925, 3.

[80] Zyromski, 'Socialisme et politique coloniale', *Nouvelle revue socialiste* 6 (1926), 182; 'Le XXIIIe Congrès national socialiste. Clermont-Ferrand, 23–26 mai 1926', *Le Populaire de Paris*, 28 May 1926, 2; and Zyromski, 'La vie internationale', *Le Combat social*, 4 June 1926, 3.

favour of placing all mandates under League control. The 'true duty of socialists', he contended, was to adapt party policy to that of the International.[81]

Unlike the SPD's Levi, Zyromski hesitated to endorse national independence for the colonial world. As with many European socialists, he viewed nationalism with considerable suspicion as a major cause of international rivalries. Throughout the 1920s, Zyromski criticized the peace treaties for having 'Balkanized' Europe, creating numerous nation states jealous of their political authority. Colonial nationalism seemingly carried the same risks. Rather than transform empires into nation states, Zyromski, much like Kautsky before 1914, envisaged a global development project knitting together the developed and underdeveloped regions.[82] A vital part of this project would be increased international control of economic exchanges and especially the distribution of raw materials. And here Zyromski initially assigned the League a leading role. Under socialist inspiration, he wrote, the League would become 'an organ of international economic and political control and naturally all colonial problems, as all international problems, would fall within its ambit'.[83] Over time, however, his suspicions of the League as an instrument of imperial power politics increased, suspicions fanned by the seeming weakness of its mandate system. Commenting in February 1927 on the League's permanent mandate commission, Zyromski deplored the success of the French and British governments in blocking efforts to expand the commission's authority; the commission, as a result, supposedly had little more power than 'neighbourhood councils' in France.[84] But the more important point is that Zyromski increasingly framed his anti-colonialism in opposition to trusteeship. His primary interest was not to reform colonialism but to transform the relations between the developed and underdeveloped worlds—a transformation that implied an end to colonial rule.

Though a minority current within the SFIO, the *Bataille socialiste* group possessed a strong base in the Paris region. No less importantly, Zyromski's anti-colonialism resonated beyond the group, a point underscored by the concerted efforts of his opponents to commit the SFIO unambiguously to the trusteeship framework at the party's congress in May 1926. Claiming a lack of time, the congress' organizers limited the debate on colonial policy to speakers from France's overseas possessions. As the socialist federations in these possessions were dominated by Europeans, the predictable result was a series of speeches praising France's civilizing mission. A delegate from Tunisia thus maintained that colonialism was 'legitimate in itself as a producer of material and moral well-being', while denouncing the 'xenophobism and naturalism of a few natives' who demanded independence. Similarly, his colleague from Algeria ruled out independence on the grounds that it would not be in the best interests of the 'natives' whose living conditions had

[81] 'Le Conseil national', *Le Combat social*, 5 November 1926, 1–2; and SFIO, CAP, 'Séance du mercredi 1er décembre 1926', *Le Populaire de Paris*, 15 December 1926, 3.

[82] Zyromski, 'La politique internationale du socialisme. L'autonomie nationale', *La Correspondance socialiste*, 13 November 1926, 2–3; and Zyromski, 'Socialisme et politique coloniale', 182.

[83] Zyromski, 'La vie internationale', *Le Combat social*, 12 June 1925, 3.

[84] SFIO, *XXIVe Congrès national tenu à Lyon les 17, 18, 19 et 20 Avril 1927* (Paris, 1927), Zyromski, 14–15.

vastly improved under French rule.[85] But the most sustained defence of colonialism as trusteeship came from Joseph Lagrosillière, an ex-deputy from Martinique. Lagrosillière began by rejecting the PCF's call for an end to colonial rule as well as Zyromski's vision, claiming that each would leave the colonies at the mercy of capitalists. Instead, socialists should pursue in the empire what they did at home—the revolutionary transformation of a capitalist society into a socialist one. Behind the anti-capitalist rhetoric, however, lay an agenda of social and economic reforms aimed at protecting and advancing the interests of natives, including the abolition of all discriminatory legislation. Significantly, Lagrosillière excluded political autonomy (let alone independence) from his agenda, insisting that only alongside France could the colonies progress towards the advent of the 'socialist civilization that we believe superior to all other civilizations'. One measure of the importance attached to Lagrosillière's position was the publication of his speech in the influential socialist journal, the *Nouvelle revue socialiste*.[86]

With the SFIO divided on colonial policy, it was left to Blum as usual to work out a consensus. But for all his subtlety, the SFIO's parliamentary leader offered not so much a compromise as confusion: sometimes he spoke of colonial independence, sometimes of France's civilizing mission, sometimes of the pressing need for reforms, and sometimes of an international solution à la Zyromski. Delphic statements, such as the one in July 1927 that the colonial question was as much a moral and psychological matter as an economic one, did nothing to clarify matters.[87] The reality is that during the mid to late 1920s the SFIO did not possess a clear-cut position on colonialism. And this absence would tempt French socialists to look to the International.

Labour's colonial policy also manifested signs of flux in the wake of the LSI's 1925 Marseille congress. Writing in *Die Gesellschaft*, a journal close to the SPD, Charles Rhoden Buxton, a prominent Labour commentator on colonial issues, complained that neither the International nor his own party possessed a well-defined position. While European socialists espoused 'vague ideas' of equality for the 'yellow, brown and black races', they did not offer any 'practical solutions'. What was socialist policy? he asked rhetorically. What did trusteeship mean? What future did socialists envisage for the colonial world in the near and longer-term future? And how did this future fit into socialist conceptions of a 'new political and economic order for the entire world'? Answers to these questions, Buxton contended, would be found neither in 'well-worn [*übliche*] Marxism' nor in 'well-worn reformism'. Haden Guest, the secretary of Labour's parliamentary group, indirectly echoed Buxton's criticism regarding the lack of precision in colonial policy. Writing also in *Die Gesellschaft*, Haden explained that Labour MPs were pressing

---

[85] 'Les débats du Congrès', *Le Populaire de Paris*, 28 May 1926, 5. For a useful study of Algerian socialists, see Claire Marynower, 'Réformer l'Algérie? Des militants socialistes en "situation coloniale" dans l'entre-deux-guerres', *Histoire@Politique* 13 (2011), 1–12.

[86] Lagrosillière, 'Le Parti socialiste et la question coloniale', parts I and II, *Nouvelle revue socialiste*, 15 July–15 August 1926, 555–62; and 15 August–15 October 1926, 80–93.

[87] Blum, 'Fin du "Voyage au Congo"', 20 July 1927, reproduced in *L'Œuvre de Léon Blum. 1914–1928* (Paris, 1972), 488–90.

for the creation of an imperial study group to examine a socialist colonial policy based on the principles of international 'cooperation and constructive socialism'. Haden, however, did not provide any indication of what such principles meant in concrete terms.[88]

As with the SPD and the SFIO, the tumult in the colonial world—the Rif War, the Syrian revolt, unrest in Egypt, India, and Iraq—fostered the impression within Labour that empire was under siege. Writing in 1928, Leonard Woolf described the mid-decade as a time of 'revolt against imperialism, against the tyranny of Western civilization and the hegemony of European states'. 'The dominance of European States in Africa and Asia,' he elaborated, 'the forcible imposition of Western civilization upon Africans and Asiatics, and the economic exploitation accompanying imperialism have welded together the various "nationalities", made them self-consciously nationalist, and taught them to use their new cohesion against their conquerors and rulers.'[89] If this phenomenon confronted all European socialists, Labourites were acutely conscious of its implications because they expected to govern Britain (and its Empire) in the very near future. The short life of Labour's first (minority) government in 1924 was viewed as a temporary setback and not as a harbinger of problems. Convinced that the party must be better prepared the next time, Labour leaders and officials set out to craft a colonial programme for an upcoming Labour government. The exercise would raise at least as many questions as it answered.

Labour thinking on colonialism during the mid-1920s centred on two issues, and on both the result was considerable uncertainty. One issue concerned India's future. Although Labour was ostensibly committed to Indian self-government, the party's colonial experts privately questioned the wisdom of this position. Thus, in 1924 the Advisory Committee on Imperial Questions (ACImQ) urged Labour to strive to persuade Indian nationalists of its determination to 'fulfil the pledges of a gradual progress towards Self-Government' in the hope that they would accept something less—'a much more moderate instalment of self-government'. Leaving aside the point that Indian nationalists were unlikely to be duped by such a cynical strategy, the ACImQ's proposal ran afoul of militants who, at Labour's annual congress in 1926, passed a resolution recognizing India's right to 'full self-government and self-determination'. 'Let no one who opposed [this motion]', declared George Lansbury, its proposer, 'stand up and say that the Labour Party did not mean Self-Determination when they used the word.'[90] Faced with this pressure, the ACImQ hesitated, seemingly uncertain how to proceed. Revealingly, two memoranda in 1927 written by the same official arrived at different conclusions. In the first one,

---

[88] Buxton, 'Der Imperialismus und die Internationale', *Die Gesellschaft* vol. 2 (1925), 217–21; and Guest, 'Die Britische Labour Party und das Imperium', *Die Gesellschaft* vol. 1 (1926), 17–28. For Haden, also see Howe, *Anticolonialism in British Politics*, 50.

[89] Woolf, *Imperialism and Civilization* (New York, 1928), 34–6.

[90] LHASC, LPA, ACImQ, memoranda: 1924–1931, 'Draft Memorandum on Indian Situation', no. 6, June 1924; and Labour, *Report of the 26th Annual Conference held ... October 11th to 15th, 1926* (London, 1926), Lansbury, 236–7.

the author argued that a Labour government must move quickly towards Indian independence by calling a conference of Indian political representatives to discuss 'the immediate application of a Constitution in accordance with the wishes of the Indian people'. Among the 'measures necessary' was 'the announcement of precise dates for the establishment of full responsible Government'. Four months later, however, he appeared less certain. Declaring that India's political situation 'bristles with difficulties', the second memorandum downplayed self-government and emphasized instead the need for unidentified 'liberal concessions' on Britain's part. Perhaps more importantly, the memorandum highlighted Labour's lack of a precise policy for India. It was 'essential', the author lectured, 'that there should be, in the minds of the members of the Labour Party...a clear understanding of the programme with regard to India which it is proposed that the Labour Party should adopt on taking over the reins of Government'.[91]

In some ways, India was an exception: Labour sympathy for Indian self-government, which stretched back to the wartime period if not before, could not easily be reconciled with the trusteeship framework favoured by many British and European socialists. But Labour officials also appeared undecided about the wisdom of trusteeship for other parts of the empire. A 1926 party pamphlet, *The Empire in Africa*, was infused with trusteeship thinking, referring to the League's mandate system as a model:

> The implication of the mandate system and its honest fulfilment must be so important that it would not only be inconsistent but practically impossible for any State to refuse to accept in non-mandated territory the same obligations as are accepted under the mandates. In a word, the principle of trusteeship under the League of Nations cannot be confined arbitrarily to particular pieces of territory; it must be extended to cover all tropical Africa, and the right of the community of nations to supervise the due carrying out by the trustee of the obligations of its trust must be frankly recognised.[92]

Doubts, however, underlay this endorsement of trusteeship. During the drafting of the pamphlet, various colonial experts had voiced misgivings about trusteeship, including Buxton, a vocal critic of the economic exploitation of native populations that he believed to be endemic to colonialism. Critiquing a draft of the pamphlet, Buxton queried the ability of trusteeship, or what he called 'the sense of imperial responsibility', to tame the 'powerful economic "drive"' towards exploitation—a drive that was 'steadily growing in intensity'.[93] Though opposed to independence for colonies, deeming them unprepared, Buxton favoured a

---

[91] TNA, Ramsay MacDonald Papers, PRO/30/68/1283, ACImQ, 'Memorandum on India', no. 39A, July 1927; and 'India and the Indian States', November 1927; both by Major D. Graham Pole. For more on Labour and India, see Nicholas Owen, *The British Left and India: Metropolitan Anti-Imperialism, 1885–1947* (Oxford, 2007), 137–69.

[92] Labour Party, *The Empire in Africa: Labour's Policy* (London, 1926), 2–3, 10.

[93] Buxton, *The Exploitation of the Coloured Man* (London, 1925), 8–9, 23. Also see LHASC, LPA, ACImQ, memoranda: 1924–1931, 'Questionnaire, Question no. 3', Buxton, undated.

more active and interventionist policy on Britain's part than that of trusteeship. Buxton, moreover, was not alone: the desire to go beyond the perceived limits of trusteeship animated the ACImQ in general; one member even suggested that much could be learned in this regard through 'consultation with foreign labour [socialist] parties'.[94] To be sure, no one on the ACImQ called for immediate political independence for the colonies. Judging trusteeship to be too passive, the committee urged Labour to elaborate a more activist colonial programme. Yet the explicit point of this activism was to hasten the attainment of self-government and, ultimately, political independence. Left unanswered was the question of Labour's attitude towards anti-colonial movements in the colonies.

If Labour evaded this question, the ILP appeared eager to address it. ILP supporters had been frustrated with what they viewed as the timidity of Labour's 1924 minority government, not least in terms of colonial policy. Keen to prod Labour in a more anti-colonial direction, the ILP in 1925 created an empire policy committee to consider the colonial question.[95] The results were soon evident. At its annual conference in 1926, the ILP committed itself to Indian self-determination without delay, a clear rebuke to Labour. The same held true for Egypt from which British troops should be withdrawn. Going beyond these two cases, the delegates approved a general statement, entitled 'Socialism and the Empire', which began by declaring that 'Socialist Empire Policy involves a complete break with many past traditions.' The break comprised a two-pronged policy. One prong, echoing Zyromski among others, consisted of approaching colonialism in terms of development—hence the call for international control of economic exchanges. The second and more immediate prong was to make self-government not simply the 'ultimate goal' of Labour colonial policy but its focal point. This would occur through League supervision of all colonial territories as well as through an extensive programme of political and economic development. Although the statement did not explicitly endorse cooperation with anti-colonial movements, its emphasis on self-government clearly implied it.[96] Perhaps more importantly, Fenner Brockway, who in 1926 became the ILP's political secretary and editor of its principal journal, was determined to pursue such cooperation. As he explained to Friedrich Adler, the LSI's secretary, in February 1926, the ILP 'urges upon the British and International Labour movements the necessity of assisting the workers of Asiatic and African countries... to organise industrially and politically for their protection against exploitation and for their ultimate emancipation'.[97]

[94] LHASC, LPA, ACImQ, memoranda: 1924–1931, 'Questionnaire on Subject Peoples', no. 22, Woolf, January 1926; no. 24, Polak, January 1926; and no. 25, Green, January 1926.

[95] Howe, *Anticolonialism in British Politics*, 68–70.

[96] ILP, *The Report of the Annual Conference...April, 1926* (London, 1926), 48–52, 53–6.

[97] IISH, 1701, Brockway to Adler, 15 February 1926, with attachment. For Brockway, also see Hazel Kent, ' "A paper not so much for the armchair but for the factory and the street": Fenner Brockway and the Independent Labour Party's *New Leader*, 1926–1946', *Labour History Review* 75 (2010), 208–11.

EUROPEAN SOCIALISTS AND THE LEAGUE AGAINST IMPERIALISM

During the mid-1920s, socialist colonial policy appeared to be in flux as European socialists questioned the trusteeship framework embodied in the League's mandate system. Although there existed little agreement on an alternative, several voices called for a more ambitious anti-colonial stance that included a more systemic approach to relations between the developed and underdeveloped/colonial worlds as well as active support for anti-colonial movements in Asia and Africa. Reflecting this flux, in 1926 the International created a colonial commission charged with formulating a common policy for the upcoming LSI congress.[98] That this exercise would not necessarily end in an endorsement of the trusteeship principle became apparent at the LSI's bureau meeting in Paris in early February 1927 that ended with a ringing denunciation of Western imperialism in Asia and especially in China. All socialists, the final resolution declared, must back the 'national and democratic freedom movement of the Chinese people'. As the SFIO's newspaper made clear, moreover, the LSI's anti-imperialist rhetoric was not confined to China.[99] But if anti-colonialism appeared to be on the rise among European socialists, during 1926–1927 a new actor emerged in international politics, the League against Imperialism (LAI), whose unintended effect would be to steer the International back towards trusteeship.

The LAI was founded in the wake of the congress against colonial oppression and imperialism held in Brussels in February 1927 and which brought together some 175 delegates from 34 European and non-European countries as well as colonies. In recent years, both the congress and the LAI have garnered considerable attention from scholars who present them as a key moment in the history of anti-colonialism and anti-imperialism—a history that would give birth after 1945 to decolonization and Third Worldism. Indeed, Vijay Prashad identifies the Brussels congress as a precursor to the famous Bandung conference of non-aligned countries in 1956, while Michael Goebel suggests that it 'made' many anti-colonial activists by endowing them not only with prestige but also with a common purpose as they inscribed their local demands onto a larger transnational critique of colonialism.[100] But the LAI also had an important influence on European socialists by effectively excluding further consideration of possible alternatives to the trusteeship framework—alternatives that included active support for anti-colonial movements. It did so, moreover, because the leading socialist parties viewed the LAI as an instrument of the Komintern and thus of Soviet policy. Recent scholarship admittedly nuances this assessment: although the LAI began as a Komintern

---

[98] IISH, SAI, 1665, LSI (Adler) circular to parties, 22 April 1926.

[99] SSAZ, SPS, Ar.1.260.5, 'Arbeiter, Sozialisten aller Länder', *Internationale Information*, vol. IV, no. 9, 13 February 1927, 75–6; and 'Appel de l'Internationale', *Le Populaire de Paris*, 14 February 1927.

[100] Vijay Prashad, *The Darker Nations: A People's History of the Third World* (New York, 2007), 32; Goebel, *Anti-Imperial Metropolis*, 199–215. Also see Fredrik Petersson, 'Hub of the Anti-Imperialist Movement', *Interventions: International Journal of Postcolonial Studies* 16 (2014), 49–71; and Derrick, *Africa's 'Agitators'*, 172–82.

initiative and received considerable financing from the Soviets, it was not a servile tool of the Bolsheviks, at least not initially.[101] Nevertheless, the pertinent point for this chapter is that European socialist leaders equated the LAI with Bolshevism.

From the outset, the LAI met with hostility from European socialist leaders who perceived the call for an anti-imperialist congress in Brussels as part of the Komintern's ongoing campaign to forge a united front by sowing discord among socialists. The fact that the LSI itself was not invited to the Brussels congress, but only Labour and the ILP (and eventually the Belgian party), confirmed the suspicion that the Bolsheviks were engaged in the same old divisive tactics. Thus as early as August 1926 the LSI's information bulletin denounced the proposed congress as a communist 'front enterprise' [*Deckfirma*]; several months later, when Adler informed Labour's international secretary that the congress 'is an enterprise of the Communist International',[102] Labour leaders needed little convincing, and the party's national executive decided not to attend the Brussels congress. By contrast, the ILP's national council accepted the invitation, naming as its delegate Fenner Brockway.[103]

Three aspects of the Brussels congress are worth emphasizing. One was its anti-colonial tone. A series of speakers, including several who would go on to become prominent anti-colonial leaders (Messali Hadj and Jawaharlal Nehru among them), denounced the colonialism of the European imperial powers. More outspoken still, the general resolution on 'colonial freedom struggles' announced that all people enjoyed a 'right to [national] self-determination', adding, in an obvious reference to the mandate system, that this right meant something else than the 'lip service' offered by the 'so-called League of Nations'. Not only must a broad-based alliance be formed to fight 'colonial oppression and imperialism', but this fight must extend beyond 'expressions of sympathy' and 'public demonstrations' to encompass 'mass action'—i.e. boycotts of goods as well as labour strikes. A second notable aspect was the presence of European socialists and especially British socialists. One of the first speakers, George Lansbury, a future Labour leader, counselled patience, explaining that anti-colonialists, though only a minority within British and European socialism, were a particularly determined and active one. Lansbury urged the delegates to join the 'ranks of socialists' as this would not only strengthen the minority but would also help to immunize anti-colonialists from the supposed dangers of nationalism. Speaking after Lansbury, Brockway expressed his 'shame' at the colonial and especially Indian policy of Labour's minority government in 1924, remarking that it was indistinguishable from that of 'a capitalist government'. The ILP, he promised, would continue to pressure Labour to adopt a more vigorous anti-colonial policy in India, Egypt, and elsewhere.[104]

---

[101] See especially Petersson, 'Hub of the Anti-Imperialist Movement'.

[102] Kowalski, *Geschichte der Sozialistischen Arbeiter-Internationale*, 82; and IISH, SAI, 1676, Adler to William Gillies, 19 January 1927. Also see Laqua, 'Democratic Politics and the League of Nations', 188–90.

[103] ILP, *The Report of the Annual Conference...April, 1927* (London, 1927), 10.

[104] Liga gegen Imperialismus und für nationale Unabhängigkeit, *Das Flammenzeichen vom Palais Egmont: Offizielles Protokoll des Kongress gegen koloniale Unterdrückung und Imperialismus. Brüssel, 10–15. Februar 1927* (Berlin, 1927), 22–31, 198–9.

The final noteworthy aspect of the Brussels congress was the decision to create a permanent organization—the LAI. In justifying the decision, Willi Münzenberg, the international communist activist and driving force behind the Brussels congress, maintained that a broad-based coalition was needed in order 'to forge a powerful weapon' against colonialism across the globe. Significantly, he indicated that one purpose of the LAI was to pressure the socialist International, which, as he deprecatingly remarked, had refused to adopt a 'clear' position at its 1925 Marseille congress. If the LSI could be expected to oppose the LAI, Münzenberg took comfort in the fact that anti-colonial activists existed in various European socialist parties who were eager to cooperate in making the 'struggle for colonial and national freedom' the 'most burning and pertinent question of world politics'. Münzenberg made clear, moreover, that he counted on Brockway to assume a prominent part in the campaign to compel the socialist International to abandon its 'lukewarmness' on the issue of colonialism.[105]

Münzenberg's confidence in Brockway and the ILP was well-placed. Earlier, in 1926, the ILP had pressed the International to open negotiations with the Komintern regarding the possibility of cooperation and, more ambitiously, of forming 'an all-inclusive International'—a goal that reflected the ILP's long-standing hope to overcome the divisions within the international socialist movement. As expected, Labour firmly rejected 'any proposal for the union of the Socialist and Communist Internationals', insisting that it was 'doomed to failure' as the 'minimum of agreement does not exist'. Brockway nevertheless insisted that the LSI discuss an approach to the Komintern, which it did at its meeting in April 1926 at which the ILP's proposal was overwhelmingly rejected.[106]

In this context, the LAI offered the ILP a means to pursue cooperation between socialists and communists at a practical level. But no less important a motive was the desire to push Labour—and European socialism more generally—in a more resolutely anti-colonial direction. An editorial in *The New Leader*, the ILP's review, thus presented the Brussels congress as an opportunity for European socialists to gain 'first-hand knowledge of the struggle against imperialism' across the globe and to 'see Capitalism as a closely knit world tyranny'. Writing in the same review several months later, Brockway elaborated on the LAI's significance. Seeking to counter socialist suspicions, he insisted that the LAI was not a communist front, accepting at face value LAI assurances that it was not financed by Moscow. But for Brockway the vital question concerned not the role of communists but socialism's response to the growing demand of colonial peoples for freedom. Put simply, European socialists could not stand aside from what he presented as a 'coloured peoples' International':

> Personally, I think it would be suicidal if Socialists refrained from association with this movement, even if it had been initiated by the Communists. It has done what the

---

[105] Ibid., 215–24. For Münzenberg more generally, see Kasper Braskén, *The International Workers' Relief, Communism and Transnational Solidarity: Willi Münzenberg in Weimar Germany* (Houndmills, 2015) for a sympathetic portrait; and Sean McKeekin, *The Red Millionaire: A Political Biography of Willi Münzenberg* (New Haven, CT, 2003) for an extremely critical one.

[106] IISH, SAI, 1702, Brockway to Adler, 6 January 1926 and 26 February 1926; SAI, 234, 'Moscow and the I.L.P. The Labour Party's Attitude', Arthur Henderson, 2 March 1926; and SAI, 239, 'Sozialistische Arbeiterinternationale und Kommunistische Internationale', undated.

Socialist International has failed to do—seriously begun the task of uniting the proletarian movements among the coloured races...even from the narrowest and most
official socialist point of view it is short-sighted and stupid, when this great development with such immense possibilities takes place, to stand aside from it and permit
the subject race organisations to gain the impression that the Communists are their
only friends.

As a sign of his commitment to the LAI, Brockway agreed to serve as the international chairman of its executive committee as well as the chairman of its British
section.[107]

Wasting little time, Brockway contacted Adler after the Brussels congress to
encourage the International to 'actively participate' in the LAI, reiterating that 'it
would be a mistake to leave such a representative movement in the hands of the
communists.' At the very least, he contended, the ILP should be allowed to affiliate. Adler replied cautiously, noting that it was a matter for the LSI's executive to
decide, though he did not disguise his suspicions of communist aims. Like many
European socialists, Adler disliked communist anti-colonialism because of its
emphasis on nationalism, which he feared would undermine socialism's real task—
to advance the international class struggle.[108] In any case, Adler soon allied with
officials from several European parties, including Gillies, Labour's international
secretary, to collect evidence of communist involvement in the LAI for an upcoming LSI executive meeting. A Labour memorandum in September 1927 summar-
ized prevailing thinking: 'There is no doubt that the initiative for the League
originated with the communists, and similarly there is no doubt that they have
tried, and will continuously try, to make use of this League for the purposes of
bolshevist politics.'[109] Meanwhile, Labour leaders pressured their members to end
their participation: thus Lansbury, who had preceded Brockway as chairman of the
LAI's executive committee, resigned after only two months.[110] Although Brockway
worked hard to defend the LAI, he soon found himself largely isolated. Tellingly,
the only open support he received came from socialists situated well to the left of
mainstream European socialism such as the ex-communist Paul Levi.[111]

Brockway's isolation was evident at the LSI executive meeting in September
1927. Opening the discussion on the LAI, Brockway asked that the ILP be
allowed to join the organization, emphasizing the opportunity to 'gain influence
with the awakening peoples' across the world. The LAI, Brockway elaborated, had

---

[107] 'At Brussels', *The New Leader*, 16 February 1927, 8; IISH, SAI, 284, Brockway, 'The Coloured
Peoples' International', *The New Leader*, 26 August 1927; and Brockway, *Inside the Left*, 168.

[108] IISH, SAI, 284, Brockway to Adler, 8 April 1927; and Adler to Brockway, 13 April 1927. Also
see VGA. Adler-Archiv, M 225/T3, 'Internationale Probleme', Adler, 16 November 1927.

[109] LHASC, LPA, LSI 14/24/1/1, 'The League Against Colonial Repression and Imperialism',
September 1927. For efforts to gather evidence, see the file in IISH, SAI, 3050.

[110] Kowalski claims that Lansbury's appointment as Labour's chairman soon afterwards was a
reward for abandoning the LAI. Kowalski, *Geschichte der Sozialistischen Arbeiter-Internationale*, 83.

[111] For Levi, see 'Der erwachenden Völker', 11 March 1927, reproduced in Charlotte Beradt, ed.,
Paul Levi. Zwischen Spartakus und Sozialdemokratie: Schriften, Aufsätze und Briefe (Frankfurt, 1969),
218–19.

'succeeded in combining the anti-Imperialist movements of the subject races' and it would be 'suicidal for Socialists to remain outside a development of such immense possibilities'. The other participants remained unconvinced, however. Speaking for Labour, Gillies dismissed the League as a 'communist front organization' and insisted that his party would have nothing to do with 'nationalists and communists'; similarly, the SPD's Otto Wels rejected all cooperation with communists and announced that his party was withdrawing membership from German socialists who had joined the LAI. The Austrian socialist, Otto Bauer, while agreeing with Brockway on the need to do more to court the 'oppressed peoples', maintained that the communists simply could not be trusted. Fully endorsing Bauer's conclusion, Adler proposed a resolution disapproving of socialist membership in the LAI. Faced with this unanimous front, Brockway promised that the ILP would respect the executive's decision, though not before warning once again that socialism's future 'depends on the colonial peoples'.[112]

At the September 1927 meeting Brockway had not promised that he would cut his own ties to the LAI, but only that the ILP would not join. Brockway, in fact, continued to be active in the LAI's British section. The ILP's aim, as he assured an LAI conference in July 1928, was to push Labour to 'be bolder in its opposition to Imperialism'.[113] As part of this effort, Brockway not only renewed his call for negotiations between the Socialist and Communist Internationals, but canvassed various socialist groups in Europe on the idea.[114] Once again, however, he met with firm opposition. Adler and the LSI executive quickly called him to order, querying Brockway on his continued involvement with the LAI and rejecting outright any approach to the Komintern. Unable to budge the International, Brockway eventually relented, distancing himself from the LAI.

The fraught relations between European socialists and the LAI had several notable consequences. In what Stephen Howe aptly describes as a self-fulfilling process, the refusal of the leading European socialist parties to cooperate with the LAI contributed to its bolshevization, even if the Komintern's adoption in 1928 of a class against class strategy (which precluded any cooperation with socialists) probably played a bigger role. In any case, over the next several years the LAI became increasingly dominated by communists—a point even the ILP eventually conceded; in 1931 the LAI would expel all members deemed insufficiently committed to anti-colonialism, a category that by then included ILP members.[115] Before then, however, the ILP continued to cooperate with the League in promoting anti-colonialism. If anything, the International's censure stoked the ardour of ILP leaders.

[112] IISH, SAI, 291, 'Protokoll', undated; and Fenner Brockway, 'At the International', *The New Leader*, 16 September 1927, 7. Also see AABS, Ssa, F02B/03, 'Tagungen der Sozialistischen Arbeiter-Internationale', *Internationale Information*, no. 48, 13 September 1927, 388–9.

[113] IISH, League Against Imperialism, 139, 'Report on the First Conference of the British Section of the League Against Imperialism...July 7th, 1928'.

[114] See the file in IISH, SAI, 1703.

[115] 'The League Against Imperialism', *The New Leader*, 27 September 1929; and Howe, *Anti-Colonialism in British Politics*, 73–5.

Much to the annoyance of Labour officials, James Maxton, the ILP's militant chairman, agreed to replace Brockway as chairman of the LAI's British section; in so doing, he signalled the ILP's intention to continue pressing Labour—and European socialism more generally—on colonial policy. As Maxton explained to an LAI executive meeting in 1928, the socialist International was 'approaching the whole colonial question from other than a Socialist point of view, not from the point of view of the working class fight for freedom throughout the world'.[116] At the LSI's congress the same year Maxton and the ILP would make one final attempt to reshape its colonial policy.

But perhaps the most significant consequence of the LAI for European socialists was to discredit anti-colonialism. The League's communist ties induced many European socialists to associate its vigorous anti-colonialism with communist internationalism; that several prominent anti-colonialist activists in the metropole were either bona fide communists or communist sympathizers did not help matters.[117] The profound suspicion of communism among socialists inevitably tainted their anti-colonialism. While clearly sympathetic to the struggles of oppressed peoples everywhere, Friedrich Adler, for example, could not detach his attitude towards the LAI from his hostility towards communism. From the outset, the LSI's secretary was convinced that the communists were exploiting the League (and anti-colonialism) to divide and weaken the International and its member parties. But for Adler the communists were anti-socialist in a deeper sense. It was not simply that he considered the Komintern an instrument of Soviet policy; it was also that he viewed communist anti-colonialism in the same fashion. In championing national independence for the colonial world, the Soviets were attempting to impose their own model of anti-colonialism, one that privileged national interests over the class interests that socialists defended and that were supposedly internationalist by definition. The League, in other words, was anathema not simply because of its concrete ties to international communism but also because its anti-colonialism appeared to be excessively nationalist in orientation—an orientation that communists had done so much to define as anti-socialist.

PREPARATIONS FOR THE LSI'S CONGRESS

To recall, at the LSI's 1925 congress the delegates had decided to defer discussion of colonial policy to the upcoming congress. Initially intended for Paris in 1927, the congress would be held in Brussels in August 1928. Meanwhile, the LSI's colonial commission, created in 1926, got down to work in September 1927 under the chairmanship of Willem Vliegen, a Dutch socialist and proponent of trusteeship. After several months of consultation and discussion, the commission produced a

---

[116] IISH, SAI, 3050, 'Press Information Bulletin', no. 2, LAI—British Section, 15 September 1928.

[117] For example, see Kris Manjapara, *Age of Entanglement: German and Indian Intellectuals across Empire* (Cambridge, MA, 2014), 182–4; and Hakim Adi, *Pan-Africanism and Communism: The Communist International, Africa and the Diaspora, 1919–1939* (Trenton, NJ, 2013).

preliminary report in February 1928. If this delay was partly due to the need to gather information, it also reflected differences within the commission on the report's content. As a Belgian member of the commission confided in June 1928, the commission encountered 'considerable difficulties' in drawing up an 'action program' for socialists because 'every delegate defended first and foremost the point of view of his country.'[118]

Despite or because of these differences, Vliegen took the lead in drafting the preliminary report. Beginning with the proposition that colonialism had enabled 'the expansion of capitalism the world over', the report argued that this process, while 'bought at the price of many evils', had nevertheless 'for the colonised peoples been the starting point of a modern evolution of the state of society and culture, rendering them accessible to modern democratic, national and social ideas'. No less importantly, colonialism had created colonies at 'varying stages of development'. For a small number, especially those possessing 'an ancient civilisation', the attainment of political independence should be relatively rapid. But for the others, who remain in a 'very primitive stage of evolution', progress would 'depend wholly on domination by foreigners'. Reflecting trusteeship principles, Vliegen's report identified the task of socialists to be to ensure that this domination worked in the interests of the natives. Socialism, it accordingly declared, 'claims efficient protection against oppression and exploitation, a systematic education directed towards preparation for these peoples' independence, and, at the same time, progressive development of their administrative autonomy, developed as far as complete autonomy'. Rather than recommending cooperation with anti-colonial forces, the statement pointed to the need to foster 'workers' socialist movements' in the colonies in order to help guide the 'struggle for national liberation'.[119]

The preliminary report's accent on trusteeship met with a mixed but generally favourable response from European socialists. On the British side, the ILP was predictably unhappy with the report. Although not represented on the colonial commission, the ILP continued to lobby the International to adopt a stronger anti-colonial position. As always, the ILP pressed for talks with the Komintern on creating a single workers' International—talks in which colonial policy could be expected to play an important part given the Komintern's insistence on national independence.[120] Meanwhile, in a short memorandum submitted to the International, the ILP outlined an alternative position on colonial policy. Having denounced the capitalist exploitation of 'backward races by the more advanced', the memorandum conceded that in some colonies 'it is not immediately practicable to extend full self-government to a subject race'. Nevertheless, it presented these as exceptional and temporary cases. The speedy attainment of self-government

---

[118] AMSAB, POB, 'Séance du Conseil Général du 13-6-1928', Mathieu. Also see 'Le Comité éxécutif de l'Internationle se réunit dimanche à Bruxelles', *Le Populaire de Paris*, 10 September 1927, 3.

[119] IISH, SAI, 297, 'Proposal of the Colonial Commission', undated but February 1928. Also see SAI, 786, 'Vorschlag Vliegen. Einleitung eines kolonialpolitischen Aktionsprogramms', undated but February 1928.

[120] For example, see IISH, SAI, 1707, John Paton (ILP) to Adler, 15 March 1928, and attached document: 'Manifesto Urging International Unity'.

would be the primary task of a much strengthened and expanded mandates system under League supervision. Indeed, in contrast to Vliegen's preliminary report, the ILP's memorandum emphasized not only the end goal of national independence, but also the need to work with anti-colonial movements. The International, it asserted, 'welcomes the growing movement among the coloured peoples of Africa to claim racial equality' and urged 'co-operation between the white and coloured workers' organisations in the common struggle for Socialism'. John Paton, an ILP leader, was blunter still: the ILP wanted the International to talk not of 'self-government' but of 'full self-determination' for all subject peoples.[121]

In his memoirs written in the 1930s, Paton spoke of the 'cold disdain' with which Labour leaders considered the ILP's colonial policy. If Paton arguably exaggerated this hostility, it is nevertheless true that Labour was increasingly sympathetic to the trusteeship framework for colonies and correspondingly doubtful about the prospects for self-determination in the foreseeable future. A 1927 paper prepared by Labour's imperial advisory committee offered a ringing endorsement of the mandates system. While admitting that the system could be faulted on practical grounds, the paper insisted nonetheless that 'in the main it is based on right principles. It represents the idea that the administration of tropical dependencies, before they reach the stage of self-government, is a <u>trust</u>; and, moreover, that it is a matter of <u>international</u> concern, and should not be left solely to the field of national exploitation.'[122] Although self-government remained the ostensible goal, in reality Labour evinced decreasing interest in it. At the British Commonwealth Labour conference in January 1928, Henry Snell, a future Labour Under-Secretary of State for India, announced that 'self-government [for India] could not be thrown at a people.' The reluctance of Labour participants to reaffirm their commitment to India's self-government prompted the Indian delegation to withdraw from the conference. Several months later, in response to ILP demands that Labour cooperate more closely with Indian nationalists, MacDonald warned Labour's annual conference against haste. Labour's 'responsibility', he lectured, 'was to see to it that India was going to be launched, properly launched, honestly and honourably launched on a sea where it was going to be captain of its ship'—a responsibility that ultimately lay with the British and not the Indians.[123]

Two related reasons explain Labour's declining interest in self-government. One reason concerned Labour's proximity to power during 1927–1928. With general elections in Britain looming, Labour leaders and officials were convinced that the party must show itself to be responsible, which meant accepting the reality of empire and the need for effective administration. Now was not the time for

[121] IISH, SAI, 57, ILP, 'The Colonial Problem'; and John Paton, *Left Turn: The Autobiography of John Paton* (London), 314–15.

[122] LHASC, LPA, ACImQ, memoranda: 1924–1931, 'Mandates', no. 55, November 1927. Emphasis in original.

[123] Labour Party, *Report of the 28th Annual Conference... October 1st to 5th, 1928* (London, 1928), 208–9, 174.

'radical' proposals, the parliamentary party warned, but for caution when it came to recognizing 'rights of self-government'.[124] The second reason concerned Labour's growing sensitivity to the dangers of white minority rule in many colonies, a sensitivity heightened by political developments in South Africa. A Labour government, another paper asserted, 'will take no steps towards so-called "responsible" government by European minorities in backward portions of the Empire'. Steps towards self-government being too dangerous, the alternative was trusteeship. As the paper concluded, the Labour Party 'frankly accepts for the whole of the backward races in the Empire, the principle underlying the Mandate system established by the League of Nations'. Tellingly, the lengthy memorandum that Labour submitted to the International in 1928 made almost no mention of self-government.[125]

Another current of Labour thinking on empire fed into the renewed support for the trusteeship framework: the rise of economic protectionism. The second half of the 1920s witnessed a growing clamour in Britain (and elsewhere) for restrictions on international trade, including calls for imperial economic blocs—calls that would culminate in 1931 with the Conservative government's introduction of imperial preference.[126] In reaction to this clamour, Labour leaders not only defended free trade in general but also opposed imperial protection in particular. European socialists, a Labour paper maintained, must affirm their 'opposition to all protectionist measures in the colonies. Such protection is against the interests of the colonies themselves and is a menace to the peaceful economic international development of the world.'[127] Indeed, Labour hoped to mobilize the International behind its anti-protectionist position at home by persuading the upcoming LSI congress to issue a forceful statement in favour of the open door in the colonial world. On this issue, Labour and the ILP shared some common ground as the ILP's memorandum mentioned above condemned the 'monopolistic control of trade or of sources of raw materials' as the leading cause of international rivalry and war. That said, whereas the ILP's opposition to protectionism was integrated into a larger critique of economic imperialism, hence its support for an international economic authority capable of counteracting the immense political-economic disparities between the developed and underdeveloped worlds, Labour focused more on the economic and political benefits of unrestricted trade.[128] But the more pertinent point is that fears of economic protectionism reinforced the need for trusteeship,

---

[124] See Labour Party, Executive Committee of the Parliamentary party, minutes, fiche 175, 'Memorandum on the Egyptian Situation', undated but 1928.

[125] Ibid., 'Points which Should be Made Clear…on Behalf of the Labour Party, in the Event of Its Forming a Government', no. 62A, June 1928; and 'The Colonial Problem', August 1928.

[126] On this issue, see Robert W.D. Boyce, *British Capitalism at the Crossroads, 1919–1932: A Study in Politics, Economics, and International Relations* (Cambridge, 1987), 83–9, 197–9, 257–68; and Clavin, *Securing the World Economy*, 39–46.

[127] LHASC, LPA, ACImQ, memoranda: 1924–1931, 'Profits of Economic Imperialism', no. 59, February 1928; also see LPA, LSI, minutes, 1921–1937, Labour, 'Draft Memorandum on Economic Tendencies Capable of Affecting the Peace of the World', March 1927.

[128] See IISH, SAI, 1702, Brockway to Adler, 3 June 1927, and attached ILP memorandum: 'The Labour Party Memorandum on the Economic Tendencies Capable of Affecting the Peace of the World'.

as neither the imperial powers if left alone, nor the colonies (if independent), could be trusted to resist the appeals of economic nationalism.

It is worth noting that considerable wishful thinking underpinned Labour's renewed embrace of trusteeship. A book published in 1928 by Woolf, a prominent ACImQ member, provides an interesting example. Like many European socialists, Woolf felt sympathy for anti-colonial movements abroad whose quest for independence could not be indefinitely denied; at the same time, he feared that anti-colonialism was feeding a 'crude nationalism' evident in racist/ethnic rivalry. If white minority rule constituted one danger, another consisted of majority rule by an ethnic group at the expense of minority ethnic groups—a concern that would resurface after 1945 in the context of decolonization. For now, Woolf argued that colonies needed guidance from Europeans during the transition 'from subjection or control to complete independence'; hence his enthusiasm for trusteeship. The problem, as Woolf and many others admitted, was that trusteeship, in the form of the mandates system, was ineffective because the mandatory powers were too self-interested to make native interests the priority. Trusteeship, in short, had been discredited by its 'dishonest application'. Woolf's response was to call for a revamped mandates system administered by a strengthened League of Nations 'free from the taint and suspicion of imperialism' and able to instruct colonies in the 'secrets of stable government, honest administration, and sound finance'.[129] Glaringly absent from Woolf's scheme, however, was any assessment of his proposal's feasibility, especially in terms of its appeal either to anti-colonialists or to the imperial powers. In the absence of a stronger League, Woolf's championing of trusteeship amounted to acquiescence in the status quo.

Other socialist parties proved no more willing than Labour to subject trusteeship to rigorous scrutiny. Within the SPD, some voices, particularly those associated with the *Sozialistische Monatshefte*, a journal on the party's right, claimed that Germany and Europe required colonies for economic reasons and presented a joint imperial project as a means of building a united Europe. Overall, however, Hermann Müller's argument that Germany had more to gain politically and economically by not pursuing colonies (or a colonial mandate) carried more weight among German socialists.[130] Reflecting this fact, the party's official response to Vliegen's draft statement made no mention of Germany's right to colonies, offering instead an endorsement of trusteeship as the only realistic option for the foreseeable future. While recognizing 'self-government' to be the eventual goal, the response dismissed it as 'useless' in practice because, with the exception of India, 95 per cent of 'colonial territories, protectorates and mandates' supposedly lacked the necessary 'civilizational level'. Self-government for these colonies risked creating a 'new slavery' in the form of a minority dictatorship (of European settlers) or of a majority dictatorship

---

[129] Woolf, *Imperialism and Civilization* (New York, 1928), 92–3, 164–6, 178–9.

[130] Max Cohen, 'Kolonialwirtschaft ist notwendig', *Sozialistische Monatshefte*, 17 December 1928, 1042–6; also see Michael Schubert, *Der schwarze Fremde: Das Bild des Schwarzafrikaners in der parlamentarischen und publizistischen Kolonialdiskussion in Deutschland von den 1870er bis in die 1930er Jahre* (Stuttgart, 2003), 349–50. For Müller, see 'Brauchen wir Kolonien? Eine alte Umfrage und eine treffende Antwort', *Vorwärts*, no. 365, 4 August 1928, 2.

(of natives). To avoid one or the other was the task of the League's mandates system, even if trusteeship had admittedly done little thus far to prevent colonial exploitation. In the end, the SPD took refuge in the vague hope that the collective weight of international socialism would somehow induce the imperial powers to apply the trusteeship framework in the best interests of colonial peoples.[131]

If Germany's lack of overseas colonies arguably made the SPD a special case, other parties from countries possessing colonies also endorsed the colonial commission's preliminary report. The Dutch party offered its wholehearted support, which is perhaps not surprising given that Vliegen was Dutch. In a memorandum submitted to the International, the Dutch party alleged that its policy remained that outlined before 1914 by Hubert van Kol; as for anti-colonial movements, Dutch socialists simply attributed demands for immediate independence to communist influence.[132] Vliegen's report did stir some opposition from Belgian socialists, with Emile Vandervelde dismissing colonial mandates as a 'hypocrisy behind which lurked permanent occupation'. In the end, however, the Belgian party approved the preliminary report because it dealt with 'grand principles' that involved no concrete commitments.[133]

The SFIO was the one major socialist party that might have challenged Vliegen's preliminary report. After all, Zyromski, among others, called for a more active anti-colonialist policy on the International's part. In a 1928 article in the Austrian socialist newspaper *Der Kampf*, the *Bataille socialiste* leader hinted at his dissatisfaction with the International's emphasis on trusteeship. While admitting that an 'immediate evacuation' of colonies might be problematic in some cases, he maintained that the principle of self-determination should not be sacrificed on the altar of so-called economic or political realities. All socialists, he continued, must work for 'the development as rapidly as possible of the right possessed by all colonial peoples to national freedom'. Aware of the lack of consensus on colonial policy, Léon Blum, the SFIO's parliamentary leader, had earlier spoken of the need for a thorough debate on colonial policy.[134] Yet such a debate never took place. One reason it did not was that for much of 1928 French socialists were preoccupied with other matters: at home there was the perennial question of the SFIO's participation in government; and abroad there was the emerging issue of disarmament—an issue that increasingly preoccupied Zyromski. But anti-communism was also a factor. In reaction to communist denunciations of trusteeship, leading French socialists swallowed their doubts and rallied to the banner of trusteeship. This dynamic is clear with Jean Longuet, a prominent member of the SFIO's left who had

---

[131] 'Unterworfene Völker: Zur Dikussion des Kolonialproblems auf dem kommenden Kongreß der Internationale', *Vorwärts*, no. 299, 27 June 1928, 2.

[132] IISH, SAI, 785, 'Historische Uebersicht über die Tätigkeit der S.D.A.P. auf dem Gebiete der Kolonialprobleme', Cramer, 11 July 1927; and 'Memorandum der holländischen sozialdemokratischen Arbeiterpartei (Juli 1927 und May 1928)', reproduced in *Dritter Kongreß der Sozialistischen Arbeiter-Internationale*, V, 148.

[133] AMSAB, POB, 'Séance du Conseil Général du 29-5-1928', Vandervelde; and 'Séance du Conseil Général du 6-6-1928', Piérard.

[134] Zyromski, 'Sozialismus und Kolonialpolitik', *Der Kampf*, vol. 12, no. 8/9, Aug–Sept 1928, 413–14; and Blum, 'Notre future programme', *Le Populaire de Paris*, 30 November 1927, 1.

numerous contacts with anti-colonial activists in Paris. Defending the assumption, essential to trusteeship, that societies could be situated on a civilizational scale, Longuet insisted that only 'Bolshevism's unbelievably bad faith and prodigious demagoguery' could suggest otherwise. Similarly, Henry Fontanier, who (together with Longuet) would sit on the ad hoc colonial commission created at the LSI's Brussels congress, framed the International's embrace of trusteeship as a response to communist attacks. Unlike the communists, Fontanier wrote, socialism 'takes colonialism as it exists rather than issuing declamations without effect... [socialism] examines and studies this complex and variegated problem and offers appropriate solutions.'[135]

In the absence of a thorough debate on colonial policy, what discussion occurred was once again dominated by socialists from the empire, a group that tended to champion colonialism. The principal speakers on the 'colonial problem' at the SFIO's national council meeting in July 1928 all came from North Africa and all criticized the SFIO (and the International) for its supposed anti-colonialism. A delegate from Tunisia thus regretted the 'negative attitude' of European socialists towards colonialism while another from Algeria asserted that the International's position revealed 'a complete ignorance of the life of the native'. In response, Fontanier sought to defend an activist interpretation of the trusteeship framework, asserting that '[w]e possess the means to protect the natives; it is just a matter of using them [these means]'; the International, he added, must take 'firm decisions' on the score. But few if any participants appeared willing to give the SFIO's delegation to the upcoming LSI congress a mandate to push for Fontanier's more activist interpretation. As a result, Longuet merely asked the national council to approve Vliegen's preliminary report, which it promptly did. No doubt the report's vague nature allowed it to satisfy all concerned.[136]

THE LSI'S BRUSSELS CONGRESS, AUGUST 1928

In preparation for the International's 1928 congress, Vliegen's colonial commission drafted a resolution on colonial policy that amounted to an extended version of its preliminary report. The resolution thus separated 'colonial races' along civilizational lines: for those that 'have under foreign rule overcome their technical and political backwardness to a large extent', it envisaged an immediate end to 'foreign domination' as there was little risk of 'their falling back from the capitalistic phase into a more ancient and primitive phase'; for those that remained 'at a very primitive level' and completely dependent 'upon the dominant foreign regime', it recommended the continuation of the 'colonial state' for otherwise the native peoples would be at the mercy of a 'minority of white settlers or... native despotism'. To curb

---

[135] Longuet, 'Le congrès international de Bruxelles', *Nouvelle revue socialiste*, no. 25, 1 August–1 October 1928, 16; and Fontanier, 'Socialistes impérialistes', *Le Populaire de Paris*, 16 August 1928, 1–2.
[136] 'Les derniers débats du Conseil National', *Le Populaire de Paris*, 16 July 1928, 2.

capitalist abuses and to protect native peoples, the colonial state would be administered according to trusteeship principles (which included the open door) with the imperial powers held accountable by a strengthened League of Nations mandate system that would be applied to all colonial possessions. While the resolution proclaimed the International's support for 'the emancipation of subject peoples', the translation of this rather generic statement into something more tangible was left to the discretion of its member parties.[137]

Although not the sole issue on the agenda, colonial policy appeared for the first time to occupy a prominent place at an LSI congress. As part of the event, the Belgian party organized a 'Day of Oppressed Peoples' to highlight the realities of political and economic oppression within and beyond Europe. Every congress delegate, moreover, received a hefty file of documents on colonial policy, which one participant enthused 'made an interesting and most stimulating study'.[138] Yet appearances notwithstanding, almost all the discussion on colonialism took place within the confines of the multi-party committee appointed at the congress. In his memoirs, the ILP's John Paton recounted how he tried to prod the committee, much to the annoyance of its Labour members, to speak of 'self-determination' rather than the more ambiguous 'self-government'. The committee's majority, however, succeeded in keeping attention focused on Vliegen's proposed resolution, thereby avoiding what another member referred to as the danger of a 'boundless colonial discussion'.[139] As a result, the final resolution differed little from the original. In presenting the resolution to the congress, Sidney Oliver, a Labour member, described it as 'a practical programme of progressive reform . . . and we regard this as a sort of textbook or handbook which should be the basis of work for Socialist Labour Parties in all countries.' Strangely, the only dissenting voice came from the Dutch socialist Charles Cramer, who pleaded with European socialists to cooperate actively with anti-colonial movements, and even suggested working with a new version of the League Against Imperialism shorn of its communist influence. But Cramer's plea, which contradicted the position of his own party, received no backing from the other delegates who approved unanimously the committee's resolution.[140]

Assessments of the Brussels congress varied. Evidently satisfied with the result, William Gillies, Labour's international secretary, pressed for the rapid publication of the colonial resolution in order to distribute it to party militants.[141] The ILP, by contrast, was disappointed. At the ILP's annual congress in spring 1929, Robert Bridgeman, a future LAI chairman, submitted a motion regretting the International's colonial resolution which, it archly noted, was the work of a commission 'none of

[137] IISH, SAI, 57, 'Motion of the Colonial Commission', undated.

[138] H.N. Brailsford, 'At Brussels', *The New Leader*, 17 August 1928, 6.

[139] Paton, *Left Turn*, 314–15; and Jürgen Rojahn, ed., *Wilhelm Dittmann. Erinnerungen* III (Frankfurt, 1995), 942.

[140] *Dritter Kongreß der Sozialistischen Arbeiter-Internationale*, VI, 98–110 and IX, 12–20. For the Dutch party, see Fritjof Tichelman, 'Socialist "internationalism" and the Colonial World. Practical Colonial Policies of Social Democracy in Western Europe before 1940 with Particular Reference to the Dutch SDAP' in Holthoon and Linden, eds., *Internationalism in the Labour Movement* I, 101–6.

[141] IISH, SAI, 1677, Gillies (Labour) to Adler, 17 August 1928.

the members of which belonged to the subject races, or, indeed, to any extra-European country'. The International's colonial policy was deemed 'un-Socialist' because it denied the inhabitants of some colonies 'any possibility of having self-determination'. Although the motion failed to pass, this failure was partly due to a concern that it would be construed as a criticism of the ILP delegation to the Brussels congress.[142] On the Continent, meanwhile, several German socialists were also wary. In reporting on the LSI congress, Arthur Crispien rehearsed terminology from pre-1914 socialist debates, warning the SPD against the 'eventual recrudescence of a [socialist] colonial policy'. The problem, as Crispien no doubt understood, was that trusteeship implied an acceptance of colonialism—and thus of a socialist policy.[143]

In reality, the International's endorsement of trusteeship committed European socialists to very little, aside from criticizing the excesses of colonialism. And this undoubtedly helps to explain why the resolution received the unanimous approval of delegates at the Brussels congress. But however open-ended it might have been, the resolution is noteworthy for what it did not contain. There was little sign of a systematic critique of colonialism of the kind that Kautsky offered before 1914 and that socialists such as Zyromski restated during the mid-1920s. The vision of a world divided into developed and underdeveloped regions, with its implicit (and sometimes explicit) call for a new international economic order, receded before the promotion of the open door in the colonies, a demand far more limited in scope and more centred on the interests of the imperial powers. As a German critic lamented, in this sense the International's 1907 Stuttgart resolution was 'clearer, more unequivocal [and] less vague' than its 1928 counterpart.[144] Equally significant, it contained no clear-cut appeal to cooperate actively with anti-colonial movements in order to accelerate the end of imperial rule. Instead, European socialists were invited to help develop the 'industrial labour movement' in the colonial world. Aside from its questionable pertinence for societies that were often overwhelmingly rural, this recommendation clashed with the reality of limited resources. An internal LSI memorandum in 1929, for example, admitted that the International lacked the financial means to aid emerging labour movements in Asia, a weakness judged particularly regrettable in light of the Komintern's greater resources. 'We must satisfy ourselves', it resignedly declared, 'with the thought that the Labour Movement in these distant countries must proceed <u>out of its force</u> to clarity on its tasks...' The interwar International, in short, would remain a predominately European and Eurocentric organization.[145]

---

[142] ILP, *The Report of the Annual Conference...March–April, 1929* (London, 1929), 63–4.
[143] SPD, *Protokoll Sozialdemokratischer Parteitag Magdeburg 1929 vom 26. bis 31 Mai*, 216–17.
[144] G. Englebert Graf, *Die Aufgaben der Sozialistischen Arbeiterinternationale in der Weltpolitik* (Leipzig, n.d.), 21–2.
[145] BA-SAPMO, II. Internationale, RY 14 I 6/2/31, 'Beziehungen zu aussereuropäischen Arbeiterparteien', July 1929. Emphasis in original.

EUROPEAN SOCIALISTS AND COLONIAL APPEASEMENT

The LSI's 1928 congress represented the high point of interest in colonialism among European socialists. Even at Brussels, colonial policy competed fiercely with other issues for attention, most notably disarmament. Afterwards, colonialism all but disappeared as European socialists became increasingly preoccupied with the deepening global economic crisis and then with the dual threat of fascism and war. Significantly, the International's colonial commission ceased to function, and efforts in 1930 to revive it met with limited success: several parties from countries without colonies politely declined to appoint a member on the grounds that the issue did not concern them.[146] But the inattention of European socialists extended to parties from countries with colonies. When a new colonial commission was finally constituted in 1931, Charles Cramer, the Dutch socialist who had pleaded in Brussels for a policy of active support for anti-colonial movements, proposed an ambitious programme. Insisting that the International could not adopt a 'hesitant attitude' towards the 'struggle of the coloured races against colonial domination', Cramer envisaged the commission as an 'action committee' charged with identifying concrete means of aiding the struggle as part of a larger effort to transform 'capitalist society into a world socialist community'. Despite Cramer's enthusiasm, it is unclear whether the colonial commission convened at all after 1932. In any case, colonial policy never once reappeared on the agenda of an international socialist gathering.[147]

For anti-colonialists, the 1930s were a period of discouragement and even despair. The ILP continued to press Labour and the International to approach the Komintern and to adopt a more forceful anti-colonial policy that included, as a 1931 memorandum affirmed, the '[c]omplete and unconditional national independence of all colonial countries'. The ILP's lack of success on both scores contributed greatly to the decision in 1932 to disaffiliate from Labour. Afterwards, the ILP's anti-colonialism became, in Stephen Howe's words, 'unequivocally revolutionary' in language; its influence on European socialists dropped accordingly.[148] Within the SFIO, meanwhile, Jean Longuet lamented the seeming indifference of French socialists to colonial matters. Writing to the SFIO's executive committee in November 1934, he warned of the 'grave consequences' attached to the growing separation between French socialists and 'the diverse national groupings in our colonies and protectorates'. The latter, Longuet explained, understood that 'we are not interested in them' and that we 'fear what we call their nationalism and [thus] we keep them at a distance'.[149]

---

[146] IISH, SAI, 790, Adler circular, 7 August 1930. For one example of refusal, see VGA, SPÖ, Sitzungsprotokolle des Parteivorstandes, 15 September 1930.

[147] IISH, SAI, 402, 'Erwägungen über die Kolonialkommission der S.A.I.', Craven, undated but July 1931; and LHASC, LPA, LSI, minutes, report on LSI Bureau and executive meetings, 21–22 February 1931.

[148] 'International Socialist Policy Basis for International Activity and Organisation', reproduced in ILP, *The Report of the Annual Conference...April, 1931* (London, 1931), 55–6; and Howe, *Anticolonialism in British Politics*, 71.

[149] OURS, Fonds Jean Longuet, 61 APO/7, Longuet to SFIO CAP, 8 November 1934.

At the same time, there were two notable exceptions to the indifference of European socialists to colonial issues during the 1930s. The French Popular Front constituted one (partial) exception: during 1936–1937 a socialist-led coalition government embarked on a well-intentioned if vague programme of colonial reform. Although the Popular Front's colonial programme is often framed in terms of failure, more recent research paints a more nuanced portrait that draws attention to its role in reshaping contemporary understandings of the relationship between French republicanism and empire, not to mention its influence on the evolution of anti-colonial activism in France and overseas. But whatever the perspective adopted, all scholars agree that the project was fundamentally reformist in orientation: consistent with the trusteeship framework, the overall aim was to 'humanize' French colonialism by reducing abuses and injustices.[150] In this sense, at least, it is possible to draw a line between the International's colonial policy as outlined at the 1928 Brussels congress and the Popular Front experience eight years later. That said, the Popular Front's experience was very much a Franco-French matter. The SFIO does not appear to have consulted with other socialist parties on colonial policy before or during the Popular Front government, nor did European socialists discuss the subject within the International.

The second and arguably more substantial exception to socialist indifference to colonialism concerned colonial appeasement. Unlike the French Popular Front experience, socialist interest in colonial appeasement was not limited to the SFIO. The scholarship on colonial appeasement focuses on intergovernmental relations and especially on British efforts to pacify Nazi Germany through the offer of colonial concessions, including the return of pre-1914 colonies in Africa. As Martin Thomas has shown, the French government was also involved not simply because France was the mandatory power in the ex-German colonies of Cameroon and Tanganyika, but also because French officials pursued their own appeasement policy.[151] The high point of intergovernmental discussions occurred during 1936–1937, after which colonial appeasement receded from view. Both London and Paris eventually realized that Nazi Germany was not sincerely interested in overseas colonies; Hitler's imperial ambitions lay in Europe.

Nevertheless, the British and French governments were not the only ones intrigued by the possibilities of colonial appeasement. So too were several prominent European socialists. Within Labour the most determined proponent of colonial appeasement was Charles Roden Buxton. Situated on the party's left, with close ties to the ILP, Buxton nevertheless regularly served as a Labour advisor on international and imperial affairs during the interwar period. Buxton also possessed numerous contacts with European socialists, which helps to explain his

---

[150] See Thomas, *The French Empire between the Wars*, 277–311; James E. Genova, 'The Empire Within: The Colonial Popular Front in France', *Alternatives: Global, Local, Political* 26 (2001), 175–209; and Tony Chafer and Amanda Sackur, eds., *French Colonial Empire and the Popular Front: Hope and Disillusion* (Houndmills, 1999).

[151] For the Anglo-German side, see Crozier, *Appeasement and Germany's Last Bid for Colonies*; for the French side, see Martin Thomas, *Britain, France and Appeasement: Anglo-French Relations in the Popular Front Era* (Oxford, 1996), 115–44.

appointment in 1930 to serve on the LSI's stillborn colonial commission.[152] Reflecting the ILP's position on colonialism, Buxton envisaged an international economic organization that would regulate relations between the developed and underdeveloped regions. But he made a name for himself as a fierce opponent of colonial exploitation. In a lengthy pamphlet in 1931, Buxton denounced the exploitation of the 'backward races' in Africa by European governments, companies, and white settler populations. As with many socialists, his solution was trusteeship embodied in a strengthened mandates system extended to all colonies. A 'very simple conception' underpinned his proposals—that of 'human equality in its broadest aspect' applied in a 'spirit of love and co-operation between human beings'. In Buxton's idealist postcolonial world, racism and inequality would no longer exist.[153] At the same time, he harboured a strong sense of injustice at Germany's treatment at the Paris peace conference, not least regarding its empire. Viewing the seizure of Germany's colonies by the victorious Allies as indefensible, Buxton was convinced that justice and wisdom dictated their eventual return. Writing to a German correspondent on the subject in 1926, Buxton argued that the return of Germany's colonies 'is just a question of time and continued efforts in writing and in other ways, in order to help the necessary education of public opinion'.[154]

If during the 1920s Buxton judged the moment not ripe for an open discussion of Germany's colonies, he had changed his mind by the 1930s. The global economic depression and the growing menace of Nazi Germany, combined with his widely shared pacifist sentiments, persuaded him that the issue was now urgent. The opportunity to express himself came with an enquiry by Labour's ACImQ into German (and Italian) claims for colonies. An unsigned preliminary paper in the autumn of 1935 kicked off the enquiry by arguing that German and Italian demands were motivated above all by economic factors, though considerations of prestige and strategy also played a part.[155] The possession of colonies, it contended, offered great powers tangible benefits in terms of access to raw materials and markets as well as in terms of fields for investment and immigration. An expanded version of the paper in July 1936 suggested as a possible solution international schemes limiting 'discriminatory or monopolistic practices' within empires. Significantly, it rejected a transfer of colonies as impractical both because the British public would likely be opposed and because the potential economic benefits to Germany would be marginal at best.[156] The latter argument became something of a maxim for Labour officials. In a statistical analysis for the enquiry, Hugh Gaitskell, an economist and future Labour leader, while accepting that colonies conferred some economic advantages to imperial powers,

[152] IISH, SAI, 789, Gillies (Labour) to Adler, 13 October 1930.
[153] Buxton, *The Race Problem in Africa* (London, 1931), 13, 47, 57.
[154] GstA, NL Heinrich Schnee, 33, Charles Roden Buxton to Mr Hauptmann, 29 December 1926.
[155] Gupta, *Imperialism and the British Labour Movement*, 237–43.
[156] LHASC, LPA, ACImQ, 'The Demand of Colonial Territories and Equality of Economic Opportunity', 159/460, October 1935; and 'The Demand of Colonial Territories and Equality of Economic Opportunity', 159/460B, July 1936.

insisted nonetheless that they were of minor importance to Britain—and thus by extension to Germany. In his recommendations, Gaitskell envisioned a revision of Britain's system of imperial preference as well as an extension of the League's mandate system to guarantee the colonial open door; but he rejected any return of Germany's colonies.[157]

Buxton, however, refused to accept this conclusion. Well aware of the disquiet provoked by the idea of transferring colonies to an avowedly racist regime such as Nazi Germany, Buxton argued in a 1936 paper that it was not necessarily true that native populations would be treated better by other European powers, Britain included; in any case, British governments in the past had transferred colonies without consulting colonial peoples. That a long-time opponent of colonial exploitation could advance such arguments is striking, and probably best explained by Buxton's horror of war. However unpalatable, colonial appeasement was preferable to another European conflict. As he asserted in the paper, 'I think we should be lacking in political realism if we did not admit that we could not resist some transfer of territory if it proved to be the only way to avert a world war.'[158]

Buxton's views carried some weight with Labour. A recognized expert on colonial matters, he had long been active in the ACImQ; during the 1930s he also chaired the ACImQ's sister body, the Advisory Committee on International Questions (ACIQ). In arguing for colonial appeasement, moreover, Buxton could draw upon the pacifist currents that ran through Labour's veins. During 1932–1935 the party was led by George Lansbury, a devout pacifist. Even after Lansbury's resignation following his defeat on the issue of economic sanctions against Fascist Italy at the 1935 party conference, pacifist sentiments continued to manifest themselves, not least within the ACIQ. But if Buxton cultivated pacifists, he was also careful to present colonial appeasement as part of a larger reorganization of the international economy—a vision long espoused by the ILP and one that resonated strongly with left-leaning socialists in other European parties. '[W]e must not forget', he remarked in his paper cited above, 'that it is not only the British Empire, but other Empires, too, that might be called upon to transfer territory—perhaps with great advantage to the Natives.' In another paper early the following year, Buxton argued that the aggressive policies of the dictator states reflected their 'economic distress' that was the product of an unfair international economic system favouring some states over others. For Buxton, colonies constituted a glaring case in point, providing advantages to Britain that aroused the understandable 'resentment and envy' of the '"dissatisfied" Powers'. The solution was a new international settlement in which colonies would benefit everyone, a solution supposedly consistent with Labour's long-standing policy as well as with trusteeship principles. The new settlement, Buxton wrote, 'can be secured by shifting international negotiation on to the plane of economic needs, including the development of the "backward regions"

---

[157] Ibid., 'Examination of the Demand for Colonial Territories and Equality of Economic Opportunity', Gaitskell, undated.

[158] MUL, Noel Edward Buxton Papers, MS 951, box 14, 'Note on Transfer of Mandated Territories', Buxton, undated.

of the world. Labour's policy of Raw Materials, Trade, and Mandates is not less, but more needed now than ever before.'[159]

During 1937–1938, intergovernmental discussions on colonial appeasement appeared to have stalled, prompting Buxton to intensify his campaign within Labour. His choice of instrument was the ACIQ. Although Buxton resigned his chairmanship of the committee in July 1937 in protest against what he perceived as the 'undue neglect… of the Party's traditional policy of economic appeasement, opposition to British imperialism, belief in the League of Nations, and the sharing of the world's resources', he continued to wield considerable influence.[160] Still more to the point, Buxton used his influence to transform the ACIQ into a voice for a policy of 'peaceful change' to the international political and economic status quo—a policy in which colonial appeasement featured prominently. In a March 1938 paper for the ACIQ Buxton maintained that Labour's support for collective security must be accompanied by an acceptance of the need for 'peaceful change', above all in the colonial domain. In addition to extending and strengthening the League's mandate system, Buxton recommended 'a re-allocation of colonial terri- tory', insisting that the 'world needs to be convinced that Great Britain recognises her own share of responsibility for the present international situation, and is pre- pared to make her own contribution'. Buxton's pressure had immediate results. The same month the ACIQ submitted a paper to Labour's executive that judged Germany's colonial demands to be 'reasonable' on political and economic grounds. While shying away from territorial transfers, the paper did propose that Britain take the initiative in 'surrendering' its colonies to the League of Nations, which in turn would ensure that all countries participated in their administration and eco- nomic development. In the ACIQ's hands, colonial appeasement became a renewed commitment to 'progressive internationalism' rather than 'bribes to others who stand for so much that we detest'.[161]

Buxton predictably viewed the ACIQ's hesitations as wrong-headed and he con- tinued to lobby for a 'scheme of colonial re-distribution'. As late as March 1939 he urged Lord Halifax, the British foreign secretary, to undertake an 'immediate British initiative in this matter'.[162] By then, however, both Buxton and the ACIQ were isolated voices within Labour. In 1937 Clement Attlee, Labour's leader, had publicly manifested some interest in the 'international control' of raw materials as an answer to Germany's colonial demands; over the course of 1938–1939, how- ever, Labour turned its back on all forms of appeasement as party leaders grew convinced that Nazi Germany's expansionist ambitions had to be resisted, if necessary

---

[159] Ibid.; and LHASC, LPA, ACIQ, memoranda 1936–1939, 'Comments on the "Memorandum on Factors in the International Situation" etc.', Buxton, no. 475, January 1937.

[160] LHASC, LPA, International Department, WG/PCE/122, Buxton to Gillies, 27 July 1937.

[161] LHASC, LPA, ACIQ, memoranda 1936–1939, 'Peaceful Change. List of Proposals', no. 489, Buxton, March 1938; and 'Proposals for Appeasement and Peaceful Change', no. 488, March 1938. Also see Labour Party, NEC minutes, fiche 236, 'International Policy and Peaceful Change', ACIQ, February 1938.

[162] MUL, Noel Edward Buxton Papers, MS 951, box 35, Buxton to Halifax, 2 March 1939; and 'A Scheme for Colonial Re-Distribution', Buxton, April 1939.

by force.[163] With the onset of another European conflict in September 1939, the question of the empire's future took a back seat to the more immediate priority of mobilizing Britain's resources behind the war effort.[164]

British socialists, however, were not the only ones attracted to the idea of colonial appeasement. During 1936–1937, Blum's Popular Front government had indicated to Berlin its willingness to consider negotiations on the colonies, but the Nazi regime did not seriously take up the French offer. The subject then lay fallow until late 1938 when French socialist interest in colonial appeasement re-emerged in the context of the deepening divide within the SFIO over France's response to Nazi Germany. While one group led by Blum advocated a policy of resistance, reluctantly accepting the possibility of war, another group, centred around Paul Faure, the party's secretary-general, rejected resistance. Recoiling at the prospect of another war, the *Faureistes* urged that everything possible be done to avoid a conflict or at least French involvement in one.[165]

Colonial appeasement became a stake in the increasingly bitter struggle between the two groups. In the wake of the Munich conference in September 1938, some *Faureistes* sought to revive US President Roosevelt's appeal to Hitler for an international conference, declaring not only that France should take the initiative but also that colonial issues—and especially the fate of the ex-German colonies that were now French mandates (Cameroon and Togo)—should figure prominently on the agenda. Much like Buxton, these socialists presented colonial appeasement as part of a larger project to reorganize the international economy. As André Philip, a future wartime resister and post-war proponent of a united Europe, explained at the SFIO's national council meeting in November 1938:

> The colonies? We cannot await for others to raise the issue. [Will we] go to war for Togo and Cameroon after having abandoned Czechoslovakia? It's psychologically impossible. The solution is to take the initiative in negotiations and to ask President Roosevelt to convoke an international conference at which all economic problems will be on the table.[166]

Soon afterwards, the SFIO's study commission on the problems of peace, created in the wake of the Munich accords, debated the issue of German colonies. While disagreeing on whether to recommend their return to Germany, the commission members all agreed that 'it is desirable to search for an international solution to the question of colonies and [that] the problem of Germany's former colonies must be the subject of a general settlement encompassing all the important questions between the great powers.'[167]

---

[163] Attlee, *The Labour Party in Perspective* (London, 1937), 244–5; and Talbot C. Imlay, *Facing the Second World War: Strategy, Politics, and Economics in Britain and France 1938–1940* (Oxford, 2003), 186–216.

[164] LHASC, LPA, ACImQ, 'Colonies in Wartime', no. 221, May 1940.

[165] Imlay, *Facing the Second World War*, 135–66; Michel Bilis, *Socialistes et pacifistes: L'intenable dilemme des socialistes français (1933–1939)* (Paris, 1979); and Michel Dreyfus, 'Pacifistes socialistes et humanistes dans les années trente', *Revue d'histoire moderne et contemporaine* 35 (1988), 452–69.

[166] 'Les débats du Conseil National', *Le Populaire de Paris*, 7 November 1938, 5.

[167] 'Compte analytique des travaux de la Commission d'étude des problèmes de la Paix et de la politique de Paix du Parti', *Le Populaire de Paris*, 29 November 1938, supplement, 3; and AN, Papiers

At the SFIO's extraordinary conference in late December 1938, called to determine the party's response to the growing threat of war, the debate centred on two motions—a *Blumiste* and a *Faureiste* one. Though by no means a central aspect of the proceedings, the colonial question did make an appearance. Predictably, Faure's motion promoted the idea of an international conference to consider all issues, including 'economic exchanges, raw materials, markets [and] colonial mandates'. In presenting Faure's motion, Félix Gouin, another future wartime resister and post-war cabinet minister, maintained that if French socialists wanted to safeguard peace they must be prepared to undertake 'a thorough enquiry into all disputed issues, [and] notably those of colonies and raw materials'. Blum's motion, by contrast, did not mention colonies; and while ostensibly supporting an international conference, it emphasized the need for France to cooperate with Britain and the Soviet Union in the construction of a solid front of opposition to Germany (and Italy). After considerable discussion, Blum's motion prevailed, receiving just over 60 per cent of the votes.[168] Afterwards, the debate on colonial appeasement petered out. The subject was not mentioned in the compromise resolution laboriously worked out by the *Blumistes* and *Faureistes* at the SFIO's congress in May 1939, even if it did call for a new international system that would ensure all peoples 'a fair distribution of resources and a fair place in a peaceful world'.[169] But if colonial appeasement receded from view it was not because of Blum's limited victory so much as Nazi Germany's evident disinterest in a negotiated settlement.

Although colonial appeasement proved to be a dead end, the interest of British and French socialists in the possibility is noteworthy for several reasons. One reason concerns the sources of socialist support, much of which came from the left.[170] To be sure, not all left socialists advocated colonial appeasement. Zyromski, for instance, rejected any idea of appeasement and allied with Blum whose reformist inclinations he had sharply criticized throughout the interwar period. Nevertheless, colonial appeasement drew on long-standing left socialist critiques of colonialism that viewed the international economic order as inherently and structurally flawed. With colonial appeasement, the primary have-nots now became the developed countries such as Nazi Germany and Fascist Italy, which did not possess an empire, rather than colonial peoples or undeveloped regions. With the onset of war, appeasement became completely discredited and some of this discredit attached itself to more systemic visions of colonialism, fostering among European socialists a renewed commitment to reformism. As we shall see in chapter 9, after 1945, this reformism initially manifested itself in calls for colonial development now shorn of any larger ambition to transform the international economic order. Another and related reason why colonial appeasement is noteworthy concerns the parochialism of European socialism. That some European socialists at least could

---

Édouard Depreux, 456/AP/4-1, 'Le rapport de la Commission pour l'étude des problèmes de la paix', 28 October 1938.

[168] 'Le Congrès national extraordinaire', *Le Populaire de Paris*, 27 December 1938, 4.

[169] 'La résolution du Congrès de Nantes', *Le Populaire de Paris*, 1 June 1939, 1.

[170] But see Benjamin Stora, 'La gauche socialiste, révolutionnaire, et la question du Maghreb, au moment du Front Populaire', *Revue française d'histoire d'outre-mer* 70 (1983), 70–3.

conceive of the Dictator states as have-nots underscores the Eurocentrism of much of interwar socialist thinking on colonialism. Individual exceptions aside, European socialist parties as a whole had very little contact with people from the colonial world and what contact there was, as in the SFIO's case, was often with the representatives of European settler communities. The empire, consequently, remained an abstract concept for many socialists, one that could be adapted and even contorted to meet political needs at home.

A final reason concerns the open-ended nature of trusteeship. That some European socialists believed it possible to reconcile colonial appeasement with trusteeship in the form of an expanded mandates system that would include Nazi Germany suggests that trusteeship was flexible enough to mean just about anything. A striking characteristic of socialist thinking on trusteeship, indeed, was its vagueness. This vagueness stemmed partly from the abstract nature of socialist discussions on colonialism that were all too often detached from colonial realities—a detachment both reflected in and reinforced by the relative absence of colonial interlocutors. But this vagueness was also due to the fact that socialists defined trusteeship less in terms of detailed policies and more in terms of opposition to what critics (socialist and communist) identified as an alternative: that of cooperating with anti-colonial movements in the colonies to bring about a rapid end to colonial rule. But whatever the reasons for this vagueness, in endorsing the trusteeship framework, interwar European socialists effectively abandoned the task of forging a collective and concrete position on colonialism. This left them ill-prepared to confront the tumultuous developments in the colonial world after 1945.

Entr'acte

Socialist Internationalism during the 1930s

In the summer of 1939, with Europe poised on the precipice of another war, Friedrich Adler, the LSI's secretary, circulated an anguished memorandum to socialist parties. Never before, he asserted, had the International been so removed from the hopes and ideals of socialists. Emphasizing the 'autonomist' and 'isolationist' tendencies within the LSI, Adler blamed the current predicament on the decline in the 'international *spirit*' within and between socialist parties. Soon afterwards, in a memorandum inspired (and most likely written) by Adler, exiled Austrian socialists spoke of the 'nationalization' of European socialism manifest in the 'absolute isolation of each [socialist] party in the specific needs of its own country'. What Adler and his Austrian comrades lamented above all was the breakdown in the practice of socialist internationalism—in the collective effort of European socialists to forge a common response to pressing issues, not least the surging threat of a new war. This breakdown, moreover, did not begin in 1939 but in 1933 with the Nazi seizure of power, if not earlier. For European socialists, the second memorandum argued, the 1930s as a whole were characterized by the failure to devise 'a shared international strategy, a shared international will in the struggle against fascism'. As a result, it concluded forlornly, 'the International no longer exists'.[1]

Much of the existing scholarship on European socialism during the 1930s directly or indirectly reflects contemporary assessments concerning its nationalization. There are thus numerous studies of individual socialist parties as well as biographies of prominent socialists.[2] There is, by contrast, very little work on the relations between socialist parties, aside from the rare institutional histories of

---

[1] Both memoranda are reproduced in Herbert Steiner, 'L'Internationale socialiste à la veille de la Seconde Guerre mondiale, juillet-août 1939: Documents de Friedrich Adler', *Mouvement social* 58 (1967), 95–112.

[2] For the SFIO see Graham, *Choice and Democratic Order*; Nathanael Greene, *Crisis and Decline: The French Socialist Party in the Popular Front Era* (Ithaca, NY, 1969); and Serge Berstein, *Léon Blum* (Paris, 2006); for Labour, see Rhiannon Vickers, *The Labour Party and the World: The Evolution of Labour's Foreign Policy, 1900–51* (Manchester, 2004); Richard Toye, *The Labour Party and the Planned Economy, 1931–1951* (Woodbridge, 2003); and Ben Pimlott, *Labour and the Left in the 1930s* (Cambridge, 1977); and for the SPD, see Michael Schneider, *Unterm Hakenkreuz: Arbeiter und Arbeitsbewegung 1933 bis 1939* (Berlin, 1999); Werner Röder, *Die deutsche sozialistischen Exilgruppen in Großbritannien 1940–1945: ein Beitrag zur Geschichte des Widerstandes gegen den Nationalsozialismus* (Bonn, 1973); and Stefan Appeluis, *Heine: die SPD und der lange Weg zur Macht* (Essen, 1999).

the International.[3] To be sure, exceptions do exist. Michel Dreyfus and Willi Buschak have examined the transnational activities of left socialists, many of whom were self-consciously internationalist. But while some of these socialist groupings formed fractions within the mainstream socialist parties, others operated outside of the latter; no less importantly, transnational left socialism was largely a marginal phenomenon, as its members found themselves squeezed between the two dominant leftist tendencies during the 1930s: reformist socialism and Soviet-dominated communism.[4] Another notable exception is Gerd-Rainer Horn's comparative examination of the response of various European socialist parties to fascism during the mid-1930s. But even Horn accepts that by mid-decade, 'European social democracy was an increasingly compartmentalized agglomeration of largely independent national parties.'[5]

The approach adopted in the previous (and in subsequent) chapters is to contrast the scholarly focus on individual socialist parties with an emphasis on the practice of socialist internationalism—and thus on the international dimension of European socialism. This entr'acte, however, eschews such an approach, which explains why it is not a chapter. In truth, the 1930s were a nadir for socialist internationalism. For various reasons, each of the three principal parties (the SFIO, the SPD, and Labour) turned inwards, dealing with pressing international (and national) issues increasingly on its own rather than collectively. If signs of this involution or nationalization of socialist internationalism can be detected towards the end of the 1920s, for example, on the issue of disarmament, the decisive factor was the growing fascist threat at home and abroad from 1933 onwards. After 1918, socialist internationalism could flourish in a post-war context in which the emphasis was on reconstructing and recasting national and international politics; but it could not during the 1930s in a situation marked by the growing threat of another European war. That said, and however dismal the situation appeared to be by 1939, European socialists never completely abandoned socialist internationalism. Even at the lowest point something remained of the collective commitment to its practice.

RESPONSES TO FASCISM

European socialists gathered in Paris in August 1933 to discuss what Adler described as the 'new situation' created by the Nazi seizure of power in Germany and by the SPD's proscription. In what proved to be the LSI's last congress, the delegates appeared divided on the national versus international orientation of

---

[3] For institutional histories, see Julius Braunthal, *History of the International* vol. II (London, 1967); and Kowalski et al., *Geschichte der Sozialistischen Arbeiter-Internationale*.

[4] Willy Buschak, *Das Londoner Büro: Europäische Linkssozialisten in der Zwischenkriegszeit* (Amsterdam, 1985); and Michel Dreyfus, 'Bureau de Paris et bureau de Londres: le socialisme de gauche en Europe entre les deux guerres', *Mouvement social* 112 (1980), 25–55.

[5] Horn, *European Socialists Respond to Fascism: Ideology, Activism and Contingency in the 1930s* (New York, 1996), 134. Also see Rapone, *La Socialdemocrazia Europea tra le Due Guerre*, which unfortunately ends in 1936; and Bruno Groppo, 'Die gelähmte Internationale: Zur politischen Entwicklung der sozialistischen Parteien in Europa nach 1933', *Geschichte und Gesellschaft* 17 (1991), 220–41.

European socialism and of socialist internationalism—a division that cut across political parties. Opening the proceedings, Adler insisted that a renewed commitment to internationalism was required: 'we need to build the International front [against fascism] on a more solid basis than before.' Léon Blum echoed Adler, arguing that 'all our [collective] efforts must be devoted to giving the International an ever more solid consistence'; similarly, the Belgian socialist Emile Vandervelde warned against a 'policy of national socialism' on the part of individual parties. The appeal to internationalism, however, was by no means unanimous. The SFIO's Pierre Renaudel asserted that socialism could not ignore the dominating reality of the nation, adding that socialists should seek 'national solutions' to fascism. Another French socialist, Adrien Marquet, who along with Renaudel would soon leave the SFIO to found a neo-socialist party, argued that socialism must be not only more active and even aggressive in its fight against fascism, but also more nationalist. Indeed, Marquet presented an accent on the nation—'the result of many centuries of history'—as the socialist answer to the Nazis' obsession with race. But it was Hugh Dalton, a Labour delegate, who perhaps best expressed the sentiments of the national-centred group in openly questioning the right of any party to intervene in the policymaking of other parties:

> My point is this; each of the Socialist parties... must judge of their own conditions in the light of the possibilities which present themselves in each country to promote Socialism and international peace, and I shall say no word which would seem to be in any way an interference in the decisions of each of those parties as to the right course to pursue to strengthen democracy, Socialism and international peace.

If strictly followed by all the parties, this principle of self-denial would spell the end of the practice of socialist internationalism.[6]

Rather than adopt a clear-cut position on the nature of socialist internationalism, the delegates preferred to sidestep the question, issuing a vague resolution that urged the 'working class' in general to 'reinforce its struggle against capitalism, against fascism and against war'.[7] Yet this vagueness notwithstanding, the dominant tendency within the International was towards autonomous decision-making by each member party. This tendency manifested itself most clearly on the contested issue of relations with the Komintern. Earlier, in March 1933, the LSI's executive had declared that any negotiations with the Communist International must take place at an official level between the two organizations and must receive the unanimous approval of all member parties—conditions that effectively ruled out any negotiations given the disagreements within and between socialist parties on the subject. Faced with the resistance of several parties to any cooperation with communists, the LSI's congress in August 1933 explicitly rejected '[communist] maneuvers for a united front'. This common position, however, came under

---

[6] *Protokolle. Internationale Konferenz der Sozialistischen Arbeiter-Internationale. Paris, Maison de la Mutualité, 21.–25. August 1933* (Glashütten im Taunus, 1976), Adler, 3–4; Blum, 160; Vandervelde, 21; Renaudel, 71–4; Marquet, 250–1; and Dalton, 80.

[7] Ibid., 'La stratégie et la tactique du mouvement ouvrier international dans une époque de réaction fasciste', 311–16.

increasing pressure not only from the Komintern, which manifested a public interest in a united front, but also from the SFIO, many of whose members sought to combine in a united (or popular) front all the anti-fascist forces at home and abroad. The result was the decision of the LSI's executive in November 1934 to leave the issue of cooperation with the communists to the discretion of each party.[8]

Across much of Western Europe over the next two years, the political momentum pointed towards united fronts of all left forces to combat the combined menace of economic depression and fascism at home and abroad. With the Komintern's abandonment of its class versus class strategy that equated socialists with fascists, communist parties in several countries became active proponents of such fronts. Meanwhile, the leadership of socialist parties faced mounting calls from socialist groups and militants to cooperate with communists and other non-socialists. This activity resulted most spectacularly in the election victory of Popular Front coalitions in Spain in February 1936 and in France in May 1936, events that the European left endowed with considerable hope and significance. Several prominent scholars have characterized these developments as an extended moment of socialist renewal. Under the anti-fascist banner, the European left in general and European socialists in particular reconfigured themselves around a commitment to democracy, economic planning, cultural flourishing, social justice, and international peace. Just as importantly, this renewal involved not simply party leaders but also encompassed an important grass-roots element as socialists militated in multiple locales. Indeed, what emerges from this scholarship is a popular and transnational movement that imposed itself on socialist parties and, in so doing, offered a potential alternative to the practice of socialist internationalism dominated by party leaders and officials.[9]

The high point of this movement came with the Spanish Civil War, triggered in the summer of 1936 by a military revolt against the legally established government in Madrid. The embattled Republic's appeal to solidarity reverberated powerfully among many European socialists. The result was a major mobilization of socialist (and non-socialist) support, three aspects of which are especially noteworthy. One concerns its centre of gravity: generally speaking, the Spanish Republican cause found its most committed advocates on the left of European socialism. Indeed, the civil war helped to consolidate the fledgling organization of leftist parties, groups, and factions, among them the Independent Labour Party, the SFIO's *Gauche révolutionnaire*, and a breakaway group from the SPD (the *Sozialistische Arbeiterpartei Deutschland*/SAPD), which sought to form a parallel socialist revolutionary International in a reprise of the Vienna Union created in 1921. This parallel International, however, remained more an ideal than a reality, partly because of the

---

[8] For LSI–Komintern relations, see Kowalski et al., *Geschichte der Sozialistischen Arbeiter-Internationale*, 178–249; and Ursula Langkau-Alex, 'Jalons pour une histoire des Internationales socialistes et l'exil dans l'entre-deux-guerres', *Matériaux pour l'histoire de notre temps* 84 (2006), 33–4. For the debates within the LSI on the issue, see the file in IISH, SAI, 438.

[9] Horn, *European Socialists Respond to Fascism*; and Eley, *Forging Democracy*, 263–8. For the cultural aspects, see Pascal Orly, *La belle illusion: culture et politique sous le signe du Front Populaire* (Paris, 1994).

marginality of many of its member groups and partly because of tensions within and between groups over issues of peace, war, and revolution.[10] The second noteworthy aspect consists of the prominent role played by militants within the mainstream European parties—Labour, the SFIO, the Belgian party (POB), etc. Working with non-socialists (as well as communists), these militants supplied the Spanish government not only with volunteers and non-military aid, but also with clandestine military material—often against the express instructions of their party leadership. Scholars have begun to research this well-organized effort, but far more work is needed to understand the dynamics of what can be seen as a popular, bottom-up practice of socialist internationalism as opposed to the top-down one that is the subject of this book.[11]

The third and final aspect concerns the missing element in this socialist mobilization on behalf of the Spanish Republic: the active participation of party leaders. Taken as a whole, the European socialist leadership refused to endorse the legitimate appeal of the Spanish Republican government for military intervention on its side. In the case of France, the Popular Front government under Léon Blum reluctantly opted to pursue a policy of non-intervention both because it feared the prospect of a possible European war and because intervention risked destroying the fragile governing coalition—and thereby jeopardizing its recently won advances in the domestic social and economic realms. Although in Britain Labour was in opposition, its leaders approved of Blum's decision due partly to a similar fear of triggering a European war and partly, as Tom Buchanan has argued, to the determination to maintain control over what they perceived as undisciplined elements within the labour movement. From the perspective of party leaders, non-military aid was acceptable and even welcome, but anything more was dangerous.[12]

In the end, the experience of the Spanish Civil War probably did more to undermine than to solidify what can be called the process of socialist renewal from below through anti-fascism. The cautious response of the SFIO and Labour leaders certainly frustrated numerous militants, but this frustration alone could not provide an enduring basis for grass-roots unity. One reason it could not do so was because the nature of the Spanish Republic's war effort—and especially the growing communist influence on and within it—provoked bitter tensions across the European left. But another reason was that the Spanish Civil War stirred anew old and divisive debates among socialists over pacifism. Military aid to the Spanish Republic might be necessary to defeat fascism in Spain, but if such aid risked setting off a European war then some socialists judged the price to be too high. Behind such calculations, moreover, lurked an even more

[10] See Buschak, *Das Londoner Büro*; and Michel Dreyfus, 'L'Internationale ouvrière socialiste, le bureau de Londres et la guerre civile d'Espagne' in Frits van Holthoon and Marcel van der Linden, eds., *Internationalism in the Labour Movement, 1830–1940* vol. I (Leiden, 1988), 355–68.

[11] For a valuable start, see Nicolas Lépine, 'Le socialisme international et la Guerre Civile espagnole', PhD dissertation, Université Laval, 2013; and Tom Buchanan, *Britain and the Spanish Civil War* (Cambridge, 1997).

[12] Tom Buchanan, *The Spanish Civil War and the British Labour Movement* (Cambridge, 1991). Also see, Groppo, 'Die gelähmte Internationale', 232.

contentious (and increasingly pressing) question: should the European democracies oppose the expansionist ambitions of the fascist states, if necessary by war? On this question the divisions ran deep within and between the principal socialist parties.

But the effects of the Spanish Civil War aside, the process of socialist renewal from below possessed important limits. Perhaps the most pertinent one for this study was its emphasis on national politics—on reforming reigning models of state–economy and state–society relations. A prominent example is the 1936 Matignon accords in which Blum's government brokered an agreement between French employers and trade unionists that accorded important material gains (and political influence) to the latter. To be sure, socialists in one country closely watched and drew inspiration from developments in other countries in what Horn identifies as a dynamic of 'ongoing cross-fertilization between social democratic movements faced with a common threat'. Nevertheless, there was almost no formal cooperation or even consultation between socialist parties on these domestic reform programmes, and this is why they are best studied in a comparative rather than interactive framework.[13] Recently, Jens Späth has drawn attention to a more informal network of European socialists that emerged after 1933, many of whose members were émigrés and all of whom were motivated by deep-seated anti-fascist convictions.[14] But the network Späth describes consisted of a handful of socialists; more importantly perhaps, it does not appear to have had any concrete influence on the principal socialist parties. In reality, these latter increasingly went their own way during the 1930s.

DEVELOPMENTS WITHIN THE PARTIES

Of the major socialist parties, the SPD obviously suffered the most from the Nazi seizure of power. Persecution and prohibition by the Nazi regime in the spring of 1933 forced the party to go underground where the vast majority of its most active members soon fell prey to the Gestapo; much of its surviving leadership fled into exile. The prolonged experience of exile proved extremely divisive. Even before the Nazi seizure of power, left- and right-leaning groups within the SPD criticized what they viewed as the leadership's paralysing and self-defeating attachment to legality and passive opposition to the Nazi threat to the Weimar Republic. Afterwards, these divisions only deepened. While the SPD's executive moved to Prague and then to Paris before finally settling in London, the 1930s witnessed the creation and consolidation of various splinter groups as German socialism fractured. A semblance of unity would have to wait until 1941 when exiled German socialists in London formed the Union of German Socialist Organisations in Great Britain (UGSOGB). For much of the 1930s, however, German socialism appeared increasingly divided

---

[13] Horn, *European Socialists Respond to Fascism*, 135. Horn's approach is comparative, as is that of Eley in *Forging Democracy*.
[14] Jens Späth, 'The Unifying Element?: European Socialism and Anti-Fascism, 1939–1945', *Contemporary European History* 25 (2016), 687–93.

not only politically but also geographically, with groups of exiles in various European countries as well as in the United States.[15]

Exacerbating this situation was the party's mounting isolation within the International. At the international socialist meeting in August 1933 in Paris, the SPD faced criticism for not having resisted more forcefully the Nazi seizure of power, prompting an irritated Otto Wels to reply that European socialists did not understand how difficult it was to oppose the 'nationalist currents' in Germany.[16] To be sure, other socialist parties extended moral support and some limited material aid to German socialists; but they were unwilling to do much more. Indeed, in 1934 and again in 1938, the International reduced the number of votes accorded to the SPD (and other exiled parties) on the grounds that it was a diminished force in German politics. In reality, many European socialists sought to reduce the SPD's influence within the International, chiefly because they disliked the drumbeat of warnings coming from German socialists regarding the Nazi danger—and thus the need for collective resistance to Nazi Germany. As early as 1934, Victor Schiff, the former foreign policy editor of *Vorwärts*, complained of the 'pacifism and humanism' of British and French socialists who seemed to believe that the combined threat of fascism and war could simply be 'wished out of existence'.[17] As with most Cassandras, German socialists found themselves shunned. Writing from Paris the same year, Rudolf Breitscheid remarked that 'for them [French socialists] we German emigrants simply do not exist'; two years later he confided that relations with the SFIO remained 'extraordinarily paltry'.[18] No doubt the dependence of exiled German socialists on the welfare of their foreign comrades did little to endear them to the latter. As chapter 6 will show, it would take some time and considerable effort for German socialists to regain the confidence of other European socialists after 1945.

As already mentioned, the SFIO during the mid-1930s entered into an electoral alliance with the communists (and the centrist Radicals), permitting the socialist-led Popular Front coalition to win the 1936 elections and to form a government with Blum as premier. The Popular Front experience, however, proved to be not only disappointing but also divisive. Greeted with widespread strikes, the Popular Front's victory resulted in the Matignon accords, mentioned above. But if the accords awarded significant gains to workers (the right to collective bargaining, the forty-hour week, paid vacations), they also represented the limits of social progress.

---

[15] See Schneider, *Unterm Hakenkreuz*, 107–18, 783–1078; Ludwig Eiber, *Die Sozialdemokratie in der Emigration. Die 'Union deutscher sozialistischer Organisationen in Grossbritannien' 1941–1946 und ihre Mitglieder. Protokolle, Erklärungen, Materialen* (Bonn, 1998); and Heinrich Potthoff and Susanne Miller, *Kleine Geschichte der SPD, 1848–2002* (Berlin, 2002), 127–69. Exile also proved divisive for Italian socialists. See Alexander De Grand, '"To Learn Nothing and to Forget Nothing": Italian Socialism and the Experience of Exile Politics, 1935–1945', *Contemporary European History* 14 (2005), 539–58.

[16] *Protokolle. Internationale Konferenz der Sozialistischen Arbeiter-Internationale*, Wels, 103–4.

[17] FES, AdsD, NL Friedrich Stampfer, 14, Schiff to Stampfer, undated but 1934.

[18] Breitscheid to Stampfer, 4 November 1934 and 7 December 1936, both reproduced in Werner Link, ed., *Mit dem Gesicht nach Deutschland. Eine Dokumentation über die sozialdemokratischen Emigration. Aus dem Nachlaß von Friedreich Stampfer ergänzt durch andere Überlieferungen* (Düsseldorf, 1968), 226, 290.

Indeed, as Robert Frank demonstrated, Blum's government sacrificed its social programme on the altar of rearmament, a decision that predictably irked many socialists who hoped for major changes to France's political order.[19] The Popular Front's ultimate demise, however, did little to reduce intra-party tensions, as French socialists grew increasingly divided over the question of whether or not France should forcefully oppose Nazi Germany's expansionist ambitions. As chapter 5 discussed, by 1938–1939 the SFIO had separated into two warring camps, one centred on Blum that advocated resistance and another centred on Paul Faure, the party's secretary general, which favoured any and all efforts to avoid a war, including colonial appeasement. In May 1939 Vincent Auriol, a *Blumiste*, privately voiced fears of a devastating 'split' within the party similar to that of 1920.[20] Although the SFIO managed to avoid a renewed schism, the process of polarization during the second half of the 1930s consumed French socialists, fostering a disinterest in international socialism. Even someone as self-consciously internationalist as Blum barely mentioned the International during this period.

Labour also distanced itself from international socialism during the 1930s. Mention was made in earlier chapters of the 'betrayal' of 1931: the fall of Labour's minority government, its replacement by a coalition led by MacDonald, and the subsequent electoral disaster. Together, these blows not only left Labour much reduced as a political force, but the resulting brooding and bitterness turned the party inwards. Reinforcing this introversion were divisions within Labour over the question of whether or not to resist Nazi Germany. The disaster of 1931 provided an opportunity for a pacifist left to flourish led by George Lansbury, who became Labour's parliamentary leader. Lansbury could count on a group of Labourites whose pacifist convictions led them to advocate efforts to appease Nazi Germany.[21] As we saw in chapter 5, this group included Charles Roden Buxton and other members of the party's Advisory Committee on International Questions, who advocated the return of Germany's pre-war colonies as part of a larger international economic arrangement. Unlike the SFIO, however, Labour did not become paralysed by division during the second half of the 1930s. Mounting internal opposition forced Lansbury to resign in 1935, and his successor, Clement Attlee, cautiously guided Labour towards a policy of opposition to German expansion in Europe and elsewhere even if this meant a European war.[22]

Significantly, however, their growing determination to oppose Nazi Germany encouraged Labour leaders to view the socialist International as at best a nuisance and at worst an encumbrance. During the 1930s, several European socialist parties, particularly those from neutral countries (Scandinavia, Holland, Belgium),

---

[19] Robert Frank[enstein], *Le prix du réarmement français (1935–1939)* (Paris, 1982). Fierce criticism predictably came from left socialists. See Hohl, *À Gauche!*, 135–58; and Jean-Paul Joubert, *Pivert et le Pivertisme: Révolutionnaires de la S.F.I.O* (Paris, 1977), 107–34.

[20] AN, Papiers Édouard Depreux, 456/AP/4-1, Auriol to Depreux, 13 May 1939.

[21] For a sympathetic portrait, see John Shepherd, *George Lansbury: At the Heart of Old Labour* (Oxford, 2002).

[22] For a good overview, see Vickers, *The Labour Party and the World*, 107–58.

resisted attempts to associate the International with anti-fascism for fear of embarrassing the neutral policies of their governments. More generally, they dreaded an ideological division of Europe into fascist and anti-fascist camps that risked dragging their countries into an unwanted war. Ironically, if these fears encouraged Labour to ally with these socialist parties in opposition to any alliance with the Komintern, which trumpeted precisely such an ideological division of Europe, they also prompted influential Labourites such as Hugh Dalton and William Gillies to work assiduously to weaken the International's voice in international politics. Lecturing Adler in August 1939, Gillies insisted that the LSI could be nothing more than a 'consultative organ' without any authority over its member parties.[23]

THE LSI'S FINAL CRISIS

By 1939, the outlook for European socialists appeared grim. While the SPD operated in increasing isolation in exile, the SFIO, prey to paralysing divisions, found itself largely excluded from political influence as an anti-labour, centre-right government led by Édouard Daladier repealed many of the Popular Front's gains in the domestic realm. In Britain, while Labour certainly appeared stronger than its French (or German) counterpart, it too remained politically isolated as the Conservative-led government under Neville Chamberlain enjoyed a sizeable majority in Parliament. If anything, the weakness of socialist parties at home paled beside the seeming powerlessness of international socialism to exert any influence on events. By the opening months of 1939, indeed, a profound malaise enshrouded both the International and international socialism—a malaise exacerbated by the final defeat of the Spanish Republic in March.

This malaise provided the background for Adler's memorandum cited at the beginning of this entr'acte. Adler was especially angry with Labour which he accused of seeking to undermine, if not destroy, the International. Abandoning his usual reserve, the LSI's secretary challenged Labour to issue a 'frank and sincere' disavowal of the International—and of socialist internationalism.[24] Labour, however, refused to take up Adler's challenge. To be sure, Labour officials continued to contest the International's claims to authority; and behind the scenes Dalton and Gillies schemed to replace Adler with someone more compliant. Yet, significantly, Labour never contemplated abandoning the International. Instead, Labour officials strove to gain greater control over the organization, attempting, for example, to move its offices from Brussels to London. However instrumentalist Labour's approach might have been, it did indicate an ongoing involvement with socialist internationalism.

[23] SSAZ, SPS, Ar.1.260.16, Gillies to Adler, 4 August 1939. For background, see Leonardo Rapone, 'La crisi finale dell'Internazionale Operaia e Socialista' in *Annali della Fondazione Giacomo Brodolini e della Fondazione di Studia Storici Filippo Turati* (Milan, 1989), 44–68.
[24] Steiner, 'L'Internationale socialiste à la veille de la Seconde Guerre mondiale', 97–102.

This involvement, moreover, was not limited to Labour. Speaking at Labour's annual congress in May 1939, the Dutch socialist J.W. Albarda reminded his hosts of the LSI's value. The International's 'very existence and activity preserve the affiliated Parties from national narrow-mindedness, national vanity, and want of appreciation for the opinions and aims of other nations'. Continuing, Albarda offered a succinct justification of the practice of socialist internationalism:

> ... it is necessary and useful that those national Parties, which are led by a common idea, should be united internationally. For through mutual contact and exchange of thoughts they will be able to profit by the insight and experience of others, to examine common problems together and to submit their own conduct to the judgment of others. Then it is not at all excluded, that they would come to a general agreement on a joint statement or even a unanimous decision, which could be of great importance in time of war as well as in peace.[25]

In a memorandum circulated to socialist parties soon afterwards, Albarda took Adler to task for his overly pessimistic views regarding the International's prospects. 'The present difficulties for the L.S.I...are enormous, and our possibilities are more than ever limited', he admitted; nevertheless this was 'not a reason to despair of the existence of the L.S.I.'. The International (and socialist internationalism), Albarda concluded, 'can be maintained on the condition that it does not desire to go beyond the frontiers of the possible'. This realistic assessment was shared by Scandinavian socialists who, like their Labour counterparts, sought to restrain the International's authority. In an article in 1939, Bjarne Braatoy, a Swedish socialist and future secretary of the Socialist International, pleaded for more frequent and more structured cooperation between socialist parties, offering the close ties between the Scandinavian parties as a potential model.[26] European socialists might disagree on what kind of International they wanted, but on the eve of another war they all agreed that an International was necessary. However fragile it was, the flame of socialist internationalism continued to flicker.

---

[25] IISH, SAI, 3404, 'J.W. Albarda's Address to the Conference of the British Labour Party', undated.

[26] IISH, SAI, 573, 'In reply to Adler's Memorandum on the "Position of the L.S.I."', Albarda, undated but August 1939; and SSAZ, SPS, Ar.1.260.16, 'Die Internationale der Arbeit in Liquidation?', Braatoy.

PART II

THE POST-WAR YEARS

6

Reconstituting the International, 1940–1951

The 1930s, as the entr'acte argued, were difficult years for international socialism. Together, the economic depression, the rise of fascism, and the growing threat of war undermined ties of solidarity between socialist parties. With the SPD forced into exile and prey to internecine squabbles and with both Labour and the SFIO preoccupied with the massive domestic challenges facing their respective countries, the principal parties increasingly went their separate ways. International socialism, however, would undergo a striking revival during the wartime and post-war years, leading in 1951 to the constitution of a new International: the Socialist International. 'The International lives', proudly proclaimed *Neuer Vorwärts*, the SPD's newspaper.[1]

This chapter traces the revival of international socialism, beginning in the early 1940s and ending with the Socialist International's founding congress in July 1951. It focuses on the efforts of European socialists to reconstitute the International, the institutional expression of socialist internationalism. One reason for this focus stems from the scholarly neglect of the subject. The Socialist International rarely figures in histories of post-war Europe or in those of international politics.[2] When scholars examine post-war international organizations, they concentrate on the United Nations and its associated agencies or on European institutions.[3] Even histories of socialism express little interest in the post-war Socialist International. Geoff Eley, for example, does not mention it in his wide-ranging study of the European left.[4] The rare scholars who do examine the International play down its significance. Guillaume Devin's study, which remains the most thorough treatment of the post-war International, describes an institution burdened with 'weak structure' and barely capable of acting as a 'mail-box'. In Devin's telling, the International operated essentially in the symbolic realm rather than in that of concrete politics, its activities limited to rituals of unity, celebration, and protest.[5] The impression

---

[1] 'Die Internationale lebt', *Neurer Vorwärts*, 6 July 1951, 1–2.

[2] For example, see Dan Stone, *Goodbye to all That?: The Story of Europe since 1945* (Oxford, 2014); Tony Judt, *Postwar: A History of Europe since 1945* (New York, 2005); Odd Arne Westad, *The Global Cold War: Third World Interventions and the Making of our Times* (Cambridge, 2005); and William Hitchcock, *The Struggle for Europe: The Turbulent History of a Divided Continent* (New York, 2004). Neither the Socialist International nor socialist (or social-democratic) internationalism receive a chapter in the three-volume *Cambridge History of the Cold War*.

[3] Mark Mazower, *Governing the World: The History of the World* (New York, 2012).

[4] Eley, *Forging Democracy*.

[5] Devin, *L'Internationale Socialiste*, 178–80, 286, 360. Also see Sassoon, *One Hundred Years of Socialism*, 210; and Rolf Steininger, *Deutschland und die Sozialistische Internationale nach dem Zweiten*

created is that neither the International nor socialist internationalism mattered to European socialists—and still less to the history of the post-war period.

Such an impression, however, distorts our understanding of post-war European socialism. The Left in general and socialists (or social democrats) in particular emerged from the war with a renewed sense of shared purpose. With much of the Right discredited by its real and perceived association with fascism, socialism in 1945 appeared poised in many countries to assume power, either alone or in coalition with other parties. As scholars have shown, various socialist parties developed ambitious programmes for post-war national renewal that included far-reaching changes to political, economic, and social structures.[6] Going further, Geoff Eley argues the period 1943–1947 offered the Western European Left (socialist and non-socialist) possibilities for 'radical democratic change, or a "third way"'—possibilities that the emerging Cold War closed off.[7] Less well known, however, is that socialists also strove to re-energize international socialism, most notably by repairing the inter-party ties that had frayed during the 1930s. The result was a renewed commitment to the practice of socialist internationalism—to working together to identify 'socialist' solutions to the pressing challenges of the post-war period. Subsequent chapters will explore this practice across several concrete issues (post-war security, European unity, and decolonization). This chapter, however, concentrates on the International in order to highlight debates within and between socialist parties on the nature and meaning of internationalism. The International in 1951 represented a compromise between various and sometimes competing visions of socialist internationalism. Just as importantly, the compromise was not fixed in stone: as always, much would depend on the collective practice of socialist internationalism.

EARLY WARTIME COOPERATION

From an international socialist perspective, the Second World War was vastly different from its predecessor. During 1914–1918 European socialists had been divided into two belligerent blocs, even if the internal cohesion of each bloc (and party) suffered as the war dragged on. No such division existed during 1939 to 1945, principally because there was no *Burgfrieden* in Germany (or Austria). When not dead, imprisoned, or intimidated into silence at home, socialists from the Axis countries were in exile, many of them in Britain. By the force of circumstances, the British played host to socialists from across Europe and beyond, placing Labour at the centre of international socialism.

Weltkrieg (Bonn, 1979). Julius Braunthal's study, by contrast, is too much of a court history. See Braunthal, *History of the International*, vol. 3, *1943–1968* (Westview, CO, 1980).

[6] The best-known case is Labour. See Geoffrey F. Field, *Blood, Sweat, and Toil: Remaking the British Working Class, 1939–1945* (Oxford, 2011); Ross McKibbin, *Parties and People: England 1914–1951* (Ocford, 2010), 106–76; and Stephen Brooke, *Labour's War: The Labour Party during the Second World War* (Oxford, 1992). For the French case, see Serge Berstein et al., eds., *Le Parti socialiste entre résistance et république* (Paris, 2000); B.D. Graham, *Choice and Democratic Order: The French Socialist Party, 1937–1950* (Cambridge, 1994); and Andrew Shennan, *Rethinking France: Plans for Renewal 1940–1946* (Oxford, 1989).

[7] Eley, *Forging Democracy*, 295.

Early on in the war, Labour came under pressure from foreign socialists to take the lead in fostering international socialist cooperation. In response, Labour's international subcommittee decided in late June 1940 to hold an 'informal and strictly confidential exchange of views and information' with European socialists. The meeting, which took place in mid-July, was attended by several prominent Labourites as well as twenty-one socialists from eight European countries. Although no minutes were taken, the participants decided to create a consultative committee that would meet 'from time to time with a view to giving advice that the Party [Labour] may invite on special questions'.[8]

William Gillies, Labour's international secretary, quickly imposed himself as the dominant voice on Labour's side. Described by one future Labour minister as the 'least social socialist whom he had ever met', Gillies aroused little affection and much hostility from foreign socialists.[9] If his brusque manner did not help, the principal cause of tension was Gillies' belief that international socialism must be entirely subordinated to Labour's needs. European socialists, he insisted in July 1940, must recognize two related realities: that the 'International can no longer function' and that Labour 'is now the only Party in Europe which is left in freedom'. Accordingly, Gillies envisaged the functioning of the consultative committee as a unilateral process in which Labour sought advice but not cooperation. Labour, he informed Camille Huysmans in this regard, had no obligations to international socialism and would simply pursue 'what is most expedient for the purposes at hand'.[10] Preoccupied with Britain's fight for survival, Labour's executive endorsed Gillies' attempt to marginalize international socialism. Officially entitled the Inter-allied Socialist Consultative Committee, it held its first meeting in November 1940. While the proposed committee would meet regularly, its gatherings were informal and confidential, with no minutes being kept. For Labour, the aim was to avoid a reconstitution of the International that could potentially hamper the party's freedom to determine policy.[11]

The problem for Labour, however, was that the European socialists resisted their marginalization. Isabelle Tombs, a leading scholar of socialist exiles in wartime Britain, has emphasized the rivalries between socialists, a product of the 'renaissance' of national as opposed to international loyalties. Yet if Continental socialists never formed a bloc, many of them shared a desire to keep alive the practice of socialist internationalism and even the International—a desire that Labour could

---

[8] LHASC, LPA, LSI 25/1/15, Gillies to Jaksch, 9 July 1940; and LSI 25/1/5, International Sub-Committee, 22 July 1940. Emphasis in original.

[9] The Labour minister is Arthur Creech Jones and is cited in Tony Insall, *Haakon Lie, Denis Healey and the Making of an Anglo-Norwegian Special Relationship* (Oslo, 2010), 55. For the reaction of one foreign socialist, see Max Buset to Camille Huysmans, 4 August 1940, reproduced in Herman Balthazar and José Gotovitch, eds., *Camille Huysmans Geschriften en Documenten VIII. Camille Huysmans in London* (Antwerpen, 1978), 37–8.

[10] LHASC, LPA, LSI 25/1/32, Gillies to Huysmans, 25 July 1940; and LSI 25/1/42, Gillies to Huysmans, 1 August 1940.

[11] CCA, Philip Noel-Baker Papers, NBKR 2/51, Labour International Department, 'The International', undated but 1941. Also see Otfried Dankelmann, 'Zwischen SAI und Sozialistischer Internationale. Zur Genesis des International Labour and Socialist Preparatory Committee in London 1940–1945', *Zeitschrift für Geschichtswissenschaft* 24 (1976), 1394–9.

not ignore.[12] Writing to Gillies in July 1940, Camille Huysmans, the LSI's president, insisted that he would not 'become complicit in the suppression of all international [socialist] activity nor forget his duties as [LSI] president':

> You can believe me! We cannot allow it to be said later that we strangled the Second International. I kept the latter alive during the war of 1914–1918. I hope to keep it alive during the current challenge and I will not allow anyone to prevent it from living, even if it is a modest life.

While accepting that regular meetings of the International had become impossible for the time being, Huysmans nevertheless argued for a more formal structure of relations directed by a small secretariat and staff. Socialist parties, he elaborated several days later, 'continued to exist as much as they could. They have their representatives. We must offer them immediate and direct help.'[13]

Huysmans received support from other European socialists. In August 1940 Marthe Lévy informed Gillies that French socialists in Britain had recently formed a 'liaison committee', soon to be known as the *Groupe Jean-Jaurès*, which proudly announced its attachment both to the 'democratic and revolutionary tradition of…international socialism' as well as to 'all socialists who remain loyal to the LSI's principles'. More concretely, the group created a secretariat to act as the SFIO's delegation to both Labour and the International.[14] Meanwhile, well aware of Gillies' hostility to the International, European socialists sought to bypass him. At the end of 1940 several of them wrote to Philip Noel-Baker, a leading member of Labour's international subcommittee. Pointing to the 'growing desire amongst international Socialists now in London to have an opportunity of coming together in an unofficial and informal way', they proposed the creation of an 'International Socialist Club'. Soon afterwards, Noel-Baker wrote to Clement Attlee, the Labour leader and deputy prime minister, in support of the idea. Members of his subcommittee had been meeting monthly with 'leading refugee socialists from the allied and conquered countries'. But while 'extremely interesting…and extremely valuable', Noel-Baker continued, these encounters 'do not, in my view, altogether take the place of proper meetings of the International'. Hence the need for something more structured.[15]

Over the coming months, pressure continued to mount on Labour's leadership to do more to facilitate international socialist relations. At Labour's annual congress in June 1941, George Dallas, the chairman of Labour's international subcommittee, thus assured the delegates that the party sought 'to keep alive the idea of International solidarity and we will keep it alive, so that when the War finished we

---

[12] Tombs, 'Une identité européenne assiégée? Les exilés socialistes à Londres', *Revue d'histoire moderne et contemporaine* 46 (1999), 263–79; and, 'L'exil socialiste européen à Londres, 1939–45: conflits et regroupements', *École française de Rome* (1991), 371–93.

[13] LHASC, LPA, LSI 25/1/40, Huysmans to Gillies, 30 July 1940; and LSI 25/1/48, Huysmans to Gillies, 6 August 1940.

[14] Ibid., LSI 25/1/55, Lévy to Gillies, 23 August 1940; and OURS, Louis Lévy Papers, uncatalogued, Henry Hauck et al. letter, 14 August 1940.

[15] CCA, Philip Noel-Baker Papers, NBKR 2/52, Arthur Wauters et al. to Noel-Baker, 31 December 1940; and Noel-Baker to Attlee, 3 February 1941.

will present a united, working-class front from the Socialist and Labour point of view'.[16] The following month, Labour's executive agreed to the creation of a 'Preparatory Committee', with Huysmans as president and Gillies as secretary, in order to 'communicate with representative Socialists of good faith in London'. As with the consultative committee, the proceedings would remain confidential and no votes would be taken or resolutions issued. But if Labour clearly intended to keep the committee on a tight leash, it only partially succeeded. Much to Gillies' annoyance, during the upcoming months the preparatory committee would hold several meetings as it extended its influence deeply into both Labour and the community of exiled European socialists.[17]

One notable feature of the preparatory committee's activities was its inclusion of socialists from enemy countries and especially Germany. With Germany's military victories in the West in 1940, Britain became the major centre of German socialism. In March 1941 several socialist groups, including the SPD's executive (SOPADE), united to form the Union of German Socialist Organisations in Great Britain (UGSOGB) with Hans Vogel as chairman. If German socialists hoped thereby to increase their influence in socialist circles in Britain, they faced determined opposition from Gillies. Labour's international secretary loathed the SPD, holding it responsible for the disasters of German politics. From the beginning of the war, he sought to exclude German (and Austrian) socialists from international socialist consultations; no Germans were invited to the July 1940 informal meeting, nor did any sit on his consultative committee. Armed with these prejudices, Gillies in October 1941 drafted a lengthy paper on the SPD's foreign policy that not only effectively accused the majority German socialists of complicity in Imperial Germany's militarism and imperialism during 1914–1918, but also insinuated that the SPD had facilitated the Nazi seizure of power. Although avoiding explicit conclusions, the implications of Gillies' paper were clear: German socialism could not be trusted and should be definitively excluded from the international socialist community.[18]

Gillies' paper, which was widely circulated, predictably provoked a strong response from German socialists. Friedrich Stampfer, a former member of the SPD's executive committee, wrote Gillies to denounce his slanderous allegations.[19] A flurry of papers soon resulted, as Stampfer, Vogel, and others penned memoranda challenging Gillies' portrait, which in turn provoked counter-memoranda from several Germans, among them Curt Geyer (a former member of the UGSOGB) and Walter Loeb, who shared Gillies' belief that German socialism had been corrupted by excessive nationalism. For support, Gillies could draw on the widespread suspicion of Germans

---

[16] Labour Party, *Report of the 40th Annual Conference...June 2nd, 3rd, and 4th 1941* (London, 1941), 152–3; and LHASC, LPA, LSI 26/2/4, Morgan Phillips to Gillies, 8 January 1942.

[17] LHASC, LPA, LSI 26/1/14, Labour, International Sub-Committee, 18 July 1941; and 26/2/5, Gillies to Phillips, 17 January 1942. Also see Dankelmann, 'Zwischen SAI und Sozialistischer Internationale', 1399–401.

[18] LHASC, LPA, International Department, ID/GER/15/47, 'German Social Democracy. Notes on its Foreign Policy in World War', Gillies, October 1941. For Gillies's anti-Germanism, see Denis Healey, *The Time of My Life* (London, 1989), 74.

[19] FES, AdsD, NL Friedrich Stampfer, 6, Stampfer to Gillies, 30 November 1941.

among European socialists. Huysmans, for example, claimed that German socialists belonged to the 'German nation' that 'is infected by the spirit of violence' and that 'will follow Herr Hitler obediently and whole-heartedly…even is [*sic*] he destroys liberty—even if he murders all the peoples around him—even if he makes a Europe of one <u>Herrenvolk</u> and numerous slave countries'. Even Adler, in exile in New York, believed that it would be necessary to create 'a new [German] socialist movement based on completely new people, who would be free from German socialism's ideological and practical mistakes'.[20]

Scholars who have examined this controversy emphasize the larger stakes involved: for Gillies and his supporters a defeated Germany must be treated harshly because the German people (and German socialists) could not be trusted.[21] But also at stake were conceptions of international socialist solidarity. From the beginning, German socialists found numerous defenders within Labour. Noel-Baker fired off a response to Gillies, accusing him of being 'unjust' to German socialists, many of whom had 'risked their lives in the struggle against the Nazis'. Continuing, Noel-Baker maintained that socialists had an obligation to work for the 'revival' of German socialism: 'Our Policy, therefore, should be to encourage now all German Social Democrats, both in Germany and outside…; and to prepare to give every assistance to a German Social Democratic Government, when the war is over…' Noel-Baker received backing from Harold Laski, a member of Labour's national executive, who denounced Gillies' paper as 'a perverse and distorted account of the facts'. While accepting the need for post-war measures to prevent Germany from renewing aggression, Laski asserted that 'it is no part of my case…that to attain this end, the record of men who have fought honourably and at grave personal risk in the Socialist cause shall be blackened by perverse and malicious innuendos.'[22] Even Labourites less sympathetic to German socialists than Noel-Baker and Laski were critical of Gillies. Commenting on Gillies' paper, Leonard Woolf judged it 'most unpleasant and inadvisable', partly because it exaggerated the nationalism of German socialists but even more so because the latter were supposedly no more or less nationalist than other socialists. This being so, Labour must cooperate with German socialism in the construction of a post-war European and international order that could prevent renewed war.[23]

---

[20] LHASC, LPA, International Department, LP/JMS (INT), box 9, 'Commentary by Camille Huysmans', 13 February 1942; and LP/JMS (INT), box 8, account of Polish socialist talk with Adler, 22 May 1942.

[21] Anthony Glees, *Exile Politics during the Second World War: The German Social Democrats in Britain* (Oxford, 1982); and Werner Röder, *Die deutschen sozialistischen Exilgruppen in Großbritannien 1940–1945. Ein Beitrag zur Geschichte des Widerstandes gegen den Nationalsozialismus* (Bonn-Bad Godesberg, 1973). Also see Isabelle Tombs, 'Socialists Debate their History from the First World War to the Third Reich: German Exiles and the British Labour Party' in Stefan Berger et al., eds., *Historikerdialoge: Geschichte, Mythos und Gedächtnis im deutsch-britischen kulturellen Austausch 1750–2000* (Göttingen, 2003), 361–81.

[22] LHASC, LPA, International Department, LP/JMS (INT), box 9, 'Memorandum Concerning the "Private and Confidential" Notes on the Policy of German Social Democracy…', Noel-Baker, undated; and CCA, Philip Noel-Baker Papers, NBKR 4/291, Laski to Noel-Baker, 19 November 1941.

[23] US, Leonard Woolf Papers, ID1a, Woolf to Gillies, 13 April 1942.

In their opposition to Gillies, Noel-Baker and Laski insisted that Labour's executive formally decide on the question of wartime relations with German socialists in Britain. In the short-term, the move backfired. In March 1942 the international subcommittee refused to refute Gillies, expressing its continued confidence in him; the following month, Labour's executive endorsed the sub-committee's decision in a close vote.[24] The upshot was a break in official relations between Labour and the UGSOGB. But although Gillies would seize on these developments to help animate a propaganda campaign against German socialism, the executive's decision was not as definitive as it might appear.[25] For one thing, the votes in the subcommittee and the national executive had been close, indicating that the party was divided on the subject. Beyond the confines of the party lead-ership, militants continued to lobby for a more sympathetic position towards German socialists, exploiting, for example, the opportunities provided by Labour's annual congress. Meanwhile, German socialists associated with the UGSOGB worked with several groups close to Labour (the Fabian Society, Left Book Club, Socialist Clarity Group, International Socialist Forum) to counter stereotypes of Germans (and German socialists) as incorrigibly militarist and nationalist.[26] A wartime pamphlet from the Socialist Clarity Group, for example, argued that Labour could count on German socialists, the 'one democratic force left as a result of German history', to work for a democratic and peaceful post-war Germany.[27] Despite Gillies' best efforts, the flame of international socialism continued to flicker within wartime Labour.

THE REVIVAL OF SOCIALIST INTERNATIONALISM

Despite or because of their official rupture with Labour, German socialists in Britain embraced socialist internationalism all the more firmly. In a speech in late 1942, Erich Ollenhauer, a future SPD leader, called for the 'union of the different socialist groups... and the most rapid reconstitution of the Labour and Socialist International'. Soon afterwards a UGSOGB report drew attention to the efforts of German socialists who were working with sympathetic Labourites for 'the speediest reactivation of the LSI'.[28] Reflecting this priority, the Union issued a declaration on international policy in October 1943 widely circulated among European socialists. Describing German socialists as first and foremost 'international socialists', it identified the UGSOGB's first goal as 'the closest cooperation of the organised workers of all lands in a new international organisation, with the task of

[24] Labour Party, NEC, 291, NEC minutes, 22 April 1942.

[25] For the campaign, see Isabelle Tombs, 'The Victory of Socialist "Vansittartism": Labour and the German Question, 1941–5', *Twentieth Century British History* 7 (1993), 287–309.

[26] Glees, *Exile Politics during the Second World War*; and Tombs, 'Une identité européenne assiégée?', 264–6.

[27] LHASC, LPA, ID/GER/2/85, Socialist Clarity Group, *Why is Germany Aggressive?* (undated).

[28] Ollenhauer speech to Mitgliederversammlung, 6 December 1942; and 'Entwurf für den Bericht des Parteivorstandes über seine Tätigkeit im Jahre 1942 von Ende Januar 1943', undated, both repro-duced in Eiber, *Die Sozialdemokratie in der Emigration*, 179–80, 656–9.

working out a common policy for the socialist labour movement and putting it into practice'.[29] It was not only German socialists in Britain, moreover, who called for a revived International. In its statement on peace aims in March 1943, the international group of democratic socialists in Sweden, among whom figured Willy Brandt, a future West German chancellor, insisted that the LSI must be 'reorganized' as part of a revamped post-war international order. For this reason, all socialist parties must devote themselves to renewing 'contact with brother parties from other countries'.[30]

By themselves, German socialists could exert little influence on Labour. This is why the support of other socialists proved so important: it amplified the call for a reconstituted International. French socialists, moreover, figured among the leading advocates of an International. In addition to proclaiming its attachment to socialist internationalism in its guiding principles, the *Groupe Jean-Jaurès* insisted that international socialist cooperation include the Germans.[31] The socialist party inside France adopted much the same position. Although most socialist militants accommodated themselves to the occupation, retreating into *attentisme*, in March 1941 a small group began the task of rebuilding the French socialist party, creating the *Comité d'action socialiste* (CAS) under the leadership of Daniel Mayer, a protégé of Blum. Marc Sadoun has argued that the CAS quickly reproduced the SFIO's traditional structure and mindset.[32] But if this process fostered some doctrinal rigidity, it also entailed a recommitment to socialist internationalism—and to the International. Before his deportation to Germany in 1943, Blum instructed French socialists in London to work with Labour and other socialist parties on a programme for the post-war world. Reflecting this emphasis on international socialism, the CAS international programme in July 1943 called for the 'reconstitution of the Labour and Socialist International'.[33]

By 1944, the clamour for an International, together with the growing certitude of Allied victory, spurred Huysmans into action. Although maintaining his hostility towards German socialists, Huysmans circulated a paper in June 1944 proposing that his committee of exiled socialists begin 'preparatory work for the New International' that would emerge from the war. Elaborating on the proposal a month later, he contended that the 'vital interests of the workers of all countries demand the speediest erection of an international organ of the Socialist movement' to foster contacts between parties and to aid in the rebuilding of Continental labour

---

[29] CCA, Philip Noel-Baker Papers, NBKR 4/295, UGSOGB, 'The International Policy of German Socialists', 23 October 1943.

[30] 'Die Friedenziele der demokratischen Sozialisten', March 1943, reproduced in Willy Brandt, *Berliner Ausgabe. Band 2. Zwei Vaterländer. Deutsch-Norweger im schwedischen Exil—Rückkehr nach Deutschland 1940–1947* (Bonn, 2000), 103–4. More generally, see Klaus Misgeld, *Die 'Internationale Gruppe demokratischer Sozialisten' in Stockholm 1942–1945* (Uppsala, 1976).

[31] For the guiding principles, see Daniel Mayer, *Les Socialistes dans la Résistance. Souvenirs et Documents* (Paris, 1968), 75; and AN, Papiers Vincent Auriol, 552/AP/3 AU8 Dr6 sdra, Lévy to Auriol, 23 February 1944.

[32] Marc Sadoun, *Les socialistes sous l'occupation: Résistance et collaboration* (Paris, 1982), 148, 227, 240.

[33] AN, Archives Léon Blum, 570/AP/19/3BL1 Dr5 sdra, Blum to Mayer, 15 March 1943; and 'Programme international proposé par le Parti Socialiste', 1 July 1943, reproduced in Henri Michel, *Les idées politiques et sociales de la Résistance* (Paris, 1954), 389–91.

movements. Huysmans accordingly suggested as a first step the creation of a 'European Emergency Council of the L.S.I.' under his direction and made up of European socialists in Britain. Although the council's authority would initially be limited, he conjectured that it would soon 'assume more importance and will [eventually] be able fully to play its part as [the] Preparatory Committee for the reconstruction of the International'. Huysmans clearly envisaged the council as the embryo of a revived LSI.[34]

Gillies responded with unconcealed scorn to Huysmans' proposal. In a paper in July 1944, he argued that the International had become an empty shell well before the war. As for the present, the socialist parties in occupied Europe no longer existed while German socialism amounted to a 'political façade designed to save Germany from the inevitable consequences of aggression, barbarism and defeat'. Another problematic factor, he claimed, was the 'national consciousness of those who were international Socialists', a trait the war had supposedly intensified across Europe. Indeed, nationalism not internationalism would likely characterize post-war socialism:

> How far … the whole conception of International Socialism may have been discredited among the masses by two great wars and the events of the last five years is still to be discovered. The resolution in the intensity of national consciousness which may be revealed after the liberation may astonish the world.

Gillies believed that European socialists would soon be preoccupied with the reconstruction of their individual parties and nations and, in this context, he doubted whether the International or international socialism could be (or should be) resuscitated. 'It would be premature and presumptuous', Gillies judged, 'to sketch the organisation of a future international.'[35] In a letter to Huysmans, he claimed that the latter's committee had no authority to create the proposed council and that any action should be left to national parties. Until then, 'There should be no plunging.'[36]

Gillies failed to bully Huysmans into abandoning his proposal. In an official letter to Gillies (and various Labour leaders), he emphasized that the International had continued to exist during the war—a continuity embodied in its executive and in Huysmans himself. More concretely, while accepting that an international socialist congress was premature, he insisted that 'common sense' pointed to the value of a provisionary committee charged with developing and overseeing relations between socialist parties. If nothing else, such a body was needed to help European socialists work out a common policy towards post-war Germany and post-war German socialism. Continuing, Huysmans dismissed Gillies' alternative—informal contacts with Labour at the centre—as a 'very poor one. It suggests to stay mute and to stimulate death.' While remaining polite in public, Huysmans was scathing

---

[34] LHASC, LPA, LSI 26/2/34, 'International Socialist Movement', 15 June 1944; and IEV, Archives Camille Huysmans, F 126/250, 'Proposal Concerning the Creation of an European Emergency Council of the Labour and Socialist International', July 1944.

[35] LHASC, LPA, LSI 26/2/34, 'The International: Points for Consideration', Gillies, 20 July 1944.

[36] IEV, Archives Camille Huysmans, F 126/205, Gillies to Huysmans, 3 August 1944.

in a private letter to Gillies, castigating his contempt for European socialists and questioning his international socialist credentials. 'You imagine yourself more and more as a sort of an "eminence grise"', Huysmans wrote, 'capable to put the whole world in his pocket and to reveal quite obviously by your manner the influence guiding you which have nothing to do whatsoever with our fundamental conceptions.' In a direct challenge, he insisted that Gillies was out of touch with Labour's leadership.[37]

Unwilling to back down, Gillies reiterated his belief that the LSI no longer existed as well as his doubts that a new International was needed. But Huysmans stood his ground, asking Gillies to refer the matter to Labour's international subcommittee for a decision.[38] In preparation for the subcommittee meeting, Huysmans and Gillies both submitted memoranda. That of Huysmans was brief, rehearsing the case for forming 'a provisional committee' that could act as 'a rallying centre' for democratic socialism. The 'continuity of international socialist action', it intoned, 'should be maintained and adapted to circumstances.' In his memorandum, Gillies warned that steps to reconstitute the International would provide German socialists with an opportunity to demand membership on any committee on equal terms. But his more basic point was that developments at the national and party levels must take precedence:

> The present writer thought that the process of reconstitution after this war would be deliberate, cautious but necessarily slow, with some regard to previous experience and the experiences and opinions of those parties which have lived under German occupation and may re-appear with rejuvenated policies and perhaps leadership. The Labour Party…would not wish to do anything that might be held to prejudge or gainsay their full Party rights in any manner whatsoever. In short, the International would be reconstructed from the bottom on the basis of living Parties.

Nothing should be done, in other words, until the dust had settled across post-war Europe, a process that would presumably take considerable time.[39]

Huysmans' insistence on referring the issue to Labour's international sub-committee was a calculated one. He knew that Gillies' contempt for socialist internationalism was not shared by most Labour leaders. In August 1944 James Walker, a leading trade unionist, intimated that Gillies 'is not representing a point of view generally endorsed by the [international] Sub-committee'. More significantly, George Dallas, the subcommittee's chair and long-time ally of Labour's international secretary, assured Huysmans that the 'little trouble with Gillies' would soon be 'put right'.[40] Although Walker and Dallas shared Gillies' anti-Germanism, they did not allow it to spill over into hostility to socialist internationalism.

---

[37] Copies of the official and private letters, dated 11 August 1944, can be found in ibid.

[38] LHASC, LPA, LSI 26/8/1, Gillies to Huysmans, 15 August 1944; and ibid., LSI 27/1/22, Huysmans to Gillies, 24 August 1944.

[39] Labour Party, NEC minutes, fiche 324, untitled note, Huysmans, 28 August 1944; and ibid., 'The International', Gillies, undated.

[40] Walker to Huysmans, 15 August 1944; and Dallas to Huysmans, 15 August 1944. Both letters are in IEV, Archives Camille Huysmans, F 126/205.

Accordingly, in early September 1944 Labour's international subcommittee accepted Huysmans' proposal. In endorsing the decision, Labour's national executive defined the preparatory committee's tasks to be 'to facilitate the resumption of contacts and the exchange of information among the Labour and Socialist Parties, and to undertake the study of the problems associated with the organisation, principles and policy of the future international association of democratic Labour and Socialist Parties'.[41] That the decision amounted to a repudiation of Gillies is evident from the fact that the subcommittee decided soon afterwards to force him to retire.[42]

To be sure, Huysmans' victory was far from complete as Labour leaders intended to keep the preparatory committee on a short leash. As Dallas informed a group of European socialists, the committee was provisional in nature and did not possess the authority to issue policy statements; nor for the time being would socialists from enemy countries be invited to attend.[43] More basically, the idea that the reconstitution of the International would take time continued to dominate Labour thinking. 'The provisional committee that has been formed will have to proceed very carefully in building up a new International', a Labour official informed a conference of commonwealth socialist parties in September 1944.[44] But if Labour leaders favoured a slow march towards an International, developments assumed a momentum of their own. The creation of the preparatory committee did little to relieve the pressure for a formalization of international socialist relations. Partly in response, Labour decided to organize informal encounters with foreign socialists during the party's annual congress in mid-December 1944. But still more was demanded. Later the same month, a long list of Labourites and foreign (including German) socialists in Britain published a letter in the *Manchester Guardian* asking Labour's executive to organize an international socialist conference, which the signatories presented as the 'first step towards establishing a world-wide unity of all the forces of Labour on the basis of true international Socialism'.[45] At Labour's annual congress several days later the debate centred not on the idea of a conference but rather on whether to invite German and Austrian socialists. After some debate, the delegates passed a compromise resolution recommending that the recently created 'preparatory Socialist International Committee' be constructed 'upon a broader basis than its present one'. Just as importantly, it called on Labour's executive to convene a 'provisional International Socialist Conference' as rapidly as possible. Soon afterwards, invitations went out to European socialists from Allied and occupied countries (though not enemy ones) to attend a conference in

[41] Labour Party, NEC minutes, fiche 324, International Sub-Committee, minutes, 1 September 1944; and LHASC, LPA, LSI 27/1/54, NEC statement, 13 September 1944.

[42] Ben Pimlott, ed., *The Second World War Diary of Hugh Dalton 1940–45* (London, 1986), 16 January 1945, 823.

[43] IEV, Archives Camille Huysmans, F 126/205, Labour, Inter-Allied Consultative Committee, 8 September 1944.

[44] LAC, CCF-NPD, MG 28 VI-I, vol. 112, 'Report of the Conference of British and Dominion Labour Parties held September 12th to 27th, 1944', John Parker, 121.

[45] For informal encounters, see SSAZ, SPS, Ar 1.260.48, Gillies (Labour) to Graber (SPS), 16 November 1944; for the letter, see LHASC, LPA, LSI 27/1/29.

London. The first item on the agenda would be the 'future of Labour and Socialist International relations'.[46]

The conference, held in early March 1945, brought together socialists from twelve parties. At the end of the three-day affair several points were clear. One was Labour's dominant position within international socialism—a dominance underscored by the financial dependence of many socialist parties. Aware of their strength, Labour participants assumed a leading role in the discussions. Another point concerned Labour's hesitant attitude towards the International. At the conference, the French delegation pushed hard for a rapid reconstitution of the International only to meet firm opposition from Labour, which the SFIO's Vincent Auriol attributed to the party's proximity to government and to its 'nationalist tendencies'. The future president of France's Fourth Republic, however, remained confident that Labour would eventually come around. For Auriol, in any case, an International would emerge from the concrete practice of socialist internationalism. And in this sense, the conference was a success. The delegates discussed a variety of pressing post-war issues, including the treatment of a defeated Germany, relief efforts, and the creation of an international economic organization to accompany the United Nations. In these discussions, Auriol reported, 'We presented precise proposals, we sowed ideas and we demonstrated the usefulness of the International.' With considerable satisfaction, Auriol underscored the final declaration announcing the collective desire to 'give new life to the Socialist International' by forming a 'Committee to prepare a plan for consideration'.[47]

DEVELOPMENTS WITHIN THE PARTIES, 1945–1947

As the war in Europe drew to a close in the spring of 1945, socialists from several parties had manifested the desire to see the International reconstituted. Yet it would take six years before the new socialist International held its founding congress. The history of relations between socialist parties during the early post-war years goes a long way in explaining how the International emerged as well as why it took so long. But before turning to inter-party relations, it is useful to consider developments within the British, French, and German parties.

Labour, as already mentioned, became the pre-eminent European socialist party during the war. This pre-eminence was reinforced by the party's decisive electoral victory in July 1945, allowing Labour to form a majority government for the first time. Socialists abroad feted the event. Labour's victory, a German socialist

---

[46] See Labour Party, Conference Report December 1944; and IEV, Archives Camille Huysmans, F 126/185, Julius Braunthal, 'The Socialist International and Its President', *The Left News*, no. 103, January 1945, 3071–2. For the conference agenda, see Labour Party, NEC minutes, fiche 328, International Sub-Committee, minutes, 20 February 1945.

[47] OURS, SFIO, Carton: Conférences socialistes internationales, 1945–1948, 'La Conférence internationale de Londres des 3, 4 et 5 mars 1945', Auriol, undated; and SFIO, Comité directeur, minutes, 15 March 1945. For the declaration, see Labour Party, NEC minutes, fiche 330, Labour Party, 'Declarations Issued at the Conference of European Socialist Parties, held in London, 3rd, 4th, 5th March 1945'.

newspaper enthused, meant that post-war reconstruction would be based on proletarian rather than capitalist principles. Similarly, Norwegian socialists congratulated Labour on its 'brilliant victory', heralding it as 'the beginning of a bright future for the British people and for democracy and socialism all over the world'.[48] But if electoral success added to Labour's lustre among European socialists, it also strengthened the party's hesitations towards international socialism and the International. Responding in August 1945 to a request for help from German socialists in Britain, Morgan Phillips, Labour's secretary, remarked that prudence was required since any promises would also bind the government. More generally, Labour leaders sought to draw a sharp line between government and party affairs; and international socialist relations clearly belonged to the latter category, a perspective that justified the Labour government in trying to wash its hands of the subject. Any 'encouragement that we should give to Social Democratic elements on the Continent', Labour's international department was curtly informed in 1946, 'should be strictly at Party level'.[49]

Two additional factors contributed to the Labour government's desire to distance itself from international socialism. One was the lack of interest in socialist internationalism among prominent cabinet ministers, including Ernest Bevin, the foreign secretary, and Attlee, the prime minister. Writing during the war, Attlee did not disguise his belief that a socialist International was essentially anachronistic in a world in which primary loyalties lay with the nation. Socialism, he speculated, was first and foremost a national phenomenon, an 'idea' that had 'to be worked out in every country in accordance with the native genius of the people of that country'. If an International could not be avoided, Attlee believed that it must limit itself to 'a forum for the exchange of socialist ideas and for the meeting together of persons'. In no circumstances must it infringe on the freedom of its member parties.[50] Such thinking only increased once Labour was in power. 'We must not move in the direction of a formal organization or an organization which makes its decisions binding', Phillips explained in 1947. So long as Labour remained in power, party leaders would recoil from the prospect of an International that might complicate the government's foreign policy. Rather than a 'more formal organization', Labour preferred to 'develop the [informal] organization we have at the present time for the purpose of contact and information'.[51] With good reason, European socialists soon identified the Labour government as a principal obstacle to the reconstitution of the International.

The second factor concerns the party. Labour ministers were not omnipotent and party officials had a word to say. In his study of Labour policy during the

---

[48] 'Die Wahlen', *Das Volk*, no. 20, 27 July 1945, 1–2; and AAOB, DNA, D. Saksarkiv. Da Alfabetisk saksarkiv (1940–71), 1945 (B-K), Norwegian Labour Party to Labour, 27 July [1945].

[49] On Phillips, see 'Notiz', Fritz Heine, 8 August 1945, reproduced in Eiber, *Die Sozialdemokratie in der Emigration*, 718; on government–party matters, see LHASC, LPA, International Department, LP/ID, box 2, letter to Healey, 13 April 1946.

[50] CCA, Clement Attlee Papers, ATLE 1/19, 'The Socialist International', undated but wartime.

[51] LAC, CCF-NPD, MG 28 VI-I, vol. 112, CCF, 'Report of the Conference of British Commonwealth Labour Parties held…September 4th to September 11th, 1947', Phillips, 32–4.

1940s, R.M. Douglas argues that the party all but abandoned its earlier inter-nationalism, defined as a willingness to participate in supranational organizations, whether at the European or international levels.[52] But there was also an international socialist aspect to Labour's internationalism, and from this perspective the post-war years are characterized not by abandonment but by a tightening web of inter-party relations. At the centre of Labour's socialist internationalism was its international department led by Denis Healey, who replaced Gillies in January 1945. In his memoirs, Healey reflected somewhat mockingly on his activities as international secretary. Yet at the time, Healey, who defined himself as a socialist and was perceived by others as extremely capable and ambitious, viewed socialist internationalism as a priority for Labour. 'The crucial principle of our own foreign policy', he avowed at Labour's annual conference in 1945, 'should be to protect, assist, encourage, and aid in every way... [the] Socialist revolution wherever it appears.' To a German socialist, Healey intimated that his 'greatest task' was 'to educate' Labour leaders, many of whom were not real socialists, about socialism and especially about international socialism.[53]

To be sure, Healey could not ignore party leaders, who generally wished to delay the reconstitution of the International. But within these admittedly limited parameters he could influence Labour policy by strengthening ties with socialist parties abroad—a process that entangled Labour more firmly in the re-emerging international socialist community. In one notable case, for example, Healey over-rode the hesitations of a cabinet minister (and Foreign Office objections) to invite a delegation of German socialists to Britain at the end of 1946.[54] More broadly, Healey lobbied successfully in favour of helping European socialist parties to re-establish themselves in the wake of occupation and defeat: Labour accordingly acted as a broker between competing factions of Italian socialists while also fur-nishing financial as well as material support (typewriters, paper, etc.) to several parties, including the SFIO and the SPD.[55] This activity is worth underscoring given Ross McKibbin's claim that Labour's socialist internationalism had 'largely disappeared after 1945'. Labour supposedly turned its back on European socialists, convinced that the latter had nothing relevant to offer.[56] But if Labour certainly had its hands full with its domestic programme of building a welfare state, two related points are worth making. First, Labour leaders were not indifferent so much as wary of international socialism, fearful that a strong International would

---

[52] Douglas, *The Labour Party, Nationalism and Internationalism, 1939–1951* (London, 2004).

[53] Labour Party, *Report of the 44th Annual Conference held... May 21st to May 25th, 1945* (London, 1945), Healey, 114; and FES, AdsD, SPD, NL Kurt Schumacher, 65, Herta Gotthelf to Ollenhauer and Heine, 19 March 1946, reporting on a private talk with Healey. Also see Healey, *The Time of My Life*, 72–93.

[54] For Schumacher's visit, see the file in TNA FO 37155374, and especially C13236, Healey to McNeil (FO), 28 October 1946. For another case, see Insall, *Haakon Lie, Denis Healey and the Making of the Amglo-Norwegian Special Relationship*.

[55] For the Italian party, see Ettore Costa, 'The Socialist International in the Cold War (1945–1951)', PhD, La Sapienza—University of Rome, 2015, 359–90. For financial help, see Labour Party, NEC minutes, fiche 331, International Sub-Committee, minutes, 18 April 1945.

[56] McKibbin, *Parties and People: England 1914–1951*, 146–7.

constrain the government. Second, they never repudiated socialist internationalism. Labour leaders presumably could have washed their hands of international socialism, refusing all contact and help. That they did not—that even Attlee and Bevin did not consider doing so—indicates that Labour leaders after 1945 continued to conceive of their party as part of a larger international movement. Labour's goal, accordingly, was not to sabotage the international socialist movement but to shape its development. And this goal provided room for manoeuvre to Healey to knit ever closer ties of mutual expectations and obligations between Labour and socialist parties abroad.

In steering Labour policy in a more international socialist direction, Healey and the international department could count on support from within the party. Jonathan Schneer has examined the groundswell of opposition from the Labour left during the post-war years, which criticized the government's foreign policy for being insufficiently socialist. Much of this criticism centred on notions of a 'third way' in which Britain (and Europe) would pursue an alternative course between the two Cold War blocs rather than allying with one or the other.[57] But an often overlooked element of this critique was a demand for closer relations with socialist parties abroad. In October 1946, several MPs who would become prominent members of 'Keep Left', a lobby group within Labour, wrote to Attlee to express their disquiet regarding the government's foreign policy and to demand that it do more to encourage social-democratic forces abroad. A few months earlier, an article in *Tribune*, a journal close to this group, maintained that the development of 'continuous links' between European socialists and trade unionists offered the best 'antidote to "the nationalisation of socialism"'.[58] The same year, Labour's parliamentary party (PLP) collaborated with French socialists in creating a 'liaison committee' charged with 'promoting close contact' between their two parties, effectively presenting Labour's executive with a fait accompli. At Labour's annual conference the following year, several speakers voiced their regret that the party leadership did not think the time 'ripe' for a new International.[59] All told, then, Labour leaders faced considerable internal pressure for a more activist international socialist policy—pressure that they could not simply ignore.

When it came to international socialist relations, Labour also had to consider the views of other socialist parties. Among them, the SPD distinguished itself as a keen advocate of socialist internationalism. That it did so might seem surprising in light of the scholarship on the post-war SPD, which typically portrays the party as imbued with nationalism. Kurt Klotzbach, author of a semi-official history of the SPD after 1945, thus accuses the party of having promoted 'national self-assertion' to a 'quasi-absolute value' and of having sacrificed its 'tradition of internationalism'

[57] See Schneer, 'Hopes Deferred or Shattered: The British Labour Left and the Third Force Movement, 1945–49', *Journal of Modern History* 56 (1984), 197–226; and Schneer, *Labour's Conscience: The Labour Left 1945–51* (Boston, MA, 1988).

[58] Parliamentary Archives, Benn W. Levy Papers, 18, letter to Attlee, 29 October 1946; and William Warbey, 'The Fight Against Nationalism', *Tribune*, no. 434, 20 April 1946, 9–10.

[59] Labour Party, NEC minutes, fiche 337, 27 February 1946; and Labour Party, *Report of the 46th Annual Conference held May 26th to May 30th, 1947* (London, 1947), 168–9.

on the altar of 'national prestige and the nation state'.[60] Dominating much of this historiography is the figure of Kurt Schumacher, the SPD's fiery leader who believed that German socialism must present itself as a fervent defender of Germany's national interests.[61] But if the German nation stood at the centre of Schumacher's preoccupations, he insisted as early as August 1945 that '[t]he policy of [German] social democracy is consciously internationalist...'[62] And Schumacher understood internationalism above all in terms of socialist internationalism, and socialist internationalism in terms of membership in an international socialist community. Schumacher's socialist internationalism was partly rooted in sheer necessity. In the spring of 1945, not only did Germany lie in ruins but the SPD was a shadow of its earlier self after years of dictatorship. Complicating the colossal task of rebuilding the party was the fact that the SPD faced powerful rivals at home both in the communists and in the Christian democrats.

In this context, the SPD desperately needed help, and Schumacher looked to foreign socialists to provide it. Much of this help was of a practical nature—assistance for exiled German socialists to return to Germany, office supplies, newspaper.[63] But as important as practical help (if not more so) was the inspiration that came from being part of a larger international socialist movement. This was perhaps less the case with Schumacher himself, who had never been actively involved in international socialist activities. But the SPD after 1945 cannot be reduced to its leader. Prominent party officials, many of whom had spent the Nazi period in exile and dependent on the aid of foreign socialists, returned to Germany after the war deeply committed to socialist internationalism. Among them was Erich Ollenhauer, Schumacher's deputy and eventual successor as party leader, who had been active in the international socialist youth movement during the 1920s and who developed close ties to Labour during the war. Writing in June 1946 to a Danish socialist, Ollenhauer described 'contact with our friends in the social democratic parties abroad' as a 'matter of survival' for German socialists; the following month he commented that the SPD's 'isolation' from other European socialists was harder to bear than even the massive material shortages afflicting post-war Germany.[64]

---

[60] Klotzbach, *Der Weg zur Staatspartiei: Programmatik, praktische Politik und Organisation der deutschen Sozialdemokratie 1945 bis 1965* (Berlin/Bonn, 1982), 195–6, 209–10. For similar arguments, see Beatrix W. Bouvier, *Zwischen Godesberg und Großer Koalition: Der Weg der SPD in die Regierungsverantwortung* (Bonn, 1990); and Dietrich Orlow, 'Delayed Reaction: Democracy, Nationalism, and the SPD, 1945–1966', *German Studies Review* 16 (1993), 77–102.

[61] For Schumacher, see Volker Schober, *Der junge Kurt Schumacher, 1895–1933* (Bonn, 2000); and Peter Merseberger, *Der schwierige Deutsche. Kurt Schumacher* (Stuttgart, 1996).

[62] Schumacher, 'Politische Richtlinien für die S.P.D. in ihrem Verhältnis zu den anderen politischen Faktoren', 8 August 1945, reproduced in Willy Albrecht, ed., *Kurt Schumacher. Reden—Schriften—Korrespondenzen 1945–1952* (Berlin, 1985), 276–7.

[63] For one example, see LHASC, LPA, International Department, LP/ID Box 2, Heine (SPD) to Healey, 1 August 1946.

[64] Ollenhauer to Hans Hedtoft-Hansen, 20 June 1946; and Ollenhauer to Karl Heinz, 12 July 1946, both in FES, AdsD, SPD, NL Kurt Schumacher, 65. For more on the SPD's socialist internationalism, see Talbot C. Imlay, '"The Policy of Social Democracy is Self-Consciously Internationalist": The German Social Democratic Party's Internationalism after 1945', *Journal of Modern History* 86 (2014), 81–123.

The SPD's socialist internationalism quickly manifested itself in efforts to renew ties with foreign socialists. Not surprisingly, closer relations with Labour was a priority from the beginning. In November 1945 Schumacher instructed Ollenhauer to consult with his 'English friends' on the question of how to construct Germany anew.[65] Taking matters into his own hands, Schumacher wrote to Healey in March 1946 of the SPD's desire for 'close contact' with European socialists, adding that '[w]e hope that we shall have a very early possibility of taking part in international co-operation with the Socialist workers' movement'. In a follow-up message three months later the SPD's executive committee pleaded for 'closer contact with the international Labour Movement', explaining: 'We feel ourselves bound up with the international Socialist Movement, of which we consider ourselves a member.'[66] More concretely perhaps, Schumacher urged Healey to invite an SPD delegation to come to Britain, a request (as we saw) that Healey accepted. In Britain, Schumacher made the most of his visit, meeting with Labour officials and MPs and enthusing to a journalist that with British comrades he felt as if he were speaking to 'his own german [*sic*] socialist comrades'. If Schumacher's enthusiasm was undoubtedly exaggerated, it does underscore the importance he attached to relations with Labour.[67]

The SPD did not woo the Labour Party alone. During the early post-war years, German socialists worked hard to knit ties to several Continental socialist parties.[68] But from the start the SFIO merited especial attention. In the autumn of 1944, German socialists in London instructed Günther Markscheffel to set up a bureau in Paris. If one of his tasks was to aid German socialists in France to return to Germany, another and more important one was to establish 'close organic and political contact' with the SFIO and to underscore the SPD's commitment to socialist internationalism.[69] Markscheffel, who had spent the war in France, was well acquainted with French socialism and he quickly gained access to SFIO leaders, including Léon Blum, allowing him to keep the SPD informed of their thinking on various issues.[70] As in the case of Labour, Schumacher took matters into his own hands, instructing Markscheffel to press the SFIO to send a delegation to Germany. Soon afterwards, Schumacher wrote to Daniel Mayer, the SFIO's secretary general, to propose a 'direct exchange of thinking'.[71]

---

[65] FES, AdsD, SPD, NL Fritz Heine, 144, Schumacher to Ollenhauer, 8 November 1945.

[66] Schumacher to Healey, 4 March 1946, reproduced in Albrecht, ed., *Kurt Schumacher*, 423–4; and LHASC, LPA, International Department, LP/ID/GER/21, 'Memorandum handed to the British Labour Party Delegation by the Executive Committee of the German Social Democratic Party, June 1946'.

[67] For Schumacher's visit, see Imlay, ' "The Policy of Social Democracy is Self-Consciously Internationalist" ', 91–2.

[68] For example, see Marc Drögemöller, *Zwei Schwestern in Europa. Deutsche und niederländische Sozialdemokratie 1945–1990* (Berlin, 2008), 52–70.

[69] See OURS, E5 180 BD, Ollenhauer to Markscheffel, 4 February 1945; and FES, AdsD, NL Günther Markscheffel, 4, letter from October 1945.

[70] Copies of Markscheffel's report are in FES, AdsD, NL Günther Markscheffel, 7; and ibid., SPD, NL Kurt Schumacher, 67.

[71] FES, AdsD, SPD, NL Kurt Schumacher, 67, Markscheffel to Schumacher, 20 December 1945; and Schumacher to Mayer, 6 January 1946.

For Schumacher, relations with the SFIO were a priority partly because, like so many socialists, he considered a Franco-German rapprochement to be essential for European peace. Working together, German and French socialists would put an end to decades of rivalry between their two countries. But more immediate calculations were also at work. German socialists understood that the SPD's reintegration into the international socialist community required the SFIO's active support. And they also understood that such support would not be easy to attain, given the general hostility of the French to all things German. In his memoirs, Markscheffel recalls that it could be dangerous to speak German in Paris following the Liberation.[72] Yet the difficulties notwithstanding, the SPD's courtship of the SFIO met with growing success. The SFIO thus agreed to send Salomon Grumbach as its official delegate to the SPD's congress in July 1947—a sign that the German socialists were no longer anathema. Grumbach, who spoke fluent German and was friends with numerous German socialists, told his hosts that the creation of an International would take time, not least because the SPD would first have to overcome the 'walls of mistrust' surrounding German socialism. But Grumbach also expressed confidence that the SPD would succeed in doing so. European socialists, including German socialists, had now entered into 'organized contact' with one another, and from this process a new International would materialize.[73]

Grumbach's presence at the SPD's congress is noteworthy for another reason: it indicated a major shift in the SFIO's international policy. French socialists perceived themselves as champions of socialist internationalism. Indeed, in his report on the March 1945 international socialist conference in London, Auriol claimed that French socialists (and some Belgian ones) were the only 'real internationalists' in attendance.[74] But behind such claims lurked doubts. Blum, the SFIO's leader, emerged from his wartime ordeal determined to root French socialism more firmly in the nation. In his extended essay, *À l'échelle humaine*, completed in 1941 but published in 1945, Blum effectively separated socialism from internationalism, defining the latter exclusively in terms of international political and economic organizations such as the League of Nations. While not denying that the SFIO was both national and international, Blum gave precedence to the former. French socialism, he now insisted, was 'ardently patriotic', conceiving of the 'international order as resting on the basis of free and independent nations'.[75] Blum's protégé and successor as party leader, Daniel Mayer, sympathized with a more national-centred orientation. A statement of party principles thus declared that the party's internationalism should never result in a neglect of 'justified national interests'.[76]

---

[72] FES, AdsD, NL Günther Markscheffel, 8, ms memoirs, dated 1976.

[73] SPD, *Protokoll der Verhandlungen des Parteitages der Sozialdemokratischen Partei Deutschlands vom 29. Juni bis 2. Juli 1947 in Nürnberg* (Hamburg, 1948), Grumbach, 30–4.

[74] OURS, SFIO, Carton: Conférences socialistes internationales, 1945–1948, 'La Conférence internationale de Londres des 3, 4 et 5 mars 1945'.

[75] Blum, *À l'échelle humaine* (Paris, 1945).

[76] FNSP, Fonds Daniel et Cletta Mayer, 1MA 2.2, 'Projet de memorandum du Parti Socialiste (S.F.I.O.). Sur l'unité organique', Auriol, undated but 1945.

Admittedly, this emphasis on the nation was partly a response to the PCF, which French socialists viewed as an instrument of a foreign country. But it also reflected a perspective that placed France at the centre of the SFIO's internationalism. French socialists, the party's internal bulletin affirmed in 1945, must pursue a foreign policy 'permitting the independence and the blooming of France'.[77]

Under Mayer's direction, the SFIO's hesitations towards socialist internationalism expressed themselves in reticence towards the SPD. There is no evidence that Mayer answered Schumacher's request for exchanges between French and German socialists. More fundamentally, the SFIO's policy towards Germany and the SPD appeared to be in flux during 1945–1946. While opposing what it took to be the Gaullist project of dismembering Germany, the SFIO demanded the imposition of far-reaching measures of control over the country, including a prolonged occupation, on the grounds that the German people (including German socialists) could not be trusted. To believe that another, better Germany would appear once Nazi Germany had been defeated, asserted an SFIO memorandum circulated to European socialist parties in March 1945, 'would be a self-deception which no reasoning whatever could justify'. Several months later, a circular to local SFIO organizations solicited opinions on whether the party should reconsider its opposition to Germany's dismemberment. More pertinently still, the circular asked whether European socialists 'should facilitate... the reconstruction of the German socialist party and accept its entry into the International'.[78] Although Mayer refrained from providing a direct answer, his deep-seated suspicion of Germans left little doubt that he preferred to exclude the SPD from the international socialist community.

The situation changed quickly, however, when a militant revolt led to Mayer's defeat at the SFIO's annual congress in the autumn of 1946. Scholars have understood this revolt as a reaction to fears that the party was losing its working-class identity, even if ironically this identity did not reflect the majority of socialist voters. Several factors stoked the fears of militants: the disappointing election results in June; the frustrating experience of tripartism (coalition with communists and Christian democrats); and Blum and Mayer's emphasis on socialist humanism rather than class struggle. At the congress, Mayer's successor as secretary general, Guy Mollet, offered doctrinal purity—defined vaguely as a 'return to Marxist analysis'.[79] Less well known, however, is that socialist internationalism constituted an important element of Mollet's socialist doctrine. Distinguishing himself from his predecessor, Mollet set out to recommit his party to socialist internationalism: the SFIO, he told its foreign affairs commission in May 1947, must place itself 'at the head of the international idea' among European socialists.[80] In his detailed

[77] Ibid., SFIO, 'Bulletin intérieur', no. 5, June 1945.

[78] LHASC, LPA, LIS 27/3/17, SFIO, 'The German Problem', undated but March 1945; and OURS, Fonds Charles Lancelle, 13 APO/1, SFIO circular, no. 29, 23 June 1945.

[79] See François Lafon, *Guy Mollet* (Paris, 2006), 255–305; and Graham, *Choice and Democratic Order*, 267–365. For Mollet, see OURS, Fonds Jacques Piette, 27 APO/6, 'Appel au Parti', undated but March 1946 and signed by Mollet among others.

[80] OURS, SFIO, Carton: Conférences socialistes internationales 1945–1948, Commission des affaires étrangères, minutes, 27 May 1947.

study of the post-war SFIO, Wilfrid Loth characterizes the commitment to socialist internationalism as insincere; it was a rhetorical device that served both to disguise a dominant nationalist perspective and to paper over differences between French socialists.[81] Loth's argument, however, is overly cynical: as subsequent chapters will show, the SFIO's position on various international issues cannot be defined simply as nationalist, if only because they were influenced by inter-party discussions. But it is also too cynical because, whatever the true motives of Mollet and his allies, their commitment to socialist internationalism was never simply rhetorical.

That something changed is evident from the SFIO's policy towards the SPD. Unlike with Mayer, the SFIO under Mollet's direction lent its wholehearted support to the SPD's reintegration into the international socialist community. In effect, this meant the victory of those like Grumbach, who argued that it would be counterproductive to abandon German socialists: if French socialists wanted a democratic Germany, Grumbach explained to the SFIO's executive committee in early 1947, they must establish 'a permanent contact' with the SPD. At a local level, German socialists now found it easier to function in the French occupation zone, a change they attributed to the SFIO's intervention.[82] Meanwhile and more generally, the SFIO under Mollet provided a new impetus to efforts to revive the International. French socialists, the SFIO's leader announced in September 1947, 'are anxious to reconstitute the workers' International because, now more than ever, there is one hope for humanity: the International'. Moving beyond rhetoric, the SFIO worked hard to organize regular exchanges of information between the parties, creating, for example, a socialist educational centre in Paris that French socialists hoped to transform into a socialist university.[83] When it came to socialist internationalism, the SFIO was unwilling to accept the status quo.

FORGING AN INTERNATIONAL: THE INITIAL STEPS, 1946–1947

With the end of the war in Europe, Labour quickly emerged as a principal obstacle to a speedy reconstitution of the International. As the pre-eminent socialist party endowed with considerable financial resources, Labour was well placed to slow down the movement towards an International. But Labour could neither freeze developments altogether nor completely control them. Socialist parties would continue to interact, and this interaction would help to institutionalize international socialist relations. During 1946–1947 two related questions dominated discussions

---

[81] Loth, *Sozialismus und Internationalismus: Die französischen Sozialisten und die Nachkriegsordnung Europas 1940–1950* (Stuttgart, 1977), 113, 135, 269, 294.

[82] For Grumbach, see OUR, Comité directeur, 28 May 1947; for the French occupation zone, see Edgar Wolfrum, *Französische Besatzungspolitik und Deutsche Sozialdemokratie: Politische Neuansätze in der 'vergessenen Zone' bis zur Bildung des Südweststaates 1945–1952* (Düsseldorf, 1991).

[83] Mollet, 'Une seule issue: l'Internationale', *Le Populaire de Paris*, 18 September 1947, 1, 4. Also see LAC, CCF-NPD, MG 28 VI-I, vol. 133, SFIO (Mollet) to CCF, 8 May 1947; and SFIO (Mollet and Pierre Commin) circular letter, 9 December 1947, with attachment: 'La Centrale d'éducation du Parti socialistes [*sic*] S.F.I.O.'.

between European socialists: what to do with the SPD and what to do with the socialist parties from Eastern Europe. Answers to both questions would be worked out over the next two years, with the Germans included and the Eastern Europeans excluded from the international socialist community. This process contributed greatly to shaping the nature of socialist internationalism. In terms of principles, the emphasis would be on democratic socialism and, as a flipside, on anti-communism. That said, it would be wrong to see international socialism simply as an instrument of Cold War politics, if only because (as subsequent chapters will argue) in practising internationalism European socialists sought to define distinct positions on concrete issues.

To recall, the international socialist gathering in London in March 1945 had decided to create a preparatory committee to examine the possibility of creating an International. Although chaired by Huysmans, Labour provided the secretariat for the committee. At a committee meeting in Paris in August 1945, the participants agreed that Labour should draw up a memorandum on the subject of the International.[84] The resulting document was notably ambivalent. On the one hand, it insisted that any new International must be more effective than its predecessors as 'it would be a grave mistake to revive the International unless it is to have some chance of successful influence.' Accordingly, it outlined an International consisting of a small secretariat housed in London; a Bureau meeting four times a year; and an annual conference. On the other hand, the memorandum envisaged an organization with strictly limited authority. Decisions would not be binding on its members 'in the sense of compelling them to take action in the direction recommended by the International or its Bureau'. Indeed, the International would function largely as a news and publicity bureau, providing information to socialists and non-socialists on the activities of its member parties.[85]

With this document in hand, Labour organized an 'informal' conference of socialist parties in May 1946 in order to 're-establish contacts broken by the war, to exchange information, and to work out, if possible, common policies on problems of mutual interest'.[86] Directing the conference proceedings would be Hugh Dalton, the Chancellor of the Exchequer, the chair of Labour's international subcommittee, and a convinced German hater. 'The German problem is very simple,' he remarked the same year, 'the problem is that there are too many Germans.' If Dalton opposed any proposals for cooperation with the SPD, he could also be counted on to defend the Labour government's position that concrete steps towards an International were 'premature and undesirable at the present time'.[87] The conference itself, held in the seaside resort town of Clacton, brought together delegates from eighteen socialist parties, all but four of which were European. Labour paid the

[84] LHASC, LPA, International Sub-Committee, minutes, 18 September 1945.

[85] LHASC, LPA, LSI 27/4/17, Labour, International Sub-Committee, 'Note on the Possible Reconstruction of the Socialist Internationale', January 1946.

[86] AAOB, Haakon Lie, Dc 0004, Labour (Phillips) to Lie, 21 February 1946.

[87] Ben Pimlott, ed., *The Political Diary of Hugh Dalton 1918–40, 1945–60* (London, 1986), 30 September 1946, 381; and Labour Party, NEC minutes, fiche 339, International Sub-Committee minutes, 12 April 1946.

expenses for all delegates, with the result, as a Canadian socialist noted, that the gathering became 'a kind of private house party put on by the British L.P.'; he added wryly that such munificence made it difficult 'to blast with sufficient vigour…a host who wines and dines you so well'.[88] As conference chairman, Dalton sought to steer the deliberations away from contentious issues, asking the delegates simply to report on 'the progress of Socialism in their own countries, their difficulties and their successes'. The SFIO's Grumbach, however, was not content with such a limited mandate. The 'purpose of this Conference is to find a means of rapid reconstruction of the Socialist International', he insisted, adding irritatedly that this was 'the third meeting here in England for this purpose'.[89]

In the ensuing debate on the International, Grumbach argued forcefully for immediate steps to be taken. He received support from the Belgian socialist Victor Larock, who warned against an International 'inspired solely by the Labour Party'. Dalton led the charge against hasty measures, insisting that they would cause difficulties for many Eastern European socialist parties as a socialist International would unlikely be welcomed by Moscow. If forced to choose between international socialism and the Soviets (whose armies occupied their countries), Eastern European socialists would find themselves in an impossible situation. That the Soviets factored heavily in Dalton's thinking was evident from his opening comments, in which he stressed that Labour's priority was on maintaining 'close relations' with Moscow. Here, moreover, Dalton could count on support from Labour's left, who feared that a new International would lead to the abandonment of Eastern European socialists. As an article in *Tribune* explained:

> An effective International today would inevitably and rightly fall under the leadership of the powerful and independent parties of the West—above all, of the British Labour Party. Those parties which are subject to Russian influence or committed to some degree of collaboration with their own Communists would find it embarrassing, if not impossible, to bind themselves by a formal tie to such a body. In particular, an International would depend on the crystallisation of zones of influence which would sacrifice the Eastern Socialist parties to Russia.[90]

But if the fate of Eastern European socialism factored into Dalton's thinking, so too did hostility to any organization that might infringe on Labour's freedom of action. Following a lengthy plea for an International, a Canadian delegate was subjected to a forty-five minute 'private conversation' with Dalton who 'explained to me why it would be unwise, nay disastrous, at this juncture to revive the International…[and] writ large across his whole statement was the obvious fact that he feared that an international [*sic*] might prove to be embarrassing.'[91] Dalton's public and private entreaties proved successful. Rather than an International, the

  [88] LAC, CCF-NPD, MG 28 VI-I, vol. 184, report, Robert MacKenzie, 21 May 1946.
  [89] IISH, SI, 234, Labour, International Socialist Conference at Clacton, 17–20 May 1946.
  [90] 'Britain and World Socialism', *Tribune*, no. 493, 7 June 1946, 9–10.
  [91] LAC, CCF-NPD, MG 28 VI-I, vol. 184, report, MacKenzie, 21 May 1946.

participants merely agreed to create a 'Socialist Information and Liaison Office' (SILO) in London whose staff would be provided by Labour.

In his official report to Labour's executive, Dalton claimed that 'valuable work had been done' at Clacton that 'would form a useful basis for future deliberations'.[92] The next international socialist conference would be in November 1946 in Bournemouth, another seaside resort in England. Topping the agenda was the question of SPD membership. Schumacher had sent a message to the Clacton conference asking for the German party to be readmitted into the 'international collaboration of socialist parties'. Dalton, who strongly opposed the SPD's request, conspired to kill discussion on the subject, ignoring the protests of several parties.[93] Dalton, however, was absent at Bournemouth, which allowed Labour officials to express a more sympathetic stance. In addition to circulating a report praising the SPD's wartime and post-war record, Morgan Phillips pleaded for the SPD's admittance, arguing that its positions corresponded to those of international socialism and that it would be counterproductive to leave German socialists isolated. Labour's case received strong backing from Western European and Scandinavian socialists who all agreed—as one Belgian socialist asserted—that 'the Germans must be invited into our confidence for the sake of the future, as Germany was very important to the International Socialist movement.' Determined opposition, however, came from Eastern European socialists who harboured deepseated suspicions of the German people (and German socialists). A Polish socialist also pointed to the SPD's anti-communism, which would likely lead the Soviets to view its membership in the International as part of a 'new [anti-communist] offensive'; Polish socialists, he added, 'could not be party to anything which could give offense to Soviet Russia, and nothing could be more offensive than such an invitation'. In the end, the delegates agreed to invite German socialists to an upcoming conference as 'observers' in order to 'state their views and to answer questions'.[94]

If the SPD's fate dominated the agenda, the participants at Bournemouth also found time to discuss the International. In many ways, the debate mirrored that at Clacton. Labour delegates resisted any concrete steps towards a reconstituted International, citing the risks of alienating both the Soviets and Eastern European socialists. The advocates of an International, meanwhile, were weakened by the absence of French socialists, who were preoccupied with national elections at home. In this situation, Labour repeated its earlier success in postponing a decision. Yet the Labour delegates were also compelled to make some concessions. Along with augmenting SILO's activities, they agreed to the creation of a consultative committee. To be sure, its powers were limited: the committee had no executive

[92] Labour Party, NEC minutes, fiche 339, NEC, 22 May 1946; and *The Political Diary of Hugh Dalton*, 20 May 1946, 372.

[93] FES, AdsD, NL Kurt Schumacher, 66, Schumacher to Healey, 12 May 1946, with attachment: 'Greetings to the International Socialist Conference in London'. For Dalton's efforts, see LAC, CCF-NPD, MG 28 VI-I, vol. 184, report, 21 May 1946.

[94] Copies of Labour's report on the SPD and of the discussion on Germany are in AAOB, Haakon Lie, Dc 0008. For the vote, see IISH, SI, 234, 'Minutes of the International Socialist Conference Bournemouth November 8–10, 1946'.

authority and all decisions had to be unanimous. Nevertheless, Labour failed to confine the committee to administrative tasks alone. At the demand of several parties, it was decided that the committee would 'act as a clearing house for all information between parties, including the exchange of views on political issues'. Those socialist parties in favour of a new International now had a forum in which to lobby for more active measures.[95]

The consultative committee's first task was to organize the next international socialist meeting, which would be held in Zurich in June 1947. As agreed to at Bournemouth, German socialists were invited to attend as observers. SPD officials initially hesitated to accept the invitation: unwilling 'to play dumb' (*die gekränkte Unschuld spielen*), they preferred to proceed by an exchange of letters rather than a personal appearance. However, when Healey reassured the SPD of Labour's support, Schumacher decided to go to Zurich.[96] For the SPD leader, the prospect of an interrogation by fellow socialists was undoubtedly galling. At home, Schumacher presented German socialism as a victim of Nazism, having himself spent almost the entire Nazi period in a concentration camp. As he liked to point out, while German socialists were being brutally hounded by the Nazi regime during the 1930s, their French and British counterparts had all too often supported the appeasement of Hitler's Germany. Angrily dismissing accusations of nationalism, Schumacher countered that it was other socialist parties and not the SPD that were 'prisoners of their national ideology'.[97] The SPD leader never doubted that his party constituted the best and, indeed, the only guarantee of democracy in Germany. In light of these firmly held convictions, Schumacher's decision to attend the Zurich conference testifies to his party's commitment to international socialism.

For the Zurich conference, the SPD submitted a document presenting the party as the 'core force' of German democracy and as the 'vanguard' of internationalism.[98] In his oral presentation, Schumacher emphasized the SPD's attachment to democratic socialism and its uncompromising opposition to nationalism and totalitarianism. 'Can international socialists', Schumacher asked rhetorically, 'renounce German social democracy as a trusted and equal member of our [international] working community?' Following Schumacher's departure, a five-hour debate ensued in which the Eastern European socialists expressed their dissatisfaction with the SPD leader's performance. In language echoing Gillies' wartime anti-German outbursts, the Polish socialist Julian Hochfeld maintained that the German people, German

[95] See LAC, CCF-NPD, MG 28 VI-I, vol. 184, M. Schulman to David Lewis (CCF), 15 November 1946; and SSAZ, SPS, Ar 1.260.48, 'Minutes of the Consultative Committee Meeting of the International Socialist Conference', 12 December 1946.

[96] FES, AdsD, Sekretariat Fritz Heine, 2/PVAJ00000083, Heine to Victor Schiff, 19 February 1947; and IISH, SI, 235, Healey to Schumacher, 23 April 1947; and Loeb (SILO) to Ollenhauer, 14 May 1947.

[97] 'Sitzung der obertsen Parteigremein am 10. und 11. Januar 1947 in München', reproduced in Willy Albrecht, ed., *Die SPD unter Kurt Schumacher und Erich Ollenahauer 1946 bis 1963: Sitzungsprotokolle der Spitzengremien Band 1. 1946 bis 1948* (Bonn, 1999), Schumacher, 137. For a good summary of Schumacher's views, see his speech, 'Wir verzweifeln nicht!', 6 May 1945, reproduced in Albrecht, ed., *Kurt Schumacher*, 203–36; and more generally, Kristina Meyer, *Die SPD und die NS-Vergangenheit 1945–1990* (Göttingen, 2015).

[98] SSAZ, SPS, Ar 1.260.17, 'Die deutsche Sozialdemokratie heute und morgen', Schumacher.

socialists, and Schumacher together represented a danger to peace, to socialism, and to German democracy. International socialists had a responsibility to combat nationalism, and this meant refusing admission to the SPD. As evidence of the SPD's inveterate nationalism, he pointed to its refusal to enter into a 'united front' with German communists. Significantly, the SFIO's Grumbach also referred to the duty of international socialists to argue instead that the SPD be admitted. Along with a moving personal defence of Schumacher, Grumbach maintained that, unlike its pre-1918 predecessor, the post-1945 SPD was untainted by nationalism. Directly addressing the Eastern European socialists, he insisted that Schumacher's refusal to unite with German communists was fully justified, adding that it corresponded to his own position vis-à-vis French communists.[99]

Schumacher's performance impressed many members. Pietro Nenni, the Italian socialist close to the communists, wrote privately of the SPD's leader 'moral vigour'.[100] But to be admitted the SPD needed a two-thirds majority, which it did not get partly because of Labour. Although publicly backing the SPD, behind the scenes, Labour officials continued to hesitate before the possibility of a definitive break with the Eastern European parties. In the run-up to the Zurich conference, Labour had rejected SFIO and POB requests for a meeting of the Western European parties to coordinate their positions because it risked creating the impression of a 'western bloc'.[101] More generally, Labour officials continued to hope that the socialist/social democratic parties in Eastern Europe could preserve some element of political independence, which in turn would help to prevent their countries from falling completely under Moscow's thumb. But whatever the precise reasons, at Zurich the Labour delegation appears to have pressured the Swiss to abstain on the vote, helping to deny the SPD a two-thirds majority.[102] But while disappointing, the vote was not a complete defeat for the SPD. At Zurich, the participants voted seventeen to two to create a liaison committee to maintain contact with German socialists and to draw up a report for the next international conference. More promising still, the committee would be presided over by the Belgian de Brouckère, a staunch supporter of the SPD, and would be composed overwhelmingly of members from the Western European parties. De Brouckère, moreover, did not hide his sympathies: in July 1947 he assured the SPD's annual congress of international socialism's duty to help the SPD.[103]

The delegates at Zurich also discussed the International, with the impetus coming largely from the SFIO. The month before, Mollet had told the party's executive committee that French socialists must push strongly for an International at the conference. British socialists attributed the enthusiasm for an International to the influence of the SFIO's left; and French police reports did highlight the

[99] Extensive but incomplete minutes of the meeting are in SSAZ, SPS, Ar 1.260.17.

[100] Pietro Nenni, *Tempo di Guerra Fredda. Diari 1943–1956* (Milan, 1981), 10 June 1947, 367.

[101] OURS, Louis Lévy Papers, uncatalogued, Lévy to Valentin, 14 May 1947.

[102] For Labour's scheming, see the French diplomatic report, based likely on SFIO information, in MAE, Série Y Internationale, DAPC, 76, Hoppenot (Suisse) to MAE, no. 1348, 18 June 1947.

[103] SPD, *Protokoll der Verhandlungen des Parteitages der Sozialdemokratischen Partei Deutschlands vom 29. Juni bis 2. Juli 1947*, 59–60.

growing dissatisfaction of SFIO militants with Labour's hesitations regarding the International.[104] Yet Mollet's socialist internationalism was also part of his campaign to bring about a doctrinal *redressement* of French socialism. At the Zurich conference, in any event, Mollet doggedly lobbied for a reconstituted International, explaining that socialists had to be better organized internationally because too many contemporary problems simply could not be solved at the national level: 'There is an urgent need, for all these problems, to determine positions that are not those of one country but of international socialism.' Mollet accordingly seconded a Belgian proposal to create a commission that would set to work at once to draw up the 'organizational basis and rules of functioning' for a new International. Thrown on the defensive, Phillips responded that Labour, while approving an International in principle, believed the present moment to be 'premature'. Revealingly, Labour's secretary remarked that the priority for his party was to build socialism at home and to win the next elections, thereby demonstrating that 'socialism was not an ephemeral creation'. For these reasons, he made clear, the Belgian proposal was unacceptable.[105]

Without Labour's support, the Belgian proposal was stillborn. Yet Phillips realized that Labour could not simply offer obstacles. He thus proposed as a compromise the creation of a commission to examine the functioning of an International. Max Buset, the Belgian socialist, eagerly embraced Phillips' proposal, interpreting it as a sign that Labour 'was not a priori hostile towards the idea of...reconstituting the International' and that preparatory work towards this goal could begin. The delegates not only endorsed the proposal in decisive fashion (seventeen to two); they also agreed that the SFIO (and not Labour) would be responsible for the commission. In his report on the conference, Mollet waxed enthusiastic about the result, claiming that the 'International is already on the march'. Although Grumbach, who would chair the commission, sought to temper Mollet's enthusiasm, he too envisaged the commission as a major step towards a socialist International.[106]

The SPD did not have to wait long for its admission into the international socialist community. Although some German socialists seethed at what they perceived as unfair treatment at the Zurich conference, Schumacher indicated his willingness to cooperate with the liaison committee presided over by de Brouckère. At the committee's first meeting, the SPD chief reiterated his commitment to 'the great fundamental principles of the Socialist International'.[107] Following two more meetings, de Brouckère drafted an interim report describing the SPD as a 'fraternal party whose activity can be linked to that of our own parties'. In refusing to offer

---

[104] OURS, SFIO, Comité directeur, 28 May 1947. For British socialists, see Francois Bondy, 'Socialism between Two Conferences', *Socialist Commentary*, July 1947, 678–9; and for police reports, see APP, BA 1959, 11 October 1946.

[105] See the minutes in SSAZ, SPS, Ar 1.260.17.

[106] Labour Party, NEC Minutes, fiche 351, International Sub-Committee, 'Notes on Minutes of the Zurich Conference', Healey, undated; and OURS, SFIO, Comité directeur, 11 June 1947.

[107] For anger at the SPD's treatment, see GstA, Nachlass Otto Braun, C.I. 276, Braun to Carl Severing, 8 July 1947; and Severing to Braun, 24 July 1947. For the liaison committee, see IISH, SI, 349, 'Sitzung der Kontakt-Kommittees in Nurnberg am 30 Juni 1947', undated.

the SPD its support, he warned, international socialism 'would bear the moral responsibility for the consequences—which may be most dangerous'. Not surprisingly, Polish socialists contested the report's analysis, insisting that German socialism remained 'imbued with a spirit of nationalism and revisionism'.[108] By then, however, any lingering hesitations about the SPD's admission among the Western European parties—and from Labour in particular—had vanished. As a result, at the international socialist conference in Antwerp at the end of 1947, the discussion on the SPD proved anticlimactic. De Brouckère presented a summary of his interim report, followed by a 'spirited but by no means bitter debate' in which the Western European socialists all endorsed the report. The SPD was then admitted by a count of twelve to four, with the Eastern Europeans voting against.[109] In a letter to Schumacher shortly afterwards, Phillips happily welcomed the SPD into 'the community of International Socialism'.[110]

The subject of the International, by comparison, proved to be more contentious. Committed to an International, French socialists worked to transform the commission created by the Zurich conference into an instrument for this purpose. As commission chairman, Grumbach worked closely with the Belgian members to force the pace of developments. At the committee's first meeting in August 1947, Grumbach thus underscored the need to pursue an International 'with a firm determination to succeed'. Echoing Grumbach, Max Buset, the Belgian socialist, declared that the POB 'will never tire in its efforts to achieve an International'. Seeking to reassure the doubters, Buset explained that the International would not function as a general staff dictating orders to its member parties but would instead facilitate the practice of socialist internationalism. Predictably, Phillips argued against precipitate action, warning against exacerbating differences with the Eastern European parties. The wiser course, he proposed, would be to improve the functioning of existing structures and especially the consultative committee formed at the Bournemouth conference in 1946. Having reached an impasse, the committee members agreed to meet again at the end of October 1947 and to ask both the Belgian party and Labour to submit memoranda on the construction of an International.[111]

Phillips' memorandum was the first to arrive. A mere two pages in length, it focused on the consultative committee, envisaging it as an administrative and not political body charged with organizing international socialist conferences and

[108] LHASC, LPA, International Socialist Conferences, SILO, 'Interim Report of the Chairman of the Liaison Committee Appointed to Keep in Touch with the German Social Democratic Party (S.P.D.)', de Brouckère, undated; and IEC, Archives Louis de Brouckère, 3, Polish Socialist Party to de Brouckère, 30 October 1947.

[109] LHASC, LPA, International Socialist Conferences, 'Summary of Proceedings', International socialist conference, Antwerp, 28 November–2 December 1947. The comment on the debate comes from LAC, CCF-NPD, MG 28 VI-I, vol. 184, MacKenzie letter (report), 7 December 1947.

[110] FES, AdsD, SPD, Internationale Abteilung, 2890, Phillips (Labour) to Schumacher, 4 December 1947.

[111] OURS, SFIO, Carton: Conférences socialistes internationales, 1945–1948, 'Procès-verbal de la 1ère réunion de la Commission internationale désignée à Zurich pour examiner les moyens et méthodes de la reconstruction de l'Internationale', 19 August 1947.

overseeing the activities of the information office (SILO). The Belgian memorandum, written by Buset, was considerably longer and more ambitious. Having rejected Phillips' proposal as grossly inadequate, it maintained that all the important political forces in the world (the Soviets, the Americans, and the Vatican) possessed an 'international structure'; only socialism did not. 'Such a weakness... gravely undermines the prestige of socialism and makes it powerless in the international realm.' The purported goal was to construct an International flexible enough in terms of doctrine and tactics to include the Eastern European parties and the parties in government (i.e. Labour). As a spur to action, Buset annexed a draft outline of a constitution for the new International.[112] Confronted with Buset's arguments, the Labour delegates refused to budge. Almost certainly on instructions from Phillips, Healey wrote Grumbach soon afterwards declaring that Labour's memorandum represented the 'unalterable basis' of its position. '[I]t is quite impossible', Healey added, 'for us to provide a different document from the one already circulated, since we are satisfied that the form of contact [between socialist parties] we preserve at present is the only basis for collaboration.'[113]

That Healey's letter did not put an end to the issue of an International became clear at the next meeting of the consultative committee in Brussels at the end of October 1947. As the manuscript notes of a Swiss participant indicate, matters came to a dramatic head at the meeting. Speaking for the absent Phillips, Healey reiterated Labour's opposition to Buset's proposals, maintaining that 'the time had not arrived' for an International. While Buset spoke of his 'disappointment' at Healey's statement, Grumbach declared that he was 'saddened, discouraged [and] very pessimistic'. Presumably in an attempt to close discussion once and for all, Healey launched into an extended attack on socialist internationalism. The widespread 'mystique of the International', he declared, had fostered illusions regarding the possibilities of international socialism; even 'a small advance forward' towards an International would heighten these illusions. The 'old internationalist spirit' was dead, Healey bluntly continued, adding that 'faith in the effectiveness of socialist internationalism is an illusion'. Not yet finished, Labour's international secretary insisted that the only reality for socialists were national parties before describing as 'unfortunate' the earlier decision to create a consultative committee on the International. Evidently shocked, Buset not only denounced Healey as the 'champion of anti-internationalism' but also castigated the 'clear and deliberate sterility' of Labour's position, which precluded any 'step forward'. Other participants, fearing a rupture, pleaded for a compromise, implicitly criticizing the apparent inflexibility of Labour's position.[114]

[112] Labour Party, NEC minutes, fiche 352, Phillips circular, 29 August 1947, containing: 'Memorandum on the Consultative Committee of the International Socialist Conference by Morgan Phillips...'.

[113] LHASC, LPA, International Department, LP/ID, Box 7, Grumbach to Healey, 16 October 1947; and Healey to Grumbach, 20 October 1947; and IEV, Fonds Max Buset, 64, Phillips to Buset, 15 October 1947.

[114] SSAZ, SPS, Ar 1.260.22, 'Séance du mercredi 29.10.47'; also see IEV, Fonds Max Buset, 67, 'Réunion du Comité provisoire chargé de considérer les possibilités de reconstruction de l'Internationale nommé par la Conférence de Zurich. Réunion tenue à Bruxelles les 28 et 29 Octobre 1947', undated.

Significantly, confronted with a possible rupture of international socialist relations, Healey (in the words of a Hungarian participant) became 'more flexible' [*nachgiebiger*]. Claiming to support 'international [socialist] solidarity and action', he announced that Labour was prepared to 'take a step forward towards international collaboration'. More concretely, Healey proposed the creation of an international socialist bureau with a more expansive mandate than the consultative commission, including the authority to name commissions to examine precise issues. After lengthy negotiation, the delegates agreed that 'the question [of the International] should remain open and should be re-examined in due course.'[115] In the meantime, the consultative committee would be replaced by an International Committee for Socialist Conferences (ICSC or Comisco) equipped with an expanded secretariat and charged with organizing twice-yearly conferences, with setting up commissions with 'specific duties', and with 'putting into action' agreed-upon measures by the member parties. As part of this structural strengthening, the information bureau (SILO) would be overhauled.[116] The following month the Antwerp conference endorsed these decisions. Speaking for Labour, Harold Laski assured the conference delegates that he welcomed 'the spirit and letter' of the decisions and viewed them 'as an important step forward in the development of international socialism'.[117]

By the end of 1947, European socialists had developed a structure of inter-party relations. It is possible to cast the story as one of failure: despite the pleas of Continental socialists, no International existed, thanks in good part to Labour's resistance.[118] Yet an emphasis on failure overlooks several noteworthy points. One is that Labour had been forced to make concessions; no less importantly, Labour officials backed down before the prospect of a break with international socialism, suggesting Labour's continued attachment to the latter, however conditional it may have been. Another point concerns the dwindling influence of the Eastern European parties. Mounting Cold War tensions, one sign of which was the creation of the Kominform in the autumn of 1947, fuelled pessimism about the likely survival of non-communist Eastern European socialism—a pessimism reinforced by the persecution of Eastern European socialists. Most European socialists, a Canadian socialist reported, assume 'that the Socialist parties within the Soviet bloc can have only a very brief life expectancy ahead of them'.[119] One by-product

[115] 'Bericht des ungarischen Sozialdemokraten A. Bán über die Sitzung der internationalen Kommission…in Brüssel', 1 November 1947, reproduced in Peter Heumos, ed., *Europäischer Sozialismus im Kalten Krieg. Briefe und Berichte 1944–1948* (Frankfurt, 2004), 483.

[116] LHASC, LPA, International Sub-Committee, 1942–1949, 'Draft Resolution unanimously voted by the International Preparatory Commission, Brussels, 29th October, 1947', undated.

[117] For the Antwerp conference, see IEV, Fonds Max Buset, 68, 'Conférence internationale d'Anvers', undated; and LHASC, LPA, International Socialist Conferences, 'Summary of Proceedings', International socialist conference, Antwerp, 28 November–2 December 1947.

[118] For an emphasis on failure, see Wilfried Loth, 'Socialist Parties between East and West' in Antonio Varsori and Elena Calandri, eds., *The Failure of Peace in Europe, 1943–48* (Houndmills, 2002), 138–42; and Steininger, *Deutschland und die Sozialistische Internationale nach dem Zweiten Weltkrieg*, 44–59.

[119] LAC, CCF-NPD, MG 28 VI-I, vol. 184, MacKenzie letter (report), 7 December 1947. For persecutions, see the files in LHASC, LPA, LP/ID/EE/1-11.

of this pessimism was that Labour found its case against an International greatly weakened. A final point concerns the practice of socialist internationalism. With a fledgling structure of cooperation now in place, a forum existed for European socialists to discuss pressing concrete issues.

PRACTICAL COOPERATION: EUROPEAN SOCIALISTS AND THE MARSHALL PLAN

Following the Antwerp conference at the end of 1947 it was unclear how to proceed. European socialists had agreed to revisit the question of the International but only in some indefinite future; and while Labour had made concessions, it remained opposed to what Healey termed any 'centralized organization'. One issue, however, would soon force the pace of developments: that of European unity. Chapter 7 will examine more closely socialist positions on Europe, including the important differences between socialists, but for now it is enough to say that the question of Europe's future provided fertile terrain for practical cooperation between the principal socialist parties—cooperation from which the International would emerge.

For European socialists (and Europeans more generally) the announcement in 1947 of what would become the Marshall Plan placed the issue of European unity squarely on the political agenda, if only because Washington insisted on important measures of political and economic coordination among countries receiving aid. The plan had been briefly discussed at the Antwerp conference, with the Western and Northern Europeans generally in favour of accepting American aid and the Eastern Europeans more sceptical, if not opposed. The resulting compromise recognized the 'usefulness' of American aid while also warning against any political strings that might be attached.[120] For the Labour Party, whose government keenly backed the American initiative, such a lukewarm endorsement was insufficient. Accordingly, at Comisco's first meeting in January 1948, Labour pressed for a conference to be held of European parties favourable to the Marshall Plan. Although the SFIO and POB would have preferred a conference open to all socialist parties, their proposal was defeated, another sign of the growing isolation of the Eastern European parties.[121] In the run-up to the conference, held in London in March 1948, Labour pursued a two-pronged strategy. One prong was to provoke a final rupture with the Eastern European parties, a goal achieved at a Comisco meeting on the eve of the London conference. At the meeting Morgan Phillips announced that a 'democratic [and] socialist Europe free from all threat of tyranny and aggression' could not be constructed in cooperation with communists, adding that the latter had 'declared war on democratic socialism'. And because the Eastern

[120] LHASC, LPA, International Socialist Conferences, 'Resolution on Peace and Economic Reconstruction', Antwerp conference.
[121] Labour Party, NEC minutes, fiche 357, International Sub Committee, 'Notes on the first meeting of the Conference of International Socialist Parties, London, January 10th, 1948'.

European socialist parties were now under the communist thumb, he continued, they could not belong to the international socialist community. Although Mollet sought half-heartedly to avoid a break, he finally backed Phillips, helping to ensure the passage of a resolution that excluded the Bulgarian, Hungarian, and Romanian parties and made the exclusion of the Czech and Polish parties little more than a formality.[122] The principal bloc of parties opposing the Marshall Plan had been eliminated.

The second prong of Labour's strategy was to insist that the success of the Marshall Plan as well as the future of Western Europe hinged on international socialist cooperation. In a lengthy memorandum prepared for the March 1948 conference and circulated beforehand to the invited parties, Labour emphasized the need for European socialists to adopt a clear and united position in favour of the Marshall Plan:

> The European Recovery Programme [the Marshall Plan] is likely to be a major factor in the political and economic life of all the countries of Western Europe for the next four years. In consequence the Socialist parties of Western Europe, most of which participate in Governments directly responsible for the programme, have a common interest in considering together some of the problems with which... the Programme is likely to confront them separately. They have too a common obligation to explain clearly the reasons why they support the... programme. Misunderstandings of the Programme's aims are already current, causing exasperation in some quarters and suspicion in others. There is here a need and an opportunity for Socialist initiative.

As the citation suggests, far more appeared to be at stake than American aid. European socialists, the memorandum propounded, had an 'obligation' to work for 'a closer association of the free countries of Western Europe' not only because democratic socialism could not survive in national isolation, but also because 'the concept of European unity' risked being hijacked for anti-socialist ends. 'Western Europe and democratic socialism stand or fall together,' it concluded. 'The ideal of European unity can only be saved from corruption by reactionary politicians if the Socialists place themselves at the head of the movement for its realisation.' Socialists, in short, must work together to build a socialist Europe.[123]

In many ways, the March 1948 conference constituted a success for Labour, as the delegates endorsed the Marshall Plan. Whatever the qualms about its possible political implications, American aid was simply too attractive a prospect to reject. As for the flipside, the appeal to European unity, Phillips was able to limit Labour's engagement to vague talk of economic interdependence and

---

[122] IEV, Fonds Max Buset, 74, 'Réunion du Comité des Conférences socialistes internationales du 19 au 20 mars 1948 à Londres', undated. For the growing divergence between Western and Eastern European socialist parties, see Jan-Arend de Graaf, 'Across the Iron Curtain: European Socialism between World War and Cold War, 1943–1948', PhD, University of Portsmouth, April 2015; and Heumos, *Europäischer Sozialismus im Kalten Krieg*.

[123] AAOB, Haakon Lie, Dc 0005, Healey (Labour) circular, 27 February 1948, with attachment: 'Memorandum of the British Labour Party on European Cooperation within the Framework of the Recovery Programme', undated.

international planning.[124] But Labour officials quickly encountered difficulty in confining discussions within these limits. Following an SFIO request, delegates from five socialist parties (Belgium, Britain, France, Holland, and Luxembourg) met in Paris the following month to 'coordinate' policies on Europe. The resulting resolution went well beyond its predecessor, extolling the benefits of European economic integration and of supranational political authorities.[125] As chapter 7 will show, the question of supranationalism in particular would stir considerable tensions among European socialists, not least between Labour and the Continental parties. But for now, the more pertinent point is that Labour had helped to place the subject of European unity at the top of the international socialist agenda.

No party was more eager to maintain the subject on the agenda than the SFIO. Committed to creating an International, French socialists sought to strengthen ties with Labour following the Antwerp conference. In January 1948 Grumbach informed Phillips that his party wanted to establish 'more regular and intimate contact than heretofore' with Labour; the following month Mollet proposed to Phillips a 'series of Liaison visits' between their two parties in order to foster 'a mutual exchange of opinion'.[126] Meanwhile, from London, the French socialist Louis Lévy advised Mollet that if the SFIO wanted to collaborate more closely with Labour, it should focus on practical issues. Labour officials, Lévy explained, 'do not want to embark [on exchanges] with a vague agenda, leading to discussions of everything and nothing'.[127] From this perspective, the question of Europe's future offered the SFIO precisely what it needed—a concrete subject for discussion. Accordingly, in a lengthy discussion paper submitted to socialist parties, the SFIO argued for greater collaboration on the subject, recommending in particular a 'permanent organism' to oversee all aspects of the Marshall Plan.[128] In an effort to avoid what one SFIO official termed 'abstract generalities' at the Paris meeting in April 1948, beforehand French socialists circulated a veritable flood of documentation on precise aspects of European unity—economic, commercial, imperial.[129] At the meeting itself, the SFIO successfully insisted on the creation of a permanent contact committee between the five participating parties. For French socialists, as an internal note remarked, European unity had become 'the motor of international socialist policy'.[130]

---

[124] Labour Party, NEC minutes, fiche 360, 'Declaration of the European Socialist Parties on the European Recovery Programme'. Also see the minutes of the conference in LHASC, LPA, International Socialist Conferences, Selsdon Park Conference, March 1948.

[125] AAOB, Haakon Lie, Dc 0005, SFIO circular, 5 April 1948; and LHASC, LPA, International Socialist Conferences, Selsdon Park Conference, March 1948, 'Resolution passed unanimously by International Conference of Socialist parties on European Unity, Paris, April 24/25, 1948'.

[126] LHASC, LPA, International Sub-Committee, 1948 file, 'Note on a Conference between Mr. Morgan Phillips and Monsieur Salamon [*sic*] Grumbach on Friday, 9th January, 1948'; and Morgan Phillips Papers, France 1951 file, Oliver Harvey (French embassy, Paris) to Phillips, 20 February 1948.

[127] OURS, Louis Lévy Papers, uncatalogued, Lévy to Mollet, 11 February 1948.

[128] OURS, SFIO, Carton: Conférences socialistes internationales 1945–1948, 'Travail préparatoire pour détérminer la position de la délégation française à la conférence des partis socialistes...(20-21-22 mars 1948)', undated.

[129] OURS, Fonds André Ferrat, 5 APO/1, Ferrat to Francis Leenhardt, 30 March 1948. For the documentation, see the file in AAOB, Haakon Lie, Dc 0005.

[130] IEV, Fonds Max Buset, 75, SFIO circular, 11 May 1948; and OURS, Fonds André Ferrat, 5 APO/1, 'Suggestion au C.D.', 29 April 1948.

As with the SFIO, the SPD was eager to collaborate with other socialist parties in the construction of a socialist Europe. Having worked hard to be admitted into the international socialist fold, German socialists had every intention of being active members. In late 1947, Carlo Schmid, a prominent SPD member, maintained that the fate of socialism at the national level depended on its 'internationalism'. Only 'when socialists of all nations stride forward hand in hand to defend against the enemies of freedom', he wrote, will 'the working classes of all countries achieve their goal'.[131] That Schmid's was not an isolated voice became clear at the SPD's annual congress in September 1948. Qualifying the present state of 'international [socialist] cooperation' as 'very inadequate', Willi Eichler, a member of the party's executive, argued that the SPD must work for the 'reactivation' of the International in order to forge an 'international socialist *Kampfgemeinschaft*'. Elaborating on Eichler's comments, Ollenhauer enthused that German socialists had recently gained 'renewed participation in these [international socialist] exchanges'. The immediate task was to translate this 'participation' into reality—a task that could best be accomplished through practical cooperation on European unity. Needed in this regard were not 'programmatic declarations', the SPD's deputy leader insisted, but 'the development' of 'practical, concrete solutions'.[132] As chapter 7 will show, the SPD's European policy would prove contentious both among German socialists and between them and other European socialists. But from early on, Schumacher committed the SPD to working with its European counterparts on the issue. The construction of Europe, the SPD's leader declared in this sense in 1947, 'is the duty of all Europeans, it is the duty of all European socialists'.[133]

It would be an exaggeration to say that by 1948 Labour had become as enthusiastic about the practice of socialist internationalism as the SFIO and the SPD. In a lecture in December, Harold Laski could claim that for most socialists 'loyalty to the nation-state' always came before 'loyalty to international socialism'.[134] Yet their hesitations notwithstanding, Labour officials were coming to appreciate the potential usefulness of international socialism. As a memorandum from the party's international subcommittee explained, although Comisco could never be a centralized organization like the Kominform, it did function as 'a moral symbol through which the policy of its members can be influenced'; Labour, it added, 'could use [Comisco] as a platform from which to publicise the British approach to problems of democratic socialism'.[135] Here, moreover, the Marshall Plan experience had been an eye-opener, as closer ties with European socialists proved its worth as a means of strengthening support for the American programme. This helps to explain Labour's readiness to agree to SFIO requests for closer relations between

---

[131] FES, AdsD, NL Carlo Schmid, 79, 'Der internationale Sozialistenkongress', ms, 3 December 1947.

[132] SPD, *Protokoll der Verhandlungen des Parteitages der Sozialdemokratischen Partei Deutschlands vom 11. bis 14. September 1948 in Düsseldorf* (Glashütten im Taunus, 1976), Eicher, 69–70; Ollenhauer, 76–80.

[133] SPD, *Protokoll der Verhandlungen des Parteitages ... 1947*, Schumacher, 36–7.

[134] Laski, *Socialism as Internationalism* (London, February 1949), 4, 8.

[135] Labour Party, NEC minutes, fiche 365, 'Memorandum on International Socialist Policy', undated but October 1948.

the two parties. Labour officials feared that French socialists, under pressure from the PCF, might waver in regards to the Marshall Plan.[136] But Labour's growing interest in socialist internationalism extended beyond such immediate calculations. In April 1948 the international subcommittee recommended that Labour 'encourage the establishment of a more peaceful and permanent Socialist organisation'; two months later, Phillips told a meeting of European socialists that Labour desired 'a strong international socialist organization equipped to fight for democracy and socialism'. More concretely, Labour decided not only to increase its financial contribution to Comisco, but also to reinforce its international department in order to 'extend and develop direct contact' between socialist parties.[137]

To be sure, Labour, sought to instrumentalize socialist internationalism: the guiding question was, how could it be used to benefit Labour? But much the same can be said of the SFIO and the SPD. That European socialist parties tended to view matters in a self-interested sense is less noteworthy than the convergence of their positions. All three socialist parties manifested a growing engagement with international socialism; and, just as importantly, for all three, this engagement translated into a desire for practical cooperation on concrete issues.

THE DEVELOPMENT OF PRACTICAL COOPERATION, 1949–1950

When it came to sites for practical cooperation, European socialists could benefit from several possibilities over the next two years. Comisco constituted one obvious possibility. While it was originally envisaged to hold one plenary conference per year and twice-yearly committee meetings, at a Comisco gathering in July 1949 the participants decided to increase the number of encounters to three or four per year; they also agreed to revamp the secretariat, appointing a permanent 'administrative officer' along with a clerical staff tasked with preparing reports, circulating information, and organizing political activities. No less importantly, the delegates approved an SFIO proposal to establish a special commission 'to examine the general lines both of doctrine and organisation which should govern the activity and ideological bases of the future International, including the powers of its Executive and Bureau'.[138] Attendance at the various Comisco meetings varied but most often included high-ranking party officials as well as prominent politicians and leaders. For Labour, Healey and Phillips were regular attendees, as were Grumbach, Georges Brutelle (party secretary), and Mollet for the French, while

---

[136] LHASC, LPA, Morgan Phillips Papers, France 1951 file, 'Note on Conversation with Mr. Brutelle 6/10/48'.

[137] Labour Party, NEC minutes, fiche 361, International Sub-Committee, 20 April 1948; IEV, Fonds Max Buset, 76, 'Conférence de Vienne (4,5,6,7 juin 1948)'; and IISH, SI, 626, Phillips (Labour) circular, 11 January 1949.

[138] Labour Party, NEC minutes, fiche 377, 'Notes on meeting of the Committee of International Socialist Conference, London, July 18th, 1949', Healey; also see OURS, Louis Lévy Papers, uncatalogued, 'Proposals by the Comisco Sub-Committee for Reorganising the London Office of the International Socialist Conference', Comisco circular, no. 30/49, 21 June 1949.

for the SPD Ollenhauer became a fixture. Equally pertinent, the initial idea of limiting discussions to administrative or informational matters was quickly waived. Almost from the start, participants grappled with pressing issues of international politics. A Comisco conference in Baarn (Holland) in May 1949, for example, witnessed extended debates on questions of international economics (trade, investments, employment) as well as on the burning issue of European unity; at a conference in Copenhagen the following year, both the Schuman Plan and colonialism figured prominently on the agenda.[139] European socialists, in short, were becoming familiar with the practice of socialist internationalism.

The proliferation of commissions under Comisco's aegis to consider specific issues reinforced this process of familiarization. A good example concerned the Saar. Now largely forgotten, at the time the Saar's future was a source of persistent European and especially Franco-German tensions. A small, coal-rich, and German-speaking area on the Franco-German border, the Saar had been occupied in 1945 by the French; under a 1947 statute it became politically autonomous but attached economically to France by a customs and monetary union, a status confirmed by the March 1950 Saar Convention negotiated between the French and Saar (but not West German) governments. As with the Bonn government, the SPD declared the Convention unacceptable, insisting that the Saar must be returned to Germany with full rights; the SFIO, meanwhile, initially supported an autonomous Saar and perhaps even its economic union with France while rejecting territorial annexation. Yet if German and French socialists disagreed on the Saar's future, both were interested in cooperating to find a mutually acceptable solution. To facilitate this goal, the SFIO and the SPD welcomed a Labour proposal in 1950 to create a Comisco commission to report on the Saar. Made up of Belgian, Dutch, and Swiss socialists, the commission quickly got down to work, issuing a report the same year that pronounced against the Saar's political and economic attachment to France and suggested either a Franco-German economic agreement or a multinational European authority to administer the region's industry.[140] Taking the report as starting point, over the next several years French and German socialists forged a framework based on the Saar's political and economic reattachment to Germany but also including economic advantages for France. Significantly, this framework prefigured the agreement eventually arrived at by the French and German governments.[141]

In addition to special commissions, European socialists organized a series of experts' conferences under Comisco's patronage. These conferences brought together small

[139] For the Baarn conference, see OURS, Louis Lévy Papers, uncatalogued, 'International Socialist Conference Baarn Holland, 14–16 May 1949: Summarised Report of Proceedings'; and IISH, SI, 240, 'Report of International Socialist Conference in Copenhagen, 1–3 June 1950'.

[140] For the Saar commission, see OURS, Fonds Guy Mollet, AGM 57, 'Rapport de la Commission de la Saare de COMISCO', undated but 1950. For bachground, see Brian Shaev, 'Estrangement and Reconciliation: French Socialists, German Social Democrats and the Origins of European Integration, 1948–1957', PhD, University of Pittsburgh, 2014, 104–9.

[141] On the Saar negotiations, see Talbot C. Imlay, 'Exploring What Might Have Been: Parallel History, International History, and Post-War Socialist Internationalism', *International History Review* 31 (2009), 550–5.

delegations from several parties to discuss issues of common concern. The first one, on the administration of nationalized industries, took place in December 1948 in Britain. Others would soon follow during 1949 and 1950 on the problems of European economic cooperation; on workers' participation in industrial management; on the international control of basic industries; on socialist propaganda; and on trade liberalization. Procedural rules were quickly established. Delegates would attend as individuals and not as party representatives, thus encouraging freedom of discussion while also avoiding formal commitments on the part of parties; the agenda would be limited in scope in order to foster focused debate; and a small 'continuing secretariat' would be created to ensure that the conference was adequately organized. Labour officials, who were active participants in the conferences from the beginning, insisted on informal discussions and resisted calls for published resolutions.[142] Some socialists found these restrictions frustrating. Writing in March 1950, the SFIO's Marceau Pivert ridiculed the practice of 'secret' meetings of socialist 'experts' whose endless discussions produced no results. The International, he pronounced, would never emerge from these 'chatterings' (*bavardages*).[143]

Pivert's dismissal of the experts' conferences was somewhat unfair. Notwithstanding the restrictions imposed, the conferences quickly gained momentum—and importance. The delegates (as well as their parties) appreciated the opportunity for open and sustained exchanges on concrete issues. A Swiss socialist thus described the September 1949 conference as 'a grounded, intensive and disciplined exchange of views... Each participant expressed his opinion that was not necessarily entirely that of his party.' Similarly, Healey welcomed the experts' conferences as 'a new technique... by which important problems could be seriously discussed by expert individuals without compromising the national parties themselves'.[144] This general satisfaction is noteworthy because it prompted socialist parties to endow the conferences with increasing significance, which in turn made it difficult to keep them within the narrow confines preferred by Labour. This became clear at the experts' conference in March 1950 in Witten, Germany. Held to consider the seemingly abstract issue of the international control of basic industries, the conference in fact amounted to an extended discussion between European socialists of the very concrete issue of the Ruhr's future status—an issue with political implications for European unity.[145] Chapter 7 will consider some of these implications, but for now the important point is that the experts' conferences quickly evolved into a prominent site of practical cooperation between socialist parties.

Comisco, however, was not the only vehicle for cooperation between European socialists. In May 1949 ten European countries signed a treaty creating a

[142] OURS, APS, circulaires ISC 1949, Comisco, 'Conference of Economic Experts, Bennekom, Holland, 14–18 March 1949. Proposals for Future Work', 14 April 1949. For Labour, see IISH, SI, 238, Phillips (Labour) to M.C. Bolle (Comisco), 2 August 1949; and 350, Fritz Heine (SPD) to Julius Braunthal, 28 February 1950.

[143] CHS, Fonds Marceau Pivert, 559/AP/9, 'Correspondance socialiste', no. 28, March 1950.

[144] SSAZ, SPS, Ar 1.260.18, untitled report, M. Oettli, 3 October 1949; and Healey, 'The International Socialist Conference 1946–1950', *International Affairs* 26 (1950), 371–2.

[145] FES, AdsD, SPD, Parteivorstand, 2/PVBT0000004, 'Bericht über die Tagung der COMISCO – Wirtschaftsexperten in Witten Ruhr vom 26.–31. März 1950', Rudolf Pass, undated.

European Council, which included a parliamentary assembly in Strasbourg that held its first session in August 1949. Socialists, who were well represented in the assembly from the outset, greeted its creation with considerable enthusiasm. Writing on the eve of the opening session, Léon Blum promised that socialists would play a prominent role in the assembly because its purpose supposedly corresponded to the 'doctrine and policies of International Socialism'. More prosaically, Schumacher justified the SPD's participation as an opportunity to interact with fellow socialists.[146] Following a suggestion from the Dutch party, socialist delegates at Strasbourg formed a group equipped with a small secretariat that met regularly during the assembly's sessions to consider the position to adopt on various agenda items. To expedite this work, the group created a 'limited commission' comprising one member from each party; equally important, the presence of high-ranking party officials and politicians, among them Mollet, Ollenhauer, and Hugh Dalton, added clout to the discussions.[147] Although the latter could be contentious, the socialist group never ceased to function, becoming a prominent site of interaction between European socialists. For committed Europeanists such as the German Willi Eichler and the French André Philip, the socialist group at Strasbourg provided an instrument for mobilizing international socialism behind the construction of a united Europe. Aware of the divisions between European socialists over Europe, Ollenhauer expressed greater caution about the group's potential. But even he spoke warmly of the personal contacts and exchanges with fellow socialists at Strasbourg.[148]

The period from 1948 to 1950 saw the development of both a structure and practice of cooperation between European socialists. Fuelling this development was a combination of pressing international issues and the emergence of several sites for cooperation, the most prominent one being Comisco. European socialist parties, as a result, found themselves being drawn closer together, a process evident in the extensive exchanges on concrete issues such as the Saar. Another such issue was 'demontage'—the seizure in the Allied occupation zones of German industrial capacity. Labour and the SPD in particular worked together to modify British policy.[149] Another sign of the strengthening ties between European socialists was the attention each party accorded to international socialism: the activities of socialist parties, for example, received extensive coverage in the principal French and German socialist newspapers during the 1940s and into the 1950s. On a more personal level, European socialists regularly helped one another in mundane matters. Thus, in March 1950, Healey wrote to the Norwegian socialist, Haakon

---

[146] Blum, 'Un grand commencement', *Le Populaire de Paris*, 8 August 1949, 1; and 'Interview Schumachers mit dem "Neuen Vorwärts": Die Entscheidung der SPD-Fraktion für eine Beteiligung an der deutschen Delegation für Straßburg', reproduced in Albrecht, ed., *Kurt Schumacher*, 802–4.

[147] IEV, Fonds Max Buset, 163a, van der Goes van Naters circular, 4 August 1949. Copies of several meetings of the socialist group in Strasbourg in August 1950 are in AAOB, Haakon Lie, Dc 0007.

[148] Eichler, 'Fraktionsbildung in Straßburg', *Neuer Vorwärts*, 25 August 1950, 2; and OURS, APS, Comité directeur, 12 September 1950, Philip. For Ollenhauer, see FES, AdsD, SPD, Parteivorstand Protokolle, 'Sitzung des PV am 16.9.50 in Stuttgart', and attachment: 'Bericht über die Tagung der beratenden Versammlung des Europa-Rates in Straßburg vom 7. bis 28. August 1950'.

[149] See the file in FES, AdsD, SPD, PV Sekretariat Fritz Heine, 2/PVAJ00000011.

Lie, asking if he could help find housing 'with a decent Socialist family' for Attlee's daughter.[150] Yet, however topical or mundane the issue, European socialists had constructed a political community characterized by formal and informal bonds. The pressing question by the end of the 1940s was not whether but when would this emerging community assume the institutional form of a fully fledged socialist International.

ADVANCING TOWARDS AN INTERNATIONAL

Of the three principal parties, the SFIO remained the one most determined to construct an International. In June 1949 Robert Pontillon, the secretary of the party's international bureau, submitted to Comisco members a memorandum on the 'reconstitution of the International'. Claiming that the time had come to reconsider the question of an International, it argued that the chief obstacles were financial and political. To overcome the political obstacles, the memorandum proposed the creation of a 'general secretariat' equipped with the resources and authority to oversee all aspects of the relations and activities between member parties; this body would also be responsible for extending relations beyond Europe to include socialist parties from Latin America, Asia, and the Pacific. To overcome the financial obstacles, it proposed an independent endowment for the general secretariat to which each party would contribute. Given the SFIO's straitened financial situation and thus its reluctance to increase its own general financial contribution to Comisco, this proposal arguably lacked some credibility. In any case, Pontillon asked for the memorandum to be placed on the agenda of Comisco's upcoming meeting in London in July 1949.[151] At the meeting, the SFIO delegates, who included Mollet and Grumbach, argued, in the words of an SPD participant, 'loudly and passionately' for a 'real International'. Labour delegates countered with their own memorandum and set of proposals for a more modest strengthening of Comisco's staff. More importantly, as a Labour report remarked, the memorandum did not (unlike the SFIO's) assume 'the desirability of reconstructing a formal Socialist International at the earliest possible moment'. After considerable debate Labour's 'sober and practical' [*nüchtern und sachlich*] memorandum was approved.[152]

French socialists, however, were not prepared to abandon the goal of an International. In August 1949, Georges Brutelle, the SFIO's deputy secretary general, wrote to Comisco of his party's dissatisfaction with the results of the recent London meeting. The 'will to reconstitute the International is so powerful in my

---

[150] AAOB, DNA, D. Saksarkiv. Da Alfabetisk saksarkiv (1940–71), 1950 (F-L), Healey (Labour) to Lie, 22 March 1950.

[151] OURS, Louis Lévy Papers, uncatalogued, Pontillon (SFIO) circular, 30 June 1949, with attachment: 'Reconstitution de l'Internationale', undated. For the SFIO's financial contribution, see ibid., Mollet to Braunthal (Comisco), 8 February 1950.

[152] For the SPD report, see FES, AdsD, NL Wilhelm Sander, 6, Sander to Ollenhauer, 10 July 1949; for the Labour report, see LHASC, LPA, International Sub-Committee, 1949 file, 'Notes on Meeting of the Committee of the International Socialist Conference, London, July 7th, 1949'.

party', Brutelle explained, 'that we believe it necessary to remind our brother parties of our initial proposals.' The 'consecration of the present situation', he added, was simply unacceptable. Over the next several months the SFIO lobbied for the question to be reconsidered, circulating to Comisco's member parties its earlier memorandum and proposals.[153] The apparent reluctance of Comisco's secretary to take up the question provoked Mollet's ire: in November 1949 he demanded that the reconstitution of the International be placed anew on Comisco's agenda.[154] As a result, at a meeting in Paris the following month, European socialists once again discussed the subject. Although no minutes of the meeting have been found, it is clear that French socialists did not succeed in convincing their fellow delegates. As a Labour report tersely noted: 'No support for the reconstruction of the Socialist International was forthcoming.'[155]

What followed can be understood as a crisis in the SFIO's commitment to socialist internationalism. Even before the Comisco meeting in December 1949, Mollet showed signs of frustration. The previous month he had complained to a gathering of French socialists that few parties aside from the SFIO were 'fundamentally internationalist'. 'A French socialist', Mollet elaborated, 'never stops being French...but he is above all a socialist. It is perhaps disappointing but a British socialist is more British than socialist, a German socialist more German than socialist.' The results of the Comisco meeting did nothing to reduce his frustration. The purpose of Comisco meetings, Mollet bitterly commented at an SFIO gathering in December 1949, was not to construct an International but simply 'to register the divergences' between parties. Implicitly referring to Labour, the SFIO's secretary general asserted that the chief problem was the nationalist impulses of socialist parties when in power:

> At present it would seem that socialist parties, once they attain partial or full [governmental] power...retreat within themselves, within the nation of which they are a part and in the name of which they operate and [in so doing] become less and less internationalist.[156]

In the spring of 1950, Mollet's frustration boiled over. Complaining that socialists exhibited 'too much the tendency to be more nationalist than socialist', he urged the SFIO's executive to consider quitting Comisco. Unless the other parties changed their ways, Mollet contended, 'there is no longer any reason to declare oneself a member of a workers' International that in reality no longer exists.' Other executive members such as Grumbach, Lévy, and Philip argued against a 'rupture' of relations with international socialism, while acknowledging that the present situation was untenable. We must find a 'solution for the sickness', Grumbach

---

[153] OURS, Louis Lévy Papers, uncatalogued, Brutelle (SFIO) to Bolle (Comisco), 23 August 1949; and LAC, CCF-NPD, MG 28 VI-I, vol. 133, SFIO (Mollet) circular, 2 September 1949.

[154] IISH, SI, 265, Mollet to Bolle, 8 November 1949.

[155] LHASC, LPA, International Sub-Committee, 1949 file, report on Comisco meeting, 10–11 December 1949.

[156] OURS, APS, Conseil National, Session d'information, 6 November 1949, Mollet, 253–4; and APS, 'Congrès extraordinaire de Paris, 13 au 14 décembre 1949', Mollet, 301–2.

opined. But Mollet's patience was clearly waning. Within Comisco, he maintained, 'one no longer speaks socialist' and the SFIO 'should not shrink from threatening a rupture'.[157]

Mollet's disillusionment with socialist internationalism found an echo beyond the SFIO's executive. At the party's national council in November 1950, Édouard Depreux, a prominent socialist and former government minister, maintained that internationalism amounted to a 'pretty gesture and a beautiful ideal but it did not exist...in the hearts and spirits' of socialist parties. As with Mollet, Depreux claimed that European socialist parties were prey to an 'awful heresy in believing it possible to construct socialism in one country alone'. And again as with Mollet, many French socialists identified the British as the principal culprits. Castigating Labour for exploiting internationalism for its own ends, Jean Le Bail, a member of the SFIO's parliamentary group, grumbled that Labourites were constantly placing 'sand in the wheels' [*batons dans les roues*] of international socialism. Socialist internationalism, he insisted, cannot be subordinate to one party in the International but must instead 'be a cooperative enterprise' in which socialist parties took 'collective decisions in an internationalist sense'.[158] Another former government minister, André Philip, spoke more alarmingly of a 'crisis' of European socialism caused by the nationalist orientations of socialist parties—a condition that also afflicted the SFIO. 'There is crisis of continental socialism,' Philip exclaimed to the party's parliamentary group in February 1950. 'It comes from the fact that of all the nationalizations [that have been undertaken] the most successful has been the nationalization of socialist parties.' Unless European socialists succeeded rapidly in creating a 'real International', he maintained in another speech the same year, developments would continue in the sense of 'national socialisms', leading eventually to 'national socialism'.[159]

For Philip, the task of European unity offered the most promising means of creating an International and, in the process, of infusing European socialism with a much-needed dose of internationalism. On the SFIO's left, Pivert shared Philip's enthusiasm for European unity though not his emphasis on the leadership of socialist parties. Pivert was convinced that nationalism blighted European socialism, writing in 1950 that 'the vast majority of workers in France, Germany, Italy [and] Britain continue to stew in their nationalist juice'; as a result, a 'tragic powerlessness' afflicted international socialism.[160] The SFIO, its sister parties, and international socialism all desperately needed to be renewed, but for Pivert this renewal would have to come not from above but from below—from militants in each party working collectively. As he proclaimed in a 1950 note:

> when one WANTS to direct organizations along the path in which they will only flourish, prosper and gain in strength and effectiveness, one must constantly intervene

[157] OURS, APS, Comité directeur, 5 April 1950.

[158] OURS, APS, Conseil National, 4–5 November 1950, Dépreux, 151; and FNSP, Groupe parlementaire socialiste, GS1, 16 November 1949, Le Bail.

[159] FNSP, Groupe parlementaire socialiste, GS2, 7 February 1950, Philip; and AN, Papiers André Philip, 625/AP/17, dossier 1950, speech to 'Cher comrades', undated.

[160] OURS, Fonds Charles Lancelle, 13 APO/1, 'Toujours le vieux style...et pourtant le temps presse', Pivert, 10 February 1950.

WHERE ONE MUST SEARCH FOR STRENGTH, that is within <u>the base itself.</u> When one is at the head of an organization that wants to advance internationalism, one cannot limit oneself to a few specialists in international activity.[161]

In an effort to practise what he preached, Pivert founded a journal, the *Correspondance socialiste internationale*, which he conceived as a rallying point for internationalist-minded socialist militants in Europe and beyond. Writing to his brother in December 1950, Pivert explained that international ties between militants were 'as valuable and useful as the large workers' organizations that don't contribute much to the forward march of events'. A truly internationalist International was possible, he declared. 'But we must begin by believing in it and wanting it.'[162]

Pivert complained that French socialist leaders opposed a real International. Whatever the truth of the complaint, Mollet undoubtedly believed Pivert's bottom-up approach to be illusory. Much like European unity, which would be created through intergovernmental negotiations, a socialist International would be first and foremost the work of elites—of party leaders and their officials. For all his evident frustration with other socialist parties, moreover, Mollet in the end was unwilling to abandon the international socialist community or the goal of an International. Socialist internationalism was simply too important to the SFIO and too integrated into its leaders' understanding of socialism. That the SFIO would continue to lobby for an International became apparent at the Comisco conference in Copenhagen in June 1950. In preparation for the latter, Mollet asked Léon Boutbien, a member of the SFIO's executive, to draft a paper on socialist inter-nationalism. The paper began by recognizing the important differences between socialist parties, rooted as they were in the diverse political, social, economic, and geographic realities in which each party operated. Nevertheless, Boutbien argued, socialist parties needed to act collectively in the international political realm to defend democracy and human rights, principally against the Soviet/communist menace; and in the economic realm in order to promote regional integration as an alternative to both the communist and capitalist blocs. European socialists, accord-ingly, must 'coordinate' their efforts in order to limit 'national sovereignty in favour of supra-national organizations'. And this coordination of activity required an International capable of exercising a 'strict control on each national section' and possessing 'sufficient authority to impose decisions'.[163]

Armed with Boutbien's note, Mollet presented a report on the 'tasks of demo-cratic socialism' to the Comisco conference in Copenhagen. The key question, the SFIO's leader asserted, was whether 'an ideological basis exists for a real socialist International'. Dismissing the claim that there existed 'no common conception of socialist action nor perhaps even of a common ideal', Mollet insisted that European socialists shared a profound attachment to the principles of democracy—principles whose application extended well beyond politics to include social, economic, and

---

[161] CHS, Fonds Marceau Pivert, 559/AP/12, dossier 1950, untitled note. Emphasis in original.
[162] Ibid., 559/AP/6, Pivert to brother, 27 December 1950.
[163] OURS, Archives Guy Mollet, AGM 53, 'Aspect international de l'idée du mouvement socialiste', Boutbien, undated but 1950.

industrial dimensions.[164] Two aspects of Mollet's presentation were noteworthy. One was the explicit search for a common denominator among the parties, for something on which they could all agree. Hence the secondary role assigned to doctrine: although viewing himself as a Marxist, Mollet knew that an emphasis on Marxism would be controversial, not least with Labour. The second aspect concerns the nature of an International. Implicit in Mollet's presentation was considerable flexibility on this score. Boutbien had insisted on the need for a centralized organization equipped with considerable authority over the member parties. In appealing to broad principles, in omitting any mention of the International's functioning, Mollet indicated that the SFIO would accept a more decentralized and far looser organization than the one Boutbien envisaged.

Regardless of an International's future form, Mollet and the SFIO could not create one on their own. They would need to convince other parties. The situation did not appear particularly promising at the beginning of 1950, as French socialists were not alone in viewing socialist internationalism with a disillusioned eye. This was certainly the case with the SPD. As chapter 7 will show, the question of Europe's future provoked heated exchanges between socialist parties, including renewed accusations that the SPD was infected with nationalism—accusations that an angry Schumacher denounced as hypocritical. 'The internationalist vocabulary [of European socialists]', he commented at the party's annual congress in May 1950, 'does not reflect real internationalism.'[165] Schumacher's bitterness owed something to his volatility and outspokenness; but he was not alone in diagnosing troubles with socialist internationalism. Two months earlier, Hermann Brill, an SPD parliamentarian, described the present period as the 'dark days of internationalism [*Internationalität*]', pointing in particular to disputes with the SFIO. A month earlier, Walter Menzel, a member of the SPD's executive, had recommended that the SPD appoint representatives to foreign socialist parties as a way of improving the woeful state of current relations.[166]

But for all the perceived problems with socialist internationalism, German socialists proved even less willing than their French counterparts to contemplate its possible demise. In what amounted to a counterpoint to Schumacher's address, Ollenhauer warned the SPD's congress in May 1950 against overly roseate assessment of international socialist cooperation: 'We know better than before how difficult the problem of international cooperation and the question of a comprehensive European [socialist] cooperation can be.' Yet, just as importantly, the SPD's deputy leader went on to underscore the SPD's determination to construct an International, drawing inspiration from the post-First World War experience.

---

[164] IISH, SI, 250, 'Report of the International Socialist Conference in Copenhagen, 1–3 June 1950', undated.

[165] See for example, Schumacher, 'Die Sozialdemokratie im Kampf um Deutschland und Europa', 22 May 1950, reproduced in Albrecht, ed., *Kurt Schumacher*, 752.

[166] 'Sitzung des Parteivorstandes am 4. und 5. Februar 1950 in Bonn', reproduced in Albrecht, ed., *Die SPD unter Kurt Schumacher und Erich Ollenhauer 1946 bis 1963*, 327; and '9.3.1950: Fraktionssitzung', reproduced in Petra Weber, ed., *Die SPD-Fraktion im Deutschen Bundestag. Sitzungsprotokolle 1949–1957* vol. 1 (Düsseldorf, 1993), 107–8.

The interwar International, Ollenhauer explained, took five years to emerge and '[e]ach step forward was difficult'; but the 'ice was broken' in 1922 with the international conference in Frankfurt at which socialist parties forged a reparations plan that not only pointed the way to the Dawes Plan but also supposedly opened an 'era of genuinely peaceful relations' in Europe.[167] Ollenhauer's comments underscore the SPD's attachment to the international socialist community: having struggled so hard to become a member, German socialists had no interest in seeing the club shut down. His comments were also rooted in the SPD's ongoing need for support to defend what it saw as Germany's interests in European and international politics, a need reinforced by the party's political isolation within Germany. But Ollenhauer's enthusiasm for the International also reflected the SPD's enmeshment in the developing web of international socialist relations—and in the practice of socialist internationalism. From this perspective, the transformation of Comisco into a socialist International appeared to be a natural and even inexorable step.

With the SPD and the SFIO pressing for an International, much would depend on Labour. Here, as well, the situation did not appear promising. In July 1949 the party's international subcommittee discussed the possibility of reconstituting a 'formal international', only to recommend that Labour 'maintain its previous position' of opposition. The following year, Hugh Dalton publicly declared that Labour would never accept any international commitments that interfered with its freedom to pursue democratic socialism at home.[168] Yet even as Dalton was speaking, several developments were pointing towards an International. One was the party's ongoing involvement with Comisco, the Strasbourg assembly, and other sites of interaction and cooperation between European socialist parties. As with the SFIO and the SPD, Labour found itself enmeshed in a thickening web of relations. No less importantly, Labour officials, as already mentioned, were coming to realize the potential benefits of this enmeshment in terms of influencing the international socialist movement as well as individual socialist parties. Influence, however, could work in several directions. The February 1950 general elections in Britain saw Labour lose seventy-eight seats, leaving it with a razor-thin majority of five seats. In this uncertain political situation, international socialism weighed more heavily on the minds of Labour leaders, who feared anything that might rock the Labour government's fragile boat. Thus, in August 1950 Dalton found himself compelled to plead with Mollet to refrain from doing anything in the Strasbourg assembly that could embarrass the Labour government. Writing as a 'Socialist and Francophil', he insisted that it was vital 'that French and British Socialists should stand shoulder to shoulder against all whom are the enemies of our common ideals'.[169] But as French (and other) socialists made clear, a precondition for international socialist solidarity was the creation of an International.

---

[167] SPD, *Protokoll der Verhandlungen des Parteitages der Sozialdemokratischen Partei Deutschlands vom 21. bis 25. Mai 1950*, Ollenhauer, 12, 15.

[168] Labour Party, NEC minutes, fiche 377, International Sub-Committee, 19 July 1949; and BLPSE, Hugh Dalton Papers, Part II, 9/8, speech, Middleton-in-Teesdale, 22 June 1950.

[169] OURS, Fonds Guy Mollet, AGM 59, Dalton to Mollet, 21 August 1950.

THE FOUNDING OF THE SOCIALIST INTERNATIONAL

In many ways, the final chapter in the story of the Socialist International's founding was anticlimactic. By the beginning of 1951, little opposition existed to a formal International, even if some ambiguity remained concerning the scope and meaning of socialist internationalism. Even Labour's resistance was waning. The initiative for the final push, in any event, came from Belgian socialists. A resolution passed at the Belgian party's annual congress in December 1950 called for an intensification of 'international socialist action' and for efforts on behalf of a 'new socialist International' in particular.[170] Wasting little time, Victor Larock, the party's Comisco representative, wrote an 'open letter' to Morgan Phillips in early January 1951 pleading for Comisco to be transformed into an International. In an attempt to allay Labour fears of an overbearing organization, Larock insisted that all socialists understood that 'National sentiment and national interests are realities which cannot be argued out of existence...' 'Nothing', he added, 'is more alien to the Socialist movement than to pretend that it could—like the Komintern in 1920—impose an "iron discipline on military lines" upon its adherents.' The new International, consequently, would respect 'the autonomy of its members' and the 'system of conferences, of resolutions proposed and not imposed' would continue. But if Larock reassured Phillips that the new International would preserve Comisco's 'structure and its functioning', he clearly envisaged what a British diplomatic report termed a 'considerable extension' of international socialism's authority.[171] And he did so, moreover, by emphasizing the new International's contribution to the practice of socialist internationalism— to the efforts to cooperate on concrete international issues. As the letter explained, socialists in all countries were confronted with problems that could not be confined within national borders, and in this situation:

> [i]t appears to us to be indispensable and urgent that the [socialist] parties together search for solutions that are consistent with their national and international interests, that they determine together their views on the ideas that unite them, and that they discuss without delay certain major questions that can crop up today or tomorrow...

To facilitate a 'larger and more regular' collective effort on the part of socialist parties, Larock concluded his letter with a series of recommendations aimed at making the new International more effective as a coordinating body—recommendations that did, in fact, imply changes to Comisco.[172]

Larock's letter received considerable acclaim from European socialists. Both *Le Populaire de Paris* and *Neuer Vorwärts*, for example, reproduced the letter with approving commentary. This reception almost certainly influenced Labour, whose national executive decided in January 1951 to accept the Belgian proposals. In a

---

[170] IEV, Fonds Max Buset, 172, 'Résolution sur la politique internationale', 2–3 December 1950.
[171] TNA FO 371/96010, British embassy Brussels to Foreign Office, 5 January 1951.
[172] Larock's letter was published in the Parti socialiste belge's (PSB's) newspaper, *Le Peuple*, on 5 January 1951. For a copy, see IISH, *Socialist International Information*, vol. 1, no. 2, 13 January 1951. Also see Larock, 'Sozialistische Aufrüstung', *Geist und Tat*, February 1951, 63–5.

public response to Larock, Phillips noted that Labour placed 'great weight' on the promise that the new International would operate by consensus rather than dictation. Phillips, in fact, cited passages of Larock's letter on this point, while also preserving Labour's right to discuss Larock's precise recommendations at a later time. Thus, if Labour endorsed the new International in principle, Phillips sought to limit the significance of this step, presenting it as largely cosmetic.[173] Healey made a similar point in private comments to a Swedish socialist, maintaining that Labour had agreed merely to a name change; its endorsement of Larock's proposals 'should not imply any change in the structure or functions of Comisco'.[174] Labour's limited conception found its way into the resolution taken at an international socialist meeting in early 1951 at which Comisco's 'change of name' received unanimous approval as did the principle that '[s]ocialist cooperation must be based on consent'. The International's decisions, the final resolution read, 'cannot constitute a binding command on Parties which are individually responsible to their own members and to a national electorate. An international Socialist body cannot claim mandatory powers.'[175] Labour, as a Canadian socialist reported, might have been forced to concede an International, but it would continue to do all it could to play down the significance of this concession.[176]

With Labour's conditional approval, the stage was set for the Socialist International's founding congress, which took place in Frankfurt in the summer of 1951. Attended by 106 delegates from 34 national parties based on 5 continents, the congress marked a milestone in the history of international socialism. For the second time in the twentieth century, socialist parties had overcome the divisions engendered by war to reconstitute an International. As the introductory chapter indicated, the dominant tone of the congress was understandably celebratory, with Morgan Phillips—the International's first secretary—leading the applause. The rebirth of the International, he enthused, confirmed Labour's 'faith in the ability of Socialism to meet the challenge of the modern world'.[177] Some of the participants likely greeted Phillips' comments with a wry smile. After all, Labour had not only been a principal obstacle to a reconstituted International but also succeeded in restricting the latter's scope. With some justice, Healey could report that 'Labour can be well satisfied with the work of the [founding] Conference and its own contribution', explaining that the International would be 'pervaded by the practical realism' of British socialists rather than the 'aggressive dogmatism of the Continentals'. The International's limited authority, in turn, helps to explain its neglect, if not dismissal, by scholars. The 'Socialist International', Donald Sassoon

[173] For the letter's reception, see IEV, Archives Camille Huysmans, I 1038a, 'La reconstitution de l'Internationale. Note au Bureau', 26 January 1951. For Phillips' reply, IISH, *Socialist International Information*, vol. 1, no. 4, 27 January 1951, Phillips to Larock, 24 January 1951.

[174] AABS, Ssa, E2B 06, Healey to Kaj Bjork, 18 January 1951.

[175] LHASC, LPA, International Sub-Committee, 1950 file, 'Report on Meeting of Comisco, March 2–4, 1951', Healey.

[176] LAC, CCF-NPD, MG 28 VI-I, vol. 135, McKenzie letter (report), 19 May 1951. Also see Devin, *L'Internationale Socialiste*, 46–7.

[177] IISH, SI, *Socialist International Information*, vol. 1, 1951, no. 27–28, 7 July 1951, 'First Congress of the Socialist International. Frankfurt am Main, 30 June–3 July 1951', Phillips, 19.

writes, 'was a Cold War organization which did little else besides formulate compromise resolutions which never had the slightest importance.'[178]

Sassoon's dismissal of the Socialist International as ineffective is arguably based on a false dichotomy between consensus and dictation. A socialist International was never going to be a top-down, centralized organization along the lines of the Komintern (or Kominform). This possibility had been decisively rejected by European socialists after 1919; all socialist parties agreed that an International could not impose positions and policies on its members. Instead, the emphasis would be—as it had been before 1914 and after 1918—on collective consultation and consensus. From the beginning, European socialists conceived of the reconstituted International as an instrument to facilitate the practice of socialist internationalism. Its effectiveness as well as its value to socialists need to be assessed in these terms.

Equally important, by 1951, the practice of socialist internationalism had been well established. As an editorial in the left-leaning newspaper *Tribune* reminded its readers in the spring of 1951, the International emerged from the activities of Comisco and its predecessors, which '[q]uietly, perhaps too quietly... [have] done much valuable work in restoring contacts between Socialist Parties... in providing machinery for mutual information and in seeking to reconcile and co-ordinate the views of various Socialist Parties on important and controversial topics'.[179] In practising internationalism since the end of the war (and even before), European socialists had woven a web of mutual expectations and obligations that, while by no means formally binding, implied some limits on their freedom of action. As Healey well knew, this web formed part of an international socialist context in which party policies operated. It was not the only context, nor always the most important one. But it was a context that all socialist parties—Labour included—could not easily ignore. A final and related point is that the Socialist International in 1951 remained very much a work in progress. Its future vitality would depend greatly on the continued practice of socialist internationalism—on the ability of European socialists to work out 'socialist' responses to concrete issues of international politics.

---

[178] Labour Party, NEC minutes, 414, 'Report on International Socialist Conference, Frankfurt a/Main, from June 30–3 July, 1951', Healey; and Sassoon, *One Hundred Years of Socialism*, 210.
[179] 'The Socialist International', *Tribune*, 9 March 1951, 3–4.

7

Constructing Europe, 1945–1960

European unity constitutes a signature development in the history of post-1945 Europe. Admittedly, there had been considerable talk of a united Europe after 1918, and in 1929 French premier Aristide Briand presented his famous plan to the League of Nations for a federal Europe. Yet for all the attention it garnered, the Briand plan produced no concrete results: during the subsequent decade the calls for Continental union echoed ever more faintly as economic and political crises fuelled rampant nationalism. After 1945, by contrast, several Continental European states experimented with forms of political and especially economic integration, an effort that included the European Coal and Steel Community (ECSC) in 1952 and the Rome Treaties in 1957 that created the European Atomic Energy Community (EURATOM) and the European Economic Community (EEC). Providing the framework for a common market, the EEC initially numbered only six countries (Belgium, France, Holland, Italy, Luxembourg, and West Germany), but in its current form, the European Union (EU), it has twenty-eight members. Although membership remains a contentious political subject in several countries, the European Union has evolved into a complex institution whose multilayered web of procedures, norms, rules, and laws has far-reaching effects within Europe and beyond.

The history of European unity after 1945 has understandably attracted considerable scholarly attention. Early studies concentrated on its political-intellectual origins, tracing the thinking of prominent individuals and movements on the subject. The impression was that of a gathering wave of support for European unity before and during the war that broke upon post-war Europe, propelling events forward. Critics, however, countered that this approach could not explain why European unity took the precise form it did when it did. The result was an expanding body of scholarship that examined the role of state actors in the emergence of the ECSC, the EEC, and other initiatives. European unity now appeared to be chiefly the work of governments, its course determined not by public debate but by rounds of negotiations between hard-headed state officials seeking to extract maximum benefits for their countries.[1] More recently, this state-centric perspective has been criticized by Wolfram Kaiser among others, who

---

[1] For useful overviews, see Wolfram Kaiser, 'From State to Society: The Historiography of European Integration' in Michelle Cini and Angela K. Bourne, eds., *Palgrave Advances in European Union Studies* (Basingstoke, 2006), 190–208; and Wilfried Loth, 'Beiträge der Geschichtswissenschaft zur Deutung der Europäischen Integration' in Loth and Wolfgang Wessel, eds., *Theoriein europäischer Integration* (Opladen, 2001), 87–106.

highlights the activities of non-state actors operating across national borders—what Kaiser calls 'transnationally networked elites'. Kaiser's own research concentrates on leading Christian democratic politicians whose transnational network, he argues, was 'hegemonic in western Europe' after 1945, dominating 'the formation of the ECSC/EEC core Europe with fundamental long-term consequences for the present-day EU'.[2] Kaiser's focus on Christian democrats reflects a recent tendency to emphasize the significance of Christian democracy as a political force in post-war Europe. Jan-Werner Müller thus speaks of the 'triumph' of Christian democracy as 'the most important ideological innovation of the post-war period, and one of the most significant of the European twentieth century as a whole'.[3]

This chapter follows Kaiser in his emphasis on transnational actors while challenging the claim of Christian democratic hegemony. Throughout the post-war years socialists participated actively in the politics of European integration. It is true that socialist parties did not dominate government as did their Christian socialist counterparts, though Britain between 1945 and 1951 is a noteworthy exception. Nevertheless, European socialists exerted a steady and sometimes decisive influence on the construction of Europe. Pertinent here is the international socialist community whose formal and informal structure was far more developed than anything Christian democrats possessed. Socialist parties worked closely together on questions of European unity, making it impossible to understand the policy of one party independently of the others. The international socialist context helps to explain the decisions of the socialist-led French government in 1955–1956, which committed France to what became the Rome Treaties; and it helps to explain Labour's growing interest in the late 1950s in a British application to join the EEC. The argument is not that consensus on Europe prevailed. European socialists disagreed on several aspects, though it is an exaggeration to say, as does one scholar, that they were 'hopelessly divided' on the subject.[4] After all, the Western European Continental parties all endorsed the Rome Treaties. Examining how they came to do so, moreover, sheds light on why European unity took the form it did. European socialists had long advocated a 'socialist' Europe, by which they meant something other than merely a common market. That they convinced themselves that the Rome Treaties were compatible with such a Europe says

---

[2] Kaiser, *Christian Democracy and the Origins of European Union* (Cambridge, 2007), 8; and Kaiser, 'Transnational Networks in European Governance: The Informal Politics of Integration' in Wolfram Kaiser, Brigitte Leucht, and Morten Rasmussen, eds., *The History of the European Union: Origins of a Trans- and Supranational Polity 1950–72* (New York, 2009), 13–21.

[3] Jan-Werner Müller, *Contesting Democracy: Political Ideas in Twentieth-Century Europe* (New Haven, CT, 2011), 130. Also see Martin Conway, 'The Rise and Fall of Europe's Democratic Age, 1945–1973', *Contemporary European History* 13 (2004), 76–88; and Conway, 'Democracy in Postwar Western Europe: The Triumph of a Model', *European History Quarterly* 32 (2002), 59–84.

[4] Kevin Featherstone, *Socialist Parties and European Integration: A Comparative History* (Manchester, 1988), 1–2. For a similar emphasis on division, see Richard T. Griffiths, 'European Union or Capitalist Trap?: The Socialist International and the Question of Europe' in Griffiths, ed., *Socialist Parties and the Question of Europe in the 1950's* (Leiden, 1992), 11, 23; and Michael Newman, *Socialism and European Unity: The Dilemma of the Left in Britain and France* (London, 1983).

something not just about post-war socialism, but also about the fate of alternative and more ambitious visions of European unity after 1945.

INITIAL SUPPORT FOR EUROPEAN UNITY

Generally speaking, European socialists had long supported the idea of a united Europe.[5] In its 1925 programme, the SPD endorsed a 'United States of Europe'; almost two decades later, the principal organization of exiled German socialists in Britain reiterated this endorsement, declaring that 'complete national sovereignty is no longer compatible with the political and economic existence for Europe'.[6] The emphasis on national sovereignty is noteworthy. While numerous non-German socialists attributed Nazism to something uniquely German, the majority of German socialists viewed it as a grossly skewed form of nationalism. The latter needed to be tamed, and for many German socialists, the best way of doing so was to place limits on the exercise of national sovereignty—hence the appeal of European federation. Klaus Voigt has argued that the enthusiasm for European federation came chiefly from leftist elements within the SPD. But in the immediate post-war years, European unity enjoyed widespread support among German socialists, who envisaged a socialist-inspired Europe as a third force between the two emerging superpower blocs. In an influential book published in 1946, the journalist and SPD member Richard Löwenthal insisted that the:

> *international mission of the socialist workers' movement is today an immediate, obvious and urgent European mission. Indeed, in today's world, the development of Europe's humanist traditions [and] the creation of an example of democratic socialist planning between the two colossuses depends so much on the preservation of Europe's independence, that precisely this European mission is the greatest historical service that socialism can offer to mankind.*[7]

If the SPD's leader, Kurt Schumacher, fully subscribed to the vision of a socialist Europe as an alternative to Soviet communism and American capitalism, his thinking on Europe was also coloured by a growing preoccupation with equality for Germany. In any 'federation of European states', Schumacher intimated in 1946, Germany must be treated as an 'equal and equally respected factor'.[8]

If anything, French socialists appeared even more committed to European unity than their German counterparts. In his wartime essay written in 1941, *À l'échelle*

---

[5] For a recent survey, see Willy Buschak, *Die Vereinigten Staaten von Europa sind unser Ziel: Arbeiterbewegung und Europa im frühren 20. Jahrhundert* (Essen, 2014).

[6] 'Erklärung der "Union" über die "Internationale Politik deutscher Sozialisten" vom 23. Oktober 1943', reproduced in Eiber, *Die Sozialdemokratie in der Emigration*, 296–8. More generally, see Tania M. Maync, 'For a Socialist Europe!: German Social Democracy and the Idea of Europe: Recasting Socialist Internationalism', PhD, University of Chicago, 2006.

[7] Klaus Voigt, ed., *Friedenssicherung und europäisacher Einigung: Ideen des deutschen Exils 1939–1945* (Frankfurt am Main, 1988), 14; and Paul Sering (Richard Löwenthal), *Jenseits des Kapitalismus: Ein Beitrag zur sozialistische Neuorientierung* (Nürnberg, 1946), 257. Emphasis in original.

[8] FES, AdsD, NL Kurt Schumacher, 70, Schumacher to C.A. Smith, 25 July 1946.

humaine, Léon Blum spoke of the need for a 'supreme state' to which 'national sovereignties' would be subordinate. While Blum was somewhat vague on the geographic extent of this state, suggesting that it would be both European and international, the SFIO's 1944 'immediate action programme' insisted that France take the lead in constructing a 'European federation' of countries tied together by 'economic necessity, a shared social identity and a common spiritual community'.[9] Like the SPD, the SFIO emphasized the need to limit national sovereignty, but French socialists did so to solve the 'German problem'. During the war, a debate raged among French socialists regarding the treatment of a defeated Germany, with several prominent socialists demanding concrete guarantees against a recurrence of aggression in the form of reparations, unilateral disarmament, and even territorial annexations. The experience of the post-1918 years, however, argued against a draconian peace: not only would France's allies likely oppose such a policy, but it also risked being counterproductive by stirring German resentment. Accordingly, thoughts turned towards alternative policies, prominent among them some form of European federation. In a lengthy memorandum submitted to European social-ists in March 1945 in preparation for an international socialist conference in London, French socialist leaders proposed a decentralized and federated Germany as the core of a future united Europe.[10] Although German socialists did not receive a copy of the memorandum, they were kept informed of the SFIO's thinking by their representative in France. French socialists, Günther Marksheffel reported to Schumacher in 1946, were convinced of the 'necessity of supranational solutions' to pressing problems—including that of Germany's future.[11] The problem was that an approach to European unity centred on security against Germany would almost certainly clash with the SPD's growing emphasis on equality of treatment.

Unlike the Continental parties, the British Labour Party initially appeared uninterested in European unity. Its June 1944 statement, 'The International Post-War Settlement', made no mention of a united Europe, envisaging instead a tripartite direction of international politics by the British, Americans, and Soviets. When, at the above-mentioned inter-allied socialist conference in March 1945, French socialists drew attention to European unity, their Labour hosts dismissed such thinking as 'too broad and idealist'.[12] But Labour's disinterest was unlikely to persist. If nothing else, the emerging dynamics of Cold War politics, which exercised a centripetal influence on (Western) European countries, would soon produce pressure for European unity that neither the Labour government nor the Labour Party could ignore. Equally pertinent, within Labour itself two groups lobbied for some form of European unity. One group consisted of European federalists, whose

[9] Blum, *À l'échelle humaine*, 171–2; and AN 72/AJ/70, 'Programme d'action immédiate', 15 August 1944.

[10] LHASC, LPA, LSI 27/17, International Meeting London 3rd, 4th, 5th March 1945, 'France'.

[11] FES, AdsD, NL Günther Marksheffel, 7, Marksheffel to Schumacher, 17 June 1946.

[12] BLPES, Hugh Dalton Papers, 7/10, Labour Party, 'The International Post-War Settlement: Report by the National Executive Committee of the Labour Party to be presented to the Annual Conference...May 29th to June 2nd, 1944'; and OURS, APS, carton: Conférences internationales 1945–1948, 'La conférence internationale de Londres 3,4 et 5 mars 1945', Vincent Auriol.

most active member was R.W.G. Mackay, an Australian-born Labour MP who believed that a European federation was imperative not only to avoid a future war but also for Britain's economic future. Convinced that the 'federation of Europe' should be 'priority number one in foreign policy', in 1947 Mackay helped to form a 'Europe Group' within Labour's parliamentary party to promote 'the political and economic integration of Europe'. Significantly, the group immediately established close 'liaison' with the SFIO's parliamentary party with the aim of pressuring the Labour leadership.[13] The second group consisted of a fairly loose band of MPs, Mackay among them, who sought to prod the Labour government to adopt more 'socialist' policies both at home and abroad. Known as the 'Keep Left' group, they published a pamphlet in 1947 that framed European unity as a means of overcoming the growing Cold War divide: 'The goal we should work for is a federation which binds together the nations now under Eastern domination with the peoples of Western Europe.' As a first step, the pamphlet proposed closer economic and especially trade relations between European states.[14] Although their aims were by no means identical, both groups sought to push Labour in a more pro-European direction.

PRACTICAL ISSUES I: THE RUHR

It was one thing to support European unity and another thing to work out concrete proposals. For European socialists the difficulties involved in the latter endeavour quickly became evident on the issue of the Ruhr. A major industrial region located close to the French and Belgian borders, the Ruhr was widely seen as a key element of Germany's economic and military potential. From the outset, the victorious Western powers discussed how to neutralize this region, with the French government generally believed to be seeking to detach both the Ruhr and the Rhineland from Germany.[15] Well aware of these intergovernmental discussions, French socialists were determined to provide a 'socialist' solution. Citing the need to ensure French security, the SFIO's 1946 'action programme' envisaged placing the Ruhr's production under the control of an international consortium.[16] Similarly, Salomon Grumbach, an SFIO expert on Germany, advocated the 'internationalization' of the Ruhr, which he conceived of in terms of some form of outside (non-German) political control combined with the expropriation of

[13] Parliamentary Archives, London, Benn Wolfe Levy Collection, LEV/64, 'Minutes of the First (Formation) Meeting of the Europe Group of the Parliamentary Labour Party held on 2nd December 1947', 8 December 1947; and BLPES, R.W.G. Mackay Papers, 2/2, Christopher Shawcross to Mackay, 2 January 1948, which includes an undated draft letter to Emmanuel Shinwell.

[14] *Keep Left: By a Group of Members of Parliament* (London, May 1947), 38–9. Also see Schneer, 'Hopes Deferred or Shattered'.

[15] Whether this was in fact the French government's policy has been challenged. Compare Alfred Grosser, *Affaires étrangères. La politique de la France 1944–1989* (Paris, 1989) and Dietmar Hüser, *Frankreichs 'doppelte Deutschlandpolitik'. Dynamik aus der Defensive—Planen, Emtscheiden, Umsetzen in gesellschaftlichen und wirtschaftlichen, innen- und außenpolitischen Krisenzeiten, 1944–1950* (Berlin, 1996).

[16] SFIO, Fonds Jacques Piette, 27 APO 6, 'Programme d'action du Parti Socialiste', undated but 1946.

German ownership of industry and mining. In an effort to strengthen the appeal of internationalization to French socialists, Grumbach claimed that it enjoyed the backing of other European socialist parties.[17]

Just what internationalization meant remained unclear, prompting Léon Blum, the SFIO's secretary general, to attempt to flesh out the proposal. In several articles during the summer of 1946, Blum rejected any 'direct or indirect annexation' of German territory while also insisting that Germany not be allowed to reconstitute its 'war capacity'. Guided by these two aims, Blum outlined what he called the Ruhr's 'international nationalization'. The Ruhr's big owners in mining and heavy industry would be expropriated, thus bridling the supposedly aggressive and expansionist impulses of German capitalism. This expropriation (or nationalization) would be followed by the creation of an international political authority to manage the Ruhr's industrial resources for the 'common benefit'. Blum conceived of the international authority not only in international terms (with representatives from several countries, including Germany), but also in corporatist terms (with representatives of workers and former owners among others). Internationalized economically, the Ruhr would remain politically German as part of a 'Rhine-westphalian state' in a larger federalized Germany.[18] Under his guidance, the Ruhr's 'international nationalization' became official SFIO policy, figuring prominently in the party's electoral campaign in the autumn of 1946.[19]

The SFIO's campaign for the Ruhr's internationalization sparked a hostile response from German socialists. At the SPD's annual congress in May 1946, Schumacher, while accepting in principle the international control of the Ruhr's production, all but rejected it in practice, contending that internationalization could not be limited to Germany. 'It is *not…a part of Germany alone that should be internationalized*', he declared, '*but all of Europe.*' Schumacher offered two additional and related arguments against internationalization. One was that international control would hamper the socialization of industry in the Ruhr and in Germany more generally. In effect, Schumacher equated internationalization with continued capitalist control, remarking: '*We don't want to replace German capitalists with foreign capitalists.*' The second argument was to insist that the internationalization of the Ruhr (and Rhineland) meant Germany's dismemberment and relegation to the status of a colony—a status that would render any socialist policy impossible. Although several speakers sought to blunt the sharp edges of Schumacher's words, no one openly challenged his message.[20] Under Schumacher, the SPD would firmly oppose the Ruhr's internationalization.

Although no longer the SFIO's secretary general, Blum returned to the charge in a series of newspaper articles in January 1948 that reiterated his proposal for the

---

[17] AN, C//15286, Commission des affaires étrangères, 9 April 1946, Grumbach.

[18] For the articles, see Blum, *L'Œuvre de Léon Blum (1945–1947)*, 225–36.

[19] See the report in APP BA 1959, 'Réunions organisées le 9 novembre 1946 par le Parti Socialiste (S.F.I.O.)', 10 November 1946; and 'Aux peuples de France et de l'Union française', resolution in OURS, SFIO, '38ème Congrès national, 29, 30, 31 août et le 1er septembre 1946', 370.

[20] SPD, *Protokoll der Verhandlungen des Parteitages der Sozialdemokratischen Partei Deutschlands vom 9. bis 11. Mai 1946 in Hannover*, Schumacher, 44–6. Emphasis in original.

'international nationalization' of the Ruhr in which the region's heavy industry would be placed under inter-allied and eventually international administration. Significantly, Blum addressed his articles to the Labour Party in the hope that it could be persuaded to pressure the Labour government to cooperate with the French government to establish international control over the Ruhr.[21] With some justice, Blum contended that his proposals corresponded to international socialist policy worked out at the Allied socialist conference in March 1945, the final resolution of which had declared that the '[h]eavy industry of the Ruhr and the Rhineland must be internationalized and administered by a co-operative organisation'. But however justified, the more important point concerned the SFIO's attempt to prod Labour to intervene. With this goal in mind, Grumbach approached Labour's secretary, Morgan Phillips, to request a meeting between their two parties in order 'to elaborate a common policy towards the Ruhr'.[22]

French socialists did not limit their efforts to Labour. At a conference of European socialist parties in Paris in April 1948, the SFIO submitted a memorandum on the Ruhr. Written by Grumbach, it emphasized Germany's responsibility for the war as well as its crushing defeat, two facts that had to be taken into account in trying to solve the 'German problem'. Going further, Grumbach argued that a revival of an aggressive and expansionist Germany could not be ruled out; France (and Europe) thus required security guarantees. Yet if this opening section was certain to anger German socialists, the following sections appeared designed to assuage them. Following a lengthy reference to the resolutions of the March 1945 Allied socialist conference, Grumbach reiterated Blum's proposal for the creation of an international control of the Ruhr's heavy industry but framed it in terms of 'international socialization' rather than 'international nationalization'. Talk of socialization would presumably render the proposal more palatable to German socialists, who were publicly campaigning for the expropriation of private ownership of all German industry. Grumbach thus portrayed the Ruhr's 'international socialization' not only as consistent with socialist internationalism, which had supposedly always championed the 'rational and equal economic exploitation' of European resources for the benefit of all peoples, but also as a 'contribution' to an 'economically united Europe'.[23]

In his opening comments to the conference, Blum argued that the impossibility of limiting German industrial production made an international control of the Ruhr and Rhineland all the more necessary for security reasons. In addition to the memorandum mentioned above, the SFIO submitted a written plea to all European socialist parties but especially to the SPD to campaign actively at home for the

[21] For the articles, see Blum, *L'Œuvre de Léon Blum (1947–1950)*, 159–64.

[22] Labour Party, NEC minutes, fiche 357, 'Note on a Conference between Mr. Morgan Phillips and Monsieur Salamon [*sic*] Grumbach on Friday, 9th January, 1948', undated.

[23] FES, AdsD, SPD, Bestand Erich Ollenhauer, 452, 'Deutschland und die Probleme der Ruhr (Vorgelegt bei der Pariser Konferenz europaeischer Sozialisten v. 24./25. April 1948)', Grumbach. For the background to the memorandum, see OURS, Fonds André Ferrat, 5 APO 1, Ferrat to Grumbach, 30 March 1948.

'international socialization' of the Ruhr.[24] Meanwhile, behind the scenes the French delegates worked to influence the commission charged with forging a shared resolution: Grumbach submitted a working draft calling for international control of the Ruhr and the Rhineland as the first stage of a larger federal structure centred on a 'vast combine of coal, steel and chemical industries in the mining region of Belgium, Luxembourg, the Saar, Lorraine and northern France'.[25] Although Grumbach succeeded in gaining the support of a majority of commission members, the SPD delegates refused to approve the resolution, arguing that one-sided internationalization discriminated against Germany. Unable to reach a consensus, the participants agreed to refer the issue of the Ruhr to an upcoming international socialist conference in June 1948 in Vienna.[26]

Reporting on the Paris conference, Erich Ollenhauer, the SPD's deputy leader, insisted that the party must prepare its own proposals regarding the Ruhr for the Vienna conference. Accordingly, in mid-May 1948 the SPD circulated a memorandum to the European socialist parties that amounted to a stark rejection of SFIO arguments. The memorandum began by accusing the SFIO of an unhelpful (and un-socialist) obsession with France's national security:

> The SPD is of the opinion that it cannot be the task of a conference of socialist parties, whose goal is the construction of a united and socialist Europe, to consider the political and economic new order of Europe…from the point of view of exploiting the power relations resulting from the war for the satisfaction of one-sided security issues.

The goal of European unity simply could not be reconciled with the internationalization of one part of German territory. Such a misuse of internationalism risked not only killing 'international thinking' in Germany, but also fatally weakening the SPD to the benefit of reactionary forces on the left and right. For the SPD, the priority must be on the socialization of German industry—a priority that the SFIO's proposal would jeopardize.[27]

Despite the SPD's uncompromising tone, French socialists remained hopeful that a compromise position could be found combining internationalization and socialization.[28] Their optimism proved to be well founded. At the Vienna conference Ollenhauer went out of his way to be conciliatory, assuring participants that the SPD was determined to work out a common 'solution'. More concretely, Ollenhauer pleaded for a policy that combined international control with the socialization of the Ruhr's heavy industry and raw materials, remarking that internationalization alone did not reflect a 'socialist perspective'. No less importantly, he presented the internationalization and socialization of the Ruhr as Germany's

---

[24] AAOB, Haakon Lie, Dc 0005, 'Conférence des partis socialistes européens. 24–25 Avril 1948. Séance du 24 avril (matin)'; and IEV, Fonds Max Buset, 167, 'La Ruhr', undated.

[25] IEV, Fonds Max Buset, 167, 'Projet de résolution…présentée par la délégation française'.

[26] See the account in FES, AdsD, NL Günther Markscheffel, 8, 'Konferenz der sozialistischen Parteien Europas, Paris, 24. u. 25. April 1948'.

[27] 'Sitzung des Parteivorstandes am 6. Mai 1948 in Springe', reproduced in Albrecht, ed., *Die SPD unter Kurt Schumacher und Erich Ollenahauer 1946 bis 1963* I, 16–18; and IISH, SI, 237, SPD, 'Die Sozialdemokratische Partei Deutschlands und die Ruhr', 15 May 1948.

[28] OURS, SFIO, Comité Directeur, 1 June 1948.

contribution to the construction of a 'European [economic] community'. Ollenhauer's plea received strong backing from the Labour delegates and especially from Denis Healey, the party's international secretary, who insisted that German socialists should be free to pursue socialism in Germany as they deemed best—i.e. through the socialization of industry.[29] The final resolution welcomed the creation of an 'International Commission for the Ruhr' while also endorsing the SPD's 'policy of putting the basic industries of the Ruhr under public ownership and socialist control'. In a report to German socialists, Ollenhauer praised the results of the Vienna conference as 'an important practical success for international socialist cooperation because we arrived there at a common position'.[30]

The apparent consensus achieved at the Vienna conference, however, did not survive the announcement at the end of 1948 that the United States, Britain, France, and the Benelux countries had agreed to create an International Authority for the Ruhr (IAR) to oversee the production and distribution of the region's coal and steel. The absence of any provisions for socialization predictably drew a scathing response from the SPD, which denounced the IAR not only as 'Diktat' but also as a victory for 'economic nationalism' that served 'neither German nor European interests'.[31] Although the SFIO initially expressed disappointment with the IAR, because of both its lack of socialization measures and its lifting of limits on German production, the SPD's hostile reaction provoked a counter-reaction. Guy Mollet privately complained that SPD leaders were 'protesting with a vehemence worthy of German Christians and nationalists', while Grumbach openly warned the SPD of the dangers of 'chauvinistic nationalism'.[32] Clearly stung by such criticisms, SPD leaders accused the SFIO of having abandoned the compromise reached at the Vienna conference. Invoking the latter, Schumacher maintained that in rejecting the IAR the SPD was acting as 'Germans, Europeans, democrats and socialists'. To a German audience, he commented that those who accused the SPD of nationalism suffered from a 'remarkable lack of [any] sense of proportion'.[33]

During 1948–1949 the tensions sharpened between French and German socialists on the issue of the Ruhr, with each side accusing the other of betraying socialist internationalism. Yet however tense their relations became, German and French socialists remained committed to the practice of socialist internationalism—of cooperating together to find a 'socialist' solution. In an effort to soothe tensions,

[29] See the untitled and partial minutes in IISH, SI, 237; and IEV, Fonds Max Buset, 76, 'Conférence de Vienne (4,5,6,7 juin 1948)', June 1948.

[30] LHASC, LPA, International Socialist Conference, Labour International Department, 'Report to the National Executive Committee on International Socialist Conference, Vienna, June 4/7 1948'; and 'Sitzung der Obersten Parteigremien vom 28. bis 30. Juni 1948 in Hamburg', reproduced in Albrecht, ed., *Die SPD unter Kurt Schumacher und Erich Ollenahauer 1946 bis 1963* I, 409.

[31] 'Sozialdemokratie gegen das neue Ruhrstatut', *Sozialdemokratischer Pressedienst*, SPD/III/157, 29 December 1948.

[32] OURS, APS, Comité directeur, 4 February 1949, Mollet; and Grumbach, 'L'Allemagne a-t-elle déjà oublié?' and L'Allemagne ne veut pas être accusée de nationalisme', *Le Populaire de Paris*, 3 January 1949, 1, 4; and 4 January 1949, 1, 4.

[33] OURS, D6 28 BD, J. Steiner-Julien to Comité directeur, 9 March 1949, with attachment, 'La réponse de Schumacher'; and Schumacher, 'Ruhrstatut und Friedensordnung', *Die Gegenwart*, 1949, reproduced in Albrecht, ed., *Kurt Schumacher*, 631.

both the SFIO and the SPD sought to encourage informal exchanges, with German socialists particularly active in this regard.[34] Meanwhile and more formally, both parties continued to cooperate under the aegis of the emerging International, and during 1949–1950 several conferences took place to examine the issues of international control of heavy industry. A final point is that other initiatives soon rivalled the Ruhr in terms of importance not only for the SPD and the SFIO but for Labour as well. The first of these initiatives was the Marshall Plan.

PRACTICAL ISSUES II: THE MARSHALL PLAN

In a speech in June 1947, George Marshall, the American secretary of state, offered European countries large dollops of financial aid for post-war reconstruction. What became known as the Marshall Plan has engendered considerable controversy. While some scholars present the plan as a model of American beneficence, rooted in enlightened self-interest, others attribute more one-sided motives to Washington, which include transforming Western Europe into a reliable ally in the emerging Cold War as well as in the expansion of global capitalism.[35] But the plan also provoked considerable controversy at the time, not least among European socialists. All too aware of post-war Britain's straitened financial situation, the Labour government responded with undisguised enthusiasm to Marshall's offer. But the Labour government could not act alone. From the beginning, the Americans attached conditions to the extension of financial aid, most notably the demand that the recipient countries provide a coordinated programme. The Labour government thus needed to work with the Continental governments. And to facilitate this cooperation, it turned to the Labour Party to mobilize the support of European socialists, who in turn could pressure their own governments to operate within the American framework. The Marshall Plan, in short, compelled Labour to seek the help of international socialism.

Pressure from within Labour contributed to this process. Mention has already been made of the *Keep Left* group, which lobbied for a more independent foreign policy and criticized what it viewed as Britain's pro-American (and anti-Soviet) slant. Its members predictably greeted the American offer with scepticism. A pamphlet published in early 1948 and signed by several *Keep Left* members declared that it was better to reject American aid than to risk a war between the superpowers. It also questioned Washington's motives, discerning behind American generosity the aim not only of rendering Europe economically dependent on the United States, but also of preventing socialist economic planning in Britain and beyond. Interestingly, however, the pamphlet did not call for an outright rejection of the Marshall Plan but instead presented the latter as an opportunity to construct a

---

[34] FES, AdsD, SPD Sekretariat Fritz Heine, 2/PVAJ00000019, Heine to Cohen-Reuß, 29 December 1948; and 2/PVA00000084, Carlo Schmid to Heine, 10 January 1949.

[35] The scholarship is immense, but a good starting point is William Hitchcock, 'The Marshall Plan and the Creation of the West' in Melvyn P. Leffler and Odd Arne Westad, eds., *Cambridge History of the Cold War* I (Cambridge, 2010), 154–74.

socialist Europe. European socialists must seize the initiative from the Americans and transform Marshall's offer into a collective project to develop socialist economic planning on a European scale. The 'prime necessity' was thus on cooperation between Labour 'and the *socialist* forces in Western Europe'.[36] In an open letter to French socialists, R.H.S. Crossman, a prominent *Keep Left* member, echoed the pamphlet's emphasis on the importance of a collective and independent socialist response to the Marshall Plan, insisting: 'What we need today is a Socialist plan of action worked out not by Civil Servants, but by us, the Socialist parties...' Like the pamphlet, moreover, Crossman framed this response in the form of a Third Force potentially embracing the capitalist and communist halves of Europe.[37] For the Labour government the message was clear: it could count on Labour militants to support the Marshall Plan, but only if it cooperated with other socialist parties in forging a common policy towards European unity.

That Crossman addressed his letter to French socialists was no accident, for the SFIO initially appeared uncertain about the Marshall Plan. Although the party's national council in July 1947 had welcomed the Marshall Plan as a 'unique opportunity' to forge a 'plan for European reconstruction', doubts could soon be heard.[38] In late 1947 the newspaper *La Pensée socialiste* kicked off an enquiry into the 'myth and reality of the Marshall plan' with a lengthy article condemning the latter as a capitalist project aimed at preventing any 'cooperation' or 'coordination' between 'European national economies'. To buttress its case against what it viewed as the 'puerile enthusiasm' of some socialists for the Marshall Plan, the newspaper highlighted the arguments of several prominent Labourites, among them Crossman.[39] Confronted with these doubts, SFIO leaders were compelled to promise that they would only endorse the Marshall Plan if no strings were attached. Earlier, in August 1947, Mollet had announced that French socialists would not accept a plan that contradicted socialist interests, whatever these might be. Several months later, Blum insisted that socialists would resist any attempts by the Americans to 'impose any compensating political or military conditions' on their aid.[40]

Aware of these doubts and eager to obtain international socialism's endorsement of the Marshall Plan, Labour proposed to hold an international socialist conference in March 1948 in London. Significantly, French socialists led the opposition to the proposal not because they opposed a conference but because Labour was unwilling to invite the Eastern European parties. To invite the latter, Healey maintained, would preclude any possibility of arriving at a common position on the Marshall Plan. The SFIO, by contrast, hoped to avoid a definitive break with these parties—a break that would undermine any prospect of socialists acting as a European Third

[36] Bodleian Library, Socialist European Group of the Labour Party, MS Eng.his.c 1127, 'Stop the War: A Plan for European Unity and Recovery', undated but early 1948.

[37] Crossman, 'Letter to a French Socialist', *New Statesman and Nation*, 27 December 1947, 506.

[38] OURS, SFIO, 'Conseil national des 5 et 6 juillet 1947', 220.

[39] Didier L. Limos, 'Mythe et réalité du Plan Marshall', *La Pensée socialiste*, no. 18, November 1947, 15–20; and Charles Ronsac, 'Il faut répondre à l'appel des socialistes anglais', no. 19, December 1947, 9–10. Also see the police report in APP BA 1959, report, 15 July 1947.

[40] OURS, SFIO, '39ème Congrès national des 14 au 17 août 1947', 2ème partie, Mollet, 111; and AN, Archives Léon Blum, 570/A/23 4BL4 Dr1, 'Discours de Stresa – 9 avril 1948'.

Force. At a meeting in January 1948, Grumbach thus proposed that Comisco rather than Labour take the initiative: as members of Comisco, the Eastern European parties would be invited. Following what a Swiss socialist described as a 'lively debate', the participants defeated the SFIO proposal by a vote of eleven to five (with one abstention).[41]

Unable to prevent Labour's proposed conference, French socialists sought to expand its scope beyond the 'excessively modest' aims of their British comrades. Rather than simply a collective endorsement of the Marshall Plan, SFIO leaders decided that the time had come for international socialism to take the offensive on European unity—to 'take control of the idea of Europe'.[42] Accordingly, and in preparation for the March 1948 conference in London, the SFIO circulated a lengthy paper arguing against a simple acceptance of aid. Reflecting the suspicion of American motives, it presented the Marshall Plan as a weapon designed to weaken and even destroy European socialism. Because non-socialist governments were more than ready to accept this outcome, opposition could only come from socialists. And opposition meant using the Marshall Plan to initiate a 'real transformation of Europe's economic life' through the introduction of economic planning on a Continental scale. Indeed, the paper was less interested in the Marshall Plan than it was in mobilizing international socialism behind European political and economic integration. The upcoming conference, it thus announced, 'must decide to take the lead when it comes to the European idea and elaborate rapid and audacious policy lines'.[43]

Well aware of the SFIO's preparations, Labour circulated its own lengthy paper in advance of the March 1948 conference. The product of considerable discussion within the party's international subcommittee, the paper reflected the recognition that Labour had to evince an interest in European unity if it wanted international socialism's acceptance of the Marshall Plan.[44] Divided into two, the first part made a case for accepting Marshall aid: in addition to emphasizing Europe's need for financial aid, it portrayed American aims in a favourable light and characterized the exclusion of Eastern European countries (and parties) as a regrettable but unavoidable necessity. The second part addressed the larger issue of Europe's future, praising the 'ideal of European unity', especially its economic aspects: 'The economic integration of Western Europe is a revolutionary aim; it must be recognised and exploited as such. The necessary redirection of national thinking cannot be

---

[41] See the accounts in SSAZ, SPS, Ar.1.260.3, 'Kurzbericht über die Sitzung des "Comité des conférences socialistes internationales" in London, 10. Januar 1948', Humbert-Droz, 17 January 1948; and BA-SAPMO, NL Viktor Agartz, NY 4140/30, 'Bericht des Sozialistischen Informations- und Verbindungsbüros über das erste Treffen des Komites der Internationalen Sozialistenkonferenzen am 10. Januar 1948 in London'.

[42] OURS, APS, Carton: Conférences socialistes internationales, 1945–1948, 'Principaux points concernant la convocation d'une conférence socialiste sur les problèmes européens', undated.

[43] OURS, Fonds Louis et Marthe Lévy, uncatalogued, 'Travail préparatoire pour détérminer la position de la délégation française à la conférence des partis socialistes... (20-21-22 mars 1948)'; and APS, Carton: Conférences socialistes internationales, 1945–1948, 'Projet d'orientation générale de la délégation du Parti Socialiste SFIO à Londres, les 21-23 mars 1938', undated. Emphasis in original.

[44] Labour Party, NEC minutes, fiche 358, 'Notes on the Memorandum by the British Labour Party on European Cooperation within the Framework of the Recovery Programme'.

maintained unless European unity is presented as a dynamic new ideal.' At the same time, the paper was notably vague. While endorsing international planning in principle, it insisted on the complicated nature of any such endeavour. Similarly and in response to the SFIO's idea of an international secretariat to oversee the Marshall Plan, the paper warned of the dangers of a 'frustrated bureaucracy'. More fundamentally, it steered away from any notion of a supranational organization, lauding instead an intergovernmental approach in which authority remained with national governments.[45]

Not surprisingly, the March 1948 international socialist conference proved to be contentious. Guy Mollet, the SFIO's new secretary general, argued forcefully for federalism, insisting that Europe could not be reconstructed on the 'old basis'; it '[m]ust be federated, and must be Socialist'. Declaring that socialists (and not the Marshall Plan) 'will create the Socialist States of Europe', he stressed the need for supranational organizations and for countries to abandon some elements of national sovereignty. Mollet received support from several delegations, including the German. Ollenhauer thus lauded the Marshall Plan not only as a 'constructive idea', but also as a first step towards a larger European integration that would facilitate 'Germany's re-integration into Europe'. In an attempt to douse Mollet's enthusiasm, Morgan Phillips preached caution, explaining that 'we must face these problems practically and study our progress step by step, and do things we believe are possible.' Hugh Dalton, who headed Labour's delegation, was far less diplomatic. Along with dismissing with contempt the very idea of supranational authority, Dalton rejected all talk of political unity as 'Utopian'.[46] With the support of the Scandinavian participants, the Labour delegation succeeded in winning approval for a resolution based on their earlier paper. Warmly embracing the Marshall Plan, it offered only a vague approval of European unity, noting banally that it 'must be based on a common faith...and a common will'. French socialists, however, did exact a price for this concession: the SFIO would hold its own international socialist conference the following month 'to determine their policy and co-ordinate their efforts towards the United States of Europe'.[47]

If Labour viewed the upcoming conference in Paris as a sop to the French, the SFIO seized on it as an opportunity to mobilize European socialists behind the project of European unity. In the invitation to the conference, Mollet identified its purpose to be to 'define a common policy...towards a federal union of European states'. Within the SFIO, a debate was underway over the most promising path for constructing Europe: while some like Blum preferred to focus on economic integration, claiming that political integration would eventually follow, others

---

[45] LHASC, LPA, International Socialist Conference, File: Selsdon Park Conference 1948, Healey note, 27 February 1948, with attachment: 'Memorandum by the British Labour Party on European Cooperation within the Framework of the Recovery Programme'.

[46] See the lengthy report from the Canadian delegate in LAC, CCF-NPD, MG 28 VI-I, vol. 184, letter dated Eastern weekend 1948; and LHASC, LPA, International Socialist Conference, File: Selsdon Park Conference 1948, minutes of meetings.

[47] Labour Party, NEC minutes, fiche 360, 'Declaration of the Fourteen Socialist Parties on the European Recovery Programme', 22 March 1940.

maintained that the two must proceed together.[48] When it came to foreign socialists, however, the SFIO presented a united front in favour of European federalism—i.e. of supranational political and economic institutions. Thus, in preparation for the conference, the French distributed a thick file that included a draft resolution presenting federation as the solution to all of Europe's problems (Germany's future, the Ruhr, overseas empire). European socialists, the resolution asserted, must work together to transform the cooperative institutions envisaged by the Marshall Plan into a truly supranational organization equipped with extensive powers. 'No perspective for a truly united Europe will open until a federal authority is created,' it defiantly concluded.[49]

In the spring of 1948, Labour's position on European unity appeared to be in flux. Although Labour leaders viewed projects for European unity with considerable scepticism, they eschewed outright opposition because of the support European unity enjoyed among some sections of Labour—not to mention the risks involved in provoking a definitive break with the SFIO and other pro-European socialist parties. But another and complementary factor stemmed from the uncertainty among Labour leaders about what they wanted. In a speech addressed to pro-European Labourites in May 1948, Attlee explained that, while Labour opposed any 'dramatic move' towards European unity, it was 'prepared in principle, in conjunction with other countries, to pool some of its [Britain's] authority'.[50] This uncertainty influenced internal Labour discussions regarding the line to take at the upcoming international socialist conference in Paris. The party's international subcommittee accordingly urged Labour delegates to steer debate away from the issue of supranational authority and towards the development of functional economic cooperation between European countries. The subcommittee even envisaged a 'real European Economic Council' to oversee 'collective action' in various fields, among them trade, transport, and the 'allocation of scarce materials like food and coal'.[51]

As with its predecessor in March, the April 1948 conference in Paris featured a clash of views between Labour and the SFIO. Speaking for the latter, Blum pleaded for a federal Europe and especially for the 'creation of a collective European economy'. This goal could not be realized 'either within a national framework or through the mere contractual coordination of national economies' but only by countries transferring elements of their national sovereignty to a supranational authority. Speaking for Labour, Dalton questioned Blum's premise that economic salvation lay at the European level, insisting that the priority for socialists must be on achieving a socialist economy at home—a priority, he added, that socialist

[48] AAOB, Haakon Lie, Dc 0005, SFIO circular letter, Mollet, 5 April 1948. For the debate within the SFIO, see OURS, Fonds André Ferrat, 5 APO/1, Ferrat to Blum, 1 April 1948; and Blum, 'Economie et politique', *Le Populaire de Paris*, 8 April 1948, 1.

[49] AAOB, Haakon Lie, Dc 0005, 'Projet de résolution de la Conférence des Partis socialistes européens...présenté par la délégation française'. Several of the SFIO's case studies can be found in IEV, Fonds Max Buset, 167.

[50] Bodleian Library, MS dep Attlee, 70, 'Federal Western Union', 4 May 1948, notes for Attlee speech.

[51] LHASC, LPA International Sub-Committee, 1948 file, 'Notes on European Unity', undated.

parties in power (Labour and not the SFIO) were best positioned to grasp.[52] This time, however, the final resolution reflected the SFIO's position more than Labour's. Affirming that 'recent international events have created new possibilities of action...to advance Europe unity', it enjoined socialists to work to augment the power of the 'permanent body' created by the Marshall Plan 'with a view to making it the nucleus of a federal power to which would accrue that part of national sovereignty voluntarily waived by the States composing it'.[53]

Blum applauded the results of the conference in public, affirming that international socialism had come out 'categorically and formally' in favour of European federalism. But behind the scenes, French socialist leaders were less convinced.[54] Soon after the Paris conference, the SFIO's propaganda bureau warned that Labour (and the Scandinavian parties) remained opposed to any supranational authority and would likely seek to promote intergovernmental arrangements. This being so, the bureau recommended a propaganda campaign centred on the value of 'federal authority' to rationalize, modernize, and harmonize Europe's economies in contrast to the liberal economic project that concentrated on a customs union. Equally pertinent, the bureau insisted that such a campaign must mobilize a mass movement, extending beyond European socialists to include all political forces in favour of a united Europe.[55]

PRACTICAL ISSUES III: THE EUROPEAN MOVEMENT AND THE EUROPEAN COUNCIL

During 1948–1950, European socialist leaders would be prodded on the question of European unity from two sources, one socialist and the other non-socialist. The socialist one initially came from the left. In early 1947 members of the Independent Labour Party (ILP), a body once affiliated with Labour but now on its own and marginalized within British politics, proposed to create a cross-party group of European 'socialist militants' committed to a socialist Europe. The proposal quickly found an echo among socialists in several countries and particularly in France where Marceau Pivert lent his wholehearted support. From his base within the SFIO's Seine federation, which included Paris, Pivert and his network of allies pursued a relentless campaign to transform the SFIO—and international socialism more generally—into a truly revolutionary force. In terms of European policy, this translated into a vision of a united and socialist Europe that would act as a third

---

[52] AAOB, Haakon Lie, Dc 0005, 'Conférences des partis socialistes européens. Paris 24–25 avril 1948. Séance du 24 avril (matin)', Blum; and BLPSE, Hugh Dalton Papers, Part II, 9/4, 'Discours prononcé à Paris, à une réunion organisée par le Parti Socialiste S.F.I.O...'.

[53] LHASC, LPA, International Socialist Conference, File: Selsdon Park Conference 1948, 'Resolution passed unanimously by International Conference of Socialist Parties on European Unity...April 24/25, 1948'.

[54] Blum, 'La conférence socialiste internationale. Un événement considérable', *Le Populaire de Paris*, 28 April 1948.

[55] CHS, Fonds Marceau Pivert, 559/AP/42, SFIO, Secrétariat général à la propagande, untitled note, 20 May 1948.

force between the Soviets and the Americans as well as between capitalism and communism. Socialists must strive collectively to construct Europe, Pivert wrote in June 1947, for otherwise the Continent will be 'Balkanized, colonized, split apart [and] [r]educed to indefinite powerlessness'; and if this occurred, socialism in France and beyond would be doomed to failure.[56] With the backing of militants such as Pivert, the ILP's proposal quickly led to the creation in February 1947 of a provisional committee, which in turn became the 'Movement for the Socialist United States of Europe' (MSEUE). The latter held its founding conference in June 1947 in Montrouge, attended by delegates from fourteen countries representing various shades of socialist thinking. 'To unite or to perish,' the MSEUE's directing committee announced soon afterwards, 'that is the clear and tragic dilemma confronting Europeanists.'[57]

From the outset, tensions existed within the MSEUE concerning the best means to promote a socialist Europe. Many of its members were extremely critical of mainstream socialist parties, which they deemed to be too reformist and too nationalist. The MSEUE, in fact, conceived of itself as the avant-garde of European socialism, indicating the way towards a truly internationalist perspective embodied in a federal Europe serving as a third force. Its role as a model for socialist parties dictated that the MSEUE remain pure from corrupting influences, which meant not only keeping its distance from 'national parties' but also from non-socialist forces. At the same time, the MSEUE hoped to mobilize a popular movement extending beyond the membership of socialist parties to encompass all proponents of a united Europe. The primary purpose of this popular movement would be to pressure socialist parties to make the building of a socialist Europe their priority. But there were risks involved in cooperating with non-socialist forces. One was that it would reopen pre-1914 and interwar disputes over whether to collaborate with non-socialists. Another and related risk was that it would dilute the MSEUE's commitment to socialism, especially if it became necessary to choose between a socialist Europe and a united Europe.[58]

Initially at least, the MSEUE concentrated on increasing its influence within socialist parties and especially Labour. In October 1947, Fenner Brockway, a former ILP member and now Labour MP, told the MSEUE's directing committee that his party was undergoing a 'major evolution' and that Third Force thinking was gaining ground.[59] Brockway and the MSEUE placed considerable hopes in Labour's Europe Group chaired by Mackay, the ever-zealous proponent of European unity. In its propaganda, the group envisioned a federated Europe bound together by a

[56] Pivert, 'Les Etats-Unis Socialistes d'Europe', *La Pensée socialiste*, no. 15, June 1947, 14–17.

[57] OURS, Fonds Jacques Piette, 27 APO/1-1, 'Appel aux peuples européens', attached to minutes of Comité d'études & d'action pour les États Unis socialistes d'Europe, Réunion du Comité international, 25 October 1947. For the MSEUE's history, see IISH, MSEUE, 1, circular, 15 May 1947; and Wilfried Loth, 'Die Sozialistische Bewegung für die Vereinigten Staaten von Europa (MSEUE)' in Loth, ed., *Die Anfänge der europäischen Integration 1945–1950* (Bonn, 1990), 219–26.

[58] HAEU, ME 87, 'Assemblée générale du Comité d'étude pour États Unis socialistes d'Europe', Puteaux, 22 June 1948.

[59] OURS, Fonds Jacques Piette, 27 APO/1-1, Comité d'études & d'action pour les États Unis socialistes d'Europe, Comité international, meeting, 25 October 1947.

common market and currency, a customs union, free movement of goods and people, and coordinated planning for major economic sectors. Although the group presented a federated Europe as vital for the future of socialism, most of its members, including Mackay, placed the priority on constructing a united Europe rather than a socialist Europe. The group was thus eager to work with non-socialists.[60] Notwithstanding its shaky commitment to a socialist Europe, Pivert wasted little time in establishing contact with Labour's Europe group through the MSEUE. In early January 1948 Pivert wrote to Mollet asking for the SFIO's 'official patronage' of the MSEUE, presenting it as a bridge between pro-European British and French socialists. Mollet readily agreed and during the opening months of 1948 a series of meetings occurred between Labour and SFIO parliamentarians.[61]

Significantly, if Mollet welcomed the MSEUE's efforts to mobilize Labour MPs, Labour leaders remained ambivalent. Some of this ambivalence stemmed from the growing prominence of the European Movement. In early 1947, Duncan Sandys, a British Conservative MP, founded the United Europe Movement (UEM). Presided over by Winston Churchill, Sandys' father-in-law, the organization brought together prominent British figures in the political, economic, and cultural realms to popularize the idea of European unity. Following similar initiatives in France and other countries, the UEM soon expanded into an international umbrella group of movements in favour of European unity regardless of their political colour. With Churchill continuing as president, the UEM's international committee set out to organize a conference in the Hague in May 1948 of all pro-European groups. Along with attracting considerable media attention, the upcoming conference stoked the hopes of European enthusiasts across Western and Northern Europe, making it impossible for socialist parties to ignore the event.[62] The MSEUE soon chose to affiliate with the UEM, increasing the pressure on European socialists to define a position.[63]

From the beginning, Labour greeted the UEM with considerable scepticism. During 1947, its national executive advised Labourites against joining the movement, maintaining that the latter's purpose was 'to create confusion in, and if possible disturb, the unity of the Labour Movement in Britain'.[64] Mackay, by contrast, viewed the UEM as an opportunity to advance his agenda of a united Europe. Eager to attend the Hague conference, he sought to persuade Labour's leadership to take the initiative. In a letter to Labour's executive, the European group thus insisted that Churchill should not be granted a 'monopoly of the United Europe idea'; instead Labour should work closely with the 'Socialist Movements in Europe' to

[60] BLPES, R.W.G. Mackay Papers, 5/1, 'Draft Statement of Policy for Europe', Europe Group, undated but 1948; and 4/3, Shawcross to Mackay, 13 December 1947.

[61] CHS, Fonds Marceau Pivert, 559/AP/42, Pivert to Mollet, 2 January 1942. For the meetings, see the file in BLPES, R.W.G. Mackay Papers, 2/2.

[62] For background, see Élisabeth du Réau, *L'idée d'Europe au XXe siècle. Des mythes aux réalités* (Brussels, 2008), 165–77; and Alan Hick, 'The European Movement and the Campaign for a European Assembly', European University Institute, PhD thesis, 1981, 79–180.

[63] HAEU, ME, 494, MSEUE circular, 2 December 1948.

[64] CCA, Philip Noel-Baker Papers, NBKR 2/78, 'Suggested Statement Issued by the National Executive Committee', undated but 1947.

forge its own socialist European policy and to use the Hague conference as a first step. Indeed, the European Group tried to force the executive's hand on the question of participation by arguing that it 'had made promises to our Socialist colleagues abroad that we should go to the Hague'.[65] Although the executive forbade Labour members from attending the conference, it did reaffirm its attachment 'to the ideal of European unity'. No less importantly, it promised that Labour would continue to cooperate with European socialists—and European socialists alone. 'As the most powerful Socialist Government in Europe', the executive's statement read, 'we have a special duty to our Socialist colleagues on the Continent—the duty of preserving a continuous initiative throughout the complex negotiations from which European unity is being born.'[66]

Labour's refusal to attend the Hague conference influenced the positions of other socialist parties. Although Schumacher had initially approved of individual participation by German socialists, Labour's position prompted the SPD to counsel against attending.[67] The SFIO was also conflicted. If Mollet disliked the idea of acting without Labour, he also believed that European unity could not be achieved by socialists alone, which meant working with non-socialists. Socialists, he tellingly remarked, 'cannot wait for Europe to be socialist before seeking to federate it'. Accordingly, the SFIO's executive approved a strictly limited participation on the part of French socialists.[68] In the end, only a handful of socialists figured among the 7,000 attendees of the Hague Conference in May 1948, including Mackay, who defied his party's edict. Perhaps the most notable achievement stemmed from the French government's proposal, backed by the SFIO, for a European assembly. After considerable negotiation, the governments of Western Europe agreed in 1949 to create the Council of Europe, consisting of a council of foreign ministers and a consultative assembly meeting in Strasbourg for one month every year and comprising members of national parliaments. Although equipped with advisory and not executive powers, the Strasbourg Assembly quickly became a central site for the practice of socialist internationalism on the issue of European unity.

With the Strasbourg Assembly's first session scheduled for the autumn of 1949, European socialists met in Baarn (Holland) in May to discuss Europe's future. Opening the proceedings, Victor Larock, the Belgian socialist, contended that a concerted effort should be made to develop the Assembly. His proposal received widespread support and the final resolution enjoined European socialists to work together 'to make a success of this experiment' [Council of Europe], which it

[65] BLPES, R.W.G. Mackay Papers, 2/2, Shawcross to Mackay, 2 January 1948, with draft letter to Shinwell; Bodleian Library, Socialist European Group of the Labour Party, MS Eng.his.c 1127, Sybil Wingate to Warbey, 21 March 1948. Also see John T. Grantham, 'British Labour and the Hague "Conference of Europe": National Sovereignty Defended', *Historical Journal* 24 (1981), 443–52.

[66] LHASC, LPA, International Socialist Conference, File: Schuman Plan, Labour circular, Morgan Phillips, 21 April 1948.

[67] See FES, AdsD, NL Willi Eichler, 1/WEAA00000110, Fritz Heine (SPD) to Eicher, 17 March 1948; and Eichler to Heine, 24 March 1948.

[68] For Mollet, see Edmond Mouret and Jean-Pierre Azéma, eds., *Vincent Auriol. Journal du Septennat* vol. II, *1948* (Paris, 1974), 9 February 1948, 79; and Loth, *Sozialismus und Internationalismus*, 209–11.

characterized as 'merely a starting point' and as a 'step on the road to a permanent European Union'.[69] Of all the parties, the SFIO placed the greatest hopes in the new assembly. On the eve of its opening session, Blum described the event as 'one of those cardinal dates that together mark and measure human progress' and called on European socialists to assume a leading role in its deliberations.[70] Having worked with the French government for the creation of the Council of Europe, SFIO leaders were determined to use the institution—and the Federalist Movement in general—to push for European union. Accordingly, the party's executive authorized Blum and André Philip to assume leading positions in the UEM; significantly, when ill health began to curtail the activities of Blum it was Mollet who replaced him.[71] From the outset, moreover, Mollet would be extremely active at Strasbourg, working tirelessly to expand the assembly's powers in order to transform it into the institutional core of European political and economic union.

Yet despite their hopes, French socialists recognized that two issues risked provoking tensions with other European socialists. One issue concerned Labour. Frustrated by what he perceived to be Labour's negative attitude, Philip wondered openly whether European unity could be achieved with the British. Mollet also had his doubts. French socialists were wrong to 'coddle' Labour, he remarked in September 1948, because it wanted to 'scupper anything contributing to European unity'. At the same time, Mollet convinced himself that the Labour Party could be persuaded to back European unity—and through the party, the Labour government.[72] The second and related issue concerned the economic orientation of a united Europe. Under Mollet, French socialists quickly concentrated on promoting economic integration, partly because it appeared to be an easier sell than political integration, not least to Labour. The challenge, however, was to reconcile economic integration with socialism. In preliminary discussions with European socialists, Mollet had outlined the bases of a socialist Europe that included ambitious social legislation as well as redistribution measures both within and between countries.[73] At the same time, he placed the priority on a united Europe, maintaining that a socialist Europe would follow. 'Europe must first be created in a democratic framework', the SFIO's leader explained in February 1949, both because a socialist Europe would take too long and because 'a democratic Europe would make possible, it would make necessary the dissemination of socialist solutions.'[74] Philip, by comparison, placed the priority on a socialist Europe, which he defined in terms of supranational economic and political institutions with the authority to plan and oversee most aspects of economic activity. Such a Europe, he recognized, required

[69] IISH, SI, 239, 'International Socialist Conference. Baarn, Holland 14–16 May 1949. Summarised Report of Proceedings', 7–18.

[70] Blum, 'Un grand commencement', *Le Populaire de Paris*, 8 August 1949, 1.

[71] CHS, Fonds Marceau Pivert, 559/AP/42, 'Rapport de la Commission des affaires internationales sur le mouvement fédéraliste', undated but September 1948.

[72] See Mollet's comments in OURS, APS, Comité directeur, 22 September 1948.

[73] IEV, Fonds Max Buset, 163a, Comité d'études pour l'Union européenne, 'Vendredi 26 novembre 1948 (après-midi)', Mollet, 9–11.

[74] OURS, SFIO, Conseil national, 27 February 1949, Mollet, 209–11.

the active support and participation of those countries pursuing socialism at home—i.e. the Scandinavian countries and above all Britain. Without them, the result would almost certainly be a liberal or capitalist Europe that Philip understood as a limited project to reduce barriers to exchange between nations. But whatever their differences, for now, Philip and Mollet agreed that the urgent task of the SFIO was to use the Strasbourg Assembly to convince Labour to cooperate on constructing a more interventionist Europe.[75]

If the SFIO invested considerable hopes in the Council of Europe, Labour's attitude remained more reserved. Predictably, the party's pro-Europeanists viewed Strasbourg as an opportunity. In a letter on the eve of the first assembly, the Europe Group urged Labour's delegation 'to play a leading part in a development which may prove to have profound historic significance'. Labour delegates, it continued, should steer debate in the 'right direction' by avoiding talk of federalism in favour of a combined 'Functional' and 'Political' approach centred on concrete economic issues of common concern. Because of the 'inter-relationship of economic problems', the practical experience of cooperation would foster a wider and deeper integration or what it termed 'comprehensive economic planning'. Not surprisingly, the Europe Group exhorted the Labour delegation to work closely with other socialists at Strasbourg. Practising what he preached, Mackay, who was a member of Labour's delegation, consulted with Mollet in the run-up to the opening session.[76]

Labour's Europe Group recognized that influencing the party's delegation to the Strasbourg Assembly would not be easy. At Labour's annual congress in 1948, Hugh Dalton, who would head Labour's delegation, criticized Mackay as 'doctrinaire' and federalism as 'a most dangerous thing to do'. Yet Dalton did not rule out some form of European union. 'I am wholly for the practical British functional approach,' he remarked.[77] Labour thinking, in fact, pointed in the direction of limited economic integration. In a lecture in the spring of 1948, for example, Denis Healey welcomed 'immediate cooperation' between European countries 'which will create a permanent common interest in collective action'. Over the coming months, Healey elaborated his thoughts in a lengthy paper on Labour and Europe that would be published as an official pamphlet in September 1949 under the title 'Feet on the Ground'. Although Healey would later present the pamphlet as an anti-federalist salvo, it was more than that: it was an effort to set the boundaries of socialist debate on Europe. And as such, it was notably open-minded. To be sure, Healey indicated Labour's dislike of European federalism and of supranational authorities. That said, he accepted the need for 'joint planning and action' in various economic sectors: coal, iron, steel, chemicals, agriculture, transport, electricity. Labour's international secretary also recognized that such 'functional' cooperation

[75] Philip, 'L'Assemblée européenne de Strasbourg', *Le Populaire de Paris*, 5 August 1949, 1. Also see Philip's speech in HAEU, ME, 366, 'IIIe Congrès européen du Mouvement socialiste pour les Etats-Unis d'Europe', 5–7 November 1949, 3–7.

[76] BLPES, R.W.G. Mackay Papers 4/1, Socialist Europe Group to Labour delegation to Strasbourg Assembly, 28 July 1949, emphasis in original; and 7/2, Mackay to Mollet, 28 July 1949.

[77] Labour Party, *Report of the 47th Annual Conference…May 17 to May 21, 1948* (London, 1948), Dalton, 177–9.

could one day 'create a vested interest in [European] union fully as binding as a federal government, without any constitutional changes in the countries concerned'.[78] Labour, in other words, appeared to be genuinely interested in discussing the possibilities and not just the limits of European unity.[79]

At Strasbourg, European socialists wasted little time in structuring their interaction. At the August 1949 session, Dutch socialists proposed that the socialist delegations meet as a group to consider common tactics. Mollet not only jumped at the proposal but added his own: that European socialists create a permanent organization with the SFIO providing the secretariat. Although Labour delegates preferred more informal contacts to a 'rigid organisation', they were compelled to accept the formation of a socialist inter-group at Strasbourg.[80] Attached to the inter-group was a small coordinating committee, consisting of one representative from each party, to guide its deliberations. Structure did not equal consensus—the discussions within the inter-group were sometimes testy as European socialists separated into two broad camps: one comprising Labour and the Scandinavian parties opposed to federalism and supranationalism; and the other made up of the SFIO and other Western European parties in favour of rapid political and economic integration.

In addition to their testiness, the exchanges at Strasbourg are important because they influenced the position of each of the major parties. For the SFIO, the exchanges sharpened the differences between Mollet and Philip, both members of the French delegation. Having concluded that Labour would never honestly cooperate on European unity, Philip urged European socialists to move forward without the British. To the question of how to build a socialist Europe without a socialist Britain, he pointed to the need for a profound renewal of European socialism to enable Continental socialists to resist the imposition of a liberal Europe. An important precondition for this renewal, it is worth adding, was a reinvigorated socialist International.[81] Though sharing Philip's frustration with Labour, Mollet refused to consider a Europe without Britain, not least because he feared leaving France alone with Germany. Mollet accordingly remained confident that the British would come around: the recent encounters at Strasbourg, he told French socialists in February 1950, suggested that Labour was undergoing 'a real transformation' in its attitude towards Europe.[82] To facilitate this process, Mollet was prepared to abandon the SFIO's support for federalism in favour of a more gradual and limited approach to European unity. 'If some countries do not want the

---

[78] BLPES, Fabian Society, J 62/5, Fabian International Bureau, Conference on Western Union and European Recovery, 30 April–2 May 1948, Healey, 'The Political Issues. Synopsis', 1 May 1948; and Labour Party, *Feet on the Ground: A Study of Western Union* (London, September 1949).

[79] Healey, 'The Strasbourg Assembly', *Tribune*, no. 654, 22 July 1949, 10.

[80] BLPES, R.W.G. Mackay Papers, 7/2, Mollet to Mackay, 7 October 1949; and Mackay to Mollet, 3 November 1949.

[81] IISH, SI, 266, Council of Europe, Socialist group, 'Réunion du 24 août 1950'; and OURS, SFIO, Conseil national. Session d'information, 6 November 1949, Philip, 194–9. For the International, see AN, Papiers André Philip, 625/AP/17, 1950 file, untitled speech to 'Cher Comrades'.

[82] FNSP, Groupe parlementaire socialiste, GS 1, 16 November 1949.

federalist method', he reassured the socialist inter-group, 'we are prepared to accept the functionalist method.'[83]

In Labour's case, the deliberations in Strasbourg had two somewhat conflicting results. The first one was to reaffirm the party's opposition to federalism and to supranationalism. Federalism, declared a Labour paper circulated to socialists, 'at this stage of European history, is a dangerous doctrine and a false scent'.[84] The second result was to highlight Labour's isolation among European socialists, a troubling situation that prodded Labourites to be more flexible. In the summer of 1950, Dalton found it necessary to appease a frustrated Mollet: in addition to appealing to socialist solidarity, Dalton promised to press the Labour government to be more forthcoming. To Bevin, Dalton warned that Mollet might resign from the French delegation, further damaging 'the already rather strained relations between our Party and the French Socialists'; he also invoked the possibility of Mollet being replaced by Philip, who, from Labour's perspective, posed greater difficulties. To Attlee, meanwhile, Dalton argued for concessions, explaining that it would be 'very bad for morale in Europe' if Labour 'seem too off-standing towards it [Council of Europe]'. Continental socialists, he explained, viewed the Labour government as 'the one great obstacle to progress' and 'I think we should go to some trouble to try to weaken this impression.'[85] The point is not that Labour's position on European unity was transformed but rather that the practice of socialist internationalism at Strasbourg entangled the party in a web of mutual expectations and obligations.

Before leaving the Council of Europe, the SPD's position merits mention. Following the creation of the Federal Republic in May 1949, the Bonn government applied for membership in the Council. From the outset, Schumacher vigorously opposed the initiative, pointing to the simultaneous entry of the Saar, a coal-rich region on the Franco-German frontier that had been part of Germany but was now politically autonomous yet attached economically to France. For Schumacher, the Saar's treatment confirmed his suspicions that European unity would disadvantage Germany. His opposition, however, stirred considerable unease within the SPD, with several prominent German socialists maintaining that the party should support Germany's membership. At the SPD's congress in May 1950, several speakers questioned Schumacher's decision, underscoring the reality that the SPD leader's suspicious stance towards European unity did not command a consensus among German socialists.[86] Schumacher, in any event, quickly shifted gears once Germany's entry became a fait accompli. In June 1950,

---

[83] IISH, SI, 266, Council of Europe, Socialist group, 'Réunion du 25 août 1950'; and BLPES, R.W.G. Mackay Papers, 7/2, Mollet to Mackay, 2 February 1950.

[84] BLPES, Hugh Dalton Papers, II, 9/8, Council of Europe, 'Contribution by some British Members...to the Study of the Problems to be Examined by the Committee of General Affairs', 28 November 1949.

[85] OURS, Fonds Guy Mollet, 110, Dalton to Mollet, 21 August 1950; and BLPES, Hugh Dalton Papers, II, 9/8, Dalton to Bevin, 21 August 1950 and Dalton to Attlee, 1 September 1950.

[86] SPD, *Protokoll der Verhandlungen des Parteitages der Sozialdemokratischen Partei Deutschlands vom 21. bis 25. Mai 1950 in Hamburg* (Bonn, 1950), Max Bauer, 100–2; Paul Löbe, 102; Brandt, 103–5; Heinz-Joachim Heydorn, 105–6, among others.

he thus recommended that the SPD send delegates to Strasbourg, adducing as a principal benefit of doing so the opportunity to develop 'contacts' with other European socialists.[87]

THE SCHUMAN PLAN

Although the European Council would continue to meet once a year, its potential as an instrument of European unity was soon overshadowed by the European Coal and Steel Community (ECSC). The latter began as the Schuman Plan, a French proposal announced in May 1950 for a joint administration of Western Europe's steel and coal industries; in 1951 it became the ECSC, grouping together the industries of Belgium, France, Holland, Italy, Luxembourg, and West Germany. During the 1940s André Philip, among other socialists, had been lobbying for the creation of a European authority for the steel industry, and Matthias Kipping has argued that Philip exerted considerable influence on French officials, especially Jean Monnet, the father of the Schuman Plan.[88] But whatever the precise role of French socialists, the Schuman Plan caught other European socialists by surprise. In many ways, their efforts to respond proved extremely divisive, with the SFIO coming out in favour of the plan and Labour and the SPD against. Inter-party tensions quickly reached new heights. Yet these tensions notwithstanding, the practice of socialist internationalism thrived during this period. Equally to the point, the leading parties managed to reconcile some of their differences, with the result that the outlines of a possible 'socialist' position on Europe began to emerge.

The initial reaction of European socialists to the Schuman Plan was one of hesitation. At an international socialist conference in June 1950, the SFIO's Grumbach lamented its lack of detail, while Hermann Veit, the SPD's delegate, feared that the plan would create an industrialist-led cartel that would preclude the socialization of German (and European) heavy industry. European socialists, Veit remarked, 'could not agree to the Schuman proposal if it meant the end of socialisation'. Speaking for Labour, Healey also emphasized the dangers of a cartel that would restrict production and consumption and thus foster unemployment.[89] The tone was more positive two weeks later at a conference in London organized by the Labour Party. Although refraining from endorsing the Schuman proposals, which 'have still to be worked out in detail', the final resolution nevertheless greeted them as a 'bold example of European initiative'.[90]

---

[87] 'Interview Schumachers mit dem "Neuen Vorwärts"', 28 June 1950, reproduced in Albrecht, ed., *Kurt Schumacher*, 803.

[88] Matthias Kipping, 'André Philip et les origines de l'Union européeene' in Christian Chevandier and Gilles Morin, eds., *André Philip, socialiste, patriote, chrétien* (Paris, 2005), 387–403.

[89] See the incomplete minutes in IISH, SI, 240, 'Report on the International Socialist Conference in Copenhagen, 1–3 June 1950', undated.

[90] LHASC, LPA, International Sub-Committee, 1950 file, 'Report on International Socialist Conference on Control of European Basic Industries...London, June 16th-18th, 1950', E.G. Farmer, undated.

Well before the final form of the Schuman Plan became known, however, the positions of the major parties began to diverge. The SFIO initially opposed the plan. At a meeting of the party's executive in May 1950, Mollet pleaded for socialists to 'clearly say no', criticizing the plan as an anti-socialist project behind which lurked the influence of Washington and the Vatican.[91] At the SFIO's congress the same month, Mollet warned against a Franco-German condominium along liberal lines in which French workers would be disadvantaged because of the higher working and living standards in France; a related danger of a liberal Europe was that it would exclude Britain with its Labour government. Well aware of Labour's suspicions of the Schuman Plan, Mollet emphasized that a united Europe without Britain meant a liberal Europe because many Continental governments were non-socialist and even anti-socialist. And a liberal Europe would preclude a socialist Europe now and in the future. Socialists, he warned, would not be able to undo the Europe created by 'conservative and capitalist governments'—a Europe created 'without us, against us and without our input'.[92]

Significantly, however, Mollet soon modified his stance, offering the SFIO's conditional backing for the Schuman Plan and eventually its wholehearted support. As early as November 1950, he described the plan as a 'grand possibility [and] a grand hope'. The following year, the SFIO's leader asked French socialists to ratify the ECSC in Parliament, arguing that its defeat would represent a 'total reversal' of socialist policy.[93] One reason Mollet reversed course was the pressure from within the SFIO. And here, not surprisingly, Philip took the lead, insisting that Mollet's hopes in Labour were misplaced and misguided. To wait for Labour to come around meant risking the construction of a liberal as opposed to a socialist Europe: while socialists did nothing, governments would negotiate limited accords to free exchanges and industrialists would re-establish cartels to limit competition and production. Alternative approaches were urgently needed, and Philip framed the Schuman Plan in these terms. In collectively managing the activities of Europe's steel and coal industries (production and investment), the plan offered an opportunity for socialists to seize the initiative on European unity. The task of socialists, he insisted, would be to ensure that the 'High Authority' envisaged by the plan took workers' interests into account, was committed to an expansionist policy guaranteeing full employment, and possessed the means to compel industrialists to comply. For Philip, moreover, this meant a supranational authority with well-defined powers independent of national governments—i.e. a 'federal European authority'.[94]

Philip's advocacy of the Schuman Plan resonated within the SFIO and as the SFIO's secretary general, Mollet could not easily ignore this reality. But Mollet had his own reasons to support the Schuman Plan. One was his emerging belief that

---

[91] OURS, SFIO, Comité directeur, 10 May 1950, Mollet.

[92] OURS, SFIO, '42ème Congrès national des 26-27-28 et 29 Mai 1950', 56.

[93] OURS, SFIO, 'Conseil national des 4 et 5 novembre 1950', Mollet, 225; and FNSP, Groupe parlementaire socialiste, GS 3, 30 November 1951, Mollet.

[94] OURS, SFIO, '42ème Congrès national des 26-27-28 et 29 Mai 1950', 71–83; and 'Conseil national des 4-5 novembre 1950', 231–2.

the best way to influence Labour was for European socialists to be 'firm', which meant moving forward and compelling the British to follow.[95] Meanwhile, Mollet's thinking on European unity and the German problem underwent revision. Mollet did not simply fear that France would find itself alone with Germany if Britain remained outside of Europe; he also worried about losing any political or economic control over a revived Germany. Philip, moreover, did all he could to stoke this latter fear with his alarming portraits of Germany's economic and industrial growth. From this perspective, the Schuman Plan offered Mollet a potential means to 'tame' Germany by internationalizing its coal and steel industries.[96] But whatever the reasons, Mollet moved closer to Philip's position. As a result, during 1950–1951, the SFIO defined a socialist Europe largely in terms of the creation of supranational authorities.

As with the SFIO, Labour initially greeted the Schuman Plan with considerable suspicion. At a high-level policy meeting in May 1950, Arthur Greenwood, a cabinet minister, described the plan as a private international cartel that the Labour government, having nationalized Britain's steel and coal industries, should not enter. 'If we weakened on this score', he added, 'we would disappoint our comrades on the continent who were looking to us for a strong lead.' With Attlee declaring that '[s]ocialist principles were relevant to our international actions', the participants all agreed that Labour 'should work for European integration on socialist lines'.[97] Another (and public) sign of suspicion came at the end of the month with the national executive's statement on 'European Unity'. Drafted over several months by Healey and Dalton, it reflected the latter's dislike of developments in Strasbourg as well as Labour's desire to force British Conservatives to end their flirtation with European federalism. Yet the statement's timing meant that it was widely seen as a response to the Schuman Plan. And if so, the tone was decidedly hostile. Rejecting all forms of federalism and supranational authority, the statement insisted that Britain must retain control of its economy and industry, equating Continental Europe with 'economic *laissez-faire*' that posed a mortal danger to the Labour government's policies of full employment and social justice at home. 'Europe's private industrialists', the statement warned, would seek to 'pervert' the Schuman Plan for 'their own selfish and monopolistic ends'. And a 'co-ordinated perversion of this type would be far worse than our present unco-ordinated competition'.[98]

The statement provoked a storm of protest from various quarters, including European socialists. Clearly annoyed, Philip openly castigated the statement as 'the expression of reactionary and nationalist isolationism that [until now] had always been the preserve of the Right'; he also described it as a 'very hard blow' against

[95] OURS, APS, Comité directeur, 13 June 1950.

[96] FNSP, Groupe parlementaire socialiste, GS 3, 30 November 1951, Mollet.

[97] LHASC, LPA, General Secretary's Papers, GS/DORK/47, 'Policy Conference at Beatrice Webb House...20 and 21 May, 1950'; and GS/DORK/58, 'Summary of discussion at the Conference..., 19–21 May, 1950'.

[98] Labour Party, *European Unity: A Statement by the National Executive Committee of the British Labour Party* (London, May 1950).

Continental socialists that their political enemies at home would exploit.[99] No less importantly, censure also came from within Labour. Predictably appalled, Mackay fired off a counter-pamphlet decrying 'its hypocrisy, its smugness, and its complacency'. More surprising, perhaps, was the reaction of *Tribune*, the newspaper of Labour's Left, which regretted the statement's effects on 'our friends on the Continent'. European socialists were searching for a 'new and positive approach' to European unity and supposedly looked to Labour to take the initiative. But rather than seizing this opportunity, the party's executive presented arguments that 'without exception...all lead up to a series of NOES'.[100] That the discontent extended beyond Labour's Europeanists and the Left was apparent from Attlee's attempts to appease the parliamentary party. Speaking to its members in June 1950, he assured them that the statement did not reflect government policy.[101]

This is not to say that Attlee or Labour in general fundamentally disagreed with the statement. Dalton's dislike of federalism and supranationalism was widely shared. But the controversy unleashed by the statement had two noteworthy effects. One was to prompt Labour to re-examine its position on European unity. Aware of the statement's negative impact on Continental socialists, Healey urged Labour to remain open to socialist proposals regarding the planning of Europe's basic industries. If any planning at the European level must remain intergovernmental rather than supranational, Healey accepted that the integration of Europe's basic industries would be mutually beneficial and that such planning 'would be a major step towards European unity'.[102] Healey, moreover, was not an isolated voice. In response to a questionnaire from European socialists, Labour admitted in 1951 that '[p]rima facie there is a strong case' for such planning authorities in transport and communications among others. This point is worth underscoring in light of the scholarship that presents Labour as categorically opposed to European unity.[103] The second and related effect of the controversy surrounding Labour's statement was to reaffirm its commitment to socialist internationalism. During 1950–1951, Labour officials met regularly with their European counterparts, a practice that subtly influenced Labour policy. At a Comisco meeting in October 1950, for instance, Morgan Phillips assured Continental socialists that Labour was not wedded to the principle of absolute national sovereignty. More concretely, Labour agreed to participate in a Comisco study group on European unity charged with working out a 'practical policy by which all the West Europeans can achieve united action in the social, economic and political fields, whatever their differences

---

[99] AN, Papiers André Philip, 625/AP/12, 'Socialisme et l'Unité Européenne. Réponse à la brochure de Labour Party'.

[100] Mackay, *Head in the Sand* (Oxford, 1950), vii; and Evelyn Anderson, 'Labour and European Unity', *Tribune*, 16 June 1950, 7.

[101] Labour Party, Executive Committee of the Parliamentary party, minutes, fiche 201, 21 June 1950; and Bodleian, MS dep Attlee, 102, minute to Attlee, 22 June 1950 and accompanying untitled note.

[102] Labour Party, NEC minutes, fiche 391, 'Background Notes for the International Socialist Conference on the Control of Europe's Basic Industries, June 16–18, 1950'.

[103] LHASC, LPA, International Socialist Conference, file: Schuman Plan, 'British Labour Party Reply to Questionnaire on European Policy', January 1951. For studies, see Newman, *Socialism and European Unity*, 127–38; and Featherstone, *Socialist Parties and European Integration*, 41–50.

of approach'. At the study group's first meeting in December 1950, its members accepted that socialist parties should 'pursue European unity by the creation of specialized authorities'—a position reconfirmed at a Comisco meeting in March 1951.[104] To be sure, Continental socialists did not succeed in converting Labour to the Schuman Plan. Nevertheless, the practice of socialist internationalism helped to keep Labour engaged in the process of European unity, even if only as a benevolent observer. In 1951, Labour reassured European socialists that it would not oppose efforts to construct a 'closer union' of Continental countries and even promised to seek Britain's 'closest possible association' with a united Europe.[105]

If Labour's position towards the Schuman Plan can be described as benevolent non-participation, that of the SPD was downright hostile. In justifying the SPD's opposition, Schumacher adduced several arguments: the Schuman Plan would create a capitalist, catholic, and reactionary Europe; it would separate Germany from Europe's socialist-led countries (Britain and Scandinavia); it would prevent the socialization of West German industry as well as the development of a new social-economic order; it discriminated against Germany; and it amounted to a stratagem to ensure France's hegemony over Western Europe. But more striking than any specific argument was the categorical nature of Schumacher's rejection. As he announced in a speech in May 1951:

> We must reject the Schuman Plan in order to keep the road to Europe open. We reject it because we are international socialists. We reject it because of the needs of the workers' movement. We reject it on the grounds of the self-assertion of the German people. We reject it equally as international socialists and German patriots. We reject it as Europeans![106]

Given such statements, it is not surprising that scholars portray Schumacher's SPD as obstructionist on the issue of European unity.[107] But while Schumacher's opposition to the Schuman Plan was certainly vigorous, not to say visceral, several points need to be kept in mind. One is that Schumacher, despite his powerful personality and dominating leadership style, was no dictator; he could not simply impose his views on the SPD. A second and related point is that Schumacher's uncompromising stance stirred considerable disquiet among German socialists. In a letter to Ollenhauer, for example, Wilhelm Kaisen, the mayor of Bremen, warned that Schumacher's views would lead the SPD's friends abroad to lose 'faith in the internationalism of German social democracy's political will'.[108] Kaisen's criticism highlights yet another point: the SPD's sensitivity to the views of other socialist parties. As with Labour, German socialists remained attached to the practice of

---

[104] LHASC, LPA, International Socialist Conference, 'Report on Comisco meeting, Paris, October 21–22, 1950'; Labour Party, NEC minutes, fiche 401, 'Report on Comisco Study Group on European Unity and Defence, London, 16–17 December, 1950', Healey; and fiche 406, 'Report on Meeting of Comisco, March 2–4, 1951', Healey.

[105] LHASC, LPA, International Sub-Committee, 1951 file, 'Labour's Aims'.

[106] BA-SAPMO, NL Viktor Agartz, NY 4140/31, 'Arbeit und Freiheit', no. 12, June 1951 which contains text of Schumacher speech to Konferenz der Sozialien Arbeitsgemeinschaften, 21 May 1951.

[107] For a review of the scholarship, see Imlay, '"The Policy of Social Democracy is Self-Consciously Internationalist"', 81–6.

[108] FES, AdsD, NL Wilhelm Kaisen, 1, Kaisen to Ollenhauer, 25 April 1951.

socialist internationalism, working closely with their European counterparts. To be sure, considerable tensions accompanied the practice, especially between the SPD and the SFIO.[109] Yet however tense the relations with the SFIO became, the SPD never considered a rupture. In fact, the reverse was truer: under the International's aegis, German socialists worked with French and other European socialists to find common ground. Thus, a meeting in May 1951 in Brussels of Continental socialists produced a 'long and fruitful exchange of opinion' between the participants as well as the decision to form a 'special commission' on the Schuman Plan that met for the first time in Frankfurt the following month. Representing the SFIO, Grumbach emphasized the need 'to create understanding for each other's attitude'. What the SFIO 'really regretted', he elaborated, 'was not so much the difference of opinion but the poisoning of the atmosphere in the public discussion. There could be nothing worse than if, in the public eye, the French and German Socialist parties used such extreme language as he found in certain German and French socialist papers or journals.' In response, German delegates energetically defended their party's position while also signalling their openness. Expressing 'how happy he was with the discussion…and the under-standing of the comrades', the SPD's Ernst Nölting left open the possibility that the SPD might accept the Schuman Plan under certain conditions.[110]

Over the next several months European socialists continued to consult on the Schuman Plan. At a conference in August 1951 it became clear that no common position was likely in the near future, principally because the SPD attached conditions that effectively precluded agreement—conditions that included the ECSC's wholesale transformation as well as British (and Scandinavian) member-ship. Yet the meeting was not necessarily a failure. Prodded to explain their rejec-tion of the Schuman Plan, German socialists admitted that domestic politics played a prominent role in their calculations: any change of policy on the SPD's part risked being construed as a retreat from its oppositional stance towards the West German government led by Konrad Adenauer. This admission, in turn, left the SPD vulnerable to the charge that it was sacrificing socialist internationalism on the altar of national politics. Recognizing this vulnerability, Herbert Wehner, a close ally of Schumacher, assured participants that the SPD was not opposed to the Schuman Plan in principle but to its precise terms. Seizing upon Wehner's argument, Grumbach pleaded for a collective endorsement of the 'principle of a supra-national authority', asserting that socialists must show the world that they could work out a common approach to European unity.[111] Although Wehner did not commit himself at the meeting, in an article soon afterwards he reiterated that the SPD

---

[109] See Imlay, '"The Policy of Social Democracy is Self-Consciously Internationalist"', 106–8.

[110] LHASC, LPA, Morgan Phillips Papers, Correspondance with Socialist International 1951–61, Comisco circular, 31 May 1951; and IISH, SI, 583, 'Minutes of the Conference on the Schuman Plan Frankfurt a/M, 27–28 June, 1951'.

[111] IISH, SI, 583, 'Bericht der Schuman-Plan Konferenz der sozialistischen Parteien der sechs beteiligten Länder, die 20. und 21. August 1951…'; and ibid., Grumbach to Julius Braunthal, 7 August 1951. For the SPD's conditions, see William E. Paterson, *The SPD and European Integration* (Westmead, Franborough, 1974), 56–7.

objected to specific aspects of the ECSC's High Authority and not to its supra-national character. Just as importantly, Wehner praised the series of international socialist gatherings, remarking that they occurred 'in a climate of factual willingness to accept and examine objections, concerns and arguments'.[112]

In the end, while the other Continental socialist parties voted in their parliaments to ratify the ECSC, the SPD voted against in the Bundestag. Yet thanks partly to the pressure from other socialist parties, the SPD did not shut the door on European unity. Equally to the point, German socialists remained intimately involved in the practice of socialist internationalism. Over the next several years, the SPD would continue to discuss the future of Europe with other socialist parties. Much of this collaborative effort would occur within the ambit of the Socialist International; but some would also occur within the confines of the ECSC. As with the Council of Europe, the SPD's initial opposition to the institution did not prevent it from sending delegates to the ECSC's assembly in Luxembourg, helping to make the latter yet another site of socialist interaction.[113]

1951–1955: FROM THE SCHUMAN PLAN TO THE ROME TREATIES

During the first half of the 1950s, the European Defence Community (EDC) dominated the debate on Europe's future—a debate, as chapter 8 shows, which divided European socialists. The EDC's demise following a procedural vote in the French Parliament in August 1954 prompted European governments to embark on a 'relance européenne', leading to the Messina conference in June 1955 that paved the way for the Rome Treaties two years later and the creation in 1957 of the European Economic Community (EEC) and EURATOM. European socialists were not passive observers of these momentous events. During the mid-1950s, both the SPD and the SFIO became vocal proponents of a common market of the six Continental European countries. For the SPD, this amounted to a major shift in its position on Europe—a shift that helped to create a political consensus around European unity in German politics. In the SFIO's case, Mollet, as head of the French government during 1956–1957, played a decisive role in keeping France involved in the intergovernmental negotiations leading to the Rome Treaties.[114] Meanwhile, if Labour refused to endorse British participation in a common market, its thinking on the benefits of European economic integration was evolving. For each of the three parties, moreover, their shifting positions on Europe were influenced by the practice of socialist internationalism.

[112] Wehner, 'Europäische Sozialisten zum Schumanplan', *Geist und Tat*, no. 10, October 1951, 313–15.
[113] On this subject, see Brian Shaev, 'The French Socialist and German Social Democratic Parties and the Future of the Working Class in the European Coal & Steel Community', *Diacronie* 9 (2012), 1–19; and Shaev, 'Estrangement and Reconciliation: French Socialists, German Social Democrats and the Origins of European Integration, 1948–1957', PhD, University of Pittsburgh, 2014, 201–28.
[114] See Lafon, *Guy Mollet*, 491–9.

For the SFIO, the first half of the 1950s were difficult years. In the 1951 elections it received 15.3 per cent of the vote, down from 18.1 per cent in November 1946; in 1956 its total would decrease slightly to 14.9 per cent. Meanwhile, the party continued to lose members, reaching 91,000 in 1955, almost four times less than in 1945. Outsiders, including other European socialists, were well aware of this decline. In a report on the SFIO's 1951 congress, Barbara Castle, a Labour MP and future cabinet minister, remarked that French socialists were suffering in both 'strength' and 'spirits'. Yet Castle was also struck by the party's outward focus. 'To a British Socialist', she wrote, 'the most marked characteristic of the French Party's annual congress is its internationalism. Attending it one feels part not so much of a national as of a European congress.'[115] As Castle recognized, a prominent element of the SFIO's internationalism was a commitment to constructing a united Europe. During the first half of the 1950s, French socialists did not disguise their dissatisfaction with the European status quo. While welcoming the ECSC, they viewed it as a stepping stone towards a larger project. Beginning in mid-decade, the SFIO would be at the centre of efforts by European socialists to answer two basic and related questions: what type of Europe to build; and which countries to include?

French socialists offered multiple and even competing answers to these questions. On the SFIO's left, Marceau Pivert and his allies in the Seine federation remained convinced supporters of a European third force between the two superpowers and between capitalism and communism. *Pivertistes* denounced the prospects of a liberal-capitalist Europe, proposing instead a Europe that was internationalist and revolutionary. If often vague on details, Pivert at least knew where the problem lay: with French (and European) socialist leaders who were too nationalist in outlook.[116] Pivert accordingly sought to pressure and even bypass Europe's socialist leadership by appealing to the masses, by which he meant the militants in each party. Europe, Pivert wrote to Mollet in March 1954, must build from the ground up by mobilizing 'the whole of European socialist militants'. In pursuit of this approach, Pivert not only remained active in the MSEUE but also developed a network of leftists (socialists and non-socialists) across Europe, using his newspaper, the *Correspondance internationale socialiste* (CSI), as a forum for transnational and even transcontinental exchanges. Pivert, in fact, envisioned a parallel socialist International that would replace the existing one that was too reformist and nationalist. Yet Pivert's hopes were always likely to be dashed. Like most socialist parties, the SFIO was a top-down and (under Mollet's leadership) an increasingly hierarchical organization. Party leaders had little difficulty in marginalizing the *Pivertistes*, pressuring Pivert himself, for example, to cease his editorship of the CSI. Although Pivert's faith in the 'socialist & revolutionary European left' remained undiminished, there was no chance of the SFIO adopting his vision of Europe.[117]

---

[115] Labour Party, NEC minutes, fiche 412, 'Report on the French Socialist Party Congress, Paris, 11th–14th May, 1951', Castle.

[116] OURS, SFIO, 'Conseil national des 4 et 5 novembre 1950', Pivert, 124.

[117] OURS, Fonds Charles Lancelle, 13 APO/1, Pivert to Mollet, 28 March 1954; and CHS, Fonds Marceau Pivert, 559/AP/16, 'Lettres aux Camarades', no. 1, April 1957. Also see Jacques Kergoat, *Marceau Pivert, "Socialiste de gauche"* (Paris, 1994), 257, 308–9.

Like Pivert, André Philip opposed the project of a liberal Europe—a Europe centred on the reduction of obstacles to exchanges between countries. European unity, he insisted in 1956, must extend beyond the 'simple liberal methods of eliminating tariff barriers or liberating exchanges' to encompass a 'positive policy' aimed at the 'progressive harmonization' of social, labour, and investment policies across Europe.[118] During the first half of the 1950s, Philip worked to expand the powers of the ECSC, convinced that supranational 'specialized institutions' offered the most promising means of building Europe. But while determined to enlarge the ECSC's authority, Philip was less interested in expanding its membership. Indeed, he sought to focus attention on the six countries of the ECSC, arguing that they constituted a European core. That this core excluded Britain (and Scandinavia) did not bother Philip, for he believed that these countries were inveterately opposed to European unity. Like Pivert, Philip hoped to mobilize socialist militants; and also like Pivert, he viewed the MSEUE as a valuable tool in this regard, becoming its president.[119] The problem for Philip, however, was that the MSEUE grew increasingly isolated from mainstream European socialism. Although the SFIO remained affiliated, other socialist parties cut their ties with the MSEUE, including the SPD. As the SFIO's interest in the MSEUE also began to wane, Philip's immediate task became to persuade Mollet to sign up to a Europe of six organized around supranational authorities.

During the 1950s, Mollet established his ascendancy over the SFIO by centralizing decision-making around a loyal coterie and by denying critics fora in which to speak.[120] As a result, the SFIO's secretary general was well placed to shape the SFIO's European policy. In some ways, Mollet's position was close to Philip's. He too wanted to build on the ECSC's model by extending it to other sectors. Yet unlike Philip, Mollet continued to reject the exclusion of Britain, arguing that a 'Europe of Six' would be clerical, reactionary, and dominated by Germany. Rather than a 'compact and exclusive [European] federation', he told a Swedish journalist, socialists must work for a looser and more flexible framework in which different combinations of countries cooperated together in specialized authorities of various types depending on the economic sector concerned. Britain, he added, need not necessarily be a full member of any one authority but instead could be associated with it. For the same reason, Mollet placed less emphasis on supranationalism than did Philip. If compelled to choose between a supranational Europe and a Europe with Britain, Mollet maintained that he would always opt for the latter.[121] His position, moreover, enjoyed considerable support within the SFIO. Thus, in 1954, over sixty socialist parliamentarians circulated a pamphlet entitled 'Against a small Europe [that is] clerical and reactionary'.[122]

[118] AN, Papiers André Philip, 625/AP/12, untitled speech, 23 March 1956.

[119] APP, P 12, André Philip, 'Conférence de M. André Philip', 27 January 1953; and IISH, MSEUE, 4, 'Pour l'étude des principes d'un socialisme européen', Philip, 1952.

[120] On this aspect, see Lafon, *Guy Mollet*, 403–43.

[121] MAE, EU-Europe 1949–1955, 47, Mollet interview with *Morgon-Tidningen*, attached to French embassy Stockholm to MAE (Bidault), no. 665, 17 July 1953.

[122] OURS, *Contre la petite Europe cléricale et réactionnaire* (May 1954); also see Archives Guy Mollet, AGM 111, Mollet to Margue, 19 November 1952.

Mollet's position on Europe, however, was not fixed in stone. And here it is worth noting that he was less opposed in principle to a liberal Europe than Philip (or Pivert). Despite the anti-capitalist rhetoric, the social aspects of European unity were not a priority for Mollet. One reason is that his fear of an independent Germany tended to crowd out other considerations. The 'German problem', Mollet publicly asserted in 1952, could only be solved by a united Europe in which all countries were bound together by 'unalterable ties'; in no case must Germany be allowed to regain the full sovereignty it possessed in 1939.[123] But another reason concerned the growing belief among French socialists that France required a dose of liberalism. Many French socialists shared the popular perception of a backward and inefficient country. From this perspective, a common market would compel economic and industrial sectors to become more modern and competitive. A study by the SFIO's economic affairs section, for example, argued that protectionism had permitted French industry to perpetuate 'antiquated structures'. The recommended solution was a progressive and collective 'freeing of exchanges' by France and its European neighbours.[124] For Mollet, this last point was critical: the liberalization of France's economy must take place in a controlled and collective fashion. Any liberalization 'would be very dangerous unilaterally', he told the Socialist International's 1955 congress, before adding that a 'common market—in which free circulation of goods, capital and labour would be assured—can only be an organised market'. A liberal Europe, in short, was acceptable if sufficient safeguards were attached. As for the charge that such a Europe constituted a betrayal of socialist internationalism, Mollet responded that the latter's meaning was collectively determined by socialist parties. If European socialists agreed on a common market then that was enough.[125]

Ultimately, Mollet also proved flexible on the question of Britain's indispensability to a united Europe. Although initially confident that Labour could be persuaded to endorse British membership in European institutions, by the mid-1950s he was no longer willing to wait, having decided that a Europe of Six was preferable to no Europe. As he explained to European socialists:

> The 'Six' represent the 'hard core' of European action. As one of the first to regret that only six countries gave their agreement to the initial form of integration [the ECSC], I continue to hope that the circle will widen. But we are forced to note that any halt in their progress towards integration would very rapidly call a halt in all European integration, and would then mean the undoing of what has already been achieved.[126]

It is difficult to exaggerate the importance of Mollet's embrace of a united Europe built on a common market limited to six Continental countries. As French premier from February 1956 to June 1957, Mollet would commit France to the

---

[123] AN, Papiers Jules Moch, 484/AP/33, Mollet speech to Consultative Assembly of the Council of Europe, 18 September 1952.

[124] CHS, Fonds Marceau Pivert, 559/AP/15, 'Projet de programme économique et social', Commission nationale des études (Section affaires économiques), undated but 1955.

[125] IISH, SI, 247, 'Speech by Guy Mollet... on the Unity of Europe', 14 July 1955.

[126] Ibid.

intergovernmental negotiations leading to the Rome Treaties. But Mollet also assumed a prominent role in inter-socialist deliberations. During the 1950s he simultaneously chaired the socialist groups of the Council of Europe and the ECSC's assemblies, while also presiding over the International's study group on European unity. The 'one common bond' between these groups, as Mollet wryly noted, was himself.[127] In all of them he strove to strengthen and institutionalize cooperation between European socialists as well as to expand the powers of Europe's fledgling institutions, especially the ECSC. Within the European socialist community (as within the SFIO) Mollet gathered a small coterie of like-minded collaborators, prominent among them the Dutch socialist Marinus Van der Goes van Naters, an ardent advocate of European unity. In an influential report on behalf of the International's European study group in January 1957, van Naters, echoing Mollet, deemed a common market to be not only 'possible, necessary and indispensable' but also in the 'interests of socialism'. But perhaps more important than the precise contents of the report was that Mollet and van Naters worked tirelessly to keep the issue of European unity at the forefront of international socialist politics and to build a solid alliance in favour of moving beyond the ECSC.[128]

At first, German socialists did not count among Mollet and van Naters's allies. As mentioned earlier, the SPD had voted against ratifying the ECSC. Afterwards, Schumacher continued to oppose concrete measures towards European unity. In an interview in August 1952, the SPD's leader declared national reunification to be 'far more urgent' than 'any form of integration with other European countries'.[129] Less than two weeks later, however, Schumacher, died, his body finally succumbing to the cumulative effects of years in Nazi concentration camps. If his death triggered an outpouring of grief among German socialists, it also cleared the way for more pro-European voices within the SPD to express themselves. One such voice was that of Erich Ollenhauer, Schumacher's successor as party leader. Having been active before 1933 in the international socialist youth movement and having spent the Nazi period in exile in Britain where he was in regular contact with European socialists, Ollenhauer was by inclination and experience more European than Schumacher, whose political life had been rooted almost exclusively in German politics. To be sure, Ollenhauer's advent did not constitute a rupture in policy. Speaking at the SPD's congress in September 1952, he decried 'a small Europe' (i.e. the ECSC) in Schumacherian tones as capitalist and reactionary. That said, under Ollenhauer the SPD would be more sympathetic to European unity. 'We are for Europe,' he insisted.[130]

[127] LAC, CCF-NPD, MG 28 VI-I, vol. 185, 'Conference of the European Socialist Parties of the Socialist International, Brussels, 27–28 February, 1954', Mollet, 47–8.

[128] IISH, Confederation of Socialist Parties of the European Union, 2, 'Der Sozialismus und der allgemeinsame Market', van Naters, January 1957. For van Naters' earlier activities, see IISH, Marinus Van der Goes van Naters, 91, report to Comisco's study group on European unity, undated but March 1951.

[129] 'Interview Schumachers mit dem Leiter des Bonner Büros des NWDR...', 6 August 1952, reproduced in Albrecht, ed., *Kurt Schumacher*, 826.

[130] SPD, *Protokoll der Verhandlungen des Parteitages der Sozialdemokratischen Partei Deutschlands vom 24. bis 28. September 1952 in Dortmund* (Bonn, 1952), Ollenhauer, 42. For Ollenhauer's early life, see Brigitte Seebacher-Brandt, *Ollenhauer: Biedermann und Patriot* (Berlin, 1984).

Under Ollenhauer, the SPD over the next several years became a staunch advocate not only of European unity but also of a common market. Pivotal to this process was the interplay of discussions between German socialists on the one hand and between German and other European socialists on the other. In this interplay, moreover, the SPD's economic 'experts' exerted considerable influence. Faced with complex political-economic realities, European socialists at the end of the 1940s instituted a series of conferences of economic experts to study specific issues. In addition to forging common positions, the aim of the conferences was to depoliticize contentious issues by focusing minds on concrete details rather than guiding principles. Thus, when in 1949 discussions on the future of the Ruhr grew tense, French and German socialists agreed to refer the question to an experts' conference, held in Witten, Germany in March 1950.[131] From the beginning, German socialists were enthusiastic participants in these conferences, helping to making them a regular feature of international socialist politics during the 1950s. Just as importantly, at the conferences the Germans involved generally espoused liberal economic approaches to European unity. Thus, at an experts' conference in December 1950 on Western European trade, a Labour report described a German delegate, Fritz Baade, as a 'heavy-weight protagonist of liberalisation'.[132]

Significantly, the economic experts' conferences provided a valuable platform for socialists such as Baade who sought to shift the SPD in a more economic liberal direction. During the 1950s, debates occurred within the SPD, and especially within its economic committee, over the best approach to European unity. Initially, the majority of committee members appeared unfavourable to the project, criticizing the Schuman Plan, for example, as a capitalist ploy to undermine the conditions of German workers.[133] But a more liberal tone could soon be detected. In a 1951 paper Hermann Veit, a committee member, emphasized the benefits of a single European 'economic space':

> The construction of a united European economic space, the removal of barriers, the forming of [external] tariffs and various standards, the free movement of labour and capital, the division and specialization of labour in a large internal market, will multiply the economic resources of Western Europe, increase significantly real incomes and thereby raise the living standards of workers.[134]

Two years later, Hellmut Kalbitzer, another committee member, submitted a paper emphasizing the need for a progressive dismantling of restrictions on cross-national commerce of various kinds, leading ultimately to a Western European 'common market'. Although some members expressed reservations about the excessively liberal thrust of Kalbitzer's paper, the majority agreed that greater economic

---

[131] FES, AdsD, SPD, Parteivorstand, 2/PVBT0000004, 'Bericht über die Tagung der COMISCO—Wirtschaftsexperten in Witten Ruhr vom 26.–31. März 1950', Rudolf Pass.

[132] Labour Party, NEC minutes, fiche 401, 'Report on the Conference held at Royaumont, December 4–8, 1950', Wilfred Fienburgh.

[133] BA-SAPMO, Nachlass Viktor Agartz, NY 4104/36, 'Protokoll über die Tagung des Wirtschaftspolitischen Ausschusses...am 9. September 1950 in Bundeshaus, Bonn', undated.

[134] IISH, SI, 267, 'Memorandum...zu Punkt 8...der Produktivitätssteigerung bei Aufrechterhaltung des gegenwärtigen Lebensstandards', Veit, 10 December 1951.

integration between European countries would be of considerable advantage to all concerned. Summing up the commission's thinking for *Neuer Vorwärts*, Kalbitzer wrote: 'Close economic cooperation in Western Europe can quickly and enduringly improve the situation; it will do so when Europe...possesses an effective common market for all goods.'[135]

The economic committee's evolving position on Europe can be seen as part of a larger transformation of the SPD from a class-based to a catch-all peoples' party (*Volkspartei*), a process marked by the adoption of the 1959 Godesburg programme with its explicitly reformist bent. One element of this transformation was the replacement of *dirigiste* and protectionist economic models by more market-oriented and competitive ones. But while this context is certainly important, the SPD's changing views also contain an international socialist dimension.[136] For much of the 1950s, the members of the SPD's economic committee were in regular contact with socialists from other European parties not only at the experts' conferences, but also in the various committees attached to the socialist groups of the assemblies of the Council of Europe and especially of the ECSC. At one such encounter of European socialists in June 1954, Gerhard Kreyssig, another committee member, praised the activities of socialists within the ECSC, remarking that for 'the first time, parliamentary group work [among socialists] was...being organised on a supra-national basis'. As a result, European socialists went beyond generalities to consider the specifics of European integration, making their 'views felt on the problem of investments, cartels, transport and the association of the Community with non-member countries'. A few months earlier, Willi Birkelbach, yet another committee member, reported that SPD members were taking the lead within the socialist group, helping to ensure that European socialists offered more than 'simple criticism' when it came to advancing the cause of European unity.[137]

In their interactions with their counterparts from other socialist parties, the SPD's economic experts framed European integration in economic liberal terms, helping to set the direction and parameters of international socialist discussions. But that is not all. Close interaction with European socialists worked to reinforce and institutionalize Birkelbach and his colleagues' status as experts within the SPD, which in turn placed them in a strong position to shape party policy. In 1953, the SPD's executive created a working group on European unity charged with coordinating policy between German socialists at the ECSC, the Council of

---

[135] FES, AdsD, SPD, Parteivorstand, 06103, 'Anlage zu Rundschreiben Nr. 20/21/1953', Kalbitzer; and Kalbitzer, 'Gemeinsamer Markt – für ganz Europa', *Neuer Vorwärts*, 15 March 1953, 9.

[136] On the SPD's economic policy, see Michael Held, *Sozialdemokratie und Keynesianismus. Von der Weltwirtschaftskrise bis zum Godesberger Programm* (Frankfurt, 1982); and Heinrich Deist, *Wirtschaft von Morgen. Beiträge zur Wirtschaftspolitik der SPD* (Berlin, 1959). For the SPD's transformation more generally, see Klotzbach, *Der Weg zur Staatspartei*, 299–494.

[137] OURS, APS, carton: circulaire I.S. 1951–1958, 'Minutes of the Conference of the European Parties of the Socialist International on European Co-operation, Paris, 26 June, 1954', Kreyssig. For Kreyssig's early support for a common market, see his *Wirtschaftliche Organisation oder Untergang Europas* (Offenbach/Main, 1947). For Birkelbach, see 'Straßburg—ein Erfolg der Sozialisten', *Neuer Vorwärts*, 22 January 1954, 7.

Europe, and the International. The SPD's economic experts wielded considerable influence on the study group, expanding its tasks to include the formulation and publicizing of party policy on Europe. The effects were soon evident. An SPD policy statement on European unity in August 1953, drafted by members of the working group, called for the 'free entry for people and free exchange of all goods and information'. The following year, the SPD's *Aktionsprogramm* reiterated the point in greater detail: 'The goal of [our] European policy is to raise the living standards of European peoples and with this [to achieve] a steady improvement in the economic and social relations in Europe and the construction of a united economic area with free movement of people, goods and information.'[138] These experts then used their enhanced status to lobby for a common market at larger international socialist gatherings. Speaking at the International's July 1955 congress, Birkelbach maintained that European socialists must 'support in every possible way the attempt to establish a common European market'. This task, he added, required not 'general discussions' but the 'study of concrete questions to which specific solutions must be found'—a task no doubt best left to socialist economics experts like himself.[139]

If the SPD came to advocate a common market, thanks partly to its economic experts, there remained the question of which countries should be members. Early on, German socialists insisted that Britain and Scandinavia must be included. A Europe without these countries, Ollenhauer lamented, would exclude the continent's 'progressive, future-shaping forces'.[140] Well aware of Labour's preference for limited integration based on intergovernmental agreements, German socialists argued that socialist ambitions for Europe should adapt to the reality of Labour's dislike of supranationalism. The SPD, Carlo Schmid confided in 1953, generally favoured a 'genuine [European] federation', but this should now be a 'distant aim' since such an organization would render impossible the membership of 'a number of countries'. For Fritz Erler, another staunch supporter of European unity, Britain's position meant that the SPD must 'choose a looser form than the supranational [one]' for Europe.[141]

In the context of ever-closer cooperation with their Continental counterparts, however, German socialists began to revise their position. Within the International's European study group, the SFIO members led by Mollet suggested that socialists might have to settle for Britain's 'association' with, rather than membership in, Europe. In 1953, the study group decided to create a smaller 'European committee', which Mollet and van Naters together steered in a decidedly integrationist direction. And such a direction, as both Mollet and van Naters recognized, meant

[138] Socialdemokratischer Pressedienst, P/VIII/200, 28 August 1953, 'Die Europapolitik der SPD', 1–2; and 'Das Aktionsprogramm der deutschen Sozialdemokratie', *Neuer Vorwärts*, 6 August 1954, 9.
[139] IISH, SI, 79, circular no. 52/55, 'Report of the Fourth Congress of the Socialist International...London 12–16 July, 1955', 30 September 1955.
[140] SPD, *Protokoll der Verhandlungen des Parteitages der Sozialdemokratischen Partei Deutschlands vom 24. bis 28. September 1952*...(Bonn, 1952), Ollenhauer, 43.
[141] FES, AdsD, NL Carlo Schmid, 634, Schmid to Marianne Gadesmann, 17 March 1953; and Nachlass Fritz Erler, 170B, Erler to Josef Winter, 16 February 1954.

leaving behind Britain—and Labour. Interestingly, Schmid, who was the SPD's representative on the new committee, eventually endorsed the common market, tacitly abandoning his earlier insistence on a Europe acceptable to the British.[142] To be sure, the SPD did not openly call for Britain's exclusion; and, as we shall see, even after the creation of a common market, German socialists continued to search with Labour for a compromise acceptable to Britain. Nevertheless, by the mid-1950s, SPD leaders had concluded that the immediate future of European unity lay with the Continental six. Writing in June 1955, Herbert Wehner, the SPD's principal foreign policy expert, urged the party to cooperate with the socialist parties of the ECSC countries in forging 'common concrete proposals' for European unity. For Wehner, the benefits of a smaller, economically integrated Europe outweighed the potential costs of excluding Britain.[143]

The SPD was not the only party whose European policy underwent revision during the 1950s. Labour's did as well, even if the change was more limited. The Labour government fell after the October 1951 British general elections in which the Conservatives won a small majority of seats. Continental socialists hoped that Labour, now free of governmental responsibilities, would adopt a more favourable attitude towards European unity. In some ways, their hopes would go unfulfilled. Prominent Europeanists such as Mackay disappeared from view, while Labour's Europe group declined into irrelevance. Meanwhile, party leaders continued to express opposition to any form of European federalism and supranationalism. 'We are not prepared to join a European federation', Dalton intoned at Labour's annual congress in 1952, '... partly because we are not prepared to hand over to a supranational authority, which might well be dominated by reactionary elements, decisions on matters which we judge vital to our national life.'[144] Referring to a meeting of Labour's executive the same year, one participant remarked that 'I thought I'd gone into the wrong committee-room and found myself in a gathering not of socialists but of Little Englanders. I could almost see the Union Jack draping the chairman's table.'[145]

Labour's position, however, was not as intransigent as these citations suggest. Party officials indicated that they were prepared to work with (though not join) existing and future European institutions. Thus, Saul Rose, Healey's successor as international secretary, assured European socialists in April 1953 that, while preferring 'inter-governmental co-operation', Labour promised to 'do its best to influence British policy towards the closest possible association with any such supra-national institutions'. In October, the delegates at Labour's annual congress

---

[142] For the committee, see IISH, SI, 583, 'Réunion du Study Group de l'Internationale sur l'unité européenne, 16–17 janvier 53'; and Schmid, 'Europa in Richtung auf mehr Einheit verändern. Die Haltung der SPD bei der Europa-Debatte des Bundestages', *Vorwärts*, 13 April 1956, 13.

[143] FES, AdsD, SPD, Bundestagsfraktion, II. Wahlperiode, 272, untitled paper, June 1955, unsigned but from Wehner.

[144] Labour Party, *Report of the 51st Annual Conference... September 29 to October 3, 1952* (London, 1952), Dalton, 113.

[145] LHASC, LPA, Jo Richardson Papers, LP/ROCH/2/2/5, 'Across the Channel', Ian Mikardo, 18 January 1952.

enshrined this position as official party policy.[146] A closer look, moreover, indicates that there was some flux in Labour's stance. In early 1952, Morgan Phillips, Labour's secretary, circulated a paper on international policy that asked whether the party's attitude towards the 'European community' required revision. Early the following year, the international subcommittee concluded that 'fresh thinking' was needed on Europe, though adding that 'it would be wrong to rush matters at this stage.'[147] To prompt the process, the subcommittee drafted a paper on Labour policy towards Western Europe that questioned the feasibility of Britain's mere association with European institutions and especially with the ECSC of which the British were not members. '[T]here appears to be a need for new Labour proposals', the paper concluded, 'which, by according more nearly with the realities involved, can offer hope of an early and positive solution to outstanding problems.'[148]

Admittedly, there was little likelihood of Labour embracing European unity in general or recommending membership in the ECSC. Too many contrary pressures operated. As we shall see in chapter 9, the promise of the Commonwealth enchanted many Labourites, who conceived of Britain as part of a global rather than merely European community—a conception nourished by close ties between Labour parties from the Commonwealth. Somewhat similarly, Hugh Gaitskell, who replaced Attlee as party leader in 1955, possessed a more Atlanticist than European vision of Britain's future. 'I should prefer to see any closer European integration taking place within a more vital and more living Atlantic community,' Gaitskell opined in 1956.[149] Nevertheless, Labour's reassessment of its European policy did have some noticeable effects. One was a willingness to work more closely with Continental socialists, whether in the economic experts' conferences or in the International's European study group. It was thus the Labour representative who first proposed that the study group establish a permanent liaison with the socialist groups at the ECSC and the Council of Europe.[150] Equally revealing, Labour's interest in the Council of Europe steadily increased. In 1951, Healey had dismissed it as a 'talking shop' in which Labour participants found themselves in the 'disagreeable and negative position of opposing Utopian nonsense or defending themselves against attack'.[151] However, as part of their reassessment of its European policy, Labour officials revised their thinking on the Strasbourg Assembly. Thus, in late 1954, Rose recommended that Labour's international subcommittee consider making the Council of Europe the centre of cooperation between European countries—and between European socialists; his recommendation received the

[146] IISH, SI, 68, SI circular no. 69/53, 'Minutes of the Conference of the Council of the Socialist International. Paris, 11–13 April, 1953', 23 April 1953; and Labour Party, *Report of the 52nd Annual Conference... September 28 to October 2, 1953* (London, 1953), 149–64.

[147] Labour Party, NEC minutes, 425, 'Memorandum on Questions of International Policy', M.P., undated but early 1952; and fiche 448, International Sub-Committee, minutes, 20 January 1953.

[148] LHASC, LPA, International Sub-Committee, 1953 file, 'Development of Labour Policy towards Western Europe 1945–1953'.

[149] Gaitskell, *The Challenge of Co-Existence* (London, 1957), 59–62.

[150] OURS, Archives Guy Mollet, AGM 110, 'Réunion du Comité européen de l'I.S.', 23 March 1954.

[151] LHASC, LPA, International Sub-Committee, 1951, file, 'Report on the Third Session of the Consultative Assembly of the Council of Europe...', undated, Healey.

backing of several subcommittee members who insisted that the Council of Europe 'should be regarded as the political centre and parliamentary forum for Western Europe'.[152] More generally, in the summer of 1956, Labour's executive approved the creation of a 'sub-committee on European co-operation' to examine policy and to 'submit conclusions and recommendations'.[153]

Once again, the point is not that Labour embraced European federalism or supranationalism. Party leaders—and a majority of militants, it appears—continued to prefer an intergovernmental approach.[154] Nevertheless, by the mid-1950s, Labour policy towards Europe had entered into a period of flux, which manifested itself not only in internal party discussions but also in discussions between Labour and Continental socialist parties.

THE ROME TREATIES AND THE COMMON MARKET

During 1956–1957, a series of intergovernmental negotiations occurred between the six Continental countries (Belgium, France, Holland, Italy, Luxembourg, and West Germany), leading to the creation of the EEC in March 1957. At its core, the EEC foresaw the progressive construction of a common market to be achieved initially by reducing customs duties between members as well as by erecting a collective tariff towards the non-members. In many ways, it was a noticeable achievement and quickly proved to be a stimulant to trade between members. At the same time, however, it is difficult to describe the EEC as a socialist success, especially if one recalls the warnings of numerous European socialists about the dangers of a capitalist or liberal Europe. After all, a mere customs union was precisely what many European socialists had said they did not want. And yet the Continental socialist parties—and the SFIO and the SPD in particular—endorsed the EEC despite the doubts of some of their members. Labour, to be sure, backed the British government's decision to remain outside of the EEC. But the latter's apparent success fuelled Labour's ongoing reassessment of its position towards Europe, laying the foundations for the decision of Harold Wilson's Labour government in 1967 to apply to join the EEC. As with the decisions of the SPD and the SFIO to endorse the EEC, the practice of socialist internationalism constituted an important (and often overlooked) element in Labour's evolving policy.

Collectively, the Continental socialist parties welcomed the creation of a common market. At a meeting in January 1957 to discuss the subject, Heinrich Deist, one of the SPD's economic experts, argued that to reject the common

---

[152] Labour Party, NEC minutes, fiches 507–508, 'The Council of Europe and Western European Co-operation', Rose, November 1954; and fiche 514, 'The Council of Europe and Western European Co-operation. Memorandum from…A. Robens…and G. de Freitas…', February 1955.

[153] Ibid., fiche 562, 'Memorandum Concerning the Sub-Committee on European Co-operation', July 1956.

[154] A poll of local Labour constituency parties in 1953 found that roughly 75 per cent opposed Britain joining a Western European federation. See ibid., fiche 453, 'Analysis of Comments on Discussion Pamphlet "Labour's Foreign Policy"', undated but 1953.

market meant abandoning any 'practical policy'. Elaborating, Deist claimed that the common market 'contains sufficient possibilities to pursue a progressive policy if we have the will and the means'. Deist accordingly emphasized the need for closer cooperation between socialist parties—a point the other participants seconded. The meeting nevertheless ended on a somewhat ambivalent note. While welcoming the efforts of European governments to advance economic integration, the final resolution lamented the proposed common market's limited scope. Socialists, it insisted, must work together to ensure that European institutions pursue a 'resolutely social policy'.[155] Similarly, at a subsequent meeting in June, an SPD delegate claimed that the common market was neither liberal nor socialist and that its final form 'required activity' on the part of socialists. In the end, the participants approved a report by the Dutch socialist Hendrik Vos that presented the common market as an opportunity provided socialists worked together:

> The [Rome Treaty]... is not in itself a treaty for the realization of a socialist European Community. It was not drawn up with this goal but it does not preclude this goal. We must therefore in the future... more than ever pursue a <u>common</u> policy.[156]

In his report on the Rome Treaty at the International's congress in Vienna the following month, the SPD's Fritz Erler echoed Vos. The treaty, he explained,

> is a starting point for progress, if we succeed in developing on the basis of this treaty a healthy social, financial and economic policy. That is the task of the Socialists. The European Community will only be healthy if the Socialists are strong. Our strength will determine whether the whole undertaking will turn out to be good or bad.

Afterwards, the delegates unanimously endorsed the treaty.[157]

Considerable disquiet, however, could be detected behind the show of consensus. When, in early March 1957, Herbert Wehner presented an assessment of the Rome Treaty to the SPD's executive, several members voiced unhappiness with its favourable tone, forcing Wehner to respond that he was simply presenting a factual report and not a recommendation. Two months later the party's parliamentary group remained undecided about what position to take in the upcoming ratification vote, wavering between 'approval, abstention or rejection'.[158] Some German socialists worried about the effects of the external tariff on trade relations with non-members; others feared that the EEC members would be forced to subsidize the maintenance of France's empire; and still others regretted the absence of Britain (and Scandinavia). Most pertinently for this chapter, several German socialists disliked the Rome

---

[155] HAEU, GSPE 15, 'Conférence des partis socialistes des pays membres de la communauté... 26 et 27 janvier 1957. Compte-rendu analytique'. For background, see IISH, SI, 584, Fernand Georges (Secretary Groupe socialiste ECSC) to Socialist International, 10 October 1956.

[156] HAEU, GSPE 17, 'Conférence des Partis socialistes des pays membres de la C.E.C.A... 3 et 4 juin 1957. Rapport... par Ir. H. Vos'. Emphasis in original.

[157] AdsD, FES, SPD, SPD Bundestagsfraktion, II. Wahlperiode, 270, 'Konferenz der sozialistischen Parteien der Mitgliedstaaten der E.G.K.S.', undated but 3–4 June 1957; and IISH, SI, 87, circular 70/57, 'Report of the Fifth Congress of the Socialist International... 2–6 July, 1957', Erler, 96–7.

[158] AdsD, FES, SPD, SPD, Parteivorstand Protokolle, 'Sitzung des Parteivorstandes am 7./8.3.1957 in Berlin', Wehner; and '2.5.1957: Fraktionssitzung', reproduced in Weber, ed., *Die SPD-Fraktion im Deutschen Bundestag*, 417–18.

Treaty's liberal economic thrust. At a meeting of European socialists in May 1957, Joachim Schöne, the chairman of the SPD's economic committee, warned that no 'automatic mechanism' [*automatisme*] existed between a common market and social progress within countries. Even Gerhard Kreyssig, a supporter of the Rome Treaty, admitted that it did 'not accord social questions the importance they merit'. Several months later, Heinrich Deist urged European socialists to clarify the 'meaning of free trade in the framework of socialist thinking', remarking that 'socialists have a tendency to adopt an overly liberal conception'.[159]

Yet despite the misgivings, the SPD in the end endorsed the EEC and the common market. German socialists, Ollenhauer advised the party's executive in May 1957, should express their 'reservations' and then vote for the Rome Treaty. Several factors influenced the SPD's thinking, including Ollenhauer's personal belief that for political and economic reasons Germany must champion European unity. Reflecting this belief, during the previous year the SPD leader had actively participated in Jean Monnet's Action Committee, a high-level and non-party group dedicated to advancing the cause of European integration.[160] But if the SPD as a whole agreed to follow Ollenhauer's lead it was in no small part because of the practice of socialist internationalism. For several years, German socialists had been cooperating with their European counterparts in several forums, fostering a strong sense of solidarity. And it was this solidarity that Erler referred to in his comments on the socialist Inter-Group's activities at the International's July 1957 congress. Working together in Strasbourg, he explained, led European socialists to realize that the only way to develop the ECSC was to take 'a forward leap... from partial integration to an amalgamation of the whole economy of these six countries'. And it was this solidarity that Wehner, a regular participant in the ECSC's socialist group, had in mind when he informed the SPD's executive that it could not simply issue a 'blank no' to the Rome Treaty.[161]

This sense of solidarity is worth emphasizing because German socialists viewed the EEC as a work in progress. From the beginning, the SPD wanted to expand the common market to include other European countries, perhaps even the Soviet bloc and East Germany in particular. Such an expansion, it was hoped, might clear the way for an eventual reunification of the two Germanys. But in the short-term at least, the SPD focused more on finding some way to integrate Britain into a united Europe. Still more to the point, the SPD seized on international socialist cooperation as a means of doing so. At a meeting of European socialists in October

---

[159] HAEU, GSPE 11, 'Compte-rendu analytique de la réunion du Groupe de travail pour les affaires économiques et sociales...8 Mai 1957'; and GSPE 19, 'Compte-rendu de la réunion du Groupe socialiste du 7 Novembre 1957'.

[160] AdsD, FES, SPD, SPD, Parteivorstand Protokolle, 'Siztung des Parteivorstandes am 30. Mai 1957 in Bonn'. For Ollenhauer's involvement in Monnet's committee, see OURS, D6 27 BD, 'Note confidentielle', Pontillon, 18 October 1956; and for the Committee, see Gilles Grin, 'Jean Monnet, le Comité d'action pour les États-Unis d'Europe et la genèse des traités de Rome', *Relations internationales* 136 (2008), 21–32.

[161] IISH, SI, 87, circular 70/57, 'Report of the Fifth Congress of the Socialist International...2–6 July, 1957', Erler, 92; and AdsD, SPD, Parteivorstand Protokolle, 'Sitzung des Parteivorstandes am 7./8.3.1957 in Berlin', Wehner.

1957, Wehner argued for more institutional cooperation between the EEC and non-EEC socialist parties. The pressing issue, he intoned, was the 'question of cooperation between [socialist] parties inside and outside the common market'. That Wehner had Britain principally in mind is evident from the importance the SPD delegates attached to considering the issue of a European free trade zone—the very issue, as we shall see, that interested Labour. The common market, Erler told another meeting of European socialists, 'would be viable and make economic sense only if it were supplemented by as large a Free Trade Area as possible'.[162]

The SPD was not the only socialist party to swallow its reservations about the Rome Treaty. The SFIO also did so. To be sure, as chapter 9 will discuss, the French party during this period was increasingly preoccupied with the Algerian War, a conflict that tore apart the SFIO and toppled France's Fourth Republic. But the question of Europe's future remained an issue of fierce debate among French socialists. Among the critics, André Philip was probably the most vocal. Philip, who had consistently opposed a liberal Europe, quickly made known his concerns about the Rome Treaties. For socialists, he wrote in 1957, a common market could never be an end in itself but only one element of a larger project of social trans- formation. More concretely, Philip continued to lobby for the creation of powerful political and economic institutions at the European level capable of coordinating the economic planning efforts of individual countries in order to generate growth, presenting them as an essential counterpart to the liberalization of commerce. The immediate problem was that the EEC lacked the supranational institutions needed to resist the forces of economic liberalism and nationalism within Europe and beyond. But for Philip the more profound problem was that French (and European) socialists had abandoned the 'idea of a complete transformation of social structures', retreating instead into a 'realism bordering on conservatism' that could only conceive of 'empirical adaptations' to the pressing problems of the day, not least that of Europe's future.[163] As a leading SFIO spokesman on economic matters, Philip's views carried considerable weight. And while not openly calling on French socialists to reject the Rome Treaty, Philip helped to foster a climate of scepticism about the EEC.

Philip would eventually be ejected from the SFIO because of his opposition to Mollet's Algerian policy. For Mollet, Philip's departure had the welcome effect of sidelining a persistent critic; yet it did not end the concern within the SFIO over the EEC. In the intergovernmental negotiations leading up to the Rome Treaties, the French government under Mollet had been compelled to make sig-nificant concessions regarding *dirigiste* measures aimed at protecting French workers—concessions that displeased many French socialists.[164] In an effort to

---

[162] AdsD, FES, NL Fritz Heine, 147, 'Internationale Sitzung 3 Gremium—20.10.57', undated; and HAEU, GSPE 7, 'Minutes of the Joint Meeting of the Bureau of the Socialist International and the Socialist Groups...Sunday 20th October 1957'.

[163] Philip, *Le Socialisme trahi* (Paris, 1957), 108–17; and AN, Papiers André Philip, 625/AP/12, untitled speech, 6 July 1957.

[164] For the Mollet government, see Laurent Warlouzet, *Le Choix de la CEE par la France: les débats économiques de Pierre Mendès-France à Charles de Gaulle (1955–1969)* (Paris, 2011), 35–59.

ensure the SFIO's endorsement of the Rome Treaty, François Lafon has argued, Mollet emphasized EURATOM, the scheme for a joint European administration of nuclear energy, rather than the common market whose domestic effects troubled French socialists.[165] There is something to Lafon's argument: in an age in which the potential dangers of nuclear power were palpable, the prospect of a collective stewardship of this resource proved attractive. Mollet, it should be added, also sought to associate the EEC with the protection of French agriculture. Indeed, the SFIO urged Continental socialists to advocate a European agricultural policy, helping to make European socialism a leading cheerleader of what would become the EEC's Common Agricultural Policy.[166] Yet just as importantly, Mollet attempted to reassure French socialists by framing the EEC itself as a socialist project. One way he did so was by reiterating the earlier demand that the common market become an 'organised market' in which workers' interests would take priority. For Liberals, he explained to the SFIO's parliamentary group in January 1957, the common market meant simply the liberalization of exchanges whereas for socialists it meant the promotion of 'social gains' for all European workers. The paucity of such social gains perhaps explains why Mollet's closest allies, such as Pierre Commin, preferred to highlight the EEC's potential benefits to French workers as consumers as much as producers.[167]

Another and significant way in which Mollet framed the EEC as a socialist project was by underscoring the practice of socialist internationalism. From early on, Mollet had striven to mobilize European socialists behind the project of a common market. In addition to prodding the ECSC's socialist group to pronounce on the 'organic development of a common market', Mollet in early 1956 pushed for an international socialist conference to consider the Messina accords.[168] Equally revealing, Mollet made his membership on Monnet's Action Committee, the non-partisan lobby group for European integration, conditional on the inclusion of other European socialists and especially SPD members.[169] To be sure, Mollet no doubt hoped that a collective socialist voice could influence the outcome of inter-governmental negotiations. But the involvement of European socialists also allowed Mollet to claim not only that the EEC possessed a socialist potential but also that the realization of this potential depended on European socialists. Speaking at the SFIO's congress in June 1957, Mollet pointed out that all the other European socialist parties approved the EEC before presenting the latter 'not as the end but as a beginning' whose eventual form would depend on the sustained and collective

[165] Lafon, *Guy Mollet*, 494.
[166] See the debate in FNSP, GSP, GS 9, 22 January 1957; also see HAEU, GSPE 18, 'Conférence des Partis socialistes des pays membres de la C.E.C.A…3 et 4 juin 1957. Compte-rendu analytique'.
[167] FNSP, GSP, GS 9, 15 January 1957, Mollet; and OURS, SFIO, 'Conseil national du 12 mai 1957', Commin, 12.
[168] AABS, Ssa, Internationella sekretarens korrespondens, E5 002, Mollet to ECSC Socialist Group, 20 October 1955, and attached discussion paper; and FES, AdsD, SPD, PV Bestand Erich Ollenhauer, 320, SFIO to Ollenhauer, 13 February 1956.
[169] OURS, Archives Guy Mollet, AGM 113, Mollet to Monnet, 16 July 1955.

effort of socialists.[170] Much of the promise of a socialist Europe, in other words, resided in the ongoing practice of socialist internationalism.

LABOUR, EUROPEAN SOCIALISTS, AND THE EEC

As Continental socialists collectively weighed the benefits of a common market during 1956–1957, they worked to include Labour in their discussions, inviting the British to attend as observers. Eager to consult with their Continental counterparts, Labour officials readily accepted these invitations. Indeed, in the spring of 1957 they pressed French and German socialists to agree to a 'three-power conference on the general problems of European policy'.[171] The ratification of the Rome Treaties did not end Labour's interest in discussing European unity with other socialist parties. At a conference of European socialists in October 1957 in Strasbourg, Labour sent a sizeable delegation that pleaded for closer cooperation between the International on the one hand and the socialist groups of the ECSC and the European Council on the other, proposing for example that representatives of both attend each other's meetings. Driving the plea for closer cooperation was what one Labour delegate described as 'the need to work out a specific socialist position on the question of European institutions'. In terms of Europe's future, Labour continued to view the practice of socialist internationalism as a useful instrument.[172]

This point is worth highlighting because much of the scholarship on Labour and Europe during this period ignores the international socialist dimension.[173] As we shall see, Labour's ongoing assessment of its European policy cannot easily be detached from its engagement with socialist internationalism. Following a high-level Labour–TUC meeting on European policy in October 1956, Harold Wilson, a future Labour prime minister, penned a note to Gaitskell underlining the need for Labour to debate a possible British entry into the common market, even if he noted that such a market would take years to construct. Other prominent Labourites were coming to similar conclusions. The same month as the TUC–Labour meeting, Kenneth Younger, the shadow Home Secretary, wrote Gaitskell that the time had come to consider 'closer ties to Europe'. 'I have always found great difficulty in clarifying my mind about the long term view of our relations with Europe and I have had the impression that the Party has never

---

[170] OURS, SFIO, '49ème Congrès national des 27, 28, 29 et 30 juin 1957', Mollet, 328.

[171] LHASC, LPA, International Department, B 35/1, Fernand Georges (Socialist group ECSC) to Labour, 16 May 1956; and Labour Party, NEC minutes, fiche 589, 'Letter from the French Socialist Party in Connection with a Conference on the General Problems of European Policy', 18 April 1957.

[172] SSAZ, SPS, Ar.1.260.32a, 'Kurzbericht über der gemeinsamen Sitzung des Buros der Sozialistischen Internationale und der sozialistischen Fraktionen…20. Oktober 1957'.

[173] For example, see Andrew Mullen, *The British Left's 'Great Debate' on Europe* (London, 2007), 43–90; and Helen Parr, *Britain's Policy towards the European Community: Harold Wilson and Britain's Role, 1964–1967* (London, 2006). An important exception is Kristian Steinnes, *The British Labour Party, Transnational Influences and European Community Membership, 1960–1973* (Stuttgart, 2014).

thought things out properly.'[174] Younger was right: during 1957–1958, Labour policy remained in flux. In early 1957, the party's executive asked the recently created European cooperation subcommittee to draft recommendations regarding both a European common market and a free trade area. After considerable consultation, the subcommittee submitted a draft statement in September 1957 contending that for political and economic reasons 'Britain cannot join the Common Market' and recommended instead that the country work to create a 'European Industrial Free Trade Area'. The following month, however, Labour's executive refused to endorse the statement, preferring to wait 'until more facts were available'.[175]

The subcommittee's recommendation regarding a free trade area was a response to the British government's attempts during the late 1950s to negotiate an agreement with those European countries belonging to the Organisation for European Economic Co-operation (OEEC), including the EEC countries. For Labour, a free trade area begged two questions. One was whether to endorse British membership. The European cooperation subcommittee, as already mentioned, answered yes, declaring in late 1957 that it would 'undoubtedly bring substantial advantages to Europe and to Britain in both the economic and political fields'. Interestingly, the subcommittee framed these advantages in protectionist terms: the creation of a 'large, protected home market' would encourage the modernization of British industries and, specifically, the adoption of 'efficient mass production'.[176] To be sure, the subcommittee was cautious in its endorsement, maintaining in early 1958 that several conditions were needed to ensure that British governments could pursue economic planning at home and that the living standards of British workers and farmers were not adversely affected. Nevertheless, the overall message was positive and emphasized the need for flexibility. In a report to Labour's executive, the subcommittee, while agreeing that intergovernmental institutions were preferable to supranational ones, accepted that 'concessions and compromise on this question [supranationalism] might be required.'[177]

The second question concerned the relationship between a European free trade area and the EEC. Labour officials generally agreed that some association between the two was necessary, if only to prevent the exclusion of non-EEC members from the common market due to the latter's external tariff. No less importantly, Labour recognized the need to work with Continental socialists on this question, welcoming the International's initiative to organize an international conference in Brussels in December 1958.[178] In preparation for the conference, Labour instructed its delegation, led by Wilson, to encourage socialists to find some arrangement ('temporary or not') for linking the two, adding that the 'emphasis should be on private discussions'. At the conference itself, Wilson spoke of creating

[174] UCL, Hugh Gaitskell Papers, C 155, 'Mr. Harold Wilson's Notes on European Common Market', 14 November 1956; and C 310, Younger to Gaitskell, 10 October 1956.

[175] Labour Party, NEC minutes, fiche 607, 'European Free Trade Area', 26 September 1957.

[176] Labour Party, NEC minutes, fiche 602, 'European Free Trade Area', F.G., September 1957.

[177] LHASC, LPA, International Department, B 25/5, 'Note on the European Free Trade Area (for discussion at the National Executive Committee, 26 March 1958)'.

[178] Labour Party, NEC minutes, fiche 643, 'Minutes of a Joint meeting of the Finance and Economic Policy Sub-Committee and the European Co-operation Sub-Committee…25th November, 1958'.

a free trade area that would include the EEC countries, thereby reducing if not eliminating discrimination against non-EEC members. Wilson received strong backing from the SPD delegates, who pointed out that they had always desired a 'larger [European] realm' than that of the EEC. By contrast, the SFIO's delegates were more cautious: a free trade area encompassing the EEC, they insisted, 'could not succeed without common disciplines [*sic*], particularly as regards tariffs to the outside world, as stringent as those laid down by the Common Market countries in the Rome Treaty'. The EEC, as one French socialist explained, represented the 'absolute minimum requirements' regarding policy coordination among European countries. From Mollet's perspective, the choice for Labour was to accept or reject the EEC as it stood, as a watered-down EEC risked provoking his critics within the SFIO. The final resolution, however, struck a more emollient note. Expressing confidence that some common ground could be found, the delegates agreed to create a 'committee' of European socialists from EEC and non-EEC countries 'to maintain continuing contact with the problem'.[179]

The intergovernmental negotiations for a free trade area broke down at the end of 1958, a result for which Labour blamed the British government's inflexibility. Negotiations between a group of non-EEC countries began the following year, resulting in May 1960 in the European Free Trade Association (EFTA). In the meantime, however, the initial breakdown of negotiations, together with the imminent imposition of the EEC's external tariff wall, triggered a renewed debate within Labour over the common market. In addition to those who were decidedly for and against British membership, it is possible to identify two additional groups whose position was less clear-cut. One group, represented and even inspired by Wilson, viewed the possibility of British membership in the EEC with sympathy. It is significant in this regard that Wilson was in regular contact with European socialists and was, in fact, Labour's principal delegate on the 'contact committee' uniting socialists from EEC and EFTA countries. It appears, moreover, that the more Wilson interacted with European socialists the more well-disposed he became towards the EEC. At a meeting of the contact committee in July 1960, he recognized that the EEC was a 'growing economic success' and indicated that Labour would be willing to endorse a British entry under certain conditions. Elaborating on a suggestion by Heinrich Deist, an SPD economic expert, regarding the progressive harmonization of tariffs between the EEC and the EFTA, Wilson affirmed that Labour would 'greatly welcome' the development of a 'wider common market' that included Britain.[180] At a subsequent meeting of the committee in July 1961, Wilson moved still closer to an endorsement of British entry. While admitting that

---

[179] AdsD, SPD, Internationale Abteilung, 2835, 'Bericht über am 17. und 18. Dezember in Brüssel staatgefundenen Konferenz der Sozialistischen Internationale zur Frage einer Europäischen Freihandelszone (FHZ)', Rudolf Pass, 6 January 1959; and LHASC, LPA, International Sub-Committee, 1958 file, 'Socialist International Conference on the European Free Trade Area, Brussels, 17–18 December, 1958'.

[180] LHASC, LPA, International Sub-Committee, 1960 file, 'Informal Discussions among Socialist Parties of the Six and Seven at Strasbourg, 8 May, 1960'; and ibid., 'Socialist International Contact Committee Between Countries of EEC and EFTA…23 July 1960'. Also see Heinrich Deist, 'Für das größere Europa', *Vorwärts*, 8 April 1960, 8.

in the 'short run' it would not be in Britain's interests to join, he accepted that in the 'long run' the economic advantages would be decisive. For Wilson, Britain's economic future lay chiefly with Europe and with the EEC.[181]

Wilson's evolving position enjoyed considerable support within Labour. An influential report by the party's research department cited Wilson in claiming that a free trade agreement would be 'a vastly inferior substitute' to the EEC. Similarly, in weighing the pros and cons of EEC membership, Labour's international department argued that the 'Socialists of the Six' would welcome Britain's entry and that Labour's influence on socialist internationalism—and, through it, international politics—would correspondingly increase.[182] At Labour's annual congress in October 1961, several speakers went further, endorsing British membership without reservations. Describing himself as an 'unrepentant believer' in the EEC, Roy Jenkins explained that it offered Britain 'a unified, expanding market', something, he observed, that the Commonwealth could not. As 'an international and adventurous party', Jenkins concluded, 'we should be moving towards and not away from Europe.' Another pro-EEC speaker, J.B. Hynd, an MP and former junior cabinet minister, also invoked socialist internationalism. 'It is the socialist governments and socialists in Europe', Hynd declared, 'who are asking us to come into this great Common Market in order that we do something we have been talking about for so long, and that is to form a solid socialist phalanx through some form of European parliament . . . in which we can play our part in the building-up of a Socialist Europe.' More significant, because of his position as deputy party leader, were the comments of George Brown. In his speech, Brown outlined a scenario in which a British Labour government joined the EEC together with the Scandinavian countries (all three of which had socialist governments). Working together, British and Scandinavian socialists would shift the balance within the EEC away from non-socialists (Christian democrats), thereby paving the way for the construction of a socialist Europe.[183]

If Wilson represented one camp within Labour, Gaitskell spoke for those who were more sceptical towards the EEC. Labour's leader did not figure among the party's anti-Europeanists, at least not at the beginning. Having trained and lectured as an economist, he tended to view the EEC as an economic project and appreciated the potential benefits of a common market. Gaitskell, in fact, professed to believe that British membership implied few political constraints. 'Of course, the Common Market implies a greater degree of unity in Europe', he wrote in July 1961, 'but the real question is not that but what particular political institutions are involved. My answer to this is so far virtually none whatever.'[184] Gaitskell's disinterest in the

[181] LHASC, LPA, International Sub-Committee, 1961 file, 'Report of the Meeting of the Contact Committee on European Co-operation and Economic Integration . . . 2 July, 1961', SI circular, 49/61, 27 July 1961.

[182] Ibid., 1960 file, 'Britain and the Common Market', Labour research department, 1960; and 1961 file, 'Britain and Europe', January 1961.

[183] Labour Party, *Report of the 60th Annual Conference . . . October 2 to October 6, 1961* (London, 1961), Jenkins, 215–17; Hynd, 220–1; and Brown, 227.

[184] LHASC, LPA, International Department, B 25/5, Gaitskell to David Ennals, 12 July 1961.

political aspects of the EEC stemmed from several sources: a strong opposition to a 'European federation'; an Atlanticist orientation that made him an avid supporter of an Anglo-American alliance; and an attachment to the Commonwealth as both a model for cosmopolitan citizenship and a force in international politics.[185] Cause and effect of Gaitskell's pro-Atlanticist and pro-Commonwealth sentiments was a relative disinterest in the practice of socialist internationalism. Unlike Wilson, Gaitskell was not in regular contact with European socialists, and when he did attend international socialist gatherings he found the proceedings to be a 'curious affair'.[186]

Gaitskell's initial position towards the EEC, then, was one of scepticism. Although interested in the economic benefits, he was unwilling to accept the potential political costs of British membership. Over the course of 1960–1962 his scepticism turned into opposition due to the combined force of several factors. One was the lobbying of David Ennals, Labour's International Secretary who was in close touch with European socialists and who underscored the EEC's far-reaching political implications. Whether socialist or non-socialist, Ennals told Gaitskell in July 1961, Continental Europeans 'are all committed to a federal approach to Europe' and will only negotiate with Britain if 'they feel that we are prepared to join with them in working for the political integration and cohesion of Britain.' Healey, Ennals' predecessor, also worked on Gaitskell in this sense.[187] Within Labour, meanwhile, anti-EEC forces actively mobilized against membership. Beginning in the late 1950s, the Commonwealth subcommittee mounted a propaganda campaign highlighting the Commonwealth's political and economic importance to Britain. If this campaign reflected rapidly changing events in the colonial world, it was also a response to intra-party debates on the EEC. Significantly, the subcommittee framed the issue in zero-sum terms, insisting that membership in the common market would undermine the Commonwealth. As a 1961 report declared: 'The alternative posed can be crystallised into a choice between Britain entering the European Community, thus inevitably weakening the Commonwealth structure; or staying out of Europe and concentrating on building up the Commonwealth association.'[188] Seeking to undercut pro-European forces, the subcommittee and its allies convinced Gaitskell to hold a conference of Commonwealth socialist parties at the same time as an international socialist gathering in London in September 1962 to discuss the EEC. The result was a clash of opinions. While Continental European socialists pressed Labour to endorse the EEC, claiming that some arrangement between the latter and the Commonwealth was possible, the Commonwealth socialists insisted that a clear choice imposed itself. If 'Britain were to enter the Common Market...', they collectively

---

[185] For a good summary of Gaitskell's views, see his *The Challenge of Co-Existence*.

[186] UCL, Hugh Gaitskell Papers, C 292, Gaitskell to David Ennals, 18 November 1960.

[187] LHASC, LPA, International Department, B 25/5, Ennals to Gaitskell, 11 July 1961. For Healey, see ibid., Box 3, 'Summary of the Discussion of the Joint Meeting of the Foreign Affairs and Economic Groups...May 4th, 1960'.

[188] Ibid., International Department, B 15/13, 'Secretary's Report June 1961', Commonwealth Sub-Committee, 8 June 1961.

announced, 'great damage would inevitably be done to many countries in the Commonwealth and therefore to the unity of the Commonwealth.'[189]

Although it would be unwise to exaggerate the influence of the Commonwealth subcommittee's campaign, it is noteworthy that at Labour's annual conference in October 1961 Gaitskell presented the choice before Labour as for the EEC or for the Commonwealth. And for Labour's leader, the Commonwealth took precedence. 'We have a different history' from that of Europeans. 'We have ties and links which run across the whole world, and for me at least the Commonwealth, the modern Commonwealth... is something I want to cherish.'[190] In his study of Labour policy, Michael Newman attributes Gaitskell's decision to internal party calculations: confident that he enjoyed the support of Labour militants, Gaitskell sought to unite the party at the expense of the pro-Europeans.[191] But if Gaitskell defeated the pro-Europeans in October 1961, the victory was not permanent. In the ensuing years, Labour would continue to debate the EEC, with the pro-European forces organized into a common market committee whose membership included numerous prominent MPs.[192] Just as pertinently, this debate was not only within Labour but also between Labour and other socialist parties. Indeed, a month after Gaitskell's speech, Labour delegates were present as observers at a conference of Continental socialist parties. In their report, the Labour delegates praised the 'useful discussions' that took place and recommended that the party 'should continue to keep in touch with the activities of the Socialist parties of the six'. During the 1960s, Labour would follow this recommendation, cooperating regularly with Continental socialists on the issue of European unity. And this cooperation would help to lay the groundwork for the decision in 1967 of the Labour government, led by Wilson, to apply for British entry into the EEC.[193]

A number of factors contributed to the decision of Continental European socialists to approve the EEC. But whatever the relative weight of each factor, it is striking how easily socialist leaders convinced themselves that the decision was compatible with socialism. Johanna Bockman has argued that socialist economics always operated in a neoclassical framework, rendering market-based approaches attractive to European socialists.[194] While intriguing, the argument does not appear to fit the case of post-1945 Western European socialism: after all, several socialists questioned the EEC precisely because it favoured a market-driven capitalism. In a

---

[189] Ibid., International Department, B 15/12, 'Socialist International and British Commonwealth Conference, London, 7–8 September, 1962', SI circular, B. 42/62, 14 September 1962.

[190] Labour Party, *Report of the 61st Annual Conference... October 1 to October 5, 1962* (London, 1962), Gaitskell, 159.

[191] Newman, *Socialism and European Unity*, 187–92; also see Steinnes, *The British Labour Party*, 67.

[192] For the membership of Labour's common market committee, see LHASC, Colin Beever Papers, Labour Committee for Europe, 'Newsbrief of the Labour Common Market Committee', no. 11, October 1962.

[193] LHASC, LPA, International Socialist Conference, file: Common Market, 'Fifth Congress of Socialist Parties of the Member Countries of the European Countries [sic]... 5th to 6th, November, 1962', Barbara Castle and Tom Driberg, 13 November 1962. More generally, see Steinnes, *The British Labour Party*.

[194] Johanna Bockman, 'The Long Road to 1989: Neoclassical Economics, Alternative Socialisms, and the Advent of Neoliberalism', *Radical History Review* 112 (2012), 9–42.

much-discussed article in August 1957, Aneurin Bevan, a leader of the Labour left, castigated the common market as an 'escapist conception in which the play of the market forces will take the place of political responsibility'. The '[capitalist] jungle', Bevan added, 'is not made more acceptable just because it is almost limitless'.[195] More concretely, European socialist leaders such as Mollet had long demanded that a common market be accompanied by powerful European institutions capable of pursuing interventionist policies across national borders. Yet as many European socialists admitted, the EEC contained little sign of these demands.

In justifying their acceptance of the EEC, European socialists emphasized two related points. One was its open-ended nature: though perhaps not socialist itself, the common market supposedly did not preclude the development of a socialist Europe. Thus, in response to Bevan's article, van Naters, the Dutch socialist and Mollet ally, claimed that the EEC 'provided opportunities' for socialists, especially regarding economic planning. The second point was that it was European socialists, working together, who would transform the EEC into a socialist project. As van Naters went on to argue, 'the policy of the socialist parties was not yet sufficiently harmonised'; but once it was, European socialists could develop the common market in a socialist sense.[196] Left unexplained was why European socialists would be more successful in shaping the EEC after its creation than before. But the faith in the future of socialist internationalism highlights another problem. Despite repeated calls to do so, European socialists never worked out a clear project for a socialist Europe, satisfying themselves instead with general references to planning or *dirigisme*. In this regard, it is worth mentioning that the MSEUE similarly failed: in 1959 it thus decried the EEC's inability to strike a balance between liberalism and socialism without defining either one.[197] Sheri Berman has argued that what defined post-war European social democracy was a belief in the 'primacy of politics' over market fundamentalism.[198] But, if so, this was a vague and open-ended principle rather than a well-defined programme. To be sure, the lack of a socialist project was not necessarily a problem: after all, a primary purpose of the practice of socialist internationalism was to elaborate such a project. But if European socialist parties failed to do so collectively then each one would be tempted to do so on its own. In the meantime, in the absence of a socialist project offering an alternative approach, European socialists focused on European unity itself, praising the EEC as a major achievement worth defending. The danger for the future was that form would trump content.

---

[195] Bevan, 'Back to Free Markets—and the Jungle', *Tribune*, 30 August 1957.
[196] HAEU, GSPE 7, 'Minutes of the Joint Meeting of the Bureau of the Socialist International and the Socialist Groups…Sunday 20th October 1957', van Naters.
[197] HAEU, ME 367, 'Thèses pour le Congrès européen du travail', May 1959.
[198] Berman, *The Primacy of Politics*.

8

The Cold War and European
Security, 1950–1960

The dominant image of Europe during the 1950s is that of a continent firmly divided along Cold War lines between the Soviet and American blocs. A variety of developments since 1945—the creation of NATO and then the Warsaw Pact, the Marshall Plan, the emergence of separate German states—drew ever-sharper lines between Western and Eastern Europe. Although some European countries succeeded in remaining formally outside of the two blocs, with few exceptions (Austria, Finland, and Yugoslavia most notably) neutrality did not appear feasible: most countries had to choose one bloc or the other, most often the American. In standard accounts of the Cold War this deepening division culminated in August 1961 with the construction of the Berlin Wall, which then symbolized the fissured continent until its fall in 1989. But for all its very real impact on Germans, the Berlin Wall reflected far more than it created the reality of a divided Europe. To be sure, there is debate concerning when this division became inevitable, even if the Marshall Plan is often identified as a key moment. But the consensus is that well before the first brick had been laid in Berlin, Germany and Europe had been partitioned between the two superpower blocs.[1]

The post-war trajectory of European socialism seemingly fits easily into the larger portrait of a Europe divided by the Cold War. While the Eastern European socialist parties found themselves excluded from the post-war international socialist community during the late 1940s, their Western European counterparts embraced the American-led Western bloc. Unable to elaborate an alternative vision of international politics, mainstream Western European socialism became 'harnessed to the Western political community of the Cold War' and the Socialist International a 'Cold War organization'.[2] Studies of individual socialist parties generally tell a similar tale, highlighting the rapid decline of third-force thinking in Labour and the SFIO. Wilfried Loth, for example, claims that French socialists chose the American side as early as 1947, abandoning the 'concept' of Europe as an independent actor between the two superpowers.[3] Admittedly, the SPD's case appears

---

[1] For general accounts, see Bernd Stöver, *Der Kalte Krieg: Geschichte eines radikalen Zeitalters 1947–1991* (Munich, 2007), 98–106, 129–38; and Melvyn P. Leffler, *For the Soul of Mankind: the United States, the Soviet Union, and the Cold War* (New York, 2007), 84–150.

[2] Eley, *Forging Democracy*, 315; and Sasson, *One Hundred Years of Socialism*, 210.

[3] Loth, *Sozialismus und Internationalismus*, 143–5. For Labour, see Schneer, 'Hopes Deferred or Shattered'; Peter Weiler, 'British Labour and the Cold War: the Foreign Policy of the Labour Governments, 1945–1951', *Journal of British Studies* 26 (1987), 54–82; and Michael R. Gordon, *Conflict and Consensus in Labour's Foreign Policy, 1914–1965* (Stanford, CA, 1969).

more complicated if only because of the party's dogged defence of German national interests, which led to frequent criticism of the Western allies. Nevertheless, most scholars agree that the post-war SPD adopted a '*Westorientierung*', a stance facilitated by a fierce anti-communism.[4] Judgements might differ regarding the political wisdom of this orientation, but the consensus is that German socialists—and European socialists in general—opted clearly and decisively for the West.[5]

This chapter does not argue that European socialists refused to take sides in the Cold War. For the overwhelming majority, socialism's attachment to democracy and individual freedom made Soviet communism anathema. Instead, in examining socialist responses to the issue of post-war European security, it seeks to nuance the image of a continent irremediably divided along Cold War lines before the Berlin Wall. Throughout the 1950s, European socialists struggled to devise a stable and peaceful security order in a world of nuclear armaments and superpower rivalries. This struggle initially centred on the European Defence Community (EDC), which began its life as a proposal for an integrated European army that would include German units. For many socialists, the EDC offered a possible means not only of avoiding an independent German army but also perhaps of overcoming Cold War divisions. Following the EDC's demise and West Germany's integration into NATO, European socialists recentred their hopes on 'disengagement'—the idea of creating a demilitarized and neutralized region in Central and Eastern Europe encompassing countries on both sides of the Iron Curtain. Indeed, during the late 1950s, European socialists emerged as the leading organized advocates of disengagement, working assiduously to keep the project in the public eye.

In grappling with the issue of security, European socialist parties constantly consulted with one another, mutually influencing their evolving positions. This point is worth emphasizing in light of the tendency to approach each party separately, whether it be in terms of the divisive debate within Labour over nuclear weapons and disarmament, the SPD's attachment to German reunification, or the SFIO's allergic reaction to German rearmament.[6] For European socialists, these

---

[4] Heinrich Potthoff and Suzanne Miller, *Kleine Geschichte der SPD, 1848–2002* (Bonn, 2002), 189–90. Also see Julia Angster, *Konsenskapitalismus und Sozialdemokratie: die Westnierierung von SPD und DGB* (Munich, 2003); and Ulrich Buczylowski, *Kurt Schumacher und die deutsche Frage. Sicherheitspolitik und strategische Offensivkonzeption vom August 1950 bis September 1951* (Stuttgart, 1973).

[5] Compare the assessments of Kurt Schumacher in Ulla Plener, *Der feindliche Bruder: Kurt Schumacher. Intentionen—Politik—Ergebnisse 1921 bis 1952* (Berlin, 2003); and Hans-Peter Schwarz, *Vom Reich zur Bundesrepublik: Deutschland im Widerstreit der außenpolitischen Konzeptionen in den Jahren der Besatzungsherrschaft 1945–1949* (Berlin, 1966), 491–588.

[6] For Labour, see Lawrence Black, '"The Bitterest Enemy of Communism": Labour Revisionists, Atlanticism and the Cold War', *Contemporary British History* 15 (2001), 26–62; Brian Brivati, *Hugh Gaitskell* (London, 1996); and Michael Foot, *Aneurin Bevan*, vol. II (London, 1975). For the SPD, see Wolfgang Schmidt, *Kalter Krieg, Koexistenz und kleine Schritte: Willy Brandt und die Deutschlandpolitik 1948–1963* (Wiesbaden, 2001); Beatrix W. Bouvier, *Zwischen Godesburg und Großer Koalition: Der Weg der SPD in die Regierungsverantwortung* (Bonn, 1990); and Gordon D. Drummond, *The German Social Democrats in Opposition 1949–1960: The Case Against Rearmament* (Norman, OK, 1982). For the SFIO, see Eric Méchoulan, *Jules Moch, un socialiste dérangeant* (Brussels, 1999); and Gérard Bossuat, 'La campagne de Daniel Mayer contre la CED', *Matérieux pour l'histoire de notre temps* 51–52 (1998), 33–45.

aspects were all interlinked, making it impossible to understand one in isolation from the others. The SPD's priority on reunification thus gained in credibility both at home and abroad in function of the support it received from other socialist parties; hence the party's determined pursuit of the International's endorsement. More generally, disengagement's appeal stemmed partly from its ability to reconcile the different priorities of the principal socialist parties as well as to soothe tensions within each one. With its ultimate refusal by the governments concerned, disengagement no longer served this function; the unity of European socialists consequently began to fracture as each party went its own way on security issues.

Efforts to conceive of a viable security order offer a new perspective not only on European socialism but also on international politics. The scholarship on postwar international security most often adopts a state-centred approach. Studies of the EDC, for example, highlight the role of national interests and calculations in Paris, London, Bonn, Washington, or elsewhere. While certainly important, a focus on governmental calculations alone risks overlooking the political drama surrounding debates on the EDC—a drama all the more pointed because many of the countries involved were liberal democracies.[7] If the response of European socialists draws attention to this dramatic aspect, it also highlights another point: that West Germany's entry into NATO resolved neither the 'German problem' nor the larger and related question of European security. The second half of the 1950s was a fertile period, replete with schemes involving the political and military configuration of Germany and its neighbouring states. On the rare occasions when scholars consider these schemes, they either dismiss them as a form of political manoeuvring between the superpowers or integrate them into a parallel history of protest movements (particularly against nuclear weapons) animated by non-governmental organizations.[8] European socialists, however, were neither governmental nor non-governmental actors. Instead, they constituted an international community of nationally rooted political parties vying to form governments in their respective countries. And it is this insider–outsider stance of European socialists that makes their advocacy of disengagement interesting, for it suggests that the possibilities of attenuating Cold War divisions during the 1950s were greater than the dominant images of the period convey.

---

[7] Examples include Michael Creswell, *A Question of Balance: How France and the United States Created Cold War Europe* (Cambridge, MA, 2006); Kevin Ruane, *The Rise and Fall of the European Defence Community: Anglo-American Relations and the Crisis of European Defence, 1950–55* (Houndmills, 2000); and Edward Fursdon, *The European Defence Community: A History* (London, 1980).

[8] For the first, see Maria Pasztor, 'France, Great Britain and Polish Conceptions of Disarmament, 1957–1964', *Acta Poloniae Historica* 90 (2004), 113–55; John Lewis Gaddis, *We Now Know: Rethinking the Cold War* (Oxford, 1997), 113–50; and Georges-Henri Soutou, *L'Alliance incertaine: les rapports politico-stratégiques franco-allemands, 1954–1996* (Paris, 1996). For the second, see Holger Nehring, *Politics of Security: British and West German Protest Movements and the Early Cold War, 1945–1970* (Oxford, 2013); and Lawrence S. Wittner, *Resisting the Bomb: A History of the World Nuclear Disarmament Movement, 1954–1970* (Stanford, CA, 1997), 44–51, 210–40.

THE PERSISTENCE OF THIRD FORCE THINKING

In many ways, the early post-war years proved fatal to the hopes of socialists that Europe might constitute an international force between the two emerging super-power blocs. The Marshall Plan, the creation of NATO, and the outbreak of the Korean War dealt powerful blows to such hopes. By mid-1950 it appeared to many observers that international socialism had firmly aligned itself with the Western camp. Speaking to an international socialist audience in June 1950, Morgan Phillips, Labour's secretary, argued that the Soviet Union's expansionist ambitions were 'dividing the world into two camps' and that only an American-led coalition could safeguard Europe. 'Socialist prejudice against the U.S.A.', he accordingly insisted, 'must be exposed as out of date.' As for talk of a European Third Force, Phillips maintained that it was a geographical and not a political idea. 'It is quite unrealistic to imagine that a Third Force based exclusively on Western Europe, or even on Western Europe and the Commonwealth, would stand politically mid-way between America and Russia....neither Western Europe nor the Commonwealth, nor both together, are strong enough to stand alone against Soviet aggression.'[9]

Significantly, several speakers at the conference contested Phillips' pro-American bias. Prominent among them was Guy Mollet, the SFIO leader, who spoke of the need for Europeans to collaborate on defence rather than to rely solely on the United States. Equally pertinent, Mollet refused 'to accept as irrevocable the division of the world in two blocks'. The SFIO leader, as a Labour delegate reported, envisaged Western Europe as a 'political Third Force throughout the world'.[10] Whether Mollet truly believed in a Third Force is open to question; as we shall see, he harboured considerable suspicions about Soviet intentions. But as the SFIO's secretary general, Mollet understood that an overly pro-Western stance would provoke many French socialists. Among the most vocal on this score was Marceau Pivert, who used his network of allies and his control of the powerful Seine federation to lobby the SFIO to adopt a balanced position between the two superpowers. The 'doctrinal position that needs to be restored', Pivert wrote a confidant in April 1950, 'is that of international socialism, that is to say essentially that of an autonomous policy for [French] socialism in terms of international politics'.[11]

Pivert's search for a Third Force led him to oppose France's membership in the Atlantic military alliance, a position that attracted only a small minority within the SFIO. But if Mollet might be tempted to dismiss the *Pivertistes* as leftist gadflies, he knew that their unhappiness with a one-sided pro-Western stance was more widely shared. Evidence of this came in the spring of 1949 in debates within the

---

[9] IISH, SI, 240, 'Socialism and Peace', Morgan Phillips, 3 June 1950.

[10] AAOB, Haakon Lie, Dc 0007, 'Report of the International Socialist Conference at Copenhagen 1–3 June 1950', SI circular no. 153/50, 14 August 1950; and LHASC, LPA, International Sub-Committee, 1950 file, 'Report on International Socialist Conference, Copenhagen, June 1–3, 1950', Healey.

[11] AN, Papiers Édouard Depreux, 456/AP/5-4, Pivert to Depreux, 13 April 1950.

SFIO's executive over whether to endorse the Atlantic pact creating NATO. Opening the debate, Louis Boutbien, an expert on international politics, argued in favour, citing the need for collective defence against the Soviet Union; Pivert predictably disagreed, pleading for an independent policy between the two super-powers rather than subordination to the United States. André Philip, meanwhile, sought to carve out a middle position. Thus, while urging ratification, Philip contended that the SFIO must also work to construct an 'international 3rd Force' that would protect France (and Europe) from dependence on the Americans and keep the door open to negotiations with the Soviets. Wrapping up the debate, Mollet also sought to bridge differences by emphasizing the importance of an international third force.[12] Although Mollet left unclear what he meant by the latter, it was nevertheless clear that many French socialists were unhappy with Europe's hardening Cold War division.

Although SPD delegates were present when Phillips delivered his hawkish speech, they did not participate in the ensuing discussion. But this does not neces-sarily mean that German socialists agreed with Labour's secretary. To be sure, the SPD was fiercely anti-communist and anti-Soviet and before 1950 it did not question the need for collective security against the Soviet Union; nor, despite the strong anti-militarist currents within the party, did German socialists rule out the possibility of a German military contribution, even if they made it contingent on equal rights for Germany.[13] Nevertheless, of the three principal socialist parties the SPD was the most committed in principle to overcoming the Cold War division of Europe for one simple reason: national reunification. Refusing to accept Germany's division as permanent, the SPD viewed reunification as a priority. At the same time, because Germany's division into two separate states reflected the larger Cold War divide, German socialists recognized that reunification depended on a con-siderable reduction of West–East tensions. The German question, remarked Kurt Schumacher, the SPD's post-war leader, must be approached as 'a problem for all Europe and for world peace'.[14] Such thinking, in turn, coloured the SPD's approach to a European Third Force. Not only must it encompass a reunited Germany, it would also have to be so configured politically and militarily as to pose little threat to either of the two superpower blocs. The challenge for the SPD was to persuade other socialist parties of the merits of such a Third Force.

Even within Labour, Phillips' hardline position did not go uncontested. As mentioned in chapter 7, Third Force thinking had been strong in Labour during the early post-war years, represented above all by the *Keep Left* group. In 1950 the group sent a fifteen-point programmatic letter to Phillips, whose third point called for an 'independent foreign policy' on Britain's part that included a concerted

[12] OURS, APS, Comité directeur, 30 March and 6 April 1949. Police reports suggested that unhappiness with Cold War divisions was also evident among socialist militants. See APP BA 2320, 'Partis Socialiste S.F.I.O.', undated.

[13] Schumacher, 'German Re-armament', IISH, SI, *Socialist International Information*, vol. 1, no. 1, 6 January 1951, 4–6.

[14] 'Sitzung der obertsen Parteigremein am 10. und 11. Januar 1947 in München', reproduced in Albrecht, ed., *Die SPD unter Kurt Schumacher und Erich Ollenahauer 1946 bis 1963* I, 142–3.

effort to 'break the East-West deadlock'.[15] Admittedly, by 1950 the *Keep Left* group had lost some of its vitality and membership. But the emergence of the Bevanites, a collection of Labour MPs and officials inspired by Aneurin Bevan, would provide Third Force thinking with renewed life. Unhappy with the Labour government's rearmament project, Bevan and two allies (one of whom was Harold Wilson) resigned from the cabinet in April 1951. Their grievance centred on the costs of rearmament, which they believed threatened Britain's welfare state created since 1945. But underlying their position was also a strong anti-Cold War sentiment, as is evident in Bevan's decision to join the *Keep Left* group and, even more so, in a jointly authored pamphlet, *One Way Only*. In addition to criticizing the 'breakneck Atlantic rearmament' against the Soviets, the pamphlet refused to abandon the possibility of forging a middle position between the two superpower blocs: it thus decried the 'lop-sided nature' of Britain's alliance with the United States and pleaded for 'peace proposals' to be made to Moscow.[16]

Admittedly, the Bevanites were never a coherent and well-organized group, partly because Bevan himself proved extremely erratic but also because its members disagreed on precise policies. Thus, if Bevan chafed at Britain's membership in the Atlantic alliance, R.H.S. Crossman, a prominent Bevanite, defined the latter as a 'necessity of survival' for socialists.[17] Yet for all their differences, Bevanites shared a desire to find some way to reduce tensions between the two blocs—hence their shared belief in the urgent need to negotiate with Moscow for a general European settlement. Equally pertinent, the Bevanites were a force to be reckoned with within Labour and especially within its parliamentary wing. Indeed, for much of the 1950s, Labour politics were dominated by the struggle between the Bevanites and the Gaitskellites (supporters of Hugh Gaitskell, who became Labour leader in 1955). If the ultimate stakes involved the direction of Labour and the nature of British socialism, a good deal of the struggle also centred on the concrete issues of British defence and European security. Unlike the Bevanites, the Gaitskellites tended to be more hawkish: firm backers of the Atlantic alliance and wary of any proposals that might weaken the latter. Both the Bevanites and Gaitskellites, moreover, sought to mobilize the support of European socialists behind their positions, lending their struggle for the control of Labour an important international socialist dimension.

THE PLEVEN PLAN AND GERMAN REARMAMENT: INITIAL REACTIONS

In June 1950 North Korea's army attacked South Korea, plunging the Korean peninsula into war, triggering a major international crisis, and exacerbating Cold War

---

[15] Bodleian Library, Barbara Castle Papers, 230, 'Draft Letter to Morgan Phillips', 17 May 1950.

[16] Aneurin Bevan, Harold Wilson, and John Freeman, *One Way Only* (London, 1951), 8–13. For Bevan's resignation, see Michael Foot, *Aneurin Bevan* vol. 2 (Frogmore, St Albans, 1975), 280–346.

[17] Crossman, 'Socialist Foreign Policy', Fabian Society pamphlet no. 287, April 1957, 9. For the disorganized nature of the Bevan group, see Crossman's comments in Janet Morgan, ed., *The Backbench Diaries of Richard Crossman* (London, 1981), 4 December 1951, 47–8.

divisions between the American and Soviet (and Chinese) led blocs. One immediate result was intensified pressure from Washington on its European allies to increase their contribution to collective defence, pressure that included calls for West Germany's rearmament. Recoiling at the prospect of a rearmed Germany so soon after the Second World War, the French government in October 1950 proposed what became known as the Pleven Plan. To forestall an independent German army, the plan envisaged an integrated European army in which German military forces would be incorporated 'on the level of the smallest unit possible'. In addition to ensuring a German contribution to collective defence, the plan was presented as a further step in the construction of a united Europe. Although the Americans had doubts about a European army's military value, they eventually endorsed a version of the Pleven Plan as the best option available to strengthen Western European security.[18] For European socialists, vague aspirations concerning a third force no longer sufficed: it became urgently necessary to define a position on the related issues of German rearmament and collective defence.

European socialists wasted little time in discussing the Pleven Plan among themselves. At an international socialist conference in October 1950, Koos Vorrink, a Dutch socialist, presented a resolution firmly in favour of collective defence and of German rearmament. In response, Mollet emphasized the SFIO's opposition to German rearmament, warning that it could result in a war because the Soviets would view it as a *casus belli* and because a rearmed Germany 'would seek unity by war'. The SPD's deputy chief, Erich Ollenhauer, also opposed German rearmament for the moment, citing among other reasons the danger of fuelling an 'aggressive nationalism' at home. While admitting that Labour had not yet fixed its position, Morgan Phillips acknowledged both the need for a German military contribution and the risks involved in arming Germany. Seeking to play the mediator, he proposed that European socialists consider approving German rearmament if it were subject to rigorous controls. Such a proposal, however, faced a fundamental problem: the SPD would only accept German rearmament on the 'basis of absolute equality' while the SFIO was unlikely to accept the mutual restrictions that equality entailed. Consequently, the participants agreed to refer the entire matter to a Comisco subcommittee for 'further study'.[19]

Before the subcommittee's first meeting in December 1950, European socialists met in November in Strasbourg for the Council of Europe's biannual session. The resulting discussion reinforced the impression that consensus would be difficult. Both Dutch and Belgian socialists presented the Pleven Plan as the best means to avoid a German army while also ensuring that Germany contributed to collective defence. Mollet appeared to agree with them, though he also underscored the need for negotiations with the Soviets to avoid an arms race. Opposition, however, came from the SPD, with Ollenhauer contending that a European army must await the

[18] For the Pleven plan, see Ruane, *The Rise and Fall of the European Defence Community*, 15–50.
[19] Labour Party, NEC minutes, fiche 398, 'Report on Comisco Meeting, Paris, October 21–22, 1950', Healey. Also see the longer version in FES, AdsD, SPD, Parteivorstand, 02517, 'Report of the Meeting of the Committee of the International Socialist Conference in Paris 21–22 October 1950', circular no, 218/50, 22 November 1950.

creation of a European government—a step unlikely to be realized in the near future. Other SPD delegates, while claiming to favour a German defence contribution, insisted on conditions that all but ruled one out, most notably full equality of status. Provocatively, Carlo Schmid defined this status to mean that Germany would not provide troops to a European army if other countries were permitted to maintain national armies. In response, the SFIO's Jean Le Bail warned that German socialists 'were playing with fire', while Mollet accused the SPD of favouring a 'neutralist policy' towards NATO. Reporting on the meeting, Denis Healey, Labour's international secretary, echoed Mollet's concerns, remarking that the SPD's position reflected 'a general emotional desire in Germany that…Germany should contract out of great power quarrels and be allowed to go its own way in peace'.[20]

Despite the SPD's absence, the Comisco committee's December 1950 meeting confirmed the elusive nature of a consensus. Ignoring Mollet's apparent approval of the Pleven Plan, Salomon Grumbach, the SFIO's German expert, castigated it as 'a Utopian formula designed to obtain France's agreement to German rearmament'. While Healey ostensibly refused to take a position, he accused European socialist parties of exploiting the issue of German rearmament to 'escape from their national defence responsibilities'. The reality, he explained, was that Western Europe could not be defended without a generalized increase in military strength. But lest this be construed as an indirect appeal for a European army, Healey added that only the presence of substantial American and British troops on the Continent could control a rearmed Germany and deter the Soviets. From this perspective, a European army was dangerous because it excluded the Americans without whom collective defence was a chimera. With no prospect of an agreement, the delegates once again deferred a decision to a subsequent Comisco meeting in March 1951.[21]

Soon afterwards, Labour Prime Minister Clement Attlee announced that Britain's support of German rearmament would depend on several conditions, including the prior rearmament of NATO countries and assurances that West Germany's military contribution would be integrated into a European army, thereby precluding any independent German military forces.[22] Labour officials seized upon the 'Attlee conditions' to try to forge an international socialist consensus on German rearmament. In a paper prepared for the March 1951 meeting, Healey reiterated the need for all countries (including West Germany) to increase their contribution to Western Europe's collective defence but left open the question of whether this should occur within the framework of the Pleven Plan. For now, the paper proposed, European socialists would support a German contribution to

---

[20] LHASC, LPA, International Sub-Committee, 1950 file, 'Supplementary Report on the Second Session of the Consultative Assembly, Strasbourg, November 18–24, 1950', Healey.

[21] Labour Party, NEC minutes, fiche 401, 'Report on Comisco Study Group on European Unity and Defence, London, 16–17 December, 1950', Healey.

[22] Saul Rose, 'The Labour Party and German Rearmament: A View from Transport House', *Political Studies* 14 (1966), 134–6; and Saki Dockrill, *Britain's Policy for West German Rearmament, 1950–1955* (Cambridge, 1991), 56–7.

collective defence subject to 'conditions already agreed by Governments'.[23] Although Healey succeeded in persuading the participants at the March 1951 Comisco meeting to endorse Labour's paper, European socialists were no closer to a common position—as became clear at the Council of Europe session in the autumn of 1951. While both Mollet and Ollenhauer accepted the need for a German military contribution (but not a German army), they disagreed on whether Germany should enjoy 'absolute equality in rights and duties' in a European army. No less worrying, Ollenhauer, when pressed, contended that West Germany's integration into the Western military alliance would eliminate any chance of national reunification by alienating the Soviets—something the SPD could not accept.[24] At a meeting of the International's council in December, the participants reiterated their positions, leading to an anodyne resolution welcoming a 'truly European army' without, however, providing any details of its make-up. Reporting on the meeting, a Canadian socialist rightly described the issue of German rearmament as 'a tangle', a situation he blamed on the absence of 'a wider viewpoint on the part of some [socialist] parties'.[25]

DEVELOPMENTS AT THE PARTY LEVEL

From the outside, the SFIO's position appeared clear: outright opposition to German rearmament. In reality, however, the situation was more confused. Within the SFIO, a small minority, comprising largely socialists on the right sympathetic to participation in non-socialist led governments, endorsed the Pleven Plan, citing the need to bolster Western Europe's security against the Soviets. Christian Pineau, a future foreign minister, figured prominently among this small minority. A larger but probably still minority group consisted of socialists such as André Philip who reluctantly supported the Pleven Plan on the ground that some German rearmament was unavoidable and that a European army was infinitely preferable to an independent German one. Making a virtue of necessity, Philip suggested that the Pleven Plan could contribute to the construction of a united Europe, especially if a European army included a supranational political authority to control it. From this perspective, the Pleven Plan appeared as the Schuman Plan's military twin. Interestingly, Philip frequently juxtaposed his position with that of the SPD: German socialists, he rightly suspected, opposed a supranational Europe in general and a European army in particular because they hoped to negotiate a deal with

[23] Healey, 'The Defence of Western Europe: Report of the Comisco Study Group on Collective Defence' in IISH, *Socialist International Information*, vol. 1, no. 11, 17 March 1951, 9–13; and LHASC, LPA, International Sub-Committee, 1951 file, 'Report on Meeting of Comisco, London, March 2–4, 1951', Healey.

[24] AABS, Kaj Björk Papers, 1, 'Rapport d'activité de l'Intergroupe socialiste à l'Assemblée consultative du Conseil de l'Europe', 26 November–12 December 1951.

[25] LAC, CCF-NPD, MG 28 VI-I, vol. 185, letter from Paul W. Fox (CCF), 16 December 1951; and LHASC, LPA, International Socialist Conference, 'Report of the Conference of the Council of the Socialist International, Brussels, 14–16 December, 1951', circular no. 15/52, 31 January 1952.

the Soviets for a reunified, demilitarized, and neutral Germany. Philip, however, rejected any idea of neutralism as 'a crime': so long as the Soviet threat existed, an integrated Europe (with West Germany) must remain a member of the Atlantic alliance.[26]

If Philip accepted the Pleven Plan, an eclectic group of French socialists rejected any idea of German rearmament. The most outspoken member was probably Grumbach, who equated German military forces with German militarism. Campaigning against Pleven's proposal, he warned that a European army would lead inevitably to a separate German army. Grumbach's deep suspicion of Germany's militarist inclinations extended to German socialists, who, he maintained, could not be trusted to keep their country on a peaceful path. But while opposing the Pleven Plan, Grumbach recognized that the SFIO needed a more constructive policy. He thus outlined an alternative: a reunified and disarmed Germany that would be subject to strict international controls. Though not explicitly invoking neutralism, such a Germany would have to be endowed with a neutral status agreed to and guaranteed by the two superpowers to prevent it from aligning with the Soviets.[27] Another member was Daniel Mayer, Mollet's predecessor as secretary general. Although fully sharing Grumbach's distrust of Germans, Mayer adroitly emphasized the SPD's opposition to the Pleven Plan, claiming that French socialists could not support a scheme that their German comrades rejected.[28] A more influential member was Jules Moch who, though also harbouring considerable anti-German sentiments, centred his case against German rearmament on the risks of undermining the prospects for general disarmament by provoking the Soviets. As a member of France's delegation to the United Nations' disarmament commission during the 1950s, Moch was convinced that an international agreement on the subject was obtainable. Numerous French socialists found his advocacy of disarmament negotiations with the Soviets appealing, partly because of the SFIO's traditional hostility to armaments but also because success might obviate the need for German rearmament. Unlike Grumbach, however, Moch baulked at the idea of a reunified and neutral Germany; the problem was that Moch's preferred alternative (a divided and disarmed Germany) appeared unrealistic in light of the pressure for a German contribution to collective defence.[29]

Finally and somewhat ironically, Grumbach could count on the support of Pivert and the *Pivertistes* in campaigning against the Pleven Plan. While Pivert loathed Stalin's Soviet Union, his pacifism stirred an even deeper antipathy towards armaments races and the risks of war they supposedly fostered. From this perspective, a European army was just as much a threat to peace as German rearmament. Predictably,

[26] See AN, Papiers André Philip, 625/AP/12, 'Les problèmes du réarmement' as well as several undated and untitled notes. Also see HAEU, ME 365, Philip, 'Le neutralisme isolationiste est un crime', MSEUE, *Bulletin de discussion*, no. 1, 15 February 1951.

[27] Grumbach, 'De Nurembourg à Fontainebleau?', *Le Populaire de Paris*, 31 August 1950, 1–2; and FNSP Fonds Cletta and Daniel Mayer, 1 MA 2.2, 'Projet de conclusions établi par Grumbach pour le Comité Directeur du 17.1.51', undated.

[28] OURS, APS, Comité directeur, 6 December 1950.

[29] On Moch, see Méchoulan, *Jules Moch*, 314–83; and FNSP, Fonds Cletta and Daniel Mayer, 1 MA 13.7, Moch to Mayer, night of 25–26 February 1952.

Pivert identified the solution in international socialist solidarity: European socialists must collectively oppose rearmament at home and abroad by building a truly socialist Europe with the help of a truly socialist International. While admittedly vague in nature, Pivert's prescriptions did draw attention to the need to cooperate with foreign socialists.[30]

With French socialists clearly at odds on the Pleven Plan, it fell to Mollet to define a position that would soothe divisions. As with most European socialists, Mollet disliked military spending in general as a diversion from social spending at home; and as with most French socialists, he disliked the idea of German rearmament, fearing a 'renascent militarism' on Germany's part.[31] At the same time, the SFIO's secretary general believed that Germany must contribute to collective defence, and hoped initially that this might assume a non-military form. But Mollet was realistic enough to realize that a military contribution was unavoidable, a realization that pointed towards acceptance of a European army in order to preclude a German army. For Mollet to say so openly, however, would antagonize the Pleven Plan's opponents; faced with this dilemma, he looked to the international socialist community for help: its endorsement of the Pleven Plan would undercut his critics at home. Yet as Mollet was forced to admit in November 1950, no consensus existed among European socialists on the subject—a situation he attributed to the 'national preoccupations' of the other parties.[32]

Unable to rely on the International, Mollet sought to avoid pronouncing on the issue of German rearmament. At the SFIO's congress in May 1951, the 'quasi-unanimity' of delegates approved a resolution submitted by Philip to postpone any consideration of German rearmament and instead to lobby for four-power negotiations aimed at creating a united Germany based on free elections, a proviso that all but ensured the country's alignment with the West and thus a Soviet refusal. In his comments on the motion, Philip remarked that he had consulted with German socialists and trade unionists, all of whom had indicated their opposition to German rearmament.[33] Soon afterwards Pivert informed a friend that the congress had 'buried' the question of German rearmament for the foreseeable future.[34] Yet even at the time Pivert's assessment seemed questionable, if only because Philip's resolution did not rule out a German military contribution. In any case, at the SFIO's national council in December 1951 the issue of German rearmament was once again the subject of heated debate. While Moch insisted that a European army with German contingents would eliminate any chance of a disarmament agreement with Moscow, Grumbach contended that all socialists must oppose the 'militarization of Germany'. Mollet, in response, sought to carve out a middle

---

[30] See Pivert's comments in OURS, SFIO, 'Conseil national des 4 et 5 Novembre 1950', 118–29; and Comite directeur, 12 December 1951.

[31] OURS, Archives Guy Mollet, AGM 53, 'Résumé du discours de Guy Mollet', undated but 1950.

[32] Mollet, 'L'heure de l'Europe', *Le Populaire de Paris*, 28 April 1950; and OURS, SFIO, 'Conseil national des 4 et 5 novembre 1950', Mollet, 53–4.

[33] OURS, SFIO, '43è Congrés national des 12, 13, 14 et 15 mai 1951', 282–305.

[34] CHS, Fonds Marceau Pivert, 559/AP/6, Pivert to Adolfo (Mexico), 25 May 1951.

position: the SFIO would accept in principle a European army but would insist on safeguards against the creation of a German army. As he explained to the party's executive two weeks later, 'My position is staunch opposition to anything that is not a genuine European army.'[35]

Meanwhile, intergovernmental negotiations had produced the outline of the European Defence Community (EDC), which envisaged the presence of German military units of division-level size within an integrated European army. In preparation for a parliamentary debate on the EDC, the SFIO in early 1952 engaged in a series of internal discussions in the aim of fixing a position. Deep divisions were apparent from the beginning. At a high-level meeting in February 1952, the vote for accepting a European army was thirty for and two against with twenty-six abstentions; the vote on German participation produced a similar result (thirty for, twenty-six against, and one abstention).[36] These divisions notwithstanding, most French socialists understood that outright opposition was unwise because the EDC's demise would likely lead to an independent German army. This explains why the SFIO's discussions in early 1952 centred increasingly on possible safeguards concerning a European army. Taking the lead, Moch proposed safeguards that he himself qualified as unattainable, most notably Britain's participation in a European army subordinated to a supranational political authority. Accepting the need for strong safeguards, Mollet tried to moderate Moch's conditions, particularly regarding the British. The vital point, Mollet maintained, was to conceive of institutional arrangements for the EDC that the British could accept—arrangements that precluded a supranational authority.[37] Ironically, the SFIO's endorsement of the EDC appeared to depend more on British than on German participation.

This being so, Mollet sought to convince Labour to support Britain's 'association' with the EDC. At Mollet's initiative, a Labour–SFIO meeting was organized in March 1952 in Paris for this purpose. Setting aside their differences, the SFIO participants jointly pressed their Labour counterparts to approve British participation in the EDC. Mollet, for example, invoked the International's December 1951 resolution in favour of a European army, claiming that it bound Labour. But pleas and arguments proved unavailing. Led by Hugh Dalton, who viscerally opposed any German rearmament, the Labour delegation made it clear that approval of the EDC was unlikely, prompting a frustrated Mollet to question the purpose of the meeting—and the practice of socialist internationalism.[38] Mollet returned to the charge the following month at a meeting of European socialists in Bonn, urging Labour to 'declare [its] position' and warning that the SFIO would reject the EDC 'if the U.K. was not prepared to enter'—a rejection that would likely entail the EDC's defeat in the French Parliament. But the Labour participants once again

[35] OURS, SFIO, 'Conseil national des 1er et 2 décembre 1951, Asnières', Moch, 61–8; Grumbach, 88; Mollet, 154–5; and SFIO, Comité directeur, 12 December 1951.

[36] OURS, Archives Guy Mollet, AGM 111, minutes of 5 February 1952 meeting; and partial minutes of 12 February 1952 meeting.

[37] Ibid., partial minutes of 12 February 1952 meeting.

[38] OURS, F6 96 BD, 'Rencontres des délégations Labour Party—SFIO (Paris, 22–23 mars 52)'. For Mollet's initiative, see IISH, SI, 605, Mollet (SFIO) to Phillips (Labour), 8 January 1952.

demurred, with Dalton telling Mollet that Labour's position on a European army must be 'left open for further discussion'.[39]

Mollet's failure to extract a Labour commitment to the EDC ensured that the SFIO's annual congress in May 1952 would be a stormy affair. While several delegates, among them Philip, spoke in favour of the EDC, many more argued against. If Mayer emphasized the SPD's opposition to the EDC, insisting that French socialists 'do not have the right to play the game of neo-Nazis against the [German] working class', Pivert pointed to the evidence of growing opposition within Labour to German rearmament, which he attributed to the influence of leftist forces. With the exception of Pivert, the anti-EDC socialists forcefully advocated negotiations with Moscow, an option rendered more attractive by the March 1952 Stalin note calling for four-power discussions on Germany's reunification and neutralization. Significantly, Labour and the SPD's fraternal delegates both echoed the call for negotiations. 'We socialists...', declared Tom Driberg, a Labour MP and Bevanite, 'reject the sterile policy of containing Communism by military means', adding: 'We should say clearly [to Moscow] that we wish not simply to co-exist but to cooperate in resolving real global problems.'[40]

Mollet found himself in a bind. The SFIO's secretary general favoured a European army not only because he believed it preferable to a German army, but also because it would tie West Germany firmly to the West. The prospect of a united, disarmed, and neutralized Germany troubled him. A militarily neutralized Germany, Mollet warned the SFIO's congress, would soon be the 'master of its destiny' and such a Germany 'will invariably not long remain neutralized'.[41] The sole means of obviating this possibility was to embed Germany (and its army) into an integrated Europe. But this is precisely what the SFIO's anti-EDCers refused to accept. By playing the card of party discipline, Mollet managed to rally a majority behind resolution supporting the EDC in principle; but he did so by attaching conditions, chiefly Britain's 'close association', which would be extremely difficult to achieve. Equally important, Mollet was compelled to swallow his suspicions of Soviet intentions and endorse negotiations with Moscow—an endorsement that placed the question of Germany's future status squarely on the agenda.[42]

If the SFIO remained divided over German rearmament, the SPD moved quickly towards determined rejection of the Pleven Plan. Initially, the SPD's criticism focused on the plan's purported discriminatory treatment of Germany—criticism that mirrored its response to the Schuman Plan. At the same time, Schumacher did not rule out a German military contribution to collective defence. The SPD, as he repeatedly insisted, did not advocate 'absolute pacifism': every

---

[39] BLPES, Hugh Dalton Papers, 9/25, 'Conference of British, French and German Socialists at Bonn, 27th April 1952', 30 April 1952.

[40] OURS, SFIO, '44ème Congrès national des 22, 23, 24 et 25 mai 1952. Montouge', Grumbach, 137; Mayer, 171; Driberg, 271. Also see LHASC, LPA, International Sub-Committee, 1951 file, 'Report of the 44th Congress of the French Socialist Party (S.F.I.O.)...', Driberg and Saul Rose.

[41] OURS, SFIO, '44ème Congrès national des 22, 23, 24 et 25 mai 1952', Mollet, 219–20.

[42] On party discipline, see FNSP, Fonds Cletta and Daniel Mayer, 1 MA 13.7, Mollet circular, 20 March 1952.

country and people had a right to self-defence by military means. More concretely, the SPD's leader accepted the need for defence against the Soviet Union, even if he also warned that the Soviet threat was being exploited by militarists in Germany and abroad. But a precondition for any German military contribution was full equality for all member states—a precondition that contradicted the plan's design to constrain Germany.[43] Other German socialists were more forthcoming. In a February 1951 article, Willi Eichler, one of the SPD's leading military experts, argued that Germany should participate in a genuine European army in which all members enjoyed equal rights and obligations. For Eichler, this army would be part and parcel of a supranational Europe anchored firmly to the Western alliance against the danger of 'Totalitarianism'.[44] Internal SPD documents from the same period echoed Eichler's article: participation in a European army required full equality of rights for Germany, which meant concretely that the role of German troops and officers corresponded to those of other countries. At this point, the SPD's position appeared similar to Mollet's: acceptance of a European army in principle but not the Pleven Plan as currently proposed.[45]

Over the course of 1951–1952 the SPD reconsidered its position on a European army, prompted partly by grumbling from party members that it lacked a 'clear principled position'.[46] The result was a clear-cut rejection of a European army, as national reunification emerged as the absolute priority trumping all other considerations. A series of internal SPD studies highlight this process. In a lengthy paper sometime in 1951, Carlo Schmid, a member of the party's executive and vocal advocate of European unity, concluded that the SPD's 'foremost goal' must be reunification—a goal that precluded the EDC. In another study, Gerhard Lütkens, a Schumacher confidant, recommended opposition not only to a European army but also to Western European integration in general on the grounds that reunification must be the SPD's 'most urgent concern'.[47] Commenting on the two studies, Herbert Wehner, the SPD's principal foreign policy spokesman, described reunification as a 'question of life and death' for the SPD and urged German socialists to work closely with foreign socialists on the issue even if he admitted that they likely did not share the SPD's 'national concerns'. For Wehner, the SPD's pressing task was to convince European socialists that reunification was in everyone's interest.[48]

What explains the shift in the SPD's position? Domestic politics certainly played a role. For Konrad Adenauer, West Germany's Christian democratic Chancellor, the guiding foreign policy principle was *Westbindung*—binding the Federal Republic to the West through both membership in the Atlantic alliance and

[43] See his comments in 'Schreiben Schumachers an Bundeskanzler Adenauer mit einer "Darstellung der sozialdemokratischen Auffasung" über einen "deutschen militärischen Beitrag"', 6 February 1951, reproduced in Albrecht, ed., *Kurt Schumacher*, 889–91.

[44] Eicher, 'Rüstung, Krieg und Frieden', *Geist und Tat*, no. 2, February 1951, 43–8.

[45] FES, AdsD, SPD, Internationale Abteilung, untitled note, 18 January 1951.

[46] FES, AdsD, NL Fritz Henßler, 5, Henßler to Schumacher, 26 December 1950.

[47] FES, AdsD, SPD, Bestand Erich Ollenhauer, 420, untitled study by Schmid, 1951; and untitled study by Lütkens, 3 January 1952.

[48] Ibid., 'Bemerkungen zu den Richtlinien für die aussenpolitischen Aktivität der SPD', Wehner, 17 January 1953.

participation in European integration. While never ruling out reunification, Adenauer did not consider it a priority as it involved an agreement with the Soviets, whose intentions he thoroughly distrusted. In any case, the likely Soviet price for reunification—a neutralized Germany—was one that he denounced as a threat to Western security.[49] In this context, an emphasis on reunification offered the SPD a means to distinguish its policy from Adenauer's while at the same time rebutting the accusation that German socialists were anti-national.[50] But international factors also contributed to the SPD's embrace of German reunification, most notably among them Stalin's March 1952 note, which, as mentioned, seemingly offered the prospect of a reunited Germany. The Soviet dictator's true intentions remain a subject of scholarly debate, though there is little reason to doubt that the Soviets hoped to prevent a rearmed West Germany integrated into NATO.[51] But whether or not Stalin would have accepted a reunited Germany, the SPD perceived the note as an opportunity. In several memoranda, Wehner claimed that Moscow's démarche merited consideration and that German socialists must 'maintain and increase our efforts' in favour of negotiations.[52]

Alone, however, the SPD could not do very much, and so German socialists turned to the international socialist community for support. Indeed, during 1952 the SPD made a concerted effort to throw the collective weight of European socialism behind a campaign for negotiations with the Soviets. At the International's council meeting in early April, Ollenhauer argued that the 'restoration of Germany's unity is a vital European concern, and it demands an East-West agreement'; socialists thus had a duty to pressure their governments to undertake four-power talks. German socialists, moreover, did not disguise their belief that a European army would preclude such talks. Speaking to the Council of Europe's socialist group the following month, an SPD delegate bluntly stated: 'We cannot reunify our country if West Germany is integrated into a defence community. This is the cardinal reason for our opposition to any such project.'[53] Earlier, Ollenhauer had urged British and French socialists to work to delay the EDC's ratification in favour of four-power negotiations. The SPD, he explained, believed that 'no treaty should be ratified, nor even signed, for a German contribution to Western defence, until the possibility of agreeing with the Russians ... had been fully tested.' As a

[49] The best study of Adenauer is the second volume of Han-Peter Schwarz's biography, *Adenauer. Der Staatsmann 1952–1967* (Munich, 1994). Also valuable is Ronald J. Granieri, *The Ambivalent Alliance: Konrad Adenauer, the CDU/CSU, and the West, 1949–1966* (New York, 2003).

[50] On this aspect, see Dieter Groh and Peter Brandt, *Vaterlandslose Gesellen: Sozialdemokratie und Nation, 1860–1990* (Munich, 1992), 248–70.

[51] For an introduction to the debate, see Wilfried Loth, *Die Sowjetunion und die deutsche Frage: Studien zur sowjetischen Deutschlandpolitik* (Göttingen, 2007), 101–74. Also see Wolfgang Mueller, 'The USSR and Permanent Neutrality in the Cold War', *Journal of Cold War Studies* 18 (2016), 148–79.

[52] FES, AdsD, NL Herbert Wehner, 1/HWAA003498, 'Bemerkungen zur Note der Sowjetregierung', undated; and 1/HWAA000106, 'Bemerkungen zur neuen sowjetische Note vom 9. April'.

[53] SSAZ, SPS, Ar.1.260.27, 'Conference of the Council of the Socialist International', 3–5 April 1952; and IISH, SI, 65, 'Compte rendu des réunions de l'Intergroupe socialiste à Strasbourg. Séance du 27 mai 1952'.

result of Ollenhauer's pleading, European socialists collectively called on Western governments to 'take seriously' the Soviet note.[54]

Although the Stalin note produced nothing tangible, the SPD remained undeterred, stepping up its campaign in favour of a four-power conference on German reunification. The 'action programme' approved at the SPD's September 1952 congress thus asserted that 'for us German unity is not a long term goal but an immediate one.' In addition to distinguishing the party's position from that of the government, the programme signalled to European socialists the SPD's determination on this score. Describing the SPD as a party of 'international social-ists', it claimed that '[socialist] internationalism' prohibited a policy of 'national abandonment'—of acquiescing to a divided Germany. For Ollenhauer, socialist internationalism required European socialists to join with the SPD in working to 'ensure the national existence of our people'.[55] The task of persuading European socialists to make German reunification a priority would not be an easy one. Cooperation with potential allies such as the SFIO's anti-EDCers, for example, was hampered by the latter's deep-seated distrust of Germans. More generally, any cooperation with the SFIO raised the issue of Germany's neutralization. SPD leaders repeatedly claimed that they did not want a neutralized Germany; hence their insistence that reunification occur through free elections, the assumption being that if allowed to vote freely, the vast majority of Germans would opt for the West. But the SPD displayed more than a little faux naiveté: it was simply inconceivable that Moscow would agree to a united Germany integrated into the Western bloc. To advocate negotiations with the Soviets implied accepting some form of German neutralism. Mollet, who opposed a neutralized Germany, understood the implica-tions of the SPD's position—hence his repeated insistence that a reunified Germany be firmly integrated into a '[Western] European Federation'.[56]

All of this helps to explain why the SPD increasingly looked to Labour more than to the SFIO for support. Initially, as we saw, Labour's policy towards a German military contribution to collective defence centred on Attlee's conditions, which included the prior rearmament of NATO countries and the exclusion of an independent German army. Attlee conceived of his conditions as a means to avoid taking a clear-cut position. 'All we have accepted so far is the principle of a German contribution...', he told Labour parliamentarians. 'The details are still under discussion.'[57] Thus, a Labour pamphlet in early 1952, while recognizing a rearmed Germany aroused considerable opposition on the Continent, not least from the SPD, explained that Germany would not remain unarmed 'particularly since the

[54] BLPES, Hugh Dalton Papers, 9/25, 'Conference of British, French and German Socialists at Bonn, 27th April 1952'; and 'Socialists français, allemands et britanniques demandent que la propos-ition soviétique soit prise au sérieux', *Le Populaire de Paris*, 28 April 1952, 1.

[55] SPD, *Protokoll der Verhandlungen des Parteitages der Sozialdemokratischen Partei Deutschlands vom 24. bis 28. September 1952 in Dortmund* (Bonn, 1952), Ollenhauer, 33, 43; and 'Das Aktionsprogramm der SPD', *Neuer Vorwärts*, 1 August 1952, 3.

[56] BLPES, Hugh Dalton Papers, 9/25, 'Conference of British, French and German Socialists at Bonn, 27th April 1952'.

[57] Ruth Winstone, ed., *Tony Benn. Years of Hope: Diaries, Letters and Papers 1940–1962* (London, 1994), 31 January 1951, 134–5.

Americans...are quite prepared to see a German national army re-established'. Accordingly, it was imperative to build a 'military framework which will be strong enough to hold an armed Germany on the Western side'. Although expressing a preference for NATO as the best-suited framework, the pamphlet did not rule out a European army. The principal message, in any case, was unmistakable: German rearmament was all but inevitable.[58]

It was precisely this drift towards German rearmament that angered Dalton. 'It should be quite wrong', he wrote Attlee in July 1951, 'that we should suddenly be faced, without warning, with a new situation in which definite decisions to arm the West Germans had been taken...' With good reason, moreover, Dalton claimed that opposition to 'West Germany's Rearmament' enjoyed considerable support within Labour.[59] Confident that he represented majority opinion, Dalton, whose views Barbara Castle, a prominent Labourite and EDC opponent, jokingly summed up as 'No guns for the Huns', sought to fix Labour's policy one time for all. In the spring of 1951 Dalton thus deftly pushed through Labour's executive a statement whose argument (that Attlee's conditions were nowhere near being met) as well as tone gave the impression that the party leadership had openly declared against German rearmament. Dalton justified the statement on the grounds not only that it commanded 'overwhelming support in the Labour movement and the country', but also that it reflected international socialist opinion—or at least that of German and French socialists.[60] Soon afterwards, Labour's parliamentary party approved Dalton's proposal to vote against the EDC in Parliament.[61]

Although Dalton was immensely satisfied with the statement, Labour's position on a German contribution to collective defence remained in flux—as became clear at the party's annual congress in October 1952. Following an inconclusive debate, the delegates passed a resolution 'so obscure', in the words of one observer, 'that it did not seem to involve any commitment'.[62] But perhaps more than anything, the conference highlighted Labour's dilemma. Practically all Labourites disliked the idea of an independent German army, a dislike that prodded some of them to consider a European army as the lesser evil. At the same time, there was a growing sense that the EDC would likely fail. Labour officials followed closely the debates on a European army in France, with Denis Healey accurately predicting in January 1952 that the French Parliament would never ratify the EDC. The problem was that if the EDC failed, the likely result would be an independent German army. By the end of 1952, in fact, a pressing question for Labour became what to do if the EDC died.[63]

---

[58] Labour Party, *Problems of Foreign Policy* (London, April 1952), 11–13.

[59] BLPES, Hugh Dalton Papers, 9/27, Dalton to Attlee, 10 July 1951.

[60] BLPES, Hugh Dalton Papers, 9/27, 'Speech for Party Meeting, Tuesday, May 13th'; and Barbara Castle, *Fighting All the Way* (London, 1993), 221.

[61] The statement is reproduced in Rose, 'The Labour Party and German Rearmament', 135–6. Also see Labour Party, Executive Committee of the Parliamentary Party, meeting, fiche 208, 29 July 1952.

[62] Labour Party, *Report of the 51st Annual Conference held on...September 29 to October 3, 1952* (London, 1952), 112–32; for the observer, see Rose, 'The Labour Party and German Rearmament', 137.

[63] For Healey, see LHASC, LPA, International Sub-Committee, 1951 file, 'Report on the Third Session of the Consultative Assembly of the Council of Europe, Strasbourg, 1951'. For pressing questions, see Labour Party, NEC minutes, fiches 444–5, 'Questions of Foreign Policy', undated.

It was in this context that Labour, much like the SPD, re-examined its position on German rearmament and on European collective security more generally. Alfred Robens, Labour's shadow Foreign Secretary, kicked off the process in early 1953. Having just returned from meetings in Strasbourg with Continental socialists, Robens drafted a paper maintaining that the question of Germany's military contribution required 'some new formula' that Labour should work out 'in association with the other Socialist parties so that when launched it would be assured of Socialist support in all the European countries'.[64] Submitted to Labour's parliamentary party, Robens' paper drew responses from several prominent members all of whom agreed that Labour should take a lead and whose proposals shared a twofold theme: that a European army was preferable to a German army and that a European army would only be possible if Britain actively participated. Healey's paper, for example, spoke of the British (and Americans) 'making a military commitment on the Continent of Europe at once more intimate and more lasting than they have so far accepted under NATO. This in fact should be the central theme of a new British initiative.'[65] Echoing Healey, Labour's international subcommittee lobbied for a 'fresh Labour Party initiative' on German rearmament. While recommending 'preliminary discussions' with the SFIO and SPD before any final decision, the committee outlined a scheme for Britain's participation in a European army that would be integrated into NATO.[66] Influential voices within Labour, in other words, were openly calling for German rearmament within the framework of a European army firmly attached to the Western bloc.

This call, in turn, provoked the Bevanites. The latter had allied with Dalton in 1952 in opposition to German rearmament—an alliance that embarrassed Dalton, who did not share their third force thinking in international politics. As a Cold Warrior, Dalton did not reject rearmament in general but only that of Germany. By contrast, if the Bevanites disliked the prospect of German rearmament, they loathed rearmament in general because of its domestic costs and because it supposedly rendered war more likely. Consequently, in response to calls for British participation in a European army, the Bevanites distanced themselves from Dalton's obsessive focus on Germany and began to lobby for a more ambitious disarmament accord that would include a reunified and disarmed Germany belonging to neither Cold War bloc. In a 1953 paper for Labour's international subcommittee, Crossman maintained that 'some informal East-West agreement is possible for slowing rearmament down…'; the EDC, accordingly, should be set aside while Labour worked 'in concert with the S.P.D.' to 'renew its demand for four-power talks'. Such an agreement, Crossman told Labour's parliamentary foreign affairs

---

[64] UCL, Hugh Gaitskell Papers, C 68, 'Memorandum from Council of Europe Delegation to Parliamentary Party', Robens, 17 January 1953.

[65] Ibid., 'Foreign Affairs Group. The Problem of E.D.C.', Healey, undated. This file also contains papers from Woodrow Wyatt and Emmanuel Shinwell.

[66] Labour Party, NEC minutes, fiche 448, International Sub-Committee, 20 January 1953; and CCA, Philip Noel-Baker Papers, NBKR 4/301, 13 March 1953 circular containing 'Memorandum on Germany and European Defence'.

group, must include 'a period of neutralization' for Germany.[67] Bevan, meanwhile, threw his considerable weight behind the idea of a neutralized Germany. In an article in *Tribune* he thus envisaged a 'general and progressive' disarmament accord allowing for a reunited Germany 'under free institutions' but outside of NATO. The Soviets, he noted in this regard, 'could not be expected to agree if a united Germany would be free to act to add her strength to that of the West'.[68]

Over the coming months, the Bevanites mobilized against the EDC (and German rearmament) and for the dual pursuit of German reunification and four-power negotiations, repeatedly citing the need to work with the SPD. Labour, Bevan lectured its international subcommittee in September 1953, should give 'its full support to the German Social Democrats in their gallant battle against resurgent German nationalism and against the ratification of the E.D.C. and the contractual agreements before a genuine effort has been made to secure the peaceful reunification of Germany'.[69] Although the subcommittee rejected Bevan's wording, the executive resolution on the subject submitted to Labour's annual conference in October reflected the Bevanite line, declaring that 'there should be no German rearmament before further efforts have been made to secure the peaceful reunification of Germany.' In his remarks on the resolution, Morgan Phillips put his finger on a key question. The Soviets, he noted, 'will not release their hold on East Germany without some return', and Labour must therefore ask: 'What can we offer?' For Phillips, the answer was to replace the EDC with a reunited and disarmed Germany attached to neither of the two Cold War camps.[70]

THE EDC AND THE PRACTICE
OF INTERNATIONAL SOCIALISM

At the same time that the British, French, and German parties each grappled with the issue of Germany's military contribution to collective defence, European socialists continued to work together in various venues to forge a common socialist position. Although consensus proved elusive, the practice of socialist internationalism helped to focus attention on the project of a reunited, disarmed, and neutralized Germany.

In October 1952, European socialists gathered in Milan for the International's second congress. Speaking for the International's committee on European unity, the Dutch socialist van Naters did not hide his sympathy for a European army (and the EDC), particularly one subordinated to a supranational political authority. Addressing German socialists, he asked how they proposed to reconcile opposition

---

[67] LHASC, LPA, International Sub-Committee, 1953 file, 'Notes on the International Situation', Crossman; and Morgan, ed., *The Backbench Diaries of Richard Crossman*, 14 July 1953, 256. Emphasis in original.

[68] Bevan, 'No Settlement of the German Problem Unless We Disarm', *Tribune*, 31 July 1953, 4. Also see Bevan, *In Place of Fear* (London, 1952), 140–6.

[69] Morgan, ed., *The Backbench Diaries of Richard Crossman*, 16 September 1953, 263–4.

[70] Labour Party, *Report of the 52nd Annual Conference held… September 28 to October 2, 1953* (London, 1953), 151, 162.

to the EDC with acceptance of a German military contribution. In response, Schmid reiterated that German reunification must be a priority for European socialists as peace was impossible without it. Rather than the EDC, Schmid advocated four-power talks that would require time and patience. Schmid received backing from the Belgian socialist (and future NATO secretary general) Paul-Henri Spaak, who urged European socialists to elaborate a well-defined position:

> the mere will to negotiate [with Moscow] is not enough, and the Socialist International must say more than this if it is to make any impression. The basis on which negotiations are to be conducted, the demands the Western Powers are willing to accept or reject, the concessions that might be made—all this needs defining.

A debate ensued regarding possible preconditions to attach to any negotiations, with Spaak insisting that German reunification be based on free elections in both Germanys and with Labour's Saul Rose counselling against anything so stringent. Interestingly, the final resolution made no mention of preconditions.[71]

The issue of a neutralized Germany figured prominently at the International's next congress in Stockholm in July 1953. Morgan Phillips opened the proceedings by stressing the need for negotiations with the Soviets, a point Ollenhauer warmly endorsed, urging European socialists to 'act in unison on this question and [to] adopt an entirely unambiguous position'. At the same time, the SPD leader insisted that a united German government 'must be free to determine the international status of the new Germany'—thus throwing into doubt its attachment to the Western bloc. And precisely for this reason, Ollenhauer's comments provoked a sharp response from Mollet. In addition to questioning the Soviet Union's peaceful intentions, Mollet cautioned against sacrificing European security on the altar of German reunification. Referring to a neutralized Germany, the SPD's leader exclaimed: 'We cannot support German unity at any price... Surely the Socialist International could never endorse such a policy.' Although van Naters, among others, reiterated Mollet's warning about the dangers of neutralism, German socialists remained adamant. 'The future status of Germany', Schmid declared, 'cannot be determined one-sidedly by either East or West.' The result, as the Belgian socialist Victor Larock admitted, was a 'heated controversy' within the committee formed to draft a resolution. After much debate, the committee finally hammered out a statement that neither approved nor ruled out the possibility of Germany's neutralization.[72]

In early 1954, representatives of the four powers met in Berlin but failed to produce any agreement on European security or on Germany's future status. European socialists gathered soon afterwards in Brussels to take stock of this failure. Predictably, Ollenhauer maintained that the Berlin conference had changed nothing: international socialism must continue to make German reunification a priority and to work for renewed four-power negotiations, both of which excluded

[71] IISH, *Socialist International Information*, vol. II, no. 47, 22 November 1952, 'The Second Congress of the Socialist International—III, Milan 17–21 October 1952', 1–20.

[72] IISH, SI, 71, 'Report of the Third Congress of the Socialist International held in Stockholm 15–18 July, 1953', SI circular, no. 115/53, 5 October 1943, 4–8, 21–5, 43–7, 54–6, 65–72.

approval of the EDC. Whereas the Labour participants appeared divided on the question of Moscow's good faith, Mollet, speaking for the SFIO, denounced Soviet aims and described neutralization as a Soviet ploy to place Germany in 'the Russian orbit'. Rather than negotiations, the West needed to strengthen its defences against the Soviet Union, which meant the EDC. Accordingly, in a lengthy report submitted to the meeting, Mollet pressed for approval of the EDC as a 'necessity'. The balance of opinion seemingly favoured Mollet: the final resolution, while nodding towards continued talks with the Soviets, called on socialist parties to 'examine very carefully the conditions for the participation or association of their respective countries with the European Defence Community as a means of ensuring European security.' Not surprisingly, the SPD participants voted against the resolution.[73]

In public, Ollenhauer played down the Brussels meeting, claiming that German reunification remained a priority for the International.[74] But in private, German socialists were angry. In a letter to Morgan Phillips forwarded to other parties, Ollenhauer complained that the Brussels resolution had been exploited by the SPD's domestic opponents to undermine the party's opposition to the EDC. 'It cannot be the goal nor the task of the Socialist International', he reproached, 'to provide arms to anti-socialists...through its action.' More generally, Ollenhauer argued that the practice of international socialism could only function if the parties respected the principle of unanimity, particularly on controversial issues such as the EDC. But behind Ollenhauer's complaint was a clear message: the SPD would not abandon the search for a European security agreement allowing for a reunified Germany.[75]

If the SPD refused to budge, the SFIO found itself prey to deepening divisions on the issue. Mollet hoped that the Brussels meeting's pro-EDC resolution would provide the legitimacy needed to overcome opposition to a European army among French socialists. But the opposite proved to be the case. Following the Brussels meeting, the SFIO's anti-EDCers stepped up their campaign. Some, like Pivert, questioned Mollet's claim to possess international socialist support, contending that the majority of European socialist militants opposed the EDC. Others, including Mayer and Moch, signed anti-EDC declarations that invoked the SPD's oppositional stance while also warning darkly of Germany's ultimate aims. Echoing German socialists, the declarations called for talks with Moscow while praising the creation of a demilitarized zone in Central and Eastern Europe.[76] Forced on the defensive at the SFIO's national council in May 1954, Mollet lashed out at the SPD for weakening the International by ignoring its resolutions on the

---

[73] SSAZ, SPS, Ar.1.260.29, 'Conference of the European Socialist Parties...Brussels 27–28 February, 1954', SI circular, no. 25/54, 19 March 1954, 8–45, annex II; and IISH, SI, 584, 'Bericht über die Europa-Armee von Guy Mollet...'.

[74] Ollenhauer, 'Perspectives internationales de la social-démocratie allemande', *Correspondance socialiste internationale*, no. 40, June 1954, 19–21.

[75] See AABS, Ssa, E2B 09, Ollenhauer to Phillips, 30 March 1954.

[76] OURS, Fonds Charles Lancelle, 13 APO/1, Pivert to Mollet, 28 March 1954; and OURS, *Contre le traité actuel de la C.E.D. Pour la liberté de vote & l'unité fraternelle du parti* (Paris, April 1954), 12–13. Also see ibid., *Contre la petite Europe cléricale et réactionnaire* (Paris, May 1954).

EDC. He also sought to discredit the anti-EDCers by equating their position with the advocacy of Germany's 'neutralization'—a proposal he described as the 'worst of follies for the party, for France and for peace'. Appealing once again to party unity and discipline, Mollet succeeded in squeaking out a majority for a pro-EDC resolution. But this victory provided pyrrhic. A few months later Mollet was powerless to prevent fifty-three SFIO deputies from withholding their support for the EDC in the French Parliament, effectively killing the treaty once and for all.[77]

Ironically, the SFIO killed the EDC at the same moment that Labour finally endorsed a European army with British participation. In late February 1954, the parliamentary party narrowly passed a motion declaring that Labour 'recognises that the conditions laid down... have been met and we should accept German rearmament in the European Defence Community'. The driving force behind the motion was Hugh Gaitskell, who would become party leader in December 1955. Gaitskell, who had long been a firm proponent of a German military contribution to collective defence, believed that the EDC integrated into NATO constituted the best option. In an article in July 1954, he not only argued that 'almost all' European socialist parties (the SPD apart) favoured the EDC, but also warned that its rejection would result in an independent Germany free to reach an agreement with the Soviets to trade reunification for neutralization. Gaitskell baulked at the prospect of a neutralized Germany, fearing that it would create 'a continual state of anxiety' in Europe between the two blocs.[78] Under Gaitskell's guidance, Labour moved towards an official endorsement of the EDC. Tellingly, in May 1954 that national executive decided to organize a pro-EDC propaganda campaign within the party. As part of the campaign, Labour issued a pamphlet, *In Defence of Europe*, which invoked the support for the EDC among European socialists, with the exception of the SPD. Rejecting opposing arguments as the work of 'an assortment of Communists and reactionary nationalists', the pamphlet identified the EDC as 'a Socialist policy'. Just as importantly, the pamphlet rejected German neutralization, warning that a reunified Germany 'isolated from the community of democratic nations' would become either the 'arbiter of Europe' or a Soviet satellite.[79]

A campaign was necessary because the executive's pro-EDC stance provoked the Bevanites. Unlike Gaitskell, Bevan and his supporters continued to view German rearmament (and the EDC) not only as dangerous but also as unnecessary because another option existed. In *It Need not Happen*, a pamphlet designed as a counter-blast to *In Defence of Europe*, several Bevanites, pointing to SPD proposals, outlined a European collective security framework that would include a reunited Germany

---

[77] OURS, SFIO, 'Conseil national extraordinaire des 29 et 30 mai 1954', Mollet, 168, 229. Also see Noëlline Castagnez, *Socialistes en République: Les parlementaires SFIO de la IVe République* (Rennes, 2004), 293–303.

[78] Labour Party, Executive Committee of the Parliamentary Party, meeting, fiche 213, 23 February 1954; and Gaitskell, 'To Arm or Not to Arm', *Socialist Commentary*, July 1954, 176–9.

[79] Labour, NEC minutes, fiche 494, NEC meeting, 26 May 1954; and Labour Party, *In Defence of Europe: Labour's View on the Question of a West German Contribution to the European Defence Community* (London, June 1954).

independent of both alliance blocs.[80] Similarly, Crossman, who had authored much of the Bevanite pamphlet, used his assistant editorship of the *New Statesman and Nation* to advocate neutralization as an alternative to the EDC.[81] In opposing German rearmament and the EDC, moreover, the Bevanites could count on considerable backing within Labour, both in the parliamentary party and among the rank and file—a situation he observed with considerable satisfaction.[82] To be sure, at Labour's annual congress in October 1954 Gaitskell secured a majority for a motion favouring a German military contribution. Yet not only was the majority razor-thin (52 per cent) but the motion had a Bevanite colouring, the result of hard bargaining: it thus called for 'further efforts…to induce the Soviet Union to permit the reunification of Germany on the basis of free elections'. If for the Gaitskellites the mention of free elections promised to scupper any negotiations, the Bevanites emerged from the congress more determined than ever to champion neutralization. Just as pertinently, they intended to do so with the International's help, for the resolution directed Labour to 'consult with the other European socialist parties in an effort to draw up a common policy'.[83]

SOCIALIST RESPONSES TO THE PARIS ACCORDS

Following the EDC's demise in the French Parliament in August 1954, the American and European governments quickly worked out their own alternative. Two conferences in September and October produced the Paris accords that called for a newly sovereign West Germany to enter NATO; Germany would be allowed its own army, albeit one subject to restrictions.[84] The immediate reaction of European socialists seemingly underscored the differences among them evident in earlier discussions on the EDC: the SPD voted against ratifying the accords, the SFIO voted in favour, and Labour abstained. Less visibly, however, European socialists were moving towards a common position on security during 1955, spurred in large part by the growing interest in disarmament and arms control. By the summer of 1955, European socialists began to sketch out the outlines of a new European security system that would permit both German reunification and a measure of (regional) disarmament. Germany's neutralization in some form, moreover, constituted a critical element of this system.

Such consensus was not evident at first. At a meeting of the Council of Europe's socialist group in September 1954, the discussion centred on the issue of a neutralized

[80] Aneurin Bevan et al., *It Need not Happen: The Alternative to German Rearmament* (London, 1954), 28–9. Not surprisingly, the SPD welcomed the pamphlet and had it translated as *Es darf nicht geschehen!* (Bovenden/Göttingen, 1955).

[81] Crossman, 'The Case for German Neutralisation', *The New Statesman and Nation*, 4 September 1954, 252–3.

[82] FES, AdsD, SPD, Internationale Abteilung, 2869, circular to Büro members, 15 February 1954.

[83] Labour Party, *Report of the 53rd Annual Conference held…September 27 to October 1, 1954* (London, 1954), 92–108; and Morgan, ed., *The Backbench Diaries of Richard Crossman*, 1 October 1954, 346–50.

[84] For details, see Creswell, *A Question of Balance*, 158–64.

Germany, with British, Belgian, and French participants resisting the SPD's argument that neither West Germany alone nor a reunified Germany should be integrated into the Western alliance. For the moment, they agreed to disagree.[85] Three months later, at the International's council meeting in Amsterdam, Mollet indicated that the SFIO would support the Paris accords because of the security guarantees provided against the Soviets and the Germans. While sympathizing with the SPD's desire for reunification, he maintained that 'preventing Germany's neutralization' was 'far more important', warning in particular of a Rapallo-type agreement between a 'neutralized Germany' and the Soviet Union. Negotiations with Moscow on Germany's future were possible, but only after West Germany's integration into NATO. Answering Mollet, Ollenhauer declared that the SPD could not endorse the Paris accords as Germany's membership in NATO would alienate the Soviets and thus preclude German reunification. Speaking for Labour, Herbert Morrison, a former cabinet minister, reported that his party was divided but that a sizeable minority endorsed the SPD's position. Admitting that this situation caused Labour 'great embarrassment', Morrison pleaded with the SPD to reconsider its policy 'so that we [socialists] can become united', which would 'be a great thing not only for our movement but for Europe and the world'. In response to Morrison's plea, Herbert Wehner urged the participants to avoid mention of a 'neutralized Germany' and instead to join the SPD in calling for immediate four-power negotiations.[86]

That the SPD would oppose the Paris accords was never in doubt. Moving beyond rhetoric, in December 1954 the party decided to organize a public campaign against the accords and in favour of reunification, the highlight of which was the Frankfurt Paulskirche gathering of socialists and non-socialists in January 1955.[87] But SPD leaders recognized that a road map was needed to indicate how to achieve a reunified Germany. Seizing the opportunity, Willy Brandt, a rising star in the party, submitted a series of memoranda arguing that the SPD must fuse the pursuit of reunification with that of a European-wide 'security system' designed to ensure peace and to offer security to both superpowers. Only by combining the two projects could reunification be rendered acceptable to all concerned.[88] Though Brandt did not mention neutralization, it was evident that a reunified Germany would have to be independent of the two alliance blocs, for otherwise Moscow would veto it. As Gordon Drummond recounts, Fritz Erler, the SPD's leading military expert, referred repeatedly to neutralization. In the Bundestag debate on

[85] IISH, SI, 76, 'Compte-rendu analytique des réunions de l'Intergroupe socialiste. Réunion du 15 septembre 1954'.

[86] FES, AdsD, SPD, Bestand Erich Ollenhauer, 111, 'Kurzbericht über die Sitzung des Generalrats der Sozialistischen Internationale in Amsterdam, 21/22. Dezember 1954'; and Labour Party, NEC minutes, fiche 512, 'Socialist International Council Meeting. Amsterdam, 20–21 December, 1954', Saul Rose.

[87] FES, AdsD, NL Herbert Wehner, 1/HWAA000907, Ollenhauer to Wehner, 30 December 1954; and Drummond, *The German Social Democrats in Oppositon*, 133–9.

[88] FES, AdsD, SPD, Bestand Erich Ollenhauer, 422, 'Grundlagen einer sozialdemokratischen Planung für die deutsche Wiedervereinigung und europäisch-globale Sicherheit', 9 November 1954; and 'Die Ausgestaltung der aussenpolitischen Haltung der SPD', 16 November 1954.

the Paris accords in February 1955, for example, Erler spoke of a reunified and democratic Germany that was neither a 'Soviet satellite' nor a 'training ground for American troops'.[89] Here, moreover, Austria appeared as a model to many German socialists: in 1955, the two superpowers agreed that the country would be officially neutral in its external relations and politically independent at home.[90]

Isolated at home, the SPD looked to European socialist parties for support in its campaign to prioritize German reunification. Indeed, committed as always to the practice of socialist internationalism, German socialists threw themselves into an effort to win over the International. Brandt had insisted on doing so in his memoranda, mentioned above. Erler, for one, needed no prodding. During the opening months of 1955, he met with leading French socialists, including Mollet and Jules Moch.[91] With Moch, moreover, Erler discovered someone who fully shared his belief that the Soviets were open to a wide-ranging agreement on European security. Similarly, German socialists sought to strengthen ties with Labour, well aware of the support for their position from the Bevanites, among others. Citing the Bevanite pamphlet *It Need not Happen*, an SPD foreign policy expert urged Ollenhauer in August 1954 to consider what could be done to strengthen the 'oppositional minority within the Labour Party'. Consequently, over the next several months the SPD organized several meetings between Labour and SPD parliamentarians to discuss pressing issues. One prominent SPD participant, Karl Mommer, publicly lauded the results of these 'exchanges of opinion' in influencing Labour thinking.[92]

The accuracy of Mommer's assessment aside, the practice of socialist internationalism certainly influenced the SPD's position. This development reflected the growing public appeal of disarmament and especially of nuclear disarmament—an appeal that concorded with the powerful anti-militarist sentiments among German socialists. Yet it also needs to be seen in the context of the SPD's effort to mobilize the International. In the spring of 1955, Wehner told the SPD's security committee that the party must find an 'entry point' [*Ansatzpunkt*] with other socialist parties.[93] And disarmament was well suited for this purpose. In a period marked by popular fears of Europe becoming a nuclear battlefield, disarmament increasingly captured the attention of numerous European socialists and (as we shall see) of Labour in particular. For German socialists, linking disarmament with reunification and a collective security agreement would help to make the pursuit of the latter two goals more palatable to socialists—and also non-socialists. This explains why SPD leaders never mentioned disarmament alone but always as part of a more ambitious security agreement that included reunification.[94] Just as pertinently, it

[89] Drummond, *The German Social Democrats in Oppositon*, 146.

[90] On this point, see FES, AdsD, NL Herbert Wehner, 1/HWAA000978, 'Zwölf Thesen als Beitrag zur weiteren Entwicklung der sozialdemokratischen Aussenpolitik', undated but 1954–1955.

[91] See Erler's comments in Deutscher Bundestag, 70. Sitzung, 25 February 1955, 3732.

[92] FES, AdsD, SPD, Bundestagfraktion, II. Wahlperiode, 19, Fritz Baade to Ollenhauer, 4 August 1954; and Mommer, 'Besuch bei Labour-Kollegen', *Neuer Vorwärts*, 5 August 1955, 5.

[93] FES, AdsD, SPD, Internationale Abteilung, 2868, 'Kurzprotkoll der Sitzung des aussenpolitischen Ausschusses des Parteivorstandes, am 1. April 1955 im Parteihaus'.

[94] For example, see Ollenhauer, 'Abrüstung', *Neuer Vorwärts*, 29 April 1955, 1–2.

helps to explain the SPD's strong advocacy of disarmament within the International. In preparation for the latter's congress in London in July 1955, Ollenhauer instructed the SPD's foreign policy committee to conceive of its proposals regarding security and reunification as a solution to the 'disarmament complex'.[95]

The SPD had good reason to look to Labour for support. Led by Gaitskell, the majority of Labour approved of the Paris accords in order to integrate West Germany into NATO and to strengthen Western defences against the Soviets. But Gaitskell could not overpower the minority, inspired by the Bevanites, who feared the accords would exacerbate Cold War divisions—and who also disliked the idea of a rearmed Germany. As a result, Gaitskell reluctantly agreed that Labour MPs should abstain from voting to ratify the Paris accords, admitting in private that otherwise 'we should have been paraded before the country as a Party hopelessly divided and unable to maintain any discipline at all.'[96] This concession, however, did little to soothe tensions. Gaitskell and his supporters continued to champion the Paris accords: at the SFIO's request, Labour even reprimanded MPs who had participated in rallies in France against the accords.[97] Meanwhile, Bevan and his supporters continued to push Labour in the SPD's direction. At a meeting of the parliamentary party in February 1955, Bevan submitted a motion calling for immediate negotiations with the Soviets 'concerning the future of Germany' without waiting for ratification of the Paris accords. The motion was defeated in a close vote (93 to 70), but the majority had to promise that it would pursue negotiations. Still dissatisfied, Bevan collected over one hundred Labour signatures to bring a similar motion before Parliament. Although the parliamentary party voted against Bevan's initiative (132 to 72), viewing it as a threat to unity, the minority's position could not be easily ignored.[98]

Labour divisions, however, were not limited to the Paris accords. During the opening months of 1955, the party faced a brewing crisis over defence policy and nuclear weapons in particular. In February, the British government announced its decision to build an H-Bomb—a decision Gaitskell and his supporters endorsed. A draft statement from the national executive explained that, while favouring general disarmament, Labour in the meantime recognized the need for national defence and thus for a British H-Bomb.[99] Many Labourites, however, baulked at the statement, preferring a more oppositional stance to nuclear armaments. Although Bevan in private appeared uncertain about his position, he quickly decided to exploit the issue of nuclear weapons (and especially the issue of first use of them) to challenge the Gaitskellite majority, prompting a bitter struggle that ended in his defeat and near-exclusion from the party. Yet Bevan's defeat was a narrow

---

[95] FES, AdsD, SPD, Parteivorstand, Sekretariat Fritz Heine, 2/PVAJ000000178, 'Kurzprotokoll. Sitzung des aussenpolitischen Ausschusses, vom 25.5.1955 Bundeshaus', 1 June 1955.

[96] UCL, Hugh Gaitskell Papers, C 117-2, Gaitskell to Geoffrey Crowther, 22 November 1954.

[97] LHASC, LPA, International Department, LP/ID/FRA/3, Mollet to Morgan Phillips, 16 December 1954 and response, 31 January 1955.

[98] For the February events, see Williams, ed., *The Diary of Hugh Gaitskell*, 19 March 1955, 364–75. Also see PAAP B31/15, London embassy to AA, no. 614-00/24, 10 March 1955.

[99] Labour Party, NEC minutes, 'The H-Bomb', Saul Rose, March 1955.

one: he lost the parliamentary party vote by 138 to 124.[100] Equally pertinent, Gaitskell recognized that a compromise on nuclear weapons would have to be found to bridge intra-party divisions. And in this context, something resembling the SPD's position offered considerable promise. Indeed, in February 1955, Richard Crossman and another Bevanite suggested that a consensus within Labour could be built around a policy combining four-power negotiations, German reunification, disarmament, and a neutralized zone in Eastern Europe.[101]

Speaking at the SFIO's congress in July 1955, Herbert Morrison declared collective security, disarmament, and the German question to be 'inseparable'.[102] That he did so in this venue was not fortuitous, for the SFIO appeared to be the socialist party most attached to a Cold War perspective. Unlike the SPD or Labour, the SFIO had voted to ratify the Paris accords. Mollet embraced the latter as a means to contain the Soviet Union as well as Germany. Along with strengthening Western defences against the Soviets, the accords would further West Germany's integration into Europe (and the West), helping to preclude the risk of an independent Germany. Significantly, there was no place in Mollet's scheme for a reunified and neutralized Germany. In a series of personal notes for the International's congress in 1955, the SFIO leader expressed the fear that a neutralized Germany would quickly fall under Soviet domination, thereby undermining NATO. But if Mollet's hostility to German neutralization mirrored the French government's position, it did not represent a consensus within the SFIO.[103] In a Europe threatened by nuclear warfare, Mollet's Cold War stance seemed unwise, if not worse, to many French socialists. On the SFIO's left, Pivert urged French socialists to take the initiative in organizing international socialism behind a 'disarmament offensive'; swallowing his hatred of Moscow, he even called for four-power negotiations to this end.[104] Well to the right of Pivert, Jules Moch, the SFIO's leading expert on disarmament, echoed the call for negotiations with Moscow, quickly becoming a much-cited reference for French and European socialists seeking an alternative to Cold War politics. More to the point, as an SPD report recognized, Moch looked 'kindly upon the idea of neutralization'—of a disarmed and neutralized Germany as part of a larger disarmament and security agreement.[105] Mollet, as a result, was forced to be more flexible. In an internal report in May 1955, the SFIO's chief

---

[100] See Brivati, *Hugh Gaitskell*, 201–4; and Campbell, *Aneurin Bevan and the Mirage of British Socialism*, 294–8.

[101] Crossman and Wigg, 'The Dilemma of the H-Bomb', *The New Statesman and Nation*, 26 February 1955, 268–71.

[102] OURS, SFIO, '47ème Congrès national des 30 juin, 1er, 2 et 3 juillet 1955', Morrison, 307.

[103] OURS, Archives Guy Mollet, AGM 53, 'IS 1955'. For the French government, see Georges-Henri Soutou, 'La France, l'Allemagne et les accords de Paris', *Relations internationales* 52 (1987), 458–9.

[104] CHS, Fonds Marceau Pivert, 559/AP/15, 'Contribution à la définition d'action internationale du Parti', Pivert, undated but 1955.

[105] FES, AdsD, SPD, Bestand Erich Ollenhauer, 422, 'Bericht über die Gespräch mit Jules Moch bei Rosenfeld…am 23. Mai [1955]'. For Moch's position on disarmament more generally, see Moch, 'Les problèmes actuels du désarmement', *Politique étrangère* 20 (1955), 127–40; and Méchoulan, *Jules Moch*, 394–7.

conceded that a neutralized Germany might be acceptable in return for German reunification but only if neutralization was extended to Central and Eastern Europe.[106]

By the spring of 1955, both Labour and SFIO appeared to be moving closer to the SPD's position. Adding to the incentives for convergence was the four-power conference scheduled for July 1955 in Geneva. If European socialists wanted to influence international politics they would need to speak with one voice. This consideration, in turn, assured that collective security figured prominently on the agenda of the International's congress in London in mid-July 1955. In the run-up to the congress, a small committee of European socialists had drafted a 'working paper' on the international situation that reflected SPD views. Characterizing the present period as 'a moment when the Cold War mold is weakening', it urged socialists to seize every opportunity to resolve 'international differences through negotiations'. More concretely, it called for high-level four-power talks on disarmament (especially on the H-Bomb), on German reunification (identified as a priority), and on a security agreement providing guarantees to the two superpower blocs. In so doing, the paper explicitly envisaged Germany's neutralization: 'A reunified Germany should not be obligated to adhere to a military alliance but should be free to determine how it will participate in international cooperation in the framework of the United Nations...'[107] During the congress itself, Mollet sought to qualify the endorsement of neutralization, insisting that a reunified Germany must not be allowed to leave the Western bloc. But the committee's proposal received strong backing from Gaitskell, helping to ensure its adoption. Although cautioning against what he termed the 'cruder notions of German neutralisation', the Labour leader entreated socialists to work for a regional security and disarmament agreement in Central and Eastern Europe that would include a reunified and demilitarized Germany.[108]

THE EMERGENCE OF DISENGAGEMENT, 1955–1957

The four-power Geneva conference in July 1955 ended without an agreement on security issues.[109] For European socialists who had eagerly anticipated the conference, the resulting disappointment tempered the gathering interest in a general collective security agreement encompassing disarmament and German reunification. In the conference's wake, the question of Soviet intentions—of whether Moscow sincerely sought an agreement—became more pressing as well as

[106] OURS, Archives Guy Mollet, AGM 60, 'Ce que devraient être les bases d'une négociation avec l'U.R.S.S.', Mollet, 18 May 1955.

[107] SSAZ, SPS, Ar.1.260.30a, 'Document de travail sur la situation internationale', SI circular no. 34/55, 20 June 1955. For the SPD's influence on the paper, see FES, AdsD, SPD, Internationale Abteilung, 2868, 'A.A. 9.6.1955', ms notes.

[108] IISH, SI, 79, circular no. 52/55, 'Report of the Fourth Congress of the Socialist International... London 12–16 July, 1955', 30 September 1955, Mollet, 17–18; Gaitskell, 35–40; and 139–42 for the resolution.

[109] Günter Bischoff and Saki Dockrill, eds., *Cold War Respite: The Geneva Summit of 1955* (Baton Rouge, LA, 2000).

more contentious. At the same time, as chapter 9 will discuss, the SFIO grew increasingly preoccupied with the Algerian War, a conflict that created tensions within and between socialist parties. Yet if these developments slowed down the momentum behind efforts to forge a common socialist position on collective security, they did not extinguish it. Over the next two years, European socialists groped towards the joint advocacy of disengagement—of creating a demilitarized and neutralized zone in Central and Eastern Europe that included a reunified Germany. Animating this process, moreover, were developments within the three principal socialist parties.

Although increasingly preoccupied with the Algerian War, French socialists could not ignore the issue of security. During 1956, Mollet strove to organize a tripartite meeting with the SPD and Labour to discuss European security and the German question, among other issues, only to see the project upended by the Suez crisis in October–November that had a chilling effect on international socialist relations.[110] Meanwhile, Moch continued to lobby socialist parties (and NATO governments) in favour of four-power disarmament negotiations that included demilitarized and perhaps neutralized zones in Europe. What 'good fortune' it was, Ollenhauer told German socialists in March 1956, that Moch was a 'committed socialist'.[111] Not all French socialists, however, shared Ollenhauer's enthusiasm. During 1955 and 1956, both Mollet and Christian Pineau, the Foreign Minister in Mollet's government, worked to undermine Moch's influence among French socialists by emphasizing (somewhat contradictorily) both the unlikely prospects of disarmament and the potential dangers of any agreement. Reflecting his suspicion of Soviet and German aims, Mollet in July 1956 raised anew the spectre of a German–Soviet agreement, telling French socialists that demilitarized and neutralized zones in Central and Eastern Europe would make another Rapallo more likely. For the SFIO's secretary general, a Germany integrated with the West was far more desirable than a reunified Germany.[112]

Mollet and Pineau also sought to counter Moch's influence among European socialists. As French premier and Foreign Minister, the two prepared a trip to the Soviet Union in the spring of 1956 to discuss international issues. Eyeing an opportunity to advance its agenda, the SPD encouraged Mollet and Pineau to press the Soviets on the importance of a combined approach to security, disarmament, and German reunification. Mollet assured an SPD official in Paris that he fully agreed with the SPD's position—and would thus presumably defend it in Moscow. The reality, however, proved to be somewhat different. Following Mollet and Pineau's return, the SFIO circulated a report to socialist parties of their visit that underscored Moscow's hostility towards a reunified and neutralized Germany,

[110] See the retrospective account in OURS, Archives Guy Mollet, AGM 59, 'Note à Guy Mollet', 13 July 1957.

[111] For Moch's efforts, see FES, AdsD, SPD, Internationale Abteilung, 2865, 'Kurzprotokoll. Sitzung der ständigen Kommission für Fragen der Abrüstung und kollektive Sicherheit, am 2. Febuar 1956, in Bonn', and attachment 'Bericht von Jules Moch'. For Ollenhauer, see AdsD, SPD, Parteivorstand Protokolle, 'Sitzung des Parteivorstandes, Parteiausschusses und der Kontrollkommission am 10. und 11.3.1956 in Bergneustadt'.

[112] OURS, SFIO, '48ème Congrès ordinaire des 28, 29 et 30 juin et 1er juillet 1956', Pineau, 29–37; and Mollet, 339–41.

which Soviet leaders had supposedly equated with its integration into the Western alliance.[113] Although there is little doubt that the Soviets were extremely sceptical about a reunified Germany, Mollet and Pineau appear to have slanted the account in order to undermine socialist support for German neutralization. When questioned by a German socialist in Paris, Pierre Commin, a close ally of Mollet who participated in the visit to Moscow, admitted that SFIO leaders had not raised the issue of a new collective security system in Europe as a means to overcome the Cold War divide; other members of the SFIO's delegation, moreover, hinted that the Soviets were perhaps more forthcoming than Mollet and Pineau's report suggested. In a private account, Édouard Depreux, a socialist deputy and emerging critic of Mollet's Algerian policy, emphasized the Soviet interest in a settlement to reduce international tensions.[114] Although German socialists did not have access to Depreux's report, they understood that the SFIO could not be counted on as an ally when it came to German reunification.

In the wake of the July 1955 Geneva conference, SPD leaders briefly despaired. The prospects for national reunification, Ollenhauer forlornly informed the party's executive, had considerably worsened.[115] But German socialists soon set aside their doubts and recommitted themselves to reunification through a European disarmament and security agreement. Writing to a friend in January 1956, Carlo Schmid refused to accept that the situation was 'completely hopeless', contending that reunification required 'good will and constructive imagination' on the part of leaders.[116] At the SPD's congress in July 1956, Ollenhauer also appeared optimistic. Declaring that reunification remained the 'most pressing task of German politics', the SPD's leader pointed to the 'decrease in international tensions' since Stalin's death in 1953 as a positive sign. Early the following year, the SPD launched a public campaign centred on the so-called 'Ollenhauer-Plan'. Predictably, it called for a reunified Germany within a larger regional security system that would replace both NATO and the Warsaw Pact.[117]

In renewing its determination to achieve German reunification, the SPD viewed the practice of socialist internationalism as a valuable instrument. German socialists, accordingly, exploited various forums (the International's disarmament commission and the ECSC's socialist group) to discuss proposals for a new security order in Europe. Once again, the focus was on Labour. An internal SFIO note admitted that its statements concerning Soviet opposition to German neutralization had

[113] FES, AdsD, NL Fritz Heine, 147, Günther Markscheffel to Ollenhauer, 28 April 1956, which includes an account of talks with SFIO leaders; and LHASC, LPA, International Department, LP/ID/FRA/3, Pontillon circular letter, 22 June 1956.

[114] FES, AdsD, NL Herbert Wehner, 1/HWAA000952, 'Bericht von der Reise nach Paris im Auftrag des PV (27. – 29.5.56)'; and AN, Papiers Édouard Depreux, 456/AP/7-2, 'Impression d'U.R.S.S.', undated.

[115] FES, AdsD, SPD, Parteivorstand Protokolle, 'Sitzung des PV und Fraktionsvorstandes am 29.11.1955 in Bonn'.

[116] FES, AdsD, NL Carlo Schmid, 653, Schmid to Kenneth Layton, 31 January 1956.

[117] SPD, *Protokoll der Verhandlungen des Parteitages der Sozialdemokratischen Partei Deutschlands vom 10. bis 14. Juli 1956 in München* (Bonn, 1957), 48–54; for the Ollenhauer plan, see Drummond, *The German Social Democrats in Opposition*, 203–5.

rankled German socialists and aggravated biparty relations, effectively pushing the SPD towards Labour.[118] Indeed, during 1956–1957 German socialists actively wooed their British counterparts. Several exchanges between Labour and SPD parliamentarians, for example, were organized under the auspices of the Anglo-German Socialist Parliamentary Group headed by John Hynd, a former cabinet minister and proponent of a neutralized Germany.[119] Probably more consequential were what Wehner described as 'confidential talks' between party leaders, which in the opening months of 1957 produced a joint 'Aide Memoire' in which the two parties agreed to work for an international disarmament accord that would include a 'zone of limited armaments in Europe' belonging to neither military alliance.[120] Admittedly, some points of disagreement remained contentious, most notably the question of Germany's eastern border: for domestic political reasons SPD leaders were loath to recognize the Oder–Neisse line. Nevertheless, as Ollenhauer enthused in early 1957, a 'far-reaching agreement' existed between Labour and the SPD on the issue of European security.[121]

On Labour's side, the budding alliance with the SPD resulted from complex political manoeuvrings. During 1955–1957, the issue of disarmament and especially nuclear disarmament risked dominating Labour debates. At the party's annual congress in October 1955, the executive argued for comprehensive and progressive disarmament through international agreement; until then, Britain would need nuclear weapons for diplomacy and defence. The executive's motion, however, met with considerable resistance from delegates who sought Labour's endorsement of immediate and more concrete measures on Britain's part, including the unilateral rejection of the H-Bomb (testing and production).[122] Afterwards, Labour's disarmament subcommittee, chaired by Barbara Castle, a fervent advocate of nuclear disarmament, worked to reshape party policy. Seeking international socialist support, Castle told a meeting of the International's Council in March 1956 that socialists must take the initiative in order to break the 'deadlock' between the two superpowers, pointing in particular to the 'cessation of hydrogen bomb tests'—a proposal, she added, that enjoyed wide support within Labour.[123] During 1957 Castle's subcommittee stepped up its efforts, consulting with experts and circulating working papers, including a lengthy one that discussed the possibility not only of a temporary unilateral British ban on H-Bomb testing but also of a 'non-atomic bloc' of Western European states that had '"contract[ed] out" of the nuclear arms

---

[118] OURS, D6 27 BD, 'Note confidentielle', 18 October 1956.

[119] CCA, John Burns Hynd Papers, HYND 1/19, Hynd to Gaitskell, 13 January 1956.

[120] FES, AdsD, SPD, Parteivorstand Sekretariat Fritz Heine, 2/PVAJ000000178, 'Aide Memoire based on conversations between members of the S.P.D. and the Labour Party', 24 May 1957; also see ibid., 'Draft. Aide Memoire on Conversations between Herr Ollenhauer and Herr Heine on the one side and Messrs. Gaitskell, Robens, Noel-Baker and Morgan Phillips on the other', undated.

[121] '28.5.1957: Fraktionsvorstands- und Fraktionssitzung', reproduced in Weber, ed., *Die SPD-Fraktion im Deutschen Bundestag*, 422.

[122] Labour Party, *Report of the 54th Annual Conference... October 10 to October 14, 1955* (London, 1955), 137–51.

[123] SSAZ, SPS, Ar.1.260.31, 'Report of the Conference of the Council of the Socialist International... 2–4 March, 1956', SI circular, no. 18/56, 29 March 1956.

race, either indefinitely or for a limited period'.[124] Resolutions, meanwhile, flowed in from local constituency parties in support for unilateral measures by Britain.[125]

Gaitskell disliked the pro-disarmament movement within Labour. Convinced of the need for collective defence against the Soviets, he basically approved of the British government's armaments programmes, both conventional and nuclear. Equally important, he feared the consequences of a pro-disarmament stance on Labour's unity and electoral chances. Yet despite his pleas to 'approach the problem [of disarmament] responsibly', Gaitskell was forced to accept the call for a temporary ban on H-Bomb testing by Britain.[126] Well aware of the dangers of an extended debate on disarmament, the Labour leader sought to direct attention to potentially less fraught issues. It is in this context that his cautious support for a demilitarized and neutralized zone in Central Europe needs to be understood. Significantly, Castle argued that disarmament should be decoupled from the search for a larger political settlement, including efforts to reunify Germany; disarmament, in fact, should have priority over all other considerations—a position Labour's international subcommittee seconded.[127] Gaitskell, however, proposed the reverse: to downplay the urgency of disarmament by adopting the SPD's position concerning the need for the simultaneous pursuit of a political settlement. In widely publicized lectures at Harvard in early 1957, he proposed what came to be known as the Gaitskell plan featuring a demilitarized and neutralized zone in Central Europe. Created by the progressive withdrawal of NATO and Warsaw Pact military forces, the zone would include a reunified Germany. The latter's neutralization, he argued in this sense, was 'a risk we ought to take'.[128]

Gaitskell's enthusiasm was probably insincere. The year before he had reacted with ill humour when Alf Robens, Labour's shadow Foreign Secretary, had spoken favourably of Germany's neutralization. 'He [Robens] gets this idea, I am sure', Gaitskell grumbled, 'from the German Socialists.' As for his plan, Gaitskell admitted to a German diplomat that he had little confidence in its feasibility and emphasized instead its value from a 'propaganda standpoint'.[129] But whatever Gaitskell's personal beliefs, the plan served his goal of shifting the focus away from disarmament. And it could so do because the idea of a neutralized Germany attracted considerable support within Labour circles. In early 1957, the TUC indicated that it welcomed Gaitskell's proposed plan and offered to cooperate in a joint publicity campaign.[130] If anything, Labour's parliamentary party was even

[124] LHASC, LPA, International Sub-Committee, B 28/3, Ad Hoc Disarmament Sub-Committee, meeting, January 1957; and B 28/2, 'Defence and Disarmament', June 1957.

[125] Labour Party, NEC minutes, fiche 589, 'Analysis of Resolutions on Foreign Policy Received for May Sub-Committee', undated.

[126] Winston, ed., *Tony Benn*, 3 April 1957, 229–33.

[127] CCA, Philip Noel-Baker Papers, NBKR 2/117, 'Amended Draft Preamble for Labour Party Policy Statement on Disarmament', March 1957.

[128] Gaitskell, *The Challenge of Co-Existence* (London, 1957), 54–8.

[129] Williams, ed., *The Diary of Hugh Gaitskell*, 14 July 1956, 539; and PA-AP B 31/27, Herwarth (London embassy) to AA, no. 1206/57, 12 March 1957.

[130] LHASC, LPA, International Sub-Committee, B 28/2, Vincent Tewson (TUC) to Morgan Phillips (Labour), 27 March 1957, which includes 'Eastern Europe and N.A.T.O.', TUC, 22 February 1957.

keener about a neutralized zone in Europe. During 1956, several memoranda proposing neutralization schemes circulated among its members. One such memorandum, written by Healey, a close advisor of Gaitskell who helped in preparing his Harvard lectures, claimed that Moscow was sympathetic to 'a reciprocal military withdrawal of Russian and Western forces in Europe as a step towards a settlement'. Pointing to recent Soviet statements in this sense, Healey argued that 'these proposals offer a more hopeful chance for negotiation for a European settlement than any since the war.' While not explicitly mentioning German reunification, he did urge that Labour 'as a first step seek agreement with the German Social Democrats on the general conditions which the West should set for such a settlement'. As Healey was undoubtedly aware, moreover, the parliamentary party's foreign affairs group was in close contact with SPD parliamentarians on security issues.[131]

For Gaitskell, a neutralized zone in Europe provided an opportunity to build bridges with Bevan and his supporters. Like many on the Left, Bevan loathed armaments and especially nuclear weapons; at the same time, he doubted the political and electoral wisdom of unilateral British disarmament. Referring to the H-Bomb, he confided in 1955 that the British people were 'not prepared to see themselves denied a modern weapon'. This being so, Bevan basically offered Gaitskell a deal: he would help to tame unilateral disarmament sentiment within the party in return for the Labour leader's backing for great power negotiations involving a collective security arrangement that included a demilitarized and neutralized zone in Central Europe. The result was what historians have called the 'Bevan-Gaitskell axis'.[132] While Bevan combatted the unilateralists, in October 1956, Labour's executive called for international negotiations to achieve German reunification through 'free and democratic elections' as well as through the 'progressive withdrawal' of Soviet and NATO military forces.[133] Speaking in Parliament two months later, Bevan emphasized that Labour policy now centred on a 'conception that might be called the policy of disinvolvement, of disengaging'. Rather than building 'an armed Western Germany into N.A.T.O', he explained, Labour sought to:

> approach this problem from a new angle, not to push the cold war up against each other but to try to establish cool areas between each other, to try to sec [*sic*] whether it is possible for the great Powers to agree that there shall be nations who would have to agree about this themselves quite independently.

Despite its vagueness, Bevan's notion of 'cool areas' clearly resembled Gaitskell's neutral zones. An article in *Tribune*, the Bevanite newspaper, underscored the

---

[131] UCL, Hugh Gaitskell Papers, C 310, Healey to Gaitskell, undated but includes 'A European Settlement', Healey, 6 December 1956. For additional memoranda, see ibid., C 311 and CCA, Philip Noel-Baker Papers, NBKR 2/113. For SPD–Labour contacts, see Hugh Gaitskell Papers, C 155, 'Agenda of Parliamentary Committee meeting... 16th May, 1956'.

[132] Campbell, *Aneurin Bevan and the Mirage of British Socialism*, 327–40; and Brivati, *Hugh Gaitskell*, 227.

[133] Labour Party, *Report of the 55th Annual Conference... October 1 to October 5, 1956* (London, 1956), 137–8, 149–50.

As SPD leaders were undoubtedly aware, an emphasis on disarmament would also resonate with Labour. The year 1958 saw the rapid growth of support for unilateral disarmament within the party. At Labour's annual conference in October 1957, the executive had proposed a motion calling on the British government to seek an international agreement on disarmament and especially on the H-Bomb. Several delegates, however, presented counter-motions committing a future Labour government to end unilateral British testing and manufacture of nuclear weapons—motions that enjoyed considerable trade union support. As a result, Bevan was compelled to intervene to argue against unilateral disarmament on the grounds not only that it would undercut a future Labour Foreign Secretary in international negotiations, but also that it contradicted the International's position. Following Bevan's plea, the executive succeeded in passing its motion but was nevertheless compelled to accept a supplementary motion for a British appeal to the super-powers to end H-Bomb testing.[152] Meanwhile, demands for a more ambitious stance on disarmament quickly multiplied. Gaitskell's position—that Britain should possess nuclear weapons so long as other powers did—left may Labourites dissatisfied. At a Labour–TUC meeting in March 1958, Gaitskell faced pressure to approve a unilateral British renunciation of first use of nuclear weapons. Despite his axis with Gaitskell, Bevan openly sympathized with the idea, while Crossman suggested that Labour would unite around a proposal 'to renounce nuclear weapons for the sake of achieving something big'.[153] Afterwards, Barbara Castle teamed with Crossman to keep open the possibility of Britain abandoning the H-Bomb in return for 'an agreement with Russia and America, [by which] no fourth power should receive or manufacture nuclear weapons'. Interestingly, Castle drew attention to the SPD's renunciation of nuclear weapons for Germany, insisting that Labour should show 'solidarity'.[154]

If Gaitskell favoured British possession of nuclear weapons, he also sought to reduce tensions within an increasingly polarized party. On foreign policy issues, Gaitskell confided to Crossman, Labour '"unity" is such a delicate plan that a good deal of care is necessary'.[155] What Labourites needed, as Crossman had suggested, was 'something big' around which to rally, and for Gaitskell this meant a neutral zone in Central and Eastern Europe that could redirect attention away from the question of unilateral British disarmament. Accordingly, with Gaitskell's blessing, Labour officials worked to make 'disengagement' official party policy. In a paper in February 1958, the international subcommittee outlined a plan for a reunified and neutralized Germany that would be gradually enlarged to include Germany's immediate neighbours in a 'neutral zone'. At a Labour–TUC meeting the same

[152] Labour Party, *Report of the 56th Annual Conference… September 30 to October 4, 1957* (London, 1957), 163–86.

[153] LHASC, LPA, International Sub-Committee, B 28/10, 'Summary Report of the Meeting between International Committees of the Labour Party National Executive Committee and the Trades Union Congress General Council…6 March 1958'.

[154] Bodleian Library, Barbara Castle Papers, 6, Political Diary, 26 March 1958.

[155] UCL, Hugh Gaitskell Papers, C 311, Gaitskell to Crossman, 13 November 1957.

month, Gaitskell waived aside talk of a unilateral British renunciation of H-Bomb testing and emphasized instead his own plan:

> ... the proposal for a neutral zone in Europe offered the best prospect for negotiation at a Summit conference. He [Gaitskell] felt that a real possibility existed that the Russians would agree to the establishment of a European neutral zone. It was realised that the most difficult problem of all would be the reunification of Germany; nevertheless there would be great relaxation of tension in the world if it were possible for the neutral zone to be established.[156]

There are two noteworthy aspects to Gaitskell's espousal of a neutral zone. First and foremost, Gaitskell and his allies presented such a zone as a step towards international disarmament and détente rather than towards a reunified Germany. In de-emphasizing reunification, they strengthened the appeal of neutral zones to the Bevanites (such as Castle) who remained deeply suspicious of Germany and who favoured unilateral British disarmament. At a meeting of Labour's parliamentary party in April 1958 to consider disarmament, Bevan insisted that the 'most important point of all was... that there should be, as soon as possible, discussions with the Soviet Union in order to bring about disengagement in Europe'; significantly, he added: 'It might be that we could not, in the meantime, settle the German problem.'[157] The second aspect concerns the TUC: a neutral zone won the TUC's backing, helping to counter the unilateralist disarmament currents swelling within the trade union movement. In April, the TUC informed Labour not only that it fully approved of Gaitskell's plan but also that measures to create a neutral zone should take precedence over steps towards German reunification. The immediate result was the launching of a joint Labour–TUC public campaign centred on 'disengagement in Europe'.[158]

To be sure, the Labour leadership's interest in a neutral zone did not stem from internal party calculations alone. Healey, a close advisor to Gaitskell and the author of a much-circulated pamphlet promoting disengagement, would later characterize the Rapacki Plan as an 'important opportunity' that the West had foolishly failed to grasp.[159] Even Gaitskell, who doubted the feasibility of a neutral zone, privately defended a regional arrangement, contending that it 'would at least mean an advance in the field of disarmament and at best progress towards an ultimate settlement'.[160] Nevertheless, it is telling that Labour leaders and officials preferred not to go into details regarding a neutral zone. In the spring of 1958, Crossman

---

[156] LHASC, LPA General Secretary's Papers, GS/DEF/50, 'Germany and the Europe Settlement', February 1958; and Labour Party, NEC minutes, fiche 615, 'Summarised Report of the Joint Meeting of the T.U.C. International Committee and the Labour Party International Sub-Committee... 13th February, 1958'.

[157] Labour Party, Executive Committee of the Parliamentary Party, meeting, fiche 225, 2 April 1958.

[158] LHASC, LPA, International Sub-Committee, B 28/10, TUC (International Department) to Labour (International Department), 13 March 1958; and 'Disengagement in Europe', joint Labour–TUC statement, 23 April 1958.

[159] Healey, *The Time of My Life*, 179. For his pamphlet, see *A Neutral Belt in Europe* (London, February 1958).

[160] UCL, Hugh Gaitskell Papers, C 312, Gaitskell to Kenneth Younger, 10 December 1958.

and several Labourites sought to use Labour's defence committee to do 'some serious thinking' on disengagement. 'Now that you and the top-level people have agreed it in vague outline', Crossman told Bevan, 'we thought we would like to decide what it really means...' Bevan, however, did not welcome the suggestion, informing Crossman that there was nothing to discuss as everyone was in agreement.[161] Nor is there any evidence that Gaitskell wanted to flesh out his plan. No doubt a certain vagueness served to facilitate international negotiations, allowing each side to place its own meaning on the initial proposal. But it also worked to postpone what promised to be a fractious debate within Labour on disarmament. In a 1958 article, Gaitskell explained that power politics posed difficulties for British socialists, particularly when Labour was in opposition. Once the party returned to power, however, these difficulties would recede as international realities compelled Labourites to accept the need for armaments and alliances. For Gaitskell, in other words, a primary purpose of security policy was to buy time until the next elections—elections, it is worth adding, that in 1958 Gaitskell and Bevan were confident that Labour could win.[162]

THE SPD, INTERNATIONAL SOCIALISM, AND THE *DEUTSCHLANDPLAN*, 1959

On the issue of security, the SPD arrived at a crossroads towards the end of 1958. German reunification, which remained the party's ultimate goal, remained as elusive as ever. Even Labour, the SPD's most important ally on the subject among European socialist parties, appeared to be wavering. For the SPD, the question was what to do now—a question international developments made all the more pressing. Between September 1958 and January 1959 the Soviets published three notes proposing four-power negotiations for a peace treaty with Germany that would include provisions for reunification based on free elections. If these notes must be seen as part of Moscow's attempt to find a solution to the existential threat posed to the East German regime by the outflow of East Germans leaving via Berlin, they reinvigorated hopes for an agreement on disengagement.[163] With these developments as a backdrop, SPD leaders embraced an Austrian proposal in late 1958 for a high-level meeting of European socialists. Ollenhauer, in particular, was eager to achieve a 'better coordination' of policy between the parties. While Mollet was willing to consider a meeting on condition that the deliberations remain private and unpublicized, Gaitskell reacted without enthusiasm, contending that socialists already met often enough.[164] It is hardly surprising, then, that no high-level

[161] Morgan, ed., *The Backbench Diaries of Richard Crossman*, 23 April 1958, 685.

[162] Gaitskell, 'Die ideologische Entwicklung des demokratischen Sozialismus in Großbritannien' in Julius Braunthal, ed., *Sozialistische Weltstimmen* (Berlin, 1958), 137–8.

[163] On Soviet policy, see Kitty Newman, *Macmillan, Khrushchev and the Berlin Crisis, 1958–1960* (New York, 2007); and Vladislav M. Zubok, 'Khrushchev and the Berlin Crisis (1958–1962)', Woodrow Wilson International Center for Scholars, May 1993.

[164] IEV, Max Buset Papers, 88, Albert Carthy (SI) to Buset (PSB), 14 November 1958, which includes 'Proposition de réunion socialiste au sommet', 14 November 1958.

meeting took place. For Ollenhauer, however, the failure to organize a common international socialist response confirmed his belief that the SPD would have to take the initiative. Maintaining that a new 'starting point' must be found, he informed German socialists in February 1959 that party officials were hard at work on the 'deepening' and 'concretization' of SPD proposals.[165]

The immediate result would be the publication of the SPD's *Deutschlandplan* in the spring of 1959, accompanied by a vast promotional campaign. The plan itself called for the establishment of a 'détente zone' comprising the two Germanys, Poland, Czechoslovakia, and Hungary through the controlled withdrawal of Warsaw Pact and NATO military forces from the area. The zone would be subject to an arms limitations agreement, guaranteed by the Americans and Soviets, which barred member states from possessing nuclear weapons and from belonging to either military alliance. Last but certainly not least, the plan outlined an extended three-phase process for German reunification. As the SPD's propaganda proclaimed, the plan 'signifies... no break but rather the continuity of the SPD's policy as well as the first sincere effort from the German side to clear the path for reunification'.[166]

Kurt Klotzbach, the post-war SPD's quasi-official historian, explains the plan largely as a response to immediate international events: SPD leaders sought to pre-empt the possibility either of an international settlement of the Berlin crisis alone or of a Soviet peace treaty with East Germany, both of which would have reinforced Germany's division.[167] But if immediate events certainly influenced its timing, the *Deutschlandplan* also needs to be seen in the context of international socialist discussions on collective security and German integration over the course of the 1950s. In many ways, it was a logical extension of these discussions. No less importantly, SPD leaders strove to obtain the International's backing so that the plan could be presented as an international socialist and not simply an SPD initiative. At the meeting of the International's bureau in February 1959, the German participants won approval for the creation of a small committee on 'European security and the German problem' to consider concrete proposals. Ollenhauer, the SPD's delegate, then used the committee to sound the other socialist parties on a collective initiative in the hope of reaching agreement at the upcoming Bureau meeting in April 1959. At the meeting, however, the French and Dutch delegates refused to endorse a 'diluted [*verdünnte*] zone' in Central and Eastern Europe— and, by extension, the *Deutschlandplan*.[168]

The absence of consensual support from the International posed problems for SPD leaders. Drawn up by a small group of party officials directed by Wehner, the *Deutschlandplan* met with a mixed response from German socialists: some resented being kept in the dark about the initiative while others had begun to question the

---

[165] FES, AdsD, SPD, Parteivorstand Protokolle, 'Sitzung des Parteivorstandes, Parteirates und der Kontrollkommission am Donnerstag, dem 12. Februar 1959 in Bonn, Bundeshaus'.

[166] 'Der Deutschlandplan der SPD', *Neuer Vorwärts*, 27 March 1959, 4. For propaganda, see 'Deutschlandplan der SPD', *Pressemitteilungen und Informationen*, no. 96/59, 10 April 1959.

[167] Klotzbach, *Der Weg zur Staatspartei*, 482–94.

[168] SSAZ, SPS, Ar.1.260.34, 'Procès-verbal de la réunion du Bureau de l'Internationale Socialiste. Londres, le 23 avril 1959', SI circular no. 18/59, 1 May 1959.

wisdom of the SPD's single-minded attachment to German reunification. At a meeting of the SPD's parliamentary group in April 1959, one participant lectured Wehner that German socialists must stop 'tilting at windmills'. Elsewhere, Willy Brandt, who was sceptical about the plan from the beginning, was groping towards a new approach that de-emphasized reunification as a short- or even medium-term aim and looked instead to foster contacts with East Germany as part of a gradual reduction of East–West tensions—an approach that would germinate into *Ostpolitik*.[169] In this situation, international socialist support for the *Deutschlandplan* offered SPD leaders a means to soothe the discontent and doubts among German socialists. And international socialism meant Labour first and foremost. In addition to underlining the *Deutschlandplan*'s similarities with the Gaitskell plan, Ollenhauer in April 1959 reassured the party's executive that both Gaitskell and Bevan stood firmly behind the SPD. In a speech to party officials the following month, he stressed the 'wide-ranging and active cooperation' with Labour on security issues that offered 'rays of light in these dark times'. While regretting the lack of consensus within the International on the *Deutschlandplan*, Ollenhauer made it clear that for the SPD, Labour was the party that mattered most.[170]

Partly by invoking Labour's support, the SPD leadership succeeded in imposing the *Deutschlandplan* on the party. Yet in the end the initiative proved to be a damp squib: neither the Adenauer government nor the governments in Washington, London, or Paris responded favourably. This negative response highlighted a fundamental weakness of socialist proposals for disengagement: the inability to translate them into government policy. The SPD, in any case, soon quietly abandoned the Plan. As several scholars have argued, its abandonment helped to pave the way for the SPD's adoption of a bipartisan approach to security policy that accepted West Germany's membership in NATO—and, by implication, Germany's continued division into the foreseeable future. In a much commented-upon *Bundestag* speech in June 1960, Herbert Wehner, a principal author of the *Deutschlandplan*, announced the SPD's new course, effectively consigning disengagement to the history bin.[171] For the SPD, the path was now free for the development under Brandt's leadership of *Ostpolitik* in which the emphasis was on détente and not on reunification. Just as pertinently, *Ostpolitik* would be the SPD's policy rather than that of international socialism.[172]

The episode of the *Deutschlandplan*, however, did not simply reshape the SPD's relations with the government: it also affected the party's socialist internationalism.

---

[169] '9.4.1959: Fraktionssitzung', reproduced in Wolfgang Hölscher, ed., *Die SPD-Fraktion im Deutschen Bundestag: Sitzungsprotokolle 1957–1961* (Düsseldorf, 1993), 252–67. For Brandt, Wolfgang Schmidt, *Kalter Krieg, Koexistenz und kleine Schritte: Willy Brandt und die Deutschlandpolitik 1948–1963* (Wiesbaden, 2001).

[170] AdsD, FES, SPD, Parteivorstand Protokolle, 'Siztung des Parteivorstandes am 24. und 25.4.1959 in Bonn'; and 'Sitzung des Parteivorstandes, Parteirates und der Kontrollkommission am 5. Mai 1959 in Bonn', with attachment: 'Rede von Erich Ollenhauer auf der Sitzung des Parteirats am 5. Mai 1959 in Bonn'.

[171] Klotzbach, *Der Weg zur Staatspartei*, 497–503; and Christoph Meyer, *Herbert Wehner: Biographie* (Munich, 2006), 225–36.

[172] See Herbert Wehner, 'Schwerer Abschied', *Neuer Vorwärts*, 25 March 1960, 1–2.

Most immediately, it deepened the gulf between the German and French parties. During the opening months of 1959, SPD leaders had expressed the hope that French socialists might be persuaded to modify their hostility to disengagement—a hope that the SFIO's July 1959 congress brutally dispelled. As an SPD observer reported: 'We cannot count on anything positive for us from the SFIO. The oft repeated statements against a neutralized Germany were clearly directed at us.' The perceived intransigence of French socialists on an issue of such importance to the SPD fuelled a sense of alienation, contributing to what became an unbridgeable divide. By December 1959, Ollenhauer's secretary could write that on many issues—and not just that of security—the SPD and the SFIO were 'moving... far apart'.[173] But it was not only the SPD's relations with the SFIO that suffered: so too did those with Labour. The failure of the *Deutschlandplan* undercut much of the common ground between the two parties, forcing Ollenhauer to admit in July 1960 that German socialists could no longer assume that the SPD and Labour shared the same 'foreign policy principles'.[174] The SPD was not simply alone; it viewed itself as abandoned by international socialism.

LABOUR AND DISARMAMENT

During 1958–1959 the interest in—and support for—disarmament within Labour continued to grow. At the party's annual conference in October 1958, the executive once again advocated multilateral disarmament through international negotiations; arguably more novel was its pledge that a future Labour government would 'give a lead to the world' by taking the initiative in ceasing to test nuclear weapons. Although Bevan underscored the significance of this pledge, not everyone was satisfied. Several motions, in fact, demanded that Labour commit itself to a more comprehensive renunciation of nuclear weapons. One trade union motion thus declared that the 'next Labour Government should cease unilaterally to manufacture and test nuclear weapons and should prohibit the use of nuclear weapons from British territory'. Clearly irritated with such motions, Gaitskell denounced unilateral disarmament as foolish and dangerous: foolish because other powers would not follow and dangerous because it would render Britain's membership in NATO untenable. At the same time, he typically sought to shift the focus away from disarmament and towards his plan for disengagement—a plan that figured prominently in the national executive's statement. Remarking that it had been discussed by both the Socialist International and NATO, Gaitskell described the plan as 'far and away the most hopeful and constructive set of proposals put forward for settling the difficult issues of Central and Eastern Europe'. Although Gaitskell and

---

[173] FES, AdsD, NL Günther Markscheffel, 8, 'Interner Bericht vom 51. Kongress der SFIO vom 9. bis 12. Juli 1959, Paris, Issy Les Moulineaux', undated; and SPD, Parteivorstand, Seketariat Erich Ollenhauer, 2/PVAH000006, Heinz Putzrath to SPD Ortsverein Wermelskirchen, 10 December 1959.

[174] FES, AdsD, SPD, Parteivorstand Protokolle, 'Sitzung des Parteivorstandes am 1.4.1960 in Bonn'.

his allies managed to secure a 'large majority' for the executive's statement, it was clear that unilateral disarmament enjoyed considerable support within Labour.[175]

In these circumstances, it is not surprising that Gaitskell welcomed the SPD's *Deutschlandplan*. Speaking privately to a journalist, he even claimed paternity for the plan, likening it to his own; to a Japanese socialist, Gaitskell conflated the two plans, insisting that they offered the best means to advance disarmament.[176] But praise for the SPD's plan extended beyond Gaitskell and his allies. *Tribune*, the Bevanite newspaper and fierce critic of Gaitskell, published a detailed outline of the SPD's proposals in April 1959, arguing that they 'deserve to be taken very seriously' as they promised 'a genuine fresh start'. The same month, the parliamentary party's foreign affairs group reported that the SPD's 'proposals' were 'much in line with Labour's disengagement policy'. Similarly, a group of Labour MPs, among them staunch proponents of unilateral disarmament, published a letter in a German newspaper championing the Labour and SPD plans and what they termed a 'policy of some form of disengagement'.[177] Gaitskell proved keen to exploit the popularity of disengagement within Labour. Under his guidance, during the summer of 1959, Labour and TUC officials prepared a joint declaration on defence and security policy. Though not explicitly mentioning the *Deutschlandplan*, the declaration reiterated support for a neutral zone in Central and Eastern Europe as 'the best hope for a long-term solution' to the 'related questions of German reunification and European security'.[178]

If Gaitskell and his allies hoped to divert attention from disarmament by emphasizing disengagement, events during 1960 conspired to sabotage their efforts. Perhaps the principal event was the government's decision to cancel Blue Streak, a programme to equip Britain with ballistic missiles and thus with an independent nuclear deterrent. Blue Streak's death raised in acute form the question of the purpose of Britain's existing nuclear weapons. Meanwhile, in May 1960, the much-anticipated four-power summit in Paris collapsed following the shooting down by the Soviets of an American spy plane. The result was a notable heightening of Cold War tensions. For numerous Labour militants, all of this confirmed both their loathing of nuclear weapons and their belief that Labour (and Britain) must seize the initiative to bring about disarmament—if necessary, unilaterally. These sentiments manifested themselves publicly in the activities of the Campaign for Nuclear Disarmament, a popular movement in which many Labourites were active. Within Labour, meanwhile, the debate over disarmament became increasingly polarized as the pressure mounted for some initiative on Labour's part. In May 1960, Labour's Defence Group, made up of MPs, discussed disarmament at

[175] Labour Party, *Report of the 57th Annual Conference held... September 29 to October 3, 1958* (London, 1958), 186–224, 259–62.

[176] BLPES, Hector Alastair Hetherington Papers, 1/8, 'Note of meeting with Mr. Gaitskell on July 23, 1959'; and UCL, Hugh Gaitskell Papers, F 21.9, Gaitskell to Mosaburo Suzuki, 29 June 1959.

[177] 'Germany: A Plan to End the Cold War Division', *Tribune*, 3 April 1959, 5; LHASC, LPA, International Department, LP/ID/GER/43, 'Some points from the Foreign Affairs Group meeting which might be raised in the debate', 22 April 1959; and UCL, Hugh Gaitskell Papers, F 21.2, letter signed by various MPs, 25 April 1959.

[178] LHASC, LPA, International Sub-Committee, B 28/10, for a draft copy of the statement.

several meetings only to conclude that no consensus was possible. As the chairman of the group remarked at the end of one meeting: 'We had had a wide canvassing of different points of view. Leaders to go back and consider. Ought not put anything in the form of a resolution. We are not in agreement.'[179]

Given organized labour's powerful and institutionalized influence within Labour, the TUC's growing support for some measure of unilateral disarmament was especially worrying for Gaitskell. As early as June 1959, Frank Cousins, head of the powerful Transport and General Workers' Union and member of Labour's executive, had written Gaitskell to argue for a unilateral cessation on the testing and production of H-Bombs as well as for a pledge of no first use of nuclear weapons by Britain (or NATO forces in Britain). In his careful reply, Gaitskell sought to appease Cousins by promising to devote further study to the issues of disarmament and defence.[180] The problem was that closer study did nothing to bridge the differences between their two positions, and by the summer of 1960 the Labour leader was close to despair. Promising privately 'to fight this thing [unilateral disarmament] right to the end', Gaitskell (and his allies) waged a rearguard action in favour of internationally negotiated and multilateral disarmament: faced with the pressure for unilateralism, they strove to limit concessions to a cessation of H-Bomb testing and the creation of a non-nuclear club in which Britain would abandon nuclear weapons if all other countries (the United States and the Soviet Union excepted) agreed to do so. With these concessions as a starting point, during the summer of 1960, Labour and TUC leaders and officials thrashed out a joint statement whose purpose, Gaitskell remarked, 'is not to <u>hide</u> but to <u>narrow</u> points of difference'.[181] While vague on disarmament, the statement underscored the value of a 'long-term plan for disengagement' whose 'first step' would be 'proposals for the limitation and control of forces in... [Central and Eastern Europe]— including an agreement to establish a nuclear-free zone'.[182]

Once the SPD buried the *Deutschlandplan*, however, disengagement lost much of its promise as a potential binding force within Labour and between Labour and the TUC. Matters came to a head at Labour's annual conference in October 1960. Speaking for the national executive, Sam Watson pleaded for a rejection of unilateral disarmament, which, interestingly, he equated with 'neutralism' and with the 'abnegation of effective influence in world affairs' by Labour. Unmoved, delegates presented several unilateralist motions, including one by Cousins that pledged a future Labour government to end the testing, making, and possession of nuclear weapons by Britain. The unilateralist motions provoked an emotional reply from Denis Healey who, like Watson, emphasized the point that the executive's statement

---

[179] UCL, Hugh Gaitskell Papers, C 206.2, 'Second Meeting of Defence Group. 16.5.1960'. The minutes of the other meetings are in the same file.

[180] UCL, Hugh Gaitskell Papers, F 21.3, Cousins to Gaitskell, 26 June 1959; and Gaitskell to Cousins, 20 June 1959.

[181] Ibid., C 206.2, Gaitskell to Alan Birch, 2 May 1960; and Gaitskell to Crossman, 13 June 1960. Emphasis in original.

[182] For the statement, see Labour Party, Executive Committee of the Parliamentary Party, fiches 235–6, 'Foreign Policy and Defence', 6 June 1960. Also see LHASC, LPA, General Secretary's Papers, Box 20, GS/DEF/99, Labour, International Sub-Committee, 'Defence and Disarmament: Some Points for Consideration', May 1960.

on multilateral disarmament and membership in NATO reflected the SPD's new position—and, supposedly, that of the International. 'The plain fact', Healey exclaimed, 'is that the Executive's policy has unanimous support from the whole of the [international] Socialist Movement.' Gaitskell himself did not refer to international socialism but instead echoed Watson in conflating unilateralism and neutralism. 'If you are a unilateralist on principle', the Labour leader contended, 'you are driven in [*sic*] to become a neutralist; you are driven to becoming one of those who wish us to withdraw from N.A.T.O.'[183] To be sure, Gaitskell did not openly renounce his earlier support for neutral zones in Central and Eastern Europe. Nevertheless, the sharp attacks on neutralism not just for Britain but in general indicate that by the autumn of 1960 much of disengagement's potential appeal had evaporated for Labour as well as the SPD.

After much debate Cousins' motion won a razor-thin majority (50.3 per cent), while that of the executive was defeated by a slightly larger margin (52.3 per cent). If Gaitskell emerged weakened from congress, it was also true, as SPD observers reported, that the closeness of the vote meant that the issue remained undecided.[184] Disarmament, in fact, would preoccupy Labour over the next several years, fuelling passions and divisions. Proposals for a neutral zone, however, played little role in this drama as disengagement became a victim of both superpower politics and international socialist politics. One result of the preoccupation with disarmament was a turning inwards by Labour on the issues of defence and security—a process accompanied by a distancing from other socialist parties. During the 1940s and 1950s the practice of socialist internationalism had constituted an important albeit rarely dominant element of Labour policymaking; afterwards, international socialism quickly receded either as an actor or as a factor. Labour would determine its position on security issues largely on its own. Appropriately perhaps, it was Healey, Labour's leading defence expert, who had begun his political career as the party's international secretary, who signalled this change. 'A Socialist foreign policy which depends on working only with [foreign] Socialists', he sniffed at Labour's annual conference in 1961, 'is a policy for hermits.'[185]

THE SFIO AND THE END OF DISARMAMENT

While Labour became increasingly preoccupied with disarmament, the SFIO embarked on the opposite course—one in favour of France's rearmament. During the late 1950s, the SFIO appeared strongly in favour of disarmament. In May 1957, French socialists signed the motion, proposed by the ECSC socialist group, calling for the suspension of all nuclear weapons testing 'as a first step towards their

[183] Labour Party, *Report of the 59th Annual Conference held... October 3 to October 7, 1960* (London, 1960), 170–202.

[184] Benjamin Carr, 'Der Kampf geht weiter. Kernwaffengegner erobern den Labour-Parteitag, aber nicht die Partei', *Neuer Vorwärts*, 14 October 1960, 9.

[185] Labour Party, *Report of the 60th Annual Conference held... October 2 to October 6, 1961* (London, 1961), Healey, 181.

prohibition by international agreement'. The following month, the SFIO's Etienne Weill-Raynal reiterated to the group Mollet's commitment to 'the exclusively pacific use of nuclear energy' as well as his proposal that France abstain from any military use of nuclear energy for at least five years in order to allow a general disarmament agreement to be negotiated.[186] Meanwhile, on repeated occasions, the Socialist International, with the SFIO's backing, affirmed its opposition to nuclear testing as well as to the proliferation of nuclear weapons.

De Gaulle's return to power in May 1958, however, quickly altered the SFIO's position. From the beginning, De Gaulle's search for *grandeur* on the international stage included not only greater independence for France from the United States and NATO but also the development of a nuclear strike force—the *force de frappe*. Although the immediate origins of France's nuclear ambitions date back to the end of 1954 and the decisions taken by the then premier Pierre Mendès-France, De Gaulle's arrival provided a new impetus. In February 1960, France would explode its first atomic bomb and the following year would begin testing a missile delivery system.[187]

The pressing question for the SFIO was how to respond. In 1958, Mollet supported De Gaulle's assumption of power as the sole means of avoiding civil war, a decision that roiled the SFIO. The immediate result was a schism, as several prominent French socialists founded a new party, the *Parti socialiste autonome* (PSA and later the *Parti socialiste unifié*—PSU). Among the PSA's policy positions was outright opposition to France's possession of nuclear weapons.[188] The SFIO, however, refused to follow the PSA's lead. Having initially served as a state minister in De Gaulle's government, Mollet (and the SFIO) returned to opposition in January 1959, increasing the pressure on the party to define a clear-cut position. At a meeting of the SFIO's national council the same month, Christian Pineau, normally a Cold Warrior, urged the rejection of De Gaulle's policy: acquiring nuclear weapons, he argued, contradicted current international trends in favour of disarmament, thus running the risk of isolating both the SFIO and France. Mollet appeared to agree, declaring that the SFIO remained attached to its 'international policy' in favour of multilateral, controlled, and progressive disarmament—a stance reflected in the council's published resolution. Interestingly, as possible steps towards disarmament, the resolution vaguely endorsed regional agreements for 'military disengagement' as well as an international agreement suspending all nuclear testing for two years, after which each country would be free to do as it pleased if no general disarmament had been negotiated.[189]

Clearly unsatisfied with the resolution, Pineau returned to the charge at the SFIO's congress in July 1959, demanding that French socialists explicitly condemn

---

[186] HAEU, GSPE 7, 'Motion for a Resolution on Thermonuclear Test Explosions', 2 May 1957; and GSPE 18, 'Conférence des partis socialistes des pays membres de la C.E.C.A...3 et 4 Juin 1957'.

[187] See Dominique Mongin, *La bombe atomique française, 1945–1958* (Brussels, 1997), as well as the chapters in Maurice Vaïsse, ed., *Le France et l'atome: études d'histoire nucléaire* (Brussels, 1994).

[188] AN, Parti socialiste unifié, 581/AP/1-3, 'Position du P.S.A. sur les questions internationales', circular no. 46, 23 November 1959.

[189] OURS, SFIO, 'Conseil National des 10 et 11 janvier 1959', Pineau, 11–12, 77–8; Mollet, 65.

De Gaulle's policy. Seconding Pineau, Jules Moch contended that France could not risk sabotaging ongoing negotiations for a cessation of testing or encouraging other countries to acquire nuclear weapons, mentioning China in particular. Another notable speaker was Eileen White, Labour's fraternal delegate, who appealed to French socialists to 'sacrifice' nuclear weapons and to work with her party in promoting a non-nuclear club encompassing all countries except the two super-powers. White's appeal, however, left Mollet unmoved. While professing support for multilateral disarmament and for a two-year ban on nuclear testing, the SFIO leader effectively dismissed the idea of French membership in a non-nuclear club. In the 'atomic domain', Mollet pointedly stated, the SFIO rejected 'all forms of renunciation and of unilateral disarmament'.[190]

Immediately after the SFIO's congress the International held its own congress in Hamburg. Labour leaders in particular were eager to use the event to press French socialists on the question of a non-nuclear club. As already mentioned, Gaitskell and his allies promoted a non-nuclear club in an effort to counter calls for unilateral disarmament within Labour and the TUC. The critical aspect of a non-nuclear club was its multilateralism: Britain would only abandon nuclear weapons if all the non-superpowers promised to do so. If Gaitskell sought international socialist support for a non-nuclear club, it was partly to strengthen the scheme's credibility. The more credible the scheme the more likely it would dampen the ardour of unilateralists at home. But for Labour leaders, the SFIO's endorsement was also valuable as a means to hamper De Gaulle's project; after all, a nuclear-armed France would end all hopes for a non-nuclear club.[191] But if German socialists offered their 'full support' to Labour, Georges Brutelle, the SFIO's deputy chairman, expressed doubts about 'a policy that left control of nuclear weapons to two powers only'. Equally worrying, Brutelle back-pedalled from the SFIO's earlier support of a two-year freeze on testing, announcing that French socialists 'are not prepared to campaign against the present plan to test a [French] nuclear weapon in the Sahara soon'. In the end and after much negotiation with Labour delegates, the SFIO agreed to work for a 'general agreement on a controlled cessation of nuclear tests over a period of two years' after which countries would regain their 'freedom of action' if no general disarmament agreement was signed. Yet given De Gaulle's obvious determination to test a nuclear weapon in the near future, this concession was meaningless.[192]

Labour delegates left the International's congress worried about the direction of SFIO policy. In an attempt to influence the latter, Morgan Phillips wrote to Mollet in November 1959 offering Labour participation in a joint campaign to pressure the French government to suspend its plans to test an atomic weapon for two years. 'We are greatly disturbed', Phillips wrote, 'that the spread of nuclear weapons to

---

[190] OURS, SFIO, '51ème Congrès national des 9 au 12 juillet 1959', Pineau, 61; Moch, 72; White, 267; Mollet, 291.

[191] See Bevan's comments in Labour Party, Executive Committee of the Parliamentary Party, meeting, fiche 230, 'Minutes of a Party meeting held on…23rd June, 1959'.

[192] LHASC, LPA, International Sub-Committee, 1959 file, 'Report of the Sixth Congress of the Socialist International. Hamburg, 14-17 July 1959'; and IISH, SI, 248, 'Resolution on Disarmament'.

more countries will make it increasingly difficult to effect an agreement that will abolish nuclear weapons forever.'[193] Phillips had good reasons to be concerned. At the SFIO's national council several days earlier, Mollet claimed that socialists had always opposed war in general but not particular weapons. Rejecting 'unilateral disarmament', he insisted that France would renounce nuclear weapons only if all countries did so, including the superpowers. No less striking was Mollet's obvious irritation with Labour:

> We have been in contact with the parties of the International that have effectively waged a campaign against the eventual possession of an atomic bomb by France. But I will never accept the argument coming from our Labour comrades that 'France must not have a bomb', as it is Labour itself when it was in power that committed [Britain] to build a bomb![194]

It is unclear whether Mollet ever answered Phillips' letter. But it does not matter, as Mollet steered the SFIO towards a tacit acceptance of a nuclear-armed France. At a meeting of the SFIO's executive in December 1959, on the eve of France's first nuclear test, Mollet brushed aside Moch's complaint that the SFIO had promised the International to cooperate on a two-year ban on testing. French socialists, Mollet argued, had had enough of the 'hypocritical arguments against the explosion of a French atomic bomb'. A year later, Mollet once again dismissed concerns about France's *force de frappe*, telling an SFIO audience that the mass of French people were indifferent to such concerns. Only the PSU militated for France's abandonment of nuclear weapons, and the PSU, as Mollet scornfully noted, was insignificant.[195] Rather than international disarmament, the SFIO under Mollet had become an advocate of French nuclear rearmament.

European socialists after 1945 devoted considerable attention to the issue of a European security order. Although often portrayed as stalwart members of the American-led Atlanticist camp, numerous Western European socialists aspired to reduce and even surmount Cold War divisions. This aspiration fuelled extended practical cooperation between Labour, the SFIO, and the SPD in order to forge an alternative approach to security centred on disengagement—an approach comprising general disarmament, German unification, and a neutral zone in Central and Eastern Europe. To be sure, no consensus was reached on the relative weight to assign to each of these elements. While the SPD prioritized national reunification, Labour was more interested in a general disarmament agreement; the SFIO, meanwhile, doubted the wisdom of neutral zones, to say nothing of German reunification. Nevertheless, during the 1950s, the three parties, together with other members of the International, carefully and collectively considered the possibilities of disengagement. On the issue of security, accordingly, the policymaking of each party possessed an important international socialist dimension that was neither all-important nor marginal. Instead, it was omnipresent

[193] LHASC, LPA, International Department, LP/ID/FRA, Phillips to Mollet, 11 November 1959.
[194] OURS, SFIO, 'Conseil national des 7 et 8 novembre 1959', Mollet, 45–6.
[195] OURS, APS, Comité directeur, 9 December 1959; and 'Congrès national extraordinaire des 21 et 22 décembre 1960', Mollet, 156.

as British, French, and German socialists all integrated the International and its member parties into their calculations.

In the end, disengagement proved to be a path not taken, chiefly because neither Washington, Moscow, Paris, nor London was prepared to make it a priority. Without four-power support, the proposal was doomed. Yet the prolonged consideration that European socialists accorded to disengagement suggests that the proposal was not as utopian as is often assumed; nor did it simply amount to the whimsical ideas of a handful of outsiders such as Kennan. European socialists were interested in disengagement because it appeared to be a practical means not only to resolve tensions within and between socialist parties but also to overcome Europe's Cold War divide. Disengagement, in short, arguably merits more scholarly attention than it has received. But whatever its potential value as a subject of study, the demise of disengagement as a feasible proposal had fissiparous effects on the practice of socialist internationalism. In the immediate term, the SPD embraced a bipartisan approach to security policy, reducing the imperative for a distinctive 'socialist' approach; in the longer term, the SPD would work out another approach (*Ostpolitik*), but it did so on its own, without collaborating with either Labour or the SFIO. Labour, meanwhile, grew more and more involuted as its members quarrelled over the merits of unilateral disarmament. No less striking was the SFIO's conversion from an opponent to a proponent of a nuclear-armed France, a conversion that marked the end of a long tradition and practice of collective socialist support for disarmament.

9

The Stakes of Decolonization, 1945–1960

Decolonization undoubtedly constituted a major development in post-war international politics. At the end of the Second World War, much of Africa, Asia, and the Pacific belonged to one of Europe's empires. A quarter of a century later, empires had disintegrated, leaving in their wake a host of new nation states. In 1945, the newly created United Nations counted fifty-one members; in 1970 the figure was 127. Constituting a growing majority in the United Nations' general assembly, the decolonized world, part of what some called the global south, appeared poised to challenge the political and economic domination of the first world, including the former imperial powers.[1] Looking back, the speed and scope of the process can make it seem inevitable—a swelling and unstoppable wave of popular resistance crashing against the rickety ramparts of empire. Yet decolonization appeared far from inevitable to many contemporaries. Rather than dismantle the empire, European states after 1945 sought to transform their imperial holdings in order to maintain them. In the British case, this effort included a revamped Commonwealth presented as a model of international and inter-ethnic/racial relations; in the French case it encompassed the *Union française*, the political-constitutional framework created in 1946 to restructure relations between metropole and colonies.[2] During the post-war years, European empires in general emphasized social and economic development, prompting scholars to speak of a trans-imperial 'developmental colonialism'.[3] While steeped in interwar trusteeship principles, which envisaged an eventual end to empire, development could also be cast as an alternative to political independence. As colonial peoples became aware of the material benefits of empire, some Europeans hoped, they would reject what French officials called 'separatism'.[4]

Recent scholarship suggests not only that decolonization was far from inevitable but also that events could have unfolded differently. The replacement of empires by

---

[1] Mark Mazower, *Governing the World: The History of an Idea* (London, 2012), 273–304.
[2] The literature is massive, but helpful starting points are Frederick Cooper, 'Restructuring Empire in British and French Africa', *Past & Present*, supplement 6 (2011), 196–210; A.G. Hopkins, 'Rethinking Decolonization', *Past & Present* 200 (2008), 211–47; and John Darwin, *The Empire Project: The Rise and Fall of the British World-System, 1830–1970* (Cambridge, 2009), 540–90.
[3] Andreas Eckert, 'Spätkoloniale Herrschaft, Dekolonisation und Internationale Ordnung', *Archiv für Sozialgeschichte* 48 (2008), 6.
[4] The standard study of development is Frederick Cooper, *Decolonization and African Society: The Labor Question in French and British Africa* (Cambridge, 1996). Also see Andreas Eckert, '"We Are All Planners Now": Planung und Dekolonisation in Afrika', *Geschichte und Gesellschaft* 34 (2008), 375–97.

multiple nation states was not the sole possibility. In an intriguing article, Todd Shepard showed French officials imaginatively reconceiving of citizenship and national identity in a quest to avoid Algerian independence. On a broader canvas, Frederick Cooper has detailed the sustained efforts of French and African politicians to transform the empire into a novel entity fostering a common identity while respecting the particularities of each member.[5] Somewhat similarly, there now exists a sizeable scholarship on *Eurafrique*, the idea of forging permanent political and economic structures between a united Europe and Africa.[6] The process of post-war European integration, in short, was not limited to Europe.[7] But however possible other outcomes might have been, it was the nation state that emerged as the heir to empire. And so the question becomes why, despite the promising alternatives, did the nation state triumph?

Although there is no simple answer to this question, examining the responses of European socialists to the issue of empire after 1945 draws attention to some of the stakes involved in decolonization for international politics. Scholars of imperialism vigorously debate the consequences of decolonization within European countries, with some claiming that imperialism's lingering effects were pervasive and others insisting that its legacy has been exaggerated.[8] But decolonization also affected international politics. Studying the Algerian War, Matthew Connelly argues that decolonization embodied a 'diplomatic revolution' in which the East–West Cold War divide was challenged by a North–South perspective emphasizing issues such as development and population growth.[9] The stakes involved, however, extended beyond the direction of global political alignments. As socialist debates suggest, the process of decolonization witnessed a struggle between competing rights: national rights, minority rights, and human (individual) rights. Each set of rights possessed far-reaching political implications, none more so than minority rights, as they were

---

[5] Shepard, *The Invention of Decolonization: The Algerian War and the Remaking of France* (Ithaca, NY, 2006); and Cooper, *Citizenship between Empire and Nation: Remaking France and French Africa, 1945–1960* (Princeton, NJ, 2014). For the British case, see Michael Collins, 'Decolonisation and the "Federal Moment"', *Diplomacy & Statecraft* 24 (2013), 21–40.

[6] Yves Montarsolo, *L'Eurafrique contrepoint de l'idée d'Europe. Le cas français de la fin de la Deuxième Guerre mondiale aux négociations des Traités de Rome* (Aix-en-Provence, 2010), 197–258; Marie-Thérèse Bitsch and Gérard Bossuat, eds., *L'Europe unie et l'Afrique. De l'idée d'Eurafrique à la Convention de Lomé 1* (Brussels, 2005); and Peo Hansen and Stefan Jonsson, *Eurafrica: The Untold History of European Integration and Colonialism* (London, 2014).

[7] Thomas Moser, *Europäische Integration, Dekolonisation, Eurafrika: Eine historische Analyse über die Entscheidungsbedingungen der Eurafrikanischen Gemeinschaft von der Weltwirtschaftskrise bis zum Jaunde-Vertrag, 1929–1963* (Baden-Baden, 2000).

[8] Much of the scholarship centres on Britain. See Jordanna Bailkin, *Afterlife of Empire* (Berkeley, CA, 2012); Stuart Ward, 'Echoes of Empire', *History Workshop Journal* 62 (2006), 264–78; Bernard Porter, *The Absent-Minded Imperialists: How British Society Really Saw their Empire* (Oxford, 2004). But more recently, scholars have begun to study other cases. See Sebastien Conrad, 'Dekolonisierung in den Metropolen', *Geschichte und Gesellschaft* 37 (2011), 135–56, which is the introduction to a special issue on the subject; and Elizabeth Buettner, *Europe after Empire: Decolonization, Society, and Culture* (Cambridge, 2016).

[9] Connelly, *A Diplomatic Revolution: Algeria's Fight for Independence and the Origins of the Post-War Era* (New York, 2002). Also see Mazower, *Governing the World*; and Guiliano Garavini, *After Empires: European Integration, Decolonization and the Challenge of the Global South, 1957–1986* (Oxford, 2012).

often associated with limits on national sovereignty. These limits could be internal, such as constitutional restraints on the working of majority rule; but they could also take the form of external constraints on sovereignty, including alternatives to the nation state itself. The victory of the nation state, in other words, was inextricably tied to the defeat of minority rights.

After 1945, as after 1918, European socialists worked to define a common socialist position on the future of empire. Yet after 1945, the practice of socialist internationalism also included non-European socialists and Asian socialists in particular. This point is important because Asian socialists compelled their European counterparts to confront the question of political independence for the colonies. Contrary to European socialists, who initially focused on development, Asian socialists insisted that socialist internationalism required an unambiguous commitment to independence. European socialists resisted this pressure, partly due to a growing concern for minorities in what were called plural or multiracial societies. In numerous colonies, they feared, a simple transfer of political power risked creating the tyranny of majority rule. The urgent task was to conceive of means to protect minorities, a goal that implied some external oversight of the postcolonial state. Among European socialists, moreover, the SFIO emerged as the leading proponent of minority rights. In the context of the Algerian War, a bloody conflict that pitted a Muslim majority against a European settler minority, French socialists desperately searched for a compromise between continued colonialism and independence; and this search led them to champion federal-type structures within Algeria, between Algeria and France, and ultimately between Europe and Africa. But if the relevance of minority rights extended beyond Algeria, the identification of these rights with a dominant white settler community helped to discredit them in the eyes not only of Asian socialists but also of a growing number of European socialists. As a result, European socialist parties eventually endorsed national over minority rights—a choice that reflected the fate of minority rights more generally during decolonization. Intriguingly, at the very moment European socialists abandoned minority rights, they began promoting human (individual) rights, which suggests that the burgeoning interest in human rights during this period stemmed in part from a search for an alternative to minority rights.[10] From this perspective, human rights were very much a second-best option.

THE PERSISTENCE OF THE TRUSTEESHIP FRAMEWORK

As we saw in chapter 5, when it came to empire, European socialists during the interwar period endorsed the trusteeship framework that emphasized the reform

---

[10] For studies of the links between decolonization and human rights that leave out minority rights, see Steven L.B. Jensen, *The Making of International Human Rights: The 1960s, Decolonization, and the Reconstruction of Global Values* (Cambridge, 2016); Samuel Moyn, *The Last Utopia: Human Rights in History* (Cambridge, MA, 2010), 84–119; and Roland Burke, *Decolonization and the Evolution of Human Rights* (Philadelphia, PA, 2010).

rather than the end of colonialism. Although purposefully vague regarding concrete policies, the trusteeship framework excluded more ambitious alternatives, among them cooperation with anti-colonial activists in the colonial world as well as demands for a profound revision of the global political and economic order. During the 1930s, several British and French socialists, who had earlier espoused these alternatives, advocated colonial appeasement, presenting the return of colonies to Nazi Germany (and Fascist Italy) as part of a larger reordering of international politics. In retrospect, a colonial deal was never likely, if only because of Hitler's disinterest. But advocacy of colonial appeasement by several prominent socialists helped to taint anti-colonialism, strengthening thereby the attachment of European socialists in general to the trusteeship framework.

No socialist party embraced trusteeship with greater ardour than Labour. An internal memorandum in March 1942 on African colonies, for example, declared that Britain administered the latter 'as a trust for the native inhabitants, the principal object of the administration being the well-being, education, and development of those inhabitants'. While trusteeship ostensibly foresaw an end to empire, the time line stretched well into a foggy future. 'For a considerable time to come', the memorandum admitted, 'these [colonial] peoples will not be ready for self-government and European peoples and states must be responsible for the administration of their territories.' Two years later, Labour's statement on the post-war settlement spoke in terms of trusteeship, insisting that colonial administrators must manifest a 'sincere determination' to work for the sole interests of colonial peoples.[11] On the eve of peace, Labour officials envisaged a renewal of the interwar mandate system complemented by new international machinery charged with supervising the imperial powers.[12] For Leonard Woolf, a leading Labour expert on empire, a 'system of this kind would be the logical result of the application of socialist principles to the colonial problem'. Similarly, Philip Noel-Baker urged Labour to seize the 'present opportunity of extending the principle of colonial trusteeship', adding 'that a number of continental socialists are ready to go a long way in this direction'.[13]

The advent of a majority Labour government in 1945 did not notably affect the attachment to trusteeship. Soon afterwards, Arthur Creech Jones, the Labour government's colonial secretary, listed a series of policy guidelines inspired by trusteeship: the colonies should be administered as 'Trusts' for the 'native inhabitants'; the priority must be the 'promotion of the welfare and the political progress of the colonial people'; and a 'cardinal principle' of Labour policy was that colonial peoples 'should proceed as rapidly as practicable to the full achievement of

[11] US, Leonard Woolf Papers, 1D2b, 'Memorandum Formulating a Policy for African Colonies and those in a Similar Stage of Development for the Labour Party after the War', International Department, no. 263B, March 1942; and BLPES, Hugh Dalton Papers, 7/10, 'The International Settlement', NEC, 1944.

[12] See LHASC, LPA, ACImQ, 'The Mandate System', March 1945; and 'The Colonies and International Accountability: An Introductory Note', April 1945.

[13] CCA, Philip Noel-Baker Papers, NBKR 4/384, Woolf, *The International Post-War Settlement* (London, September 1944), 20; and LHASC, LPA, International Sub-Committee, 1945 file, 'Memorandum on the Principle of Colonial Trusteeship', undated.

responsible self-government'. Accordingly, Labour officials studied how to reconcile the maintenance of empire with what a 1947 Labour paper described as the 'awakening to self-conscious' of colonial peoples. Its answer was to develop the limited trustee provisions under the UN Charter.[14] Underlying such thinking was a vision of gradual progress towards political autonomy and self-government but not political independence, which was excluded as a realistic possibility for the foreseeable future. Three years later, Creech Jones, now no longer colonial secretary, reiterated that Labour's mission was 'to make the colonies less dependent and to fulfill the conditions so that colonial status can merge into responsible self-government'. While recognizing the reality of 'an emotional "nationalism"' in the colonies, he remained confident that trusteeship could succeed.[15]

To be sure, the trusteeship framework did not apply to all cases. Under the Labour government, India and Pakistan became independent in 1947, followed the next year by Burma and Palestine (Israel). Afterwards, Labour would hold up India as a model—as a colony that under careful British guidance had attained political maturity and independence. As Nicholas Owen argues, however, at the time the Labour government reluctantly accepted Indian independence for lack of a workable alternative. Although during the war Labour had publicly committed itself to Indian self-government, this was to occur in association with Britain. The demand of Congress, the dominant political party and movement in India, for complete political independence frustrated Labour officials, prompting them to look to other options, including Indian socialists who favoured continued ties with Britain. Congress' decisive victory in the general elections of December 1945, however, effectively made political independence unavoidable.[16] In some ways, Labour's recasting of itself as a champion of Indian independence reflected a larger process, outlined by Stuart Ward, in which post-war Europeans reconciled themselves to the loss of empire by 'inventing' decolonization as an irresistible phenomenon carried forward by history's *forces profondes*.[17] But it is also worth emphasizing that Labour viewed Indian independence as an exception. Writing in 1947, James Callaghan, a future Labour prime minister, discounted the idea that India 'contains lessons' for the colonial world and for Africa in particular. For Africans to have any future, he continued, they must 'bind themselves closer together in partnership' with Britain. 'It will be a tragedy for the people of Africa if we are diverted from the task of conquering poverty, ignorance and disease by sordid political squabbles'—by which he meant demands for political independence.[18]

But if India was an exception, the events surrounding its independence (as well as the end of the Palestine mandate) influenced Labour's perspective. Labour officials

[14] BLCAS, Arthur Creech Jones Paper, ACJ 16/3, 'The Elements of a Labour Colonial Policy', Creech Jones, 1946; and LHASC, LPA, ACImQ, 'International Accountability in Colonial Affairs', W. Benson, March 1947.

[15] Creech Jones, 'A Colonial Policy for Today', *Tribune*, no. 709, 11 August 1950, 9–10.

[16] Owen, *The British Left and India*, 271–98. For Indian socialists, see IISH, SI, 657, 'Extract from letter from Madhu Limaye—Foreign Affairs Department of the Indian Socialist Party, dated 7.6.48'.

[17] Ward, 'The European Provenance of Decolonization', *Past & Present* 230 (2016), 228–59.

[18] Bodelian Library, James Callaghan Papers, 238, Callaghan to editor (Daily Guardian), 7 August 1947.

were shocked by the communal violence involved—a shock that heightened sensitivity to the state of what were designated as plural or multiracial colonies. Even before Indian independence, members of the Fabian Colonial Bureau (FCB), a think tank closely associated with Labour, had been considering the question of how to protect minority rights in a democratic regime based on majority rule.[19] In the wake of the massive violence in India and Pakistan, the FCB issued a lengthy pamphlet on 'self-government and the communal problem', which a press release described as 'the most difficult of political problems—how self-government is to be achieved in a Colony where the population is divided within itself by race, nationality or religion'.[20] Thanks to its close contacts with Labour, the FCB circulated a slimmed-down version of the pamphlet within the party. Pointing to the recent experience in India and Palestine, it warned that similar 'difficulties' could be expected to 'arise in some British Colonies' unless concrete measures were undertaken to break down group identities. Although the FCB avoided any sense of urgency, it had planted a seed within Labour that was destined to grow.[21]

For now, Labour officials concentrated not on the potential problems of plural societies but on colonial development. The lead had been given by the Attlee government, which inherited the priority on development embodied in the April 1945 'Colonial Development and Welfare Act'. Reflecting the government's orientation, a 1949 Labour party statement on colonial policy suggested that 'progress towards self-government' should take a back seat to improving the material conditions of life for people. Insisting that 'we cannot hope to build up sound political institutions on a foundation of poor material resources, of imperfect health or of inadequate education', it sketched an ambitious development programme for the empire in general as well as particular colonies.[22] Such a programme, explained Rita Hinden, an FCB member, would take at least a decade to produce any results, a prediction that reflected the widely held assumption that self-government was a distant prospect at best for most colonies.[23] Just as significantly, party officials understood that Britain alone lacked the resources for such a programme. An international effort would clearly be required involving both the United Nations and a united (Western) Europe. And Labour officials also understood that they would need allies abroad to promote such an effort—allies they expected to find among socialists in Europe.

[19] See the file in BLCAS, Fabian Colonial Bureau, 49/2, and especially 'Comments on Communal Electorates and other Forms of Minority Protection, with Special Reference to Experience in India', 20 October 194?. For the FCB, see David Goldsworthy, *Colonial Issues in British Politics 1945–1961* (Oxford, 1971), 255–64.

[20] BLCAS, Fabian Colonial Bureau, 32/1, Margaret Nicholson, *Self-Government and the Colonial Problem* (London, April 1948); and press release, 13 April 1948.

[21] LHASC, LPA, Commonwealth Sub-Committee, B 12/1, 'Self-Government in the Colonies and the Problem of Plural Societies', ACImQ, no. 319A, undated but July 1948.

[22] LHASC, LPA, ACIQ, 'Statement on Colonial Policy: Economic Development of Colonial Territories', undated but 1949.

[23] For the force of this assumption, see Ronald Hyman, *Britain's Declining Empire: The Road to Decolonisation 1918–1968* (Cambridge, 2006), 94–167. For Hinden, see BLPES, Fabian Society, 62/5, 'The Imperial Aspect: Synopsis', Hinden, undated but May 1948.

If anything, the SFIO was even less prepared than Labour to imagine an end to empire in a foreseeable future. For the vast majority of French socialists, the empire was an integral part of France. In early 1946, Oreste Rosenfeld, a party spokesman on foreign affairs, spoke admirably of France's 'radiance' and its ongoing 'civilizing activity' in the colonies. Three years later, Rosenfeld informed French socialists that, when it came to the empire, the critical question was whether 'France wants to remain what it is or to drop to the level of a country like Portugal'.[24] If Rosenfeld excluded political independence, he was no die-hard colonialist. Rather, French socialists like him pleaded for a reformed colonialism that placed the interests of colonial peoples first and foremost. The instrument for this reformed colonialism, moreover, would be the *Union française*, the political-constitutional framework created in 1946 to reshape relations between France and its empire. Despite its embryonic nature and limited reach, French socialists invested considerable hopes in the *Union française*. Addressing the SFIO's national council in March 1947, Guy Mollet envisaged it as a 'fraternal community' of fully autonomous and equal members organized along federalist lines in which 'more and more authority will be attributed to local assemblies'. The SFIO's leader presented the *Union française* as an alternative to 'separatism' (political independence), which he dismissed as 'a defensive reaction against trusteeship...and which does not constitute a means of genuine liberty'.[25]

The problem for the SFIO was that its vision of the *Union française* ran up against the reality of events in the empire, most notably in Indochina. The French government's determination in 1945–1946 to reimpose control over Indochina triggered armed resistance on the part of the Viet Minh, a nationalist and communist movement, which quickly developed into a war. Early on, the SFIO proclaimed its sympathy for the oppressed Indochinese masses, its opposition to colonial exploitation, and its dislike of the government's use of military force; at the same time, French socialists viewed askance the Viet Minh because of its communist affiliation and demands for national independence. The SFIO therefore called for a negotiated settlement that would maintain Indochina within the *Union française*. Even as inveterate an anti-colonialist as Marceau Pivert agreed that Indochina could only be 'independent within the *Union française*, and tied to us by economic accords freely entered into'.[26] The challenge for French socialists was how to reconcile the right of self-determination for the Indochinese with a rejection of 'separatism'. In a lengthy report in July 1949, Paul Alduy, a close associate of Mollet, proposed a revised *Union française* in which the links between its

[24] Rosenfeld, 'La France et l'Indochine', *Le Populaire de Paris*, 23 February 1946, 1; HIL, 'Rapport d'Oreste Rosenfeld', *Bulletin intérieur du Parti Socialiste SFIO*, no. 39, February 1949, 51–4.

[25] OURS, SFIO, 'Conseil national 19 et 20 mars 1947', Mollet, 43–4; and Mollet, 'Une union largement consentie', *Le Populaire de Paris*, 20 September 1947. For French socialists and the *Union française*, see James I. Lewis, 'The Tragic Career of Marius Moutet', *European History Quarterly* 38 (2008), 68–77.

[26] OURS, Fonds Charles Lancelle, 13 APO/1, Pivert to Lancelle and Henri Barré, 21 December 1946.

members would be 'rather loose'.[27] But Alduy's vague formulation left unanswered the question of how to persuade the Viet Minh to accept his proposal. Mollet was no more helpful, maintaining that the *Union française* embodied an alternative between military victory, deemed unattainable, and 'evacuation', judged unacceptable.[28]

Unable to define an alternative for Indochina, French socialists reluctantly acquiesced in the 'internationalization' of the conflict—a code for France's growing dependence on American financial and military support. However frustrating this development might be, it did allow French socialists to claim that Indochina was an international and not a colonial issue. Yet even so, the SFIO could not avoid taking a position on national independence for the colonies. In justifying their opposition in principle, French socialists insisted that national independence contradicted the realities of international politics. After 1945, as we saw in chapter 7, the SFIO emerged as a leading proponent of European unity based on supranational political authorities. With the Viet Minh demanding political independence, French socialists quickly persuaded themselves that what made sense for Europe made even more sense for the empire. Addressing French socialists in March 1947, Mollet argued that the colonies such as Indochina were too weak to survive as independent states in an age of 'interdependence of interests and needs'; left alone, they 'risked becoming the prey of the two great imperialist powers'. Similarly, Alduy in his report claimed that a truly 'revolutionary formula... consisted of eliminating the stage of absolute [national] independence... in favour of a subtle system of inter-dependence'.[29] Significantly, such statements reflected a consensual view within the SFIO and not simply that of the right or centre. European socialists, Pivert thus wrote in 1947, must convince the Vietnamese people that 'in today's world there is no genuine national independence for small non-industrialized countries'.[30]

In the meantime, French socialists recognized that something was needed to appease the mounting anti-colonial forces in the empire. One possibility was to promote the *Union française*; but it remained a shell, existing, as one French socialist admitted, only 'on paper'.[31] And so—like Labour—the SFIO turned towards development. In 1946, the French government had created an investment fund (FIDES), chiefly for France's African colonies. But however welcome, FIDES was insufficient. As Mollet explained at an international socialist conference in 1950, a major programme was needed to improve the material conditions of colonial peoples—'to educate them, to provide them with human dignity, to allow them to benefit from the riches of the colonizing countries'.[32] The familiar problem, however, was that France alone lacked the resources to develop its empire. And this consideration fuelled the SFIO's interest in integrating empire into the project of

[27] HIL, Alduy, 'Rapport de politique générale', July 1949 in *Bulletin intérieur du Parti Socialiste SFIO*, no. 43, supplément, Août 1949, 12–13.

[28] For Mollet, see FNSP, GPS, GS 2, 18 October 1950; and OURS, SFIO, 'Conseil national des 4 et 5 novembre 1950', Mollet, 45–7.

[29] OURS, SFIO, 'Conseil national 19 et 20 mars 1947', Mollet, 44.

[30] CHS, Fonds Marceau Pivert, 559/AP/11, 'Correspondance socialiste', no. 1, July 1947.

[31] OURS, SFIO, 'Conseil national 19 et 20 mars 1947', Gaston Deferre, 51.

[32] OURS, Archives Guy Mollet, AGM 53, 'Situation du socialisme démocratique dans les territoires d'Outre-Mer' in 1950 Comisco dossier.

European unity: colonial development would become a European rather than strictly French endeavour (or burden). The pressing task for French socialists was to persuade European socialists to conceive of European unity more broadly. A 'Western Europe federation will only be a federation of remainders', asserted an SFIO paper circulated to European socialist parties in 1948, 'if it is confined to Europe geographically'.[33]

Among the major socialist parties, the SPD was the least attached to empire. Unlike their British and French counterparts, German socialists initially had little to say on the subject. The reasons for their reticence are obvious: Germany had no overseas colonies and German socialists were preoccupied with the gigantic task of reconstruction at home. Consequently, the SPD at times appeared remarkably clueless about the colonial world. In his spirited defence of German rights, Kurt Schumacher occasionally likened the treatment of Germans by the Western allies to that inflicted on colonial peoples.[34] More revealing perhaps was the reaction of party officials to proposals in 1951 to organize an international socialist conference on overseas development. Fritz Baade, a Bundestag deputy and SPD economic expert, commented that there was no need to submit a position as Germany's 'under-developed areas' lay at home and not overseas. Not surprisingly, the subject of colonial development was almost entirely absent from the SPD's public discussions.[35]

The SPD, however, would soon reconsider its position, as the colonial world became a subject of growing importance to international politics—and thus to international socialist politics. In this context, moreover, German socialists began to view Germany's lack of colonies as an asset: unburdened by the weight of empire, the SPD supposedly possessed greater moral authority among colonial peoples than other socialist parties. Already in 1950, Schumacher had suggested that the demands of colonial peoples for freedom resonated with German socialists because the German people were also struggling for political freedom and equality.[36] Under Erich Ollenhauer, Schumacher's successor, the idea that the SPD enjoyed a privileged political-moral position vis-à-vis the decolonizing world became an operating assumption.

EUROPEAN SOCIALISTS CHAMPION DEVELOPMENT, 1950–1952

As we saw, Labour and the SFIO exhibited a growing interest in colonial development during the late 1940s. In this sense, European socialists reflected their time, as the task of developing the undeveloped or underdeveloped world moved to the

[33] AAOB, Haakon Lie, Dc 0005, 'L'Intégration des empires coloniaux dans les États-Unis d'Europe', documentation française, no. 19, 1948.

[34] Schumacher, 'Aufgaben und Ziel der deutschen Sozialdemokratie', reproduced in Albrecht, ed., *Kurt Schumacher*, 407.

[35] FES, AdsD, SPD, Parteivorstand, 2/PVBT0000007, Baade to Pass, 15 August 1951; and Pass to Fritz Heine, 23 August 1951.

[36] FES, SPD, 'Dr. Schumacher zur Kolonialfrage', *Sozialdemokratischer Pressedienst*, 4 September 1950, 4–5.

forefront of international politics. Although American historians often identify Truman's Point Four Program, announced in January 1949, as the starting point of international concern for development, scholars of empire have traced the origins of the post-war engagement with development to the interwar and wartime periods.[37] In addition to a sincere desire to reduce global poverty and inequalities, proponents of colonial development hoped to appease anti-colonial sentiments in the colonies that could provide fertile ground for communism and/or for armed struggles for national independence. As Frederick Cooper showed for the British and French empires, moreover, development as a discourse and practice had unintended effects, most notably the rapid expansion of political and economic claims by groups within the colonies—claims whose burden Britain and France were increasingly loath to bear.[38] Attention to socialist debates regarding development highlights another aspect of the subject: the refusal from the outset of non-European and especially Asian socialists to accept development as an alternative to immediate national independence for colonial peoples.

Among European socialists, Labour took the lead on development. At the time, the party enjoyed immense prestige among socialists because of the Labour government's colonial policy, which was seen as having 'set free' India, Pakistan, and Burma and as moving towards self-government elsewhere.[39] Exploiting this prestige, Labour sought to mobilize international socialism behind economic development. During 1950–1951, party officials worked on a comprehensive statement of colonial policy. While trusteeship principles 'still held good', Labour's Commonwealth subcommittee pronounced, 'there is a need for a statement of a less negative and more positive character with greater emphasis on the problem of the post-war world and the colonial setting on which policy has to be worked out.'[40] It quickly became clear, moreover, that colonial development would figure prominently in any statement. Reflecting on Labour policy at the time, Anthony Crosland, an MP, future minister, and emerging party intellectual, argued that reducing global inequality was a pressing task. 'The most obvious fulfillment of socialist ideals to-day', Crosland wrote, 'lies in altering not the structure of society in our own country, but the balance of wealth and privilege between advanced and backward countries.' Similarly, Rita Hinden, describing the reduction of global inequality as 'one of the meanings of international socialism', urged Labour to champion a 'World Plan' for development. Strong support came from the Labour left, especially the Bevanites, who decried current proposals for tackling world poverty as 'woefully inadequate'. If outrage at global inequalities motivated the

---

[37] The scholarship on development is rapidly expanding. For two useful overviews, see Joseph Morgan Hodge, 'Writing the History of Development', parts 1 and 2, *Humanity* 6 (2015), 429–63; and 7 (2016), 125–74; and Frederick Cooper, 'Writing the History of Development', *Journal of Modern European History* 8 (2010), 5–23.

[38] Cooper, *Decolonization and African Society*.

[39] See the letter to Labour from the International's secretary and vice-chairman, dated 31 October 1951, in Labour Party, NEC minutes, fiche 418.

[40] LHASC, LPA, Commonwealth Sub-Committee, B 14/2, 'Need for a New Policy Statement on Colonial Affairs', undated.

left, a massive development effort was also attractive as an alternative to increased defence spending.[41]

These converging currents of support soon produced results. In early 1951 a lengthy paper circulated within Labour entitled 'A Mutual Aid World Plan' outlining an international development programme for 'underdeveloped countries', financed by the wealthy countries and administered by the United Nations. Combining public investment and planning, the programme would reach down to the local level to improve the conditions of 'every peasant and worker in that vast two-thirds of the world which we call "underdeveloped"'. This initial paper, in turn, provided the basis for 'Towards a World of Plenty', a statement adopted at Labour's annual conference in 1952. The statement called for a comprehensive and global effort to reduce poverty and its concomitants ('squalor and disease...famine and epidemics...ignorance and misery') through limits on population growth, agricultural reform, and some industrialization, all of which would fuel increases in production and productivity. The responsibility of the wealthy countries was to furnish finance and technical assistance. Introducing the statement on behalf of Labour's executive, James Griffiths, a former colonial secretary, insisted that it 'deals with the central challenge of our time' and warned that the 'world cannot find peace while one-third are rich and two-thirds are poor'.[42]

The executive designed the statement not only for a Labour audience but also for an international socialist one. At the Socialist International's founding congress in July 1951, Morgan Phillips, Labour's secretary and chairman of the International, argued that socialism meant the search for equality both within and between nations. In this regard, he emphasized, 'Some such bold new policy as in envisaged by the Labour Party's World Plan for Mutual Aid is absolutely vital...'[43] Several months later, Labour seized on the occasion provided by a socialist economic experts' conference on development to prod the International. In preparation for the conference, Julius Braunthal, the International's secretary, had asked the SFIO to draw up policy proposals. Rather than do so, the SFIO submitted a paper listing political reforms aimed at making the *Union française* more effective.[44] The SFIO's omission provided Labour with the opportunity to circulate its own paper—'Towards a World of Plenty'. At the conference itself, several participants questioned the feasibility of a large-scale economic development programme, maintaining that Western Europeans would baulk at the sacrifices entailed. Nevertheless, the conference's conclusions, reflecting Labour's statement, declared

[41] BLPES, Charles Anthony Raven Crosland, 4/1, undated and untitled note; Hinden, 'Challenge of the Undeveloped Areas', *Socialist Commentary* May 1951, 114–17; and LHASC, Jo Richardson Papers, LP/RICH/3/2/3, 'Draft of First Half of Tribune Pamphlet', undated but 1950.

[42] LHASC, LPA, International Sub-Committee, 1951 file, 'A Mutual Aid World Plan', February 1951; Labour Party, NEC minutes, fiche 433, Commonwealth Sub-Committee, 'Towards a World of Plenty'; and Labour Party, *Report of the 51st Annual Conference...September 29 to October 3, 1952* (London, 1952), Griffiths, 141.

[43] IISH, Socialist International Information, 'First Congress of the Socialist International...30 June–3 July, 1951', no. 27–28, 7 July 1951, Phillips, 18.

[44] OURS, APS, carton: Conférences IS 1952–1961, Braunthal to Georges Brutelle (SFIO), 24 May 1951; and 'Rapport de la Délégation française', undated.

that 'it is necessary for all countries to join in a great co-operative effort to create the prerequisites for better living conditions in the under-developed areas.' The task for European socialists, they underscored, was 'to attempt to bring about in their countries a public opinion favourable to an active participation in a programme for economic development in less advanced countries'. No less importantly, the conference report recommended the creation of an international socialist commission to draft a statement of colonial policy based on these conclusions in time for the International's next congress scheduled for Milan in October 1952.[45]

In the British elections in October 1951, Labour lost its parliamentary majority, ceding power to the Conservatives. With the party now freed of governmental responsibilities, the international socialist context assumed a larger place in the making of Labour policy. One sign of this came at the International council meeting in December 1951 to which Labour sent a high-level delegation to press its views on development. Opening the discussion, Phillips warned that people in 'under-developed areas' expected help in achieving 'a high standard of living and between health and physical well being'. Echoing Phillips, Griffiths warned of the dangers of disappointing such expectations:

> Two-thirds of the people on the earth live in poverty, but they are rising to emancipate themselves and to improve their conditions. What road are they going to take? This question may be the most vital question of our time. It is up to us to help them in taking the road that leads to democratic Socialism. We must avoid the disaster which threatens if they choose the totalitarian way and become part of the Communist world of suppression and slavery.

Reporting on the conference, a Canadian socialist praised Griffiths' 'warm and moving speech', calling on 'Socialist parties everywhere [to] devise and press for plans to improve the lot of two-thirds of the world's population'. Regardless of whether all the participants shared his enthusiasm, they endorsed the proposal to create 'a small drafting committee' to prepare a statement for the International.[46]

Not surprisingly, Labour officials were determined to shape the work of the committee. With this goal in mind, E.G. Farmer, Labour's commonwealth officer and committee member, drew up a statement in January 1952 that sought 'to preserve the propaganda value to Socialists of a "World Plan for Mutual Aid" and the economic realities which have to be faced'. The resulting declaration predictably called for a 'World Plan for Mutual Aid' organized on a global, regional, and bilateral basis.[47] But another motive also stirred Farmer: to use the discussion within the International to compel Labour to think harder about development. 'What I wanted', he confided to Griffiths, 'was the realisation...that there is <u>much</u>

---

[45] See the partial summary of the conference's deliberations in IISH, SI, 352; and OURS, APS, carton: IS circulaires 1951–1958, 'Preliminary Report on the Seventh Economic Experts Conference. Vienna, 12–16 November, 1951', SI circular, no. 119/51, 23 November 1951.

[46] LHASC, LPA, International Socialist Conferences, 'Report of the Conference of the Council of the Socialist International, 14–16 December, 1951', SI circular, no. 15/52, 31 January 1952; and LAC, CCF-NPD, MG 28 VI-I, vol. 185, Paul Fox (CCF) report, 16 December 1951.

[47] LHASC, LPA, Commonwealth Sub-Committee, B 19/4, Farmer to W. Burke, 10 January 1952; and B 14/4, 'Socialist Policy for the Underdeveloped World: A Declaration of Principles', undated.

work to be done by the Party on the World Plan idea before we really have "a policy".'[48] Labour experts, in fact, harboured reservations about development and especially about the feasibility and consequences of large-scale economic aid. Drawing on his experience as colonial secretary, Creech Jones commented that 'human nature' was 'much more intractable than the argument [in favour of economic development] supposes...', adding that in any event it 'is a very long term policy'.[49]

For now, however, Farmer's draft statement became the starting point for discussions within the International's committee. Not all the participants were fully satisfied with the final result: German socialists, for example, complained that it was overly vague and might commit European socialists to defend the perpetuation of imperial control.[50] Labour's draft, nevertheless, emerged relatively unscathed from the process. Presenting the statement at the International's congress in October 1952, Hendrik Vos, a Dutch socialist and committee chairman, asserted that socialism championed welfare not only within but also between states. European socialists, Vos elaborated, must work to 'persuade our own people that it is our duty to provide the underdeveloped countries with the means to satisfy the direct human needs and to reach full development in the future'. Interestingly, towards the end of his presentation, Vos admitted that the declaration might disappoint 'comrades' from non-European and especially colonial areas who wrongly believed that it reflected 'the old colonial mentality'. Nevertheless, he resisted the idea that political independence for the colonies should be the priority, remarking: 'National independence does not always mean a higher standard of living.' The vast majority of participants appeared to share Vos's priorities, and the statement was accepted after only a brief discussion.[51]

In some ways, the statement was a noteworthy achievement. With its adoption, the International became one of the first international political organizations to promote global development as a political and moral obligation of wealthy countries. European socialists thus helped to place the issue on the agenda of international politics. That said, Vos's comments about national independence pointed to future difficulties. In the run-up to the congress, the committee had sought the views of Asian and particularly of Indian socialists. In their response, the latter insisted that national independence be given priority. 'Socialists', the Indian Socialist Party announced, 'must demand immediate freedom for all dependent countries from imperialist bondage and colonial exploitation, and they should actively work for it. There cannot be any gradualness.' In defending the committee's work, Morgan Phillips claimed that it was not easy to arrive at a text that 'would not only express the views of European Socialists, but which would appeal

[48] LHASC, LPA, Commonwealth Sub-Committee, B 19/4, Farmer to Griffiths, 18 January 1952. Emphasis in original.

[49] LHASC, LPA, Commonwealth Sub-Committee, B 19/3, Creech Jones to Farmer, 21 March 1952; also see Labour Party, NEC minutes, fiche 421, 'Notes on the "World Plan for Mutual Aid"', undated.

[50] BA-SAPMO, NL Viktor Agartz, NY 4104/40, Pass to Agartz, 8 July 1952, which includes the SPD's proposed revisions to the statement.

[51] IISH, Socialist International Information, 'The Second Congress of the Socialist International – II. Milan, 17–21 October, 1952', no. 45–6, 8 November 1952, Vos, 2–11.

to Socialists in the under-developed territories and help bridge the emotional gap which still divides Western and Asian socialists'.[52] As we shall see, this 'emotional gap' was considerably larger than Phillips suspected.

EUROPEAN SOCIALISTS AND THE ASIAN SOCIALIST CONFERENCE

The participants at the International's October 1952 congress included eleven Asian socialists from five different parties. Several observers considered this Asian contingent noteworthy, even if a handful of Asian socialists had attended the International's founding congress the year before. For the SPD's Carlo Schmid, the presence of Asian socialists signified the end of the International's Eurocentrism.[53] Although unstated, Schmid's reference point was the interwar LSI, which had been dominated by its European members. During the 1950s, by comparison, European socialists made a concerted attempt to enlarge the International, most notably by wooing Asian socialists. Guillaume Devin has judged the results 'particularly slim', with relations between European and non-European socialists 'limited, fragile and shot through with misunderstandings'. Although Devin's assessment rings true, an emphasis on failure overlooks the fact that the interactions between European and Asian socialists profoundly affected the response of the former to the accelerating process of decolonization.[54]

In the immediate post-war years, European socialists had made sporadic attempts to get in touch with non-European socialists. Perhaps the most spectacu-lar attempt came from left-wing socialists, grouped in the *Mouvement socialiste pour les États-Unis d'Europe* (MSEUE), who in June 1948 organized a 'Congress of European, Asiatic and African Peoples' in Paris. Gathering together almost three hundred participants (socialists and non-socialists), the congress adopted a strongly anti-colonialist line. 'International socialists', it declared, 'accept unequivocally, and absolutely, the right of every people to national self-determination, and consider this to be the fundamental right of the colonial peoples.'[55] Significantly, however, the congress had almost no impact on European socialist leaders, who basically ignored it. Their reaction reflected not only a hostility to claims for national independence, but also the ongoing Eurocentrism of socialist internation-alism. Although Braunthal had expressed some interest in transforming the International into 'a great association of the Labour and Socialist Parties of the

---

[52] IISH, SI, 65, 'Amendments by the Indian Socialist Party', SI circular no. vii/52, 18 September 1952; and AABS, Ssa, E2B: 07, Phillips to Kaj Björk, 12 July 1952.

[53] AdsD, FES, NL Carlo Schmid, 95, 'Der Mailänder Sozialisten-Kongress', 25–26 October 1952.

[54] Devin, *L'Internationale Socialiste*, 51–60; also see Peter van Kemseke, *Towards an Era of Development: The Globalization of Socialism and Christian Democracy, 1945–1965* (Leuven, 2006), 141–52.

[55] HAEU, Mouvement européen, 704, Congress of European, Asiatic and African Peoples, 'Political Report'. Also see Anne-Isabelle Richard, 'The Limits of Solidarity: Anti-Colonialism and Socialism at the Congress of Europe, Asia and Africa in Puteaux, 1948', *European Review of History* 21 (2014), 527–32; and Howe, *Anticolonialism in British Politics*, 178–82.

world', the principal European socialist parties, preoccupied with events in Europe, did not view the project with any urgency. Reporting on the International's 1952 congress, a Canadian socialist could complain that the organization remained '[i]n essence...a European International'.[56]

This lack of urgency regarding relations with non-European socialists soon changed. One reason was the growing belief that the non-European world and Asia in particular was awakening from a long slumber. A 1952 Labour pamphlet described the ongoing 'revolt in Asia' in the following terms:

> The people of Asia, for centuries the passive objects of international dispute, were beginning to take the world stage in their own right. Conscious of their rights and dignities as nations, they were demanding freedom from control by European peoples who too often regarded their white skin as a badge of superiority. Behind this national revolution an economic revolution was also stirring. The people of Asia were becoming conscious of their wretched poverty.[57]

If a dawning awareness of the non-European stirred the International's promotion of a global development programme, it also fuelled the search for like-minded partners beyond Europe. As early as 1951, the International's bureau asked Braunthal to gather information on the 'strength of Socialist Parties in the under-developed countries'; several months later he reported that five non-European parties were affiliated with the International, thirteen were in regular contact, and another thirty or so received its newsletter.[58] Braunthal, meanwhile, set out to woo Asian parties. Writing to the editor of *Janata*, an Indian socialist newspaper, he argued that the 'moral and political force of international Socialism in the world' would be much greater if Asian parties adhered to the International. Several months later, Braunthal told U Ba Swe, the Burmese socialist, that he was 'very anxious' for the Burmese socialist party 'to join the Socialist International' because the latter 'cannot become a world organisation without the Socialist Parties of Asia'.[59]

Braunthal's focus on Asia was not arbitrary, for Asian socialists were in the process of forming a regional organization—the Asian Socialist Conference (ASC). The ASC's origins can be traced back to the Asian Relations Conference held in New Delhi in spring 1947. Hosted by India's provisional government, the conference was meant to herald Asia's emergence from two centuries of Western imperialism that had, in Jawaharlal Nehru's words, fostered 'the isolation of the countries of [the continent] from one another'.[60] Eager to stamp a socialist imprint on this emerging sentiment of Asian solidarity, several socialist delegates discussed the possibility of a separate conference of socialist parties. Taking the lead, in August

---

[56] IISH, SI, 735, Braunthal to M.P.D. Nair (Labour Party of Singapore), 31 January 1950; and LAC, CCF-NPD, MG 28 VI-I, vol. 185, John S. Burton to Lorne Ingle, 25 November 1952.

[57] Labour Party, *Problems of Foreign Policy* (London, April 1952), 3.

[58] OURS, APS, carton: circulaires I.S. 1951–1958, 'Memorandum on the Socialist Parties in Under-Developed Countries', Braunthal, SI circular, no. 118/51, 22 November 1951.

[59] IISH, SI, 657, Braunthal to Rohit Dave (*Janata*), 1 September 1950; and SI, 547, Braunthal to U Ba Swe, 16 March 1951.

[60] Asian Relations Conference, *Asian Relations, being report of the proceedings and documentation of the First Asian Relations Conference* (New Delhi, 1948), Nehru, 22.

1947 the executive of India's Congress Socialist Party (CSP) instructed two of its members to make 'preliminary preparations for calling in India a world Socialist Conference'. Not much happened before 1951, however, when Rammanohar Lohia threw himself into the task of preparing a conference on behalf of the Indian Socialist Party (ISP), founded in 1948 as a successor to the CSP following the latter's disaffiliation from the Indian National Congress. Eager to distinguish the fledgling ISP from the politically dominant Congress and convinced that European socialism was a spent force, Lohia sought to create a distinct Asian socialist movement.[61] Thanks in no small part to his efforts, Burmese, Indian, Indonesian, and Japanese socialists met in Rangoon in March 1952 and agreed to form a preparatory committee charged with organizing a plenary conference to be held in the same city in January 1953.[62]

Lohia's initiative had a galvanizing effect on European socialists. In a memorandum to the International's bureau in 1952, Morgan Phillips warned that the organization 'is in imminent danger of becoming a "Western" or "white" International'. Pointing to the possibility of an Asian socialist congress, he insisted that the 'undesirability of having two Socialist Internationals divided...on racial lines cannot be over-stressed'. Phillips reiterated his warning at the International's Milan congress in October, sketching out a vision of an International in which 'East meets West on an equal footing' and in which the 'accidental divisions between races and between nations are transcended by our united dedication to the cause of International Socialism'.[63] The pressing task, Phillips averred, was to dissuade Asians from creating a separate organization; and to this end Labour urged the International to create an Asian Socialist Fund whose declared purpose was to contribute to 'forging closer links between the Socialist movements of the white men's Continents and the Socialist movements of their coloured brothers'.[64] Phillips himself was confident that European socialists would succeed, chiefly because the International possessed allies among Asian socialists. In addition to Japanese and Israeli socialists (Asian socialists considered the Middle East as West Asia), the International's chairman counted on the support of Indian socialists, who reassured European socialists of their desire to cooperate. Attending a meeting of the International's council in October 1952, Madhav Gokhale, the secretary of the Indian party's foreign affairs bureau, commented that Asian parties strove not to form a 'rival International' but to 'integrate the Socialist movements of East and West'.[65]

---

[61] Lohia believed that Asians must regenerate socialism. See his 'Doctrinal Foundation of Socialism', May 1952 in Lohia, *Marx, Gandhi and Socialism* (Hyderabad, 1950), 320–41; and 'Foreign Policy Report' in Lohia, *The Third Camp in World Affairs* (Bombay, 1950), 8–10. For Lohia's activities, see V.K. Arora, *Rommonohar Lohia and Socialism in India* (New Delhi, 1984).

[62] See IISH, 'Asian Socialist Conference', *Socialist Asia*, vol. 1, no. 1, 6 August 1952, 1–7.

[63] LHASC, LPA, International Sub-Committee, 1952 file, 'The Socialist International', Phillips; and IISH, SI, *Socialist International Information*, vol. II, no. 43–4, 25 October 1952, 'The Second Congress of the Socialist International. Milan, 17–21 October, 1952', Phillips, 2.

[64] OURS, SFIO, carton: circulaires I.S.C. 1951, 'Fund for the Socialist Movements of the Under-Developed Countries', SI circular, no. 1/52, 3 January 1952.

[65] SSAZ, SPS, Ar.1.260.28b, 'Minutes of the Council of the Socialist International...Milan, 17 & 18 October 1952', SI circular no. 72/52, 28 October 1952.

At the meeting, Gokhale remarked that Asian and European socialists had 'differences of approach' on how to integrate East and West. The differences, in fact, were as much between Asian socialists as with European socialists. Several issues divided Asian socialists, including the relevance of European socialism to Asian conditions. Whereas Lohia insisted that Asian socialism must chart its own course, proclaiming in 1952 that '[n]o greater disaster could befall socialism than if the historical peculiarities of its career in Europe were sought to be universalized and reproduced in the other two-thirds of the world', Asoka Mehta, another prominent Indian socialist, rooted Asian socialism in a longer and largely European tradition. European socialism, Mehta explained, had been developing over a century and a half, and its 'study can yield a fresh insight and a deeper outlook'.[66] Not surprisingly, Mehta was more open to cooperation with the International than Lohia. Another—and more immediate—issue involved Cold War politics. While the Japanese (Right) and Israeli parties were generally pro-Western, the Indonesian and Burmese socialist parties criticized European socialists for aligning with the American camp—an alignment that precluded an international third force. As Braunthal reported on a preparatory meeting for the ASC in spring 1952, Burmese and Indonesian socialists believed that the European-dominated International 'is too strongly tied up with the anti-Russian bloc'.[67]

Asian socialists barely mentioned their disagreements on European socialism and on a third force in the statement issued following the preparatory meeting. By contrast, the statement was far less reserved on the issue of anti-colonialism, ending with a ringing call for the 'complete emancipation of the broad masses of Asia'. Anti-colonialism, indeed, quickly emerged as a dominant theme for Asian socialists, no doubt because it was one in which consensus was possible. The demand for a rapid end to empire struck powerful emotional chords in Asian socialists, many of whom had been and were active in resisting colonial rule. Addressing Asian socialists, the Burmese socialist U Kyaw Nyein spoke of the 'common ties that bind us together, the bonds of common suffering and exploitation that we have experienced in our struggle for freedom against the colonial Powers'.[68] The appeal of anti-colonialism, moreover, extended beyond Asia to Africa and other parts of the colonial world. Revealingly, in July 1952 the Indian Socialist Party teamed up with the Tunisian Destour Party to entreat European socialists to support Tunisia's 'battle of freedom' against French imperialism. 'By identifying themselves in act and deed with the yearnings and suffering of slave humanity', it read, '[European] socialism can add a glorious chapter to humanity's endeavour to create a world of peace, progress and plenty.' Reporting to Braunthal on his talks with various Asian socialists in the spring of 1952, a Labour official underscored the anti-colonial sentiments of his hosts, which he attributed to

---

[66] For Lohia, see his 'The Doctrinal Foundation of Socialism'; for Mehta, see his *Studies in Asian Socialism* (Bombay, 1959), 8; and *Democratic Socialism* (Bombay, 1959).

[67] IISH, SI, 65, 'Preparatory Meeting for the Plenary Congress of the Asian Socialist Parties', SI circular B 14/52, Braunthal, 29 May 1952.

[68] IISH collection, U Kyaw Nyein, 'Common Ties that Bind Us Together', *Socialist Asia*, vol. 1, no. 3, 16 September 1952, 1.

'emotional motives rather than rational'. In dealing with Asian socialists, he warned, the International must consider the 'psychological aspect'.[69]

It is with this 'psychological aspect' in mind that the International decided to heed the advice of Indian socialists and to send a high-level delegation to the ASC's founding congress in January 1953. Led by Clement Attlee, the Labour leader, the delegation attended the congress as observers with the aim of quietly influencing the deliberations.[70] Two aspects of the congress impressed the Europeans. One was the apparent youth and enthusiasm of their Asian counterparts. 'There was a fresh-ness and youth in the aspirations of Asian socialists,' noted André Bidet, a French socialist and delegation member. It is hard not to see in such descriptions the hope that Asian socialists would contribute to regenerating a European socialism whose zeal and idealism had suffered from the passage of time and from the realities of government.[71] European socialists, in any case, were even more struck by the second aspect—the congress's anti-colonial tone. Back in London, Attlee reacted with irritation at the 'under-current of anti-Colonialism', regretting the 'tendency' of Asian socialists 'to go off the deep end, and deliver some well worn speeches on anti-Colonialism which had probably done service twenty or thirty years ago'.[72] Bidet's assessment, however, was probably closer to the mark. Reporting to French socialists, he characterized the event as 'an anti-colonial congress' in which the anti-colonial convictions of European socialists were repeatedly questioned. The 'hyper-sensitivity' of Asian socialists regarding colonialism, Bidet warned elsewhere, meant that the International's relations with the ASC would centre on this issue.[73]

Rather than affiliate with the International, Asian socialists opted to create a separate organization made up of ten parties from Asia and the Middle East. Notwithstanding their disappointment with this result, European socialists were determined to create a single global International. With this goal in mind, the Swedish socialist Kaj Björk recommended a series of measures to knit closer ties between the two organizations, including regular meetings as well as the exchange of information and delegates. While not denying that basic disagreements existed between Asian and European socialists, most notably on colonial issues, Björk remained sanguine that as the two groups 'become better acquainted with one another' the 'psychological conditions' would emerge for closer collaboration.[74] The International's bureau quickly responded, creating a subcommittee on rela-tions with the ASC that in June 1953 presented a set of proposals mirroring those of Björk while adding one of its own—the establishment of a joint publishing house. A degree of apprehension underpinned the reaction of European socialists.

[69] AABS, Ssa, E2B: 07, Indian Socialist Party (M. Gokhale) to Swedish Democratic Party, 26 July 1952; and IISH, SI, 65, 'Bernard's Report on the Socialist Parties of Burma and India', SI circular no. B.21/52, 4 July 1952.

[70] For the deliberations, see ASC, *Report of the First Asian Socialist Conference* (Rangoon, 1953).

[71] OURS, APS, carton circulaires I.S. 1951–1958, 'Rapport de la délégation de l'Internationale à Rangoon. Observations d'A. Bidet, France', SI circular, no. 60/53, 2 April 1953.

[72] RIIA, 8/2125, Attlee, 'The Asian Socialist Conference at Rangoon', 17 February 1953.

[73] OURS, SFIO, 'Conseil national des 23 et 24 janvier 1953, Asnières', Bidet, 71; and Bidet, 'Le colonialisme et le féodalisme', *Le Populaire de Paris*, 31 January–1 February 1953, 1.

[74] OURS, APS, carton circulaires I.S. 1951–1958, 'La Conférence socialiste asiatique de Rangoon. 6–15 Janvier', Circulaire no. 50/53, 19 March 1953, Björk.

If left to itself, they feared, the ASC might develop into a rival International, appealing to the discontented masses not just in Asia but also in Africa. Hitherto, the International had evinced little interest in African socialism, with Braunthal remarking in 1951 that one should not expect socialism to thrive 'among illiterate peoples'. Two years later, however, Morgan Phillips framed the ASC's mounting interest in Africa as a threat. 'I believe that the African continent', he told the International's bureau, 'is one in which the Socialist International should take the initiative and seek to bring them [*sic*] into its ranks, otherwise we are in great danger of the coloured people outside the continent of Asia automatically linking up with the Asian Socialist Conference without giving the necessary consideration to joining the Socialist International.'[75] Were the latter to happen, the International's limited scope—or its whiteness as Phillips reiterated in November 1953—would be evident for all to see.[76]

While apprehensive about the ASC's ambitions, European socialists were confident that they could persuade Asian socialists of their good intentions—and especially of their anti-colonial bona fides. Committed to reformism and gradualism, European socialists viewed the ASC's uncompromising anti-colonialism as unrealistic, a product of political immaturity. The urgent task was to guide Asian socialists towards a better understanding of the complexities of colonial and international politics. As Bidet informed the SFIO's directing committee, the ASC's anti-colonialism reflected its 'one-sided information'. 'Better informed, I believe that they [Asian socialists] will be able to adopt a more understanding attitude.' Bidet, accordingly, proposed a campaign to educate the ASC. 'It is the duty of the Socialist International and its member parties', he reported in June 1953, 'to make a propaganda effort to enlighten the Asian Socialist Conference... first of all about Socialist solidarity, then about the aims and means of democratic world Socialism.'[77] Saul Rose, Labour's international secretary, agreed with Bidet on the need for a 'propaganda effort', complaining that the ASC 'showed little awareness that any problems existed'. Rose, indeed, believed that Labour was particularly well positioned to undertake such an effort because of the prestige and contacts it enjoyed among Asian socialists (as well as English as a common language).[78] Unwilling to leave matters to the International, Labour in early 1953 created the British-Asian Socialist Fellowship (BASF) to encourage exchanges not only between British and Asian socialists in Britain but also between Labour and the ASC. With Attlee as its president, the BASF organized an impressive series of activities, including the visit of prominent Asian socialists to Britain to meet with Labour leaders and officials.[79]

[75] IISH, SI, 605, Braunthal to Brutelle (SFIO), 16 October 1951; and SI, 73, 'Morgan Phillips' Report on the Bureau Meeting of the Asian Socialist Conference', SI circular, no. B.19/53, 24 September 1953.

[76] LAC, CCF-NPD, MG 28 VI-I, vol. 185, 'Memorandum of the Meeting of the Bureau of the Socialist International of November 19th, 1953'.

[77] OURS, APS, Comité directeur, 4 February 1953; and IISH, SI, 73, 'Memorandum on Cooperation between the Socialist International and the Asian Socialist Conference. Submitted by André Bidet (France)', Circular no. xx/53, 27 June 1953.

[78] LHASC, LPA, International Sub-Committee, 1953 file, 'Socialism in Asia', Rose, undated.

[79] LHASC, BASF, 1, 'British-Asian Socialist Fellowship', Labour circular, Phillips, March 1953. The LHASC possesses four uncatalogued boxes of records on the BASF's activities during the 1950s.

The International's didactic approach proved ineffective as the ASC's anti-colonialist position soon hardened. Invited to a meeting of the International's general council in April 1953, Madhu Limaye, an ASC secretary, complained that debates on colonialism failed to mention the 'unfettered freedom of colonial peoples to have national governments of their own choice'. Three months later, at the International's congress in Stockholm, Prem Bhasin, another Indian socialist, criticized the anti-colonialism of European socialists as 'a modified and more polished form' of the 'proverbial white man's burden'. Talk of gradual progress towards independence was unacceptable: all socialists, he maintained, must support immediate political independence for colonies, adding tellingly 'that people smarting under the heels of foreign rule prefer self-government to good government'.[80] At a meeting of the ASC's bureau the following month, Asian socialists, rejecting Phillips' plea for a merger, decided instead to create an Anti-Colonial Bureau (ACB) whose initial declaration announced that the 'right of peoples to self-determination is a basic principle of the democratic system of society'. Following its first meeting in May 1954, the ACB pursued an anti-colonial programme designed 'to encourage, guide and help the freedom movements to speed the attainment of Independence in their own countries according to Socialist lines as adopted by the [January 1953] Rangoon Conference'.[81] The ASC, meanwhile, made it clear that anti-colonialism would be a determining factor in its relations with the International. At a meeting of the ASC's Bureau in August 1955, James Markham, a Ghanese socialist and ACB joint secretary, castigated the 'socialists of the Metropolitan countries' for failing to 'adopt an uncompromising anti-colonial attitude and to sympathise [*sic*] and help the national freedom movement'. European socialists, he admonished, must 'awake in time and rise to the occasion'.[82]

European socialists responded to the ASC's criticisms by reiterating their commitment to gradualism centred on development—a commitment that all but ruled out political independence in the foreseeable future. In a discussion paper for the International entitled 'A Socialist Policy for Asia', Georges Brutelle, the SFIO's deputy leader, identified the 'awakening' of colonial peoples as the 'vital problem of our epoch'.[83] But while insisting that socialists must oppose 'all forms of colonialism', Brutelle argued that Asia urgently needed economic development rather than national independence. The following year, an International study group questioned the ASC's single-minded focus on national independence for Asian and African peoples. 'National independence', it reported, 'does not in itself provide a

[80] IISH collection, 'Report on the S.I. Council', *Socialist Asia*, vol. II, no. 1, 1 May 1953, Limaye, 18; and IISH, SI, 71, 'Report of the Third Congress of the Socialist International held in Stockholm', 82–3, 86–9.

[81] For the ACB's founding, see 'Decisions of the Bureau Meeting of Asian Socialist Conference', *Janata*, 20 June 1954, 9–10. Also see BLCAS, Fabian Colonial Bureau, 149/1, 'Declaration on Colonialism' in ACB, *Newsletter*, no. 2, July 1954; and TNA CO 936/351, 'Program' in ACB, *Newsletter*, no. 12, August 1955.

[82] Markham, 'The Heart of the Matter' in IISH collection, *Socialist Asia*, vol. 3, no. 9–10, 1955, 11–13.

[83] Brutelle, 'A Socialist Policy for Asia' in IISH, *Socialist International Information*, vol. IV, no. 20, 15 May 1954, 355–61.

solution to the economic and social problems afflicting the region [Asia]. A vigorous program of economic and social development is everywhere an urgent necessity.'[84] European socialists, in short, refused to accord national independence the priority.

The contesting views on colonialism came to a head at the International's congress in London in July 1955. Opening the proceedings, Morgan Phillips claimed that no 'basic differences' divided European and Asian socialists. In response, Wijono, an Indonesian socialist and the ASC's general secretary, pointed out that 'two major factors' prevented unity: 'the approach to world politics and the question of freedom of the dependent peoples.' In terms of world politics, Asian socialists continued to criticize the International's adherence to the Western camp—a criticism boosted by the recently held Bandung conference that heralded the advent of the non-alignment movement. In London, however, the ASC speakers focused far more on colonial policy. Taking issue with gradualism, Wijono insisted that socialist policy must 'pass the test of immediacy'. Gokhale was still more direct. It is 'useless to say merely that the colonies will be freed step by step', he asserted. 'At this stage we must declare much more concretely and definitely how we are going to achieve this end.' More concretely, Gokhale proposed the creation of a joint ASC–International commission to 'draw up a concrete and time-bound programme for the freedom of the colonial peoples'. After much negotiation, European and Asian socialists quietly agreed to implement Gokhale's proposal for a study commission. The ASC had succeeded in pushing the issue of rapid transfers of power in the colonies to the forefront of the international socialist agenda.[85]

EUROPEAN SOCIALISTS AND MINORITY RIGHTS

Meeting in October 1955 the International's bureau not only confirmed the decision to create a study group with the ASC on the future of European colonies but also accepted Morgan Phillips' proposal that Labour prepare a discussion paper for the group.[86] Written by John Hatch, Labour's commonwealth officer, the resulting paper was submitted to the International in December. Having announced the commitment of socialists to the right of self-government and of self-determination, the paper then qualified this commitment. It began by describing three types of colonies: the ethnically homogenous, the ethnically mixed, and those too small to exist independently. If 'development towards independence' posed little problem for ethnically homogenous colonies, this was not so for ethnically mixed ones, principally because of the existence of minorities possessing disproportionate

---

[84] SSAZ, SPS, Ar.1.260.30a, 'Document du travail sur la situation internationale', SI circular, no. 34/55, 20 June 1955.

[85] IISH, SI, 79, 'Report of the Fourth Congress of Socialist International held in London, 12–16 July, 1955', 2–3, 6–7, 80–1, 123–4.

[86] LHASC, LPA, Commonwealth Sub-Committee, B 19/11, 'Secretary's Report. November 1955', Hatch, 3 November 1955.

power. In all likelihood independence in these colonies would mean minority rule and perhaps even white minority rule—a likelihood underscored by the case of South Africa and the Central African Federation (created in 1953 between Rhodesia and Nyasalan). But whatever the ethnic make-up of the groups concerned, the establishment of democracy based on one person one vote would not preclude the danger of minority domination. As the paper explained:

> Political power is not solely dependent upon a universal franchise, nor does the universal right to vote suffice alone to represent the will of the people. The standard, strength and experience of political organisation, the participation of all sections of the community in economic life, and the stage of development of social organisations, all influence the control of political power. At present it is obvious in most multi-racial societies that minorities control not only political power itself but the means by which such power can be gained.

Consequently, the colonial powers had a responsibility to pursue policies aimed at reducing 'communal barriers' and creating 'a national as opposed to communal loyalty'; only then could political power be conceivably transferred. Well aware of the magnitude of the task, the paper shied away from fixed timetables and instead spoke vaguely of a period of ten to fifteen years.[87]

Labour's initiative in drafting a paper for the International's study group was rooted in internal party thinking on colonial policy. During the 1950s, the Fabian Colonial Bureau remained preoccupied with the problems of 'multi-racial societies'. In a 1952 report, the FCB discussed the concept of 'partnership' anchored in political and constitutional arrangements between 'Africans' and 'Europeans' in the same colony. Interestingly, the statement framed the challenge posed by multiracial societies in terms not only of defending the majority from a (white) minority but also of minority protection against majority rule. No less interestingly, FCB members conceived of partnership as a 'double concept' implying political-constitutional arrangements within a territory as well as between Britain and the territory, with London acting to safeguard different ethnic groups from one another. 'If [ethnic] cohesion is not secured in a country through a common will', one member commented, 'it can only be secured through an authority external to the groups which constitute the population.'[88] The FCB eventually dropped the concept of partnership, fearing that it would be perceived by anti-colonialists in the empire as a stratagem for the maintenance of imperial rule. Nevertheless, the problem of 'multi-racial societies' remained present for FCB members. In 1955 Creech Jones thus warned that the 'problem of the Mixed Territories' must be addressed when considering the future of empire. 'Is democracy attainable?' he asked. 'Are there alternative policies to the creation of the nation-state?'[89]

---

[87] Labour Party, NEC minutes, fiche 543, 'Memorandum on Colonial Problems. Submitted by the British Labour Party', SI circular, B. 24/55, 24 December 1955.

[88] BLCAS, Fabian Colonial Bureau, 34/4, *Advance to Democracy: A Report to the Colonial Bureau on the Implications of 'Partnership' in Multi-Racial Societies* (London, June 1952); and the comments of various FCB members and especially those of Marjorie Nicholson.

[89] BLCAS, Arthur Creech Jones Papers, 16/4, 'Anglo-Belgian Colonial Conference. Synopsis of Paper by…A. Creech Jones', 1 April 1955.

The FCB worried that Labour might endorse rapid transfers of power without regard for the situation in multiethnic colonies. At the party's annual congress in 1954, several motions were presented in support of the 'fixing of times and dates' for colonial independence. Although the national executive successfully argued against 'target dates', the pressure from militants was clearly mounting. For the FCB, which viewed 'time schedules' as 'crude and dangerous', the International's decision to create a joint study group to 'draw up a concrete and time-bound programme for the freedom of the colonial peoples' constituted a dangerous development.[90] Yet the study group also offered a potential means to mobilize international socialism behind the effort to sensitize Labour to the problems posed by 'multi-racial societies'. The FCB could do so, moreover, because overlapping membership gave it considerable influence on Labour's Commonwealth subcommittee. Under FCB influence, the subcommittee in early 1955 prepared a statement on multiracial societies for Labour's executive. In drafting his statement for the International's bureau, Hatch, who was active in the FCB, drew on drafts of the subcommittee's document. Meanwhile, Labour's Commonwealth subcommittee formed a 'working party' on 'multi-racial policy' whose four members included Creech Jones and Hinden from the FCB. If one purpose of the working party was to spur work on a Labour statement, another one was to oversee the deliberations of the International's study group to ensure that it took account of 'multi-racial societies'. The International's support, in turn, would make it easier for the FCB/Commonwealth subcommittee to influence Labour's evolving colonial policy.[91]

Having received Labour's paper on colonial policy, the International's bureau created its own subcommittee made up of Belgian, British, and French socialists to consider its contents. The Belgian party generally endorsed the paper, which is not surprising given that British and Belgian socialists had consulted with each other the previous year on the issue of multi-ethnic colonies. Belgian socialists, in fact, assumed that the colonial power would have to play an active role as protector of minorities and majorities. Accordingly, they gently criticized Labour's paper for not going far enough in conceiving of alternatives to the nation state for multiracial colonies—alternatives involving some form of federalist arrangement for the empire and according important responsibilities to the colonial power. Pointing to Africa, the Belgians argued that for some colonies, 'the federal idea constitutes... a happy solution to delicate political problems that are difficult to resolve in a so-called national framework that encompasses diverse "nations" with artificial borders.' Although the SFIO responded more tepidly, with Robert Pontillon, the party's international secretary, commenting that the 'spirit and letter' of Labour's paper 'does not correspond exactly to what we ourselves wish', French socialists were far from opposed either to the focus on 'multi-racial societies' or to federalist

[90] Labour Party, *Report of the 53rd Annual Conference... September 27 to October 1, 1954* (London, 1954), 124–38. For timetables, see Labour Party, NEC minutes, fiche 508, Creech Jones to Hatch, 11 September 1954.

[91] LHASC, LPA, Commonwealth Sub-Committee, B 14/13, 'Preliminary Draft of Labour Party Policy on the Multi-Racial Territories', April and September 1955; and B 19/11, 'Secretary's Report. December 1955'.

solutions as an alternative to national independence.[92] Pontillon thus proposed that Belgian, British, and French socialists continue to meet in order to amend Labour's paper, meetings that took place in June 1956 and that produced a final, slightly revised version.

Assured of the support of European socialists, Labour's Commonwealth subcommittee received the approval of the party's executive in the summer of 1956 to publish a statement on multiracial societies. Subtitled *Plural Society*, the resulting pamphlet defined the subject as 'the major international problem of the mid-twentieth century' for the simple reason that the 'world is inhabited by a multitude of peoples of varying races, colours, religions, languages, customs and traditions'. When it came to empire, the pressing challenge was to reconcile three imperatives: ending colonial rule; respecting the rights of inhabitants of each colony to determine their political system; and balancing 'the rights of powerful minorities with those of weak majorities and the rights of weak minorities with those of powerful majorities'. Several additional points are worth underscoring. First, the pamphlet focused on internal political arrangements and safeguards for minorities and majorities, refraining from any mention of federalist structures linking Britain and its colonies. Second, much like Labour's paper for the International, it proposed a series of policies aimed at breaking down group identities in order to forge common identities. Third, if the pamphlet identified the final goal as the establishment of democracy based on one person one vote, it also insisted that a lengthy transitional period would be required during which British authority would be paramount: '*It is, therefore, the responsibility of Britain to retain ultimate control in all these plural societies until such conditions for the establishment of full democracy exist.*' Fourth and finally, the memorandum made no mention of 'target dates' for the transfer of power.[93]

The publication of *Plural Society* highlighted the growing gap between Asian and European socialists on colonial policy. Whereas Asian socialists emphasized national rights, insisting that international socialism must support immediate independence for colonies, European socialists were increasingly sensitive to minority rights, a concern that worked against any rapid transfer of power. It is in this context that European (and Asian) socialists confronted the growing crisis provoked by the Algerian War.

INTERNATIONAL SOCIALISM
AND THE ALGERIAN WAR

In November 1954, the *Front de Libération Nationale* (FLN), an organization dedicated to attaining full political independence for Algeria, launched an armed

---

[92] IISH, SI, 376, 'Avis de la Commission coloniale sur le memorandum présenté à l'Internationale socialiste par le Parti Travailliste Britannique', POB, 27 February 1956; and Pontillon (SFIO) to Braunthal (SI), undated.

[93] Labour Party, *Labour's Colonial Policy: I Plural Society* (London, July 1956), emphasis in original. For the decision to publish the pamphlet, see the file in LHASC, LPA, Commonwealth Sub-Committee, B 19/10.

revolt against French rule. Initially of limited scope, the revolt soon widened as French authorities proved unable to suppress the FLN. But it was during the tenure of a socialist-led government under Guy Mollet (February 1956 to June 1957) that the revolt expanded into a large-scale anti-insurrectionary conflict on France's part. Although Mollet's Republican front government came to power with an ambitious programme of social and economic reforms, the Algerian War came to dominate its existence. Under the triptych 'cease-fire—negotiations—elections', Mollet's government embarked on the dual project of defeating the FLN by military means and of convincing the Muslim population that Algeria's future would best be served by remaining within France's orbit. In practice, the project manifested itself in a vertiginous increase of violence—an increase that included a doubling of French troop levels to 400,000, the large-scale resettlement and internment of Algerian Muslims, the imposition of martial law, and the systematic use of torture.[94] As several scholars have recounted, Mollet's Algerian policy provoked considerable unease and criticism among French socialists, fuelling a brewing crisis within the SFIO.[95] Less well known is that the crisis possessed an international socialist dimension that would profoundly shape the response of European socialists to decolonization.

Even before the FLN's revolt, Asian socialists had expressed support for the national independence of North Africa (Tunisia, Morocco, and Algeria) in general. The ASC's founding congress in January 1953, for example, had announced its 'full sympathy and solidarity with the people of North Africa in their present struggle for national liberation'.[96] But with the revolt, the attention of Asian socialists focused increasingly on Algeria. Beginning in 1955, the Anti-Colonial Bureau (ACB) produced a steady drumbeat of propaganda denouncing French repression and championing Algeria's right to national self-determination. Proclaiming the Algerian people's 'right for freedom', a joint ACB–ASC statement in February 1955 appealed to 'the socialists of Europe and the Socialist International and in particular the French socialists to express their solidarity with North Africa's urge for freedom and independence which is their birthright'. In July of the same year the ACB called for a week of protest in Europe and elsewhere under the title 'Stop Colonial Aggression in Algeria Week'.[97] Writing to the Socialist International in August 1956, Wijono, the ASC's secretary, insisted that support for Algeria's national independence was an imperative for all socialists. 'As Socialists', he

---

[94] For an excellent overview of the Algerian War, see Martin Evans, *Algeria: France's Undeclared War* (Oxford, 2012). Also see Stephan Malinowski, 'Modernisierungskriege: Miltärische Gewalt und koloniale Modernisierung im Algerienkrieg (1954–1962)', *Archiv für Sozialgeschichte* 28 (2008), 213–48; and Raphaëlle Branche, *La torture et l'armée pendant la Guerre d'Algérie* (Paris, 2001).

[95] See Lafon, *Guy Mollet*, 506–653; Gilles Morin, 'De l'opposition socialiste à la Guerre d'Algérie au Parti Socialiste autonome (1954–1960). Un courant socialiste de la S.F.I.O. au P.S.U.', thèse, Université de Paris I, 1990–1991; and Etienne Maquin, *Le Parti socialiste et la guerre en Algérie: la fin de la vieille maison, 1954–1958* (Paris, 1990).

[96] 'Tunisia, Algeria and Morocco' in ASC, *Resolutions of the First Asian Socialist Congress* (Rangoon, 1954), 25.

[97] IISH collection, 'The Fight in North Africa' and 'Stop Colonial Aggression on Algeria', *Anti-Colonial Bureau Newsletter*, no. 6, February 1955, 1 and no. 10, June 1955, 5–6.

contended, 'we should support this right for freedom' and should 'appeal to the French government to recognise Algerian independence immediately'.[98]

Not surprisingly, Algeria figured on the agenda of the ASC's second conference in Bombay (Mumbai) in November 1956. Although the proceedings occurred under the shadow of the Suez crisis triggered by Anglo-French military intervention against Egypt, Asian socialists took the time to reiterate their demand for Algerian independence and to denounce the French government's 'use of force' in Algeria as 'incompatible with the Socialist ideal'.[99] Criticism of Mollet's government, which was not only pursuing a violent policy of 'pacification' in Algeria but was also responsible for the country's participation in the Suez expedition, fortified the ASC's anti-colonialism. One result, as the British journalist and ASC sympathizer Alex Josey observed, was to fuse together anti-colonialism and nationalism. So long as independence struggles continued, Josey reported, Asian socialists and nationalists would be 'brothers in arms'. Another and a related result was a renewed rejection of a progressive approach to independence—an approach favoured by European socialists and expressed in Labour's pamphlet on plural societies. As the ASC conference's resolution on 'dependent territories' declared:

> The Conference desires to emphasise that the most peaceful solution of the colonial problem must include the immediate independence of the colonial people. It rejects categorically the emphasis upon phased and constitutional developments, as history has recorded in this context that the colonial powers have utilised this policy in order to break up national states and to create antagonistic societies in order to maintain or prolong their own domination over these people. It reiterates that the struggles for freedom that are at present being waged do not accept any phasing of their progress towards independence.[100]

Summarizing the conference, Bjarne Braatoy, the Norwegian socialist who replaced Braunthal as the International's secretary, reported that Asian socialists 'have come out flat in favour of independence without any sort of delay'—a position, he added, that 'raises all sorts of difficulties' for the International.[101]

European socialists, by contrast, initially evinced considerable sympathy for the SFIO and the French government's Algerian policies. At an international socialist conference in March 1956 the participants voted a resolution applauding 'the courageous efforts of the French Socialists to reach a lasting solution of France's present difficulties'.[102] The SPD, moreover, figured among the Mollet government's staunchest supporters. To be sure, several German socialists criticized French policy in Algeria, among them Rolf Reventlow, one of the few SPD members with first-hand knowledge of North Africa, and Peter Blachstein, who

---

[98] IISH, SI, 513, Wijono (ASC) to Bjarne Braatoy (SI), 30 August 1956.

[99] SSAZ, SPS, Ar.1.260.60, 'Resolution on Algeria' in ASC, *Information Bulletin*, no. 4, November 1956, 6.

[100] Alex Josey, *Socialism in Asia* (Singapore, 1957), 20; and 'The Statement of the A.S.C. on Dependent Territories', *Janata*, 18 November 1956, 11–12.

[101] IISH, SI, 376, 'Colonial Problems', Braatoy, 13 August 1957.

[102] FES, AdsD, NL Herbert Wehner, 1/HWAA001044, 'Report of the Conference of the Council of the Socialist International. Zurich, 2–4 March, 1956'.

actively aided Algerian refugees in Germany.[103] SPD leaders, however, refused to heed calls for a more critical stance towards the SFIO. Their refusal stemmed partly from the demands of international socialist solidarity and partly from political calculation: SPD leaders feared that the 'loss' of Algeria might doom the Fourth Republic with incalculable consequences for Franco-German relations and for Western security. Revealingly, an internal report likened France's political situation to that of Weimar Germany, warning of the threat of fascism if the regime fell.[104] But SPD leaders were also motivated by an awareness of the complexity of the situation in Algeria—a complexity rooted in the divide between a Muslim majority and a European minority. Algeria, Ollenhauer lectured SPD parliamentarians in September 1956, was an 'enormously complicated question' and it was 'too simple' to expect 'everything to be alright' if national independence were achieved.[105]

An appreciation of the complexity of the Algerian situation also influenced Labour's response. Speaking at the SFIO's congress in June 1956, Morgan Phillips recognized that Mollet's government had 'inherited a complex situation, fraught with difficulties and perils', adding that it was unfortunate that criticism tended 'to submerge the sincere and immediate efforts you [French socialists] are making to find a solution' to Algeria.[106] Underpinning Phillips' sympathy for the SFIO's difficulties was Labour's growing sensitivity to the challenges posed by plural societies. This sensitivity manifested itself at a conference of commonwealth socialist parties organized by Labour in the spring of 1957. While James Griffiths identified the most pressing task as that of forging 'a real sense of nationality' in colonies divided along ethnic and other lines, Patrick Gordon Walker, a former commonwealth secretary, went further, calling for a policy of 'socialist imperialism' in 'multi-racial territories'. Labour, he explained, 'cannot yield up British power until there is true political partnership between the races. The steps towards independence of the central government must be accompanied by progress towards political equality, franchise, etc... Then, and only then, can we yield up power.'[107] Although Griffiths and Gordon Walker were discussing British colonies, Algeria, with its multi-ethnic make-up (and divisions), fit easily into this framework of analysis. That European socialists in general sympathized with this framework, moreover, is suggested by the fact that within the International the only formal criticism of the SFIO during 1956 came from the Uruguayan party.

The sympathies of European socialists, however, began to change in the wake of the Suez crisis at the end of 1956. Following Egypt's decision in July to nationalize the Suez Canal, the French and British governments colluded with the Israeli government to provoke a military confrontation aimed not only at securing the

[103] See Thomas Scheffler, *Die SPD und der Algerienkrieg (1954–1962)* (Berlin, 1995).

[104] FES, AdsD, SPD, Internationale Abteilung, 2868, Putzrath circular, no. 2/56, 28 February 1956 with undated attached report.

[105] '10./11.9. 1956: Fraktionsvorstands—und Fraktionssitzung', reproduced in Weber, ed., *Die SPD-Fraktion im Deutschen Bundestag*, 352–3.

[106] OURS, SFIO, '48ème congrès ordinaire des 28, 29, 30 juin et 1er juillet 1956', Phillips, 303.

[107] LAC, CCF-NPD, MG 28 VI-I, vol. 133, 'The British Labour Party Commonwealth Conference. Monday, 27th May to Thursday, 6th June, 1957. Conference Report', Griffiths, 10; Gordon Walker, 24.

canal but also at inflicting a major military defeat on Egypt that would lead to the overthrow of President Gamel Abder Nasser. Consequently, on 29 October Israel invaded Egypt, providing the pretext for an Anglo-French military intervention on 5 November. But despite their military success on the ground, Paris and London were forced to withdraw their troops soon afterwards under strong pressure from the Americans and Soviets. In a longer perspective, the Suez fiasco underscored in public and humiliating fashion the reality that Britain and France were no longer global powers. But in placing the Mollet government and the SFIO in the dock, a more immediate result for European socialists was to call into question the French government's Algerian policy.

During the run-up to the Suez crisis, Labour took the lead in calling for a peaceful settlement with Egypt. Although Labour leaders disliked Nasser's decision to nationalize the canal, they opposed military action. Indeed, during the autumn of 1956, Labour waged a vocal campaign on this score. An SFIO analysis attributed Labour's oppositional line chiefly to domestic political calculation: as an opposition party, Labour needed to distinguish itself from the Conservatives, many of whom were clamouring for a military response. But the analysis also recognized that Labour's traditional pacifism and support for collective security through international institutions (the United Nations) enjoyed a near-consensus within the party. For Hugh Gaitskell, whose leadership was constantly contested, the promise of a consensus was undoubtedly attractive.[108] But whatever his precise motives, Gaitskell made it clear to European socialists that Labour would not accept a military solution. At a tête-à-tête with Gaitskell in mid-September 1956, Mollet admitted that he was searching for an 'excuse' for military intervention, prompting the Labour leader to plead for a recourse to the United Nations and for economic sanctions against Egypt. Unhappy with Gaitskell's answer, Mollet sought to organize a more formal meeting between British, French, and German socialists to discuss Suez, but Labour leaders declined, warning that the public revelation of their differences with the SFIO would be 'highly embarrassing'.[109]

In the wake of Suez, the SFIO pressed for a meeting with Labour to reduce tensions between the two parties. Once again, the British declined a bilateral meeting, citing the 'wide divergence of opinion between the parties'.[110] But Labour leaders were not content merely to shun French socialists: they also sought to mobilize the International against the Mollet government's policies. The opportunity soon came at a meeting of the International's council in Copenhagen in December 1956. Attending in person, Gaitskell presented a resolution sharply condemning French and British military intervention during the Suez crisis. Although Robert Pontillon, the SFIO's international secretary and head of the French delegation, reported afterwards that Labour and Gaitskell in particular

---

[108] OURS, Archives Guy Mollet, AGM 80, 'Le mouvement ouvrier britannique et le conflit de Suez', Henry Hauck, 8 September 1956. For Labour's campaign, see the file in LHASC, LPA, General Secretary's Papers, GS/SUEZ.

[109] Williams, ed., *The Diary of Hugh Gaitskell*, 24 September 1956, 599–600.

[110] IISH, SI, 605, Pontillon (SFIO) to Phillips (Labour), 15 November 1956; and LHASC, LPA, International Department, LP/ID/FRA/3, Labour to Pontillon, 25 November 1956.

distinguished themselves by their 'partisan preoccupations', the other European parties were also angry with the SFIO, even if they rejected a Uruguayan proposal to eject the French party from the International. Tellingly, what a Canadian socialist called Gaitskell's 'outspoken resolution' received unanimous support, prompting the French delegation to storm out in protest.[111] The Copenhagen meeting, however, did not simply underscore the SFIO's isolation within the International. It also focused attention on Algeria. Ironically, this was partly the SFIO's doing. Although the Mollet government had hitherto striven to safeguard the Algerian War from outside scrutiny, insisting that it was an internal French matter, Pontillon, in defending the SFIO in Copenhagen, insisted that military action had been necessary to combat Pan-Arabism, a movement that supposedly encompassed North Africa and Algeria in particular. Algeria, Pontillon contended, could not be isolated from international politics—and thus from the socialist International. German socialists were clear on this point. The International, the SPD's *Neuer Vorwärts* intoned in this sense, could not remain silent while an SFIO-led government violated the 'fundamental principles of the socialist world view' in Egypt and Algeria.[112]

That Algeria had become a subject of debate became evident at the International's congress in Vienna in July 1957. The initiative to place the Algerian War on the agenda came from the Norwegian party. In May Haakon Lie, the Norwegian party leader, had written to Morgan Phillips complaining that reports of French violence against Muslims provoked 'great damage to the cause of socialism and democracy' not only in Europe but also 'in all the countries of Asia and Africa that look to the Socialist International as a force that should lead the way in the struggle against imperialism and for national emancipation of the peoples who are not yet independent'.[113] But if the Norwegians took the initiative, the other European parties were not far behind. In the SPD's case, Ollenhauer, recently returned from a trip to Asia, explained in early 1957 that a wave of national independence was sweeping away colonial empires and that Asian socialists expected their German counterparts to contribute to the emerging new international order. European socialists, the SPD leader counselled, must be careful not to be 'dragged into' France's colonial policy in North Africa.[114] In Labour's case, Gaitskell warned that French policy in Algeria risked alienating Asians and Africans. There is 'a feeling of strong resentment, sometimes leading to bitter hatred, felt by millions of Asian and African people against the white races and the powerful Western countries', he lectured to an American audience in January 1957. 'But what precisely is it that is

[111] OURS, D5 41 BD, 'Note sur la réunion du Conseil de l'Internationale à Copenhague', Pontillon, undated, emphasis in original; and LAC, CCF-NPD, MG 28 VI-I, vol. 185, Jean Chapman to Lorne Ingle (CCF), 13 December 1956.

[112] OURS, D5 41 BD, 'Le Parti Socialiste Français et l'Affaire de Suez', undated memorandum circulated to socialist parties; and 'Die Labour-Party zu Kopenhagen', *Neuer Vorwärts*, 21 December 1956, 8.

[113] AAOB, DNA, D.Da. Alfabetisk Saksarkiv 1957 (I-K), Lie to Phillips, 21 May 1957.

[114] AdsD, SPD, Internationale Abteilung, 2686, 'Kurzprotokoll der Sitzung des aussenpolitischen Ausschusses, am 19.1.1957'; and SPD, Parteivorstand Protokolle, 'Sitzung des Parteivorstandes am 8. und 9.2.1957 in Bonn'.

resented and hated? In the first place, of course, it is direct colonial rule against the wishes of the inhabitants. Algeria is the most obvious example of this in the minds of the people of the uncommitted areas today...'[115]

With criticism of French policy mounting, the International's Vienna congress promised to be a difficult experience for the SFIO. Opening the debate with what a Labour report described as 'a remarkable speech that was courteous, scrupulously fair and lucidly argued', the Norwegian socialist Finn Moe reiterated his party's unease with French violence in Algeria. But Moe's more important argument concerned national independence. The presence of a sizeable European minority, he acknowledged, rendered the Algerian situation complex; yet this complexity could 'not render null and void our solemn pledges to non-independent peoples to give them their independence'. All socialists, he continued, must 'recognise the right of the people of Algeria to their independence'. To buttress his argument Moe insisted that non-Europeans viewed Algeria as a 'test case' for socialism:

> The unfortunate Suez intervention last year revived the old suspicions of Western imperialism everywhere in Asia and Africa. If Socialism fails to make it clear that we shall liquidate as soon as possible whatever remnants there may be of military, political and economic imperialism, the teeming masses in Asia and Africa will lose their faith in Socialist methods for the liberation of humanity.

In response and speaking for the absent Mollet, Pierre Commin, a close ally, under-scored the multi-ethnic nature of Algeria and the Mollet government's determin-ation to ensure the peaceful coexistence of the European and Muslim communities. More intriguingly, Commin maintained that the 'liberation of man' and not national independence had always been the basic goal of socialist policy. National independence, indeed, was dangerous, because behind it lurked nationalism—a destructive force antipathetic to liberty. Socialists, consequently, had a duty to 'help [colonial peoples] avoid that dangerous phase [of nationalism] and, instead, to advance towards a higher form of co-operation between colonial and metropol-itan peoples'. In the Algerian case, this meant a close association with France that could also serve to 'link Europe with Africa' in a larger grouping—what some called *Eurafrique*.[116]

Commin's comments drew a blistering response from Aneurin Bevan, Gaitskell's chief rival for Labour's leadership, who reiterated Moe's point that Algeria's 'pecu-liarities' could not justify the denial of national independence. In what amounted to an implicit repudiation of Labour thinking on plural societies, Bevan argued that the existence of a European minority changed nothing, as there were minor-ities in all colonies. More generally, he rejected Commin's claim that nationalism was necessarily dangerous or somehow incompatible with internationalism. International cooperation, Bevan explained, was only possible when all nations

---

[115] Gaitskell, *The Challenge of Co-Existence*, 75.

[116] IISH, SI, 87, 'Report of the Fifth Congress of the Socialist International held in Vienna on 2–6 July, 1957', SI circular, 70/57, 6 December 1957, Moe, 41–5; Commin, 45–50. For the Labour report, see Labour Party, NEC minutes, fiche 597, 'Report of the Vth Congress of the Socialist International. Vienna, 2–6 July, 1957'.

had won their independence. For international socialists, any 'solution [to the Algerian problem] must be consistent with the principles of [national] independence'. Anything else—and especially Commin's vision of a Franco-Algerian entity— amounted to 'enforced imperial association'. Although several participants resented Bevan's sharp tone, few disagreed with the contents of his speech. Well aware of this and eager to stave off a resolution criticizing the Mollet government, Commin sought to buy time by proposing that the International send a 'fact-finding mission for an on-the-spot investigation of the Algerian drama'. With Labour's grudging acceptance, the proposal passed.[117]

For Mollet and his allies, the danger was that criticism of the French government's Algerian policy from socialists abroad would encourage the SFIO's internal critics. For much of 1956, these critics were few in number. To be sure, there was considerable unease within the party—an unease evident at the SFIO's national congress in Lille in the summer at which several speakers voiced concern about the wisdom of attempts to suppress the FLN by military means. Nevertheless, the final resolution, endorsed by the SFIO leadership, received 90 per cent of the votes. The result, as a German embassy report noted, represented an 'overwhelming victory' for Mollet.[118] In many ways, his victory rested on a consensus behind a policy of combating extremism on both sides (the FLN and among the European population) and, more ambitiously, of forging a third way between continued colonial domination on the one hand and national independence on the other. At the same time, the speeches at the Lille conference indicated that the stakes involved went beyond the future of Algeria to include the meaning of socialism—and of socialist internationalism. For almost all speakers, an underlying question was whether the Mollet government's policies were consistent with socialist principles. And this was a question for all socialists and not just the French.

By the end of 1956, Mollet's carefully crafted consensus on Algeria began to unravel. Mounting evidence of massive violence (and torture), together with the Suez fiasco, stoked critiques of the government's policies from French socialists. Significantly, moreover, the critics often pointed to the SFIO's isolation within the International. In an article in December 1956, Marceau Pivert urged socialist militants to denounce the government's Algerian policy, whose nationalism and militarism betrayed international socialist principles. The previous month, Pivert had signed a collective letter from prominent French socialists to Pierre Commin that criticized the Mollet government's Middle Eastern and Algerian policies. In demanding a change of policy in Algeria, the signatories affirmed 'our solidarity with the majority of foreign socialist parties and particularly that of Britain'. Copies were sent to the International and to the European socialist parties. Soon afterwards, in an open letter addressed to 'comrades', Pivert contended that only a

---

[117] IISH, SI, 87, 'Report of the Fifth Congress of the Socialist International', Bevan, 53–60; and 'Resolution on Algeria', 150. For Labour, see IEV, Papiers Max Buset, 89, J, Bracops to Buset, 16 July 1957.

[118] PAAP, B 24/262, Paris embassy to AA, no. 2733/56, 2 July 1956. For the conference, see OURS, SFIO, '48ème congrès ordinaire des 28, 29, 30 juin et 1er juillet 1956'.

'European revolutionary and socialist left' could save the SFIO's 'soul', and pointed to 'Bevanism' in Britain as proof that the building blocks for such a left existed.[119]

Mollet could ignore Pivert, a gadfly on the SFIO's left. But it was harder to disregard another signatory of the collective letter, André Philip, a party stalwart. Although Philip had long been troubled by the government's repressive methods in Algeria, the Suez crisis propelled him into open conflict with Mollet. When the latter sought to sanction him, Philip refused to be silenced. In a declaration to the party's executive in December 1956, he castigated the Mollet government and the SFIO for sacrificing socialist internationalism to a 'pre-fascist, jingoist nationalism' and for 'losing the confidence of European socialist parties'. It was not the SFIO, he defiantly concluded, but a minority within it 'that remains loyal to socialist traditions in solidarity with the great majority of parties in the International. In censuring me you are censuring the workers' International.' In a further provocation, Philip published the declaration shortly thereafter.[120] Meanwhile, in January 1957, Philip and other SFIO dissidents formed a *Comité socialiste d'étude et d'action pour la paix en Algérie*, which consistently invoked the International in its claim that the SFIO leadership had abandoned socialism.[121] That Mollet perceived the nexus of external and internal party criticism as a threat is apparent from his growing frustration with the International and with Labour in particular. Speaking to French socialists in December 1956, he insisted that Labourites were not true socialists but religious zealots. In terms of socialist internationalism, Mollet added bitterly, 'there is nothing, and the little that there is notably impoverished. It is religion that guides them.' The same month, Pontillon, Mollet's deputy, warned that Labour's criticism jeopardized the future of the International, which could operate only on the basis of solidarity between its member parties.[122]

THE SFIO, ALGERIA, AND SOCIALIST INTERNATIONALISM

Frustrated sarcasm would not disarm Mollet's critics within the SFIO. More was needed, and scholars have highlighted the internal disciplinary methods employed by Mollet and his allies: the centralization of power around the position of secretary general; a de facto censorship of party publications; and the threat of disciplinary sanctions. What Pivert denounced as a 'Stalinist conception of discipline' failed to stifle criticism.[123] And so Mollet sought to mobilize international socialism

---

[119] OURS, Fonds Charles Lancelle, 13 APO/1, 'Les Fossoyeurs', Pivert, undated but December 1956; FNSP, Fonds Cletta et Daniel Mayer, 1MA 17.1, collective letter to Commin, 24 November 1956; and CHS, Fonds Marceau Pivert, 559/AP/16, 'Lettre aux camarades', April 1957.

[120] AN, Papiers André Philip, 625/AP/12, 'Déclaration', 19 December 1956, emphasis in original; and Philip, *Le socialisme trahi*, 219–26.

[121] For the Comité, see the file in FNSP, Fonds Alain Savary, SV 1.

[122] OURS, SFIO, 'Conseil national des 15 et 16 décembre 1956. Puteaux', Mollet, 235; and OURS, D5 41 BD, 'Note sur la réunion du Conseil de l'Internationale à Copenhague'.

[123] For the measures, see Lafon, *Guy Mollet*, 535–52, 634–46. For Pivert, see CHS, Fonds Marceau Pivert, 559/AP/16, Pivert letter to several French socialists, 12 February 1958.

behind his government. One way he did so was through appeals to international socialist solidarity in the hope of restraining pressure from other parties—pressure that the SFIO's internal critics continued to exploit to undermine Mollet. During the Suez crisis, for example, Mollet wrote to Gaitskell explaining that the SFIO had studiously refrained from publicly criticizing Labour when it was in government and that 'simple courtesy' and 'solidarity between socialists' justified the SFIO in expecting the same. Similarly, Mollet complained to Ollenhauer of attacks on the SFIO by SPD members, arguing that they weakened both the SFIO and international socialism.[124] Interestingly, Mollet's appeals had some effect, a point that testifies to the bonds of mutual obligations and expectations between socialist parties. As Gaitskell informed a particularly vocal Labour critic in September 1956, 'I think it is not unreasonable of Mollet to ask that leading speakers of the Labour Party in Britain should bear in mind the existence of a Socialist Government in France.'[125]

Direct appeals to other socialist parties, however, were a wasting asset. As opposition to the Mollet government's policies mounted, Labour and SPD leaders became less willing (and able) to preach moderation to their members. Mollet, in any case, wanted something more ambitious: the International's official endorsement of his Algerian policy. And, here, the SFIO's leader seized on the decision taken at the Vienna congress to send a fact-finding mission to Algeria. In his study of the commission, Jean-Paul Cahn judged it a success for Mollet; but this overlooks the commission's effects on other parties, particularly Labour and the SPD.[126] Immediately following the Vienna Congress, Alsing Andersen, the Danish socialist and International President, wrote to the British, French, and German parties suggesting that the SFIO be asked to establish the commission's scope and mandate. The suggestion provoked a sharp response from Labour's international secretary, who pointed out to Gaitskell that the French 'are automatically disqualified [from participating] as an interested party'. Gaitskell concurred, prompting a lengthy discussion at the meeting of the International's bureau in October 1957.[127] The result was the creation of a 'small commission' consisting of a British, Danish, and Belgian member to undertake 'an objective and constructive investigation'. The ASC was also invited to participate but could not for reasons of time and money. The commission's make-up worried SFIO leaders: while confident that they could count on Belgian support, they doubted that of the British and Danish parties. Nevertheless, the SFIO's international secretary reassured sceptics that the

[124] UCL, Hugh Gaitskell Papers, C 310, Mollet to Gaitskell, 3 September 1956; and OURS, Archives Guy Mollet, AFM 58, draft letter to Ollenhauer, undated.

[125] UCL, Hugh Gaitskell Papers, C 310, Gaitskell to John Strachey, 5 September 1956.

[126] Jean-Paul Cahn, 'Die SPD und der Bericht der Internationalen Sozialistischen Algerien-Untersuchungskommission (1957–1958). Einige Bermerkungen über die internationale sozialistische Fact-Finding-Mission', *Internationale wissenschaftliche Korrespondenz zur Geschichte der deutschen Arbeiterbewegung* 32 (1996), 172–203.

[127] IISH, SI, 507, Andersen (SI) to Labour, SFIO, and SPD, 20 July 1957; LHASC, LPA, Morgan Phillips Papers, Correspondence with Socialist International 1951–61, Ericsson (International Department) to Gaitskell, 26 July 1957; and Gaitskell's response, same date.

International could be trusted to 'take into account' [*ménager*] French socialists and to maintain a 'certain equilibrium' between Labour, the SPD, and the SFIO.[128]

Having spent two weeks in Algeria in November and December 1957, the commission members returned divided in their analyses. If the Belgian Jules Barry basically endorsed the SFIO's position, placing the burden of responsibility on the FLN's 'intransigence', Sam Watson, the Labour member, concluded that it was unwise for the French to reject the principle of national self-determination for Algeria, while the Norwegian John Sanness warned against excluding the FLN from any future negotiations—a point the ASC predictably echoed. The ensuing report studiously avoided a clear-cut position, preferring to compromise: in addition to rejecting military pacification as an enduring solution, the report called for a negotiated end to the war and expressed the desire to avoid a complete 'rupture' between France and Algeria. The unsatisfactory nature of the compromise was evident from the attached rider, which stated that it did not reflect the 'unanimous agreement' of the commission's members. At the International bureau meeting in February 1958, a tense discussion occurred over whether to publish the report, with the vast majority voting to defer a decision to an upcoming meeting of the International's council.[129] Although the report was meant to remain confidential, soon afterwards several French and British newspapers, including the Bevanites' *Tribune*, leaked details of the meeting, creating the impression that its non-publication was due to criticism of Mollet's policy. Furious at this 'indiscretion', Mollet demanded that the International publish the full report as well as the conclusions. Andersen, however, refused to do so unless the 'observations' of the commission's three members were included.[130]

Deft politician that he was, Mollet exploited the situation to his advantage. At the SFIO's national council in March 1958, he claimed that the report was not published because it reflected the SFIO's position, particularly its refusal to negotiate with the FLN. Mollet attributed the confusion to intrigues by Bevan, who supposedly had prodded an ally to draft a report that was 'a bit hard' on the SFIO, only to have the three commission members append a conclusion that 'validated the cause of France and of the SFIO'. So thwarted, Bevan then persuaded the bureau members to keep the report and its conclusions under wraps. Significantly, Mollet framed the affair in terms of loyalty towards socialist internationalism. Unlike Bevan, who had no notion of 'fair play', Mollet told his audience that he could not divulge the precise contents of the report's conclusions because he had given his word at the bureau meeting. But in Mollet's telling, the intrigues extended beyond Bevan. The International, he warned, would eventually produce conclusions

[128] Labour Party, NEC minutes, fiche 608, 'Report on Meeting of the Socialist International Bureau…10 and 11 October 1957'; and OURS, Archives Guy Mollet, AGM 54, Pontillon to Lacoste, 23 October 1957.

[129] For the report's conclusions, see OURS, Fonds Maurice Deixonne, 1 APO/44, 'Rapport de la Mission d'information en Algérie, au Congrès de l'Internationale socialiste. Conclusions', 17 January 1945; and for the members' views, see IISH, SI, 91, 'Report of the Fact-Finding Mission to Algeria. Note of Statement', SI circular, B.13/58, 10 February 1958.

[130] OURS, Archives Guy Mollet, AGM 54, Mollet to Andersen, 24 February 1948; and Andersen to Mollet, 19 March 1958.

drafted by socialists who had never been to Algeria—conclusions, he added sardonically, that it would hasten to publish. Outraged by this account, Mollet's supporters and critics united to demand that the International publish the mission's conclusions. With good reason, a British Foreign Office report marvelled at Mollet's success in 'turning an apparent political set-back to his own advantage'.[131]

If Mollet's account of events convinced the majority of French socialists, European socialists proved to be another matter. The commission's report was meant to serve as the basis for a resolution on Algeria for the International, and a small committee dominated by Labour and the SPD was charged with crafting a statement. Taking the lead, Morgan Phillips circulated a draft in February 1958 that, while favouring a 'durable working partnership' between the Europeans and Muslim communities in Algeria, urged negotiations with all parties without pre-conditions, mentioning in particular those that 'imply capitulation in advance'— i.e. the FLN's military defeat. Going further, it insisted that all possibilities must be considered, including Algeria's integration with France but also its 'self-determin-ation'. Interestingly, the SPD was unhappy with Phillips' draft, with Fritz Heine, Ollenhauer's deputy, remarking that many German socialists wanted the 'disap-proval of France to receive clearer expression'.[132] Phillips accordingly added a statement condemning 'all acts of torture, terrorism, intimidation and suppression of civil liberties in Algeria'. Unhappy with developments, Mollet told the SFIO's directing committee on the eve of the International's meeting in April 1958 that he expected a 'real battle' over Algeria. At the meeting, the SFIO delegation, led by Mollet, grudgingly accepted the resolution, well aware of its isolation among European socialists. A well-informed British Foreign Office report underscored the significance of the result. 'It is true that the magic word "independence" does not feature in the resolution', it noted, 'but acceptance of the phrase "self-determination for Algeria" as a possibility which must not be excluded is quite a significant step.'[133]

Less than two months after the meeting, events in Algeria and France risked undoing the International's recently forged consensus on Algeria. Following a military coup in Algiers in mid-May, Charles De Gaulle returned to power with the declared purpose not only of ending the crisis but also of ushering in a new republican regime. The question of how to respond deeply divided French socialists, with forty-nine deputies (including Mollet) voting in favour of De Gaulle's investiture and forty-two against. European socialists closely followed these developments, expressing considerable sympathy for the SFIO. The latter, a Labour analysis asserted, 'was faced with an incredible human drama in having to make such a choice in such circumstances'.[134] Importantly, however, this sympathy did not translate into a willingness to reconsider the International's emerging support for Algeria's

---

[131] OURS, SFIO, 'Conseil national des 15 et 16 mars 1958', Mollet, 176–80; and TNA PRO 371/131701, James Murray (Paris embassy) to J.H.A. Watson (FO), 24 March 1958.

[132] OURS, Archives Guy Mollet, AGM 54, 'Draft Resolution on Algeria', Phillips, 25 February 1958; and IISH, SI, 506, Heine (SPD) to Albert Carthy (SI), 11 March 1958.

[133] OURS, APS, Comité directeur, 23 April 1958; and TNA PRO 371/131701, J.G.S. Beith (French embassy) to Watson (FO), 3 May 1958, which includes the text of the resolution on Algeria.

[134] Labour Party, NEC minutes, fiche 631, 'Report on the French Crisis', June 1958.

national independence—a point the SPD's position illustrates. Worried about developments, Ollenhauer sought to 'postpone' an SPD resolution on Algeria. At the SPD's annual congress in May 1958, however, the majority of participants refused to do so. Faced with demands for a statement in favour of Algeria's national rights, Ollenhauer gave way, presenting the Algerian War as an anti-colonial conflict and announcing the SPD's support for the 'self-determination and self-government of the Algerian people'.[135] Clearly, Mollet could not count on international socialist support in his efforts to prevent Algerian independence.

THE SFIO, MINORITY RIGHTS, AND *EURAFRIQUE*

Over the next few years, events moved rapidly in France and Algeria. For outside observers, French socialists often appeared as passive actors, swept along by the winds of change. But this appearance was misleading. Led by Mollet, the SFIO sought to frame the future of Algeria and of Franco-Algerian relations in terms of minority rights, a framework that had implications for the response of socialists (both French and non-French) to decolonization. No less importantly, Mollet employed this framework with both French and foreign audiences in mind.

To be sure, the interest in minority rights was not entirely new. In 1957, Mollet announced to French socialists that in Algeria, 'national rights cannot be of a kind to bully [*brimer*] the rights of minorities.'[136] Beginning in 1958, however, the SFIO's concern for minority rights became a preoccupation, a change that needs to be seen in the context of the growing interest in Algerian independence among French and other socialists. In a book published in 1958, Mollet criticized the very right to national self-determination, equating it with an 'integral nationalism' that contradicted the 'spirit of the times'—a spirit working to 'blur national sovereignties' and to foster 'interdependence between nations'. The pressing task for socialists became '*to make it unnecessary for dependent peoples to go through a nationalise phase*'. These people, Mollet explained, must be made to understand that their 'desire for emancipation and their will to be free' could be satisfied 'without giving way to the reactionary isolation and turning inwards that characterizes nationalism'. Significantly, in emphasizing the dangers of national self-determination, Mollet pointed to its monolithic tendency to ignore the rights of minority groups.[137] The SFIO leader returned to the subject of minority rights at the SFIO's congress in September 1958. In response to French socialists who invoked the International's support for Algerian national self-determination, Mollet maintained that national rights could not be separated from minority rights. In a future Algeria, the majority

[135] FES, AdsD, Parteivorstand Protokolle, 'Sitzung des Parteivorstandes am 16.5.1958 in Stuttgart'; and SPD, *Protokoll der Verhandlungen des Parteitages der Sozialdemokratischen Partei Deutschlands vom 18. bis 23. Mai 1958 in Stuttgart* (Bonn, 1958), Ollenhauer, 44–5, 84. Also see Jean-Paul Cahn, 'Le Parti social-démocrate allemand face à la Guerre d'Algérie (1958–1962)', *Revue d'Allemagne* 31 (1999), 589–602.

[136] OURS, Archives Guy Mollet, AGM 54, 'Déclaration de Guy Mollet au cours de l'entretien avec le Bureau de la SFIO…', undated but 1957.

[137] Mollet, *Bilan et perspectives socialistes* (Paris, 1958), 44–6. Emphasis in original.

must 'respect the fundamental rights of individuals making up the minority'. Going further, Mollet presented the 'desire to protect individuals of European origin' as the principal stake in the conflict, one he described as 'an absolutely dramatic problem' that 'complicated the positions of all concerned'.[138]

In highlighting minority rights, Mollet admitted that reconciling such rights with majoritarian democracy would not be easy. As a result, during 1957, the SFIO considered the partition of Algeria along communitarian lines or what one advocate called an 'Israeli-type solution'.[139] But partition was never a viable option, as Algerian nationalists would reject it out of hand. Soon afterwards, Mollet dismissed integration, another possibility and one that French socialists had promoted in the immediate post-war years in the context of the *Union française*, as no longer feasible because it would almost certainly mean the European minority's absorption by the Muslim majority. With partition and integration off the table, Mollet began to envisage a federal arrangement for Algeria in which the European and Muslim communities would coexist. Federalism, of course, was in the air: in 1956 Gaston Defferre, the socialist Minister of the colonies, had introduced the *loi-cadre*, a legal framework for francophone Africa that combined a devolution of power to local assemblies (*territorialisation*) with federalism among the various territories. In November 1957, the French national assembly passed a specific *loi-cadre* for Algeria that foresaw the creation of separate political assemblies (*Conseils des communautés*) for Europeans and Muslims.[140] Equally pertinent, France was expected to play the role of guarantor of both the European minority and the Muslim majority. In order to 'guarantee the rights of minorities' and to safeguard the country's 'Algerian personality' [its Muslim majoritarian character], Mollet argued in September 1959, it was imperative 'that all interested parties accept that their ties to metropolitan France should not be broken'.[141]

Mollet's argument for the maintenance of formal political ties between France and Algeria was vulnerable to the accusation that it amounted to a stratagem to preserve l'*Algérie française*. Not surprisingly, Asian socialists accused French (and European) socialists of precisely this aim. So too did some French socialists. In a letter to the International in June 1958, Oreste Rosenfeld, a former SFIO executive member, insisted that Mollet's position on national self-determination for Algeria violated the 'elementary principles of socialism': to contend that nationalism was obsolete amounted to a 'neo-colonialist doctrine'.[142] To counter such charges Mollet wrapped his vision of permanent Franco-Algerian ties in a larger European-African package—*Eurafrique*. Much of the scholarship on *Eurafrique* focuses on the

---

[138] OURS, SFIO, '50ème congrès national des 11, 12, 13 et 14 septembre 1958. Issy-les-Moulineaux', Mollet, 45, 309.

[139] OURS, Fonds Etienne Weill-Raynal, 40 APO/1-2, Weill-Raynal to Mollet, which includes 'Note sur la question algérienne', 3 September 1957.

[140] See Cooper, *Citizenship between Empire and Nation*, 226–46; Tony Chafer, *The End of Empire in French West Africa: France's Successful Decolonization?* (Oxford, 2002), 163–92; and Evans, *Algeria*, 222–3.

[141] OURS, SFIO, '50ème congrès national des 11, 12, 13 et 14 septembre 1958', Mollet, 244.

[142] IISH, SI, 513, Wijono (ASC) to Carthy (SI), 25 May 1959; and AdsD, NL Günther Markscheffel, 8, Rosenfeld to Socialist International, 7 June 1958.

negotiations for the Rome Treaties of 1956–1957 during which the Mollet government demanded the French Empire's association with the EEC. The goals were to 'Europeanize' the burden of colonial development, which France alone could not afford, and, more fundamentally, to preclude a choice between Europe and empire.[143] Yet Mollet continued to speak of *Eurafrique* well after the Rome Treaties, describing it in July 1959, for example, as an 'urgent necessity'.[144] This enduring interest in *Eurafrique* reflected the need to convince French and non-French socialists that *France-Algérie*—and the protection of minority rights it promised—was not designed to perpetuate French colonial rule or the dominance of the European settler community. Instead, talk of *Eurafrique* allowed Algeria's future to be enfolded into a more ambitious vision not only of peaceful coexistence between ethnic groups, but also of a world in which nationalism was tamed, national sovereignty blurred, and the nation state replaced by regional and transregional associations. For Mollet, as for many Western European socialists, the ongoing process of European integration provided proof that this vision was not utopian.

Towards the end of the 1950s, Mollet's SFIO emerged as a vocal advocate of minority rights. If this advocacy was inextricably connected to the Algerian War and the need to find a solution acceptable to all the parties involved, French socialists presented their proposals as an alternative to national self-determination not just for Algeria but for the postcolonial international order in general. The future, they insisted, lay with larger transnational groupings and not with the proliferation of nation states. To be sure, French socialists were not alone. In 1953, the British academic Max Beloff observed that proponents of 'federal solutions' could be found not just in Europe but also in Africa and Asia. More recently, Michael Williams has proposed viewing the 1950s as a 'federal moment' in international politics marked by a widespread interest in federations as 'alternatives to imperial rule that resisted the logic of sovereign states on national lines'.[145] But if the search for alternatives to the independent nation state was a popular activity during the 1950s, the SFIO's fusion of *France-Algérie*, *Eurafrique*, and minority protection appears to have been unique. More pertinently to this chapter, in positing a conflict between national and minority rights, the SFIO prodded European socialists to look for ways to reconcile the two. In doing so, British, French, and German socialists would come up with different solutions.

THE ASC'S DECLINE

Following its second congress, held in Bombay in November 1956 and attended by a high-level delegation from the Socialist International led by Ollenhauer, the

---

[143] In addition to the studies cited in fn 6, see Louis Sicking, 'A Colonial Echo: France and the Colonial Dimension of the European Economic Community', *French Colonial History* 5 (2004), 207–28; and Rik Schreurs, 'L'Eurafrique dans les négociations du Traité de Rome, 1956–1957', *Politique africaine* 49 (1993), 82–92.

[144] OURS, SFIO, '51ème Congrès national des 9 au 12 juillet 1959', Mollet, 292.

[145] Max Beloff, 'The "Federal Solution" in its Application to Europe, Asia, and Africa', *Political Studies* 1 (1953), 114–31; and Michael, 'Decolonisation and the "Federal Moment"'.

ASC began to lose steam. Its propaganda efforts, for example, notably declined, reducing the ASC's visibility. Despite these signs of weakness, European socialists remained committed to expanding the International into Asia, and the immediate result was a renewed effort to improve relations with Asian socialists. At the meeting of the International's council in June 1958, the Israeli socialist Reuven Barkatt reported that 'there can be little doubt that the Socialist movement in Asia is in the throes of a serious crisis' marked by the individual and collective weaknesses of its member parties. At the same time, Barkatt claimed to detect a 'radical change' in the ASC's position towards European socialists. Although still staunchly anti-colonialist, the ASC's 'lack of trust, bordering on subconscious hostility, which existed towards the Socialist International is disappearing'. Barkatt attributed this change to two factors: a growing awareness among Asian socialists of the dangers of communism; and the growing belief 'that the European Socialist movement could be of real help to them in solving their own problems'. Urging European socialists to seize the opportunity, Barkatt recommended several measures to encourage closer cooperation between the ASC and the International, including more frequent meetings, financial help, joint study groups, and a combined publicity effort.[146] Several months later, the International's secretary wrote the ASC's secretary and vice-chairman expressing the 'International's earnest desire to develop and to extend to the fullest possible extent co-operation between the two organisations and between their respective member parties'.[147]

Over the next two years, little of Barkatt's ambitious list of recommendations would be realized. One problem was money. As Barkatt was well placed to know, the ASC lacked reliable funding and was in constant deficit. Its earlier publicity campaign relied heavily on subsidies, some of which came from European socialist parties; any new effort would require the same. The International, however, functioned on a shoestring budget. The ASC's own financial problems, in turn, exposed its organizational weaknesses. 'I could hardly venture to say that that organisation [ASC] exists in practice today', Barkatt admitted to Arthur Carthy, the International's secretary, adding that he 'did not know if it could be party to any negotiations [with the International]'.[148] In fact, by the end of the 1950s, the ASC appeared to be little more than a post office box, dependent on the activities of a two-person secretariat comprising U Hla Aung (Burma) and Wijono (Indonesia). Although Wijono managed to keep up a regular correspondence with Carthy over the next two years, the ASC as an organization became a shadow of its former self, even if a handful of Asian socialists continued to attend International meetings in its name.[149]

---

[146] IISH, Hein Vos Papers, 44, 'Minutes of the Meeting of the Council of the Socialist International. Brussels, 12–14 June, 1958', Barkatt, 20–4; and OURS, APS, Carton: Circulaires I.S. 1951–1958, 'Summary of Report by Reuven Barkatt of Meeting of Asian Socialist Conference Bureau', SI circular, no. B 25/58, 28 April 1958.

[147] IISH, SI, 513, Carthy (SI) to U Hla Aung and Wijono, 7 November 1958.

[148] IISH, SI, 513, Barkatt to Carthy (SI), 26 October 1958.

[149] For the two-man secretariat, see ibid., Aung to Carthy, 4 January 1959. For the ASC's decline, see Rose, *Socialism in Southern Asia*, 245–66.

The ASC's organizational (and financial) weakness stemmed from several factors. A prominent one was divisions within its member parties. Both the Indian and Burmese parties, two pillars of the ASC, suffered from schisms and splits during the 1950s, reducing the influence of both. Another factor consisted of ongoing disputes between member parties, whether on specific local issues (between Indian and Pakistani socialists on the future of Kashmir), or on more general issues, such as Cold War alignments and the role of Asian socialism as an international third force. But these disputes highlighted a more basic factor: the national rootedness of Asian parties. Notwithstanding their internationalist pretensions, Asian socialists proved susceptible to the pull of national politics. In a speech in August 1958, the celebrated Indian socialist Rammanohar Lohia contended that the International was merely a 'composite body of national socialisms' and that, sadly, Asian socialists were imitating their European counterparts in this regard:

> One might have expected Asian socialists to pursue the straight and revolutionary line in regard to native as well as foreign affairs, to persevere in the midst of seeming defeats and not to lose the soul in the search of expediency and office. They did not have to carry burdens of imperialist privilege. Nor were they like the tired third-general social-ists of Europe. And yet they proved to be worse than the socialists of Europe, than even the neat nationalists and conservatives of their own lands.[150]

Interestingly, the sole exception to the nationalist curse that Lohia identified among European socialists was Marceau Pivert, who by then had been marginal-ized within the SFIO. In a world in which the number of nation states was rapidly increasing due to decolonization, Lohia arguably posited an unattainable ideal of socialist internationalism. After all, as Asoka Mehta, another Indian socialist, plausibly contended, the pressing problem for socialists was to reconcile socialism and nationalism. And, as Mehta avowed, it was a problem that 'remained to a con-siderable extent unresolved'—for both Asian and European socialists.[151]

But whatever the explanation for the difficulties of Asian socialism, the ASC's decline meant that European socialists would debate the relative importance of national versus minority rights largely among themselves, without an organized non-European interlocutor. From the beginning, Asian socialists had insisted that European socialists accord national rights the absolute priority. The ASC's waning voice helped to create space for alternative conceptions.

FRENCH SOCIALISTS AND MINORITY RIGHTS

Mollet and the SFIO continued to privilege minority rights over national rights. This preference manifested itself in the ongoing interest for some form of perman-ent political-constitutional link between France and Algeria. In June 1959, Max Lejeune, a Mollet ally, told the SFIO's parliamentary group that France must avoid

---

[150] 'Inanity of World Socialism' (August 1958), reproduced in Rammanohar Lohia, *Notes and Comments*, vol. 1 (Hyderabad, 1972), 163–5.
[151] Asoka Mehta, *Studies in Asian Socialism* (Bombay, 1959), 47–8.

any solution to the Algerian War that 'leads ever so gently towards independence'. Needed instead was a 'statute' that would allow Algeria to be integrated into France. At the SFIO's congress the following year, Mollet elaborated on Lejeune's point, contending that a negotiated end to the war should be based on 'self-determination' (and not independence) for Algeria as well as on an 'internal federal structure' with 'guarantees for the rights of ethnic communities and individuals'. An 'associative accord' with France would provide assurances that the Algerian government actively protected these rights.[152] Mollet's talk of association was not fortuitous. The constitution of the newly minted Fifth Republic provided for the creation of a *Communauté française*, a political-constitutional structure between France and its empire freely accepted by each of its members and that ruled out national independence. While it is unclear whether De Gaulle believed Algeria could be fitted into this community, Mollet and the SFIO clearly hoped that it offered a means to preserve French-Algerian ties—and thus to safeguard the European minority. The community, loftily declared André Bidet, 'unites in equality the former colonized and their colonizers, creating between them a solidarity equally beneficial to all'. More prosaically, Mollet insisted that De Gaulle and the community represented the sole means of preventing a 'blood bath' in Algeria.[153]

In privileging minority over national rights, the SFIO faced renewed pressure from European socialists. In July 1959, Gaitskell privately commented that since the Suez crisis 'French socialists have been the odd man out in the Socialist International'.[154] The International's congress the same month indicated that the SFIO's position on Algeria and national self-determination more generally explained much of this ostracism. At the congress, several participants criticized French socialists on this score, including the SPD's Carlo Schmid, a long-time proponent of Franco-German rapprochement. Socialists, Schmid pointedly pleaded, cannot allow themselves to become 'co-responsible for putting the brakes on the "universal and inevitable" process of emancipation of people under [foreign] control'. Although the SFIO's delegation succeeded in excluding mention of Algeria from the resulting resolution, the latter nevertheless expressed socialist support for the 'rapid achievement of emancipation and genuine independence' for all peoples.[155]

The SFIO's success, however, proved fleeting. At the international socialist conference in April 1960 in Haifa, Israel, the first such meeting held outside of Europe, the majority of participants were determined to extract a clear-cut statement on Algerian independence. Before the conference the SFIO had circulated a statement emphasizing the need for guarantees to be attached to Algeria's exercise

---

[152] FNSP, GPS, GS 11, 4 June 1959, Lejeune; and OURS, SFIO, '52ème Congrès national des 30 juin, 1er, 2 et 3 juillet 1959. Issy-les-Moulineaux', Mollet, 252–60.

[153] Bidet, 'Fédération ou Confédération? Pour un effort d'imagination', *Revue socialiste* 127 (November 1959), 561; and OURS, SFIO, 'Conseil national des 10 et 11 janvier 1959. Puteaux', Mollet, 60.

[154] BLPES, Hector Alastair Hetherington Papers, 1/8, 'Note of Meeting with Mr Gaitskell on July 23, 1959'.

[155] See the report in MAE, EU-Europe 1956–1960, 224, Hamburg (Conseil Général) to MAE, no. 272, 16 July 1959; and IISH, SI, 249, 'Resolution on General Problems', July 1959.

of self-determination—guarantees designed to protect the existence of the European and Muslim communities. At the conference itself, however, the SFIO's position received almost no support.[156] The Labour delegation submitted its own draft resolution on Algeria that urged the SFIO to accept immediate negotiations with 'Algerian nationalists' (the FLN) for a peace founded on 'the full application of the principle of self-determination'. Significantly, the final resolution went even further, implicitly placing national rights over minority rights: the International, it read, believes 'in the right of all people to self-determination and to equal rights, on the basis of "one man, one vote"'. On Algeria in particular, the resolution declared that the application of this principle was 'long over-due'.[157] Afterwards, Labour officials continued to press Mollet on Algeria, making it clear that their party would not accept any backsliding on the SFIO's part. With Labour's firm backing, at the International's congress in Rome in October 1961 the delegates reconfirmed the position taken at the Haifa conference.[158]

The SFIO also faced growing pressure from dissident French socialists. Increasingly frustrated with Mollet's leadership, in September 1958 a group of prominent French socialists, many of whom belonged to the *Comité socialiste d'étude et d'action pour la paix en Algérie*, founded a breakaway party, the *Parti socialiste autonome* (PSA). From the outset, moreover, the new party appealed to international socialism for support. The PSA, Edouard Depreux, the party's chairman, declared at its opening congress, 'does not want to limit itself to socialism in one country . . . We cannot work for peace without contact with other socialist parties who everywhere wage the same struggle.'[159] The PSA immediately set out to woo the International. In a letter to European socialist parties in 1959, Vincent Auriol, a former Fourth Republic president, condemned Mollet's SFIO for having 'compromised the future of socialism'. Invoking his past activities as a socialist internationalist, Auriol claimed that the International had a duty to admit the PSA as a member as it alone reflected the true face of international socialism in France. Depreux, meanwhile, worked assiduously to cultivate contacts with other parties. In interviews in *Tribune* and *Vorwärts* in the spring of 1959, for example, he assured British and German readers that the PSA, unlike the SFIO, aligned itself with the principles of socialist internationalism.[160]

The SFIO rightly perceived the PSA's internationalist claims as a potential threat that must be opposed. Denouncing the PSA for its 'crypto-communist orienta-tion', Mollet in June 1959 wrote to Gaitskell asking that Labour not receive Depreux and another PSA member who were in Britain. Although Gaitskell agreed,

---

[156] 'French Socialist Policy in Algeria' in IISH, *Socialist International Information* vol. X, no. 12, 19 March 1960, 175–6.

[157] LHASC, LPA, International Sub-Committee, 1960 file, 'Draft Resolution on Algeria', April 1960; and 'Report of the Conference of the Socialist International, Haifa, April 1960'.

[158] See UCL, Hugh Gaitskell Papers, C. 293.1, David Ennals (International Department) to Gaitskell, 16 November 1960; and HAEU, GSPE, 'Algeria', 1961.

[159] AN, Parti socialiste unifié, 581/AP/1/5, Montrouge congrès, 1 May 1959, Depreux.

[160] LHASC, LPA, International Department, LP/ID/FRA/5, Auriol letter, undated but July 1959. For Depreux, see 'French Socialism is not Dead says Edouard Depreux', *Tribune*, 5 June 1959, 5; and 'Depreux vertraut auf die Einheit', *Vorwärts*, 20 April 1959, 9.

he could not prevent Labour's parliamentary party from meeting with them. As the meeting suggests (and as PSA leaders recognized), the new party aroused considerable interest among European socialists.[161] Both Labour and the SPD sent observers to the PSA's founding congress in 1959. In his report, David Ennals, Labour's international secretary, lauded the 'excellent spirit throughout the congress' and stressed in particular the strong presence of young socialists—a presence apparently absent at SFIO gatherings. Similarly, Heinz Putzrath, Ennals' equivalent in the SPD, confided in December 1959 that the PSA contained 'long-time and genuine social democrats' and that 'there is much that ties us to this party'. Much of this sympathy, moreover, stemmed from the PSA's more flexible position on Algeria and on national independence in general. As European socialists were well aware, the PSA (unlike the SFIO) strongly denounced French atrocities in Algeria, most notably the use of torture, demanded immediate negotiations with the FLN, and recognized what it called Algeria's 'national vocation'. More generally, the PSA repeatedly proclaimed its attachment to the 'right to national independence and to the free self-determination of all peoples and in particular to "colonized" peoples'.[162] In a book published in 1960, Depreux invoked Bevan's criticisms of Mollet in castigating as anti-socialist the argument that the Algerians (and all colonial people) should follow Europeans in rejecting nationalism and the nation state. 'Overly deft casuists', Depreux scornfully remarked, 'tell us that one can skip the national phase...and pass directly from colonialism to membership in a [larger] community.' For Depreux and the PSA, the latter were conceivable only after and not before Algeria had achieved national independence.[163]

Interestingly, in sympathizing with the PSA/PSU British and German socialists overlooked the reservations that Depreux and his allies attached to Algeria's right to national self-determination. At first, most PSA supporters hoped to avoid an independent Algeria. As Alain Savary, a PSA founder, had admitted to Mollet in 1957, he favoured Algerian independence but not the 'exercise of this right for as long a period as possible'.[164] Animating Savary's comment was a concern for Algeria's European community: its preservation would be difficult in an independent Algeria. For this reason, the PSA, like the SFIO, spoke initially of the need to protect minority rights in a future Algeria. This need led André Philip, another SFIO exile and PSA founder, to conceive of Algeria's future much as Mollet did. As late as 1960, Philip envisaged the 'integration...of *the two communities that together constitute the Algerian homeland*', with France acting as the '*arbitrator* ensuring that the legitimate interests of each one are equally safeguarded'. But if this vision resembled Mollet's, it was also one that the majority of PSA leaders realized had been overtaken by events. As Depreux conceded, such conceptions were only

[161] UCL, Hugh Gaitskell Papers, F 21.12, Mollet to Gaitskell, 19 June 1959; and Ennals (International Department) to Gaitskell, 26 June 1959. For the PSA's assessment, see AN, Parti socialiste unifié, 581/AP/1/5, 'Réunion de la Commission administrative permanente élargie aux responsables des fédérations au samedi 13 Décembre 1959. Résumé des débats'.

[162] AN, Parti socialiste unifié, 581/AP/1/5, 'Préambule', 1959.

[163] Depreux, *Renouvellement du socialisme* (Paris, 1960), 129.

[164] OURS, Archives Guy Mollet, AGM 82, Savary to Mollet, 20 January 1957.

possible if Algerians agreed—and by the time Philip wrote there was no chance of the FLN doing so.[165]

For Depreux and others, the pressing question was how to reconcile Algeria's national independence with the protection of minority rights. Their answer lay with human (individual) rights. Partly in reaction to the spiralling violence in Algeria and partly in an effort to distinguish itself from the SFIO's more doctrinaire Marxist rhetoric, the PSA highlighted the importance of the individual. Thus, in 1959, Philip claimed that 'socialism rests on the primacy of the human individual and the affirmation of his eminent dignity that is superior to all group interests and morals'.[166] But the interest in individual rights also needs to be seen as a third option between minority and national rights—and one compatible with Algeria's impending independence. In his speech at the PSA's 1959 congress, Depreux underscored the link between national and individual rights, insisting that '[national] independence needs to be viewed as something as sacred for nations as human rights are for the simple citizen'. The PSU's 1960 programme reiterated the point:

> [The PSU] declares its unequivocal support for the right of peoples to self-determination and independence—a right as sacred to nations as human rights are to citizens. It promises to support and promote all action aimed at respecting democracy and human rights and the complete emancipation of all people who remain colonized.[167]

Although embryonic, it is possible to detect in such statements a compromise between national and minority rights in which the members of a minority in post-colonial independent nation states possessed a right to protection as individuals. One advantage of this compromise was that it did not imply any limits on Algeria's national sovereignty, as a minority rights-centred approach appeared to do. One disadvantage was that the respect for individual (and, by extension, minority) rights would depend almost entirely on an independent Algeria.

Significantly, the SFIO also exhibited a growing interest in human rights for much the same reasons as the PSA. Here, moreover, Jules Moch and his *Groupe d'études doctrinales* (GED) played a key role. Best known for his activities in favour of disarmament, Moch, an ally of Mollet, felt increasingly uneasy about the course of the Algerian War: as early as October 1958 he privately admitted that Algeria would become independent. Repeating the prediction two years later, Moch argued that the best the French could hope for was to negotiate 'guarantees' for the Europeans in Algeria and for the Algerians in France. '[E]verything else', he added, 'was an illusion'.[168] Given the unlikelihood of attaining any such guarantees, Moch needed an alternative solution that might offer some safeguards, however fragile, to

---

[165] Philip, *Pour un socialisme humaniste* (Paris, 1960), 109. Emphasis in original.

[166] AN, Parti socialiste unifié, 581/AP/1/4, 'La sitiuation politique française', Philip, PSA circular no. 23, 17 April 1959.

[167] AN, Parti socialiste unifié, 581/AP/1/5, Depreux speech, Montrouge congress, 1 May 1959; and 'Éléments du programme du Parti socialiste unifié', 1960. Text available at: http://www.institut-tribune-socialiste.fr/wp-content/uploads/1960/04/60-CONGRES-PROGRAMME.pdf.

[168] AN, Papiers Jules Moch, 484/AP/35-1, minutes of GED meeting, 5 October 1958; and OURS, APS, Comité directeur, 16 November 1960.

the European community. This need helps to explain his activities as head of the GED, which the SFIO created in 1958 to modernize French socialist doctrine. In some ways, the GED belonged to a larger transformation of European socialism during the 1950s and 1960s away from Marxist and class-centred approaches to politics and towards a more reformist and inclusive politics. The emblematic case is that of the SPD, which in 1959 endorsed the Godesburg programme in which references to class struggle were notably absent.[169]

But the GED also needs to be placed in the context of the immediate dilemma facing French socialists—that of protecting minority rights in an independent Algeria. Under Moch's guidance, the GED undertook an extended enquiry into the question of national self-determination. After much debate, its members agreed that the SFIO must endorse this right for all peoples, even if some did so reluctantly. Once agreement was achieved on this principle the GED turned to the question of national sovereignty and, more precisely, to that of what if any limits could be placed on the internal exercise of authority by governments. All agreed that some limits were desirable. One member, Pierre Bonnal, insisted that socialists must propose 'a new conception of state sovereignty', though he recognized that this would not be easy as 'states are more and more numerous and jealous of their rights'. Bonnal expressed the hope that De Gaulle's *Communauté française* might provide a solution, but few of his collaborators were confident on this score. Some pointed to democracy as a possibility, suggesting that democratic institutions could restrain governments and thus protect Algeria's European minority. But this raised the question of how to ensure that postcolonial regimes would be or remain democratic in this sense. Gilbert Garcin, who drafted the GED's report on national self-determination, all but admitted that he had no answer in arguing that democracy could only function in nations with a homogenous population—a category that excluded Algeria.[170]

Faced with this impasse, Moch steered the GED towards an emphasis on individual rights. 'Socialism', he announced at the group's first meeting, 'is a doctrine that fosters the self-fulfillment of the individual.'[171] In summing up the lengthy debate on national self-determination, Georges Maleville, who was close to Moch, fused together national and individual rights. Having declared that the 'fundamental goal of socialism is to liberate the human individual from formal oppression', Maleville explained that 'national emancipation contributes to individual emancipation in so far as it creates new responsibilities and rights in conferring...citizenship to members of a collective promoted to the rank of nation.'[172] Published in December 1960, the GED's proposed new programme for the SFIO placed human liberty—and the individual—at the centre of socialism's concerns. In presenting the programme to the SFIO's congress the same month, Maleville underscored the

---

[169] See Carl Cavanaugh Hodge, 'The Long Fifties: The Politics of Socialist Programmatic Revision in Britain, France and Germany', *Contemporary European History* 2 (1993), 17–43.

[170] Garcia, 'Du droit des peuples à dispoer d'eux-mêmes', and accompanying dicussion in *Revue socialiste*, no. 137, November 1960, 320–54.

[171] AN, Papiers Jules Moch, 484/AP/35-1, minutes of GED meeting, 5 October 1958.

[172] Garcia, 'Du droit des peuples à dispoer d'eux-mêmes', and accompanying dicussion, 348–51.

link between national and human rights. The right to 'national freedom', which all peoples possessed, 'would be contrary to the socialist ideal if it did not also favour individual freedom'.[173] Although Mollet continued to insist that concrete 'minority guarantees' were required for Algeria's European minority, the majority of delegates at the SFIO's May 1962 congress endorsed a new programme based on the GED's draft. The SFIO's preoccupation with minority rights had given way to an emphasis on individual rights.[174]

THE SPD, NATIONAL RIGHTS, AND DEVELOPMENT

Whereas French socialists replaced a focus on minority rights with a mounting interest in human rights, German socialists ultimately subordinated minority rights to national rights. The solution to inter-group tensions within postcolonial nation states would be found not in human rights but in a renewed commitment to development. The end of the 1950s witnessed rising strains between the SPD and the SFIO, due principally to the latter's refusal to recognize Algeria's right to national self-determination. As Thomas Scheffler and Jean-Paul Cahn have shown, SPD militants continued to pressure party leaders to repudiate French/SFIO policy on Algeria.[175] Responding to this pressure, Heinz Putzrath, the SPD's international secretary, confided in October 1958 that a 'mighty clash' with French socialists on colonial policy was inevitable as the SFIO's stance 'stood in contradiction to the declared goals and principles of the Socialist International'. The SPD, Putzrath added, would not 'shrink' from this clash because to do so would lead to an 'enormous loss of prestige [for socialism] not only in Europe but also and above all in Asia and Africa'.[176] As Putzrath's comments suggest, the SPD's embrace of national rights encompassed the colonial world in general. In some ways, the SPD's advocacy of national independence reflected its pursuit of German reunification—a pursuit expressed in the *Deutschlandplan* and framed in terms of the right of the German people to national self-determination. Willy Brandt, the SPD's rising star who would succeed Ollenhauer as party leader, presented German reunification and decolonization as elements of a larger process ushering in a new international order founded on national rights for all peoples and equality between nations.[177]

That said, the SPD's embrace of national rights for the colonial world also stemmed from a belief that history was surging in this direction. 'It is not a question

---

[173] OURS, SFIO, 'Congrès national extraordinaire des 21 et 22 décembre 1960. Puteaux', Maleville, 22.

[174] OURS, SFIO, 'Programme fondamental de la S.F.I.O', 1962.

[175] Scheffler, *Die SPD und der Algerienkrieg*, 56–61, 66–71; and Cahn, 'Le Parti social-démocrate allemand face à la Guerre d'Algérie (1958–1962)'.

[176] AdsD, SPD, Internationale Abteilung, 2847, Heinz Putzath to Werner Gregor, 16 October 1958.

[177] Willy Brandt, *Plädoyer für die Zukunft: Beiträge zur deutschen Politik* (Frankfurt am Main, 1961), 40–3.

of principle', Brandt wrote in 1961, 'but of time for the coloured peoples in gen-eral to achieve their independence.'[178] But well before then the belief that colonial independence was inevitable had taken hold among German socialists; and, just as importantly, the SFIO's refusal to endorse national rights helped to crystallize the SPD's thinking. Thus, in March 1959 the party's press service issued a statement entitled 'Africa in Revolt' in which decolonization was presented as inevitable and French attempts to prevent it as futile. Dismissing talk of an 'association' between France and its colonies as illusory, the statement affirmed that the only question was 'whether the separation [of colonies] from the mother country would occur peacefully or bloodily'.[179] Ollenhauer provides a useful bellwether of SPD thinking. At the party's 1958 congress he had limited his comments on national self-determination largely to Algeria; when it came to the larger colonial world he spoke vaguely of a 'positive partnership' with the peoples of Asia and Africa—a partnership that did not exclude formal ties between Europe and its colonies. Yet only a year later, much of this vagueness had disappeared. Underscoring the SPD's unconditional support for national rights in general, Ollenhauer declared: 'Colonial domination in all its forms must be ended...without bloody confrontation through the recognition of the right to [national] self-determination for all peoples without consideration of class, faith or colour.' Tellingly, the SPD's new programme approved at the congress envisaged a world of sovereign and equal nation states all of which would be members of the United Nations.[180]

If the Algerian War pushed the SPD to embrace national rights for the colonial world, it also spurred German socialists to reject minority rights. Illustrative, here, is the case of Hellmut Kalbitzer, a Bundestag deputy and leading SPD expert on the developing world. In a book published in 1961, Kalbitzer castigated socialists such as Mollet who 'looked down their noses' at colonial nationalism. Rather than a phase that could be skipped, he presented nationalism as 'a necessary phenom-enon for the achievement not only of external but also and more importantly of inner independence'. Kalbitzer did not deny that colonial nationalism could be dangerous, noting that it was 'full of resentment, and excesses were not unknown'. But for him, minority rights were illegitimate. Invoking the Algerian War, he equated claims to minority rights with attempts by settler communities to perpetu-ate their colonial domination with the backing of imperial authorities. Insisting that the European community in Algeria was the instrument of a 'reactionary fas-cist ideology', Kalbitzer not only rejected its right to a separate existence but also denied the reality of multi-ethnic societies in principle. Rather than threaten minority rights, he maintained, decolonization would merely end the 'parasitical [and] exceptional status' of a small number of people.[181] Although few German socialists were as outspoken as Kalbitzer, the almost total absence of interest in minority rights within the SPD is telling. Ironically, in identifying minority rights

[178] Ibid., 40.   [179] FES, AdsD, *SPD Pressedienst*, 'Afrika in der Revolt', 7 March 1959.
[180] SPD, *Protokoll der Verhandlungen des Außerordentlichen Parteitages der Sozialdemokratischen Partei Deutschlands vom 13.-15. November 1959 in Bad Godesburg* (Bonn, 1972, reprint), Ollenhauer, 66; and 'Entwurf für ein Grundsatzprogramm der Sozialdemokratischen Partei Deutschlands', 538–9.
[181] Hellmut Kalbitzer, *Entwicklungsländer und Weltmächte* (Frankfurt am Main, 1961), 77–91, 132.

so closely with Algeria and its European (settler) community, the SFIO discredited these rights in the eyes of German socialists.

A commitment to national rights, however, did not answer the question of how to protect people (whether minority groups or individuals) from their own governments. The SFIO's seeming faith in democracy and individual rights appeared unconvincing to German socialists, many of whom doubted the democratic prospects of postcolonial states. Referring to the latter, Putzrath counselled against expecting 'democratic state structures' to emerge. 'I believe', he explained, 'that the authoritarian stage is a necessary transitional phase in the development of nationalism in these countries [former colonies]'; even if democracy eventually developed, he added, it would not resemble our 'Western conceptions'.[182] Instead of democracy and human rights, the SPD turned to development. During the early 1950s, as we saw, the International had championed social-economic development as an alternative to national independence. By the end of the decade, however, for the SPD development was no longer an alternative but a necessary accompaniment to national rights. At the party's 1959 congress, Ollenhauer framed development in familiar Cold War terms, as a means to prevent the new postcolonial states from veering into the communist camp.[183] But the Cold War was not the only factor. In 1960 the SPD created a high-level working group, headed by Kalbitzer, to formulate the party's position on development. Along with recommending a substantial effort on the West's part, Kalbitzer insisted that development would reduce the social and economic inequalities within what he (like Labour) called 'multi-racial societies', thereby fostering an underlying equality that would override any ethnic differences. At the same time, development would reduce the inequalities of power between states, which Kalbitzer viewed as the true source of national and international tensions.[184]

Two related points are noteworthy regarding the SPD's advocacy of development. The first is that it was intimately connected to a strong suspicion of French colonial ambitions that dated from the time of the Mollet government. As part of the EEC negotiations in 1956–1957, the French had demanded that their empire (including Algeria) be incorporated into the common market, pushing in particular for an ambitious overseas development fund. German socialists reacted strongly to this demand, fearing that European integration would be tainted by French colonialism. The SPD must be 'attentive', Fritz Erler, a leading member of its executive, warned in early 1957, that the common market does not become 'the heir of French colonial policy'. Not surprisingly, the Algerian War factored into the SPD's hostility to French proposals. At meetings of European socialists in early 1957, SFIO delegates argued for a European effort to develop Algeria, warning that

---

[182] FES, AdsD, SPD, Internationale Abteilung, 2848, Putzrath to Hermann Bremer, 7 August 1958.

[183] SPD, *Protokoll der Verhandlungen des Außerordentlichen Parteitages der Sozialdemokratischen Partei Deutschlands vom 13.–15. November 1959*, Ollenhauer, 67.

[184] Kalbitzer, *Entwicklungsländer und Weltmächte*; FES, AdsD, SPD Bundestagsfraktion, III Wahlperiode, 48, 'Arbeitsgruppe Entwicklungsländer', Putzrath circular, 23 March 1960; and 48, 'Imperialismus und Entwicklungsländer', Kalbitzer, undated.

if Europe refused to do so the Soviets or the Americans would step in. In reaction, the SPD took the lead in resisting Algeria's eligibility for aid, with Willi Birkelbach, a prominent SPD economic expert, insisting that 'the construction of Europe absolutely cannot lead to a new form of collective imperialism'.[185] Afterwards, German socialists remained highly suspicious of the EEC's overseas development programme. In addition to questioning the wisdom of aid to Algeria, Kalbitzer maintained more generally that any development funds to African countries must be free of political conditions.[186] Kalbitzer's suspicions were not groundless: as Véronique Dimier has shown, in the early years, French officials dominated the EEC's development bureau, making it difficult to distinguish European from French policy.[187]

Lingering suspicions of the French, in turn, influenced the SPD's approach to development, the second noteworthy point. Beginning in the late 1950s, the SPD came to consider development more as a party project rather than an international socialist one. One sign of this tendency was the growing role of the party's think tank, the Friedrich Ebert Stiftung (FES), in cultivating ties with socialists and non-socialists in Africa, Asia, and beyond. Increasingly, the SPD worked through the FES rather than the Socialist International, organizing activities such as work-shops and visits, scholarships to foreign students to come to Germany, and studies of local conditions.[188] Mirroring this change, German socialists viewed develop-ment first and foremost as a West German effort, which meant that the political discussions over its aims and scope took place between German socialists and non-socialists more than they did between German and other European socialists. Writing in 1960, Brandt argued that West Germany (and, by extension, the SPD) must forge its own development policy for the newly decolonized countries, one that avoided a 'misunderstood solidarity' with former colonial powers—i.e. France.[189] While German socialists continued to discuss overseas development with other European socialists in the context of the EEC, for the SPD, the national realm assumed increasing importance during the 1960s as a site of policymaking. In this sense, its development policy was nationalized—an ironic outcome of the exten-sive international socialist cooperation on colonial issues that had marked the previous decade.

[185] FES, AdsD, NL Fritz Erler, 171B, Erler to Hans Darmstadt, 7 March 1957; and HAUE, GSPE 17, 'Compte rendu de la réunion du Groupe socialiste: Strasbourg...13 Mai 1957'.

[186] FES, AdsD, *SPD Pressedienst*, Kalbitzer, EWG—Afrika und Gleichberechtigung, 3 May 1961.

[187] Véronique Dimier, *The Invention of a European Development Aid Bureaucracy: Recycling Empire* (Basingstoke, 2014). But also see Martin Rempe, *Entwicklung im Konflikt: Die EWG und der Senegal 1957–1975* (Köln, 2012).

[188] On the FES, see Patrick von zur Mühlen, 'Entwicklungspolitische Paradigmenwechsel am Beispiel der Friedrich-Ebert Stiftung vom Ende der 1950er bis zu den 1990er-Jahren', *Archiv für Sozialgeschichte* 48 (2008), 411–32.

[189] Brandt, 'Aussenpolitische Kontinuität mit neuen Akzenten', *Aussenpolitik* 11 (1960), 722. Also see Bastian Hein, *Die Westdeutschen und die Dritte Welt: Entwicklungspolitik und Entwicklungsdienste zwischen Reform und Revolte 1959–1974* (Munich, 2006).

LABOUR, MINORITY RIGHTS, AND THE COMMONWEALTH

To recall, during the first half of the 1950s, Labour had been increasingly concerned about the future of plural or multi-ethnic colonial societies. Party officials feared that the transfer of power based on majority rule would leave minority groups vulnerable to abuse. Labour, moreover, had been responsible for placing the issue of minority rights on the international socialist agenda, even if it was the SFIO that became the principal champion of these rights in the context of the Algerian War. During the second half of the 1950s, however, Labour moved towards the support of national rights—of the right of colonies to national self-determination. This movement continued during the late 1950s and early 1960s, prodded in part by dissatisfaction with France's Algerian policy. Reporting on his visit to Tunisia in the spring of 1959, David Ennals, Labour's new International Secretary, under-scored the country's commitment to an FLN victory in particular and to 'the cause of national independence and anti-colonialism' in general. Shortly afterwards, Tony Benn, an anti-colonial activist and future minister, attended a meeting in Tunisia of the All-African People's Conference (AAPC), a Pan-Africanist grouping founded in 1958 and dedicated to achieving immediate independence for all colonies in Africa. In his report, Benn argued that the Algerian War remained a touchstone not only for Tunisians but for almost all African leaders. But Benn's larger point was that events were assuming a 'quickened pace' and that Labour would be wise to embrace the reality of national independence.[190] He reiterated his point the following year in a report on the AAPC's second conference:

> The pace of change in Africa has accelerated so fast that we are in danger of getting out of touch with events there. We no longer can dictate the speed at which independence will come. Non-violence by the Africans does not mean that they are willing to wait, nor does it rule out other compelling types of force. And violence is always in reserve—as we see in Algeria.[191]

Benn's advocacy of national rights resonated among prominent Labourites. At the International's July 1959 Congress in Hamburg, Tom Driberg, a Labour colonial expert, rejected the argument that national rights must be subordinated to good government. No colony would ever be fully 'ripe' for independence; it must learn from doing. 'That is why even the best intentioned paternalism is futile,' Driberg noted. Similarly, at the meeting of the International's council in Haifa in April 1960, Gaitskell remarked that events were moving quickly in Africa and that socialists must unite around a 'passionate belief in racial equality and an equally strong support for colonial freedom'.[192] At Labour's annual conference in October

---

[190] LHASC, LPA, International Department, LP/ID/FRA/15, 'Report on Visit to Tunisia March 1–5, 1959', Ennals; and 'Report of Visit to Tunisia—27th May/2nd June, 1959', Benn.

[191] Labour Party, NEC minutes, fiche 671, 'The Second all African People's Conference in Tunis', Benn, 4 February 1960; also see Bodleian Library, Barbara Castle Papers, 6, Political Diary 1957–1963, 9 February 1960.

[192] IISH, Socialist International Information, 'Sixth Congress of the Socialist International . . . 14–17 July 1959', Driberg, vol. 9, no. 51–2; and Gaitskell, 'The International Situation', vol. 10, no. 21, 21 May 1960, 315.

1961, Barbara Castle, speaking for the executive, announced that the 'world was witnessing the final manifestation of a dying colonialism' and that 'large numbers of former Colonial territories are moving forward steadily to independence and to self-government'. Although in North Africa, 'the Colonialist Powers [i.e. France] are putting up a last fierce resistance in Algeria', the process could not be stopped or even delayed. For Labour, national rights had become paramount.[193] Revealingly, a year earlier the party's Commonwealth subcommittee had quietly decided against reissuing 'Plural Society', which focused on minority protection in multi-ethnic colonies, 'because of the progress of events since this policy pamphlet was written four years ago'.[194]

Consigning the pamphlet to history, however, did not resolve the potential tensions between minority and majority rights in multi-ethnic societies. Algeria was a case in point, but so too were South Africa, where a white minority regime pursued a systematic policy of discrimination (apartheid) towards the black African majority, and the Central African Federation (Rhodesia and Nyasaland), an entity Labour had vigorously opposed since its creation in 1953 and that appeared to be heading in a direction similar to South Africa. But the problem was not limited to colonies with a white settler minority. During the late 1950s, the Fabian Colonial Bureau (renamed the Fabian Commonwealth Bureau) continued its efforts to sensitize Labour to the issue of minority protection in general. However unrelenting the demands for national independence, Creech Jones wrote in this regard, the 'Western colonial powers' could not shirk their responsibilities 'if race conflict is to be avoided in the future' within colonies.[195] Similarly, Rita Hinden, another FCB activist, warned in 1959 that the 'insistent demand' for national independence offered no solution to the problem of 'plural societies' defined as 'those colonies—particularly in East and Central Africa—where different races live side by side and refuse to mix, let alone coalesce, into nationhood'. The following year, Hinden deplored the tendency to equate political independence with majority rule, maintaining that 'one-man-one-vote' was a dangerous principle. The FCB must make Labour understand that 'democracy also means civil liberties, opposition parties, and full rights for minorities.' To this end, in a 1961 FCB pamphlet she underscored the 'difficult conditions prevail[ing] in many Asian and African countries, with religious, tribal and linguistic divisions often superimposed on social and economic under-development'. Groping for a solution, Hinden concluded that governments in newly independent countries should be subject to a 'series of controls', even if she recognized that the principle of national sovereignty would make this difficult.[196]

The FCB's activities indicate that behind the mounting support for national rights lurked continuing unease within Labour regarding the protection of minorities.

---

[193] Labour Party, *Report of the 60th Annual Conference held… October 2 to October 6, 1961*, Castle, 195.
[194] LHASC, LPA, B 15/8, Commonwealth sub-committee, meeting, 10 May 1960.
[195] LHASC, LPA, BASF, 3, 'Colonial Policy and the Labour Party', Creech-Jones, June 1959.
[196] Hinden, 'Socialism and the Colonial World' in Arthur Creech Jones, ed., *New Fabian Colonial Essays* (London, 1959), 14–18; BLCAS, Fabian Colonial Bureau, 29/1C, 'Future Work of the Fabian Commonwealth Bureau', Hinden, May 1960; and Hinden, *Principles of Socialism: Africa and Asia* (London, April 1961), 8–11.

No less importantly, Hinden's arguments suggest that in a system centred on sovereign nation states the respect for minority rights (or individual rights for that matter) would ultimately depend on the willingness and capabilities of national and subnational governments. The awareness of this reality, in turn, helps to explain Labour's growing interest in the Commonwealth towards the end of the 1950s. The signs of this interest are numerous. In 1957, Labour organized a conference of Commonwealth socialist parties, the first one since 1947; afterwards, it took the lead in creating a 'Commonwealth Association' in order to facilitate contacts between its member parties.[197] In 1958, Labour's international subcommittee recommended that the Commonwealth section be hived off from the international department to become an independent department with its own secretary. The following year the new department began publication of *Commonwealth: A Socialist Review*, a quarterly journal aimed at socialist parties within the Commonwealth. 'We socialists', Morgan Phillips wrote in the first issue, 'believe that the Commonwealth offers great opportunities for developing a common understanding between our parties and we believe that this new Review will help to bring us all closer together.' During 1961, John Hatch, Labour's Commonwealth Secretary, set about organizing another socialist conference, which was held in September 1962.[198]

At Labour's annual conference in October 1962 Gaitskell presented the turn towards the Commonwealth as the counterpart to the rejection of the EEC. Britain's membership in the latter, he famously declared, would mean 'the end of the Commonwealth'. But a presumed choice between Europe and the Commonwealth was not the sole consideration at work. Labour's growing interest in the Commonwealth also needs to be seen as a response to decolonization. In a stimulating article, Stuart Ward argues that Harold Macmillan's famous 'wind of change' speech in 1960 marked the beginning of the end of notions of a Greater Britain—of an empire based on 'global British racial kinship' linking together the white Dominions and the colonies with white settler communities. The result was a 'conceptual vacancy that was not easily filled'.[199] But this conclusion overlooks the fact that Labour possessed its own alternative vision of empire as an international multiracial/ethnic society. As early as February 1957 Gaitskell privately praised the Commonwealth's 'multi-racial character'. Over the next several years, Labour propaganda emphasized the Commonwealth as an instrument of racial harmony. As a draft statement by Hatch in late 1958 explained:

> Since 1945 Britain has taken the lead in building a Commonwealth which represents the greatest multi-racial community mankind has ever known. Its influence for world peace is immeasurable and it offers to present and future generations of British people

---

[197] LAC, CCF-NPD, MG 28 VI-I, vol. 133, Hatch (Labour) to CCF, 20 July 1957.

[198] LHASC, LPA, *Commonwealth: A Socialist Review*, no. 1 Jan–March 1959, iii–iv; and B 19/9, Commonwealth sub-committee, Hatch (Labour) to Praja Socialist Party, 28 April 1961.

[199] Ward, 'Run Before the Tempest: The "Wind of Change" and the British World', *Geschichte und Gesellschaft* 37 (2011), 218. Also see Kathleen Paul, '"British Subjects" and "British Stock": Labour's Postwar Imperialism', *Journal of British Studies* 32 (1995), 233–76.

particular opportunities as a world-wide family of nationalities. In this Commonwealth, as throughout the world, race relations is a continually exposed nerve. Failure in these relations can destroy all hope of peace and international friendship. Unless peoples of different races and colours can learn to live together in harmony, the future of our children in this rapidly shrinking world will be one of extreme danger. The Commonwealth has a unique opportunity to create racial understanding, confidence, and co-operation.[200]

For Labour, this roseate vision of the Commonwealth served the useful purpose of displacing the problem of multi-ethnic societies to the international realm. The pressing challenge was no longer to reconcile minority and majority groups within a nation state, but to foster harmony between them as equal members of the Commonwealth. To be sure, this vision did not preclude harsh criticism of South Africa and its apartheid regime, which was forced out of the Commonwealth in 1961. But South Africa was an exception. In Labour's conception, the Commonwealth constituted a community of sovereign nation states.[201] There was some hope that membership might exert a normative force on governments, encouraging them to respect basic freedoms. But the paramountcy of national rights meant that the Commonwealth's members would be largely free to determine on their own their internal affairs—and thus what if any protection they accorded to minorities.

Not all Labourites were comfortable with the Commonwealth as a solution to the problems posed by postcolonial states that were also multiracial societies. Some, such as Fenner Brockway, the anti-colonial militant and staunch advocate of national rights, placed their faith in the spread of democratic socialism in the decolonized world, which would eventually create more just and equal societies in which group tensions gradually disappeared. Others, such as Hinden, hoped that the Socialist International might contribute to the development of socialism in the postcolonial world, though she admitted that it was 'inadequately equipped' for such a task.[202] If Hinden's hopes were strained, so too were those of Brockway, whose faith in the future of African socialism appeared excessive even at the time. But arguably more representative was John Strachey, a Gaitskell supporter and former cabinet minister, who argued that poor countries would require a 'strong central authority' to bring about development. While admitting that it would be unfortunate if such an authority became arbitrary, violating the rights of its citizens (whether as individuals or minority groups), Strachey could see no better option.[203] In the end, Labour, like the SFIO and the SPD, had abandoned the advocacy of minority rights.

---

[200] UCL, Hugh Gaitskell Papers, F 21.2, Gaitskell to T.R. Bradbury, 9 February 1959; and LHASC, LPA, B 15/3, 'Alternative Draft Statement on Racial Prejudice', Hatch, September 1958.

[201] LHASC, LPA, B 15/13, 'Draft Statement on the Commonwealth', Labour, Commonwealth Department, January 1961.

[202] Fenner Brockway, *African Socialism: A Background Book* (London, 1963), 22–3, 124; and BLCAS, Fabian Colonial Bureau, 29/1C, 'Future Work of the Fabian Commonwealth Bureau', Hinden, May 1960.

[203] John Strachey, *La fin de l'Impérialisme* (Paris, 1961), 139.

As mentioned in the introduction, scholars emphasize the open-ended nature of decolonization after 1945. There was nothing inevitable about the dissolution of European empires into multiple nation states. Until late in the day, numerous contemporary actors in Europe and in the colonial world conceived of alternatives, including federations of various sorts linking together metropoles and former colonies. In some ways, the thinking of European socialists on the fate of empire reflected this search for alternatives. Prompted by the SFIO, during the 1950s, European socialists contemplated the possibility not only of a *France-Algérie* but also of *Eurafrique*—the proposal to widen the project of European unity to include Europe's former African colonies. In the end, nothing came of this socialist thinking, as independent nation states soon replaced empire in Africa as the dominant form of political organization. There are obvious reasons why the nation state proved so attractive to anti-colonialists and to postcolonial rulers—the fact that most European (and Western) countries were nation states and that the United Nations Charter recognized national sovereignty as the bedrock of post-war international politics. But the discussions of European socialists point to two additional reasons. One concerns the vagueness of alternatives. Unlike federalist projects, which were rarely well defined, everyone knew what the nation state looked like if only because Europeans themselves provided the model. The second reason concerns the taint of colonialism. *France-Algérie*, *Eurafrique*, and all such proposals aimed at bypassing national independence could not escape the suspicion that their chief purpose was to perpetuate colonialism in another guise.

Socialist efforts to grapple with decolonization highlight the issue of minority rights. Because so many colonies constituted what Labour officials called 'multiracial societies', the possibility and then reality of decolonization raised the issue of minority rights—of how to protect ethnic, religious, linguistic, and other minorities from the majority. Neither socialists nor non-socialists found an answer. In retrospect, minority rights suffered a severe blow at the hands not only of national rights but also of human rights. Indeed, in this chapter, human rights appear as something of a second-best alternative to minority rights as French (and some European) socialists promoted them in the forlorn hope that they might afford some protection to minorities in postcolonial independent states. There is much to regret in the sidelining of minority rights during decolonization. After all, divisions between majority and minority groups were a reality in many colonies and postcolonial states; worse still, when it came to minority protection, the record of many former colonies was dismal.[204] Another reason to regret the fate of minority rights is that they arguably encourage greater sensitivity to social-economic inequalities than do national or human rights, both of which have tended to be defined in political terms. But as the extended exchanges between European and Asian socialists indicate, the basic problem with minority rights is that they entailed limits on national sovereignty. And this was something that postcolonial leaders were unwilling to accept.

[204] Henry Carey, 'The Postcolonial State and the Protection of Human Rights', *Comparative Studies of South Asia, Africa and the Middle East* 22 (2002), 59–75.

Conclusion

In examining the practice of socialist internationalism, this book has sought to combine three fields of historical scholarship (socialism, internationalism, and international politics) in the aim of contributing to each one. The contribution to the first area, socialism, is perhaps the most obvious. Contrary to numerous claims, socialist internationalism did not die in August 1914 but survived the outbreak of war and afterwards even flourished at times. Indeed, during the two post-war periods, European socialists worked closely together on a variety of pressing issues, endowing the policymaking of the British, French, and German parties with an important international dimension. This international dimension was never all-important: it rarely, if ever, trumped the domestic political and intra-party dimensions of policymaking. But its existence means that the international policies of any one socialist party cannot be fully understood in isolation from the policies of other parties. The practice of socialist internationalism was rarely easy: contention was present and sometimes rife. Equally pertinent, idealism could be in short supply. Often enough, European socialists instrumentalized internationalism for their own ends, whether it was Ramsay MacDonald with the Geneva Protocol during the 1920s or Guy Mollet, who hoped to discredit internal party critics of his Algerian policy during the 1950s. Nevertheless, the attempts to instrumentalize socialist internationalism underscore the latter's significance. After all, such attempts would be inconceivable unless socialist internationalism meant something to European socialists.

In terms of internationalism, this book has focused on its practice—on the efforts of European socialists to cooperate on concrete international issues. This focus stands in contrast to the tendency of scholars to approach internationalism as a project, the best-known example being liberal internationalism. Such an approach, however, runs up against the amorphous nature of the liberal internationalist project (and all internationalist projects, for that matter): scholars either disagree on its precise contents or offer broad principles (peace and prosperity) that border on the vacuous. A focus on practice, by comparison, directs attention to the contested, contingent, and changing nature of an internationalist project, the definition of which is the product of ongoing negotiation between a set of actors grappling with real issues. No less importantly, attention to practice can help to explain the waxing and waning of internationalism. For European socialists, the active practice of internationalism breathed life into the latter, preventing it from becoming an abstract shell.

Approaching internationalism as a practice also provides insights into the relationship between the international and the national. As Glenda Sluga argues, the histories of nationalism and internationalism have been entangled for much of the twentieth century; and this entanglement seemingly obviates the need to privilege one or the other: actors can operate simultaneously in both the national and international realms and they can identify both with their nation and with something larger.[1] The practice of socialist internationalism, however, suggests that the relationship between the nation and the international is not only more fraught than the image of entanglement conveys, but also more unequal. The pull of the nation was and is powerful. It took a self-conscious and concerted effort on the part of European socialists during the two post-war periods to resist this pull by working together to forge 'socialist' responses to pressing international issues. In doing so, they remained embedded in their nations: the international dimension of policy-making never eclipsed the national and intra-party contexts. Nevertheless, the practice of internationalism did prod socialists from one country (and party) to define national interests in interaction with socialists from other countries, helping to counter the temptation to adopt an exclusive (or more national) perspective. In this sense, European socialists sought not so much to do away with the nation as to internationalize it by shifting the vantage point abroad: national interests would be considered from the outside-in and not solely from the inside-out. This intriguing experiment ultimately failed, however, as socialist internationalism became nationalized during the 1930s and again from the 1960s. One reason for this failure lies in the practice of socialist internationalism itself, which, by underscoring and exacerbating differences, pushed socialist parties to work out international policies on their own, independently of other parties. But it is probably also the case that, in the long term, the pull of the nation was simply too powerful in a world of nation states.

The book's contribution to international history is arguably less direct. During the two post-war periods, European socialists sought not only to work out shared 'socialist' positions on international issues, but also and more ambitiously to fashion a new model of international relations that would reduce the seemingly endemic tensions and rivalries between nations leading to recurring wars. Their success in this latter endeavour was admittedly limited at best. Collectively, European socialists were never in a position to impose a new model; more substantively, it would be difficult to identify a clear-cut socialist model of international relations. Instead, European socialists pronounced their adherence to broad principles such as peace, disarmament, and European unity—principles whose practical application needed to be defined. In addition to being vague, these principles were often shared by many non-socialists, fostering the impression that there was little distinct about socialist internationalism. Hence the temptation to dissolve socialist internationalism into liberal internationalism.[2]

This temptation is worth resisting, however, because the extended efforts of European socialists to wrestle with pressing international problems offer a novel

---

[1] Sluga, *Internationalism in the Age of Nationalism*.
[2] Laqua, 'Democratic Politics and the League of Nations'; and Sluga, *Internationalism in the Age of Nationalism*.

perspective on the latter. Viewing the post-1918 period through an international socialist lens highlights the fragility of the so-called second peace settlement achieved in the mid-1920s as well as the intractable nature of disarmament during the late 1920s and early 1930s. When it comes to interwar colonialism, such a lens throws into relief the contested and unstable nature of the League of Nations' mandate system as well as the idealist origins of proposals for colonial appeasement, rooted as they were in earlier systemic visions of a world divided into developed and undeveloped (or have-not) regions. In the case of the post-1945 security order, an international socialist lens underscores the dissatisfaction with the Cold War divide of Europe—a divide often presented as a fait accompli by the end of the 1940s. Galvanized by the SPD, during the 1950s, European socialists became prominent advocates of a neutral zone in Central and Eastern Europe that would cut across and transcend a divided Germany and a divided continent. The same lens also helps us to understand how the project of European unity came to centre on a common market. Although European socialists initially envisaged something more ambitious, their inability to define what this might be left them susceptible to the argument that the priority should be on a united Europe and that a socialist Europe could come later. Finally, an international socialist lens draws into sharper focus the role of minority rights in the process of decolonization—rights whose emphasis had important implications for the postcolonial order at the national and international levels. All told, European socialists might have failed to transform international politics, but their prolonged engagement with concrete issues encourages us to reconsider—and perhaps even reframe—familiar aspects of the two post-war periods.

THE FATE OF SOCIALIST INTERNATIONALISM

This book argues that the practice of socialist internationalism flourished during the two post-war periods and declined afterwards. It was not that European socialists grew disinterested in international politics. Instead, socialist internationalism was nationalized, as the principal socialist parties increasingly preferred to work out their positions on international issues on their own, independently of other parties. To be sure, a socialist International never officially ceased to exist in some form, although in 1939–1940 it was clearly moribund. Still, during the 1930s and again from the 1960s, the International lost much of its vitality. As both a cause and effect of this process, the International became increasingly marginal to European socialists. *Vorwärts* (or *Neuer Vorwärts* from 1948 to 1955), the SPD's chief newspaper, offers a telling example. During the 1940s and into the 1950s, international socialist gatherings garnered considerable attention, often appearing as front-page news. By the end of the 1950s, however, such events had migrated to the newspaper's back pages. Today, the socialist International continues to function, even if seventy or so socialist and progressive parties—including Labour, the SPD, and the French *Parti socialiste*—met in May 2013 to create an alternative: the Progressive Alliance. It remains to be seen whether the new organization, which its founding statement describes as a global 'network which is open to progressive, democratic, social-democratic, socialist and labour parties and party networks', can reanimate socialist internationalism. But for the time being, the prospects do not appear promising.

There are at least two related objections to the argument that socialist internationalism declined from the 1960s onwards. One is that the 1970s supposedly witnessed an international socialist renaissance. This renaissance is often associated with Willy Brandt, the former SPD chancellor, who served as the International's president from 1976 to 1992 and who worked to strengthen links with the socialist and democratic forces across the developing world stretching from Asia to Africa and to South America. Together with the Swedish Olaf Palme and the Austrian Bruno Kreisky, moreover, Brandt formed a highly visible socialist triumvirate that sought to influence international politics, principally by advancing the new international economic order aimed at reducing the global North–South divide and by encouraging a peace settlement in the Middle East.[3] But while it would be unfair to discount Brandt's influence, the renaissance of socialist internationalism proved temporary, waning during the 1980s. No less importantly, it was driven by personalities rather than being firmly rooted in the various socialist parties; indeed, Brandt's international activism can be seen as an attempt to compensate for his declining influence in German politics and within the SPD, both now dominated by Helmut Schmidt.[4] In any event, the unrooted nature of this renaissance helps to explain why the activities of the Brandt–Kreisky–Palme triumvirate proved ephemeral.

The second objection concerns the European Union. The argument here is not that socialist internationalism declined but that its locus shifted from the International to European institutions. This shift, which began in the early 1950s with the European Council and the ECSC, was reinforced in 1957 with the creation of the EEC. The practice of socialist internationalism, in short, continued within a more strictly European context. Christian Salm's recent and well-researched study offers an excellent example. During the 1970s, Salm insists, 'transnational socialist networks' decisively shaped the policies of the European Community (EC), particularly in the areas of development aid and of southern enlargement. Building on the work of Wolfram Kaiser, he emphasizes the role of informal networks whose influence is obscured by a focus on more formal structures of cooperation.[5] Yet if Salm certainly shows that European socialist cooperation continued during the 1970s, he arguably exaggerates the impact this had on the EC—an aspect he treats in hasty fashion in his chapters. But for this book,

---

[3] See Rother and Schmidt, eds., *Willy Brandt. Über Europa hinaus Brandt*; and Oliver Rathkolb, 'Brandt, Kreisky and Palme as Policy Entrepreneurs: Social Democratic Networks in Europe's Policy towards the Middle East' in Kaiser et al., eds., *Transnational Networks in Regional Integration: Governing Europe, 1945–83* (Houndmills, 2010), 153–75.

[4] For tensions between Brandt and Schmidt, see Bernd Faulenbach, *Das sozialdemokratische Jahrzehnt: Von der Reformeuphorie zur Neuen Unübersichtlichkeit. Die SPD 1969–1982* (Bonn, 2011).

[5] Salm, *Transnational Socialist Networks in the 1970s*. For Kaiser, see his 'Bringing History Back in to the Study of Transnational Networks in European Integration', *Journal of Public Policy* 29 (2009), 223–39.

a more pertinent reservation concerns the limits of networks. Salm and Kaiser among others praise networks for their loose, flexible, and adaptable features, but the networks that Salm describes were notably diffuse and even nebulous; still more to the point, they were largely unrooted in—and detached from—socialist parties.[6] These networks are best viewed as creatures of a distinct and isolated institutional environment (the EC) that fostered highly specialized and ultimately narrow exchanges between the socialists involved. Commenting on a meeting of socialist members of the Community's assembly in June 1977, Roy Jenkins, a pro-European Labourite, privately complained that 'they are not an inspiring group and most of the conversation was about some incredibly detailed, pointless, trivial matters between the Commission and the Parliament.'[7] The practice of socialist internationalism might have continued into the 1970s and beyond, but it did so in a very circumscribed manner.

This leaves the question of more formal cooperation between socialists within the European Community/Union. That such cooperation existed (and exists) is clear. As early as 1957, the EEC's socialist parties formed a liaison bureau in Luxembourg charged with coordinating the activities of socialist members of the assembly; in 1974, the bureau became the Confederation of the European Parties of the European Union and in 1992 the Party of European Socialists. But despite occasional optimistic assessments regarding the emergence of a cohesive socialist bloc (and even party), these changes did not amount to a renewed commitment to the practice of socialist internationalism.[8] As Salm admits, the creation of the Confederation 'resulted in marginal institutional improvements' in inter-party cooperation. Greater cooperation, he adds, required a 'decisive change in the decision-making process'—a change that the parties fiercely resisted. As a result, socialist parties invested less and less effort in cooperating with one another, privileging, in Claudia Hiepel's words, 'national strategies for the handling of problems'. Without some 'binding structure', Hiepel concludes, more informal 'transnational [inter-] party cooperation' (of the kind Salm emphasizes) is 'hardly fruitful'.[9] Whether such structures constitute the critical factor is debatable, but what does seem clear is that, to thrive, the practice of socialist internationalism needs to be rooted within socialist parties—in their day-to-day functioning, in their politics, and in their identities. Neither networks nor more formal structures are enough.

[6] For a useful discussion of networks, see Madeleine Herren, 'Netzwerke' in Jost Düffler and Wilfried Loth, eds., *Dimensionen internationaler Geschichte* (Munich, 2012), 108–28.

[7] Jenkins, *European Diary, 1977–1981* (London, 1989), 14 June 1977, 117.

[8] For example, see Simon Hix, Abdul Noury, and Gérard Roland, 'Power to the Parties: Cohesion and Competition in the European Parliament, 1979–1991', *British Journal of Political Science* 35 (2005), 209–34.

[9] Salm, *Transnational Socialist Networks in the 1970s*, 28; and Claudia Hiepel, '"Europa gehört keiner Partei": Die SPD und der Weg vom Socialist Information and Liaison Office zur Sozialdemokratischen Partei Europas' in Jürgen Mittag, ed., *Politische Parteien und europäische Integration: Entwicklung und Perspektiven transnationaler Parteienkooperation in Europa* (Essen, 2006), 280, 287. Also see Simon Hix and Urs Lesse, *Shaping a Vision: A History of the Party of European Socialists, 1957–2002* (Brussels, 2002); and Kristian Steinnes, 'The European Turn and "Social Europe": Northern European Social Democracy 1950–1985', *Archiv für Sozialgeschichte* 53 (2013), 1–22.

THE LOST PROMISE OF SOCIALIST INTERNATIONALISM

Socialist internationalism was not a singular species: other internationalisms emerged during the twentieth century centred on nationally based political parties. The two most prominent, as mentioned in the introduction, were Christian-democratic and communist internationalism. Nevertheless, socialist internationalism distinguished itself from its two chief rivals in noteworthy respects. Organized in networks, Christian-democratic internationalism lacked socialist internationalism's more formal structures. Indeed, for leading Christian democrats such as Konrad Adenauer, international socialism served as a goad by highlighting their own organizational weakness.[10] Socialist internationalism also distinguished itself from communist internationalism, most obviously in its voluntary element. Although recent work on the international communist movement questions the extent of Moscow's coercive authority over foreign communist parties, few would deny that both the Komintern (1919–1943) and the Kominform, its successor from 1947, were, in the final analysis, instruments of Soviet policy. In terms of structure and functioning, neither organization can be compared to either the interwar or the post-war socialist Internationals. This difference is fundamental, for it underscores the point that the practice of socialist internationalism was a matter of choice and not of imposition.

The combination of structure and voluntarism, of organizational capabilities and political legitimacy, not only distinguishes socialist internationalism from its Christian-democratic and communist rivals; it also offers something of a counterpoint to contemporary internationalism. The introduction presented European socialist parties as hybrid entities, incorporating aspects of both state and non-state actors. If so, socialist internationalism can be seen as a compromise between the two dominant forms of internationalism today (a state-centred and a non-state-centered one), combining many of their strengths while avoiding some of their weaknesses.

The strengths of a state-centred internationalism are considerable. In addition to commanding extensive authority and resources, its principal actors (governments) are deeply rooted in—and therefore in principle more sensitive to—national realities and needs, a notable asset in a world in which the nation state continues to command substantial loyalty. A major weakness, however, is the tendency of governments to conceive of national interests in exclusive and often competitive terms. Even if one accepts the argument concerning the obsolescence of major war between developed states, contemporary international politics abound with examples of rivalry and strife below the threshold of armed conflict. In mirror image fashion, an important strength of a non-state-centred internationalism is the refusal of international non-governmental organizations (INGOs) to allow states

---

[10] See Adenauer's comments in 'Genfer Kreis, 22.12.1948, Protokol Koutzine', reproduced in M. Gehler and W. Kaiser, eds., *Transnationale Parteienkooperation der europäisachen Christdemokraten: Dokumente 1945–1965* (Munich, 2004), 149–50.

alone to dictate the nature and agenda of international politics. Although one can exaggerate the irenic effects of non-state actors in general, many of these organizations do seek, directly or indirectly, to reduce the sources of discord within and between states. At the same time, a prominent weakness of this internationalism is its diffuse, almost kaleidoscopic make-up in which a myriad of groups promote a shifting array of issues—a weakness that neither more INGOs nor denser links between them will easily overcome. No less problematic is the lack of national rootedness of many INGOs, which sometimes makes it difficult to influence national policy.

By contrast, because socialist parties were deeply embedded in national politics and, indeed, sought to form governments, their internationalism remained closely attuned to local conditions while also ranging widely in scope. Socialists could neither limit their attention to single issues nor ignore the imbrications of international and national politics. Equally pertinent, because post-war European socialists possessed a powerful sense of collective belonging and purpose, they strove to conceive of national interests in inclusive and cooperative ways. To be sure, the shared commitment to socialist internationalism never eclipsed the national loyalties of the individual parties during the twentieth century. Still, the deliberate effort to escape the mental confines of the nation set the post-1918 and post-1945 international socialist community apart from international governmental organizations such as the United Nations, the IMF, or even the emerging European Union, whose basic function was (and arguably remains) to mediate between competing national interests. Simply put, post-war socialist internationalism amounted to something unique: a well-structured and voluntary community of nationally rooted political parties that were self-consciously internationalist. And as such it offered a potential means not of doing away with the nation, but of internationalizing it through the collective forging of an international as opposed to national-oriented internationalism.

In the end, socialist internationalism fell short of this potential. But rather than simply write off socialist internationalism as a failure, we might be better served by reflecting on its achievements. For an extended moment after 1918 and again after 1945, European socialists not only imagined but also sought to practise among themselves an internationalized internationalism, one which considered the world not simply from the nation outwards but also from the outside-in. That they were able to do so offers some grounds for hope that others might do so as well.

List of Archives

AUSTRIA

Verein für die Geschichte der Arbeiterbewegung (Vienna)
    Adler-Archiv
    Socialdemokratische Partei Österreichs

BELGIUM

AMSAB—Institut voor Sociale Geschiedenis (Antwerp)
    Archives Camille Huysmans
    Parti ouvrier belge
Institute Emile Vandervelde (Brussels)
    Archives Emile Vandervelde
    Fonds Louis de Brouckère
    Fonds Max Buset

CANADA

Library and Archives Canada (Ottawa)
    Co-Operative Commonwealth Federation and New Democratic Party Fonds
McGill University Libraries (Montreal)
    Noel Edward Buxton Papers

FRANCE

Archives de la Préfecture de Police (Paris)
    Cabinet du préfet de police
Archives diplomatiques (La Courneuve)
    Série Y Internationale
Archives nationales (Paris)
    Archives Léon Blum
    Archives du Comité d'histoire de la Deuxième Guerre mondiale
    Commissions parlementaires
    Ministère de l'Intérieur
    Papiers Vincent Auriol
    Papiers Édouard Depreux
    Papiers Jules Moch
    Papiers Joseph Paul-Boncour
    Papiers André Philip
    Papiers Marcel Sembat
    Papiers Albert Thomas
    Parti socialist unifié
Centre d'histoire sociale du XXè siècle (Paris)
    Fonds Marceau Pivert
    Fonds Jean Zyromski

Fondation Jean Jaurès (Paris)
    Fonds Robert Pontillon
Office universitaire de recherche socialiste (Paris)
    Archives de Guy Mollet
    Archives du Parti socialiste-SFIO
    Fonds André Bidet
    Fonds Georges Brutelle
    Fonds Ernest Cazelles
    Fonds Maurice Deixonne
    Fonds André Ferrat
    Fonds Albert Gazier
    Fonds Charles Lancelle
    Fonds Loui Lévy
    Fonds Jean Longuet
    Fonds Jacques Piette
    Fonds Etienne Weill-Raynal
Sciences Po. Centre d'histoire (Paris)
    Fonds Daniel et Cletta Mayer
    Fonds Alain Savary
    Groupe parlementaire socialiste

GERMANY

Auswärtiges Amt—Politisches Archiv (Berlin)
    Botschaft Bern
    Botschaft London
    Bostschaft Paris
    NL Brockdorff-Rantzau
    Politisches Archiv
Bundesarchiv Koblenz
    NL Eduard David
Bundesarchiv Lichterfelde (Berlin)
    Auswärtige Amt. Zentralstelle für Auslandsdienst
    NL Paul Löbe
    Reichskanzlei
    Reichsministerium des Innern
Bundesarchiv SAPMO (Stiftung Archiv der Parteien und Massenorganisationen der DDR im Bundesarchiv)
    II. Internationale
    NL Viktor Agartz
    NL Eduard Bernstein
    NL Emil Eichhorn
    NL Kurt Eisner
    NL Karl Kautsky
    NL Paul Levi
    NL Hermann Müller
    Sozialdemokratische Partei Deutschlands
    Unabhängige Sozialdemokratische Partei Deutschlands

Friedrich Ebert Stiftung. Archiv der sozialen Demokratie (Bonn)
  NL Eduard Bernstein
  NL Peter Blachstein
  NL Arthur Crispien
  NL Wilhelm Dittmann
  NL Willi Eichler
  NL Fritz Erler
  NL Fritz Heine
  NL Fritz Henβler
  NL Wilhelm Kaiser
  NL Karl Kautsky
  NL Waldemar von Knoeringen
  NL Adoplh Köster
  NL Paul Löbe
  NL Günther Markscheffel
  NL Walter Menzel
  NL Karl Mommer
  NL Hermann Müller-Franken
  NL Rolf Reventlow
  NL Heinrich Ritzel
  NL Wilhelm Sander
  NL Carlo Schmid
  NL Kurt Schumacher
  NL Carl Severing
  NL Friedrich Stampfer
  NL Herbert Wehner
  Parteivorstand Bestand Erich Ollenhauer
  Sozialdemokratische Partei Deutschlands
  USPD Fraktionsprotokolle
Geheime Staatsarchiv Preuβischer Kulturbesitz (Berlin)
  Geheimes Ministerialarchiv
  NL Otto Braun
  NL Heinrich Schnee

ITALY

Historical Archives of the European Union, European Union Institute Archives (Florence)
  Fonds Paul-Henri Spaak
  Groupe socialiste au parlement européen
  Mouvement européen

NETHERLANDS

International Institute of Social History (Amsterdam)
  Alexandre Bracke Papers
  Archief Johan Willem Albarda
  Archief Marinus van der Goes van Naters
  Archief Pieter Jelles Troelstra

Archief Hein Vos
Bureau Socialiste International Archives
Confederation of Socialist Parties of the European Union Collection
Fritz Adler Papers
Jules Guesde Papers
Julius Braunthal Papers
Labour and Socialist International Archives
Labour and Socialist International. London Secretariat Archives
League Against Imperialism
Mouvement socialiste pour les États-Unis d'Europe Collection
Rudolf Breitscheid Papers
Second International Archives
Socialist International Archives

NORWAY

Arbeiderbevegelsens Arkiv og Bibliotek (Oslo)
    Haakon Lie Papers
    Norske Arbeiderparti

SWEDEN

Arbetarrörelsens Arkiv och Bibliotek (Stockholm)
    Kaj Björk Papers
    Hjalmar Branting Papers
    Alva and Gunner Myrdal Papers
    Sveriges socialdemokratiska arbetareparti

SWITZERLAND

League of Nations Archives (Geneva)
    Disarmament Section
Schweizerisches Sozialarchiv (Zürich)
    Sozialdemokratische Partei der Schweiz

UNITED KINGDOM

Bodleian Library, University of Oxford
    Clement Attlee Papers
    James Callaghan Papers
    Barbara Castle Papers
    Gilbert Murray Papers
    Arthur Ponsonby Papers
    Socialist European Group of the Labour Party
British Library of Political and Economic Science Archives (London)
    Charles Roden Buxton Papers
    Charles Anthony Raven Crosland Papers
    Hugh Dalton Papers
    Ernest Davies Papers

Fabian Society Papers
Hector Alastair Hetherington Papers
Independent Labour Party Archive
R.W.G. Mackay Papers
David Mitrany Papers
E.D. Morel Papers
Christ Church College, University of Oxford
Tom Driberg Papers
Churchill College Archives, University of Cambridge
Clement Attlee Papers
John Burns Hynd Papers
Philip Noel-Baker Papers
National Library of Wales (Aberyswyth)
Ron Davies Papers
Thomas Jones Papers
Parliamentary Archives (London)
Benn Wolfe Levy Collection
Lloyd George Papers
People's History Museum, Manchester (formerly National Museum of Labour History)
Colin Beever Papers
British Asian Socialist Fellowship
Labour Party Archive
Morgan Phillips Papers
Jo Richardson Papers
John Rylands University Library, University of Manchester
Guardian Archive
John Ramsay MacDonald Papers
C.P. Scott Papers
The National Archives (Kew Gardens)
Foreign Office Records
James Ramsay MacDonald Papers
University College London
Hugh Gaitskell Papers
University of Sussex
Leonard Woolf Papers
Weston Library (formerly Bodleian Library of Commonwealth and African Studies, Oxford University)
Charles Roden Buxton Papers
Arthur Creech Jones Papers
Fabian Colonial Bureau Papers

UNITED STATES

Hoover Institute Library, Stanford
Bulletin intérieur du Parti socialiste—SFIO
Karl B. Frank Papers

Index